MUSIC AND THE RACIAL IMAGINATION

MUSIC
AND THE
RACIAL
IMAGINATION

EDITED BY
RONALD RADANO AND
PHILIP V. BOHLMAN

WITH A FOREWORD BY
HOUSTON A. BAKER, JR.

THE UNIVERSITY OF CHICAGO PRESS
CHICAGO AND LONDON

Ronald Radano is associate professor of Afro-American studies and music at the University of Wisconsin, Madison. Philip V. Bohlman is associate professor of music and Jewish studies at the University of Chicago.

The University of Chicago Press, Chicago 60637
The University of Chicago Press, Ltd., London
© 2000 by The University of Chicago
All rights reserved. Published 2000
Printed in the United States of America
09 08 07 06 05 04 03 02 01 00   5 4 3 2 1

ISBN (cloth): 0-226-70199-9
ISBN (paper): 0-226-70200-6

Library of Congress Cataloging-in-Publication Data

Music and the racial imagination / edited by Ronald Radano and Philip V. Bohlman;
    with a foreword by Houston A. Baker, Jr.
        p.   cm.
    Includes bibliographical references and index.
    ISBN 0-226-70199-9 (alk. paper) — ISBN 0-226-70200-6 (pbk. : alk. paper)
    1. Music and race.   I. Radano, Ronald Michael.   II. Bohlman, Philip Vilas.
ML3795.M782   2000
780'.89—dc21   00-23672

For those voices silenced by racism

CONTENTS

PART III

REPRESENTING/DISCIPLINING

PART IV

HISTORY/MODERNISM

PART V
POWER/POWERLESSNESS

FOREWORD

Conventional, academic aesthetic common sense suggests that music is to race as fine wine is to taste. Both offer undiluted, transcendent pleasures of consumption. For example, there is a traditional and remarkably intractable insistence by musicology that cultivated sound consumption consists precisely in a tasteful, raceless listening. Such audition buoys a universal spirit that is good to the last drop—or, the final encore. Lesser vintages—which is to say the varied soundings of "primitive," "folk," "ethnic," or "racial" communities—have been relegated by a high musicology to the bargain bins of ethnomusicology. Even the work of a traditional ethnomusicology, however, has striven for at least an arriviste immunity from race, claiming "culture" in sound and liberal "relativism" in taste as refuges from race: *chacun à son bruit*, as it were.

In a classic formulation on art and value, David Hume provides a succinct account of matters. In "Of the Standard of Taste," Hume seems to open the field of valuation and consumption to all comers: *de gustibus non disputandum est*. We can all, on equal terms and with apt perceptiveness, help Jeremiah drink his wine. Turns out, however, that for Hume only the grand sommelier is sensitive enough to pick up that "off taste" left by a key accidentally dropped into the barrel. Hence, "each to his own taste" reveals itself to mean: it is all right to consume "ethnic" or "racial" music if you are an ethnomusicologist, not a music man. For the key to music and musicology's greatness is iteration, returning again and again and again—indeed timelessly—only to the vintage without keys. Music for musicology is Europe and European of an inventively bounded cast, caste, and cask.

The great aesthete Walter Pater had something of this in mind when he wrote that all "art" aspires to the condition of music, which Pater held to be the most "abstract" of all the arts. Ronald Radano and Philip V. Bohlman have such matters very much in mind when they write: "A specter lurks in the house of music, and it goes by the name of race."

The following collection of boldly analytical essays is meant as an exorcism (at the very least, an "outing") of ghosts, an extraction of keys to the hoops and barrels of musicology, a tugging brilliantly into real space and time of abstract and haunting demarcations of race and music. The implicit claim of editors and essayists alike is that disciplinary protocols of musicology are distillates of Western imperialism's genocidal desire for self-sameness. In short, once the Other has been silenced through slaughter, domination, conversion, and "Indian schooling," then one "music" reigns supreme, tasteful, abstract, and alone in its self-definition of the *Ding an sich*.

Of course, mine is a great oversimplification of the present volume's sophisticated interventionist theory and poetics of music and the racial imagination. Still, the courageousness of editors and essayists in harmony seems to lie in their relentless refusal to blink away the specter or ignore the trace of those sounds and deafening silences that have rendered much of musicology's invention a barren or, at best, barely cultivated vineyard. Editors and essayists alike are as unafraid of "race" as they are unforgiving before imperializing shibboleths of "taste." What seems clear after reading the following essays and the editors' magnificent introduction is that the traditional "music" of a traditional musicology represents a pretty corked vintage, well past its prime. Cultivated in the soil of "race," it has frequently left a dull residue of stereotype, condescension, and error as a substitute for useful knowledge.

Commencing with the methods and spirit of a vigorous cultural studies, the following essays give new point to the implicit "racial" significations of the old chestnut: Let me write the songs of a nation and I care not who makes its laws. Well, yes, especially if the songs are thoroughly racialized products, defining both the "citizen self" and the limits of available good "taste" that constitute "civilization." Here is no easy listening. The following meditations, reflections, and analyses are soundings that rigorously critique visible disciplinary exclusions by exposing the formative spectral lines of race that must be reckoned with everywhere. All who are committed to the best offices of the current cultural studies project in its global dimensions must lift a glass to this work. Cheers.

Houston A. Baker, Jr.
Durham, N.C.

PREFACE

Music and the Racial Imagination is the product of our commitment to a musicology and ethnomusicology of engagement. We seek to engage music's place within history, within politics, within the realm of ideas, all toward giving some semblance of voice to those silenced by racism and prejudice. Similar engagements, of course, have characterized cultural studies for many years, and in this respect the essays in the present volume follow a parallel mode of analysis within specifically musical dimensions. Our hope is to stimulate new forms of engagement between the fields embraced by musical scholarship and cultural studies, fields we believe must enter into direct conversation and exchange.

Still, though we take interdisciplinarity as a given and as our point of departure, *Music and the Racial Imagination* is not primarily a volume about theory and theorizing the relation between music and race. Rather it takes an activist stance, and we mean the volume to serve, above all else, as a call to an intellectual activism within the domains of musicology and ethnomusicology. From the beginning, both the editors and the authors were struck by the paucity of literature on music and race within musical scholarship. And it is our collective aim to interpellate the aesthetics and politics of neglect that have led to that paucity. Indeed, it is precisely because musical scholarship has so rarely embraced activist approaches (particularly to matters of race) that the "silence" these essays aim to rend may seem so deafening.

It is hardly surprising, then, that this project began as a formal move within the disciplines to redress what we might call the racial quietude of musical scholastics. It first took the form of a double session, also named "Music and the Racial Imagination," at the 1993 annual meeting of the Society for Ethnomusicology at the University of Mississippi.

The editors were joined at the session by Jocelyne Guilbault, Christopher Waterman, and Ethan Nasreddin-Longo. Responses to that panel ranged from open enthusiasm to equally open outrage. We had touched a raw nerve, and we quickly realized that the topic would take us far beyond a paper session at an SEM meeting. Over the next few years, preparations for the volume virtually consumed us as we discussed the volume with our authors, and as we shuttled back and forth between Madison and Chicago. The shaping of the volume helped us to conceive of a place for race in the musical conversation, a topic about which we did not have, nor do we yet have, simple answers. We offer it as a launching point from which, we hope, conversation and study will ensue.

During the years the volume was taking shape, both editors had the good fortune to benefit from research fellowships that afforded opportunities to travel, to meet, and to think about the issues critical to the book. Ronald Radano wishes to express his gratitude to the Rockefeller Foundation, the Guggenheim Foundation, and the Smithsonian Institution for funding that advanced this and other projects on music and racial ideology, and Philip Bohlman gratefully acknowledges fellowship support from the Council for the International Exchange of Scholars (Fulbright Commission), the International Research and Exchanges Board (IREX), and the Internationales Forschungszentrum Kulturwissenschaften in Vienna, all of which afforded opportunities for extended research in Central and Eastern Europe. As our own commitment to a musical scholarship of engagement developed, *Music and the Racial Imagination* itself took shape. We brought our authors into the project, and we secured the interest of David Brent at the University of Chicago Press, whose own musical and intellectual interests resonate in countless ways with those of the authors who have contributed to the book. For his encouragement over the long haul, we extend to him our special thanks. We also wish to thank the editorial staff at the University of Chicago Press, especially Claudia Rex, Peter T. Daniels, and Matthew Howard, for their willingness to tackle the "big book," rendering it infinitely clearer during the editorial process. We learned much from the anonymous readers who, too, tackled the manuscript, and we wish to express special gratitude to Bruno Nettl, Co-General Editor of "Chicago Studies in Ethnomusicology," for his support and enthusiasm for the book.

Without the contributors there would be no "big book" whatsoever. Our authors have been a terrific lot, at once patient and impatient, occasionally argumentative and acquiesent, both stubborn and remarkably willing to take their essays through numerous revisions. We are fortunate indeed that they have been so unflagging in their own commitment to a scholarship of engagement.

When we met for working sessions in Madison and Oak Park, Colleen Dunlavy and Christine Wilkie Bohlman generously left us to our own affairs. They are surely happy that the "big book" is now complete, as they share our commitment to living humanly and purposefully.

R.R.
Madison and New York
P.V.B.
Chicago and Vienna
June 1999

INTRODUCTION

Music and Race, Their Past, Their Presence

RONALD RADANO & PHILIP V. BOHLMAN

THE OCCLUSION OF RACE IN MUSIC STUDIES

Ghostbusting

Aspecter lurks in the house of music, and it goes by the name of race. For most observers, it hovers and haunts barely noticed, so well hidden is it beneath the rigors of the scholarly apparatus. The racial specter, nonetheless, has an enormously powerful, nearly palpable effect: welling up from the depths of the discipline of musical scholarship, it casts a shadow across this putatively "objective" enterprise. The specter of race is not the edifice of "black music" to which the musical disciplines, when acknowledging the racial, reflexively turn. It is, rather, the ideological supposition that informs this reflex. The specter of race is neither the root cause of the music historian's enduring commitment to the sameness of European studies nor the reason for the ethnographer's preoccupation with the performance of difference. It is, rather, the commonsense opinion that what distinguishes the musically racial from the not-racial is as simple as telling the difference between black and white.

Race lives on in the house of music because music is so saturated with racial stuff; it inhabits the semiotic site supporting what Wahneema Lubiano calls "The House That Race Built." As a key signifier of difference, music for America—in its wonder, in its transcendence, in its affective danger—historically conjures racial meaning. As a matter of course, so too has musicology, in its various guises, "grown up" in this racial house. It is part of the fabric of the social; and its approaches, concerns, and orientations necessarily reflect the force of that experience. As

1

a modern discipline, however, musicology—in its historical, structural-analytical, and ethnographic expressions—has sought to deny the racial dimension. Indeed, it has done so vigorously, to the point where claims of a "racial dimension" must now run against the common logic of musical disciplines as viewed and taught today.

To recognize the racial in historical musicology, music theory, and ethnomusicology, however, is not to say that their interpretive strategies are necessarily predetermined by racial tenets, nor is it to defame a scholastic tradition as patently "racist." It means only to acknowledge the enduring effects of a racial imagination that has grown within the contexts of modernity to take on a peculiarly American cast in the twentieth century. Without committing to foundationalist premises, one might argue that the racial as it has been variously constituted within the contested spaces of difference is the Western ground on which the musical experience and its study has been erected. Like the Jubilee Hall of W. E. B. Du Bois's famous depiction, it is a house "ever made of the songs themselves, . . . full of the voices of [our] brothers and sisters, full of the voices of the past" (Du Bois [1903] 1989: 177–78).

Since the rise of the "new musicology" in the late 1980s—a term reserved principally for historical rather than ethnographic studies—scholars have sought to advance a more critically informed kind of scholarship, largely by turning to the realm of what has been rather casually labelled "postmodern theory." In the work of Carolyn Abbate, Philip Brett, Lawrence Kramer, Susan McClary, Ruth Solie, and others—and in the wake of Joseph Kerman's call for the end of tenacious positivism in *Contemplating Music* (1985)—musicology has widened the range of possibilities determining what critical practice may mean. So has it broadened the landscape of viable musical arenas, building on the important work in ethnography and American music history appearing since the 1950s (e.g., Alan Merriam, Bruno Nettl, Richard Crawford, Charles Hamm).

Historical musicology has, nonetheless, still remained remarkably committed to the affirmation of what is and is not racial, most typically by adhering to an easy binary of what is and is not European. This commitment, so commonly grounded in aestheticist assumptions about "the music itself," continues to determine the norms of scholarship as they are reflected in presentations at annual meetings, in essays featured in academic journals, and in patterns of academic hiring still committed to perpetuating the European canon.[1] These regressive tendencies have had an adverse effect on what the new musicology has thus far been able to achieve, constrained as it has been to maintaining a still rather narrow, politically uncontested realm of inquiry.

The political is, indeed, one of the principal motivations for the expansion of new musicological practice. Many successes have been achieved, and it is in this light that the new musicology continues to voice its challenges. Yet despite these advances, musicology endures the burdens of aestheticism and commitment to repertory that preclude a more radical refiguring of scholarship. Even when employing destabilizing strategies owing variously to poststructuralist practices from Foucault to Derrida or celebrating the subversive tactics of queer theory, scholars have commonly remained committed to a historically and musically centered "Europe" whose cultural and artistic boundaries, despite centuries of global encounter, remain tidy and distinct. Indeed, musicology continues to embrace a kind of invented tradition of Continental coherence and absolute value, together with modes of reception that go hand in hand with them, in apparent ignorance—notwithstanding the important contributions of Gary Tomlinson (1995) and V. Kofi Agawu (1995)—of the decisive challenges of postcolonial theory to these European constructs first articulated thirty years ago, most forcefully by Edward Said's assault on orientalism (Said 1978; see also Spivak 1988, Gilroy 1993, Bhabha 1994, Gikandi 1996).

Living in a world fraught with racial and social conflict, so overwhelmed with the intertext of "popular" and "artistic" mediations, musicological reception studies still remain largely limited to presentist constitutions of art and modes of experience based in the narrow subculture of the concert hall. To hear beyond this center would mean simply to position the invented tradition of "European music" within the world around us. To hear the social and racial in the European canon would mean to take seriously Adorno's account of modern listening (1978), to observe intertextually those other "unsung voices" of the global constellation in which we live (Abbate 1991).

Within the ethnographic initiatives that constitute the musical subdiscipline of ethnomusicology, a similar kind of selectivity has burdened scholarly engagement. In part this selectivity repeats historical musicology's musician-centered orientation, which has produced a similar kind of aestheticism in the unrelenting internalist fascination with the complexities of non-Western musical "form." But instead of devoting attention to a body of musical works, ethnomusicologists have more often committed to the sanctity of a well-worn methodological procedure based in mid-century scientism (Bohlman 1991). In this way, they follow another version of "positivism" in their commitment to objective scientific analysis and to the collecting of "world music" largely uncomplicated by the new hermeneutical challenges of history, philosophy, and anthropology (e.g., Hans-Georg Gadamer, Paul Ricoeur, and James Clifford). Particularly problematic is ethnomusicology's investment in rather fixed concepts of ethnicity, culture, and subjectivity that extend from the legacy of area studies and which have been subjected to critique in many humanistic studies.[2]

As we argue in this essay, ethnomusicology's commitment to "culture," in particular, developed as a response to the pernicious theories of race that had consumed musical thought in the early twentieth century. And yet the tenacity of this commitment has ultimately had a limiting effect on the kinds of questions ethnomusicologists now allow themselves to ask. Despite a laudable political activism nearly absent in mid-century Europeanist music studies, scholars have typically pursued a narrow interpretive focus that leaves out important, sustained debates of racial and cultural concepts. Indeed, ethnomusicology—notwithstanding the important individual contributions of Kenneth Gourlay (1978, 1982), David Coplan (1994), Anthony Seeger (1987), and others—seems as a whole at once to acknowledge and even to welcome political and racial debates while simultaneously displacing them. Because of its dual allegiances to methodological orthodoxy and area studies, it avoids the more slippery critical problems facing contemporary social theorists, even when those racial matters become centralized within the ethnographic encounter now consuming so much attention in global and post-colonial studies.[3]

As the various musicological projects move into the twenty-first century, they reflect, each in their own way, an emerging openness to the most pressing issues facing cultural investigation while nonetheless remaining constrained by the burdens of valuative assumption and disciplinary procedure. In their orthodoxy, they perpetuate the invisibility of race in musical studies while reinforcing the discipline's place on the margins of contemporary scholarship. With *Music and the Racial Imagination* it is our explicit goal to formulate and advance new thinking about musicological practice as it seeks to situate the discipline more explicitly within the existing conversation about cultural politics and race.

The essays in the book build from the body of work on the study of race in contemporary cultural studies as it foregrounds the importance of music within these lines of inquiry. Working from the legacy of African-American social and cultural criticism which first identified the important linkages between the musical and the racial—Frederick Douglass,

W. E. B. Du Bois, Zora Neale Hurston, Ralph Ellison, James Baldwin, Amiri Baraka, to name the most obvious—*Music and the Racial Imagination* proceeds from the many versions of post-black–arts movement criticism that have flourished in the wake of Houston Baker's seminal study, *Blues, Ideology, and Afro-American Literature* (1984).[4] So does it acknowledge its debt to the many important studies of the social construction of race, perhaps most notably Henry Louis Gates's *"Race," Writing and Difference* (1986). Aggressively multidisciplinary, *Music and the Racial Imagination* offers a forum for scholars outside musicology to direct their prior consideration of racial matters onto musical questions, as it encourages music scholars to begin to speak to racial ideas from their specialist perspectives. In this way, we hope to broaden the conversation about the associations between race and music, while also widening the range of musical reflection—to explore the range of possibilities of what "talk about music" can actually mean.

In this book we define "racial imagination" as the shifting matrix of ideological constructions of difference associated with body type and color that have emerged as part of the discourse network of modernity. As a crucial aspect in the constitution of identities and groups, it carries profound social meaning. As an ideology, however, the racial imagination remains forever on the loose, subject to reformation within the memories and imaginations of the social as it blurs into other categories constituting difference (Fields 1982; Eagleton 1991; Scott 1991; West 1987, 1994; Bhabha 1994). As such, "race" defines not a fixity, but a signification saturated with profound cultural meaning and whose discursive instability heightens its affective power.

The focus on race's musical aspect in *Music and the Racial Imagination* will centralize something curiously missing from social- and cultural-studies analyses, despite the common lip service paid to its importance. The imagination of race not only informs perceptions of musical practice but is at once constituted within and projected into the social through sound. Intersecting the musical and discursive, it becomes a "soundtext" that circulates within as well as across national boundaries. The subjects explored by the scholars whose essays are gathered in this collection speak to musical power as those scholars, collectively, call for engaged musicological reflection on the critical and historical study of race and culture.

Hearing Racially

One might comprehend this special racial significance by observing the "social situation of music" according to the classic Hegelian dialectic of

Self and Other (Adorno [1932] 1988). While this relation describes a patently European construct, still it provides, at least for the purposes of analysis, a way of observing the effects of musical and racial experience in which European concepts are inextricably linked. The longstanding metaphysical properties associated with music enhance the imagination of racial difference: race contributes fundamentally to the issues of belonging and ownership that music articulates. At individual, group, and broader social levels alike, few deny that one type of music can be possessed and claimed as one's own, while there are other musics that belong to someone else. The music of this variously constructed Self is different from the music of the Other, therefore making it possible to articulate and even conceptualize the most basic differences through our musical choices.

One can conceive of at least two kinds of metaphysics of ownership that establish the conditions of difference. The first of these results from the need to make music understandable, which is more often than not achieved through the attribution of linguistic properties to music; that is, to hear in music communication, signification, and meaning. The second derives from the technologies of music's production, which further control its distinguishing characteristics of selfness. Selfness therefore accrues to the objects and material culture of music, that is, bodies and instruments, but also the technologies and objects that represent music and allow it to be passed on from one member of a group to another (e.g., print culture). By possessing the objects containing music, one acquires the power to own and control the ways in which music bounds the group for which it has meaning.

Race is imagined as a component of these issues of music because it is connected with understandability, belonging, and ownership, all of which is encapsulated as forms of identity. The Other cannot or should not own or occupy the music that the Self purports to own. In European music history, Richard Wagner was surely the most visible, though only one among legions of anti-Semites, to make claims that Jews distorted the language of European opera and vocal music because of their inability to control its language. Wagner's claims, however steeped in biological prejudice, addressed the linguistic distinctiveness of music as he understood its current historical and social presence. The metaphysics of musical technology takes obvious racialized form in South Asia, where only privileged castes, especially Brahmins, could perform certain types of instruments (e.g., the *vina* in Karnatak music). Historically, other instruments were left to the lower castes, for example drums to untouchables such as the pariahs. The instruments of both Karnatak and

Hindustani musics functioned as a racial mapping of the caste system it-self, even as these categories have been increasingly subjected to critique by the musicians themselves (White, forthcoming).

Race is also fundamental to the ontologies of music, in other words to shaping basic concepts of what music is. Music's ability to represent essential metaphysical qualities enters profoundly into the discourse of race. Accordingly, music contributes substantially to the vocabularies used to construct race. The putative inseparability of dance and music in the African diaspora is an obvious case in which music participates in the construction of race. The metaphysical essence of "African music" is, therefore, physical and bodily. It derives from rhythmic patterns ob-served in the West as "complex" and from extensive improvisation that requires the participation of the entire body. One might argue that the more Africans are perceived as dancing, the more problematic the on-tology of African music as a bounded metaphysics of sound has become. So have these same racialized discourses cast about to define ownership and otherness among non-Africans: whirling dervishes, Native Ameri-cans, "naturally rhythmic" gypsies.

The racialization of musical metaphysics rarely ceases with simple stereotypes that support claims of difference. By its very "nature," in fact, the ontological mapping of music onto race leads to stereotype and prej-udice. In European music history, the most obvious case of a metaphys-ical otherness is the essentialized connection between speech and melody in Jewish music. On the one hand, Jewish histories of Jewish mu-sic (e.g., cantorial traditions of historiography that fill cantorial journals or monographs analyzing performance practice and repertory in the synagogue; cf. Baer 1883 and Friedmann 1908) stress that the mainte-nance of a truly Jewish music in the synagogue through centuries of sep-aration from Israel could only have been possible because of the inter-dependence of Hebrew texts with the esoteric knowledge and ritualized performance of those texts. Knowledge of Jewish music required spe-cialized knowledge and practice of a language unique to Jews. On the other hand, the view of an essentialized (or, to borrow from Baker et al., "referential"; Baker, Diawara, and Lindeborg 1996: 9) Jewish music as a bounded form of language spawned myriad prejudices about the inabil-ity to translate a Jewish musical metaphysics to a tradition where a knowledge of different languages was necessary. In the extreme forms of racial prejudice, a music would "sound Jewish" because its performer could not escape a race-specific predilection to a Jewish metaphysics of music.

In the racial imagination, music also occupies a position that bridges or overlaps with racial differences. Music fills in the spaces between racial distinctiveness, and when it does, it undergoes another, albeit no less racialized, metaphysical transformation, which in this book generally falls under the rubric of hybridization or hybridity.[5] Thus, music is a domain that different races, depending on interpretation and case, can potentially share, appropriate, and dominate; or that contains common syncretic practices. During the early centuries of European conquest and subjugation in Latin America, for example, missionaries, above all the Jesuits, and other colonizing forces used music to convert and control (Aracena 1999).

In these and many other colonial instances, however, domination quickly destabilizes, turning the direction of "influence" back upon the oppressors, and consequently unseating the simple logic of colonizer/colonized. The modern historiography of British-Pakistani music, for example, has depended on both the ontological uniquess of South Asian and Western popular musics, and on the neat ways in which they fit together when they come into contact in transnational public culture, such as when European harmonic structures provide the syncretic template for the *bhangra* style of the Safri Boys. The same can be said about the formations of Nigerian and Ethiopian forms of funk, which, in their homage to James Brown, define a crossnational racial meaning while simultaneously establishing local forms of musical significance. Music thus occupies a domain at once *between* races but has the potential of embodying—*becoming*—different racial significations. The concept of hybridity, then, does not signal a move away from racialized metaphysics, but rather serves to reinforce that metaphysics.

Music participates in many of the aesthetic and discursive constructions of race, and race provides one of the necessary elements in the construction of music. It might be useful to compare the difference between the ways music has been used discursively to construct the African diaspora with the ways music has provided the tools for mapping the landscape of ethnicity. Here, we deliberately distinguish between ethnicity and race, despite the effects of racial discourse in defining ethnic categories (Sollors 1986). Ethnicity, as we witness it on the American musical landscape, is constructed through choice and the exercising of options, whereas the racialization of music's metaphysics functions also to limit choices and options. Our concern, however, is primarily with the epistemes of musical discourse. Our basic argument is that discourses about music fundamentally derive from the construction and deployment of racial categories, just as these same categories grow ever more complicated and confused as a result of their sonic-discursive projection within the metaphysics of music. It is through music that the "new ethnicities" proposed by Stuart Hall—identities of conditional difference rather than identities of unbridgeable separation—may be enacted by such theorizing of the musical within the racial (Hall 1987).

Looking at the effects of a globalized public culture provides a final way in this preliminary analysis to comprehend the discursive roles of music and race. "World beat," as it has been constructed and commodified via the effects of a transnational capitalism, depends on deracinated languages about music, just as it derives its "authenticity" from the significations of racial difference manufactured in modernism. The condition of ownership has, after all, been stripped from world music, for anyone able to buy CDs or turn on the radio or television can possess it. The juxtapositions and unlimited possibilities brought about through the deracination of world music suggest that music represents the heightened repetition and destabilization of meaning associated with the "postmodern condition" by calling attention to difference only to deny its political presence in the CD anthologies of "Planet Soup." The enduring debates over the collaborations of Western pop stars and non-Western locals—such as Paul Simon's seminal album, *Graceland*— show it to be perhaps the supreme example of a world music whose racial character augments the mediation attendant upon collaboration through deracination (Meintjes 1990, Hamm 1988). World musics, with all their pretense toward hybridity, are therefore no less constructions of race and music, both of which continue to depend on a mutual inseparability.

The new, deracinated racial discourses of today's postcolonial soundworld bring us back to the history of racial denial that has long informed the musicologies. The paradox is particularly striking because neither historical- nor ethno-musicological discourses could have taken shape as modern disciplines without the crucial element of race itself (see, for example, Blum 1991). These historical and historiographical issues will emerge throughout the present introduction, and they are evident in most of the essays in this book. The disciplinary dilemma faced by historical musicology when it confronts race and music is its preoccupation with sameness; that of ethnomusicology is its dependence on difference. Ethnomusicology in particular is implicated in this analysis largely because of its commendable effort to broaden the scope of musicological inquiry. And yet it constructs its ontologies of music by accepting—and celebrating—differences as if they were givens, as if world music were dependent on them. While it is true that ethnomusicology's embrace of difference has broadened the landscape of musical research—which might otherwise have been left to the assumed supremacy of modern Europe—so has it reified forms of difference in ways no longer consistent with comprehensions of subjectivity and culture. Race, as the generating force of difference, is actually neutralized—or "eraced"—because difference is shifted from human differences to musical differences, to the object of music itself. By locating race "on music," both race and music become fetishized and denied.

At the end of the twentieth century, race is one of the most enduring factors contributing to the formation of musical difference. It is a component of the multiplex of musicological discourse, and one might argue that its import is repeatedly heightened with each attempt to secure its neutrality. It is therefore part of a litany of differences that is all too familiar: race, gender, class, ethnicity. Who dares to weight one more than the others? We are not arguing for or against any of these elements in the litany; on the contrary, close scrutiny reveals that they interact and interfere with each other's signification. Rather we are pointing out how the occlusion of race in a liberal musical discourse has meant that those realities have actually been denied. And we shall not deny the ironic cruelty that this paradox implies when the field denies those concerns it publicly claims as its own. Our concern, then, is to address the ways in which discourses about music can be constructed in order not to deny race.

THE PLACES OF RACE IN
EUROPEAN MUSICAL HISTORY

The Place of Race 1: Premodern Terminologies

The concept of race, as a construct distinguishing one group of humans from another on the basis of shared biological appearances, emerges from a legacy of human difference-making that traces across humanity. Indeed, determining difference appears to be a common if not universal quality of human consciousness, showing up across diverse contemporary cultural circumstances as it reaches back to the recesses of antiquity (Appiah 1992: 11–14; Hannaford 1996). But it is not until the early modern era, and then more precisely during the second half of the eighteenth century, that the modern concept of race is canonized. As Anne McClintock compellingly argues, this modern concept becomes constituted as part of a process of naming in which distinctions between race and gender blur into a discursive mix of male appropriative desire. What is more, naming records not only the intent of subjugation but expressions of fear that populate the colonial imagination: of cannibals, licentious savages, violent creatures that together construct a monstrous rhetoric or "porno-tropics" (McClintock 1995: 2–24; see also Pratt 1992, Wiegman 1995). Music comes to play a key role in this imagination of difference, as the multiplex significations of a metaphysical resonance share in the making of the context from which race emerges. The early discursive history of race and music, then, implicates Europe in its extent—at its margins and along geographical boundaries of interaction and conflict with the world beyond (e.g., Lafitau 1724). From the beginning of any historiography of music and race, Europe is there, and its interaction with those it imagines as Others secures its places in that historiography (see Stocking 1968).

The word "race" first appears in Europe during the thirteenth century, when several Romance languages exhibit forms of it: *raza* (Spanish), *raça* (Portugese), *razza* (Italian), and *race* (French). Philological evidence suggests that its usage in Romance languages, specifically Spanish and Portugese, derives from the Arabic as a result of the Muslim presence in the Iberian Peninsula and further contact and cultural exchange between the European and North African sides of the Mediterranean littoral (Geiss 1988: 16). In Arabic usage, the term *ras*, whose Semitic etymology is the same as that of Hebrew *rosh*, refers to the "head" or the "leader," specifically the leader of a tribe or social collective. The Arabic concept of *ras* enjoyed widespread currency in North Africa after the Muslim conquest in 711 c.e., especially among Bedouin groups, where usage more broadly signified affiliational choices among group members. *Ras* applied to a collectivity whose members recognized relatedness to their "leader,"— relatedness, that is, in both biological and cultural senses. The biological genealogy of the group became to a large extent isomorphic with the cultural genealogy (see the essays in Fischer and Wölflingseder 1995). This isomorphic relation is, moreover, evident in one of the first distinctions of musical difference based on racial difference, namely that made by the North African polymath Ibn Khaldun in his "Introduction to a history of the universe" ([1377], trans. Rosenthal, 1958). The geographical zones, running from east to west, into which Ibn Khaldun divided the world determined human differences because of characteristic influences of climate on the humors and, by extension, human disposition. In warmer, more southerly climates, sub-Saharan Africa for instance, the humors flowed more freely and yielded more animated expression of culture. Music, it followed in Ibn Khaldun's ethnographic imagination, was more excited and impassioned in the lands of the south, less so in the lands of the north.

When the term *raza* appears in Spain during the Reconquista (1064–

1492), it already reflects both senses explicit in the Arabic *ras.* Increasingly during the Reconquista, however, *raza* came to imply noble bloodlines, that is, group connections to the head of a particular court, in some cases to royal courts (Geiss 1988: 17). The appropriate genealogy, based on familial ties, allowed one certain privileges vis-à-vis those unable to claim that genealogy. On the Iberian peninsula, race made a transition from Semitic/North African applications to emerging European/Christian modes of classification. Because concepts of race in North Africa continued to designate affiliation to tribal genealogies, traceable eventually to a leader and through the leader's family, such concepts engendered mobility—in other words, a capacity to carry race with one or empower it to give coherence to a group, tribe, or extended family wherever these constituted themselves. European/Christian modes of classification depended much more intensively on the institutionalization of a polity and of the connection of polity to place. Racialized genealogies were relatively immobile and centralized, with racial selfness accruing to the structures at the center (e.g., of court or monastic culture) and with otherness characterizing peoples beyond the periphery, those without properly institutionalized polities. In a very literal, that is, geographic, sense, European/Christian modes of human classification had become Eurocentric on the eve of the Early Modern era.

The term "race" itself found its way into other European languages relatively slowly, appearing in English first in the sixteenth century—figured in Shakespeare's Caliban *(The Tempest)* and the Jewish Shylock *(The Merchant of Venice)*—and in High German only in the eighteenth century; the modern Germanized spelling *Rasse* (or, in the Old High German, *Reiza;* see Hannaford 1996: 5), shows up only in the early nineteenth. As a concept, it served mainly as a term of classification, attributed commonly to the late seventeenth-century writings of François Bernier. Bernier was a physician and author of travel accounts— a proto-physical anthropologist, we might say —who employed the term "race" (in this case, the French *race*) as a correlate of "species" *(espèce),* to delineate and bound a larger human collective. From this usage emerged the biological extensions of the concept, that is to the species classification of animals (e.g., *Rasse* in modern German, which describes both human races and animal species; cf. Geiss 1988: 17–18).

The etymological history, of course, should not be taken to mean that modern European determinations of difference had not already existed. Jews had been banished from England by the late thirteenth century; religious determinations traced across early modern and modern engagements with the Other and served to justify a legacy of violence, war, and

African enslavement (first by the Portuguese and Spanish, then the English); color, if not a biological determinant, nonetheless figured into more malleable constructions of intellect and character (Hannaford 1996, Horsman 1981, Pieterse 1992). In music, moreover, references to difference informed the derogatory projections of Jewishness in early eighteenth-century opera. It also served as a signifier of the magical in the Renaissance, a formulation reinforced as Europeans encountered similar music–social correlations among those whom they colonized (Tomlinson 1993).

Since the eighteenth century, the biological–cultural tension in genealogies of race has persisted. Indeed, with the emergence of canonized and institutionally implemented forms of racism, biologically determined genealogies have won the upper hand. In the philological and discursive histories of race, the specific rhetoric of "racism" is quite recent, reformulated through theories of Social Darwinism and appearing in a concerted form in the twentieth century, specifically to designate social and political action against Jews (Geiss 1995: 103–6; Gould 1981). The point we wish to make here is not that European languages were not filled with a surfeit of terms to express racial prejudice and hatred, but rather that the modern discourse of racism, which transformed the ways we must now understand the full history of the racial imagination, was constructed from the local and global events that determined European modernity (see Stocking 1994). Historically, modernity contained contexts that refocused and intensified many aspects of the European racial concepts as racism. Prevailing genealogies of music must take into account the ideological contexts in order to understand the full complexity of contemporary disciplinary praxis.

The Place of Race 2: Modern Conceptions

Race found its way into new spaces with the Enlightenment. These were the spaces of the mind, of scientific categories, of forms of desire, and of a world observed, processed, and remapped on the imagination of Europe (see, e.g., the readings in Eze 1997; see also Stafford 1991). Race was a common trope of Enlightenment observation encompassing the variety of discursive formations of imperial desire. So too was music part of this constitution, and in its ineffability, it signified the danger zones of global encounter. Together the matrices of race and music occupied similar positions and shared the same spaces in the works of some of the most lasting texts of Enlightenment thought. A historical continuum emerges, coalescing around the musical works of Jean-Jacques Rousseau and Johann Gottfried Herder, so much so that, by the end of the eighteenth century, music could embody differences and exhibit race. Once reified as a modern object or thing, it could undergo scientific observation because of its differences. Music's differences became as evident as those of color and the other human distinctions of a racialized world. The reification of that racialized "world," with its full geographical totality, becomes key to this racio-musical formulation. As Europe looks outward, so does it position music at the foreground of its modern racialist perspective.

Just as nature gave birth and form to race, so music exhibited remarkable affinities to nature. Nature was a source of difference, a gendered "virgin territory" that lent itself to control and male classification. Rousseau's *Dictionnaire de la musique* provides a place for difference in music by lexicographically opening and plotting a complex glossary of terms that provide the scaffold for a new musical discourse. The *Dictionnaire* pried open the language about music to make space for language about race. For Rousseau it was language and its presence in music that most represented racial difference. Especially in song, one observed distinctive ways in which the people of different nations and cultures sang; in voice, because of its embodiment of the physical, one could actually hear human difference. In one of the most frequently cited definitions, for the Swiss *ranz des vaches* (songs used in and derived from cattle-herding practices), Rousseau goes so far as to perceive semiotic attributes in song, which in turn transcend music by transforming vocal expression into the embodiment and exercise of memory:

> We shall seek in vain to find in this air any energetic accents capable of producing such astonishing effects. These effects, which are void in regard to strangers, come alone from custom, reflections, and a thousand circumstances, which retrac'd by those who hear them, and recalling the idea of their county, their former pleasures, their youth, and all their joys in life, excite in them a bitter sorrow for the loss of them. The music does not in this case act precisely as music, but as a memorative sign. (Rousseau 1975: 267; cf. Seeger 1991: 347–48)

In Rousseau's *Dictionnaire*, French music was unlike Italian music because the French language allowed the singer to formulate sound in ways unlike the Italian language. Rousseau went a step further, however, because he made a case for those languages that were more natural than others, as well as those musics that demonstrated more direct connections to nature than others. Accordingly, nature provided for Rousseau a privileged site for the connections between music and language. As with language, the origins of song were rooted in nature; it was the artifice of modern musical practices that violated the naturalness of human vocal expression. It was the human interaction and intervention with nature that unleashed the processes of racial difference and encoded them through music and language. Through song, the racial difference immanent in nature was given voice.

Herder took the categorization of music and human difference several steps further. In his two-volume compendium devoted to *Volkslieder* (Herder 1778–79) he gathered a diverse cross section of genres and repertories. In this first and eventually canonic use of the term *Volkslied*, Herder cast his conceptual nets as widely as possible, attempting to gather in what we would today describe as examples of world music. There are song repertories from throughout Europe, from both center and periphery (e.g., Gaelic and Baltic songs), and from accounts of missionaries and other travelers. These determinations of "folk," however quaint today, nonetheless grew from the same impulse of colonial desire and determinations of difference occupying early modernity. Jean de Léry's collections (1585) of indigenous songs from the Bay of Rio de Janeiro (see de Léry 1990; cf. Greenblatt 1991: 14–20), which Montaigne mediated in a form that resituated them in the burgeoning colonial discourse of Europe (see Montaigne 1952 and Bohlman 1991), belong no less to the discursive space of European folk song than do ballads anthologized by Bishop Thomas Percy in his *Reliques of Ancient English Poetry* (1765) and Walter Scott's *Minstrelsy from the Scottish Border*. As a genre, Herder's *Volkslied* includes songs from oral tradition, popular street repertories, and the works of famous poets, among them Shakespeare and Goethe. Not only are folk songs drawn from the historical past and philologically determined present, but they construct a history of musical difference that connects societies of the past with those of the present. This universalizing effect gave to song a source of power that encouraged new melding of musical languages within the racial. Music's magic, indeed, spoke of an alchemical effect, and colonialist reports of an audibly fantastic otherness invited similar projections of the native danger.

In its transcendence, music could amplify points of contact within and without social groups; it reinforced group and (later) "national" boundedness as it enabled imagined transgressions linking peoples, only to increase its danger. Because of their transhistorical vision of song, whose origins are scattered about the world (though especially about Europe), folk songs came to create their place in a classical space of Enlightenment thought. At the end of the eighteenth century, however, this space was anything but classical; indeed, one might argue that it was overtly anti-classical. It gave language a new power by creating a new conceptual space for thinking about "music itself." And Herder's notion of *Volkslied* was music in the broadest and most diverse sense, whose absoluteness gave it historical potential. As "music itself," folk song substantially intensified its displacement from the places in which its social functions relied on localized concepts of human distinctiveness rather than on the increasingly globalized concepts of racial difference.

The Place of Race 3: Europe Looks Outward
(the Emergence of "World Music")

Race, as we have seen, accrues meaning around spaces of Otherness. In these other spaces, race *sounds* different, that is, foreign and distant—displaced from the familiar. It has, nonetheless, an arresting quality because, its foreignness notwithstanding, race enables access. Its "logic of form" seems to sound across temporal and social distances, fulfilling for a legacy of Western observers an appropriative desire for the authentic, the universal. Throughout histories of culture contact—in travel accounts, in colonial encounters, in missionary and military excursions—music has arrested the attention of observers because of its putative accessibility and universality of meaning. For colonizing listeners, the music in spaces of Otherness seemed both remarkable because of its primordial foreignness, which identified the site of an original culture, and unremarkable because of its "primitiveness," which precluded its value as a cultural form. This paradox would inform cultural reports into the twentieth century, as European expansion brought with it new, contradictory imaginations of global sound.

The "looking outward" that constitutes the third place of race in this section extends from the European historical forces that were essential to constructing racial difference musically. With the escalation of imperialism, missionaries and colonial officials encountered music in the spaces of Otherness, that is, the music of "races" other than their own, and with this music they were able to imagine for the first time in European history a truly global music. Indeed, global travel profoundly influenced the European imagination of music, and the new discourses on music came to represent both the ideation and the repression of a newly displaced, transmutated European subjectivity. For just as difference broadened the musical imagination of the foreign and Europe's relational aspect to the same, so did it vitalize theories of a universal sound in which Europe remained centrally situated. One might even argue that the modern comprehension of "music" as such would not have come about without the emergence of a relational circumstance that positioned a European practice above and beyond the more authentic, yet ultimately lesser, forms of "emerging" peoples. This European musical supremacy, in turn, would be reinforced by a new musical economy of public concert listening, guided by critics who provided determinations of meaning for an increasingly music-conscious bourgeoisie.

Representations of the musics of Others occupied the pages of European encounter, documented in the accounts of venturesome travelers and in scholarly musical monuments. Noteworthy examples were already appearing in the seventeenth and eighteenth centuries, among them Athanasius Kircher's encyclopedia *Musurgia universalis* (1650) and Joseph-Marie Amiot's *Mémoire sur la musique des chinois* (1779); the world voyages of Johann Georg Adam Forster (1772–75) and Jean François Galaup de la Pérouse (1785–88); together with ethnographic compendia such as Guillaume Chenu de Laujardière's *Relation d'un voyage à la côte des Cafres* (1686–89), Joseph-François Lafitau's *Mœurs des sauvages américains* (1724), and William Hamilton Bird's *The Oriental Miscellany* (1789). Within the context of the slave trade, moreover, several French and English writers documented the performance practices among blacks populating Africa and the islands of the Caribbean (Abrahams and Szwed 1983). If these commentaries were commonly and, into the eighteenth century, increasingly limited by supremacist assumptions of blacks' social, racial, and religious inferiority, they nonetheless revealed an emerging propensity to correlate difference with distinctive forms of sonic production This recognition of difference grew into a veritable industry of "colonial desire" (Young 1995) that gave rise to a surfeit to texts, including a seventeen-volume historical compendium depicting musical and other cultural practices (Pinkerton 1808–14).

If seventeenth- and eighteenth-century commentaries identified the makings of European chronicles of musical Others, the publications appearing in the nineteenth century revealed a new dimension of fascination. What had appeared in large numbers during the first decades would swell by mid-century, particularly after the European occupation of Africa in the 1870s (e.g., Corry 1807, Laing 1825, Beecham 1841, Ellis 1883). Whereas prior accounts variously depicted musical accomplishments, these later studies commonly positioned foreign musics in a decidedly inferior status in ways consistent with the growing orthodoxy of racialist opinion, laden as it was with the pernicious claims of Social Darwinism. Paraphrasing a considerable body of philosophical speculation on the character of Africans, François-Joseph Fétis wrote: "Cette race n'a ni histoire, ni littérature, ni arts qui méritent ce nom" (1869, 1: 28). Despite the assertions of irreversible inferiority, however, writers continued with their labors, vividly documenting "peculiarities," and sometimes providing detailed transcriptions of what were routinely portrayed as heathenish practices (Amiot 1779, Bowdich 1819, Brinner 1993).

This contradictory discourse of discipline and desire appears consistent with the rhetoric of masculinized conquest that narrated modernity's colonial mapping. Yet the intrusion of a Rousseavian conception of "natural ability" into a prior discourse of heathenish, black "noise" made for a peculiarly schizophrenic projection when attention focused increasingly on African and African-American musical practices (Radano, in press). In "Negro music" Europeans identified a kind of mimetic genius: despite their intellectual limits, blacks produced imitations of European singing that seemed to exceed the value of the "original." Such characterizations already appeared in texts from the seventeenth century, such as Richard Ligon's incredulous account of an African in Jamaica making music on a makeshift marimba. By the nineteenth century, however, they had become widespread, as observers sought to coordinate a racialist ideology of denigration with their own empirical observations of the creativity of human Others.

In *Histoire générale de la musique* (1869), for example, Fétis took pains to argue European superiority through a rationalist equation of beauty, intelligence, and harmony while working carefully through the details of non-European practices that so obviously fascinated him. In another influential text, *Primitive Music* (1893), Richard Wallaschek sought similarly to establish European superiority through a fine-combed analysis of a world of musical difference. Significantly, Wallaschek begins his study with a discussion of the musics of Africa, which form the locus of primordial ancestral expression and the base of humanity's intellectual and creative hierarchy. As the lowest of the low on the hierarchical level of civilization, African-American music was viewed as nothing more than "poems" set to European song.[6] As the epitome of "racial music," the black voice identified both an origin and an absence coeval with an earlier, primitive moment.

THE UNSPOKEN HISTORY OF MUSIC
STUDIES IN THE UNITED STATES

The development of American musicological research is commonly portrayed as an extension and elaboration of German scholarly practices of *Musikwissenschaft* which emerged in the late nineteenth century (Krader 1980). Within the scheme proposed by Guido Adler (1885), historical procedure takes form as a scientific quest for natural law couched in an epistemological frame of organicism (Allen 1939, Kerman 1985). Ethnomusicological practice develops in its turn from a related comparative orientation (*vergleichende Musikwissenschaft*, or "comparative musicology"), which Adler classifies as part of the analytical development of systematic musicology. The histories of the discipline that appear subsequently—and particularly after World War II—commonly build on this perspective, concentrating on the evolution of methodological procedure set apart from the vagaries of social and ideological change. "Intellectual history" is thus consistent with the internalist histories of music that have occupied the discipline for decades. That European music studies are now becoming better situated within the history of ideas gives hope for a more reflective, critical outline (e.g., Bohlman 1987, Thomas 1995, Bent 1996). And the appearance of new historiographic studies that specify the racial dimension in Germany's own musicological development—such as Pamela Potter's (1998) groundbreaking work on music studies during the Nazi era—encourages a similar reassessment of the social circumstances surrounding musicology's emergence in the United States. To this end we offer here some brief reflections on the specifically American social arena in which U.S.-based musicologies take form. Contrastive though they may be, one can identify in each a discernible racialist background giving way to attempts to mask racial matters.

Musicology emerged during the early twentieth century alongside the institutions of culture that defined America's coming of age (DiMaggio 1982). As patrician classes forged institutions to propagate an elite sense of refinement, so did colleges and universities introduce a pedagogy that reinforced the liberal ideology of Enlightenment through the appreciation of cultivated arts. From the beginning, the directive was to edify and educate, to build on nineteenth-century affirmations of "taste" in response to the aesthetically and morally deficient "popular arts" overtaking public culture at the time. Institutional founders focused specifically on securing a canon comprising the major works of the European commonpractice era, (eighteenth and nineteenth centuries), together with genres of choral music and American composition that reinforced a common aesthetic judgment. As expressions of culture, these repertories seemed to rise above matters of ideology and race. And yet they did so by limiting representation to those emblems of civilization that, as we have seen, grew up within racial frames of whiteness.

Whiteness, in fact, is key to the formation of musical appreciation in American culture (Hill 1997), just as music occupies a key role in the making of the color line. With the rise of evangelical movements in the early nineteenth century, for example, music served as a crucial vehicle for conversion, and its power was equally and enthusiastically embraced by blacks and whites. As the liminal states of racial and religious transgression began to intersect in belief and song, prohibitions were constructed to segregate along racial lines (Radano, in press). With the rise of blackface minstrelsy in the 1830s, moreover, "whiteness" specified a class position for those most vulnerable to association with African-Americans— notably, Irish immigrant workers. According to David Roediger, the Irish-American workers helped to solidify a conception of racial whiteness as a means of distinguishing themselves from those racially and socially beneath them. The means by which these same workers accessed whiteness through the performance of blackness revealed the contradictions inherent in a racial ideology that limited identification to only a portion of humanity (Roediger 1991; see also Ignatiev 1995).

The widespread appeal of black music meant that its effects were more than trivial; to be sure, black music had a transforming effect that entered into the very recesses of social experience (Michaels 1995). By the mid nineteenth century it had overwhelmed Euro-American public culture, informing the new interest in slave autobiographies, and, after the Civil War, in spirituals, coon songs, ragtime, and the courtly jubilees which Dvořák proposed as a vernacular "coloring" to spruce up America's musical blandness (Lott 1993, Fishkin 1993). Significantly, these "black musics" were never racially pure but, more typically, relationally determined. While performances sought overtly to signify one racial category or the other, their reception and comprehension commonly articulated something in between. The power of black music derived from this racial instability. It was, as Werner Sollors (1997) has described a similar phenomenon in the context of literature, "neither black nor white, yet both."

The contradictions inherent in the racial construction of music in America had profound repercussions on the emerging disciplines of musicology. Notwithstanding the work of Oscar Sonneck and other nation-minded (yet exclusively white-centered) writers on folk and band musics, historical musicology remained most obviously committed to the study of European and Euro-American art musical achievements. This orientation no doubt developed from multiple incentives, social, experiential, geographic, and otherwise. As a commitment to art, to *Musik an sich*, it expressed above all a progressive desire to move beyond the racial stereotypes contaminating public consciousness, to transcend the regressive impulses of America's own colonizing, imperial past. In so doing, however, musicology did not solve these issues but merely deferred them. Possessing the option to focus beyond race, white scholars could claim an enlightened racelessness that only betrayed privilege and, in certain circumstances—particularly when the conversation turned to nationalist musical practices—a clear desire to maintain a Euro-centered racial preserve (Elson 1900, Sonneck 1927). Indeed, it is precisely the tenacity with which historical musicology has claimed the European and Euro-American traditions as its principal purpose that reveals the racial specter lurking in its house. What might a racial critique of this past mission say about our own desires and claims? What would it mean to hear Elliot Carter's rhythmic practices as responsive to the aesthetic challenges of jazz, to observe Copland's music beyond the Turneresque narratives of frontier freedom that so consume the public imagination?

Ethnomusicology's historical narrative similarly shares a genealogical relation with a nineteenth-century racial music. Whereas historians, however, resisted the power of racial ideas in musical experience, ethnographers embraced it, above all, to exalt difference. The first musical ethnographers openly acknowledged music's difference along racial lines: In the depictions of ballads collected by Francis James Child and his Cambridge colleagues, in the forms of blackness that preoccupied the Wisconsin historian William Francis Allen (Allen, Garrison, and Ware 1867) and other students of slave song (Radono 1996), in the "imperialist nostalgia" that characterized the multitude of essays on Native Americans' music appearing directly after their massacre (Rosaldo 1989). In their pursuits, ethnographers sought to locate the "missing link" of authenticity that had since Rousseau defined the completion and unraveling of civilization. Yet whereas for Rousseau such contradictions developed from a sturdier sense of superiority and as a challenge to aristocratic confidence, for American ethnographers they revealed the contradictions of racial logic in a divided nation. The desire for and contempt of racial Others pervaded ethnographic texts that rapidly proliferated after the Civil War, leading a well-known observer of Native American music to dismiss strategically in a final paragraph of one of her monographs the artistic value of "primitive" song (Densmore 1909). Such contradictions were also at work when W. E. B. Du Bois himself cast disparaging comments about the "brothers and sisters" who had invented the music he proclaimed "the greatest this side the seas" (Du Bois 1903; see also West 1989: 143). The unrelenting power and appeal of "race music" would increasingly complicate the emergence of scholarly ethnographic practice, as the exaltation of science intersected with racial fantasies establishing America's social common sense.

These trajectories of popular "race music" were perhaps more important in the making of modern musical ethnography than any other single influence. Their appeal established the frames of reference in which modern narratives of difference would be written, refashioned according to nineteenth-century racialist assumptions to express the musical imaginations of early modernism. Accordingly, the distinctions one makes between "scholarship," "journalism," and "entertainment" grow complicated, given the extent to which their rhetorics betray racial sensibilities consistent with early modernism (Torgovnick 1990). In Dorothy Scarborough's *On the Trail of Negro Folk-Songs* (1926), for example, one hears the voice of blackface, just as it bears resemblances to the authenticities that inform the primitivist rhetoric of Harlem writers. The 1932 cartoon image of Betty Boop traipsing across the African jungle (in fear of the "spook" image of a disembodied Louis Armstrong) carries forth significations of exoticism and danger that define the black image in anti-Negro social criticism, and even in fieldwork depictions of the WPA and Library of Congress (Gabbard 1996: 205). These racialisms, moreover, informed even the most scientific observations. In his early exercise in mechanical transcription (phonophotography), for example, Milton Metfessel chose as his laboratory specimen the "Negro voice," dissecting, like Walter Benjamin's camera, the physicality of African-American sonic renderings (Metfessel 1928). This is not to conflate the many dimensions of musical representation, whose purpose, quality, and achievement varied widely, but rather to identify the discourse network in which the conversation about racial music was taking place. Indeed, it seems not too much to say that racial difference consumed talk about music, a fact that carries profound significance when observing the growth of academic studies in ethnomusicology.

It is against this social background that the modern discipline of ethnomusicology emerges. At once it embodies these racial notions as it works purposely to establish a higher ground of representation. Recognizing the racialisms that so preoccupied scholars in the 1920s and 1930s, those of the post-War era worked to remove racial matters form the academic discourse. Unlike Europeanists, however, who merely displaced "racial music," scholars of world music were forced to face it directly while searching strategically for better analytical models. For this they turned to the discipline of cultural anthropology, and particularly to the perspective of "cultural relativism" established in the work of Franz Boas, which offered a way of disrupting the aesthetic hierarchy that had preoccupied Europeanist studies. In its stead they proposed a kind of cultural egalitarianism that relegated aestheticist concerns—beyond intracultural explorations of David MacAllester, Alan Merriam, and others—to mere judgments of taste.[7] Stressing above all the objective claims of "science," ethnomusicology provided for music studies the outlines of a new Enlightenment Project, consistent with the calls for the "end of ideology" that would emerge in the late 1950s and 1960s (Bell 1960). That these calls, however laudable, also revealed a new kind of imperialism consistent with America's world dominance rarely entered into the reflections on the discipline's mission (for noteworthy exceptions see Gourlay 1982, Keil 1982, Agawu 1992). Discussion of race was absent as well: it seemed to evaporate from the scholarly discourse in the attempt to reach to higher intellectual order.

An important text in this "unspoken history" was Melville Herskovits's monumental *Myth of the Negro Past* (1941), which outlined a culture-based way of expressing essentialist positions once framed in racial terms. His dual emphases on culture over race and on the processes of transmission enabling diasporic continuities helped scholars to maintain arguments about musical essence without succumbing to the problematic views of bilogical determinism. Although Herskovits himself devoted only marginal attention to musical matters, his students, notably Alan Merriam and Richard Waterman, were instrumental in transposing this interpretive apparatus to the emerging ethnomusicological discipline. In the work of both Merriam and Waterman one observes a commanding devotion to scientific objectivity as a way of transcending racial pitfalls together with versions of the modern racial–musical intertext. Waterman's theories of "hot rhythm" (1948) reflect an unmistakable legacy of racializing music (Radano, this volume), just as his musical applications of the anthropological theory of syncretism (1952), in which African-American music was observed as a melding of European and African similarities, may be read as a metaphor of the integrationist debates consuming mid-century American liberal thought. Merriam's vigorous demands for scientific practice similarly revealed progressive political sentiments. Yet in the end they could not obscure the extent to which he succumbed to the primitive myth of African ferocity—such as when he proposed Henry Stanley's narrative of "Bandussuma at Usiri" as an unparalleled depiction "of the emotional impact of African rhythm" (Merriam 1959)—anymore than the achievements of Alan Lomax (1959) can deny the "pornotropic" rhetoric of his early studies of folk-song style.

One must certainly commend the early figures of a discipline in their progressive commitment to a bolder kind of musical scholarship than that which characterized commentaries of non-European music before.

They sought to chart an ambitious, democratic vision that expressed as much a new sympathy for realms of difference as it reflected an imperial self-confidence after America's world victory.[8] It is certainly not our intention to denigrate their mission, but only to observe how their scholarship reinforced as it reflected ideologies pervasive in an academy still dominated by white, male privilege.[9] In these positions toward race, we can now recognize, from a distance, the extent to which they carried the denial of race forward. To dismiss this body of scholarship would be an injustice. But to overlook its racialist rhetoric would be equally unjust, leaving us hopeless of ever moving beyond it.

CONSTRUCTION OF RACE IN (AND BY) THE "NEW EUROPE"

During our discussions with potential contributors to this volume, our colleagues who worked at the greatest distance from Europe and the United States were most adamant in their insistence that "race in its European sense" just did not apply; it was "foreign," for example, in many countries in Southeast Asia or the Caribbean, whereby our interlocutors meant that no one described musical and cultural differences with discourses distinguished as racial. As this introduction has sought to show, however, "music," is a European construct exhibiting a European metaphysics that has variously extended into non-Western realms. As a marker of racial differences, it is overwhelmingly implicated in European colonial history. The more extensively categories and constructs of "music" solidified—became exclusive rather that inclusive in their metaphysics—the more European concepts of music insinuated themselves into non-Western cultures. In music cultures of Islamic societies, for example, the terms $mūsīqā$ and $mūsīqī$ are consciously borrowed from European terminology and enter Arabic musical ontologies to mark not only otherness but that which is foreign to Muslim discourses of sound and language. All these forms of historical evidence and vehement criticism were unsettling, for we also struggled against the ever-present danger of essentializing race. Did we face a dilemma, then, in which talking about music *and* race ineluctably trapped us in European history, even as it drove the engines of transnationalism?

Not to devote a section of our introductory essay to Europe in the 1990s would also be inexcusably irresponsible. Whatever else can be said about race in Europe since the collapse of communist governments in Eastern Europe, it is impossible to ignore the sharp rise of racism. In a continent where radical political change has a truly global impact, the brutal results of racist histories are everywhere palpable. Whatever else can be said about music in the New Europe, it is impossible not to recognize the proliferation of musics outside the Western canon—indeed, music that gives voice to the peoples politically and ideologically excluded from European history. Music gives voice to this postmodern European otherness; the new musics of the New Europe insist that we confront race and racism.

Fundamental to European concepts of race is an opposition between musics that historically participated in the construction of a European canon and those that did not. Such a "fundamental" opposition sounds straightforward enough, but in fact European constructs of otherness are anything but straightforward. The Other may be outside Europe, different by dint of not being European. The Other may also dwell within Europe, different therefore by dint of being all-too-European. Racial difference accrues to the Others because of the nature of the gap between them and Europe. When they dwell beyond the borders of Europe, that gap in an impediment to understanding and a source of misunderstanding. When they dwell within Europe, the gap diminishes so completely that its potential implosive effect concentrates and intensifies fear. The gap, internal and external to Europe, historically assumes the form of aporia—for our purposes, a gap or suspension of understanding and tolerance—and it is in the spaces of this aporia that Europe construct its forms of race and racism.

The hegemony of the European canon of music and by extension European music history notwithstanding, concepts of race do not necessarily predominate in the discourses on European art music, or, for that matter, on European folk and popular music. With the exception of the anti-Semitic language that characterized German musical discourse during the Nazi era, race is very difficult to distinguish from other attributes of Otherness in European music (Elscheková and Elschek 1996). Stated more bluntly, the quartet of socio-aesthetic attributes that Americans are wont to insist upon—race, ethnicity, class, gender—does not apply, or rather, is not applied, to European musics. Ethnicity, for example, takes on several other forms, bracketed on one side by "minority group" and on the other by "nationalism."[10] Minority music culture, moreover, stands in a dialectical relation with national music culture, which, it follows, represents the majority of the nation's residents.

Austria, to take one nation in which the musical constructs of difference are historically very complex, contains many different minority music cultures. There are border provinces in which linguistic minorities have their own musics, such as Slovenians in Carinthia. There

are urban neighborhoods in Austria's larger cities that have historically contained immigrants from outside Austria, such as the largely
Czech district, Favoriten, or the Jewish Second District, Leopoldstadt,
in Vienna. There are musics of religious minorities—for example, Jews,
but also Protestant Christians and Muslims—and these too constitute
minority musics. Roma peoples, even when they are the most prevalent
performers of urban popular music, are designated as minorities who
produce minority music. By no means is the mapping of musical difference onto minorities an atavistic holdover from the Habsburg Monarchy and its colonial control of Eastern Europe. In 1994, designated
as the "Year of the Minorities" in Austria, gays and lesbians also acquired the designation of minority, and institutions of minority culture
within the gay and lesbian community were officially recognized (see
Initiative Minderheitenjahr 1994). The crucial point here is that, as
more and more groups were sanctioned as minorities, discourses on
race, ethnicity, and even gender became more and more contradictory.
The situation is not simply one of semantics, because Austria has undergone a dramatically sharp rise in racism during the mid and late
1990s (e.g., terrorist bombings and murders in Roma communities) that
has been almost impossible to sort out from the parallel rise of nationalism emblematized by Jörg Haider's Freedom Party. Under such circumstances, when anything and everything can be minority, many become blinded to even the most overt displays of racism.

By and large, the European rhetorics of nationalism do not include a
semantic place for race, often because they affirm a history in which race
did not exist as a separate category. The new language of ethnicity derives and then tautologically confirms a history that was blind to racial
difference. Even in the 1990s, the concept of ethnicity largely extends to
previous forms of national and regional alignment. Beginning in the
1960s, for example, a new concept of "interethnicity" began to apply
to the interaction between and among linguistic and ethnic minorities
in Eastern Europe (see Weber-Kellermann 1978). Interethnic cultures,
according to this theory, formed in regions such as Transylvania,
which contained (and still does contain) Romanian, Hungarian, German, Ukrainian, Roma, and Jewish communities. Interethnicity may
well account for the historical uniqueness of the region (e.g., the deliberate settlement of German farmers after the retreat of the Ottoman
Empire from Europe in the seventeenth and eighteenth centuries), but
it utterly ignores the presence of race in that historical uniqueness (e.g.,
the full impact of the Holocaust on one of the largest concentrations of

Jewish and Roma communities in Europe). Race simply fails to make an appearance on the modern landscape of interethnic exchange.

It would be unfair, however, to suggest that race does not appear in the racial imagination of Europe in the late twentieth century. It does, and it bears the markers of a moral dilemma in modern society. According to many, however, race is not Europe's problem, but America's. In the European racial imagination, race and racism afflict American music; race is, moreover, often fetishized as an American condition, whose impact is all the more intense because of the absence of tradition, that is, of a sustained music history that can be claimed nationalistically as German, French, or Hungarian. By fetishizing race in American music, European music undergoes a process of deracination. To speak of "Jewish music in Austria" is to employ a contradiction; to talk about "Gypsy music in Hungary" is to make a sweeping generalization about a minority group that distinguishes itself only by playing the music of others. There is, in other words, no lack of terms to apply to the presence of music in the European racial imagination; those terms simply fail to separate race from other categories of difference.

It would be tempting to attribute European distantiations of race as a semantic problem or at least a discursive dilemma. It is, as many essays in this volume demonstrate, far more complicated than that. At root, the European racial imagination is most profoundly affected by what we might call an ecological dilemma: a failure to provide economic, physical, cultural, and religious space for all those seeking it. Minority groups share what remains after the majority has sufficiently managed to implement a hegemonic culture; racial groups, however, are denied even the spoils. It is the failure to win a place in the ecology of European culture that undergirds the racialization of certain groups. Throughout much of European history—well into the nineteenth century—Jews were denied the right to own land; Romas, as the European historical narrative tells it, wander from place to place, and therefore require none of their own; Turkish guest workers in modern Germany cannot become citizens, even when they are born in Germany of Turkish parents. The more space is at a premium, the more racial exclusion insinuates itself into the European imaginary of selfness.

In the New Europe at the end of the twentieth century, there may be no better evidence that music is more intensely present than ever in the European racial imagination than the tendency to look beyond the borders of Europe for race and racism. Just as history—and music history—provide a rhetoric of displacement, they also have the power to identify the rupture that displacement leaves. Historically, Europe has been implicated as no other place in the ways music has been employed to construct race and to undergird racism. Music and race interact far too often in the history of Europe and in the history of Western art music to sustain attempts to deny race and to silence the ways in which music calls attention to racism.

GLOBAL CIRCUMSTANCES

It would be misleading and dangerous to limit our discussion of music's presence in the construction of race to the American and European conditions outlined in previous sections. As a signifier within the broad discursive space of the imperium, race casts its lot variously, assuming new appearances from station to station. The historical interplay between the musical and the racial has in turn fostered new, global interpolations that have heightened the effects of both. Race, one might say, also inhabits the world's musical house. It is the modern's realization of an imagined premodern unity, the artificial construct of the mythic "universal language."

In this section, therefore, we shift our attention from the West to the racialized conditions of music that do not primarily depend on American and European history. This shift in focus, however, should not lead the reader to believe that we are trying to cover the rest of the world. Whereas we may have attempted certain gestures during the long course of editing this volume that we hoped would enhance the inclusivity of representation, we eventually determined that this strategy would fail. As such, we seek merely to account for the broader determinations of racial-musical meaning that inform local practices, and to acknowledge how these articulations emerge rationally from the interplay of indigenous inventions within the legacy of the colonial project. Rather than moving horizontally—across the globe, so to speak—we have chosen to make a series of moves that identify what we believe are the most crucial circumstances affecting music with a postcolonial racial matrix.

Origins and Authenticity

The power of musical ownership that is so essential to the racial imagination has an extraordinarily global presence. In the most universal sense, the condition whose presence is most global is that of authenticity, the assertion that a particular music is ineluctably bound to a given group or a given place.[11] In the diverse historiographies of music, authentic music is that which bears witness to the "origins" of music—geographical, historical, and cultural. The assertion that certain traits of African-

American music are fundamentally African is fundamental to claims of authenticity in the African diaspora, whether in North America and South America, or along the Atlantic littoral. The claims for authenticity for Jamaican reggae and Brazilian *capoeira*, the first connected to Ethiopia, the second to Angola, are different only in kind, for both depend more extensively on historically fluid notions of the larger African diaspora.

Place has an even more specific role in the ways authenticity was claimed for Jewish music, for it was not only the music of *Eretz Yisrael* ("Land of Israel") but the Temple that contexutalized true Jewish music, particularly in a diaspora where the authentic had been lost. By returning to the point of origins, it would be possible again the reclaim authenticity. Indeed, the concern for authenticity lends itself to a complex of metaphors about origins and their unalterability, for example, when the "African elements" are identified in the musics of the Americas, or when music of the Ashkenazic synagogue in the diaspora was thought to maintain liturgical music linked directly to the Temple in Jerusalem, whereas the less authentic liturgical music of post-reconquista Sephardic synagogues in North Africa had been polluted by Arabic musical influences.

The musicological resonance of the term "authenticity" might at first seem to imply an objectification and potential commodification of music itself—for instance, "early music" as an essentialized and technologically reproducible object—and we would argue that this modern, if not postmodern, use of authenticity is not irrelevant to the ways in which authenticity contains the conditions of racialized musics. The rhetoric of origins is designated by a vocabulary that is rich in its diversity yet subtly nuanced in the ways that vocabulary is employed and understood. We further recognize global conditions for the authentication of race in music through terms such as biologicism, organicism, naturalness, or species specificity (cf. Blacking 1995b). In the language of nationalism, music that grows organically from the soil of a particular nation is *ipso facto* more natural, more authentic, because it is nourished by sources to which no other nation has access. Musical talent and certain types of physical disposition—dance, rhythm, even heightened mystical capacities—are similarly confused as being more natural for some races than for others.

The globalization driven by the world-music motor of transnational recording industries has rather unabashedly reinvented earlier forms of authenticity, remolding these into postmodern journeys in search of the "natural musician." World-music collectors, therefore, appoint themselves as the saviors who will rescue what is left of musical origins. The vocabulary of the postmodern search for authenticity makes it possible to construct a neomythology of musical and racial origins. The origins that one identifies and saves by bounding a world music is imagined to be a condition of prehistory. The origins of an authentic music existed prior to the construction of race, in a timeless world when the conflicts between different peoples did not affect the racial purity of music. We question whether the postmodern search for authenticity is fundamentally distinct from earlier attempts to racialize music by insisting on the naturalness of its origins. Their similarities, quite the contrary, lead us to argue strongly for a larger, more variegated music history that accounts for as many global circumstances as possible in the intersection of music with the racial imaginary.

Migrations

"Migration," on the surface, suggests the antithesis of origin, for in music's transmission it is necessarily decentered, displaced from that which is first and authentically "real." In fact, displacements have been as much a part of world music's history as the emergence of firsts from native soil (MacAllester 1979). We know that people have always traveled, bringing with them customs and habits, and those habits have changed as part of the process. Indeed, the observed linguistic and "racial" variations that change gradually across geographical space reflect patterns of contact as much as they have served to demarcate difference. So, too, with music can we observe points of stability identifying "native expression," just as they reveal upon a closer look prior entrances and exchanges—those trajectories of influence which ethnomusicology has historically defined as "transmission." Court practices and instrumentations of Japan owe to the influence of China; instrumental prototypes of Europe trace to the Middle East; scalar forms and rhythmic patterns of India bear resemblances to those found in Arabic, Persian, and Central Asian cultures. With the rise of colonialism, moreover, transmissions escalated with the repetition of exchanges between the colonizer and colonized, while also influencing processes of intracultural borrowing. The mestizo musics of the Americas reflect intersections of Spanish and native practices as they identify the emergence of new expressions (and corresponding racial specifications) specific to New World encounter; the endurance of the court gamelan in Java may be attributed as much to the European reification of "high culture" as to its importance within a local hierarchy (Sumarsam 1995). These are but a few examples in a world history of countless cross-referential engagements.

Historically, studies of migration have commonly stressed continuities over their disruptions. In this way, they have perpetuated the "salvage" approach first forged in nineteenth-century folkloristics, which sought to establish the vernacular essences and authenticities from which new versions proceeded (Bendix 1997). As we have seen, music has played a central role in this formulation, largely owing to its proposed metaphysical uniqueness as an artifact of the racial imagination. As part of the critique of racial essences, cultural studies scholars, particularly those working in Afro-American studies, have more recently challenged this devotion to continuity in order to expose the inevitably hybrid "forms" that occupy nearly all cultural terrain (e.g., Gilroy 1993, Adell 1994, Awkward 1995). That this process of encounter has quickened as a result of colonial contact should not obscure the extent to which it also describes a pre-colonial and possibly "natural" human state. This is no less so for music—despite theories of slow processes of change proposed by Lomax (1959: 930), Blacking (1977), and others—whose placeness and fixity must always be seen as a momentary pause extending from prior intersections and shifts. That music has nonetheless served as a kind of center within even "postmodern" interpretations reveals the extent to which a racial metaphysics lives on in the very efforts to demystify the interpretation of culture.[12]

Simultaneously centers of new belonging and products of a prior realm, musical migrations express a paradoxical concentration of sameness and difference consistent with the ontologies of form discussed above. That each new center reveals a prior past is never enough to cease the process of centering and naming, for these truth claims remain central to the musical constitution of identities. Such formations of the authentic develop from the image of diaspora long associated with Jewish history. More recently, in the United States particularly, they are most frequently drawn in reference to African-American music, which owns a legacy of authentic sites: the totalized "slave culture," the Mississippi Delta, a succession of urban terrains from early modern New Orleans to the late twentieth-century Bronx. Significantly, these sites of the authentic grow from a textual web narrating other, prior racial realms: the Jewish shtetl, the Scottish border, the Italian-American ghetto. So too have they contributed to new discourses of authenticity constructing new origins across the transnational soundscape: heavy metal in Jakarta, rock-based performance experiments in Ljubljana, polka in Wisconsin, a romanticized Sinatra heralded as the icon of hip hop masculinity (Gennari 1996). "Origins" necessarily give way to prior positions which destabilize fixities of place.

Mediation

If migrations challenge musical continuity as they narrate new memories of a "changing same" (Jones 1966), mediation destabilizes those centers as it magnifies their invented coherences. First through the circulation of 78-rpm recordings, then via radio and television transmission, and now with the distribution of the compact disc and a Third-World black market of cassettes, music has become increasingly disembodied from its modes of production, enabling new processes of consumption together with new forms of colonization. Listeners may now acquire these recorded musics and give them specific, local meaning; yet so do they comprehend these musics within a global economy that provides, free of charge, matrices of meaning articulated, if not regulated and controlled, by the transnational institutions of mass-marketed entertainment (Erlmann 1996). Significantly, the saturation of culture that this electronic-age circulation provides is for the consumer at once more distant and more familiar: as the artist moves further from the listener through the economy of purchase, so does the consumer imagine a more intimate connection to the totality of "global sound." It is in this ever-increasing proliferation of sonic fragmentation—and the new densities of space and place it constructs—that one finds attached corresponding formations of the authentic and real; with each displacement the "truth" of place and origin seems to rise in value (Harvey 1989).

And so are revealed in the many versions of popular music tracing across the metropoles new rhetorics of the folk vernacular which repeat as they reinscribe modernity's never-ending quest for the authentic. That these rhetorics of authenticity have been occupied with discernibly American racial figures betrays the colonizing effects of a United States empire without colonies. In popular forms from Tokyo to Cairo, Havana to Brazzaville, the imagic power of "blackness" appears as a dislocated, fragmentary hypertext of post–World War II American popular sound—soul, rock 'n' roll, disco, jazz, funk, hip hop. Yet in their affecting rhythmic projections they colonize as they inhabit (Feld 1996). For in rhythm one finds not simply the "groove" that regulates all global sound, but the figure of liberation inextricably linked to a highly problematic romance of race (Keil and Feld 1994). If, moreover, these musics speak to the globalizing effects of a worldbeat and the various local articulations that they inform, so do they communicate the success of a State Department agenda to populate the music market with American signifiers of "freedom" created by the progeny of those this nation had once enslaved (Von Eschen 1997). The "difference" of Othered sound speaks at once to a new kind of mediated closure and the absolute fracture of prior coherences, which, in turn, inspire new imaginations of belonging.

Public Sphere/Public Culture

At the end of the twentieth century, then, musical instantiations of race flood the public sphere in countries throughout the world. If no music is excluded from world music, then the globalization of world music would seem to have created a set of postmodern conditions in which space and place are no longer a problem. Any given music might take its place in numerous racial imaginations, might participate in countless struggles against hegemony. The globalization of Celtic music, for example, has resulted from far more than filiopietistic celebration in an imaginary Celtic diaspora. Politically charged in many of its local forms, Irish folk music can and does potentially resist anything from the British presence in Northern Ireland to the Palestinian struggle in the Middle East (e.g., the band Men of No Property) to Spanish colonialism in the New World (e.g., the Chieftains on their Grammy-winning CD, *Santiago* [1996]).

To some extent, we have reached what then appears as the farthest extreme from the point at which we began this section. If any world music can occupy any space or, for that matter, innumerable spaces, then what is the meaning of authenticity? On the global musical marketplace, race is a slippery signifier, for its musical capital is considerable. Musics whose origins would seem irrefutibly racial are no longer bounded by a locally relevant racial framework. In what ways have the blues, for example, not been appropriated? Which national and linguistic popular music has not spawned "its own" forms of rap music? We might ask the question whether the local conditions of music, those that are most potently constitutive of racial resistance, have ceased to exist, or whether the local in music is inevitably propelled along a global trajectory. Is the public culture of music actually a new hegemony, albeit a palpable field that opens itself to resistance for the local at all times?

This welter of questions, some rhetorical, others begging for answers that we are not yet fully prepared to offer, is surely unfair, but it brings new perspectives to the sea change that informs so many of the essays in this book and that was the primary motivation for our decision to undertake the book in the first place. At the end of the twentieth century, all evidence indicates that music is playing an even more powerful role in the construction of racial imaginaries. The sea change is a result of realignments between the local and the public, between the musics of place and the musics of displacement. The global circumstances for world music are radically different today from those a generation ago. Just as race is more evident in the globalization of music, however, contemporary musical scholarship and the disciplines mustered under the umbrella of cultural studies are only beginning to struggle with the task of sorting out meaning from the explosion of musical practices and their dissemination across a global landscape. These new musics should provide a means of shaping a new chapter in a music history of the present. To do so, however, would require the radical realignment of disciplinary boundaries, the challenge of which we address in the next section.

AFTER THE SILENCE OF THE HOLOCAUST

As the new millennium approaches, the call for an end to racism and to the modern and postmodern preoccupations with race has crescendoed into an almost deafening cacophony. It would seem as if almost no modern scholarly discipline, whether in the humanistic, social scientific, or biological studies, wants to be denied a place in the debate, and yet the motivation for staking that claim is to state conditions for ending the debate itself. To enter into the debate requires that one also have some strategy, or formula, for ending the debate. From the Right, from the Left, and from the middle, the voices arguing for an end to racism are louder and more public than ever. They are also more political than ever, which has also reconfigured the ways in which they influence the political discussions and policies of the public sphere.

It is hardly surprising that the voices from the Left have intensified their battle against racism. African-American scholars and scholarship, which have so very much at stake in the race debates, have taken the lead in restating the ways in which race concentrates the most critical intellectual questions of the 1990s. In much continental European scholarship, it is the "Old Left" that has most aggressively raised the banner in the fight to end racism. The Old Left is, of course, the loose coalition of Marxist scholarship that has reconfigured its most pressing intellectual and political agendas for a post-communist Europe and a post-nationalist world. The activist engagement with race is fundamental to what has become a transition of the Old Left into the New Left, which has shifted its activities from localized political tactics to globalized moral imperatives (see, e.g., the essays in Fischer and Wölflingseder 1995).

The entrance of the conservative and reactionary Right into the debates about ending racism, on the other hand, was for many quite surprising, if not disturbing. In the United States, the Right has turned to race as a means of bolstering its arsenal in the culture wars. Insisting that

American culture continues to bear the scars of a history of racial differences, so the argument goes, only perpetuates the destructive influences of that history. The spokespeople for the Right's call for an end to racism, notably Dinesh D'Souza (1995), appeal to an objectification of race and a rationalization of the conditions of racism. The insidious message behind the Right's argument is that American society is now "multiracial," thereby reflecting an organic transformation of racism itself. In D'Souza's "new vision for a multiracial society," therefore, he would like Americans to place race in a somehow gentler perspective. "Racism," according to D'Souza, "undoubtedly exists, but it no longer has the power to thwart blacks or any other group in achieving their economic, political, and social aspirations" (1995: 525). The Right's claim, therefore, is that racism will die a natural death, and so, again, nature is invoked to obfuscate the reasons that American society historically failed to stem its racialization of itself.[13]

The different political perspectives and motivations in the voices raised against racism notwithstanding, there is also a rather disturbing sameness that inflects the message they bear. One reason for what might arguably be called a discursive gray-out is the hopefulness—indeed, a shockingly optimistic, almost millennial belief that it has become possible really to implement an end to racism—that pervades all perspectives. Even the most radical of the African-American feminist voices, bell hooks, takes an unabashedly positive stance when looking toward the future.

> Progressive feminist writing on the issue of race and racism . . . is fundamentally optimistic even as it is courageously and fiercely critical precisely because it emerges from concrete struggles on the part of diverse groups of women to work together for a common cause, forging a politics of solidarity. . . . In counter hegemonic race talk I testify in this writing—bear witness to the reality that our many cultures can be remade, that this nation can be transformed, that we can resist racism and in the act of resistance recover ourselves and be renewed. (hooks 1995: 6–7)

Hooks calls for a "politics of solidarity," a middle road for the struggle against racism. It is the middle road, moreover, that all calls for the end to racism would take as their own, and this is what is most remarkable, for it is on the middle road that differences really do cease to exist, where racism disappears by dint of its alternative, hybridity.

In contrast to the pre-millennial rhetoric calling for an end to the weight of race's presence in postmodern society, an alternative strategy for facing race today has also emerged in recent scholarship, a strategy that can best be understood by returning again to the historical framework David A. Hollinger (1995) has proposed for the post-multicultural era in the United States. Whereas Hollinger has suggestively recast the diversity and difference that variously constituted ethnicity as "postethnicity," it would seem no less compelling to extend this framework beyond the American geographical and cultural borders to consider the possibility of a "postracial" world. In the postethnic America described by Hollinger the borders separating one ethnic group from another are simply no longer relevant. The mix and remix, the hybridity and realignment of ethnic cultures are too extensive. It is simply a given in an America where choosing between ethnicities results from affiliation, not from biological, linguistic, or religious predetermination. So why shouldn't race also involve choice and affiliation as responses to the global collapse of borders and boundaries, and to transnational realignments?

It would be very convenient if the answer to this question were a simple and easy affirmation of a globalization of its application to the United States. But it is precisely because ethnicity and race are not isomorphic categories that allow a shift from American to global perspectives that the essays in this book do not lead us to that affirmation. The logic speaks for itself: the breaking down of racial boundaries and differences has been one result of postcolonial histories. It is the question of realignment and, more to the point, of affiliation that gives us pause. Moreover, whereas the recourse to a rhetoric of hybridity is indeed attractive, it becomes more fragile—and not less fully convincing— through its globalization. Is all hybridity the same?

The postmodern and postmulticultural appeals for rapprochement with race depend to a rather remarkable degree on a contemporary willingness to accept that a world, once marked by differences, has now undergone a sea change to become a world unraveling into hybridities. At some time in the 1990s, the sea change whose tides brought an undertow of hybridity with them rather completely washed away the distinctions within world music. The late 1990s rhetoric about world music, like the late 1990s reimagination of a postethnic America, takes hybridity in music as a given. The attempts from only a half-decade ago to articulate the historical conditions for music that was hybrid, say, because of the transnationalism of the African diaspora (see, most notably, Gilroy 1993), today seem, well, unexceptionable. No one really denies the transnational mix. It comprises what ethnomusicologists and the recording industry alike call "world music." It provides new genres and classificatory systems for popular-music scholarship, the study of mass culture, and cultural studies. The transnational mix has not erased race from music, but rather it has recontextualized it. We argue that this recontextualization has brought about an even more critical confrontation between race and music.

Surely, no essay in this book accepts any racial or ethnic boundedness in the musics the authors interrogate. To talk about race and music means crossing boundaries, embracing the mixture of genre and repertory, and accepting that race is everywhere in music. Race is everywhere in music, and it is precisely this given that has the potential of seducing us into being deaf to its presence. The question that his book raises at this millennial juncture in the musical scholarship that addresses race and ethnicity, difference and hybridity, is whether it, too, has an end in sight, such as the "end of racism" that both the Right and the Left are calling for. The essays in this book militate against the rhetoric that foresees an end to race and racism. When the authors turn to music in the racial imagination, the evidence just isn't there. World music and postmodern hybridities have yet to eliminate racial barriers, and they show no signs of masking the conditions that give rise to racial differences.

Seen in this light, the musical scholarship that the different authorial perspectives in this book represent is not resonant but dissonant when compared with the premillennial call for ending racism. Rather than closing the spaces around the human suffering wrought by racism, the musics examined here suggest that music may provide one of the most powerful media for listening to and understanding what it is that racism continues to do on a global scale. Music gives voice to racial difference, and music ring with the rupture and fragmentation that afflicts humans because of their race throughout the world. We don't deny that there is an alternative to listening to the music that is so inseparable from the racial imagination, but we would struggle against invoking it. That alternative is, of course, silence.

It is silence that has historically posed the greatest danger to confronting the insidious destruction of racism, silence as the hopeful belief that racism will just come to an end. Music, of course, resists silence, and music has the power to undo the historical aporia of silence. The danger posed by silence is most evident in the memory-politics that confront assertions that the Holocaust was a unique historical phenomena, utterly irreplicable and thus irrelevant as a means of representing racism in post-Holocaust Europe. The resistance to silence acknowledges the real-life, contemporary effects of centuries of slavery in the United States. To look above and beyond these realities is to invoke

the privilege of silence. Silence pushes the racism of slavery into someone else's history, and it insists on the distance between that history and
our own.

Such notions of historical silence, however, neglect the traces of
racism that refuse to be silenced because their audibility survives. More
specifically, music gives voice to those silenced by racism. We witness
such a returning of voice in the hip-hop movement that has overtaken
American popular music since the early 1980s. We witness such a returning, too, in the music of the Holocaust, in Viktor Ullmann's 1943
opera *Der Kaiser von Atlantis* [The emperor of Atlantis], composed in the
concentration camp Theresienstadt/Terezín without hope of performance because of the modeling of the character of Death [der Tod] after
Hitler in Peter Kien's libretto. Indeed, *Der Kaiser von Atlantis* was the
final major composition of Ullmann, who would be killed in Auschwitz
in 1944. To rescue such a work from silence therefore confronts racism
because it forces us to take into consideration the very racist attitudes
toward music that play a role in narrating the Holocaust.[14]

Silence has also served as a racialist weapon because of the power ac-
crued to it through the failure to listen to the music of powerless and
voiceless peoples. We mean to call here for the imperative of listening
to the musics of Roma peoples or the sacred practices of Muslim peoples,
whose needs are erased by the silencing gestures of nationalism in the
1990s. We mean to draw attention to the silencing of resistance groups
in Indonesia and Chile, to the invisibility of America's "truly disadvan-
taged," whose socio-economic position and cultural stigma are inseparable from racial differences. The silence of the underclass is unques-
tionably a racial silence, which nonetheless has the potential to gain a
new voice in the Hispanic and African American urban musics of the
1990s. Listening to or into the silence powerfully forestalls us from
imagining that an "end to racism" is on or just beyond the horizon; the
audible evidence convinces us that the history of racism just does not
end in this way. In essence the essays in this book argue for a sort of
racial listening that accounts for a "postsilence," thereby reconfiguring
the history of music and the racial imagination to include the present
and the future.

MUSICOLOGY'S RECONSTRUCTION

What role might the musicologies play in this call for a new racial hearing? Despite some notable exceptions, our discipline presently manages

still to avoid the more pressing controversies surrounding the legacy of cross-determinations between the musical and the racial. To an extent this reflects the endurance of established paradigms of scholarship and the personal choices scholars make in their quest for knowledge. Too often, however, musicological investigation appears content with its circumscribed agendas of musical meditation and exotic isolationism. Scholars increasingly complain about their position on the margins as they resist an outward focus; the rigors of formal musical training prove limiting when we are asked to face the larger social matters in which the subject of music increasingly finds itself. And so, we leave to our colleagues in other disciplines—in literature, history, sociology, philosophy—the challenge of establishing the place of the musical within the wider study of politics and culture. There is, of course, no reason to seek a reversal of this arrangement, to bully our way in and establish musicological authority. As the essays in this volume reveal, some of the most compelling research on musical meaning comes from those working beyond the bounds of music schools and departments. And yet it is our hope that the musicologies might rise, so to speak, to the occasion and find their way in the emerging national and international conversation on race, for it is in music that the racial resonates most vividly, with greatest affect and power.

It is, of course, reasonable for musicologists to exclude themselves from these more pressing social concerns. For, as we have shown, to face them brings with it the necessity of acknowledging the racialist background of the discipline's own making. To address the racial qualities behind the modern conception of musical power would mean observing the formation of the discipline within this same ideological background. And to face this would also mean recognizing the legacy of exclusion that still privileges Europe and those seemingly static non-Western "music cultures." It would mean ultimately rewriting what Du Bois called in his study of Black Reconstruction the "propaganda of history," those "lies agreed upon . . . [which] allow no room for the real plot of the story" (Du Bois [1935] 1992: 714–15).

In our call for musicology's reconstruction, then, we imagine something more than the common practices of newness of recent years. The newness we propose is one that begins with the revelations of the racial in order to foster interpretive procedures that reveal the ideological underpinnings of our enduring disciplinary color line, of the distance we maintain between "the West and the rest." We seek to do so not to cast blame—whom could we blame, in any case?—but rather to unseat this division's regressive, debilitating effects. Newness after the silence would mean the opening of the musical disciplines to face matters of race directly as a way of framing new territories of musical exploration and observing the dynamics of difference that so profoundly inform music's affective power. The call for reflexive methodologies reveals, in turn, the need for tools that meet the challenges of critical study of society and culture. And yet in its effort to catch up with others so long after the linguistic turn, musicology risks its own deracinated "race for theory" (Christian 1987), of reaffirming the hierarchies of privilege and difference as it shifts focus from the cloistered realm of aesthetic enchantment to a putatively political yet ultimately exclusionary infatuation with post-structuralism's magic. We hope for more pragmatic, socially grounded, and broadly populist engagements that recognize the real-life consequences of musical experience within the cross trajectories of a diverse historical past—richly populated beyond the court and church—and the diverse locales of the global present. As musicology emerges after the silence, it will no doubt re-invent itself variously. Yet within this range we hope for no small measure of attention focusing on the concerns of those millions outside the concert hall for whom music plays such a profound, constitutive role.

So begins the imagination of a new musicology emerging from "the space-clearing gestures" of a transnational, postcolonial world (Appiah 1991). The "posts" of musicology identify its legacies: the European, the ethnic. These are legacies not to disavow, but to determine within a new relation, between a prior racial supremacy that nonetheless establishes modes of critical reflection and analytical rigor, and a darker complected, self-reflexive avenue of exploration of a mulatto "new." Such calls for a post-Europeanist, post-ethnic musical scholarship seek not to do away with the legacies of interpretation that have become us, but to clear a space for the inclusion of new, progressive programs that speak to the multiplex considerations revealing the musical within the racial. It is a call for a space-clearing that enables the exploration of a cultural phenomenon that still today can sustain collective dreams of universal language as it serves to demarcate color-bound difference. Through such working from within the racial/musical complex, we might begin to comprehend the motivations of our own aesthetic desires, to understand how we as a nation could proclaim an invisible, seemingly inconsequential sonic phenomenon "the most beautiful expression of human experience born this side of the seas" (Du Bois [1903] 1989: 178).

Epilogue

The Place of Race 4: Millennial Transit

Wherever one turns in the post-Holocaust Europe of the 1990s, one encounters klezmer music. No weekend passes in Berlin without the opportunity to attend several different, which is to say, countless, klezmer concerts. Klezmer has been all the rage for the past few years, since the *Wende,* and klezmer bands have become a ubiquitous marker of a reunified Germany. Klezmer music, moreover, fits any context. Nightclubs and sundry street festivals are obvious contexts; intermission entertainment at the opera or appearances at village wine and beer festivals are less obvious contexts. Similarly, klezmer can be a context for just about any music. Though traditionally an instrumental music, European klezmer includes extensive repertories of Yiddish song, especially songs and sounds marked "Hassidic."

The political message and the cultural imperative of postmodern Europe is that it is in transit. There is little doubt about what it is in transition *from;* there is little consensus about what it is in transition *to.* The omnipresence of klezmer is a metonym for Europe's millennial transit, for it arises from and depends on the stasis of Europe's current transitory postmodernism. The public traces of klezmer are notable for the ways they adhere to billboards, to the pages of free newspapers cluttering subway stops, and, above all, to the pedestrian passageways that wend their ways through construction zones. These are the *Passagen*—the Benjaminian arcades (Benjamin 1982)—of a reunified Europe, as it recovers its past to rebuild its future. "The Chicago–Berlin Express— Klesmer aus der Neuen Welt [Klezmer from the New World]" announces the repetitious litany of posters wallpapering the passageworld that connects East Berlin's socialist–realist past to its capitalist future, via the memorialization of the Nazi Era. As "Jewish music," klezmer has special meaning for Germans, and in the 1990s it has become the music that symbolizes race and racism in the public sphere of post-Holocaust Germany more than any other.

And yet, that public sphere of a unified Europe is itself transitory. It is as if race and its music are best accommodated to the present by fitting them to the spaces in-between, to those transitory surfaces that are always present but which one briskly puts behind oneself. The spaces of transit, however, are themselves everywhere, and these are the spaces that music empowers race to occupy. The spaces of race are those of the racial imagination, the spaces where races refuse to go away.

In the New Europe klezmer nostalgically contextualizes the Old World—the American band "Brave Old World" enjoys enormous success—especially the 1920s and 1930s, when jazz and other black musics putatively resisted a Europe spinning uncontrollably down the road toward fascism. In 1990s Europe the difference between black music and Jewish music blurs in klezmer. It's both. And it's more, for there's Roma music in the new mix. No one says there's Roma music in the mix, but rather that it has a "Gypsy flavor."[15] Then again, no one would say that it is Jewish or black music. The music masks such racial categories. They are present but they are also invisible and inaudible. Everyone knows they are present, but the music makes it possible to imagine they are not. The music provides a site for unleashing the racial imagination, but it serves as a reminder of the consequences of the racial imagination unchecked. In post-Holocaust Europe klezmer has become a public site for confronting and reimagining the disastrous consequences of a century given historical meaning by the struggle with and against race. Klezmer, in the Old World or the New Europe, does not exist alone. Klezmer is therefore one of the metonyms for the ways in which music and race open the historical spaces of the racial imagination throughout this book.

Klezmer in the United States, however, passes along quite a different millennial transit, for rather than the geographical passageways of postmodernity, American klezmer provides the crucial temporal element in the construction of Jewish modernity. Klezmer proliferated in the United States earlier than in Europe, and in doing so it was motivated by the belief that it functioned as a metonym for survival in the diaspora during the Holocaust. In the United States, klezmer musicians who had immigrated early in the twentieth century provided revivalists the opportunity of learning the old traditions (see Slobin 1982). The oral traditions of klezmer music therefore provided a simulacrum for authenticity writ large. Learning at the feet of Dave Tarras, for example, allowed one to bridge the past and the present.

That bridge, nonetheless, crossed over the aporia of the Holocaust. The authenticity that sometimes becomes obsessive for American revivalists lies in the music itself, and we witness another case in which claims for a musically grounded authenticity requires deracializing. The authenticity of klezmer, moreover, depends on a willingness to dehistoricize it, which is achieved by returning it to the ghetto, to the "Judengasse,"[16] and to the temporalized public spaces of ritual. Circumcisions and weddings, the signifiers of birth and reproduction, become the sites for klezmer, but so too do the pathways of death, also given metaphorical meaning by the Judengasse. The place of race, therefore, is again transitory, but it enters history not as the narrative of race and racism that would silence European klezmer musicians, but rather as the dehistoricized, deracialized music of timeless ritual (see *Klezmer Music* 1996).

Why race? It's not simply that klezmer is Jewish music, with Roma and black histories running through it. More to the point, in the European public sphere Jews, Roma, and blacks largely do not play klezmer music. Indeed, there are rarely Jews, Roma, and blacks in the audiences at klezmer concerts. Klezmer in Europe is a music made by the Other for the Other—it constantly affirms its Old World status—and as such it confirms a deracialized Self. The racial mix that complicated the history of klezmer prior to the Holocaust's historical assault on racial difference disappears in the 1990s, effaced as the New Europe recuperates some histories and erases others. In post-Holocaust Europe, there is little public discourse about race. Which is not to say that the history of race is never present, but rather it accrues to a politics of the Right and its aggression and violence against guest workers in Central Europe, and against immigrants from former colonies in western and northwestern England. The economic conflict between South and North is everywhere reduced to black vs. white—that is, to a racial and racist vocabulary that Europe shares with the rest of the world. It is hard to talk about race because that would admit to the reality that the horror of the Holocaust might again be possible. Calling it race makes it real again, today, not yesterday.

Why music? That's the question that this book eventually poses. Is race embedded in music and related expressive practices, such as dance, in particularly powerful ways? Does music mark race? Or does music reproduce the traces of race, thereby perpetuating the racial imagination itself? For many it may seem that making a case for music's culpability in the reproduction of racial stereotypes is empirically unsound because music is music, not race. Music is, one might argue, no more than a nonsignifying, free-floating, essentialized object. But the question "why music?" is particularly unsettling precisely because of its banality. To dismiss music as non-signifying is possible only when one ignores the power that accrues to musical practice. Music acquires power because it can be used to attribute and ascribe multivalent meanings. The moment when it seems not to signify, music becomes most significant; music acquires its very powerlessness as an object. In grappling with the question "why music?" then, the editors and many of the authors contributing to this book rethink several of their own positions in the ethnomusicological debates of recent years, particularly the forceful arguments made against essentializing music (e.g., Radano 1993, Bohlman 1993, Monson 1995). There is, instead, a political and moral imperative that necessitates returning music to contemporary discussions of race and the racial imagination. As the reality of heightened violence against racial difference forms at those borders of the social spaces that exclude the Other, music may be one of the few social practices that can truly fill those spaces. Black music fills the racialized landscape of America and the ceaseless crossings of the African Diaspora; Roma music charts historical journeys from the South Asian past no longer inhabited by Roma to the European present that is simply uninhabitable by Roma because of its always already imminent danger; and klezmer music is everywhere to be heard, indeed, in the transitory spaces of an everywhere that collapses in a history of musical silence and racial exclusion.

NOTES

1. For a critique of the ways in which musicology relies on a commitment to the music itself to deny its political and racial ideologies, see Bohlman 1993.

2. Appiah 1992, Herbert 1991, Scott 1995, Bhabha 1994, Clifford and Marcus 1986.

3. That ethnomusicological discourse still frequently relies on the uninterrogated mid-century concepts of "etic" and "emic"—derived from the linguistic theory of Kenneth Pike—makes manifest the discipline's "resistance to theory." Significantly, Pike himself was very concerned with the relational aspect of this study, which he proposed dialectically in ways that implicated the observer (see Pike 1967 [1954]).

4. This has been pursued subsequently by a range of creative scholars: among others, Robin D. G. Kelley, Tricia Rose, Herman Gray, Evelyn Higginbotham, Cornel West, Bruce Tucker, George Lipsitz, Hazel Carby, John Szwed, and others. In the musicologies, there has been a growing body of thoughtful critical work in some cases inspired by black cultural studies. See esp. Floyd 1995, Monson 1995, and Keil and Feld 1994. The bibliography of racial studies is massive. Among the noteworthy titles are: Gossett 1997, Jordan 1968, Davis 1975, Appiah 1992, Gilman and Remmler 1994, Delgado 1995, and Fishkin 1995.

5. Our use of these terms should be understood as avoiding scientistic affiliations.

6. Wallaschek's dismissal—claiming the spirituals to be mere poems set to Euro-American song—probably reflects his dissatisfaction about the enormous popularity of Fisk and other jubilee singers from the 1870s. Such views show up into the twentieth century, notably in the work of George Pullen Jackson (1943).

7. Significantly, Boas himself rarely spoke of specifically African-American

racial matters, and when he did, he voiced the patronizing rhetoric informing a legacy of thought. See Szwed 1969.

8. This imperialism was acknowledged in Merriam's depiction of the "white-knight syndrome" in ethnomusicology, as well as in Mantle Hood's highly personal portrayal of the discipline in his book *The Ethnomusicologist* (Hood 1982 [1st ed., 1971]: 1–23).

9. For a seminal challenge to the masculinization of musical analysis, see Herndon 1974.

10. For a discussion of the difficulty of establishing meanings for ethnicity in European musics, see Hemetek 1996.

11. For a rich set of essays devoted to the musical construction of place, see Stokes 1994.

12. Such mystifications can be observed, for example, in two otherwise important books on black music: Tricia Rose's *Black Noise* (1994) and Paul Gilroy's *The Black Atlantic* (1993). Gilroy, it is true, works to historicize black music's various projections. And yet in the end he adheres to a purely sonic projection of black music that enables proposals of transhistorical consistencies of transhistorical consistencies of meaning.

13. For a blisteringly brilliant interpellation of D'Souza's call to end racism, see Bérubé 1996.

14. Several performances of *Der Kaiser von Atlantis* took place in 1998, the centenary of Ullmann's birth.

15. There are several interesting exceptions, such as the "Austrian" trio, Ensemble Klezmer, whose accordionist, Mario Koutev, is Bulgarian-born Roma. The Hungarian world music ensemble Muzsikás makes a point of learning its klezmer repertory for Romas living in Transylvania, who claim themselves to have learned Jewish pieces from klezmer musicians prior to the Holocaust (see Muzsikás 1993).

16. The Judengasse [lit., "Jewish street"] was the traditional border between the Jewish quarter and the non-Jewish sectors of European cities and villages. In the historical imaginary created for klezmer music, the Judengasse was the site of most performances, even those accompanying, for example, weddings.

REFERENCES

Abbate, Carolyn. 1991. *Unsung Voices: Opera and Musical Narrative in the Nineteenth Century.* Princeton, N.J. Princeton University Press.

Abrahams, Roger D., and John F. Szwed, eds. 1983. *After Africa: Extracts from British Travel Accounts and Journals of the Seventeenth, Eighteenth, and Nineteenth Centuries Concerning the Slaves, Their Manners, and Customs in the British West Indies.* New Haven, Conn.: Yale University Press.

Adell, Sandra. 1994. *Double Consciousness, Double Bind.* Urbana: University of Illinois Press.

Adler, Guido. 1885. "Umfang, Methode und Ziel der Musikwissenschaft." *Vierteljahrsschrift für Musikwissenschaft* 1:5–20.

Adorno, Theodor W. [1932] 1988. "The Social Situation of Music." Trans. Wes
    Blomster. *Telos* 35 (Spring): 128–64.
———. 1978. "On the Fetish Character in Music and the Regression of Listen-
    ing." In Andres Arato and Eike Gebhardt, eds., *The Essential Frankfurt School
    Reader*, pp. 270–99. New York.
Agawu, V. Kofi. 1992. "Representing African Music." *Critical Inquiry* 18:
    246–66.
———. 1995. "The Invention of 'African rhythm.'" *Journal of the American Mu-
    sicological Society* 48: 380–95.
Allen, Warren Dwight. 1939. *Philosophies of Music History*. New York: American
    Book Company.
Allen, William Francis, Lucy McKim Garrison, and Charles Pickard Ware, eds.
    1867. *Slave Songs of the United States*. New York: A. Simpson and Co.
Amiot, Joseph-Marie. 1779. *Mémoire sur la musique des chinois, tant anciens que
    modernes*. Paris: Nyon.
Appiah, Kwame Anthony. 1991. "Is the Post- in Postmodernism the Post- in
    Postcolonial?" *Critical Inquiry* 17: 336–57.
———. 1992. *In My Father's House: Africa in the Philosophy of Culture*. New York:
    Oxford University Press.
Aracena, Beth. 1999. "Singing Salvation: Jesuit Musics in Colonial Chile, 1600–
    1767." Ph.D. diss., University of Chicago.
Awkward, Michael. 1995. *Negotiating Difference: Race, Gender, and the Politics of
    Positionality*. Chicago: University of Chicago Press.
Baer, Abraham. 1883. *Ba'al Tefillah, oder der practische Vorbeter*. 2nd ed. Gothen-
    borg, Sweden: Abraham Baer.
Baker, Houston A., Jr., 1984. *Blues, Ideology, and Afro-American Literature: A Ver-
    nacular Theory*. Chicago: University of Chicago Press.
Baker, Houston A., Jr., Manthia Diawara, and Ruth H. Lindeborg, eds. 1996.
    "Black British Cultural Studies." In *Black British Cultural Studies: A Reader*.
    Black Literature and Culture. Chicago: University of Chicago Press.
Beecham, John. 1841. *Ashantee and Gold Coast*. London: Dawsons of Pall Mall.
Bell, Daniel. 1960. *The End of Ideology: On the Exhaustion of Political Ideas in the
    Fifties*. Glencoe, Ill.: Free Press.
Bendix, Regina. 1997. *In Search of Authenticity: The Formation of Folklore Studies*.
    Madison: University of Wisconsin Press.
Benjamin, Walter. 1982. *Gesammelte Schriften*, vol. 5, *Das Passagen-Werk*. 2 parts.
    Ed. Rolf Tiedemann. Frankfurt am Main: Suhrkamp.
Bent, Ian, ed. 1996. *Music Theory in the Age of Romanticism*. Cambridge: Cam-
    bridge University Press.
Bérubé, Michael. 1996. "Extreme Prejudice: Dinesh D'Souza and the Coarsen-
    ing of American Conservatism." *Transition* 69: 90–98.
Bhabha, Homi K. 1994. *The Location of Culture*. New York. Routledge.
Bird, William Hamilton. 1789. *The Oriental Miscellany: Being a Collection of the
    Most Favourite Airs of Hindostan, Calcutta*. London.
Blacking, John. 1995a. *Music, Culture, and Experience: Selected Papers of John
    Blacking*. Chicago: University of Chicago Press.

———. [1977] 1995b. "The Study of Musical Change." In Blacking 1995a: 148–73.

Blum, Stephen. 1991. "European Terminology and the Music of Africa." In Nettl and Bohlman 1991: 3–36.

Bohlman, Philip V. 1987. "The European Discovery of Music in the Islamic World and the 'Non-Western' in 19th-century Music History." *The Journal of Musicology* 5: 147–63.

———. 1991. "Representation and Cultural Critique in the History of Ethnomusicology." In Nettl and Bohlman 1991: 131–51.

———. 1993. "Musicology as a Political Act." *The Journal of Musicology* 11: 411–36.

Bowdich, T. Edward. 1819. *Mission from Cape Coast Castle to Ashantee*. London: John Murray.

Brinner, Benjamin. 1993. "A Musical Time Capsule from Java." *Journal of the American Musicological Society* 46: 221–60.

Carby, Hazel V. 1986. "'It jus be's dat way sometime': The Sexual Politics of Women's Blues." *Radical America* 20 (4): 9–24

Chieftains. 1996. *Santiago*. RCA BMG 09026 68602.

Christian, Barbara. 1987. "The Race for Theory." *Cultural Critique* 6: 51–63.

Crafts, Susan D., Daniel Cavicchi, and Charles Keil, eds. 1993. *My Music*. Hanover, N.H.: Wesleyan University Press.

Clifford, James, and George Marcus, eds. 1986. *Writing Culture*. Berkeley and Los Angeles: University of California Press.

Coplan, David B. 1994. *In the Time of Cannibals: The Word Music of South Africa's Basotho Migrants*. Chicago: University of Chicago Press.

Corry, Joseph. 1807. *Observations upon the Windward Coast of Africa*. London: W. Bulmer.

Davis, David Brion. 1975. *The Problem of Slavery in the Age of Revolution, 1770–1823*. Ithaca: Cornell University Press.

Delgado, Richard, ed. 1995. *Critical Race Theory: The Cutting Edge*. Philadelphia: Temple University Press.

Densmore, Francis. 1909. "Scale Formation in Primitive Music." *American Anthropologist* 11: 1–12.

DiMaggio, Paul. 1982. "Cultural Entrepreneurship in Nineteenth-century Boston: The Creation of an Organizational Base for High Culture in America." *Media, Culture, and Society* 4 (January): 33–50.

D'Souza, Dinesh. 1995. *The End of Racism: Principles for a Multiracial Society*. New York: Free Press.

Du Bois, W. E. B. [1903] 1989. *The Souls of Black Folk*. Repr. ed. Henry Louis Gates, Jr. New York: Bantam.

———. [1935] 1992. *Black Reconstruction in America, 1860–1880*. Repr. with introduction by David Levering Lewis. New York: Atheneum.

Eagleton, Terry. 1991. *Ideology: An Introduction*. New York: Verso.

Ellis, A. B. 1883. *The Land of Fetish*. London: Chapman and Hall.

Elscheková, Alica, and Oskár Elschek. 1996. "Theorie und Praxis der

Erforschung der traditionellen Musik von Minderheiten." In Hemetek 1996a: 17–30.

Elson, Louis Charles. 1900. *The National Music of America and Its Sources*. Boston: L. C. Page.

Erlmann, Veit. 1996. "The Aesthetics of the Global Imagination: Reflections on World Music in the 1990s." *Public Culture* 8: 467–87.

Eze, Emmanuel Chukwudi, ed. 1997. *Race and the Enlightenment: A Reader*. Oxford: Blackwell.

Feld, Steven. 1996. "pygmy POP: A Genealogy of Schizophonic Music." *Yearbook for Traditional Music* 28: 1–35.

Feld, Steven, and Dennis Tedlock, eds. 1996. *A Sense of Place*. Albuquerque, N. Mex.: American School for Social Research.

Fétis, F.-J. 1869. *Histoire générale de la musique*. Paris: Librairie de Firmin Didot Frères.

Fields, Barbara. 1982. "Ideology and Race in American History." In *Region, Race, and Reconstruction: Essays in Honor of C. Vann Woodward*, ed. J. Morgan Kousser and James M. McPherson, 143–76. New York: Oxford University Press.

Fischer, Gero, and Maria Wölflingseder, eds. 1995. *Biologismus, Rassismus, Nationalismus: Rechte Ideologien im Vormarsch*. Vienna: Promedia

Fishkin, Shelley Fisher. 1993. *Was Huck Black? Mark Twain and African American Voices*. New York: Oxford University Press.

———. 1995. "Interrogating 'Whiteness,' Complicating 'Blackness': Remapping American Culture." *American Quarterly* 47: 428–66.

Floyd, Samuel A., Jr. 1995. *The Power of Black Music: Interpreting Its History from Africa to the United States*. New York: Oxford University Press.

Friedmann, Aron. 1908. *Der synagogale Gesang: Eine Studie*. 2d, expanded edition. Berlin: C. Boas Nachf. 1st ed. 1904.

Gabbard, Krin, ed. 1996. *Jammin' at the Margins: Jazz and the American Cinema*. Chicago: University of Chicago Press.

Gates, Henry Louis, Jr., and Kwame Anthony Appiah, eds. 1986. *"Race," Writing, and Difference*. Chicago: University of Chicago Press.

Geiss, Imanuel. 1988. *Geschichte des Rassismus*. Frankfurt am Main: Suhrkamp

———. 1995. "Rassismus." In Fischer and Wölflingseder 1995: 91–107.

Gennari, John. 1996. "Passing for Italian." *Transition: An International Review* 6, 4 (no. 72, Winter): 36–49.

Gikandi, Simon. 1996. *Maps of Englishness: Writing Identity in the Culture of Colonialism*. New York: Columbia University Press.

Gilman, Sander L., and Karen Remmler, eds. 1994. *Reemerging Jewish Culture in Germany: Life and Literature since 1989*. New York: New York University Press.

Gilroy, Paul. 1993. *The Black Atlantic: Modernity and Double Consciousness*. Cambridge: Harvard University Press.

Gossett, Thomas. 1997. *Race: The History of an Idea in America*, 2d ed. Race and American Culture. New York: Oxford University Press.

Gould, Stephen Jay. 1981. *The Mismeasure of Man*. New York: W. W. Norton.

Gourlay, Kenneth A. 1978. "Towards a Reassessment of the Ethnomusicologist's Role in Research." *Ethnomusicology* 22: 1–36.

———. 1982. "Towards a Humanizing Ethnomusicology." *Ethnomusicology* 26: 411–20.

Gray, Herman. 1995. *Watching Race: Television and the Struggle for "Blackness."* Minneapolis: University of Minnesota Press.

Greenblatt, Stephen. 1991 *Marvelous Possessions: The Wonder of the New World.* Chicago: University of Chicago Press.

Hall, Stuart. [1987] 1996. "New Ethnicities." In Baker, Diawara, and Lindeborg 1996: 210–22. University of Chicago Press.

Hamm, Charles. 1988. *Afro-American Music, South Africa, and Apartheid.* Brooklyn: Institute for Studies in American Music.

Hannaford, Ivan. 1996. *Race: The History of an Idea in the West.* Washington and Baltimore: The Woodrow Wilson Center and The Johns Hopkins University Press.

Harvey, David. 1989. *The Condition of Postmodernity: An Enquiry into the Origins of Cultural Change.* Oxford: Blackwell

Hemetek, Ursula, ed. 1996a. *Echo der Vielfalt/Echoes of Diversity: Traditionelle Musik von Minderheiten/ethnischen Gruppen—Traditional Music of Ethnic Groups/Minorities,* Vienna: Böhlau Verlag.

Hemetek, Ursula. 1996b. "Einführung." In Hemetek 1996a: 11–16.

Herbert, Christopher. 1991. *Culture and Anomie.* Chicago: University of Chicago Press.

Herder, Johann Gottfried. [1778–79] 1975. *"Stimmen der Völker in Liedern"* and *Volkslieder.* Stuttgart: Reclam.

Herndon, Marcia. 1974. "Analysis: The Herding of Sacred Cows." *Ethnomusicology* 18: 219–62.

Herskovits, Melville. 1941. *The Myth of the Negro Past.* New York: Harper and Brothers.

Hill, Mike, ed. 1997. *Whiteness: A Critical Reader.* New York: New York University Press.

Hollinger, David A. 1995. *Postethnic America: Beyond Multiculturalism.* New York: Basic Books.

Hood, Mantle. 1982. *The Ethnomusicologist.* 2d ed. Kent, Ohio: Kent State University Press.

hooks, bell. 1995. *Killing Rage: Ending Racism.* New York: Holt.

Horsman, Reginald. 1981. *Race and Manifest Destiny.* Cambridge: Harvard University Press.

Ibn Khaldun. [1377] 1958. *The Muqaddimah: An Introduction to History.* Trans. by Franz Rosenthal. 3 vols. New York: Pantheon.

Ignatiev, Noel. 1995. *How the Irish Became White.* New York: Routledge.

Initiative Minderheitenjahr. 1994. *Wege zu Minderheiten in Österreich: Ein Handbuch.* Vienna: Verlag der Apfel.

Jackson, George Pullen. 1943. *White and Negro Spirituals.* Locust Valley, N.Y.: J. J. Augustin.

Jones, LeRoi. 1966. "The Changing Same (R&B and New Black Music)." In *Black Music*, 180–211. New York: Morrow.

Jordan, Winthrop D. 1968. *White over Black: American Attitudes toward the Negro, 1550–1812*. Chapel Hill: University of North Carolina Press.

Keil, Charles. 1982. "Applied Ethnomusicology and a Rebirth of Music from the Spirit of Tragedy." *Ethnomusicology* 26: 407–11.

Keil, Charles, and Steven Feld. 1994. *Music Grooves*. Chicago: University of Chicago Press.

Kelley, Robin D. G. 1994. *Race Rebels: Culture, Politics, and the Black Working Class*. New York: Free Press.

Kerman, Joseph. 1985. *Contemplating Music: Challenges to Musicology*. Cambridge: Harvard University Press.

Kircher, Athanasius. 1650. *Musurgia universalis, sive ars magna consoni et dissoni*. Rome: Francesco Corbelletti.

Klezmer Music. 1996. *Klezmer Music: A Marriage of Heaven and Earth*. Ellipsis Arts 4090.

Krader, Barbara. 1980. "Ethnomusicology." In *New Grove Dictionary of Music and Musicians*, 6th ed. London: Macmillan, 6: 51–63.

Kramer, Lawrence. 1990. *Music as Cultural Practice*. Berkeley and Los Angeles: University of California Press.

Lafitau, Joseph-François. 1724. *Moeurs des sauvages amériquains, comparées aux moeurs des premiers temps*. 2 vols. Paris: Saugrain et Hochereau.

Laing, Major Alexander Gordon. 1825. *Travels in the Timannee, Kooranko, and Soolima Countries*. London: John Murray.

La Pérouse, Jean François de Galaup. 1799. *A Voyage Round the World in the Years 1785–1788*. Trans., 2d ed. London.

de Laujardière, Guillaume Chenu. 1996. *Relation d'un voyage à la côte des Cafres (1686–1689)*. Paris: Les Éditions de Paris.

de Léry, Jean. [1585] 1990. *History of a Voyage to the Land of Brazil, Otherwise Called America*. Trans. Janet Whatley. Berkeley and Los Angeles: University of California Press.

Lipsitz, George. 1994. *Dangerous Crossroads: Popular Music, Postmodernism, and the Poetics of Place*. New York: Verso

Lomax, Alan. 1959. "Folk Song Style." *American Anthropologist* 61: 927–54.

Lott, Eric. 1993. *Love and Theft: Blackface Minstrelsy and the American Working Class*. New York: Oxford University Press.

Lubiano, Wahneema, ed. 1997. *The House That Race Built: Black Americans, U.S. Terrain*. New York: Pantheon

MacAllester, David. 1979. "The Astonished Ethno-Muse." *Ethnomusicology* 23: 179–89.

McClary, Susan. 1991. *Feminine Endings: Music, Gender, and Sexuality*. Minneapolis: University of Minnesota Press.

McClintock, Anne. 1995. *Imperial Leather: Race, Gender, and Sexuality in the Colonial Context*. New York: Routledge.

Meintjes, Louise. 1990. "Paul Simon's *Graceland*, South Africa, and the Mediation of Musical Meaning." *Ethnomusicology* 34: 37–73.

Merriam, Alan P. 1959. "African Music." In *Continuity and Change in African Cultures*, ed. William R. Bascom and Melville J. Herskovits, 49–86. Chicago: University of Chicago Press.

Metfessel, Milton F. 1928. *Phonophotography in Folk Music: American Negro Songs in New Notation*. Introduction by Carl E. Seashore. Chapel Hill: University of North Carolina Press.

Michaels, Walter Benn. 1995. *Our America: Nativism, Modernism, and Pluralism*. Durham, N.C.: Duke University Press.

Monson, Ingrid. 1995. "The Problem with White Hipness: Race, Gender, and Cultural Conceptions of Jazz Historical Discourses." *Journal of the American Musicological Society* 48: 396–422.

Montaigne. 1952. *Essais*. Paris: Éditions Garnier Frères.

Muzsikás. 1993. *The Lost Jewish Music of Transylvania*. Hannibal HNCD 1373.

Nettl, Bruno, and Philip V. Bohlman, eds. 1991. *Comparative Musicology and Anthropology of Music: Essays on the History of Ethnomusicology*. Chicago: University of Chicago Press.

Pieterse, Jan Nederveen. 1992. *White on Black: Images of Africa and Blacks in Western Popular Culture*. New Haven: Yale University Press.

Pike, Kenneth L. 1954. *Language in Relation to a Unified Theory of the Structure of Human Behavior*. Glendale: Summer Institute of Linguistics. Rpr. The Hague: Mouton, 1967.

Pinkerton, John, ed. 1808–14. *A General Collection of the Best and Most Interesting Voyages and Travels in All Parts of the World: Many of Which Are Now First Translated into English; Digested on a New Plan*. 17 vols. London: Longman, Hurst, Rees, and Orme.

Potter, Pamela M. 1998. *Most German of the Arts: Musicology and Society from the Weimar Republic to the End of Hitler's Reich*. New Haven: Yale University Press.

Pratt, Mary Louise. 1992 *Imperial Eyes: Travel Writing and Transculturation*. New York: Routledge.

Radano, Ronald M. 1993. *New Musical Figurations: Anthony Braxton's Cultural Critique*. Chicago: University of Chicago Press.

———. 1996. "Denoting Difference: The Writing of the Slave Spirituals." *Critical Inquiry* 22: 506–44.

———. in press. "Black Noise, White Mastery." In *Decomposition*, ed. Philip Brett, Sue Ellen Case, and Susan Leigh Foster. Bloomington: Indiana University Press.

Roediger, David R. 1991. *The Wages of Whiteness: Race and the Making of the American Working Class*. New York: Verso.

Rosaldo, Renato. 1989. "Imperialist Nostalgia." *Representations* 26: 107–22.

Rose, Paul Lawrence. 1992. *Wagner, Race, and Revolution*. New Haven: Yale University Press.

Rose, Tricia. 1994. *Black Noise, Rap Music and Black Culture in Contemporary America*. Middletown, Conn. and Hanover, N.H. University Press of New England.

Rousseau, Jean-Jacques. 1975. *A Complete Dictionary of Music*. New York: AMS Press. Reprint of the 1779 English translation.

Said, Edward. 1978. *Orientalism*. New York: Pantheon.

Scarborough, Dorothy. 1925. *On the Trail of Negro Folk-Songs*. Cambridge: Harvard University Press.

Scott, Joan W. 1991. "The Evidence of Experience." *Critical Inquiry* 17: 773–97.

———. 1995. "Multiculturalism and the Politics of Identity." In *The Identity in Question*, ed. John Rajchman, 3–14. New York: Routledge.

Seeger, Anthony. 1987. *Why Suyá Sing: A Musical Anthropology of an Amazonian People*. Cambridge: Cambridge University Press.

———. 1991. "Styles of Musical Ethnography." In Nettl and Bohlman 1991: 324–55.

Slobin, Mark. 1982. "How the Fiddler Got on the Roof." In *Folk Music and Modern Sound*, ed. William Ferris and Mary Hart, 21–31. Jackson: University Press of Mississippi.

Solie, Ruth, ed. 1993. *Musicology and Difference: Gender and Sexuality in Music Scholarship*. Berkeley and Los Angeles: University of California Press.

Sollors, Werner. 1986. *Beyond Ethnicity: Consent and Descent in American Culture*. New York: Oxford University Press.

———. 1997. *Neither Black Nor White Yet Both*. New York: Oxford University Press.

Sonneck, Oscar. [1927] 1983. "An American School of Composition: Do We Want and Need It?" In *Oscar Sonneck and American Music*, ed. William Lichtenwanger, 158–66. Urbana: University of Illinois Press.

Spivak, Gayarti Chakravorty. 1988. "Can the Subaltern Speak?" In *Marxism and the Interpretation of Culture*, ed. Carey Nelson and Lawrence Grossberg, 271–313. London: Macmillan.

Stafford, Barbara. 1991. *Body Criticism: Imaging the Unseen in Enlightenment Art and Sciences*. Cambridge: MIT Press.

Stocking, George W., Jr. 1968. *Race, Culture and Evolution: Essays in the History of Antrhopology*. Chicago: University of Chicago Press.

———. 1994. "The Turn-of-the-Century Concept of Race." *Modernism/Modernity* 1: 4–16.

Stokes, Martin, ed. 1994. *Ethnicity, Identity and Music: The Musical Construction of Place*. Oxford: Berg.

Sumarsam. 1995. *Gamelan: Cultural Interaction and Musical Development in Central Java*. Chicago: University of Chicago Press.

Szwed, John F. 1969. "An American Anthropological Dilemma: The Politics of Afro-American Culture." In *Reinventing Anthropology*, ed. Dell Hymes, 153–81. New York: Pantheon.

Thomas, Downing A. 1995. *Music and the Origins of Language: Theories from the French Enlightenment*. Perspectives in Music History and Criticism. Cambridge: Cambridge University Press.

Tomlinson, Gary. 1993. *Music in Renaissance Magic: Toward a Historiography of Others*. Chicago: University of Chicago Press.

———. 1995. "Ideologies of Aztec Song." *Journal of the American Musicological Society* 48: 343–79.

Torgovnick, Marianna. 1990. *Gone Primitive: Savage Intellects, Modern Lives.* Chicago: University of Chicago Press.

Tucker, Bruce. 1989. "'Tell Tchaikovsky the News': Post-Modernism, Popular Culture, and the Emergence of Rock 'n' Roll." *Black Music Research Journal* 9: 271–95.

Von Eschen, Penny M. 1997. *Race against Empire: Black Americans and Anti-Colonialism, 1937–1957.* Ithaca: Cornell University Press.

Wallaschek, Richard. 1893. *Primitive Music: An Inquiry into the Origin and Development of Music, Song, Instruments, Dances and Pantomimes of Savage Races.* London: Longmans, Green.

Waterman, Richard. 1948. "'Hot' Rhythm in Negro Music." *Journal of the American Musicological Society* 1: 24–37.

———. 1952. "African Influence on the Music of the Americas. In *Acculturation in the Americas,* ed. Sol Tax, 207–18. Chicago: University of Chicago Press.

Weber-Kellermann, Ingeborg. 1978. *Zur Interethnik: Donauschwaben, Siebenbürger Sachsen und ihre Nachbarn.* Frankfurt am Main: Suhrkamp.

West, Cornel. 1987. "Minority Discourse and the Pitfalls of Canon Formation." *Yale Journal of Criticism* 1: 193–201.

———. 1988. "On Afro-American Popular Music: From Bebop to Rap." In *Prophetic Fragments,* 177–87. Grand Rapids, Mich., and Trenton, N.J.: Eerdmans/Africa World Press.

———. 1989. *The American Evasion of Philosophy: A Genealogy of Pragmatism.* Madison: University of Wisconsin Press.

———. 1994. *Race Matters.* New York: Vintage.

White, H. Roger. forthcoming. "Caste and Patronage in Hindustani Musics." Ph.D. diss., University of Wisconsin, Madison.

Wiegman, Robyn. 1995. *American Anatomies: Theorizing Race and Gender.* Durham, N.C. Duke University Press.

Young, Robert J. C. 1995. *Colonial Desire: Hybridity in Theory, Culture, and Race.* New York: Routledge.

PART I

Body/Dance

1

The Asian American Body
in Performance

DEBORAH WONG

> Our major political preoccupations are how to regulate the
> spaces between bodies, to monitor the interfaces between bod-
> ies, societies and cultures, to legislate on the tensions between
> habitus and body.
> (Bryan S. Turner)

> The body is the Achilles heel of hegemony.
> (John Fiske)

Asian American and African American bodies have problematic relationships. I immediately think of violence: those terrible grainy
images of Soon Ja Du shooting Latasha Harlins;[1] Korean Americans arming themselves in Los Angeles in 1992. These recent memories lead almost immediately to others—the Asian-owned convenience
store in the Black neighborhood—into a racialized loop of asymmetrical
opportunities and surveillances. The Asian American cannot come into
proximity with the African American without activating metaphors of
encroachment and use—metaphors that are all situated in ontologies of
embodiment.

Put simply, I'd like to offer some thoughts—explicitly, self-
consciously Asian American thoughts—on cultural appropriation and
the presence of Asian American performers in two traditions, jazz and
hip hop, that have been racially constructed as African American. More
broadly, I want to consider the relationships between the body, race,
and performance, and the racialization of bodies *through* performance.
The performances of those bodies in question have trajectories that
reach into ideologies of labor in a late capitalist world. I especially want
to offer some thoughts on the somatic process through which Asian

57

American jazz musicians and rappers have sometimes been constructed as a problem—in short, as inauthentic—and to propose some ways of rescuing such constructions by exerting what might be called a positive hermeneutics.[2]

This essay is in part a response to Ingrid Monson's trenchant exploration of ethnic authenticity in her article "The Problem with White Hipness: Race, Gender, and Cultural Conceptions in Jazz Historical Discourse" (1995). Looking closely at the interface between Whiteness, Blackness, music, style, modernity, and cultural ownership, Monson reveals certain alignments of difference that have created possibilities for resistance and cooption in contrasting communities. Boldly focusing on the dangerous performatives through which White Americans have borrowed African American style and thus constituted rebellions of their own, Monson productively refigures naturalized connections between race, gender, and resistance. My essay might be considered a parallel conversation to hers—another encounter between bodies where performance is a constitutive moment for an activist response to racialized inequities.

The absent body in the Asian American/African American "problem" is of course White, always present yet rendered invisible by ideologies that create marked and unmarked categories. The larger, controlling cultural performances that place Asian American and African American bodies in conflict rely on what Peter McLaren has called "White terror" and its unmarked frameworks, its naturalized terms (1994: 59–62). To be an American and to think about race means engaging with Whiteness and all its performances, yet this encompassing racialization is perhaps the most under-theorized embodiment of all, and therein lies its power and narrative definition. In its most complete form, I might attempt that theorization in this essay. But I choose not to reinscribe its historical power that directly; instead, I leave it in the wings, watching, defining, but deliberately unvisualized.

THE BODY POLITIC: THE BODY, POWER, AND DIFFERENCE

There's a moment in *Yankee Dawg You Die*, Philip Gotanda's deeply reflexive play about Asian American representations in film, in which several bodies collide. Two Asian American actors, playing Asian American actors, break into a song-and-dance number from a famous World War II–era nightclub in San Francisco's Chinatown. As they do a soft shoe shuffle, they sing about tea cakes, moon songs, and strolling down Grant Avenue, and they light into a classic pentatonic Oriental lick that any of us would recognize anywhere, in the soundtrack of any movie. The younger of the two characters suddenly stops in his tracks, looks at his companion, and says (Gotanda 1991: 21):

> Wait, wait, wait, what is this—WAIT! What am I doing? What is this shit? You're acting like a Chinese Steppin Fetchit. That's what you're acting like. Jesus, fucking Christ . . . *A Chinese Steppin Fetchit.*

This moment of recognition—forcing a character to see his own body moving through representations, of corporeally enacting the cultural memory of other racialized representations—is a key moment in a profoundly reflexive play. Seeing his own body evoke an African American body literally stops him in his tracks and stops the dramatic action of the play. The problem of impersonation opens up to him, to us, in all its regulatory might. This moment is emblematic of Asian American/African American encounters through other kinds of performance as well, and I mean to trace the ideological histories of some Asian American performatives that draw on African American forms. This will necessarily create some theoretical uneasiness over verbs. How to describe that ethnicized encounter? Do Asian Americans borrow, appropriate, incorporate, absorb, transform, evoke, or steal African American forms? Without retreating from the politicized nature of that encounter, I want to look closely at its character in jazz and hip hop. And, as Susan Foster has suggested, to think about performance and difference without taking their corporeal histories into account is a particular kind of ideological denial,[3] so I begin with the body.

Thinking about the body can only take place between two paradigms: the body as a site of regulation, or the body as a site where hegemony is evaded and resisted. Recent theory suggests that bodies are socially constructed, often through performance; that gender, sexuality, and race are inter-constitutive and dialectically related; and that the performative reality of such interpenetrations is often deeply contradictory.

Foucault, of course, looms large in recent theories of the body. Though he never explicitly addressed race or performance, his positioning of the body between ideology production and the effects of ideological structures has had a profound impact on all subsequent theories of the body. He posits a "political economy" and "political technology" of the body (1977: 24–25) in which the state exerts or subtly brings to bear power and mastery over the materiality of bodies. In his view,

knowledge is produced by power, not vice versa, and this enables his reworking of the Hobbesian body politic:

> One might imagine a 'political anatomy'. This would not be the study of
> a state in terms of a 'body' (with its elements, its resources and its forces),
> nor would it be a study of the body and its surroundings in terms of a
> small state. One would be concerned with the 'body politic', as a set of ma-
> terial elements and techniques that serve as weapons, relays, communica-
> tion routes and supports for the power and knowledge relations that in-
> vest human bodies and subjugate them by turning them into objects of
> knowledge. (1977: 28)

The body, power, and knowledge are thus directly linked, and the "anatomy" of power is not abstract at all, but rather material, situated in bodies. To know a body is to produce the possibility of controlling, disciplining, or instructing it.

Strongly influenced by Foucault, the sociologist Bryan Turner has
devoted several books to exploring the social constitution of bodies, particularly in terms of regulatory schemes such as science, medicine, diet,
and so forth. He points out that "in addition to the metaphor of politics, the human body has been conceived either as a work of art or as a
machine" (Turner 1992: 182). Although he too does not address race, he
shows how public anatomical dissection, diet, and *anorexia nervosa* are all
ideologically tied to concerns of class and social control, though in historically distinct ways.[4]

Foucault's linking of the body, discipline, and the fade-away of its
public spectacle marks an important moment in bodily history—in fact,
in the history of bodily performance. As torture, execution, and even incarceration were slowly and methodically removed from the public gaze
(beginning in the early nineteenth century), the theater of the disciplined
body has been redefined. But it certainly hasn't disappeared. The social
drama of the body is the focus of much interesting recent work that has
prompted new ideas of performativity linking corporeality and social
transformation. While Foucault located bodies in submission, scholars
working in postindustrial, postmodern contexts look intently for signs
of revolt, and performance has been identified by some as a means for
locating agency.

The theorist of popular culture John Fiske, for instance, has consistently regarded the body as an important site of reception and agency.[5]
His recent work has focused on the material and social bodies of African American slaves, Rodney King,[6] homeless men watching (and responding "incorrectly" to) the movie *Die Hard*, Elvis, and Elvis fans.

Fiske proposes a poststructuralist model for power and resistance based on dynamics of "locales" and "stations": localizing moves are cultural strategies for gaining control over "the immediate conditions of everyday life," while stations are the opposite but equivalent of locales, i.e., a physical and/or social space in which "the social order is imposed on an individual" (1993: 12). Though this model may at first glance seem uncomfortably structuralist (is the social order so easily, well, located?), Fiske carefully reroutes assumed connections between the social and the material body, suggesting that localizing moves afford the possibility of agency (288):

> In slavery, the technologies of . . . power were applied to the physical body; in "the new racism" their application is as much upon the social body. Environmental and economic racism work on the black social body as did the whips on the physical body. Retelling the atrocious narratives of slavery . . . evokes shudders in the bodies of those who hear them. These shudders are experiences of affective intensity of the body's recognition that what it touches *matters*, and they are theoretically comparable to the homeless men's cheers at *Die Hard* or Elvis fans' ecstasy, even though their intensity is of horror rather than pleasure. This bodily affect enables the power that oppressed the bodies in the narrative to be taken into the bodies of the listeners and turned against its origin.

Fiske is thus able to trace the channeling of power through time, through bodies, and to chart its transformation from imperializing power into localized agency. As I will suggest later, moments of performance could thus be seen as moves that establish important locales for reracializations.

While Fiske focuses on the body's relation to the enactment of power, Judith Butler posits gender, sex, and the body as exceptionally mobile constructions. Her work has tremendous potential for theories of racialization and performance. Refiguring sex and gender as discursive possibilities, Butler posits sex as an aspect of a "regulatory norm" that performatively moves the materiality of the body into expected shapes. Linking the body to discourse, she joins and extends Foucault and Derrida, focusing closely on the "reiterative power of discourse to produce the phenomena that it regulates and constrains" (1993: 2). Suggesting that sex is phantasmatic, she grapples directly with the "problem" of materiality, refusing to explain it away as "mere" discourse.[7] No mere construction, corporeality is rather "a process of materialization that stabilizes over time to produce the effect of boundary, fixity, and surface we call matter" (9). Butler thus rescues the reality of the body from Derridean disappearance, placing it firmly at the intersection of

power, control, performance, and agency. Refusing to romanticize performance as an enactment of agency and opposition, Butler instead insists on an intimate relationship between agency and control: "The paradox of subjectivation," she notes,

> is precisely that the subject who would resist such norms is itself enabled,
> if not produced, by such norms. Although this constitutive constraint does
> not foreclose the possibility of agency, it does locate agency as a reiterative
> or rearticulatory practice, immanent to power, and not a relation of ex-
> ternal opposition to power. (15)

Most importantly, Butler makes the jump to race. In her discussion
of passing (that is, the regulatory possibility of masking/performing
race), she shifts her focus to difference, musing that feminist theorists
have at times been overly intent on the social force of sexual difference.
"This privileging of sexual difference," she notes, "implies not only that
sexual difference should be understood as more fundamental than other
forms of difference, but that other forms of difference might be *derived*
from sexual difference." Instead, she repositions sexual difference within
a broader sphere of relationships which must "be understood as articulated through or *as* other vectors of power" (167). She suggests
that homosexuality and miscegenation could be seen as analogous, as a
"constitutive outside" to the normative, whether sexuality or race. In
her analysis of Nella Larsen's novel *Passing*, the heroine's masked race,
miscegenation, and an attraction to another woman can be resolved only
through death—through "the success of a certain symbolic ordering of
gender, sexuality, and race" (183). Just as performativity assigns sex, gender, and sexuality to bodies, it also creates, maintains, and transforms a
racialized body. Racializing norms thus "exist not merely alongside gender norms, but are articulated through one another" (182). As she puts
it, whiteness is therefore not a form of racial difference (ibid.), and the
performative creation of unmarked bodies constitutes "the currency of
normative whiteness" (171).

How, then, can we even begin to talk about race and the body? Having
admitted that race is a social construct, how can we meaningfully look
at its signs without reinscribing its violence?[8] In *The Body in Pain*, Elaine
Scarry suggests that the body always creates narratives of time and place
and that is it always political, whether in war or peacetime. Scarry muses
that the body doesn't reflect winning or losing: "It is not (after a war) as
though the winners were alive and the losers are dead," she says (1985:
114). Instead, she proposes "some surrogate form of objectification, . . .
a vehicle of memorialization" (114–15), such as a thread worn on the

upper arm or a change in walking habits that might be adopted by both populations, winners and losers, to signify the past presence of war. Let me turn her proposal around and suggest that seeing racialized bodies is another vehicle of memorialization, though an involuntary one. If we defamiliarize the topography connecting body, race, class, gender, and sexuality, then race begins to look much more like a vehicle of memorialization dedicated to terror. The network of connections emanating from race function to maintain some bodies as injured, in pain.

In other words, Scarry's extended meditation on the body at war can easily be read allegorically—if we read war as "a surrogate form of objectification" for the cultural maintenance of racial difference, then the mechanisms through which racialization occurs become clearer. As Scarry notes, "injuring works in part by the abiding signs it produces" (115). One might say that racialization is a convenient feedback loop, in which race is the sign that promotes past and continued injury by its very presence. Scarry says that one of the functions of injury is that it "provides a record of its own activity" (116), which is precisely how a racialized body functions in, and is maintained by, the state. "Injuries-as-signs point both backward and forward in time," she says: they have a "reality-conferring" function (121) that makes them unstable but nearly impossible to argue with.

Seeing performance and the body in dynamic relationship has emerged most strongly from medical anthropology. In the introduction to their recent volume *The Performance of Healing*, Carol Laderman and Marina Roseman suggest that healing rituals are perhaps *the* performative of the body (1996: 3, 8–9). After all, what other cross-cultural behavior is as rooted in the belief that performance, however defined, will fundamentally change the status of the body? Healing ritual, almost always performed, is directed toward physiological change —"real" change, often conceived as material change. In the same volume, Thomas J. Csordas, looking closely at Charismatic Christian beliefs about healing, notes that the performance of healing "works" in that context because

> for Charismatics, efficacious healing is predicated not only on a cultural legitimacy that says healing is possible, but on an existential immediacy that constitutes healing as real. The immediacy of the imaginal world and of memory, of divine presence and causal efficacy, have their common ground in embodiment. (1996: 108)

Performatives of healing can connect different spheres—e.g., cosmology, imagination, and the body. One might say that the most serious regard for the performative may be located in medical anthropology. The connections thus made between performance, change, the body, and social reality can be effectively extended into theoretical frameworks for race.

The injuries of race are acted out all the time in performance. In her marvelous ethnography of dance in small-town Greece, Jane Cowan shows us bodies in motion—men, women, dancers, musicians—and as she unfolds their dialectic relationships and their mutual dependencies, the constellation of instrumental music, Gypsies, and the not-human emerges vividly, overshadowed somewhat by Cowan's interest in gender but striking nonetheless. Men lead the dance, women watch; men dance in public, women in private; women sing, men make instrumental music; instrumental music drives the dance. The musicians who specialize in instrumental music are in fact Gypsies—not-Greek, deeply Other— referred to by the Greek townspeople not as "the musicians" but as "the drums" *(daulia)* or "the instruments." In continuous dynamic interaction with the male dancers, these musicians are essential but held at arms' length, necessary but despised. Cowan mildly notes "the Greek contempt for Gypsies" and the Greek townspeople's "tendency to ignore the humanity of the musicians" (Cowan 1990: 102). Deeply suspect, the musicians are nonetheless the source of the most intense physical and emotional experience of dance *(kefi)*: their music literally sends dancers into a heightened state, yet the money pressed upon them in the heat of such moments confers status not on them but on the giver: as Cowan puts it, the townspeople rarely remember which musicians were playing, nor do they see the bills as special evidence of the musicians' skill (105–6). She says:

> I have stressed the hierarchical interdependence between Gypsy musicians and male youths in the performance of gender. These youths need the Gypsies' tunes in order to structure their dances and, thereby, to structure their emotions. And they need to appear to dominate the Gypsies in order to enhance their own masculinity. (126)

Focusing all her analytical interest on gender, Cowan misses the chance to see racialization in process, through performance. It is clear from her energetic descriptions that the bodies in her ethnography are busily being engendered and racialized with great intensity, in performance. Men behave with physical abandon while women enact decorum (showing enthusiasm only in their faces and gestures). The Gypsy musicians, however, "are always upright, physically composed, their faces often expressionless as they play" (127). They are wordless, gentle, dignified, but not respected. Cowan translates their racialization as not-Greek into the language of gender:

> The Gypsies' comportment is a total inversion of [the] explicit, stylized, slightly parodied sexuality [of Greek townsmen]. In a symbolic sense, then, the Gypsies appear not as feminine but as sexless, neutered men. In this play of gender, gender is a code of power as well as of difference.
>
> The symbolic position of the Gypsy musician in the performance is thus complex. He is at once, paradoxically, a man, a socially inferior and thus unsexed man, and an instrument. . . . He is, through his music, the one who constitutes the performance itself, and at the same time his performance, according to [Greek townspeople's] norms, is and should be in a gestural sense invisible, neutral, without qualities, symbolically reflective. The performances of the [Greek] dancer and the Gypsy musician are a subtle, uneasy choreography of mutual interdependence. (ibid.)

The musicking Gypsy body thus provides a record of its own activity by driving Greek dancers. The injury of race renders the Gypsy less than human, and Cowan's insistence on the deep relationality of all these performing bodies is astute despite her overly tight focus on gender. In fact, the Gypsy body as subordinate, as a body that serves and labors, has deep resonance with the performative constitution of other racialized bodies in other historical and cultural contexts.

I am interested here in exploring two metaphors, that is, in seeing *and* hearing race in the performing body. The shaping presence of "visual economies" in ideologies of the body is undeniable. Much of Robyn Wiegman's book *American Anatomies* (1995) is focused on making these economies theoretically visible: she suggests that race and gender have been rendered "real" via "naturalizing discourses of the body, . . . discourses that locate difference in a pre-cultural realm whose corporeal significations supposedly speak a truth which the body inherently means" (4). Technologies of representation, she argues, have been technologies of vision which have fundamentally shaped contemporary cultural politics as well as "the investigative terrain of modern disciplinarity itself" (3). Indeed, Wiegman argues that color has been a visible economy since the late seventeenth century and the colonial encounter, and race has subsequently become overdetermined—the condition for subjection. The Western production of race emerged directly from imperialism and world trade; as such, the cultural reliance on visual signs of race is deeply situated.[9] Wiegman insists that "we must take seriously the notion of race as a fiction . . . in order to jettison the security of the visible as an obvious and unacculturated phenomenon" (24). Race became an overdetermined sign through specific historical processes that joined scientific, industrial, and technological "revolutions" and constituted certain racialized bodies as subjects, as objects of knowledge (36). The reliance on visible race was, and is, central to both an economic system and a representational economy. As Wiegman explains,

> In Western racial discourse, for instance, the production of the African subject as non- or subhuman, as an object and property, arises not simply through the economic necessities of the slave trade, but according to the epistemologies attending vision and their logics of corporeal inscription: making the African "black" reduces the racial meanings attached to flesh to a binary structure of vision, and it is this structure that precedes the disciplinary emergence of the humanities and its methodological pursuits of knowledge and truth. (4)

Susan McClary and Robert Walser have argued that the visible sign of the Black body in performance has been central to American epistemologies of racial subjection. In their essay "Theorizing the Body in African-American Music" (1994), they note that the body generally has not been "a prestigious topic among scholars of the arts" (75) because of the Cartesian mind/body split and the body's conception as precultural. McClary and Walser demonstrate how a chain of relationships— the body, to dance, to African and African American aesthetics connecting music and dance—has enabled a dismissal of African American musics from scholarly consideration. These perceived connections allow celebration-in-dismissal:

> African and African-American musics [have been perceived] as sites where the body still may be experienced as primordial, untouched by the restrictions of culture. . . . The mind and culture still remain the exclusive property of Eurocentric discourse, while the dancing body is romanticized as what is left over when the burdens of reason and civilization have been flung away. (76)

One way of resisting or intervening in this epistemology is to try to get the body back into scholarship on Euro-American musics, or to focus on "the more intellectual aspects of African-American music" (77), though, once again, the interventionist paradox of reinscription raises its head. Still, I would like to engage with McClary's and Walser's suggestion that

> The challenge is to assess the international impact of African-American articulations of the body without falling into the usual traps—neither

undervaluing physicality as a complex artistic terrain nor celebrating it as a site where one pushes reason aside to come in contact with (fantasies of) universal primal urges. (82)

In the remainder of this essay, I would like to rise to that challenge by looking at, and trying to hear, Asian American bodies articulated through African American bodies, and even articulations of Asian American and African American bodies that perform together, against/ through/with each other. Robyn Wiegman notes how the rhetoric of contemporary identity politics has often elided and collapsed discussions of difference to a consideration of "blacks and women": this rhetoric "simply weds these identity categories together, writing 'blacks and women' as the inclusivist gesture of post-1960s politics" (1995: 7). Somewhat playfully, then, I will turn my attention to a kind of body excluded from such gestures—the Asian American man in performance—and I will consider how such bodies sound as well as look.[10] The elision of music and the body (and race, labor, and the body) means that the musicking body is necessarily racialized. If these performing bodies necessarily enact historical memories of subjectivation and injury (as I think they do), then I also mean to rescue those memories by refashioning their labor as cultural work.

THE RACIALIZATION OF JAZZ

It is increasingly difficult to write or talk about jazz in unracialized terms —or rather, to do so looks increasingly naive, reconstituting jazz in a language too close to the discourse of art music to go unchallenged. Questions of who speaks, who ought to be speaking, and who has spoken too much already are more and more frequently cast in racialized terms. These are by no means new issues.[11] The first sentence of Amiri Baraka's *Black Music* reads: "Most jazz critics have been white Americans, but most important jazz musicians have not been" (Jones 1967: 11). Though not new, moving discursive discussions about race from a background murmur into the front lines indicates that jazz has been reconfigured as something eminently worth owning. The tug-and-pull over ownership has centered on who is making the music and who is writing about it. Both arguments have been cast in Black and White terms; the racialization of jazz has been aggressively binary because it is a ventriloquist, metonymic stand-in for control over an American Elsewhere. The long history of Other colors in jazz—that is, Asians and Latinos—is consistently refigured as absence. If the very idea of an Asian

American jazz is new or strange, this demonstrates—successfully—the American hermeneutics of race as binary: either/or, Black/White. Any other kind of jazz simply isn't.

Much writing on the cultural politics of jazz has indeed been produced by white men.[12] How Whites regard jazz has been of on-going concern to White critics.[13] A recent compendium, *Reading Jazz* (1993), edited by David Meltzer, is a collection of White writings that dramatically points out how nearly a century's worth of White musings on jazz has served as a lens on cultural mores and anxieties at different historical moments. Meltzer openly acknowledges his modus operandi: he admits that the collection "is a deliberate one-way street, a display of re-creation" (30). Meltzer, a White poet and critic, has framed these writings with an impassioned, impressionistic "pre-ramble" in which he takes on the racialization of jazz in all its historicized might. "This [book]," he writes,

> is about the white invention of jazz as a subject and object. . . . While the music is the creation of African-Americans, jazz as mythology, commodity, cultural display is a white invention and the expression of a postcolonial tradition. . . . This is a source-book of forms of permissible racism. (4–5)

Meltzer argues that consumers, fans, and critics have a different experience and in fact a different history from that of jazz performers (21), and that the political economy of jazz and its artifacts are controlled by White consumer society. No liberal apologist, Meltzer points to the structural roles of capitalism in the racialization of jazz, and in talk about it. Control over the flow of material goods around jazz enables a kind of racist forgetfulness that allows jazz to be owned: "Jazz," Meltzer writes, "has entered the elaborate interweaving maze of the archive; it's fixed in an upwardly mobile museum culture; a branch of nostalgia and amnesia" (29). The centrality of jazz in the Japanese American internment camps or the fame of San Francisco's Forbidden City are thus easily forgotten because those jazz sounds were neither produced nor heard by the right kind of Americans.

The very attempt to "get at" jazz is more and more consistently framed by jazz historians as an exercise in discursive representations.[14] Getting at race in jazz has been most creatively refigured by Gary Tomlinson (1992) and Ingrid Monson (1995). I will address Monson's argument for a racialized understanding of appropriation and participation below. Tomlinson focuses on African American theories of intertextuality and dialogics on music and thus disarms essentialist arguments for a core of African American identity in jazz. Rather than try to clear a space for himself or even for White historians, Tomlinson instead provides an argument that allows jazz discourse (whether musical or scholarly) to move beyond assertions of Black purity and nationalism. Vernacularism and Signifyin(g) create meaning by attempting to "keep sight, so to speak, of the other modes of thought around it by keeping them above [their] horizon" (1992: 66). Meaning thus emerges from engagement with difference, not retreat or isolation from it.[15] He outlines a resituated and re-racialized way of approaching jazz and, indeed, any form of located expression, allowing for encounter and dialogical complexity. Dialogical knowledge, he says,

> is unsettling precisely because it works against our natural impulse to be settled in the complacency of our own rules and terms. It threatens because it relinquishes the comforting idea of mastering a fully cleared space with open horizons in order instead to scrutinize uneasily the mysterious others crowding in on it. (93)

I turn now to some of those mysterious Others crowding in on jazz— Others who have always been there, always listening, participating, and consuming the musics imagined to be jazz. In the Bay Area around San Francisco, a small but widening circle of Asian American jazz musicians have been performing, composing, and recording since the mid-1970s; though they have not been acknowledged in the racialized discourse of jazz capital, they themselves have placed ethnicity and identity politics at the center of their activities from the beginning. Mark Izu, Jon Jang, Francis Wong, Glenn Horiuchi, and Anthony Brown may not be familiar names to jazzheads, but they are to those who follow Asian American arts and performance. All five are composers and performers; all five have recorded extensively, especially on the Asian Improv label, which is devoted to Asian American musical expression; all five have collaborated extensively with African American jazz musicians; and all five have been, and continue to be, involved with Asian American activism.

As McClary and Walser have pointed out, it is especially in African American musics that the body has been emphasized in order to enable its containment and dismissal. Jazz has been especially subject to location in an im/amoral body, a body beyond the control and humanity of culture. Still, virtually no criticism or scholarship has ventured beyond the African American or the White jazz body, maintaining instead two social anatomies in continual struggle with each other. Where might yet another kind of racialized body find a place where it is still allowed to produce jazz sounds?

These are precisely the kinds of questions that engage activist Asian American musicians. Most are involved with local Asian American community organizations. Their expressive activities are diverse: they perform in festivals and nightclubs; they manage recording companies; they compose the scores for (primarily) Asian American plays, films, and documentaries; they arrange for Asian musicians to visit the U.S. and to collaborate with them; and of course they teach. They try to shake up racialized and racist social structures through a variety of activities, but the connecting thread is an effort to use performance as a force in social transformation.

Collaboration with African American jazz musicians is explicitly important to many of the Asian American musicians. Jon Jang, for instance, studied with the African American composer and performer Wendell Logan as an undergraduate at Oberlin College, where he was introduced to the identity politics of jazz. Francis Wong, Jang's longtime friend and collaborator, describes Jang's experience of the jazz culture wars as follows:

> [Jon had] experiences at Oberlin where people really tried to challenge that fact—students just couldn't get behind acknowledging that the [jazz] innovators were African American. You know, they'd be arguing with Wendell Logan and stuff like that. And I think there's also a basic playing off—like Jon said there were two big bands at Oberlin, one that was the official one under Wendell's direction that played interesting or creative music—Charlie Parker, and stuff like that—and then . . . I guess some of the white students organized another band that featured mainly white arrangers. The thing is that that whole stage band movement—big band—in colleges is primarily white. I mean, a lot of it came out of the Stan Kenton thing, and then people made it business—like Sammy Nestico and a lot of these arrangers. So a lot of the white players really want to play that, and there wasn't an interest in learning from the [African American] masters, basically.[16]

According to Wong, Jang's interest in acknowledging and collaborating with African American musicians was thus established early in his career. Most of the long-lived Asian American jazz ensembles expressly include African American musicians. Fred Ho's group, the Afro-Asian Music Ensemble, has always been multiracial. Anthony Brown's ensemble, the Afro-Asian Eclipse, refers not only to Ellington's "African-Eurasian Eclipse" but also to Brown himself, who is half Japanese and half African American. James Newton, the well-known African American wind player who appears on many Asian American jazz albums, is a childhood friend of Brown's. The African American/Asian American musical encounter is thus self-conscious, though, I hasten to add, it is imagined and pursued in different ways by different Asian American musicians. Many agree, though, that musical collaboration enacts political coalition as well as respect for the African American origins of jazz.

Non–Asian American musicians may not "read" or hear this music in the same way that an Asian American might. I once sat down with Charles Sykes, an African American musician friend, and listened with him to part of Jon Jang's *Reparations Now!*, a multi-movement "Asian American concerto for jazz ensemble and taiko" that addresses Japanese American political efforts to attain reparations from the United States government for unconstitutional internment during World War II.[17] Jang's ensemble, the Pan-Asian Arkestra, is multiracial though mostly Asian American, and its name alludes to Horace Tapscott's Pan African People's Arkestra. The name of the suite *Reparations Now!* is politically as well as musically referential, pointing to Max Roach's *We Insist! Freedom Now Suite* (which had addressed the racist administration of South Africa).

At the time I listened to this work with Charles, I found the music extremely exciting—it was stirring to me in ways that I was just beginning to articulate. A historian of African American popular musics and a gifted performer, Charles listened intently and provided a running commentary identifying all kinds of musical references to particular African American jazz musicians and even to famous performances of particular works. He was able to hear an intertextuality that was beyond me, and he was thus as engaged with the work as I but in a very different way. He wasn't listening blind: he knew that the musicians were ethically diverse but mostly Asian American, and he understood the activist base to the work itself and more broadly to the musicians' work as a whole. At one point, however, he observed that the musicianship was technically good but "stiff"—that the musicians consistently maintained a rather close metronomic sense of the beat that "revealed" them as not African American.[18] He even stopped the tape at one point to demonstrate how an African American musician might realize a particular phrase with a looser, more fluid sense of rhythm and even timbre. I never felt that he was criticizing the Arkestra's technical skill or musicianship; rather, he was pointing out certain moments in which he felt he could hear the racialized conditioning of bodily and musical behavior. He didn't attempt to identify an Asian American sound—instead, he was hearing the absence of an African American musicking body, and this in itself was an assertion that such a body was somehow identifiable.

But what exactly *was* he hearing, and why? Rhythm, of course, is what

Black bodies are supposed to have, and this innate quality has been mapped onto the African American body as surely as Reason has been central to the White cartology of Western racial theory. Ronald Radano (1993b) has outlined an archeology of rhythm and blackness, suggesting that the connections between the two are deeply discursive. Getting through the representations that have constructed blackness to begin with is an exercise in racialization, he contends, and he opts instead to unpack a single allegorical category:

> By focusing on a single discursive gesture, the value-saturated sign of rhythm, we can observe a formative device in the construction of musical blackness. Rhythm, as the central modernist figure of African-American culture, has typically been inscribed as something beyond the grasp of whites; accordingly, it offers performers and insiders a powerful tool for inventing an exalted racialized space. (1–2)

Radano proposes that rhythm is "a fundamental discursive feature of modern racial consciousness" (4) that, once established in the eighteenth century, has only been reworked, revised, and reinscribed through "countless manifestations" and many African American genres. Rather than try to assert the corrective power of specific methodologies (e.g. Signifyin[g]), he calls for "new listening practices (in the spirit of postmodern anthropology) that negotiate between the racialisms of black musical romance and our efforts to deconstruct them" (10)—in other words, for closely located interpretations that enable constructive engagement with representations *and* resistance to them, history *and* our response to it.

I don't think that Sykes was deliberately or self-consciously clearing out an aural space beyond Asian American reach, nor do I think he was drawing lines in the sand. I think he heard what he heard, but the next step is, of course, to theorize what he thought he heard, or what he was expecting to hear and didn't. What he heard is beyond discussion at a certain level. When I told Francis Wong about the incident, he didn't try to "explain" the sound of the Asian American musicians on the album, nor did he try to move Asian American performers into a shared space with African American bodily experience. Instead, Wong said:

> Well, I don't have any problems with that, because people hear whatever they hear, you know. Eastern philosophy [suggests that] you can't second-guess someone's perception. If that's what he hears, that's what he hears. I don't have any issue with that.

Can one hear race? [19] I asked Wong if he could tell whether a musician was African American just by listening. Wong is articulate about the social and political dimensions of Asian American jazz, though the language he uses to describe the racialized musical encounter is a curious mixture of social activism and Western art ideologies. He said,

> In the past, I used to try to think about that, but now I just kind of listen to [musicians'] influences.
>
> DEBORAH WONG: OK. Does that mean you can tell sometimes?
>
> FRANCIS WONG: Yeah, well, usually I can just tell who they are, at this point. After listening to the music for over twenty-five years, I can hear who they are or who they're coming from.
>
> DW: Do you notice that more consistently with Black musicians, or White musicians, or even Asian American musicians?
>
> FW: Well, it's still a pretty new thing with Asian American musicians, so it's a little harder. That's why it's not so much their color: you can hear what they *stand* for, you know. There's certain kinds of approaches that reflect more of a world view, I think.
>
> DW: What do you mean?
>
> FW: It's more about hearing how people think about creativity, how they think about spirituality—things like that. So you could maybe take it to the next level and say, well, they're probably black, or they're probably this. But myself, I'm not as interested in doing that. That's not that important to me.

So Wong apparently once listened for race, but now hears particular histories and politicized, aestheticized stances; he hears what a musician "stands for," that is, *whose* influences sound through a particular performance. "Who they're coming from" is a matter of choice as well as personal history—he suggests that jazz musicians are well aware of who they're coming from, and that these aural autobiographies are constituted selectively, with emotional and political awareness. He resisted the question of whether race is musically audible, recognizing the essentialist shape of the question and answering, instead, that "playing" race is a matter of conscious choice; linking oneself to particular musicians represents a performative of political and ethnic coalition. We went on, and I persisted in posing essentializing questions:

> DW: So sometimes, depending on who he or she is quoting from, or styling themselves on, or whatever—
>
> FW: Sure, whatever tradition their feet are planted in.
>
> DW: —will tell you something, sometimes.
>
> FW: Yeah. You know if their music seems to be kind of heady, that doesn't mean that they're White—it just means that it's heady.

DW: Oh, really? "Heady" as in, like, abstract?

FW: Not necessarily abstract, but intellectual. I don't really look at abstract and intellectual as the same thing.

DW: What's "heady," then?

FW: Well, heady is to me, like, intellectual—you know, like they're thinking about the stuff too much.

DW: How can you tell when someone's playing in an intellectual way?

FW: Well, I think it's a lot of time like a lack of feeling, or it just doesn't have a grounded feel to it. So it can be pretty abstract and still feel pretty grounded, you know. People always used to feel Coltrane was abstract, but I never felt his music was abstract.

DW: Really? You felt it was grounded?

FW: It was always grounded.

In short, Wong resists both of the ways that African American musicians have long been tied to their bodies. He disallows a simple, nativist explanation connecting rhythm or, for that matter, any specific musical behaviors to race: music may be produced by a body, but that body's racial history is not, to him, the source of its characteristic sound. He then resists the narrative force of the mind/body split, refusing to place headiness in White bodies.

Wong, Jang, and many of the other Asian American musicians oscillate between calling their expressive activities "jazz" and "creative music." In this, they quite deliberately model themselves on the Association for the Advancement of Creative Music (AACM) and its innovative mix of free jazz, avant-garde modernist improvisation, and Black nationalism. The inspiration for Asian Improv and the annual Asian American Jazz Festival also comes from the AACM: though never formally organized as a repertory group or an association, Asian Improv represents an effort to carve out an explicitly ethnic space in the recording industry, though in less nationalist terms than those espoused by the AACM in the 1960s and 1970s. This particular mixture of economic self-determination and avant-gardism is the direct ideological legacy of the AACM. The Asian American musicians' connection to the AACM is sometimes enacted even more directly: Joseph Jarman (a founding member of the AACM) was the featured guest artist at the 1996 Asian American Jazz Festival in San Francisco, where he performed with Glenn Horiuchi and Francis Wong. Ronald Radano's thoughtful account of the AACM's formative years pinpoints some of the same ideological contradictions and challenges faced by these Asian American musicians thirty years later. He notes that it would be hard to ignore the contradiction between the musicians' efforts to distance themselves from Western artistic notions while simultaneously pursuing exceedingly Western, progressivist goals. There is no doubt that the AACM players embraced modernist ideas of style and greatness. (1993a: 104)

I must emphasize that the musical and ideological language of the Asian American musicians is based on a 1990s admiration of and delight in cultural hybridity, so their gestures toward an imagined Asia bear little resemblance to the Afrocentric purity and authenticity that AACM members sought to create. Yet the end results have interesting parallels. Just as the radical Black artists' "beliefs inspired something quite profound" (ibid.), the Asian American musicians' respectful use of the AACM's aesthetic language and musical styles relies on discomfiting notions of African American cultural authenticity even as it enables startling new sounds. That "the formation of grassroots organizations . . . could accommodate radical creative pursuits" (77) while still asserting identity politics is the AACM's legacy. Sitting at Asian Improv's headquarters in San Francisco in May 1996, I listened to Izu, Wong, Horiuchi, Jang, and other Asian American musicians talk with Joseph Jarman and agree that neither identity politics nor "jazz" could contain their musical vision any longer, though each was essential to their development as musicians, collectively and individually.[20]

For them, the use of the category "jazz" is both connecting and confining. The tie to African Americans is important to all of them, and jazz is the genre they have chosen to speak for and to that community. To some extent, jazz is valorized by the Asian American musicians as emblematic of African American experience but illustrative of particular parts of that experience—as an expressive response to attempted subjectivation. As Francis Wong said to me:

Some of it has to do with our own political maturity—[becoming active] in that period of the late 60s and the 70s, where there was a developing perspective about black music and its relationship to the struggle for freedom and things like that. And the recognition that the major innovators in jazz were African American [was part of that]. So I think in that sense, in trying to both play the music and learn the music, there was an important emotional and intellectual desire to be connected to that tradition, in a very direct way.

The Asian American political identification with jazz is thus as an African American music. On the other hand, Asian American musical experimentation sometimes stretches beyond anything immediately recognizable as jazz, and Wong, among others, has noted the tug and pull between an identification with politically racialized music and an ideology of original, expressive creation. I've wondered, too, if this isn't a protective gesture, meant to insulate them from suggestions that what they're making isn't *jazz*. Radano suggests that "the development free jazz may be seen as a kind of dialogue taking place between white and black in the context of artistic modernism" (1993a: 109), but a modernism transformed by Black aesthetics. Similarly, the Bay Area musicians' "creative music" has emerged from an Asian American/African American encounter tempered by a politicized avant-gardism.

Monson (1995: 406) has described similar politics in the 1940s between the use of re-bop, be-bop, bop, and the term "modern music." Of all innovations in jazz music, bop was a supremely self-conscious response to jazz traditionalists. Monson notes that the use of the term "modern" had at least two associations. The "structural and artistic elements of the music itself" was impenetrable to many traditional jazz performers. (Interestingly, Louis Armstrong likened bop's utter strangeness to "Chinese music.") Second, bop's practitioners deployed its "modern" face as a political and social response to racist containment of jazz as entertainment. Instead, they insisted on bop's modern character, its status as "art," not entertainment; the body held at bay, the uneasy truce between resistance, self-determination, and reinscription. Rhetorically, at least, bop was cast in a radically intellectual mold. When Asian American musicians gesture toward their own "creative music," they too negotiate a new territory, in a language of newness—drawn from modernism—that introduces other depoliticizing ideologies.

Asian American jazz musicians approach the problem of White hipness in other ways, however. Tricia Rose has noted the phenomenon of "young white listeners trying to perfect a model of correct white hipness, coolness, and style by adopting the latest black style and image" (Rose 1994: 5). Any appropriation of African American expressive modes is fraught with problems; as Rose puts it, "Young white listeners' genuine pleasure and commitment to black music are necessarily affected by dominant racial discourses regarding African Americans, the politics of racial segregation, and cultural difference in the United States" (ibid.). Monson identifies gender and masculinity in particular as channels that mediate White notions of race, class, and African American cultural authenticity. Identifying African American musics as a source for Asian American expression becomes a way for Asian American musicians to rescue certain possibilities made so difficult by racializations that muffle and silence them. White hipness was (and is) an expression of imagined racial authenticity—an attempt to borrow racial markers in order to create White sites of rebellion and resistance. Identifying those racial markers is an exercise in reduction that, Monson says, "has caused many white Americans to perpetuate unwittingly primitivist assumptions about African American cultural authenticity" (1995: 422). Asian American jazz musicians approach this dangerous territory in yet another way. Whereas hip as a style became a marker for White liberal youth, Asian American musicians see their own activities as an expression of an important political moment when the Asian American movement emerged from Black activism during the Third World Strike at San Francisco State University in 1968–69 (Wei 1993: 15). Many Asian American musicians are overwhelmingly concerned with creating performatives of coalition and connection, and their historical awareness (unforgetfulness) of political indebtedness prompts their ongoing discursive use of (what they regard as) African American musical expressions. I would argue—more bluntly, less gracefully than Monson—that hipness is a top-down proposition. And yet, relative dominance and subjectivation is slippery ground. Who's on the bottom? Who's on first? The shape of the questions exposes their critical clumsiness. If hipness is a kind of slumming, i.e., a playacting of the privileged founded on essentialist, classist logic, are color-ful performatives of resistance then forever beyond the reach of anyone else? The notion of "people of color" is tricky on several counts and powerfully possible on several others. Grouping encourages totalizing gestures, but informed, unforgetful coalition is another story. If, as Anthony Braxton suggested, it's no longer hip to be hip anyway,[21] perhaps we need to rethink the politics of appropriation in ways that will allow for combustion as well as colonization.

RACIALIZING THE RAPPING BODY

On 29 October 1995, I sat in the back room of a community organization's headquarters in Philadelphia and listened to the Mountain Brothers, a three-man Asian American hip hop group, answer questions about the performance they had just given. Their audience was a group of some twenty Asian American teenagers who had listened intently as the Mountain Brothers rapped over the "beats" they'd brought on a cassette. Chops (Scott Jung), Peril (Chris Wang), and Styles (Steve Wei) were relaxed and funny as the audience asked questions about how the rappers had gotten started, what their parents thought, and whether they'd gotten signed yet. A young woman asked,

Q: What does "The Mountain Brothers" mean?

PERIL: It comes from a Chinese legend. But we're not real familiar with the details. *[everyone laughs]* The Mountain Brothers were a bunch of bandits that lived on a mountain. They stole from the rich and gave to the poor. Each one had special powers—there was actually one hundred and eight of them.

Q: One hundred and eight mountain brothers?

PERIL: Yeah. There was actually a girl, too.

STYLES: There was a girl.

CHOPS: She kicked some ass. *[everyone laughs]*

PERIL: They had these powers, and we just liked that. We extended the concept. *[He gestures toward Styles.]*

STYLES: The mountain is part of the ground, you know, but it's like taking it to a higher level. *[As he says this, he outlines a mountain with his hands, gestures upward, lets it go.]* But it's still part of the ground—it's still true to the ground—it still has its roots in the ground.

Styles's evocation of the trio's groundedness was a typical moment for the Mountain Brothers: easily explained but a bit esoteric, with much left unsaid.

Rap is a site where the body and ground (i.e. history, community) can come into conflict. It is one of the most transnational of popular music genres, yet even outside the United States it is perceived as closely linked to African Americans. In a global context, rap is consistently associated with youth and social criticism, though the form that such criticism takes is extremely contingent. In American contexts, rap is performed by Whites, Latino/as, Native Americans, and Asian Americans as well as African Americans. Its bodily language, its sartorial style, its gender politics, and its technological base all originated in African American performance practice.

Despite the international and interethnic spread of hip hop, matters of cultural ownership are constantly and passionately contested by some African American performers and producers. Tricia Rose has addressed these matters in the most depth and with the most consistent insight into African American youth culture and its aesthetics. Moreover, she has seriously engaged with the looming political problem of rap's transformations as it moves out of African American communities and into others. She allows for this movement within certain bounds. "To suggest that rap is a black idiom that prioritizes black culture and that articulates the problems of black urban life does not deny the pleasure and participation of others," she writes (1994: 4). Just as Dick Hebdige has used the idea of incorporation to describe the manipulation and absorption of subcultural elements by dominant institutions, Rose refers to the "bifocality" of African American culture in general, i.e. its longstanding ability to address, simultaneously, an African American audience and an enfolding White social framework (5). The "ideological recuperation of black cultural resistance" is not a matter of semantics or subtle political analysis for many African American rappers: they are well aware of the potential for appropriation and, as Rose points out, "some rappers have equated white participation with a process of dilution and subsequent theft of black culture" (ibid.). Vanilla Ice is a particularly clumsy and specious example, though his fifteen minutes of fame suggest that White appropriations of Black authenticities continue to have ideological and commercial force. His fabricated childhood in the Black inner city reduced the ghetto to a code for authenticity, a sign of hipness, and this naturally brought the wrath of the rap community down on him (11–12). The appropriation of rap by other youth communities of color speaks in a very different direction, though. A horizontal identification along class lines has generally occurred without conflict or challenge from African American rappers. Vanilla Ice's error lay not only in race but in class, which may be a category that allows for no contingencies.

Theo Chung, a first-year undergraduate at the University of Pennsylvania in 1995–96 and a Korean American DJ and MC, grew up in Los Angeles in a community that was half Asian American and half African American. The racial politics of rapping at Penn has been a source of amusement as well as concern to him. Performing in an environment that continues to be perceived in terms of Black/White relations despite a large Asian American student population has been a puzzle to him, but even stranger from his perspective is the relative lack of engagement between Asian American and African American students. He began to rap in the ninth grade; the hip hop group with which he continues to perform in LA is interracial, Asian American and African American. At Penn, his fellow MC was an African American student named Aaron Jones; the two of them hosted a weekly hip hop show on the university radio station, and they frequently DJed and MCed together. I asked him if the two of them made their interracial partnership part of their performance in any way, at any level, and he responded that race matters, but a respect for and immersement in hip hop culture is the main thing for him:[22]

THEO CHUNG: I guess a lot of Asians around here never hung around
    with Blacks, but I'd have to say the majority of my friends at home—

half my friends are Asian and half my friends are Black. I know I live
in a world that's a little different from everyone else. I don't treat anyone different just because they're Black, or just because they're Asian.
You know, if you rap, that's all I care about. You know, if you're White,
if you're Black, Hispanic, Jewish—if you rap well, and you respect hip
hop, if you're living it, then I'll support you all the way.

DEBORAH WONG: Do you and Aaron ever freestyle,[23] you know, about
race? about ethnicity?

TC: Oh, I see—you really want [to talk about] that racial thing! *[laughs]*

DW: I'm really curious about it. I don't mean, you know, to keep bringing
the conversation back to that!

TC: My partner's Black also, he goes to North Carolina Central right
now, and whenever we went to talent shows, everyone would ask, well,
how did you get an Asian kid and a Black kid to rap together?

DW: So you've had these questions before.

TC: Yeah, a million times.

DW: *[laughs]* OK, good.

TC: Yeah, we rap about it. We rap about it when we feel that people are
watching out for that. I'm not going to say it because it's, like, nothing
unusual to me, right. So I'm not going to say it just to impress you. But
if I can feel that the crowd feels kind of funny about it . . . then I'm
gonna say it, so I could stick it in your face, so you're gonna be like,
OK, I guess it's accepted.

DW: So they have to deal with it.

TC: Yeah. I'm not going to be, like, leaving you wondering whether or
not him and I are really friends. I'll tell you straight out—like an Asian
and a Black kid rapping together—but only for the means of like sticking it in their face, like, here you go, take it, you know?

In other words, Chung makes race an issue on a proactive basis, when he
feels it's needed, and then does so assertively.

"Respect" for hip hop is frequently cited by rappers as an important issue. Few rappers describe hip hop as *only* an African American tradition,
but many acknowledge its origin and vital location in African American
communities. The Mountain Brothers' publicity packet, for instance,
features the following statement, summing up some of the salient issues
of hip hop authenticity, ownership, and participation:

Because of [the Mountain Brothers'] dedication to the art, they (like the
originators and true keepers of hip-hop) bring the kind of material that
will add to hip-hop music, *not* steal from it or cheapen it. **No shallow
gimmicks, *no* karate kicks, *no* horror movie blood splattering, *no***

"songs that sound like the group that went platinum," just straight up self truth. What the Mountain Brothers represent most of all is *a deep love, respect, and ability* for true "rewind the shit over and over in your walkman" hip-hop.

"The originators and true keepers of hip-hop" are of course African Americans, and the Mountain Brothers' ready acknowledgment of African American ownership *and* their own place in that "art" are up front and matter-of-fact. Even as they align themselves with African Americans, they dissociate themselves from Orientalisms and mass culture commercialism. They express "focused anger on vital issues." In other words, they carve out a space assertively their own, "a viewpoint which has yet to be represented in hip-hop," an Asian American voice and perspective.

The Mountain Brothers, Theo Chung, and Aaron Jones first encountered each other on College Green, an open public space at the center of the Penn campus. It was 27 October 1995, the final day of Penn's Asian Pacific American Heritage Week, and much of that day was filled with Asian American performances on an outdoor stage in front of the library. A Japanese American folk-rock singer strummed on a guitar and was mostly ignored. Various student clubs—Thai, Filipino, Chinese, South Asian—performed traditional dances and drew their respective constituencies to the Green. A local Japanese American performer did modern dance. Hip hop ended the day. By the time the rappers came on, the student clubs were closing up their foodstalls and the crowds were waning.

My presence that day was neither accidental nor disinterested. Wanting to encourage a broader spectrum of Asian American performances and particularly eager to bring local, non-university Asian American performers onto the campus, I had arranged for the Mountain Brothers to appear.[23] Before they came on, though, two young men—Aaron Jones and Theo Chung—leaped up and took the stage, freestyling in such a spirited manner that the crowd began to gather all over again. It was the first time that day that an African American appeared onstage. The student crowd laughed and cheered at their clever sexual jokes, and some began to sway and clap in time with the beat. Two young African American women suddenly climbed up on stage and demanded the microphones—they gave it back to the young men verse for verse, prompting pleased cheers from both women and men in the audience.

I was riveted, torn between capturing it all on videotape and wanting simply to experience the moment. Between 1993 and 1995, the Penn campus was the stage for some of the uglier racial performatives in the country, including the infamous "water buffalo" incident (which was a Jewish student's response to African American sorority sisters doing a stepping routine outside a dorm). Virtually any Penn student will tell you that the campus is deeply segregated, and that socializing across racial and ethnic lines is unusual and difficult. Seeing African American and Asian American students onstage together, in the context of an Asian American performance event, was thus a commanding sight.

By the time the Mountain Brothers came on, word was going up and down Locust Walk, the main crosswalk on campus, that *Asian* guys were rapping on the Green; by the time they finished up, the crowd included a group of local Asian American high school students who were on campus for the day. They wanted more and asked for it. As the stage was struck behind them, all five rappers pulled into a circle and began to freestyle.

Clear differences in style and emphasis stood out in these moments. For one thing, Jones and Chung were much more comfortable with freestyling than the Mountain Brothers, but this is a matter of chosen focus. The Mountain Brothers are entirely directed toward getting signed and releasing an album, so all their work is carefully scripted; they never DJ, though they do perform at some parties. Jones and Chung have only just begun to think about recording; instead, their work is placed within the university party scene and some local clubs. They are used to performing spontaneously and responsively; their audience is integral to their resulting performance. Their interaction with each other is clearly central to what they do; they may cite its explicitly interracial character as an occasionally necessary performative, but in fact it is there continuously. They look at each other, they respond verbally to each other, they egg each other on in any number of ways. The more introspective nature of the Mountain Brothers' hip hop did not come off as well in this context: although willing to engage with Jones and Chung, freestyling simply isn't what they do; all of them struggled with the beat at times, and after a certain point, two of them weren't freestyling at all but instead uttered the texts of their set pieces. The Mountain Brothers' texts are in fact extremely complex, dense with metaphors and intertextual references and designed for repeated listening.

Yet, for the late afternoon audience gathered around them, that was less important than the fact that Asian American guys were rapping. The presence of Aaron Jones introduced a certain wariness that wasn't lost on Chung. Months later, I asked him:

So tell me about the crowd that day—it was almost entirely Asian American—there must have been about fifty Asian American Penn students standing around staring at the two of you. How was it?

TC: I mean, it's cool! I mean, any time they can get a chance to see that, you know . . . I mean, I think it's a positive thing. And you're always going to get people walk away from it, be like, jeez, I can't believe, like, that Asian guy raps, that's so stupid, that's for Black people. You know, you're always going to have that. So the more people you can—show that's more natural—it's *good* to have the Mountain Brothers come out, and it's *good* to have us come out, and whatever the groups, because in society, people take Asians—it's not even for granted—they take you—it's a subliminal thing, but like—they just don't want to accept you into anything. If you see a Black kid doing White music—if you can call it White music—like Hootie and the Blowfish, you know what I'm saying? People, like, accept it, they're like, it's cool that a Black kid would want to get into rock music. I mean, rock music's Black music anyways, but people forgot that.

DW: Right, right, right.

TC: People say that, but then, like, if you see an Asian kid doing rock music, then people are, like, what a stupid Asian kid, you know? There's just a certain negative vibe, and the more you stick it in their face, the more they're just gonna have to accept it.

DW: I see. OK. That sounds like a good strategy to me. I sensed a bit of caution from the crowd that day . . .

TC: There was . . .

DW: I wasn't sure where it was coming from, though. Part of it was that they didn't seem to know how to respond to you—I mean, they didn't seem to know enough to dance, to move their bodies.

TC: That's another problem. I don't think Asian people—at least at Penn—especially on the East Coast—because on the West Coast, hip hop—I mean, I'm glad I was born on the West Coast and lived there because hip hop is much more diverse. For example, I go to all the Pharcyde shows on the West Coast—and actually Tray from the Pharcyde is our group's manager—and we went to all the shows, and half, maybe a third of the audience is White, a third of the audience is Asian, a third of the audience is Black. I went to the Pharcyde show here two months ago, and it was *all* Black, you know it's *much* more segregated over here. And all the Asian kids here—you know, if you go to the Asian frat dances that I DJ—like, if I play hip hop, they don't like that, you know? Whenever you go to any quote-unquote Asian party or Chinese Students Association you always hear, like, Euro music, techno. That's the kind of music that, like, I guess Asians are generally interested in. So they just didn't know hip hop, you know.

The East Coast/West Coast politics of hip hop are thus racialized in different ways. On the East Coast, at least in contrast to California, hip hop is strongly identified with Blackness, so much that Chung sometimes finds himself off balance, resisted in ways he is not used to. The manner in which his performance activities are collapsed into Blackness is both puzzling and exasperating to him, though not threatening; his sense of his own position in the tradition is quite certain.

What happens to race, voice, and the body in hip hop? Chung says that he uses his body in very particular ways when he raps: different parts of his body do different parts of the beat. One hand, as he explained it, "may be doing quarter note, quarter note, quarter note, the other is doing beats one and three, and my feet might do the *and-and-and* part of the beat." His hands operate in another way as well: when he points at the audience, especially during freestyling, it's to draw them in, to address them directly. His body is doing several things, then. It keeps the beat, and the beats within the beats, and it even enacts the relationships between some of those beats. In other words, his rapping body is rhythmicized in all the complex, driving ways that dancing bodies have always been. If African American bodies have been epistemologically confined to the physical enactment of rhythm, and if that embodiment of rhythm is directly keyed to historicized social interactions, then the insertion of an Asian American body into that discursive moment is troubling for some witnesses. The literal absorption of an Asian American body into an older conversation, and one so central to historical anatomies of White/Black difference, can't occur without challenge and confusion. Indeed, I can't help but wonder about the perceived Asian/Asian American predilection for techno, as if the coolie body were drawn to music evoking postindustrial technologies.

The possibility of racial impersonation is essentially at center stage in hip hop. If the body—any body—can rap, then where does African American authenticity lie? Take the case of Theo Mizuhara, a *sansei* (third-generation Japanese American) DJ in Los Angeles: he has made his name by sounding Black (Della Cava 1996). "The king of LA drive-time" can be heard on 92.3 The Beat, and his voice has also been featured as the DJ in the film *Waiting to Exhale;* he has attracted spots for his show by Snoop Doggy Dogg and Ice Cube and has appeared in music videos by Shanice (in whose "I Wish" video he appears as a rose-bearing suitor) and Easy E. His "tag," frequently uttered, is "No color line." In fact, his ethnicity was a station secret until a local TV station broke the news a year after he had gone on the air. One magazine editor has dismissed Mizuhara as complicit with the tradition of "white jazz jocks and others, like Wolfman Jack, who played black music. Radio is a theatre of the mind" (ibid.). Mizuhara himself reacts to discussion of his color-crossing voice "with distaste and dismay" and doesn't think of himself as bridging race relations (ibid.). What does it mean to have a voice that passes? Mizuhara may insist on "no color line" but appears to have crossed it successfully and convincingly. Yet, when pressed to justify his radio presence, he too falls back on the language of cultural authenticity (Tazuma 1996):

I'm being prejudiced against because I'm not Black. It's kind of crazy. . . . The thing is that I understand. I may not agree. I may not think it's fair. Black people have been fucked with as long as they've been in the United States. They, I think, have been raped and robbed of their identity. I think they look at Black music as one of the last, maybe, unbastardized—to use a strong word—art forms that they possess, and they want to keep it as pure as possible. I understand that.

The coalescence of the Asian American and African American voice/body in hip hop is, for some, a newly threatening phenomenon. Asian Americans have traditionally been more easily absorbed into Whiteness. The American color line is Black and White, so an Asian American can be a banana (Yellow on the outside but White on the inside), and a White rapper can be accused of posing as a Wigger (a White nigger) (Rose 1994: 11–12), but for Asian Americans to *choose* to move in the direction of color is literally unimaginable. When it happens, it's suspicious, uncomfortable, hermeneutically impossible. And when that bodily movement coincides with rap—one of the most oppositional performatives now at play—everyone is put on the alert except, perhaps, most hip hoppers themselves. Hip hop culture recognizes ownership, owns up to racialized authority, and yet allows encroachment on those terms. So Asian Americans rap and engage in a kind of racialized shape-shifting that is unsettling, not unproblematic, but inherently seated in identity politics. Asian American rappers are watched and heard with pleasure and discomfiture; the cultural tropes they rely on create a discursive environment in which, by rapping, they can't be White.

SOMATIC SOCIETY: RACE,
PERFORMANCE, AND CULTURAL WORK

What might an authentic Asian American cultural performance be, then? Locating an authentic cultural space from which Asian Americans might signify is no small task. Looking to Asian soundscapes has been a recurring experiment: Glenn Horiuchi incorporated his *nisei* (second-generation Japanese American) aunt, Lilian Nakano, playing shamisen into his "Poston Sonata"; Mark Izu has played the Chinese sheng in several of his jazz compositions; Jon Jang has made abundant use of Chinese musicians and Chinese melodies in his many works. As Francis Wong has said, "I think you open yourself up to some problems if you just come in and take the form and you don't bring anything to it." The question remains, what *can* an Asian American bring to jazz or hip hop, and must it be Asian? The *nisei* Hollywood composer Paul Chihara, for instance, balks at drawing on Asian sounds in his scores. The musical sounds he remembers from his childhood years in the Minidoka internment camp were big band, and this is the soundscape that he deliberately chose to evoke in his score to the film *Farewell to Manzanar*.[24]

The problem of an authentic Asian American musical sound is, I think, directly related to the problem of locating an Asian American body vis-à-vis Whiteness and Blackness. Neither authentically Asian nor American, this body is held at arm's length by history, by legislation. Its Oriental ability to work is needed but suspect; in times of economic recession, the Asiatic body becomes a satisfying site for violence and refusal. If healing rituals are a central performative of the body, then performatives of racial violence are their inversion, equally dedicated to real, material change. Vincent Chin becomes a metonymic performance for holding back the Yellow Peril, for resisting the successful Oriental who labors unceasingly, perfectly, consumingly. Yet seeing Soon Ja Du shoot Latasha Harlins is shocking in a different way because it suggests the bottomlessness of the regulatory schemes maintaining race in America. The theater state is indeed terribly close at hand; the social drama of race is played out in endlessly creative and damaging ways. Just as every American of a certain age remembers where they were and what they were doing when Kennedy was shot, every Los Angeleño knows where they were when news broke of the verdict in the first Rodney King trial. Such moments are neither emblematic nor encapsulating; rather, they are constitutive sites for how racialized bodies come into being. Just as turn-of-the-twentieth-century conceptions of the Asiatic body were a response to modernity and capitalist industrialization, so have the results of three large-scale American wars in Asia, coupled with an increasingly global economy and stepped-up Asian immigrations, prompted a similar return to fin-de-siècle anxiety.

I suggested above that race is a constructed sign of historical injury that must be productively maintained and refashioned over time. The body will not stay still. I further suggest that the body is a somatic site for a society's most extreme visions of itself. Certainly it is difficult to forget the opening pages of Foucault's *Discipline and Punish*. The body is built up and broken down again and again, whenever the stakes are high. Race is not disinterested, let alone natural—it's hard work to maintain its categories. The Cartesian paradigm has tried to convince us that a psychosomatic symptom isn't real—not "really" of the body—but I suggest instead that the somatic realization of race is one of the great performative, destructive accomplishments of any society. Turning again to the anthropology of healing, I can conceive of performatives whose purpose is not to "fix" race but rather to shift racialized materialities. Robert R. Desjarlais (1996: 159) notes that, among the Yolmo of Nepal, "Healing transformations take place not within some cognitive domain of brain or heartmind, but within the visceral reaches of the eyes, the skin, and the tongue." He calls for "less cerebral" models of healing, citing how a Yolmo shaman creates physiological change by altering a patient's sensory environment: the shaman's "cacaphony of music, taste, sight, touch, and wild, tactile images activates the senses and the imagination" (160). Desjarlais suggests that the shaman "jumpstarts a physiology" (ibid.), and I unashamedly borrow from him to suggest that racialized performance has a physiology of its own that can result in social healing or disaster. By taking the body seriously, and by acknowledging its ongoing social construction, we are afforded the possibility of imagining other performatives. As Bryan Turner has suggested,

> We might define the somatic society as a social system in which the body, as simultaneously constraint and resistance, is the principal field of political and cultural activity. The body is the dominant means by which the tensions and crises of society are thematized; the body provides the stuff of our ideological reflections on the nature of our unpredictable time. (1992: 12)

In bringing the Mountain Brothers to perform at Penn, I certainly hoped for a material response from the complex body politic of the university's undergraduates. The cultural technologies that created racialized global flows of people represent a kind of cultural labor in its own right. Race might well be regarded as a condition for labor in a postindustrial world, the somatic indication of modernity's success. The question remains whether the reconfigured identities proposed by identity politics can move beyond the conditions that set it in motion to begin with. This is the juncture where hermeneutics and cultural work converge—where performance is operationalized.

Racial performatives like lynching or the exhaustive telecasting of the Simpson trial rely on a hermeneutics of suspicion which allow surveillance to become direct, actual control over troublesome bodies (Gabbard 1995b: 17). One might say that the American culture wars from the Reagan era onward have hinged entirely on such a hermeneutics, where the very parameters of discussion have been defined as tightly as possible. Looking at performance, however, allows the formulation of a positive hermeneutics, or a glimpse at activities that redefine their own terms as they emerge. Theorizing race through performance might perhaps even be regarded as a tautology—a full circle reflexive look at that-which-is-made-through-performance.

What are the points of contact between these Asian American performers and nineteenth-century minstrelsy, Stepin Fetchit, or Al Jolson? As Asian American jazz musicians and rappers move toward Blackness, their self-conscious movement away from Whiteness is unequivocal. Passing and impersonation are, after all, performatives of privilege and longing. Impersonation takes place from the top down, and passing from the bottom up. When Asian Americans explore African American performance traditions, they describe their transit as lateral. Moving toward color can be a reclamation of race and labor; the laboring body instead discovers that it is engaged in the class-conscious cultural work of social and political transformation.

As Monson has noted, there exists "a range of options within which African Americans have situated themselves with respect to twentieth-century urban modernity" (1995: 419). I suggest that some Asian American men use performance to mediate ideas of Asian American ethnicity, and they too have a range of options between which they choose strategically. They draw freely and imaginatively on particular cultural forms for particular reasons. Jazz and hip hop speak in many directions and are radically contingent traditions, historically positioned at ground zero in the culture wars of the American twentieth century. These are not the only forms that Asian American musicians encroach on and appropriate, but they are proving important sites for a certain recouping of race and ethnicity. The close alignment of these traditions with African American history, experience, and identity politics is not coincidental, nor is it unproblematic. Still, the choice to move away from Whiteness is a racial performative that is anti-assimilationist and potentially bridge-building.

The White musicologist Gary Tomlinson writes that "dialogical knowledge consists in this precarious maneuver of clearing space and building in it a discourse that never pushes other ways of knowing beyond its own horizon" (1992: 73). As an Asian American scholar, I want to believe that Asian American incursions into African American forms are conscious attempts to link different ways of knowing and reconfiguring race. This activation of the body politic is no small thing. If we regard these performers' efforts as pedagogical rather than appropriating, we can see anger, interrogation, coalition, action, revolution, in motion.

NOTES

I would like to thank Irene Nexica and Marina Roseman for help and advice as I explored theories of the body. The graduate students in the Dance Program of the Department of World Arts and Cultures at UCLA and participants in the 18th Annual Dance Ethnology Conference, 17–18 February 1996, offered comments and made suggestions on an earlier draft of this essay; members of the Department of Music at UC Riverside also made useful suggestions on an earlier version. Ingrid Monson, Ron Radano, and Philip Bohlman offered detailed criticism of the best sort—the final shape of this essay owes much to their careful readings.

1. In March 1991, a Korean-American grocery store owner, Soon Ja Du, got into an argument with an African American teenager, Latasha Harlins, in Du's convenience store in South Central Los Angeles. Mrs. Du accused the girl of trying to steal a $1.79 bottle of orange juice and, after a brief tussle, Mrs. Du shot and killed Ms. Harlins. Mrs. Du was charged with murder, but a jury convicted her of voluntary manslaughter and Compton Superior Court Judge Joyce Karlin sentenced her to five years probation, four hundred hours of community service, and a five hundred dollar fine. The verdict outraged members of the South Central community who saw the sentence as evidence of the low value that American society places on Black life. The Rodney King trial in 1992 exacerbated these resentments and led to the Los Angeles uprising of 1992, when Korean Americans and African Americans came into direct conflict.

2. I am indebted to Roger Savage for giving me the opportunity to think about a political hermeneutics and for pushing me to engage with it even when I resisted.

3. Foster (1995: 11–12) writes: "The body shares with women, racial minorities and colonized peoples, gays and lesbians, and other marginalized groups the scorn and neglect of mainstream scholarship. The canonical thrust of Western scholarship has worked at every turn to deny and repress or else to exoticize the experience of these peoples just as it has dismissed body-centered endeavors and the participation of the body in any endeavor. The critiques of canonical scholarship established in feminist and queer theory, postcolonial and minority

discourses of inherent racial, class, and gendered biases have immediate relevance for a scholarship of the body. These critical inquiries explicate techniques of dismissal used in canonical scholarship that find direct analogues in scholarly approaches to body-centered endeavors."

4. Turner suggests that theories of diet, for example, have almost always been tied to matters of class: the aristocratic body and the laborer's working body have been imagined through very different working metaphors, and the working-class body politic has been conceived as a machine. Since the Enlightenment, ideas of diet have been closely tied to interests in working-class efficiency: first developed for prisons and asylums, dietary regimes have been created to effect maximum efficiency through minimum sustenance—i.e., the working-class body has been constructed as a site that can be maintained in many ways, including the materiality of its sustenance.

Turner also suggests that *anorexia nervosa* stands in direct contrast to such dietary regimes of social control, though still rooted in matters of class formation and maintenance (1992: 214–28). He posits that anorexia is an "overdetermined disease, . . . peculiarly expressive of the personal and social dilemmas of educated, middle-class women, because it articulates aspects of their powerlessness within an environment that also demands their competitive success" (224–25). In essence, he suggests that the disorder may be pathological in nature but is still characterized by individual agency.

The first epigraph to this chapter comes from p. 12 of Turner's book.

5. In his earlier work, Fiske connected the body and pleasure, suggesting that "bodily pleasures offer carnivalesque, evasive, liberating practices—they constitute the popular terrain where hegemony is weakest" (1989: 6). At that point, he conceived of pleasure as a kind of experience beyond the reach of dominant ideology, as "the least politically active" kind of resistance (8). Analyzing surfing and video arcade games as social performances, Fiske described pleasure as a moment when "ideological subject reverts to the body"; he suggested that "the body becomes the site of identity and pleasure when social control is lost" (93). His conception of pleasure as resistance, though, was rooted in a model of hegemony as homogeneous in character, and resistance (especially popular culture) as heterogeneous (7–8). Rather than posit a body in interaction with dominant ideologies, Fiske froze it in an oppositional stance and invested it with a modernist individuality as a primary site of agency. His subsequent work is quite different, strongly inflected with poststructuralist theories of the body.

The second epigraph to this chapter comes from p. 76 of Fiske's earlier book.

6. The body of Rodney King has prompted a number of scholarly and political responses, most notably in Gooding-Williams 1993.

7. Turner (1992: 41) is similarly unwilling to do away with the reality of the body: "It would be wrong to construe my sociology of the body as *merely* a social constructionist viewpoint. In arguing that the body is socially constructed (by language, ideology, discourse or knowledge), it has been assumed, wrongly in my view, that one could not in addition believe that there is such a topic as the phenomenology of pain. . . . In short, I do not believe that reality is *discourse*, that is, I do not believe that social reality is merely an issue of representation."

8. This central problem has been acknowledged by many theorists. Wiegman (1995: 6), for instance, notes that "a politics based on identity must carefully negotiate the risk of reinscribing the logic of the system it hopes to defeat."

9. See, of course, Said's *Orientalism* (1978) for more on these connections.

10. See Wong 1996 for more on issues of Asian American masculinity and performance.

11. I am grateful for bibliographic help from Andrew Weintraub and Matthew Butterfield in this section.

12. One of the most recent such books, subtitled *Jazz, Black and White* (1995), by the White jazz critic Gene Lees, is the latest, rather clumsy attempt to write against race. Much of this rambling study profiles jazz musicians, mostly African American, and addresses in sympathetic White liberal mode the brutality of the racism encountered by African American musicians. At times, Lees's own role as empathetic White friend to these musicians is heavy-handed; in that sense, he plays out White angst in awkward but well-meant terms. More damaging, though, is his final chapter, "Jazz Black and White," in which he takes on anti-White racism among African American jazz musicians, and suddenly one realizes that this is where he's been headed all along—the moment when he can take on the Black nationalist stance of Stanley Crouch and Wynton Marsalis. Lees complains that "anti-white racism is showing increasing signs of being institutionalized" (190) and proceeds to show how White musicians have been ignored, excluded, and expropriated from jazz then and now. In the end, the language of liberal humanism (can't we all just get along?) simply doesn't allow him to take Black nationalism seriously.

13. Frank Kofsky opens his book *Black Nationalism and the Revolution in Music* (1970) with the reflection: "There is a curious dichotomy that reigns among white Americans. If they are in the jazz world proper, then they will tend to deny that, whatever else jazz *may* be, it is first and foremost a black art—an art created and nurtured by black people in this country out of the wealth of their historical experience. On the other hand, if they are not part of the jazz milieu, white Americans will automatically and virtually without exception assume that jazz is black—though not an art—and therefore, though this may go unstated, worthy of no serious treatment or respect" (9–10).

14. Krin Gabbard's dynamic paired collections, *Representing Jazz* and *Jazz among the Discourses*, are devoted to a poststructuralist questioning of how jazz comes to carry meaning, presenting particular moments in jazz history as radically contingent. Gabbard himself directly addresses the political economy of writing about jazz, noting that "ever since the first serious writings about jazz appeared, critics have sought to become organic intellectuals, who would theorize themselves and the music into importance" (1995b: 7). Most of the case studies in these two volumes address the institutional structures and apparatuses surrounding jazz, with fascinating but often unexamined implications for race.

15. Tomlinson notes, too, the potentially transformative effect that Signifyin(g) can have on what it touches: by locating meaning in the interstices of place, expression, and movement, the nature of those materials shifts. "By naming [for instance] the black tradition from within itself we revise and rename

all the other traditions with which it . . . interacts," he says (1992: 69). Presenting Miles Davis as a figure through whom African American and White critics (Crouch, Litweiler, Williams, and Baraka) have Signified their abiding concerns with jazz as they imagine(d) it, Tomlinson reconfigures Davis as problematically racialized and problematically true to the Signifyin(g) strategies of the blues.

16. From a telephone interview with Francis Wong in San Francisco, 29 January 1996.

17. This suite is on the album *Never Give Up!*, Asian Improv Records AIR 0007, 1989.

18. A year later, when I asked him if I could refer to his reaction in this essay, my friend, Charles Sykes, expanded on his original comments in an e-mail note as follows: "I liken 'stiff' to a metronome, an electronic one that plays an exact pulse. Music that grooves always seems to have a push and pull—there is a sense of the 'beat,' that constant, abstract metric pulse, but the groove is established on 'top' of the beat (slightly before) or by 'laying back' (slightly after the beat)."

19. Hearing race in music is of course heuristically related to hearing sexuality and sexual orientation in music: both are ontologically grounded in a conception of difference vis-à-vis the normative. For a number of essays that explore (among other things) the problems of "hearing" sexual orientation, see *Queering the Pitch* (Brett, Wood, and Thomas 1994).

20. I would like to thank Mark Izu for including me in that roundtable discussion during the weekend of the 1996 Asian American Jazz Festival, which he curated.

21. Pers. comm. from Anthony Braxton to Ronald Radano.

22. All of Theo Chung's comments are from a telephone interview conducted in Philadelphia on 1 February 1996.

23. Freestyling is impromptu, improvised rapping that often takes place between two or more rappers in contexts of live performance; like the dozens and other forms of African American oratory, it can have a competitive frame. Each rapper takes a turn, rapping for a moment or two until s/he either hands the floor over the next rapper or has it forcibly (verbally) taken away. Freestyling rarely appears in audio recordings or in music videos.

24. The Mountain Brothers' appearance at Penn was sponsored by the Department of Music, the Theater Arts Program in the Department of English, and the Graduate Student Associations Council Multiculturalism Committee.

25. Interview with Paul Chihara in Pittsburgh, 23 January 1996.

REFERENCES

Bourdieu, Pierre. 1977. *Outline of a Theory of Practice*. Trans. Richard Nice. Cambridge: Cambridge University Press.

Brett, Philip, Elizabeth Wood, and Gary C. Thomas, eds. 1994. *Queering the Pitch: The New Gay and Lesbian Musicology*. New York: Routledge.

Butler, Judith. 1993. *Bodies That Matter: On the Discursive Limits of "Sex."* New York: Routledge.

Cipriano, Ralph. 1996. "The Skinny: Buddha Aims to Wing It." *Philadelphia Inquirer* (27 January): B1, 5.

Cowan, Jane K. 1990. *Dance and the Body Politic in Northern Greece*. Princeton, N.J.: Princeton University Press.

Csordas, Thomas J. 1996. "Imaginal Performance and Memory in Ritual Healing." In *The Performance of Healing*, ed. Carol Laderman and Marina Roseman, 91–113. New York: Routledge.

Della Cava, Marco R. 1996. "DJ's Voice Cuts Across Color Lines." *The Nation* (8 February): C6.

Desjarlais, Robert R. 1996. "Presence." In *The Performance of Healing*, ed. Carol Laderman and Marina Roseman, 143–64. New York: Routledge.

Fiske, John. 1989. *Reading the Popular*. Boston: Unwin Hyman.

——. 1993. *Power Plays, Power Works*. London: Verso.

Foster, Susan Leigh. 1995. "Choreographing History." In *Choreographing History*, ed. Susan Leigh Foster, 3–21. Bloomington: Indiana University Press.

Foucault, Michel. 1977. *Discipline and Punish*. New York: Vintage.

Freer, Regina. 1994. "Black–Korean Conflict." In *The Los Angeles Riots*, ed. Mark Baldassare, 175–203. Boulder, Colorado: Westview Press.

Gabbard, Krin. 1995a. "Introduction: Writing the Other History." In *Representing Jazz*, ed. Krin Gabbard, 1–8. Durham, N.C.: Duke University Press.

——. 1995b. "Introduction: The Jazz Canon and Its Consequences." In *Jazz among the Discourses*, ed. Krin Gabbard, 1–28. Durham, N.C.: Duke University Press.

Gilroy, Paul. 1991. "Sounds Authentic: Black Music, Ethnicity, and the Challenge of a *Changing* Same." *Black Music Research Journal* 11: 111–36.

Goldberg, David Theo, ed. 1994. *Multiculturalism: A Critical Reader*. Oxford: Blackwell.

Gooding-Williams, Robert, ed. 1993. *Reading Rodney King/Reading Urban Uprising*. New York: Routledge.

Gotanda, Philip Kan. 1991. *Yankee Dawg You Die*. New York: Dramatists Play Service.

Hanna, Thomas. 1970. *Bodies in Revolt: A Primer in Somatic Thinking*. New York: Holt, Rinehart and Winston.

Johnson, Carolyn Schiller. 1995. "'Freaks of Imagination' and 'Brown Women Dancers': The Racialization of Foreign Dancers at Century's Turn in Chicago." Paper presented at the 40th Annual Meeting of the Society for Ethnomusicology, 19–22 October. Los Angeles.

Jones, LeRoi. 1967. "Jazz and the White Critic." In *Black Music*. New York: Morrow.

Kofsky, Frank. 1970. *Black Nationalism and the Revolution in Music*. New York: Pathfinder Press.

Laderman, Carol, and Marina Roseman. 1996. "Introduction." In *The Performance of Healing*, ed. Carol Laderman and Marina Roseman, 1–16. New York: Routledge.

Lees, Gene. 1995. *Cats of Any Color: Jazz, Black and White*. Oxford: Oxford University Press.

Lye, Colleen. 1995. "American Naturalism and the Asiatic Body: Fin-de-siècle Encounters on the Pacific Rim." Paper presented at the University of Pennsylvania, 23 October.

McClary, Susan, and Robert Walser. 1994. "Theorizing the Body in African American Music." *Black Music Research Journal* 14: 75–84.

McLaren, Peter. 1994. "White Terror and Oppositional Agency: Towards a Critical Multiculturalism." In *Multiculturalism: A Critical Reader*, ed. David Theo Goldberg, 45–74. Oxford: Blackwell.

Meltzer, David, ed. 1993. *Reading Jazz.* San Francisco: Mercury House.

Monson, Ingrid. 1995. "The Problem with White Hipness: Race, Gender, and Cultural Conceptions in Jazz Historical Discourse." *Journal of the American Musicological Society* 48: 396–422.

Radano, Ronald M. 1993a. *New Musical Figurations: Anthony Braxton's Cultural Critique.* Chicago: University of Chicago Press.

———. 1993b. "The Bounds of Black Musical Significance." Paper presented at the annual meeting of the Society for Ethnomusicology, Oxford, Mississippi, 29 October.

Rose, Tricia. 1994. *Black Noise: Rap Music and Black Culture in Contemporary America.* Hanover, N.H.: Wesleyan University Press and the University Press of New England.

Said, Edward W. 1978. *Orientalism.* New York: Pantheon.

Scarry, Elaine. 1985. *The Body in Pain: The Making and Unmaking of the World.* New York: Oxford University Press.

Smith, Arthur H. 1894. *Chinese Characteristics.* Repr. Singapore: Graham Brash (Pte) Ltd., 1986.

Takagi, Dana Y. 1992. *The Retreat from Race: Asian-American Admissions and Racial Politics.* New Brunswick, N.J.: Rutgers University Press.

Tazuma, Larry J. 1996. "Double Prejudice in Urban Radio." http://www.yolk.com/magazine/iss1/theo.html.

Tomlinson, Gary. 1992. "Cultural Dialogics and Jazz: A White Historian Signifies." In *Disciplining Music: Musicology and Its Canons*, ed. Katherine Bergeron and Philip V. Bohlman, 64–94. Chicago: University of Chicago Press.

Turner, Bryan S. 1992. *Regulating Bodies: Essays in Medical Sociology.* London: Routledge.

Wei, William. 1993. *The Asian American Movement.* Philadelphia: Temple University Press.

Wiegman, Robyn. 1995. *American Anatomies: Theorizing Race and Gender.* Durham, N.C.: Duke University Press.

Wong, Cynthia. 1996. "'Asian for the Man!': Stereotypes, Identity and Self-Empowerment in Asian American Rap." Paper presented at the annual meeting of the Mid-Atlantic Chapter of the Society for Ethnomusicology, Peabody Conservatory, Baltimore, 22 March.

2

Ethnifying Rhythms, Feminizing Cultures

FRANCES R. APARICIO

mi negra no te molestes	[my black woman, don't get upset
si te dicen sabrosona	if they call you tasty
por ese andar que tú tienes	because of the tremendous and playful
tan tremendo y retozón.	way you walk.]
	(Orquesta Aragón, "Sabrosona," 1956)

The song "Sabrosona" (Very tasty woman), interpreted by the Cuban Orquesta Aragón, makes explicit one of the most predominant ideologemes in the Afro-Caribbean musical tradition: the figure of the mulatta and/or the black woman dancing, walking, or moving to the musical rhythms of the Caribbean. This iconic tradition is ever-present in Latin salsa, Dominican merengue, and Afro-Latin rap. It permeates the discourse of male composers and musicians as well as of male Caribbean writers, from turn-of-the-century essays to the contemporary postmodern renderings of Antonio Benítez Rojo and Edgardo Rodríguez Juliá.[1] Also imbued with racial and class implications, this patriarchal discursive figure has been an important site for negotiating national and cultural identity. Moreover, it has been appropriated, fetishized, and reconverted in instances of transcultural discursive and physical encounters.[2] Its synesthesic texture, that is, its multiple sensorial suggestiveness —her color and visually desirable shape and body, her bodily movements, and the rhythms that she necessarily evokes—makes this cultural icon a productive interartistic site for the study of patriarchy, colonialism, and globalization. Briefly put, the rhythmic mulatta has become a cultural sign or signifier that, in its national and transnational circulation, reveals the tensions, contradictions, and inner workings of patriarchy in (post)-colonial, intercultural contexts.

In this essay, I trace some of the diverse meanings of this culturally complex figure who lays bare the imperial processes of ethnifying

rhythms and feminizing cultures. While the icon of the rhythmic mulatta builds on the social and patriarchal imaginary of nation, particularly in the Caribbean, it is also deployed interculturally to ethnify
and feminize Third World cultures. Within the boundaries of nation,
the female is constituted as Other; in larger, transnational cultural trans-
actions the (Caribbean or Latin American) nation itself becomes feminized by an imperial, colonizing gaze. To be ethnified, then, is to be
constructed and displaced as Other, as "heathen alterity." [3] Concomi-
tantly, to be feminized is to be re-presented with feminine attributes,
or as woman, in order to be depoliticized, to be rendered invisible,
mute, as a passive, erotized object rather than an active subject or agent
of culture.

Obviously, this is not a new approach. Feminist incursions in post-
colonial studies have already engaged in fruitful analyses of such processes, and this study, in fact, owes much to this strong critical tradition. [4]
Yet, except for Vera Kutsinsky's feminist perspectives in *Sugar's Secrets*, [5]
a study of the erotic desire for the mulatta in the discourse of the Cuban
nation, scholarship on nationalism and sexuality has elided this figure in
the context of the Hispanic Caribbean. Emphasizing rhythm as an allegory of nation, this cultural icon needs to be examined across various
cultural texts, such as music, literature, and media.

This essay attempts to understand how and why the rhythmic mulatta
continues to be in currency despite an increasing consciousness about
patriarchy, racism, and colonialism. Through such an analysis, we can
also understand the central role of discourse in the hegemonic processes
of negotiating power. Rather than limiting my study to a seemingly uni-
lateral, feminist denunciation of the rhythmic mulatta as constructed
by male Caribbean subjects, I also want to destabilize the national and
cultural fixity of approaches to machismo by looking at other writing subjects. The transcultural and transnational connotations of this
signifier are evident in the Concert of the Americas, produced in 1994
for the Third Hemispheric Summit of Presidents, which illustrates the
current, revitalized role of feminizing and erotizing Latin American nations during the emergence of NAFTA. This construct has also been internalized and deployed by U.S. Latinas. For the Puerto Rican poet
Judith Ortiz Cofer, reflecting on the body of her mother and on the way
she walks is a way of negotiating between, on the one hand, the traditional, patriarchal discourse underlying the meanings according to her
self-tropicalized mother and, on the other, the process of enculturation
and the forging of new, modern identities for second-generation U.S.
Latinas.

Desiring the Rhythmic Mulatta

Listening to Orquesta Aragón's "Sabrosona," we are reminded of the visual erotic fixation of the male gaze on the hips and pelvic movements of the mulatta and black woman, which has become, in the culture of the Hispanic Caribbean, a national fetish. Throughout numerous salsa songs, merengues, and rap; in popular jargon and in the urban folklore of male-authorized *piropos* addressed to women;[6] and even in the postmodern cultural texts of male Caribbean writers, the visual reference to the mulatta's hips, *caderas*, and pelvic movements constitutes an ever-present patriarchal synecdoche in the Hispanic Caribbean. According to Vera Kutzinski, in the case of the mulatta, this icon surreptitiously reveals that she disrupts the ordered, masculine political and national body based on a paradigm of mestizaje that attempts to naturalize a stable, harmonious image of the nation in its racial relations:

> For what the mulatta, unlike the ideology of mestizaje, represents is not a stable synthesis but a precarious and tenuous multiplicity, "a concentration of differences," of "insoluble differential equations." The mulatta indexes areas of structural instability and ideological volatility in Cuban society, areas that have to be hidden from view to maintain the political fiction of cultural cohesion and synthesis. The key signifier of such instability and volatility is the nonwhite woman's body conceived as the site of troubling sexual and racial differences. As much as this site has all the attractions of a mythic place of intellectual and psychological refuge and "epistemological consolation" in a society like Cuba, it is simultaneously feared as the locus of potential change, disruption, and complication. (*Sugar's Secrets*, 172)

As Kutzinski also observes, the literati of Cuban white male poets have represented the mulatta as "pure rhythm," thus constructing her as another instance of black primitivism, foregrounding her physicality and body rather than her whole self as a thinking, rational subject. By commodifying blackness, these poets also isolate issues of race and racist social practices from their political and social implications. What Kutzinski suggests, then, is that by fixating on the mulatta body and particularly her *caderas*, her genitalia, her vagina, as a locus of desire and pleasure for the Cuban male subject, writers and musicians systematically detract attention from racist and violent practices in Cuban society. However, the irony behind this synecdochal erasure is that it is precisely the woman's *caderas* that have been subjected historically to racism through rape and sexual violence and should, precisely, evoke rather than erase the past of violence against women of color. This displacement, then, is one of signifieds: by celebrating and trivializing her *caderas* only as a rhythmical and musical pleasurable entity, then Caribbean patriarchy can erase from the body of the mulatta any traces of violence for which it has been responsible throughout history.

For instance, in a recent piece titled "Salsa × 2," the Cuban American journalist Enrique Fernández introduces Latino culture to an Anglo readership as the essentialist expression of an erotic gastronomy.[7] He capitalizes on the double discourse that the word "salsa" suggests: the sensuality of both the rhythm and the food. He illustrates his point by emphasizing the desire for the "yummy Negress" that the male singing subject expresses in the popular Dominican merengue "El negrito del batey" (The black man from the sugarmill), a male desire that elides any history of violence against black women in the Caribbean. Fernández reads this merengue exclusively as an articulation of an essentialized Latino sensuality that, according to him, is "our finest Hispanic heritage" (7) and an answer to the Anglo Other's "sensory vacuum" which he also problematically constructs. Most revealing, however, is the author's total silence regarding the subaltern subjectivity of the slave that this merengue articulates. In the merengue, the voice of the black male complains about hard physical labor and humorously suggests that work was invented by God for the ox and the animals, not for human beings, a contestatory utterance against the exploitations of slavery and the dehumanizing and animal-like practices to which slaves were subjected. In this song, dancing is not just about an essentialized erotics that all Latinos embody, as Fernández puts it, but rather suggests itself as a political practice engaged by the subaltern in an attempt to survive the oppressive conditions of forced labor. As Jesús Martín Barbero reminds us, Afro-Caribbean rhythms and dances need to be contextualized as traces of a symbiosis of work and rhythm that allowed slaves to survive. The "gestural style" of blacks in Brazil, for instance, was seen by society as a "double indecency," yet for the enslaved black communities the hypnotizing effects of such rhythms allowed them to endure long working hours and rigorous physical exertion.[8] Fernández's reading of this merengue illustrates how mainstream society decontextualizes the historical uses of Afro-Caribbean rhythms and dance, rendering them invalid as politically informed practices, as resistance, and celebrating them, as Fernández does, as objects to be consumed for the benefit of patriarchy.

In *The Repeating Island*, Antonio Benítez Rojo also exemplifies the naturalizing effects of this discursive tradition and its implications for cultural criticism. In his introduction, the author invokes the image of two older, wise black women whom he observes from a window above during an apocalyptic afternoon in Havana at the beginning of the Missile Crisis:

> While the state bureaucracy searched for news off the shortwave or hid behind official speeches and communiqués, two old black women passed "in a certain kind of way" beneath my balcony. I cannot describe this "certain kind of way"; I will say only that there was a kind of ancient and golden power between their gnarled legs, a scent of basil and mint in their dress, a symbolic, ritual wisdom in their gesture and their gay chatter. I knew then at once that there would be no apocalypse. The swords and the archangels and the beasts and the trumpets and the breaking of the last seal were not going to come, for the simple reason that the Caribbean is not an apocalyptic world; it is not a phallic world in pursuit of the vertical desires of ejaculation and castration.[9]

In this passage, Benítez Rojo establishes a master metaphor that will recur throughout the rest of his analysis: he finds the polyrhythms of the Caribbean embodied in that "certain kind of way" of walking of these two black women. The visual image is thus transformed into an aural reference, it becomes rhythm evoked, impossible to define, elusive, ineffable, a source of pleasure for the male subject who gazes at the women from a superior and vertical location (despite the author's reticence to recognize the Caribbean as a phallic world "in pursuit of the vertical desires of ejaculation and castration"). The ineffability of these rhythms is further developed in the first chapter, where Benítez Rojo discusses the difficulty of writing and inscribing African rhythms and dances within the boundaries and through the codes of a Western musical system.[10] After quoting Fernando Ortiz's observations in this regard, Benítez Rojo adds nothing more to this analysis.

This silence is not unique, but part and parcel of the systematic erasure of African codes and meanings in westernized writings about the mestizo culture of the Caribbean. Antonio Pedreira, in his foundational essay about Puerto Rican culture, *Insularismo*, describes the African-based syncopated rhythms of the *danza* as "*disparate*" (nonsense) and only alludes to the African elements of Puerto Rican culture with adjectives such as "singular" and "particular."[11] Under Western eyes and ears, any differences from the systems of musical notation or from Spanish grammatical norms, as the *jitanjáforas* also illustrate, have not been accorded culturally based meanings but instead are emptied of meaning, rendered as nonsense. In his book, Benítez Rojo does not even question the implicit hierarchies in this supposed "difficulty" of transposing one musical system to another. In other words, why transpose an oral tradition into a written system that imposes its own measures, codes, and values on African-based performances? Who benefits ultimately from these transpositions? The implicit deficiencies, if anything, are located in the Western system of musical notation, in the divisions of measures and beats that cannot accommodate the total and simultaneous coexistence of heterogeneous beats and rhythms. These politics of musical notation continue in conservatories and music education programs, where improvised, popular music is still not considered worthy of being included in the curriculum. Meanwhile, the mimetic act of "reading" written music is privileged as the dominant mode of learning and of becoming a musician. In this light, Benítez Rojo's discourse continues to render Afro-Cuban rhythms and music as a mysterious site, as a locus of an essentialized, impenetrable authenticity. Rather than proposing new ways of approaching this musical tradition as a system of knowledge in conjunction with its religious, social, and cultural contexts, he renders it always already unknowable.

Music, as performance, may invest the cultural icon of the rhythmic mulatta with potentially oppositional meanings. For instance, Toña La Negra's interpretation of "La negrita Concepción," composed by Cuates Castilla, imbues the lyrics with instances of feminist and racial revisionings.[12] Her vocal rendering of the black woman or the negra as text suggests a self-ironic appropriation of her own dark-skinned body in Mexico whose very artistic name—Toña La Negra—strategically essentializes herself as a "racial Other" within a Mexican social imaginary that has excluded blackness from the national body. In the song, la negrita Conceptión is described as a famous rumbera who moves in extraordinary ways: "Hay que ver cómo se mueve. . . . Ay mamá qué tembladera. . . . Cómo mueve la cintura . . ." (You have to see how she moves. . . . Oh, woman, what shaking. . . . How she moves her waistline). In Toña's singing, the imperative male gaze, which usually mediates the fashioning of the rhythmic mulatta, may become a rather undefined or plural gaze; that is, the impersonality of the "hay que ver" refers us not only to male voyeurs but also to possible female "gazers." The object of the gaze, the negrita Concepción, also becomes doubled in the musical performance of a black female singer, Toña La Negra, who is simultaneously being seen while she sings. Thus, this particular musical utterance, in the voice of Toña, destabilizes and pluralizes the gendered semantics evoked by the patriarchal discursive tradition of the rhythmic mulatta.

The dialectics between the centripetal forces (the waistline) and the centrifugal movements of la negrita Concepción reaffirm Kutzinski's analysis regarding the instability and volatility that the mulatta's movements represent to patriarchy. Yet Toña La Negra's interpretation does emphasize the refrain to the song—"Esta negra es una fiera / que no tiene domador" (This black woman is a beast / without a tamer)—which, if read literally, may suggest the primitivist construct of blacks as beasts, a construct historicized in and through the institution of slavery. Yet, from a feminist perspective, this refrain simultaneously may allude to the independence of black women, to their agency as subaltern subjects who resist being "domadas" (domesticated) or controlled. Within the strong, brassy sounds of the mambo rhythms that frame the lyrics, the black woman is named Concepción, a meaningful name that remits us to the female black body as the origins of mestizaje and mulatismo in the Caribbean and to the figure of the Virgin. She becomes a reaffirmation of the power of the mulatta to control her own life and her own body as text, to be the sole agent of her rhythmical movements, and to reject any possibilities of being owned by a male.

Resisting Polyrhythms

Other Caribbean subjects, both male and female, have "resisted" the hybridization of rhythms and the icon of the rhythmic mulatta as an index of racial confrontation, violence, rape, slavery, and national "impurity." The Puerto Rican Positivist thinker Salvador Brau, for instance, wrote at the turn of the century against the creollization—read Africanization —of the European country dance, the contradanza in Puerto Rico. In his important essay "La danza puertorriqueña" (1885), he bemoans what he deemed the intrusion of the upa or merengue from Cuba that began to displace the traditional country dance.[13] While other musicologists have proposed different explanations for this instance of musical transculturation—for instance, the influence of upper-class venezolanos who migrated to Puerto Rico around 1835–40—what is clear is that, whether from Cuba or Venezuela, the influence of African-based rhythms was transforming what was deemed a pure, European cultural practice into a creolle, Afro-Caribbean dance.[14] Brau opposed the two major changes that this phenomenon effected: first, the shift from figure dancing to couple dancing, and second, the dismissal of the *bastonero* (the guide or leader who led the dance with his cane). These two changes transformed the danza into a more democratic practice. By dismissing the strongly rooted authority of the bastonero, who in many cases assured a degree of "purity" between the man and the woman, now the Puerto Rican danza could be danced by couples who could embrace and whisper to each other. Most significant about the merengue is that it penetrated the ballrooms of the Philharmonic Society by 1846, and by 1854 the original eight measures of the merengue had extended to 34 and later to 130. Thus Salvador Brau appropriately describes the merengue as an "invading or invasory march," a "revolution" that indeed threatened not only Brau but Spanish-born Puerto Ricans, the gachupines.[15]

Brau's reaction against the transgressive presence of the "timbales" in the salon orchestras textualizes the social meanings that instruments, rhythms, and musical structures do evoke:

[El timbal] recuerda los sacudimientos peculiares de la bomba africana, acentuando la cadencia de baile de un modo obsceno, adaptable a las contorsiones grotescas y lascivas de esos abigarrados botargas que recorren las calles en la época de nuestro extraordinario carnaval.[16]

(The timbal reminds us of the peculiar rumblings of the African bomba, accentuating the cadence of the dance in an obscene manner, adaptible to the grotesque and lascivious contortions of those who traverse the streets during the season of our extraordinary carnival.)

This quote is worth noting, not only for the ways in which it inscribes "Africanness" as exotic sensuality, as a dehumanized expression bordering on the animalesque and as amoral obscenity, but also because it reveals a fissure in Brau's ambivalence regarding his own membership in the Puerto Rican national imaginary. The use of the possessive in referring to the "extraordinary carnival" signals that contradiction, for if Brau totally disavows the African elements of Puerto Rican culture, how come he inscribes himself as a part of the most African-based Puerto Rican collective feast, the Carnival? My guess is that this is no linguistic slip, but rather a clear moment of reasserting power by a writer who is struggling for the ownership and control of a culture that is visibly and musically slipping away from the pure, European mold.

While national and racial purity are central to Brau's discourse, it is also significant that Brau is willing to celebrate hybridity only when the interaction, or marriage, is characterized by the appropriation of Puerto Rican *creolle* music by European or U.S. composers. Thus, the model of transculturation that Brau privileges is evident in his discussion of Louis Moreau Gottschalk, who was "intoxicated by the voluptuosity of this hybrid music," and of Don Félix Astol, also seduced by the eroticized rhythms of the Puerto Rican danza. For Brau, evidently, transculturation can only be textualized within a discourse of seduction whereby the Puerto Rican hybrid danza is rendered as a female, erotized body that seduces the masculine creative thrust of First World composers. The inverse, the African musical signifiers penetrating European culture, represented an excessive discursive transgression and an inversion of gendered power for Brau to accept.

Ironically, this resistance is also articulated by U.S. Latinas, although at a different sociohistorical moment and from an opposite subject position from Brau's, as hybrid subjects themselves. Let me examine three brief texts: one short letter written by the daughter of a Cuban-born woman that appeared in a San Diego newspaper on 6 April 1994, and a prose passage and a poem from *Silent Dancing* by the Puerto Rican poet Judith Ortiz Cofer. The authors of these texts share a common subject location as second-generation U.S. Latinas who resist, obviously for different reasons than Brau, the social implications of the Latina's body and movement. Yet in all these texts the metonymic value of the body of the Caribbean woman as a site of exotic, erotized rhythm is connected to underlying anxieties about national "purity" and cultural hybridity.

The daughter of a Cuban-born woman in San Diego, California, wrote the following short letter to the *San Diego Union Tribune*:

> My family was at Seaport Village and we were approaching a restaurant called Papagayo. A strong Latin beat pulsed from inside. As we got closer, it became clearer.
>
> "What a rhythm," my mom said.
>
> My mom was born in Cuba, and she has pure Latin American blood. When she hears some of her native music, she just can't control herself. So there we were, in the middle of the boardwalk at Seaport Village, and my mom was dancing like she was at the Festivale [*sic*] in Cuba. I couldn't believe it. Has she no pride? People were starting to stare, some were trying to hide their snickering. They could have started throwing money at any minute. I resumed walking faster and faster, saying to myself over and over again, "I don't know this woman."

This second-generation Cuban American woman disavows her Cuban-born mother's body as the latter dances publicly to Latin rhythms. The resistance on the part of the daughter, a hybrid U.S. Latina (given her Anglo last name), to being identified with her "native" dancing mother reveals significant underlying constructs about Latin American racial identity and culture as Other. First, her reference to her mother's "pure Latin American blood," an unsurprisingly homogenizing tendency in United States racial categorizing, remits us, however unwittingly, to the central signifiers of racial politics in the colonial history of Latin America, the "pure blood" (*sangre limpia*) necessary for survival in Inquisitorial Spain and its territories. Yet, in this daughter's discourse, the pure blood serves to signal an essentialist view of culture as rhythm. Her mother is a pure Latin American, a "native," because she has not cleansed herself from the impulsive, primitivist, irrational forces of these rhythms. "She just can't control herself," observes the daughter, as if these rhythms were evil forces that overpower Reason and civilization. Thus, in the process of ethnifying Latin rhythms, the daughter necessarily ethnifies her own mother. This double ethnification is, in turn, necessary for the speaking subject to differentiate herself as "pure" American, un-ethnic, a disavowal expressed in the last line, "I resumed walking faster and faster, saying to myself over and over again, 'I don't know this woman'." Herself a descendant of that very same ethnified body, the daughter fashions herself as separate by walking away, despite the unexpressed pain.

The space where this incident occurs and from where the Latin beat emerges is a restaurant called Papagayo, one of many Californian postmodern versions of primitive South of the Border culture as reimagined by United States capitalism. Thus, the juxtaposition of the ethnified native woman dancing to her rhythms and the restaurant that appropriates Latin American food, cultural icons, and natural resources, resemanticizing them to the exigencies of a First World taste and desire, articulates the colonial fixation on Latin culture as object to be consumed and the simultaneous disavowal of the very people who embody and produce the culture desired by the dominant Other.

Judith Ortiz Cofer, in *Silent Dancing*, shares the shame of having an "ethnic" mother who looks too Latina, too tropical, too erotic for the cultural environs of Patterson, New Jersey:

> I would walk home every day from school. I had fifteen minutes to get home before my mother panicked and came after me. I did not want that to happen. She was so different from my classmates' mothers that I was embarrassed to be seen with her. While most of the other mothers were stoutly built women with dignified grey hair who exuded motherliness, my mother was an exotic young beauty, black hair down to her waist and a propensity for wearing bright colors and spike heels. I would have died of shame if one of my classmates had seen her sensuous walk and the looks she elicited from the men on our block. And she would have embraced me in public, too, for she never learned moderation in her emotions, or restraint for her gesturing hands and loud laughter. She kept herself a "native" in that apartment she rarely left, except on my father's arm, or to get one of us from school. (126–27)

Having internalized the dominant patriarchal binary of woman as either whore or virgin mother, the young Cofer contrasted the American mothers, seemingly asexual and thus "dignified," and her own self-tropicalized mother whose "sensuous walk" was a source of shame for the young daughter. Like the Cuban American woman, Cofer also describes her mother as "native," yet unlike the former, she clarifies the constructedness and strategic nature of this identity. It is the mother's objective, as Cofer puts it later, "to remain 'pure' for her eventual return to the island by denying herself a social life . . . , by never learning but the most basic survival English; and by her ability to create an environment in our home that was a comfort to her, but a shock to my senses" (127). Unlike Judith's bicultural socialization, the mother refuses to integrate herself into U.S. society and thus attempts to keep her body "pure" from hybridization or assimilation. Thus the Puerto Rican national body, allegorized in the body of her mother, is also inscribed as erotized rhythm which Cofer, as daughter, refuses to embody by virtue of her contact with U.S. society and values.

In both texts, second-generation daughters negotiate between the traditional, pre-modern, and primitivist connotations of their mothers' bodily movements and gestures, and the process of enculturation to which they are objected. Moreover, their writings re-inscribe the binaries of tradition or primitivism (located in Puerto Rico or Cuba) versus the modernization that Anglo-American society promotes. These Latinas insert themselves in a modernity reached through the rejection of individual time and bodily rhythms and through the assimilation of a new organization of time "which is mechanically fragmented and unrelated to context," the "time of objects" rather than that of "subjects," a rhythm of productivity akin to urban, industrialized society.[17]

As a writer whose works reaffirm the relativity of truth, Cofer offers us another vantage point to her mother's body as erotized rhythm. In the poem "The Way My Mother Walked," the daughter, from the outside, can only guess her mother's anxiety over the ways others define her as embodied, erotized rhythm. While Cofer describes her as

the gypsy queen of Market Street,
shuttling her caramel-candy body past
the blind window of the Jewish tailor
who did not lift his gaze,
the morse code of her stiletto heels sending
their Mayday-but-do-not-approach into
the darkened doorways where eyes hung like mobiles in the breeze,

(Silent Dancing, 99)

she also shows how her mother communicated to her, woman to woman, the dangers of possessing, and being possessed by, a female body: "Alleys / Made her grasp my hand teaching me / the braille of her anxiety." Only in the privacy of their apartment, "where her needs and her fears could be put away / like matching towels on a shelf," her mother finds the sense of safety as a Latina whose body is erotized by the surrounding male gaze as well as by the long history of colonialist discourse vis-à-vis Puerto Rico.

Yet, like the Cuban-American woman, in the prose passage above, Cofer disavows her mother's effusiveness and affective lack of control, another allegorical instance of the discourse that allows for the feminization of Third World cultures, a social construction that justifies the need for intervention, containment, reason, and civilization. As Kelvin Santiago-Valles has summarized in *"Subject People" and Colonial Discourses*, since 1898 the U.S. colonizers represented "the Porto Rican majorities as needy children and women in distress" precisely to "socially construct the colonizers as the manly protectors and the teachers/masters of an 'enlightened civilization' that had arrived on Island shores under the auspices of U.S. battleships, soldiers, and generals." [18] Cofer's mother, from the colonial U.S. perspective voiced by the daughter, "never learned moderation in her emotions, or restraint for her gesturing hands and loud laughter"; the Cuban mother in San Diego, according to her U.S. Latina daughter, "just can't control herself" and thus ridiculed her family by performing and enacting the very gestures and bodily movements that have been defined as disorderly, centrifugal, and thus colonizable. Although deracialized, the Cuban woman dancing and Cofer's mother symbolize "the Other country" to a dominant or colonized (daughters' gaze) that "project[s] beyond its own borders the sexual practices or gender behaviors it deems abhorrent." [19]

FEMINIZING LATIN AMERICA

These mothers also constitute a "spectacular body" for a dominant audience. As defined in the introduction to *Nationalisms and Sexualities*, "newspapers, film, novels and theater all created sexed bodies as public spectacles, thereby helping to instill through representational practices an erotic investment in the national romance." [20] In this light, the feminization and erotization of Latin American countries continue to be articulated by the United States media, as a constellation of signifiers reinvigorates the colonizability of the Third World through global economies. As I mentioned earlier, the Concert of the Americas in 1994, held in conjunction with the Third Hemispheric Summit of Presidents, serves as a productive instance of how rhythms, gender, and colonial discourse converge in dramatizing and enacting the contradictory positionality of Latin America in the newly emerging context of NAFTA and globalization. Not unlike Antonio Pedreira, who in *Insularismo* equates the feminine, docile rhythms of the Puerto Rican danza with the passivity and colonizability of the Puerto Rican peoples; not unlike films such as Disney's *The Three Caballeros;* and not unlike the hegemonic tradition of political cartoons, the official discourse of the Concert of the Americas feminizes and erotizes the cultures south of the border.[21] It ethnifies and differentiates them in a displacing logic in order to justify the economic penetration of U.S. capital in many countries with previously nationalized industries. Thus, the discourse of national unity, as "family," is extended to the Americas, to a hemispheric "family of nations," in Bill Clinton's words. As García Canclini has asserted, this "conception of the rupture of the borders—between cultural fields and between nations—is equivalent to subordinating local forces to transnational chains of production and circulation of symbolic (and, I would add, material) goods."[22] Indeed, corporate advertising in Puerto Rico reveals how transnationals have appropriated and recirculated the allegory of nation as rhythm. Coca-Cola's campaign for "Menea la cola" (Move your butt) and Budweiser's "El virazón" (The great turn) deploy the characteristic patriarchal synecdoche of the rhythmic butt as an icon of "local" culture which also becomes transnational. The Americas, then, is constructed as a (trans)national body for safeguarding the corporate interests of the paterfamilias, that is, of the United States.

While in many Latin American countries private industry has replaced the State as the main producer of national culture, the Concierto de las Américas was the collaborative creation of both private corporations and the U.S. federal government. Co-sponsored by Ford, PULSAR International, Texaco, and American Express, and produced by Quincy Jones and David Saltzman Productions in conjunction with There Goes the Neighborhood Productions, this performance was clearly informed by the convergence of mainstream and corporate conceptions of multiculturalism as a deracialized, harmonious unity, with the economic interests of transnationalism. In the closing comments to the concert, the actor Michael Douglas summarized the purpose of the performance: "to redefine the music of all the Americas in a broader multicultural context"; yet immediately after, he revealed the symbolic value of music in relation to economics when he said that at this Third Hemispheric Summit "never before is so much at stake." Emphasizing a discourse of "love and freedom for you and me" at an unprecedented historical time when many Latin American nations are under "democratic" governments, the Concert articulated a utopian view of open borders, cooperation, and equality within the hemisphere and celebrated, as Clinton put it, what "this splendid community of democracies can yet become." Unity within diversity and a respect for cultural differences were, on the surface, the predominant themes. Yet given a post-NAFTA perspective that has revealed the egregious inequities and unprecedented monopolization of power that globalization has made possible, phrases like "Let us work together, trabajemos juntos," which the Nicaraguan salsero Luis Enrique voiced in his performance, can only now be read as the unifying, (trans) national discourse needed to pave the way for consent to economic domination.

Once more, rhythms, music, and erotics were the central signifiers of cultural difference. A closer analysis of the language by which different regions, including the United States, were defined and represented in the Concert unveils the patriarchal, colonial, and imperialist motivations behind this spectacular dramatization of globalizing economies. The concert's repertoire was structured according to regions and/or countries, each being represented by a characteristic singer or folkloric dance. Introductory statements were presented by famous personalities, and it is this framing discourse that lays bare the economic and political interests being played out. Canada, for instance, was celebrated as a "cultural mosaic," in contrast to previous discourses about the balkanization of the French in Quebec. The United States, strategically represented by an African-American and a Cherokee, was "the embrace of 240 million people," "a garden rooted with a little bit of each of us," again asserting national identity as multicultural harmony. The countries south of the border, however, continued to be homogenized and essentialized, fashioned with the discursive tools that have constructed Latin America since the turn of the century: Mexicans "are the song and fire of life"; the Caribbean is "a potpourri of tropical spices," "mystical islands," "tender, succulent mangos"; Brazil is "unimaginable in its riches," "197 million people" whose destiny, quoting poet Carlos Drummond de Andrade, "is to love, more love and more love." South America, introduced uncoincidentally by Maria Conchita Alonso, is "exotic and hypnotic lands"; "land of pulsing rhythms, saucy sambas, sensual bossa nova, and the tantalizing feast of the tango."

The transnational unity summoned by the Summit and the Concert is rooted precisely in the patriarchal gaze mediated by Latin music and under which all Latin American countries are subsumed. Speaking of Brazil and of its paradigmatic song "Girl from Ipanema," a Hawaiian actor commented that there was no need to understand Portuguese, since listening to this song "we could all envision that tall and tanned and lean, lovely girl walking down the beach and swinging so gently . . . and the Americans will say aaah! . . . and the Japanese, oooh! The language of music is truly, truly universal." The "we" uttered here refers to a patriarchal gaze that transcends geopolitical boundaries, one very much analogous to the "camaraderie with the caballeros from Brazil and Mexico" that *The Three Caballeros* portrayed.[23] Yet national identity and difference continue to be noticeable, surfacing in and through the distinctions between the Americans' reaction and the Japanese's.

Yet this feminizing discourse is far from being seamless. While the official script erotized these countries as vast deposits of natural and human resources waiting to be tapped or penetrated by transnationals, some of the Latino actors and musicians managed to create moments of transgression that would remind the audience of the asymmetries of power still at play within the Americas. As performance, the Concert of the Americas enacted the struggles and tensions inherent in intercultural, colonial encounters; in this case, the reconversion and resemantization of language made present the struggle for discursive power. For instance, the Chicano comedian Paul Rodríguez, introducing Mexico to the audience, read his script about the strong, pre-Columbian heritage in Mexican culture, an expression of the official Mexican discourse on nation. As an aside, he turned to Vicky Carr, ironically the other icon of Mexican authenticity, and said, "Of course, Vicky, that was before Proposition 187." A nervous and tardy laughter ensued. Later, the Nicaraguan salsero Luis Enrique evoked the history of resistance scripted by the slaves as he played the congas; yet he simultaneously recited a formal tribute to the Central American region that calls for unity among all "Americans," exhorting us to "work together" and "reason together." This new call for all Americans included decolonizing the term and stripping off its imperialist usage: "When I say American I mean everybody in this hemisphere, from Tierra del Fuego to the Arctic."

At the other ideological pole, Celia Cruz, the Queen of Salsa, sang José Martí's *versos sencillos* in her rendering of "Guantanamera," while she exhorted all presidents to free Cuba from communism and to get rid of Castro. It was ideologically meaningful that the cameras would close up on Violeta Chamorro during Celia Cruz's performance. President Clinton, in his closing statement, quoted Pablo Neruda's poetry to make the point that there should be no lone struggle and no solitary hope, a call that, in Neruda's poetry, was clearly informed by his active participation as a communist in Latin America. While the United States was introduced as a harmonious, multicultural nation free from conflict, violence, and imperial colonialism, a discourse strategically articulated by an African-American and a Native American, their discourse was also laced with intertexts from the Pledge of Allegiance. Thus, two racial minorities performed, by their very presence, the ultimate act of articulation and co-optation; they uttered the significant contradiction between the utopian view of a nation in racial harmony and the history of slavery and genocides, scripted on their own bodies, that has victimized their respective communities. Yet this dominant multiculturalism was also offset by the gospel music that followed, as singers reaffirmed black culture and resistance through religious rhythms and the racialized rhythms of spirituality.

The Concert's final message, "Teach to sing each other's songs and dance each other's dances," encapsulates the allegorical role of music and rhythms and their mediating role in naturalizing ideology, in inscribing cultural difference, and in paving the way, in 1994, for economic globalization in Latin America. The circulation of the cultural icon of the rhythmic mulatta, as traced in this essay, is closely tied to the feminizing discourse on Latin America. However, as this partial genealogy also reveals, the centrifugal movements of the body of the Caribbean woman not only disrupt the project of maintaining national purity, they also serve as a disturbing reminder to U.S. Latinas of our own unstable location as hybrid members within the dominant boundaries of nation.

NOTES

1. The overarching presence of the rhythmic mulatta is evident in popular songs as well as in "high art" and literature. Earlier Afro-Caribbean songs ("Sabrosona," "La negrita Concepción"), popular merengues ("El negrito del batey"), contemporary rap (Gerardo's "Rico Suave"), and the literary and scholarly works of the Cuban-American critic Antonio Benítez Rojo (*The Repeating Island: The Caribbean and the Postmodern Perspective*, trans. James Maraniss; Durham, N.C.: Duke University Press, 1992), the Puerto Rican writer-chronicler Edgardo Rodríguez Juliá (*El cruce de la Bahía de Guánica;* Rio Piedras: Editorial Cultural, 1989), and Luis Rafael Sánchez's China Hereje in *La guaracha del Macho Camacho* (Buenos Aires: Ediciones de la Flor, 1976), are some of the numerous sites where this cultural icon is inscribed.

2. I use the term "reconversion" with a different twist from Néstor García Canclini as he defines it in *Hybrid Cultures: Strategies for Entering and Leaving*

Modernity, trans. Christopher L. Chiappari and Silvia L. López (Minneapolis: University of Minnesota Press, 1995). While García Canclini focuses on reconversion as a process, like resemantization, that enacts the struggles for power between the dominant and the popular sectors and between "traditional" and "modern" forces within the nation, I deploy it here in an intercultural and transnational context that is, of course, not devoid of the dialectics of power summoned by García Canclini.

3. In his introduction to *An-Other Tongue: Nation and Ethnicity in the Linguistic Borderlands* (Durham, N.C.: Duke University Press, 1994), 2, Alfred Arteaga reminds us of the etymology of "ethnos" as opposed to "nation": "Nation, in the singular, in 1300 signified people of a common place, but nations, in plural, in 1340 signified heathen, that is, non-Jewish, non-Christian, peoples. Ethnic, from its first occurrence in 1375, so thoroughly denoted non-Jew, non-Christian, that ethnos was erroneously assumed the etymological root of heathen."

4. See, among others, Judith Williamson, "Woman is an Island: Femininity and Colonization," in *Studies in Entertainment: Critical Approaches to Mass Culture*, ed. Tania Modleski (Bloomington: Indiana University Press, 1986), 99–118, repr. in *Theorizing Feminism: Parallel Trends in the Humanities and Social Sciences*, ed. Anne C. Herrmann and Abigail J. Steward (Boulder, Colo.: Westview Press, 1994), 382–400; and the useful introduction and collection of essays in *Nationalisms and Sexualities*, ed. Andrew Parker, Mary Russo, Doris Sommer, and Patricia Yeager (New York: Routledge), 1992.

5. Vera Kutzinski, *Sugar's Secrets: Race and the Erotics of Cuban Nationalism* (Charlottesville: University of Virginia Press, 1993).

6. A *piropo*, part of Hispanic oral tradition, is a compliment to women usually characterized by a pun or wit; for example, once I was told by a male passerby that he desired to be the seat of the bike I was riding.

7. Enrique Fernández, "Salsa × 2," in *Currents from the Dancing River*, ed. Ray Gonzales (San Diego: Harcourt Brace, 1994), 1–10.

8. Jesús Martín Barbero, *Communication, Culture and Hegemony: From the Media to the Mediations*, trans. Elizabeth Fox and Robert A. White (Newbury Park: Sage Publications, 1993), 172.

9. Benítez Rojo, *Repeating Island*, 10. See Vera Kutzinski's feminist analysis of this same passage. In *Sugar's Secrets*, 174–78, she foregrounds "the highly ambivalent disposition of Benítez Rojo's narrative toward the kind of feminine knowledge it extols," an ambivalence inscribed in the juxtaposition between his "reason" and the women's "wisdom." Kutzinski goes on to argue that the two black women, as "initial signifier," become "expendable" later as Benítez Rojo associates the Caribbean with carnival.

10. *Repeating Island*, 76.

11. Antonio Pedreira, *Insularismo* (Rio Piedras: Editorial Edil, 1973), 155, nonetheless ultimately recognizes that in the rhythm "está encerrado un singular aspecto de nuestra conciencia" (resides a singular aspect of our conscience). Under Western logic, the juxtaposition of two against three notes in the danza does not make sense, and Pedeira cannot ultimately give it meaning. He even refuses to define overtly Puerto Rican culture or "nuestra conciencia" as African.

12. *Toña La Negra: La sensación jarocha* (Mexico, D.F.: Discos Peerless, S.A.), MCP 2519–7, 1991.

13. Salvador Brau, "La danza puertorriqueña," in *Disquisiciones sociológicas y otros ensayos* (Rio Piedras, P.R.: Ediciones del Instituto de Literatura, Universidad de Puerto Rico, 1956), 189–206.

14. Braulio Dueño Colón, "Estudio sobre la danza puertorriqueña," in *Ensayos sobre la danza puertorriqueña*, ed. Marisa Rosado (San Juan: Instituto de Cultura Puertorriqueña, 1977), 14–22.

15. In "Vida y desarrollo de la danza puertorriqueña," in *Ensayos*, ed. Rosado, 23, Amaury Veray identified a significant resistance against the merengue among the "ciudadanos peninsulares que se escandalizaron con tan deleznable atrevimiento" (many Spaniards who were scandalized by this daring, unacceptable behavior). This is significant not only because it reveals an underlying morality imposed on the youth, but also because it reveals the tensions between gachupines who saw themselves as gatekeepers of national purity and a younger generation of criollos.

16. Brau, "La danza," 206.

17. Barbero, *Communication*, 90.

18. Kelvin A. Santiago-Valles, *"Subject People" and Colonial Discourses: Economic Transformation and Social Disorder in Puerto Rico, 1989–1947* (Albany: State University of New York Press, 1994), 63. Santiago-Valles carefully shows how these processes of gendering were strategic and contingent on the historical moment. For instance, the Puerto Rican masses were not always feminized, but at times gendered as masculine in their representation of conflicts with Puerto Rican landowners and educated bourgeoisie.

19. Andrew Parker, Mary Russo, Doris Summer, and Patricia Yeager, eds., *Nationalisms and Sexualities* (New York: Routledge, 1992), 10.

20. Ibid., 12.

21. I mention Antonio Pedreira's *Insularismo*, originally published in 1934; Walt Disney's *The Three Caballeros*, first distributed in 1945 and now sold as part of the Disney Classics Series; and the tradition of U.S. political cartoons that has represented Latin America as female in order to emphasize the diverse sites in which these representations emerge and the complicity between U.S. imperialism and Latin American elite interests. See Julianne Burton's essay, "Don (Juanito) Duck and the Imperial-Patriarchal Unconscious: Disney Studies, the Good Neighbor Policy, and the Packaging of Latin America," in Parker et al., *Nationalisms and Sexualities*, 21–41, and John J. Johnson, "Latin America as Female," in *Latin America in Caricature* (Austin: University of Texas Press, 1980), 72–115.

22. García Canclini, *Hybrid Cultures*, 277.

23. Burton, "Don (Juanito) Duck," 35.

3

"Ain't I People?": Voicing National Fantasy

BRIAN CURRID

THE CINEMA FIRMAMENT

"**P**eople? I ain't people! I am a 'shimmering, glowing star in the cinema firmament.' It says so. Right there." Inverting Sojourner Truth's famous phrase, "ain't I people?," Lina Lamont speaks, or rather, shrieks these words as her position as star is clearly at risk in the penultimate sequence of Singin' in the Rain (Kelly/Donen, 1951). In this film, set during the traumatic conclusion of Hollywood's "silent" era, Lamont (Jean Hagen) represents one half of the leading romantic duo of the silent screen at Monumental Pictures, Lockwood (Gene Kelly) and Lamont. The "coming of sound" to Hollywood produces a moment of crisis, and Lamont, with her high-pitched "Bronx" tones, is at risk of rupturing her stardom—her public iconicity—with the excessive materiality of her vocal production.

In both the metaphoric and a more literally economic meaning of the phrase, the plot of the film offers a "face-saving" solution to this problem, a frugal redirection of resources for the studio and for Don Lockwood that will require the later devaluation of Lina's soon-to-be outdated "currency." By secretly dubbing the voice of Kathy Selden (Debbie Reynolds) for that of Lamont, the studio hopes to retain its own prestige and appeal, as well as that of its central star, into the new world of sound film. When Lamont discovers her planned instrumentalization as dummy, she attempts to reverse or revise the relations of production that such a ventriloquism requires, while endorsing its own terms and economic logic. Lamont momentarily blocks Monumental Studio's attempt to disarticulate her spectacular body from her new voice, that of Kathy Selden. In so doing, Lina thinks she can reclaim her body as her *own*

Figure 3.1. *Singing' in the Rain* (Kelly/Donen, 1951): Lina's decadent publicity

capital and trademark while mobilizing Kathy Selden's voice as appropriated labor and public prosthetic.[1] Masquerading as the studio chief,
R. F. Simpson, Lamont sends out a press statement, an "exclusive to *all*
the papers in town," marking the release of *The Dancing Cavalier*, to claim
possession over both her "singing pipes and dancing stems"; Lamont
believes that she has learned to work the contradictory nature of publicity, which on the one hand uses the female subject while also offering
limited possibilities of agency to that subject. She thinks that through
her manipulation of the apparatus of publicity (represented by the shot
of the newspaper, fig. 3.1), her retooling of the differentially distributed
prosthetic operativity that (according to Lauren Berlant and Michael
Warner) publicity represents,[2] she has attained a space of agency outside
the popular, a space entailed by her legal-juridical interpellation,[3] secured by her contract ["the party of the first part, that's me . . ."] and
the guarantee of control over her public iconicity that it supposedly
offers. Paradoxically, Lina also believes that by submitting to the surplus embodiment that American national publicity requires of its female citizens/subjects she has secured a form of "absence-to-her-body"
(Berlant 1993: 173) behind the prosthetic voices of Kathy Selden and the
entire publicity apparatus that "bad" Hollywood represents in this film.

But through her shrieking ventriloquism of the public voices of both the studio and a newspaper, her own desperate and degenerate publicity, Lina points to the intersection of two trajectories marking a strategic moment of rupture and crisis within an American national fantasy: her dually disruptive roles in relation to both the *hierarchy* of gender (the star who does not know her place) and the *horizontality* of nationality (the scandal of an inappropriate display and fetishization of class power) puncture the affective utopia that the film and the multiple films within the film are all attempting to piece together.[4]

As we learn from Simpson directly prior to Lina's sacrificial dismemberment as star body before a metonymically national theater public in the final scene of the film, this time she has gone "too far." For the purposes of this chapter I will tendentiously overinvest Simpson's statement with literal meaning: Lina has gone too far outside the always excessively metaphoric borders that secure the National Symbolic and the fantasy that it enables.[5] Her travels outside that space and her counter-progressivist temporality as relic of a silent, decadent, and implicitly antinational past of pre-sound film serve as a clear moment of what Homi Bhabha has termed "national pedagogy," while at the same time pointing toward the limits and contradictions that the nation produces and polices in its performativity (Bhabha 1990: 297).

Speaking of a quite different form of publicity, Hortense Spillers (1987) has made clear the centrality of the operation of race in articulation with gender to the public strategies that secure national fantasy and make operable its symbolic instruments, its pedagogy:

> Let's face it. I am a marked woman, but not everybody knows my name. "Peaches" and "Brown Sugar," "Sapphire" and "Earth Mother," "Aunty," "Granny," God's Holy Fool, a Miss Ebony First, or Black Woman at the Podium: I describe a locus of confounded identities, a meeting ground of investments and privations in the national treasury of rhetorical wealth. My country needs me, and if I were not here, I would have to be invented. (65)

This national need is especially revealed by the histories of "American" popular and/or "folk" music. Eric Lott's work on the minstrel show and blackface explores how, in the nineteenth century, the production and reproduction of an American "national popular" depended on the double movement of a simultaneous mobilization and disavowal of race (1995: 91–100). Peter Antelyes (1994) has similarly argued that the terms of embodiment and agency available to the "red hot mamas" Sophie Tucker and Bessie Smith were entries in a thesaurus that registered similarity and difference along the axes of race, gender, and ethnicity and required the syntactical possibilities of a national grammar for their iteration. Antelyes further suggests that the performative deployment of those terms of agency and embodiment—their iteration—simultaneously endorsed and undermined the limits and contradictions of the systems of equivalence that gave them "meaning," illustrating both the productivity and failure of the nationalizing grammar that served as the rules of enunciation.[6]

In a third critical examination of the relationship of American nationality to race in music, Ronald Radano (1996) has argued persuasively that "black music"—"less a formal continuity grounded in the vernacular than a series of socially constituted expressive practices emerging from the complex discursive matrices of post–Civil War, public culture" (508)—represented the "supplement or missing link of American national identity" (522). Echoing Lott's explication of the paradoxical doubleness of music in the American racial imaginary, Radano suggests that the very formal constitution of "black music" is thoroughly implicated in the commodification of both the black body and of "music" itself (523). He points out that "black music" at the same time, contrary to its necessary function in securing the romantic temporality of "America" as progressivist and continuous, remained nonetheless a site of contestation where the very materiality of race secured a contradictory ground of critical agency for the black American subject in the staging of American collectivity (544). "It is through the idea of difference that black America would finally hear its cultural past, discerning the echoes of an ancestral world saturated with textually invented 'Negro Sound'" (544).

These and other studies point toward the repetitiveness which characterizes the role that popular music and its racial imagination have played in the production and productivity of the national imaginary. I want to stage as a case of this compulsive repetition a moment in the history of American cinema which dramatized in a particularly resonant way how the Americanness of that cinema was dependent on that repetition for its intelligibility and cohered only insofar as it was able to produce yet another iteration of its terms or instantiation of its logic. By sketching out the symptoms, I do not mean to imply that this obsessive repetition is without tension or contradiction. To the contrary, I hope to show that this particular moment of national crisis reveals the repetition precisely as a symptom,[7] the necessity of which testifies profoundly to the contingency of national iterability itself (Bhabha 1990: 297).

One of the theoretical moves that any consideration of popular music, and especially popular music in Hollywood film, needs to make when concerned with issues of national affect is a move toward thinking about popular music less as a body of musical texts and more as an element of a broader apparatus of publicity, whose very nature determines the contingent meaning and locus of its popularity (Bennett 1986).[8] Michael Warner makes the point that publicity in the West, which might be rethought as the dialectical relationship between the subjectivities of spectatorship/citizenship and stardom, requires iconicity for its intelligibility (1992: 385). We might say as well that to be public in the West, or "here," in "America," means to have a resonance, to resonate, to reverberate. The differential access to publicity that Warner (and others) argue is central to its historical trajectory and function in real existing democracy is marked (or unmarked) by its audibility as much as by its visibility. The kind of voices that are heard in the institutionalized public sphere, the very way voice is constructed as a locus of agency and subjectivity, the registers of the material conditions of certain forms of embodied publicity, and the relationship of voice to body: each contribute to the way we think about publicity as both a differentially distributed resource and a selectively localizable burden. While theorists like Warner have begun to explore the visual culture of publicity, the acoustics of publicity remain largely untheorized.[9]

In this chapter, I will explore how the acoustics of national publicity can be described, and suggest in broad outlines the ways such a diagnostic or physics [10] of publicity might more precisely locate—or indeed, critically dis-locate—the reverberations and resonances within the "cinematic apparatus" and the temporality of film history that are the voicing of national fantasy. With this goal in mind, I will be looking at a particular moment in the historical narrative that we recognize as "Hollywood," or "American" cinema. *Singin' in the Rain* and *A Star Is Born* (Cukor 1954), two American film musicals from the early 1950s, thematized the historic constitution of sound film and its relationship to a national affect of "authenticity" by coupling, in a nostalgic gesture, the classical Hollywood sound film and vaudeville; in the first, by deploying Hollywood's institutional history, and in the second by producing star (auto)biography as the working out of that history and its contradictions. The contours of this thematic were shaped through the deployment of "race" (in the figure of blackface) as constitutive of an American public personhood, and illustrate a strategic displacement of a racial logic onto a cinematic portrayal of gender. Linking critically the modes of nostalgia produced by these two films suggests that any rethinking of the history of sound film needs to critique the hegemonic articulation of the materiality of race and gender and the relationship of this articulation to the production of "Americanness" that this nationalizing and naturalizing history served to secure.

UN-AMERICAN ACTIVITIES: HOLLYWOOD IN THE 1950s

There are three major issues or events to confront in talking about the period of the 1950s in "American" cinema as one of crisis in the national character of its address—in the "American" address of Hollywood as an institution and as a style. By exposing Hollywood's dependence on certain modes of production, practices of everyday life, and the limiting nature of the properly political power of the state, these issues or events crystallize the heterogeneous development and weakness of Hollywood's claim on "America," that is, Hollywood's role as the American mode of publicity par excellence and its concomitant role as ultimate arbiter of representability in the national popular.

In this chapter, my primary objective is to illuminate the obsessively ahistorical and repetitive nature of the centrality of race in the production and policing of "America" as national fantasy. To clarify the epistemological status of my contextualization of the problem I should first state that the uses of history are here to be understood as at most provisional interventions rather than final pronouncements on a period of American film history. The historicism of such a formulation is one of the locations where the theoretical object here under investigation, America, coheres most profoundly. Taken as axiomatic for these readings is Bhabha's theorization of the national as constantly in crisis, and an exploration of how Hollywood was implicated in a critically demarcated moment of national crisis will allow a more productive disarticulation of the ways that national crisis was made legible and ameliorated through strategies historically specific to Hollywood as an institution. It will allow us as well to see those strategies as effective precisely because of their constitutively repetitive nature in American national fantasy.[11]

The first event that defines this moment is the separation of production and exhibition. The American motion picture industry in the 1930s and 1940s was characterized by an increasing drive toward monopolization and centralization. Crucial in this historical shift was the increasing control of the so-called "Big Five" (Paramount, Loew's/MGM, Warner Bros., Fox, and RKO) of key theaters in all major American cities. As

Douglas Gomery explains, the control over exhibition was not a mere matter of collecting profits but reveals an entire technology of publicity (the "run-zone-clearance system") that seems to approximate total manipulation. "By carefully manipulating trade arrangements for the booking of films, the Big Five were able to reduce risk, ensure continuity of operation, and almost guarantee regular profits" (Gomery 1992: 67).[12] The *Paramount* decision in 1948 changed all this when the courts deemed the practices that secured the Big Five's control over both production and exhibition as monopolistic. The conclusion to an antitrust suit filed by the federal government already in the 1930s, this decision of early May 1948 caused a radical break with past Hollywood practice (ibid.: 89).

This event is interesting not only for the economic effect it would have on Hollywood as an industry; it also marks a shift in the way Hollywood as a publicity apparatus operated in relation to an "America" conceived as a series of locales or a geographical dispersion of place. The shift from the Big Five and the stratified concentric circles of publicity that constituted its audience produced new ways of configuring the audience, or the public. The "address" of Hollywood needed to be redefined. The place of the public would also be radically (if indirectly) altered by this decision, as the decline of the centrality of the movie palace[13] in American viewing practices was accelerated and new forms of exhibition (drive-ins, shopping center theaters) began to dominate and dissect the film market in the opening of access to independent exhibitors (Gomery 1992: 91ff.).

In and of itself, the *Paramount* decision might not have had such a great effect on Hollywood but together with the second factor, the installation of television and changes in what commentators called "lifestyle" that it marked and encouraged, Hollywood was seriously under question as the major form of national publicity. Between 1950 and 1952, the motion picture industry experienced a sharp loss of income owing to the inroads of television into the entertainment market.[14] Lynn Spigel (1992) has pointed to the very real transformations in everyday practice that the "installing of the television" represented. The coming of television was not only about the suburbanization of "America," but also replaced the centrality of American cinema as the central locus for the production of national simultaneity and altered the way the relationship between family and community was understood. While, as Gomery has pointed out, any simple argument about television as a substitute for the cinema depends on "the assumption of the economics of the substitution effect" (1992: 83), Spigel suggests that the architectonics of national affect and public discourse around television were indeed increasingly central themes in the late 1940s and early 1950s:

> By the early 1950s, floor plans included a space for television in the home's structural layout, and television sets were increasingly depicted as everyday, commonplace objects that any family might hope to own. Indeed the magazines included television as a staple home fixture before most Americans could even receive a television signal, much less consider purchasing the expensive item. The media discourses did not so much reflect social reality; instead they preceded it. (Spigel 1992: 39)

One of the key ways television claimed its centrality as the new or future form of utopic publicity was through the trope of the home theater, directly asserting the superiority of this new form of private publicity to the irredeemable publicness of theatrical exhibition, not only because of convenience but also according to a logic of verisimilitude (ibid.: 106–9).[15] In other words, while the increasingly home-bound nature of suburban society lent itself to the decline in movie attendance, Spigel shows that the very conception of the home space was from the late 1940s deeply invested with the utopic communitarian possibilities that television was supposed to provide.

While these first two issues pertain to the technologies of national affect, and as such seem abstractly concerned with the constitution of the national itself, the final aspect of Hollywood's crisis directly relates to claims about what is and is not "American" political behavior: the persecution of Hollywood (now understood as a localizable minority population) by the House Un-American Activities Committee. The political climate of the early 1950s was primarily concerned with the redefinition through excision of what "Americanness" was. Gene Kelly and the makers of MGM musicals were among the primary subjects of investigation for the committee; taking this into account, the claim on authenticity that especially the musicals and most particularly the show musicals seem to have represented had to have been thrown severely into question by the HUAC investigations. Peter Wollen (1992) describes in some detail the implications of the activities of the committee for the making of *Singin' in the Rain*. But the more central issue is the way the public denunciations and accusations of Communism in Hollywood strained the relationship between the production of a politically sanctioned national publicity in "Washington" and publicity as it was produced in "Hollywood." The national claim of Hollywood as an institution was something that, like the allegiances of its stars, needed to be proven; this was especially true in the realm of the musical, which, as

Wollen points out, was inordinately subject to the nationalist surgery of Washington's anticommunist fervor.[16]

SINGIN' IN THE RAIN, OR THE DUELING MAMMY

Through an almost obsessively repetitive reference to Al Jolson and *The Jazz Singer*, *Singin' in the Rain* consistently equates a vaudevillian blackface as both the origin and the goal of an authentic sound film art, without ever bringing his well-known (black)face into view. Understood in this context, the central problem of the film, that is, the mismatching of body to voice in the figure of Lina Lamont and the difficulties that it engenders with the authenticity of sound film, become legible as not merely a problem with gender, but rather, a displacement of what seem to be quite other concerns. The opposition between Lockwood and Lamont that the film explores might be read productively as the simultaneous fetishization and excision of racial impersonation as a guarantee of the naturalized/nationalized affect of "American" sound film, or of Hollywood.

Cosmo Brown (Donald O'Connor), the vaudeville pole in the overdetermined field of entertainment that is the subject of *Singin' in the Rain*, suggests *The Dueling Mammy* as the title for Monumental Pictures' first musical film. This is but one odd example of the way *Singin' in the Rain*, at central moments of crisis within its plot, posits *The Jazz Singer* as both the first sound film (as historical background) as well as the catalyst toward the "sound revolution" (as narrative device).[17] In a sequence prior to Cosmo's odd inspiration, the premiere of Monumental Pictures' nonmusical Lockwood–Lamont talkie, *The Dueling Cavalier*, we witness failure on a grand scale. This failure is not only one of a screenplay that failed to adapt to actually being heard but, more interestingly, is also the failure of the technology itself to preserve the illusion of synchronization for the character played by Lina Lamont. All this brings a representative audience member to register his frustrations comparatively: "They should make more movies like *The Jazz Singer*."

The fact that the audience's demand is provoked by the failure of synchronization, made legible by the mismatching of gender in *The Dueling Cavalier*, suggests that the model of synchronization and its "American" address *needs* to be *The Jazz Singer*. While it might be written off as merely a repetition of the historically dubious narrative of progression that Hollywood tells about itself,[18] this fails to explain its insistently present absence within the diegesis of the film. The repetitive invocation of blackface as *the* model of synchronization, and the naturalized, nationalized,

and heterosexualized progress that synchronization allegorizes in *Singin'*
in the Rain, is matched by the failure of blackface to appear. This non-
appearance is enabled by the transformation of the contradictions and
problems of blackface as a model for an authentically transparent *national*
public prosthetics, into the non-synchronous figure of Lina Lamont.
Lina Lamont's removal from the Hollywood narrative allows for the recuperation of the authenticity that blackface seems to represent without
articulating its dependence on racial impersonation and the especially
"American" use of black bodies or their simulacra.

Carol Clover (1995) has interpreted the film as symptomatic of disavowal: the repressed that Clover sees as returning in *Singin'* is the history of the appropriation of black musics and dance so central not only
to this film, but to Hollywood more generally. But appropriation as a
descriptive tool both limits our interpretation of these kinds of practices
as a disorder in cultural property relations and implies a kind of liberal
cultural politics where the relations of cultural production can be reformed through the proper attribution of cultural creativity. It doesn't
allow us to see the way appropriated forms become available as a source,
a raw material for the production enabled by relationships of appropriation, only within the systematic logic of appropriation itself. There is, in
other words, no moment *prior* to appropriation that can claim an ontological locus external to the symbolic economy of appropriation. The
production of a prior moment of fully self-present, intact, coherent
"culture" is always retroactive in its temporality, contemporaneous with
the process of appropriation itself. Further, a focus on appropriation
cannot allow us to interpret the profoundly national stakes of a film like
Singin'. Blackface can and should be read as a symptom and an instance
in mass culture of the economics of appropriation that have determined
the relationship between the black subject and the regimes to which s/he
is subjected, and Hollywood's implication in that system certainly should
be made available for critique. I would submit, however, that this is but
a first step. *Singin'* allows us to see the regime of racial imagination as a
requirement for the operation of a national fantasy, by insisting on its effectivity in securing a specifically American authenticity.

I suggest that the disavowal of *Singin'* is a double, national disavowal,
simultaneously requiring, first, the performative erasure of the non- or
anti-national specificities that make impersonation and, ironically, the
specificity of "Americanness" intelligible; and second, the excision of impersonation (or its public traces) from the mise-en-scène of "American"
collectivity. In other words, two Linas need to be publicly removed

before the national audience: the first Lina is the Lina with the Bronx accent, an overly embodied, vocally disruptive specificity, the materiality of whose voice disrupts the acoustics of national publicity. But another Lina poses a threat that requires national(ist) surgery, the Lina who stars only in aristocratic costume dramas and mimes de-ethnicized Americanness through the appropriation of Kathy Selden's voice. This Lina threatens a national acoustics in that it implicitly places that acoustics under suspicion, in that it represents publicity as a decadent form of impersonation.[19] The multiple Linas that determine the logic of this film in its production of American national fantasy, when read alongside the film's dependence on/disavowal of blackface, serve as the contorted working through of the difficulties of specificity and impersonation in regard to American national identity that blackface, and indeed, blackness itself, historically represents.[20]

A number of film historians have pointed out that *The Jazz Singer*, the model of successful sound film in *Singin'*, can hardly be taken as a model for the perhaps always oxymoronic "realist" musical cinema that is implicitly privileged in the plot of *Singin'*. But it is clear that this is not at issue: *The Jazz Singer* serves as an index for a certain kind of national simultaneity ("The people are clamoring for more") and a national progression (Anderson 1983). *Singin' in the Rain* articulates an isomorphism that maps the history of cinema onto a history of national progress. The past (the decadent 1920s) is marked by secrets and deception; this past is represented only to be overcome in the passing of national time through the institutionalization of a new unitary public. In the "simultaneity" of the coming of speech, this new public is a reenactment of what Derrida describes as the Rousseauian "micro-society of non-violence and freedom, all the members of which can by rights remain within range of an immediate and transparent, a 'crystalline' address, fully self present in its living speech" (Derrida 1976: 119) after the decadence and perfidy of "writing" represented by the silent film.

Returning now to the character of Lina Lamont: this woman whose "voice" refuses to be recorded, and who "ain't people," serves as a hieroglyph for the dangers of obfuscation and illusion that prevent the success of national consensus. But witness the way in which the perfidy of writing is produced and registered: by a woman with a Bronx accent, with clear ambitions of power (her final failure is her attempt to "speak for" R. F., the producer, owner of the studio), and whose future success, we are led to believe, relies on the alienation of another's voice from her body. Lamont becomes the blackface character, if a blackface with a very different relationship to value than Al Jolson or Jakie Rabinowitz: a Bronx woman playing a French aristocrat. Her excision from the studio family, her sacrificial dismemberment and abjection, allows the final statement of heteronormative love to be sung, without microphones, without French costumes, without secrets, in the fantasy public world of the cinema become stage.

This "American" utopics literally resonates in the last scene of the film when Don and Kathy, having disposed of Lina Lamont, can sing their "true" feelings to one another by ironically miming fandom: the song they sing, "You Are My Lucky Star," makes love intelligible in the vocabulary of commercial stardom. Fan publics, as opposed to the general audience, are marked continuously in the film as excess, screaming hysteric distortions of proper public decorum, or manipulated victims of studio direction; here, fandom is transformed into the normative space of a mutual yet stratified heterosexual erotics. The spectacle of degeneracy that fan culture and its fetishistic relationship to star bodies represents in the rest of the film seems to be obliterated in the acoustic fullness of the moment. There are now no acoustic problems, symbolic or "actual," and "truth" is accessible without technological assistance: what we see and hear is supposedly what we get. This is even marked by the lack of reverberation in the last song; the "echo" that haunts Lina's ventriloquism of "Singin' in the Rain," actually sung by Kathy Selden behind the curtain, seems to comment on the visual demarcation of space that the scene makes available (Kathy backstage, Lina in front of the curtain) and the excess of technology required to pull it off. But for the last words of love, no mikes are required. Listening to the final chorus that resonates during the last shot, as Kathy and Don stare up longingly at their star bodies, displayed on a billboard advertising a film entitled *Singin' in the Rain*, becomes a utopic acoustics of national publicity, where audience and stars are each properly resonant points in the unisonance of the national public. As vaudeville and cinema are (re)united in Gene Kelly's character[21] and his rediscovery of the pleasures of the stage, so is the phantasmatic audience reunited into the spectacle, to see its secrets, and to be in some sense the concluding nondiegetic chorus which concludes the soundtrack of the film. Not only does the screen disappear, but the stage curtain, and finally the stage, as the horizontality of audience and star is reasserted even as the film ends with another sight of strangely reminiscent dismemberment: gazing up at their own billboard, the stars become audience, representative of the public iconicity and operativity that the American national fantasy pretends to make equally available to all. Simultaneously, the horizontality of nationality and the hierarchy of gender are reproduced; and dissonance between them is registered unproblematic by the consonance of the background chorus echoing the harmonic duet of love between Don Lockwood and Kathy Selden: properly resonant stars.

Throughout the film, Lina finds herself increasingly isolated. Signifying at the end only a sort of obstreperousness in relation to the new technologies of sound film, her role is most strikingly contrasted early in the film with the easy transition of a nameless male performer, where cinematic filming/recording is configured as a direct analog of seeing and hearing. While this nameless male singer performs an elaborate Busby Berkeley-esque number with the aid of a strategically placed anachronism, the mike boom, the difficulties surrounding Lina's resonance center around the impossibility of finding a location for the mike that promises intelligibility and invisibility. But before restricting our reading here to any simply gendered conception of the logic of the film, it seems important to complicate the issue and think how gender is invoked and revoked as a mark of inclusion or exclusion at different points in the film. These technologies are in fact only visible as clunky wires in Lina's case; Kathy Selden has a very different relationship to technology.

In the sequence where Kathy dubs "Would You?," the final song in *The Dancing Cavalier*, we witness this crucial difference played out visually and aurally.[22] The sequence begins on a dissolve, marked on the soundtrack by the orchestral introduction to the song, and in which R. F. Simpson is replaced as the central figure in the shot by a strikingly elegant microphone. The shot widens to the left to include, first, Kathy standing beside that microphone, and then Cosmo directing the orchestra. Kathy turns to her right to sing, and the camera leads us, panning right, to the focus of her look: Don Lockwood, seated, smiling back at her (fig. 3.2). Seen in relation to the content of the musical number, the mise-en-scène and the camera movement bring home the central point that Kathy is singing for Don as much as for the microphone. Or rather, that singing for Don and the microphone become inseparable actions. After focusing a moment on the love-smitten Lockwood, the camera follows him as he moves in front of Kathy. With a close-up on Selden's singing, the image dissolves to a shot of a spinning record, accompanied by Lina's voice and the hiss of inscription. With the camera panning up and to the right, the spectator finds first Miss Densmore, Lina's vocal coach, then a large recording horn labeled "Monumental Studios," held in place by an anonymous assistant, and finally Lina

Figure 3.2. *Singin' in the Rain* (Kelly/Donen, 1951): Kathy singing "Would You?"

Figure 3.3. *Singin' in the Rain* (Kelly/Donen, 1951): Lina singing "Would You?"

herself, accompanied by an anonymous worker (fig. 3.3). The shot moves to focus on Lina, and we witness the diva having great trouble singing her part, despite all the assistants around her, in a painful dissonance that fails in its vain attempts to approximate Selden's continuous voice-over. As was the case earlier in the film, when the mike boom was available to an anonymous male star but clearly not a possible solution to Lina's technical difficulties, the technology available to Lina is again strategically nonsynchronous with the easy modernity relayed by the scene of Kathy's recording. With Lina, we see the machine itself as it inscribes, and, more importantly, we hear that machine making a hiss, commenting itself on the nature of the work it seems forced to do.[23] This is *work* for Lina, clearly in contrast to the easy melodiousness witnessed in Kathy Selden.

Following another dissolve, we see and hear the motion of the camera filming the final shot for the film. But continuous over the action is Kathy's voice. After a cut to a closer shot, we hear only the vocal track. With the climax of the song we achieve the unity of Lina's character, a unity which is now perceived to be finally and completely Kathy's, and the shot turns to black and white, with a more moderate hiss indicating its status now as projected. We see the final cut and hear the reaction of the men (Cosmo, Don, and Simpson) gathered in Simpson's office to witness synchronization. Kathy's relationship to technology is clearly one which effaces technology. The final film version of *The Dancing Cavalier* becomes in a sense pure ventriloquism, but as ventriloquism it preserves the coherence of Kathy's voice beneath the shadow play of Lina's acting. Additionally, Kathy's "untrained" voice holds this sequence together, without being "wired" for sound. The production of a coherent sound space for Kathy is here registered as unproblematic: no balance problems, no fuzz. Further, Kathy's installation as real replacement for Lamont in the heterosexual duo and the "vaudeville" trio is finally concluded in this scene; Kathy's voice coming through the cinema apparatus signifies more than anything its transparency.

Kaja Silverman argues that *Singin'* exhibits the high stakes laid at the synchronization of the female voice with the female image. Lina Lamont becomes the site where sexual heterogeneity is displayed, only to be exorcised in the last moments of the film, as she literally runs from the exhibited space on the screen. But Silverman's brief analysis of the "array of female voices marshalled at both the diegetic and the extradiegetic levels" (1988: 46) that makes *Singin'* work remains trapped in the naturalized binarism of gender which the film seeks to police. In other words, Silverman fails to ask why the binary frame of gender is made the site for the exposure and recircumscription of the cinematic and recording apparatus.

At first this might seem a mundane and obvious point. When Cosmo's voice replaces Selden's in the public display of live dubbing at the end of the film, it only serves to enact rupture, breaking the "unity of the fictional character" by raising the "specter of sexual heterogeneity," when it is understood that sexual homogeneity is represented by the properly married synchronization (ibid.: 47). Further, it is not clear that Cosmo's appearance in this last scene is about the specter of sexual heterogeneity at all, as the audience and the cinematic spectator, understood to be in some sense "identified," witness not a confusion of gender, but rather its clear distinction. The moment when the very idea of making *Dueling Cavalier* into a dubbed musical pops into the protagonists' heads, when the invention of dubbing itself is explained, we witness a similar configuration of gender, but with a crucial difference. This time, Kathy Selden is singing, while Cosmo is mouthing the words. His instructions to Don, "Watch my mouth," echo both the pedantic demonstration of synchronous sound at the beginning of the film and, more provocatively, the emphasis on the mouth that blackface performance (and Cosmo's imitations of blackface performance) requires for its semantics of racial impersonation.

An interpretation of *Singin' in the Rain* limited to the axis of gender fails to understand other odd points about the film, in that it fails to explain the proficiency that other women in the diegesis of the film exhibit in relation to recording technologies and vocal performance. It seems that voice is used to dramatize a number of issues: How is gender used to make these other problems legible? Lina Lamont's problem, while obviously articulated through the frame of gender, might not itself "be" gender, as Silverman's brief analysis seems to insist, and a reading which does not site her gender as operative within a logic that is implicitly racial and national reduces the complexity of the film as case and fails to see the complex overdetermination of gender and race in the American national imaginary that can be read off its surface.

Lina's voice marks not only gender, but importantly class as well. *Singin' in the Rain* argues that the world of sound cinema is a wonderland of classless consumerism, directly in contrast to the "un-American" extravagance of the silent cinema, its royal and aristocratic titles, and its overly accessorized stars. Lina's accent becomes as ontologically secure a part of her identity as her gender. Indeed, its class signification *does* her gender, and in so doing, must be removed (she runs from the stage). Her gender is only one register of her excessively minoritized body (Warner 1992), an excessive minoritization sounded by her overly accented voice.[24] The contours of her body (understood here as a resonant body, a sound problem in the acoustics of national publicity) come to approximate, if not analogize, precisely the way "race" is located in the National Symbolic; her particularity far exceeds and overperforms her gender.

If, as Michael Rogin (1992) has argued, *The Jazz Singer* uses blackface to narrate the success of a national pedagogy by which the Jew becomes an American, Rabinowitz becomes Robin, *The Jazz Singer* as an index for transformation within *Singin' in the Rain* signals the "putting on" of sound, and in its narrative relationship to popularity and "naturalness" becomes an iconic representation, or perhaps a fetishistic reflection, of the utopic success of a collective national performativity[25] Lina Lamont exhibits the dissonance between the pedagogical and the performative, only to be excised from the stage, from Monumental, from a (metonymically) national history and present tense. The staging of this failure is enacted through gender and class and masks the operations of race and ethnicity central to the "American" address of sound film under the hieroglyph of Lamont's character. In other words, to borrow Berlant's term, the *mnemotechniques* of *Singin' in the Rain* secure both the collective amnesia of specificity *and* its erasure required for the acoustic realization of a fantastically performative national public, and serves pedagogically to render unproblematic the history of impersonation and appropriation on which a utopically "American" specificity is grounded.

A STAR IS BORN: "JUDY SINGS LENA?"

While *Singin' in the Rain* concerns itself with the history of Hollywood and sound film as institutions, securing their centrality as *the* mode of American publicity through the re-narration of that history in a nostalgic mode, *A Star Is Born* resites that nostalgia in the figure of a single star represented by an impressive heterogeneity of names: Judy Garland/ Frances Gumm/Esther Blodgett/Vicki Lester/Mrs. Norman Maine. This heterogeneity demands alternative solutions to the national problematic and requirement of impersonation. Judy Garland's character lays claim to her authenticity as a star by doing Al Jolson in drag in the elaborate and (we are to presume, autobiographical) "Born in a Trunk" number. The fact that this scene dramatizes the "naturalness" of Esther Blodgett/Vicki Lester/Judy Garland/etc. by citing blackface traditions in a drag number without seeing this dramatization as in any way a problem suggests that it is again indeed precisely blackface that secures the authenticity of this more than thrice named persona; it is the reference to blackface that makes the fantasy of an especially American authenticity possible. The Garland character in the film shuttles between two distinct historical moments of racial impersonation, in both these moments arguing that it is precisely the racial impersonation that secures the Americanness and authenticity of her stardom and by extension the very star system that the seeming self-reflexivity of the film supposedly brings into question (Feuer 1993). By articulating the historical moment crystallized in the torch song and the subjectivities that it requires and produces with the earlier national moment of blackface, already a prism of mutliple moments of nostalgia, *A Star Is Born* replicates the national claim for racial impersonation that we have seen operative in *Singin'*, but this time across the star text of a single star.

But to begin by fast-forwarding to another moment in the archive, in a 1963 episode of the ill-fated *Judy Garland Show*, Garland appeared with Lena Horne, with whom she did a "medley of songs they made famous" (Watson and Chapman, 1986: 100).[26] In a still taken from that television appearance (fig. 3.4), we see Lena Horne and Garland sitting on a strange object of furniture emblazoned with the words "Judy sings Lena sings Judy sings. . . ." Judy looks to the gesturing Horne as she sings. This episode captures the shape of the problematic I'd like to discuss: How did Garland's voice achieve its status as authentically American through the "appropriation" of forms that can be glossed as African American, in particular as blues or jazz? How is this appropriation achieved through impersonation, and how does this impersonation produce the very specificity of racial difference in musical practice? How can we read the production of the "real" off the impersonation that makes its operation possible?

"The Man That Got Away" is, according to Richard Dyer, the key sequence in *A Star Is Born* that first establishes Esther Blodgett/Vicki Lester/Judy Garland/Frances Gumm/Mrs. Norman Maine as an "authentic star" (1991: 138). Esther Blodgett has just finished singing with her band (named the "Glen Williams" Orchestra) at a gig in a nightclub, and retires with the band to a dive on Sunset Boulevard for a jazz session. Norman Maine (James Mason) is out in search of Blodgett, whom he had met while in a drunken stupor at a benefit for the Shriners. Maine arrives at the nightclub, and is told by the manager there that the band goes off to play on their own after their gig in the club: "They're crazy people, you know. They blow their heads off here all night and then instead of going to bed they go off to this little place and they blow their

Figure 3.4. From *The Judy Garland Show*, 1963

heads off *for themselves*." Maine goes to this dive, named (we later learn) the "Downbeat Club," and enters to the strains of the band playing "The Man That Got Away."

Dyer points to a number of factors in this sequence that serve as markers of that authenticity: lack of control, spontaneity, and privacy. The second of these three markers, spontaneity, Dyer associates with the staging of Esther and her friends as jazz musicians:

She and the other musicians have already been described as jazz musicians, thus linking them to a music tradition that is assumed to be based on unpremeditated musical expressivity (as it is assumed that improvisations in jazz just happen, immediate and spontaneous, unrehearsed); and behind that, there is the link with black culture, which has always functioned as a marker of authenticity and naturalness in white discourses. (139)

To spend some time on Dyer's last point, this scene mobilizes historic modes of film signification to designate this a "jam session."[27] The mise-en-scène focuses on the after-hours nature of the session, particularly on the chairs which have been piled up on tables. The disorganization of the club after closing and the way the musicians occupy this disorganization (the way they move through the leftover chairs) insist that this is not a performance for an audience, but that the voyeuristic pleasures which the cinematic spectator and, indeed, the character of James Mason, receive from the privileged view into this scene are not part of the vulgar (prostituted) world of entertainment, but rather an accidental witnessing of music for music's sake, a form of *authentic* artistic expression. Cukor uses a sequence shot for the song, beginning with Garland's vocal entrance (fig. 3.5); this shot is intended to at least give the impression of

Figure 3.5. *A Star is Born* (Cukor, 1954): Esther Blogett (Judy Garland) singing "The Man that Got Away"

being a POV shot from Maine.[28] The associations with realism that the use of the sequence shot engenders and the way this shot sutures the spectator in the position of Maine reinforce the "music for music's sake" nature of the session.[29]

Complicating the racial politics of the jam session is its musical opposition to the preceding scene. The club in which Blodgett's band had played earlier and where Maine finds himself looking for Blodgett has a mambo band playing. The conversation between Maine and the club manager focuses on the manager's pimp-like role, looking for a new woman to fill Maine's sexual appetite. "No young ones. I had a young one last week." When this atmosphere is taken into account, the playing for money that Blodgett's band engaged in is at least metonymically associated with a kind of prostitution (metonymically through the sign of money and its transaction). This association is continued later in the film, when in the "Born in a Trunk" number her first real job is singing "The Peanut Song" with a Latin-style band. The position of an American authenticity that is secured by reference to black musics is clearly predicated on the devaluation of the expressive potential of other musical forms and the labeling of them indeed as un-American and inauthentic. Judy can and should do Lena, and as we will later see, Al Jolson as well, but when she does Carmen Miranda, the mimicry is framed as counterfeit and is proscribed as a form of excess.

This "art for art's sake" effect that the scene produces is accomplished in the musical material as well. The number seems to negotiate between three modes of jazz performance and aesthetics: big band, smaller swing combos, and finally bebop. But of course the most obvious form of musical signification mobilized by the diegesis of the film at this point is indeed the song itself and Judy Garland's performance. Its use of chromaticism in the first phrase, incorporating both the minor and the major third of the scale, and Garland's style of delivery, rhythmically off the beat and excessively torchy, make the racial semantics of this quite clear. These semantics were commented on at the time and made an explicit part of the Garland star text. *Time* magazine revealingly described Garland's singing: "Her big dark voice sobs, sighs, sulks, and socks them out like a cross between Tara's harp and the late Bessie Smith" (cited by Jablonksi [1961] 1985: 180).

The impersonations in the film and in the Garland star-text do not stop with "Judy sings Lena," however. *A Star Is Born* further complicates the issue of impersonation by having Judy "do" Al Jolson. Garland's body in *A Star Is Born* becomes the site of (at least) two impersonations, one of which is presented as problem, and the other as almost not an impersonation at all, but more a channeling, a form of "natural" expressivity that finds its roots in "American" tradition. Judy, to simplify her name, becomes metonymically the teleological endpoint of an implied history of "American" entertainment as a whole. The excision of excess and artifice that is enacted by the diegesis of *Singin' in the Rain* across the figure of Lina Lamont happens in *A Star Is Born* within Garland's character itself. As Esther Blodgett is "discovered" by Norman Maine to have that "little something extra," Maine attempts to arrange a screen test at the studio, Oliver Niles Studios. Esther enters the studio for the first time in this sequence and is sent to the Make Up Department in preparation for her debut on film. The makeup artists attempt to make Blodgett into a typical starlet, so much so that she later passes anonymously for a moment as a typical starlet in the eyes of Mason; and the film stresses the point that this makeover is not the authentic Esther, or the authentic Judy. Blodgett is given layers and layers of makeup and a blonde wig, and the makeup artists even think of giving her what they term a "Crawford mouth." The style of the gaudy pink dress she is given to wear is clearly out of fashion, and as such marks its artificiality by re-marking on its own ephemeral nature *as* fashion—as costume (fig. 3.6). The film makes the claim here that it is exposing the artifice of bad

Figure 3.6. *A Star is Born* (Cukor, 1954): A star is manufactured?

Hollywood, and the quasi-surgical production of stardom on which it depends; but bad Hollywood is only mobilized to mark the authentic star quality of Esther as even more real. The danger to the hetero-masquerade that is normative gender that this scene briefly incites, by dramatizing the ways femininity (in its star register) is a historically specific form of masquerade and quasi-surgical construction, made and not born, is resolved later in the film by the oscillating avowal and dis-avowal of that masquerade on a different plane of materialization.[30]

The "Born in a Trunk" number is presented as a stage production (with cinema-like memory sequences made coherent through Judy's voice-over)—within a film (Vicki Lester's first film, with Vicki Lester nervously in the audience watching)—within *the* film. The dizzying array of *mise-en-abyme* that this sequence mobilizes serves ironically as a method of securing the coherence of Judy/Esther/Vicki, a coherence that is achieved not only in the diegesis of the film but also by accessing material from the stylized vaudevillian biography of Judy Garland/Frances Gumm herself. But the key moment in the number is Garland's version of Al Jolson's "Swanee."

By the early 1950s, Jolson's blackface was a central figure of nostalgia in "American" mass culture, not only due to its role in the history of cinema from *Singin' in the Rain*, but also in relation to the very popular new Jolson films of the late 1940s, *The Al Jolson Story* and *Jolson Sings Again*, the latter being the top grossing film of 1949 (Rogin 1992: 450). Not only was Jolson's figure a central mnemonic for an imagined national past, but Garland's stardom was intimately associated with the nostalgia that this mnemonics guaranteed. Garland did a tribute to Jolson in her concerts of 1951 at the London Palladium and at New York's Palace Theater. Both concerts were central to this first of Judy Garland's many comebacks (Fricke 1992; Watson and Chapman 1986), and centered around her impersonation of Al Jolson and revival of vaudevillian "tradition." Fricke quotes Garland as saying about the Palladium: "I suddenly knew that this was the beginning of a new life. . . . Hollywood thought I was through; then came the wonderful opportunity . . . to appear at the London Palladium, where I can truthfully say, Judy Garland was reborn" (1992: 66). The song "Swanee," then, as it appeared in *A Star Is Born*, was clearly identified with its blackface history; but further, Garland performing "Swanee" in her odd vocal drag of Jolson makes a claim about the relationship of this blackface tradition to the star's own comeback, to the "rebirth" of Garland as star.

As Garland does "Swanee" in the film within the film, the connection to Jolson is made explicit in a number of ways. The dance number

Figure 3.7. *A Star is Born* (Cukor, 1954): Esther/Vicki/Judy does Jolson

features what are referred to in the shooting schedule for the scene as "six colored dancers." These dancers might well not be whites in black-face, but the dance moves they do behind Garland are clearly intended to be impersonations of vaudevillian minstrels (fig. 3.7). Four of the dancers are playing large tambourines, and the other two are holding stylized banjos as they dance. Each of the dancers smiles his way through the number, to make the impersonation of minstrel performance practice complete.

As the black dancers are doing impersonations of whites in blackface, Judy Garland is doing a drag impersonation of Jolson—not in blackface. Dressed with a top hat, a jacket and tie, and white gloves, her costume is a stylized version of the Jolson attire. The crossing of gender that Judy's drag performs stands in for the black face she is prohibited from putting on. But the story doesn't end here: her drag as Al Jolson is guaranteed a position as authentic and real by the implied blackface that his/her character enacts, by the claim to American folkishness that minstrel traditions in cinema seem to represent. If *Singin' in the Rain* uses the unseen black-face of Al Jolson as a fantastic icon of the authenticity of sound film and disposes of the contradictions that blackface represents through the exci-sion of the figure of Lina Lamont, Garland's drag rendition of "Swanee" resites the claim to authenticity on the grounds of race ironically through a drag impersonation of the historical moment of blackface. *Singin' in the Rain's* two Linas (impersonation and specifity) become in *A Star Is Born* the multiple characters that circulate around/in Judy Garland. The American claim is finally here located in naming, as these multiple figures become in the last scene of the film retroactively local versions of a new, hyperreal, majestically national public persona: "Mrs. Norman Maine."[31] The contradictions that impersonation and specificity present to the national imaginary seem to disappear behind the abstraction of the heterosexual moniker, while, at the same time, preserving the productiveness of both for the acoustics of national publicity.[32]

Both *A Star Is Born* and *Singin' in the Rain* exhibit a concern for the relationship of star bodies to national fantasy, and both use race articulated through gender as their relay toward both the specificity and generality that the national paradoxically requires. Reading these two films as a test case of the ever-recurring crisis in national publicity, a crisis legible in its material conditions of reproduction as much as in its seemingly less material ideological requirements, allows us to witness dramatically the way the repetitive productivity of race has functioned to secure the naturalized and nationalized affect of "America" understood as Hollywood audience. Garland sites this affect (auto?)biographically in the "Born in a Trunk" number discussed above as stretching temporally and geographically from the Princess Theater in Pocatello, Idaho, to the asymptotic "here, today" phantasmatically secured by the point of view of the audience within the film to which we find ourselves irrevocably sutured. *Singin' in the Rain* makes its geographic address less specific, but from the similarly constructed pseudo-autobiographical moments in the film that depict the move from small town to big city, through the film's opening focus on the national address of radio, and finally to the failure or success of Hollywood film, the national audience is invoked both temporally and geographically and is essential to the claims the film makes. Thinking about the ways film musicals functioned to police and produce this affect—the way in which popular music was an implicitly contested site for the repair of the acoustics of national publicity—leads us in new directions in thinking not only about the musical content of national temporality and geography but also about the issue of race in the popular musical imagination.

A great deal of recent work on popular music has wittingly or unwittingly relied on a grammar of racial stereotype rather than examining the ways popular music as a form of publicity produces race as a historical and political phenomenon. For one example, in his work on the semiotics of popular music, Middleton has suggested that the structure of small-scale, or "musematic," repetition, links black musics somehow directly to the experience of embodiment (1990: 267–93). I would argue that the way these commentaries seem intuitive points directly to the ways public discourse about race in popular music is one of the primary sites of race's reproduction. I hope that by thinking through the way "the voice," and especially the black voice, is secured *not* by the nature of "the music itself," but rather in what I have termed the acoustics of national publicity—the terms and logics by which race is given "voice" in American popular music—we might, as Radano suggests, configure black music not only as a popular, naturally expressive vernacular, but also as a space produced by the racial imagination of what the popular, expressively vernacular is. This is not to disallow the possibility, the necessity, of the concept of black music, but rather to realize its profound contingency within the operation of a National Symbolic and the effects of its operation within the differential gendered access to publicity that its terms and logics require.

NOTES

Material used in this chapter has been presented in the Lesbian and Gay Studies Workshop at the University of Chicago, the Colloquium series in the Music Department at the University of Chicago, and Feminist Theory and Music III: Negotiating the Faultlines, held at the University of California, Riverside, in June 1995. My thanks to the participants at these events for their support and helpful commentary, and to the organizers for the opportunity to participate.

Additionally, I would like to acknowledge those whose assistance and suggestions were crucial during various stages of my work in this project: Mary Carbine and the staff of the Film Center of the University of Chicago, James Lastra, Arthur Knight, Miriam Hansen, Dana Seitler, Ingrid Monson, Hank Sartin, Wilhelm Werthern, Robert Devendorf, and finally, the editors of this volume.

1. I am borrowing Berlant's (1993), and Warner's (1992) use of the term "prosthetic" here. For a further development of the prosthetics of publicity, see Berlant and Freeman 1993.

2. For *Öffentlichkeit* as a theoretical tool, see the first two chapters of Habermas ([1962] 1989) and the preface and first two chapters of Negt and Kluge ([1972] 1993). For a thorough outlining of the German debates about *Öffentlichkeit*, see Miriam Hansen's introduction to the translation of Negt and Kluge. Hansen (1991) also offers a thorough exploration of the use of the theoretical tools developed in these debates for the study of cinema history in her monograph on American silent cinema. Following the work of other scholars, I prefer the use of "publicity" to "public sphere" as a translation for both its useful

ambiguity and the somewhat less spatialized and territorialized ontology of the social than the more frequent translation "public sphere" suggests.

3. See Althusser's (1971: 170–77) development of the concept of interpellation.

4. On the contradictory field of utopic fantasy in Hollywood musicals, see Richard Dyer's (1992) account: "[Entertainment] presents . . . what utopia would feel like rather than how it would be organized. It thus works at the level of sensibility, by which I mean an affective code that is characteristic of, and largely specific to, a given mode of cultural production" (18).

5. Berlant (1991: 4–5, 21ff.) develops these concepts in her study of Nathaniel Hawthorne.

6. In my own work on house music and queer performativity (1995), I attempt to discuss the figure of the black disco diva in the production of queer communal affect, examining the ways race structures the experience of queer sonic space and the possibilities of embodiment and agency that it locates.

7. See Žižek's (1989) work on the symptom: "This, then, is a symptom: a particular, 'pathological,' signifying formation, a binding of enjoyment, an inert stain resisting communication and interpretation, a stain which cannot be included in the circuit of discourse, of social bond network, but is at the same time a positive condition of it" (75). See also Butler's critical appraisal of Žižek's work, where she mobilizes a similar concept of symptom: "Indeed any attempt to totalize the social field is to be read as a symptom, the effect and remainder of a trauma" (1993: 192).

8. Bennett suggests reconfiguring "the popular" in critical work: "Popular culture can be defined only abstractly as a site—always changing and variable in its constitution and organisation" (1986: 8). He further suggests that any critical concept of hegemony and "resistance" needs to locate the hegemonic "in the points of confluence between these opposing tendencies whose contradictory orientations shape the very organisation of the cultural forms in which they meet and interpenetrate one another" (19). Bennett's theory, marking a move in British cultural studies that seems in many ways parallel to Negt and Kluge's in critical theory, reclaims the "people" and "the popular" as a political field of contestation, rather than an arena of folklike expression or cultural administration. It should also be pointed out here that my thinking about the contingency of the audience is primarily indebted to Hansen's (1991) work on the formation of the audience of Hollywood film.

9. For an attempt at tracing through the ways social orders are produced in sound, see Attali 1985. My thinking about the acoustics of the nation and its publicity is indebted to a number of sources. Anderson (1983) already gestured toward thinking about the nation as having an acoustics: "Take national anthems, for example. Sung on national holidays. No matter how banal the words and mediocre the tunes, there is in this singing an experience of simultaneity. At precisely such moments, people wholly unknown to each other utter the same verses to the same melody. The image: unisonance. Singing the Marseillaise, Waltzing Matilda, and Indonesia Raya provide occasions for unisonality, for *the echoed physical realization of the imagined community*." (132; emphasis added).

A more convincing and evocative approach to this acoustics, focusing on the audibility of national modernities in specific architectures, is evident in Philip Bohlman's work on the "New Germany" (1993); his interesting retooling of Benjamin's optics of modernity for a study of its acoustics, and particularly the acoustics of a specifically national modernity, both spatial and temporal, has been central to my thinking on this subject. He undertakes a Benjaminian examination of the *Fußgängerzone* as a site appropriate for studying the acoustics of national public-ness and the possibilities and contradictions it enables, even requires, for its resonance, in time as well as in space. "Music fills the streets of the New Germany. *Straßenmusik* . . . is everywhere to be heard. . . . Street music marks and remarks upon many of the conditions that have made the New Germany possible and that establish the historical connections between the New Germany and its past" (122). See also Johnson's (1995) recent work on listening in Paris.

10. Thinking about the "acoustics of national publicity" requires a physics, an investigation of "the constraints of what is materializable and whether there are modalities of materialization" (Butler 1993: 35).

11. Žižek and others have discussed the dangers of "over-rapid historicization" (Žižek 1989: 50). See also Butler's discussion of this point (1993: 198ff.).

12. Gomery further argues that Hollywood "publicity" (in the banal sense) was standardized at the same time ownership of theaters was consolidated (1992: 69).

13. Parenthetically, the forms of cinema public that appear (in idealized form) in films like *A Star Is Born* and *Singin' in the Rain* are indeed those on the way out in the 1950s. See Gomery's discussion of these issues (1992: 83–102).

14. Gomery argues directly against this line of reasoning, suggesting that TV substituted for radio rather than film, and that the chronology it is based on is incorrect: movie-going attendance was already in decline before 1950, and thus contradicts the "blame TV" approach for the historical change in the American mass cultural landscape (1992: 83–88). Taking Gomery's well-argued point, it still seems that a new kind of publicity and new sets of social practices that can be shorthandedly described as "television" did replace the cinema as the central site of phantasmatic Americanness at this historical juncture.

15. See Bordwell, Staiger, and Thompson (1985: 330–32) for discussion of additional changes in Hollywood as a mode of production, specifically the decline of the studio system, its causes and effects.

16. Wollen further suggests that *Singin'* might allegorize the national political scene, with Kathy Selden "blacklisted" (51).

17. See Clover 1995: 729–30 for a different discussion of the same issue.

18. An increasingly popular move to the history of cinema has mobilized positivist notions of evidence and event for its narratives. This seems especially clear in the history of the conversion to sound; while a number of scholars have empirically shown the progressivist fable of Hollywood's transition during this period to be a just-so-story (Williams 1992; Altman 1992; Bordwell, Staiger, and Thompson 1985), little thought has been given to the ideological function of this fable and specifically its relation to the racial calculus of a National Symbolic.

Looking at *Singin' in the Rain* provides a chance to work through some of these concerns.

19. Lina becomes the site for the conflation of two forms of national fantasy, which Žižek (1996: 116) has described as symbolic fiction (fantasy[1]) and spectral apparition (fantasy[2]). Lina, the hyperspecific disturbing body, the gap in the complete acoustics of national publicity, represents the irritation that is displayed by the nation. Simultaneously, Lina serves as the constitutive outside to the fantasy of national self-presence, allowing that symbolic fiction to cohere.

20. Radano (1996) describes the tension between the construct of racial difference and the production of Americanness as a national paradox, which would lead "whites ironically to blame blacks for the partiality and incompleteness of American society as a whole while continuing to look to black otherness for the cure of a national ill" (521).

21. This might be the revelatory moment when the formalist in us all locates/produces the dual focus narrative, which according to Rick Altman (1987: 16ff.) constitutes the generic structure of the American film musical.

22. Debbie Reynolds herself did not "actually" sing this song in the film—the song was dubbed for Debbie/Kathy dubbing Lina by Betty Noyes (Silverman 1988: 46; Clover 1995: 725).

23. My thanks to Jim Lastra for drawing my attention to this issue.

24. On the issue of accent, see Silverman 1988: 61–63, Lawrence 1992, Antelyes 1994. On speech barriers and their role in the relationship between proletarian and bourgeois publicity, see Negt and Kluge [1972] 1993.

25. That is to say, as a national pedagogical tool: "The people are not simply historical events or parts of a patriotic body politic. They are also a complex rhetorical strategy of social reference. . . . In the production of the nation as narration there is a split between the continuist, accumulative temporality of the pedagogical and the repetitious, recursive strategy of the performative. It is through this process of splitting that the conceptual ambivalence becomes the site of writing [recording? filming?] the nation" (Bhabha 1990: 297).

26. Judy actually "does" Lena in the number "Get Happy" in the film *Summer Stock* (Walters, 1950), at least according to an account in John Fricke's biography: "'Get Happy' was the last routine Garland filmed at MGM. (To put her at ease, Walters [the director] gave her the image of Lena Horne to use as her attitude for the routine)" (Fricke 1992: 121).

27. This point will have to remain only tangential for the scope of this paper. Arthur Knight (1996) outlines the historic production of a form of Hollywood representation of jazz in the 1940s.

28. On the shot, see Dyer (1991: 138).

29. Radano (1996: 515–17) has illustrated the relationship between ideas of "absolute" and "black" musics, a relationship on which the intelligibility of this sequence depends.

30. See Butler's (1990) now classic account of gender performativity and heteronormativity.

31. Of course, it might be pointed out that the Norman Maine (James Mason) figure voices an extranational form of Hollywood stardom. But the crucial point

here is that, at the end of the film, Mr. Norman Maine is no longer with us, having drowned himself off a California beach. Mrs. Norman Maine takes on this name only as a widow: the force of the name is less a claim about her husband than an assertion in the public sphere of her domesticity. The fact that *A Star Is Born* is itself part of a complex series of remakes further complicates the issue of national temporality and its relationship to stardom. But a discussion of this aspect would exceed the limits of this chapter.

32. *Singin'* and *A Star Is Born* can be compared in many more ways than those discussed here. The "Born in a Trunk" number, for example, corresponds quite well to two numbers in *Singin'*: the autobiographical sequence as the Kelly character tells his story to the radio audience, and the "Broadway Melody" number, again film (or film idea) within the film about a stage actor. This, and other points of similarity, are first of all to be attributed to simple considerations of genre—both are back stage musicals. But the concern in these two films with connecting the history of "American" entertainment to autobiography is more than just a genre device; it makes clear that the central issue in both these films was the mobilization of a national history to justify a certain configuration of national publicity.

WORKS CITED

Althusser, Louis. 1971. "Ideology and Ideological State Apparatusses." In *Lenin and Philosophy*, trans. Ben Brewster, 127–88. New York: Monthly Review Press.

Altman, Rick. 1987. *The American Film Musical*. Bloomington: Indiana University Press.

———. 1992. "Introduction: Sound/History." In *Sound Theory, Sound Practice*, ed. R. Altman, 113–25. New York: Routledge.

Anderson, Benedict. 1983. *Imagined Communities*. New York: Verso.

Antelyes, Peter. 1994. "Red Hot Mamas: Bessie Smith, Sophie Tucker, and the Ethnic Maternal Voice in American Popular Song." In *Embodied Voices: Representing Female Vocality in Western Culture*, ed. L. C. Dunn and N. A. Jones, 212–19. Cambridge: Cambridge University Press.

Attali, Jacques. 1985. *Noise: A Political Economy of Music*. Trans. by Brian Massumi. Minneapolis: University of Minnesota Press.

Bennett, Tony. 1986. "The Politics of 'The Popular' and Popular Culture." In *Popular Culture and Social Relations*, ed. T. Bennett, C. Mercer, and J. Woollacott, 6–21. Philadelphia: Open University Press.

Berlant, Lauren. 1991. *The Anatomy of National Fantasy: Hawthorne, Utopia, and Everyday Life*. Chicago: University of Chicago Press.

———. 1993. "National Brands/National Body: *Imitation of Life*." In *The Phantom Public Sphere*, ed. B. Robbins, 173–208. Minneapolis: University of Minnesota Press.

Berlant, Lauren, and Elizabeth Freeman. 1993. "Queer Nationality." In *Fear of a Queer Planet: Queer Politics and Social Theory*, ed. M. Warner. Minneapolis: University of Minnesota Press.

Bhabha, Homi K. 1990. "DissemiNation: Time, Narrative, and the Margins of the Modern Nation." In *Nation and Narration*, ed. H. Bhabha, 291–322. New York: Routledge.

Bohlman, Philip. 1993. "Music, Modernity and the Foreign in the New Germany." *Modernism/Modernity* 1: 127–58.

Bordwell, David, Janet Staiger, and Kristin Thompson. 1985. *The Classical Hollywood Cinema: Film Style and Mode of Production to 1960*. New York: Columbia University Press.

Butler, Judith. 1990. *Gender Trouble: Feminism and the Subversion of Identity*. New York: Routledge.

———. 1993. *Bodies That Matter: On the Discursive Limits of "Sex."* New York: Routledge.

Clover, Carol. 1995. "Dancin' in the Rain." *Critical Inquiry* 21: 722–47.

Currid, Brian. 1995. "'We Are Family': House Music and Queer Performativity." In *Cruising the Performative*, ed. Sue Ellen Case, Philip Brett, and Susan Foster, 165–96. Bloomington: Indiana University Press.

Derrida, Jacques. 1976. *Of Grammatology*. Baltimore: Johns Hopkins University Press.

Dunn, Leslie C., and Nancy A. Jones, eds. 1994. *Embodied Voices: Representing Female Vocality in Western Culture*. Cambridge: Cambridge University Press.

Dyer, Richard. 1991. "*A Star Is Born* and the Construction of Authenticity." In *Stardom: Industry of Desire*, ed. C. Gledhill, 132–40. New York: Routledge.

———. 1992. "Entertainment and Utopia." In *Only Entertainment*, 17–34. New York: Routledge.

Feuer, Jane. 1993. *The Hollywood Musical*. 2d ed. Bloomington: Indiana University Press.

Fricke, John. 1992. *Judy Garland: World's Greatest Entertainer*. New York: Holt.

Gomery, Douglas. 1992. *Shared Pleasures: A History of Movie Presentation in the United States*. Madison: University of Wisconsin Press.

Habermas, Jürgen. [1962]. *The Structural Transformation of the Public Sphere: An Inquiry into a Category of Bourgeois Society*. Trans. Thomas Burger, with the assistance of Frederick Lawrence. Cambridge: MIT Press, 1989.

Hansen, Miriam. 1991. *Babel and Babylon: Spectatorship in American Film*. Cambridge: Harvard University Press.

Jablonski, Edward. [1961]. *Harold Arlen: Happy With the Blues*. New York: Doubleday, 1985.

Johnson, James H. 1995. *Listening in Paris: A Cultural History*. Berkeley: University of California Press.

Knight, Arthur. 1996. "Jammin' the Blues, or the Sight of Jazz, 1945." In *Representing Jazz*, ed. K. Gabbard, 11–53. Durham: Duke University Press.

Lawrence, Amy. 1992. "Women's Voices in Third World Cinema," In *Sound Theory/Sound Practice*, edited by R. Altman, 178–90. New York: Routledge.

Lott, Eric. 1995. *Love and Theft: Blackface Minstrelsy and the American Working Class*. New York: Oxford University Press.

Middleton, Richard. 1986. "In the Groove, or Blowing Your Mind? The Pleasures of Musical Repetition." In *Popular Culture and Social Relations*, ed.

T. Bennett, C. Mercer, and J. Woollacott, 159–76. Philadelphia: Open University Press.

Negt, Oskar, and Alexander Kluge. [1972]. *Public Sphere and Experience*. Trans. Peter Labanyi, foreword by Miriam Hansen. Minneapolis: University of Minnesota Press, 1993.

Radano, Ronald. 1996. "Denoting Difference: The Writing of the Slave Spirituals." *Critical Inquiry* 22: 506–44.

Rogin, Michael. 1992. "Blackface, White Noise: The Jewish Jazz Singer Finds His Voice." *Critical Inquiry* 18: 417–53.

Silverman, Kaja. 1988. *The Acoustic Mirror: The Female Voice in Psychoanalysis and Cinema*. Bloomington: Indiana University Press.

Spigel, Lynn. 1992. *Make Room for TV: Television and the Family Ideal in Postwar America*. Chicago: University of Chicago Press.

Spillers, Hortense. 1987. "Mama's Baby, Papa's Maybe: An American Grammar Book." *Diacritics* 17: 65–82.

Warner, Michael. 1992. "The Mass Public and The Mass Subject." In *Habermas and the Public Sphere*, ed. C. Calhoun, 377–401. Cambridge: MIT Press.

Watson, Thomas J., and Bill Chapman. 1986. *Judy: Portrait of an American Legend*. New York: McGraw-Hill.

Williams, Alan. 1992. "Historical and Theoretical Issues in the Coming of Recorded Sound to the Cinema." In *Sound Theory, Sound Practice*, ed. R. Altman, 126–37. New York: Routledge.

Wollen, Peter. 1992. *Singin' in the Rain*. London: British Film Institute.

Žižek, Slavoj. 1989. *The Sublime Object of Ideology*. New York: Verso.

———. 1996. "'I Hear You With My Eyes'; or, The Invisible Master." In *Gaze and Voice as Love Objects*, ed. Renate Sglecl and Slavoj Žižek. Durham, N.C.: Duke University Press.

4

"Sexual Pantomimes," the Blues Aesthetic, and Black Women in the New South

TERA W. HUNTER

"The dance halls are the curse of the day."
(quoted in W. E. B. Du Bois, *Morals and Manners Among Negro Americans*)

It was Saturday night on Decatur Street in Atlanta and the dance joints were jumping. In a makeshift cellar of a building, women and men crowded onto a dance floor, swinging their bodies to the rhythms of a piano player in one corner banging ragtime tunes and nascent blues, accompanied by another musician "patting juba" to the beat. "The lights were so low, you couldn't recognize a person ten feet away," and the "smoke was so thick you could put a hand full of it into your pocket" (Thomas Dorsey in Harris 1992: 60).

Delia Mitchell, Helen Henry, Grace Huley, Victoria Reed, and Emma Pitts were typical among the women who would arrive together and pair off with male friends and strangers to perform movements that varied in mood and tempo from the "itch" to the "slow drag" on any given night. Dressed in their nightclub finery, the women signaled that they were out to have fun, to escape the daily hardships of manual labor that drove their preoccupations nearly every day of the week.

The era was the 1910s, a transformative moment in American history when commercial leisure outlets were on the rise. African-Americans in Southern cities were among those who eagerly sought the pleasures offered by cheap theaters, moving picture shows, vaudeville acts, and amusement parks. But dance halls and dancing had a distinctive appeal especially for the working class, in that it rejuvenated the spirits and the bodies of people whose normal physical exertions were devoted to productive activities, the benefits of which they could little enjoy. Dancing was growing in popularity everywhere in urban America as neophyte and veteran devotees "danced like mad."

Dance halls as sites of pleasure generated controversy between the mostly black working-class patrons and their middle-class critics, however. The public record is replete with women like Mitchell, Huley, Reed, and Pitts, who may have left home anticipating an evening of frivolity, but encountered tussles on the dance floor, conflicts with the police, and arrests. Continuing pressures from critics eager to close the dance halls indicated that much more was at stake in dancing than simply having fun. The halls, the activities, and the people were often associated with urban "vice"—crime, drinking, and illicit sex. Broader tensions and anxieties about race, class, and sexuality were articulated in the contests between workers and the middle class. These tensions were especially pronounced regarding who had the prerogative to control black, especially female, laboring bodies. African-American working-class expressions of creativity and resilience in their dancing and their refusal to follow the dictates of the elites exemplify the emergence of a modern culture. The substance, style, and form of black vernacular dancing were profound expressions of an emergent cultural aesthetic grounded in the nascent blues. The blues and dance formed a symbiotic link that offers clues to African-American working-class self-understanding in a modern industrial world. This essay explores the parallel philosophical underpinnings of these two cultural forms as they were enacted and contested in the first two decades of this century, particularly in the context of Atlanta, the self-proclaimed model of the New South.

By the turn of the century, Atlanta was en route to becoming the metropolis that urban boosters had been aspiring to create. From the antebellum period when the city was a mere hamlet in the foothills of north Georgia, through its soaring growth as a strategic transportation point for the Confederate Army during the Civil War, and through its continued rise as a regional center of commerce and industry over the next several decades, Atlanta had traveled far. Ambitious young businessmen, journalists, and politicians had colluded since the 1880s to create Atlanta as the model of the "New South." They promised to uplift the South from its sullied reputation for plantation slavery and one-crop agriculture, by diversifying economic development and harmonizing race relations. They accomplished the former by building cotton mills, rolling mills, and manufacturing plants for a multitude of consumer products on the market—including the world-renowned Coca-Cola, other food products, clothing, pianos, and furniture. They accomplished the latter by codifying a modern system of segregation to control inter-racial commerce, residency, and mobility in the interests of whites.

The fortunes of African-Americans in the city dovetailed with the city's overall development. The black population soared during the Civil War and especially afterward as slaves and ex-slaves sought to find work and respite from the debilitating economic and social conditions of the rural plantation life. Like most urban black populations, women out-numbered men. As adjustments were made in the reorganization of agri-culture, women who were single, divorced, or otherwise unattached to adult men were the most easily disposed out of the rural economy that put its highest priority on hiring family units with male heads of house-holds. Thus, black women moved to cities like Atlanta in disproportion-ate numbers to find work to support themselves or to feed their families.

What they hoped to find was a city amenable to the fulfillment of their dreams for unencumbered freedom. What they encountered was some-thing less. Despite the diversity of the burgeoning economy, African-Americans were relegated to the bottom of the labor market in the worst paid and least desirable manual jobs. Black women were confined to do-mestic work almost universally from adolescence until disability or death. They labored as cooks, maids, or child-nurses in the homes of white em-ployers; and as laundresses in their own homes, on behalf of white clients. Black men were only slightly better off in some ways and worse off in others. They found a more diverse offering of jobs open to them in the railroads, civil service, hotels, restaurants, and a variety of businesses that hired common labor. Their wages were higher than women's, on av-erage, but they faced more frequent layoffs and firings in the capricious capitalist labor market.

By the turn of the century, black residents were jammed together in enclaves on the worst topography of the city, in the valleys that were subject to floods and sewerage spills and beyond the boundaries of mu-nicipal services such as running water and sewer connections.

Despite the fundamental limitations imposed on African-Americans' pursuit of economic self-sufficiency, they created a dynamic culture to meet the exigencies of urban life. Women played a central role in the creation of this culture as wage workers, wives, mothers, and neighbors. A large proportion of black women, especially those who were married or with children, worked as laundresses. The social organization of this work held some relative advantages for black families and communities. Since the labor was performed in the homes of the workers or in com-munal spaces within their neighborhoods, it enabled women to have some flexibility in juggling wage-earning with their other responsibilities

as mothers and wives. The communal character of laundry work encouraged the extension of social networks that sustained women through
commiseration about shared struggles and the exchange of vital resources. These kin-like networks of reciprocity and the intimacy they inspired could cut both ways, however. They caused friction as well as solidarity, and conflicts had to be negotiated as in all complex human
relationships. Women sometimes resorted to public brawls and fights to
air their grievances with each other (and with men) to seek support and
resolution within their communities.

African-American women who spent most of their time in white
workplaces also contributed to community development. They insisted on living in their own homes, rather than with employers, which
gave them some space of their own to engage in the non-remunerative
labor that helped to enhance their livelihoods, group survival, and personal enrichment. They fed into the informal networks of laundresses;
women combined across occupations not only to insure everyday
subsistence but also to protest injustices such as surreptitious boycotts,
strikes, and spontaneous retaliations against police brutality. All these
instances of community-building contributed to the development of
formal organizations like churches, schools, social clubs, and mutual aid
societies—the latter sometimes serving as trade unions. By the turn of
the century, African-Americans were linked to one another through kinship, friendship, and affiliations with organizations across the city wherever they were concentrated as de facto segregation hardened into de
jure Jim Crow.

Wage labor and subsistence tactics consumed most of working-class
women's time. But they sought balance and respite; they worked to live
rather than the reverse. They looked for outlets to replenish their souls
and renew their energies. Many of their economic strategies served multiple purposes and rewarded them in edifying sociability. But as work
and leisure increasingly resided in separate spheres, and leisure time was
seen as a right by American workers and middle-class professionals
alike, African-Americans sought to find ways of enjoying their leisure in
other contexts.

By the 1910s, the array of commercial entertainments had widened
considerably. African-Americans enjoyed a flourishing leisure life in saloons, billiard rooms, restaurants, gambling dens, vaudeville, and motion picture houses. Most of these outlets were headquartered on the infamous Decatur Street, the epicenter of the urban leisure milieu. Its
resemblance to other seamy metropolitan districts sometimes conjured
comparisons with Canal Street in New Orleans, the Bowery of New

York City, the Champs Élysées of Paris, and Chinatown of San Francisco. While one could encounter a wide variety of commercial and social activities in progress at any given moment, Decatur Street was "a kaleidoscope of light, noise and bustle from dawn to dawn," especially on Saturdays (Garrett 1969: 607–9). On the weekends, local residents and country transients flocked in large numbers to conduct business with street vendors or auctioneers waving their wares, as the smells of peanuts, tobacco, near-beer, hot dogs, fried fish, horse manure, and cheap perfume mingled in the air. Second-hand clothing stores and a multitude of shoe and boot stores attracted scores of astute consumers looking for snazzy outfits at bargain prices. Others brought items to exchange for cash in the pawnshops—the places where victims of larceny headed hot on the heels of thieves in hopes of reclaiming stolen property. Dozens of bars, eateries, pool rooms, bordellos, barbershops, drugstores, delicatessens, grain merchants, seafood vendors, and dry goods stores lined the street awaiting customers. Meanwhile, one could take an instant tintype photograph with a street camera fakir, catch up with passing friends and trade news, or perhaps sneak a jig of moonshine from the Appalachian farmers who sequestered the contraband between piles of fresh corn, peas, and greens brought to market.[1]

The conspicuous presence of Chinese laundrymen, Jewish and Greek shop owners, Yankee spielers, Italian chorus men, and moonshine mountaineers rubbing shoulders with one another reinforced the street's reputation as the "melting pot of Dixie." One of the few avenues of escape for black women seeking non-domestic work was petty entrepreneurship, such as running lunch carts on busy streets like Decatur. Ella Jackson and Nettie Penn, two black women lunchroom owners, were located in the same block with Fred Ketchum's jewelry store, Nathan Weitzman's barbershop, and Luna Park, an amusement business. Similarly, Lina Richardson, a black lodging house owner, ran her business a few doors away from Isaac Sinkovitz's pawnshop, Evan Williams's grocery store, and Lula Edwards's brothel. The reputation of Decatur Street as a "melting pot" meant more than the coexistence of a diversity of ethnic businesses, however. Decatur Street was also one of the few places where different racial and ethnic groups mingled relatively freely. Yet despite this reputation for the intermingling of people from diverse nations and cultures, Decatur street was best known as a "negro playground" based on the prominence of an "African majority."

African-American working-class people were especially devoted to the dance halls located on Decatur as well as other downtown streets, such as Peters, Marietta, and Harris Streets. Some dance halls continued

earlier traditions of sharing quarters with saloons, though they were
mostly makeshift rooms, usually located in basements—ergo the name
"dives"—that were devoted primarily to music and dance.

The seamy reputation of Decatur Street in general and the close proximity of legal and illegal merriment were undoubtedly factors that tainted
the reputation of dance halls in the minds of middle-class reformers. For
patrons of some dance halls, dancing was not the main attraction. The
combination of gambling, alcoholic drinks, and excited bodies moving
in time to the music was intoxicating, and sometimes the misunder-
standings that could occur in festive crowds on any occasion would lead
to petty skirmishes or mushroom into spirited melees. Police records
in Atlanta are replete with examples of lively partying gone awry, and
fights that included women domestic workers were commonplace. Pinkie
Chandler, for example, was injured by a beer glass thrown in her face by
Helen Henry when she accidentally brushed up against Henry's partner
while dancing; Delia Mitchell created trouble when she tried to squeeze
onto an already crowded dance floor and another woman pushed her
out of the way. The action outside the dance halls could generate a theater of its own as couples necked or said their farewells and youths gathered for the last brouhaha. Light-hearted fraternizing on the way home
could turn sour as well, embroiling women in fights with each other or
with men.[2]

Black vernacular dance also generated controversy because of its distinctive physical characteristics, which challenged Euro-American conceptions of proper bodily carriage and etiquette. African-American dance
emphasized the movement of body parts, often asymmetrically and independent of one another, whereas Euro-American dance demanded
rigidity to mitigate its amorous implications. Black dance generally exploded outward from the hips; it was performed from a crouching position with the knees flexed and the body bent at the waist, which allowed
a fluidity of movement in a propulsive rhythmic fashion. The facial
gestures, clapping, shouting, and yelling of provocative phrases reinforced the sense of the dancer's glee. A woman might shout, for example, "C'mon Papa grab me!" as she enjoyed the music.

Middle-class people who saw working-class black dance performed
or who conjured images of what it must look like from the descriptions
of observers (whites "slumming" in the dance halls or conducting journalistic investigations) discerned cultural differences that they interpreted to fit ideas about black inferiority.[3] Some middle-class blacks
were not immune from seeing black vernacular dance through the
lens of dominant, pejorative assumptions. As Henry Hugh Proctor, the

pastor of the First Congregation, stated bluntly: "In the name of Anglo-Saxon civilization, remove these things that are ruining the character of our young men and stealing away the virtue of our young women" (*Atlanta Constitution*, 7 July 1903). Proctor's choice of words—Anglo-Saxon civilization, character, and virtue—were loaded constructions; they were part of a powerful ideology predicated on whiteness as supreme and blackness as a throwback to the primitive. Proctor saved white Atlantans the trouble of articulating the perceived racial threat of black expressive culture to Victorian notions of self-restraint.

Yet Proctor's appraisals, though based on narrow cultural standards, recognized the sexual connotations that permeated black working-class dance. The sultry settings, dimmed lights, and prolonged musical renditions invited intimacy as couples swayed together. The "slow drag," one of the most popular dances, was described by one observer this way: "Couples would hang onto each other and just grind back and forth in one spot all night." The Itch was described as "a spasmodic placing of the hands all over the body in an agony of perfect rhythm." The Fish Tail put the emphasis on the rear end, as the name suggested; the "buttocks weave out, back, and up in a variety of figure eights." The names of other dances had erotic overtones also: the Grind, Mooche, Shimmy, Fanny Bump, Ballin' the Jack, and the Funky Butt. Skirt-lifting, body-caressing, and thrusting pelvic movements all conveyed amorous messages that offended moral reformers (Stearns and Stearns 1968: 1–12, 21, 24, 27).

Vernacular dance assumed these characteristics in large part from the inspiration of the music, reflecting the fact that in black culture, music and dance were virtually inseparable. African-American music has been an engaging social practice where audience and performers are expected to respond to one another with oral and physical gestures. The complex rhythmic patterns of voice and instruments prompt the desire to mimic the emotions they evoke through bodily movement such as foot-stomping, hand-clapping, and leaping around (Stuckey 1987: 57–59; Levine 1977: 16, 203; McClary 1991: 8–25, 54–57, 153).

The music enjoyed in the dance halls was varied and fluid, typically characterized as ragtime or "lowdown" blues, performed live before the advent of records and the radio. The blues, which were rooted in the field hollers, worksongs, and spirituals of the South, were formulated toward the end of the nineteenth century. The blues grew to maturity in the dance halls, rent parties, and vaudeville theaters and became more formalized in the 1910s and 1920s. In Atlanta, the Eighty One Theater, owned by a white businessman, Charles Bailey, and located on Decatur

Street, was one of the most influential nightclubs to popularize the blues. An endless litany of celebrities, such as Ma Rainey, Ethel Waters, Skunton Bowser, and Buzzin' Burton, would perform there, especially in the 1920s and 1930s.[4] More importantly, it served as a launching pad for local talent. Bessie Smith, the "Empress of the Blues," regularly hung out at the Eighty One as a teenager in 1913. The young Smith practiced her craft in the backyard of the club during the day, trained chorus girls using the expertise she had acquired in the road shows she performed in before moving to Atlanta, and sang on stage at night. Once she began her professional singing tour on the Theater Owners' Booking Association (TOBA) circuit a few years later, the Eighty One Theater served as her home base (Albertson 1972: 28–32, 56; Barlow 1989: 166; Harris 1992: 30, 42). Thomas Dorsey, though later known as "the father of gospel music," also began his career as an adolescent in the secular world of the Eighty One Theater. Dorsey used his job as a "butch boy" selling soft drinks and popcorn during intermission to learn from veteran piano players in the early 1900s. By the time he was sixteen years old, he was already a sought-after musician, playing at the Eighty One, the Ninety One Royal Theater, other vaudeville clubs, movie theaters, social halls, house parties, and dance halls (Rusch 1978; Harris 1992: 19–20, 26–46).

In some dance halls, the blues were generated by a pianist like Dorsey, a fiddler, or by one or more individuals "patting juba"—a practice dating back to slavery that involved clapping hands, snapping fingers, and patting limbs rhythmically. In other instances, a piano was the sole instrument driving the rhythmic beat. The dancers themselves would shout and yell as they moved (*Atlanta Constitution*, 6 August 1900, 13 July 1902; Oliver 1960: 1–11; Levine 1977: 221–39; Jones 1963: 50–94; Abrahams 1992: 94–95).

While the sights and sounds of black music and dance meant one thing to middle-class critics, they meant different kinds of racial imaginings for black working-class people. The blues and popular dance reflected a new aesthetic that was beginning to emerge in black cultural life. They were positive affirmations of cultural memories and racial heritage, and the envisioning of new possibilities and new racial realities. Like its ancestors, the blues inspired active movement rather than passive reception, and dance provided the mechanism for the audience to engage the performer in a ritual communal ceremony. Despite the connotations of its name, the blues were "good-time" music that generated a profound positive rhythmic impulse to divert and drive away depression and resignation among a people whose everyday lives were filled with adversity. The blues served as the "call" and dance as the "response" in a symbiotic performance in which ecstatic bodily movements mocked the lyrics and instrumentation that signified pain and lamentation (Jones 1963, Murray 1976, Neal 1972, Oliver 1984: 18–46).

The close relationship between the blues and dance was especially evident in Atlanta, where musicians and vernacular dancers had long-lasting influences on both art forms. "Didn't no dance go on without the blues," Dorsey recalled from his days in the city (Harris 1992: 31). This close association was further reinforced by songs that originated in the city with lyrics describing particular steps. Atlanta's own Perry Bradford was known for composing tunes with detailed instructions for dances he witnessed both at home and in his travels. Included in this reper-toire were "Ballin' the Jack," "Walkin' the Dog," "Bullfrog Hop," "Messin' Around," and "the Original Black Bottom Dance."

This close link between the blues and dance was disconcerting to middle-class and religious people as African-Americans renegotiated the relationship between sacred and secular culture. The latter assumed a larger significance as blacks faced the exigencies of a new material, mod-ern, industrial world. The tensions that resulted were most pronounced in the evolution of music and dance and their relationship to religion and the church. The shared pedigree of sacred and secular music and dance complicated matters for the pious, who emphasized the differ-ences between shouting for the Lord and shouting for the Devil. The similarities in the ritual, cathartic, communal, and expressive purposes of secular and sacred music and dance threatened the province once oc-cupied primarily by religion in African-American life. For middle-class Christians like Proctor, this close resemblance between raucous secu-lar dancing and ecstatic religious worship made the former doubly ob-jectionable. The most elite black religious denominations and individ-ual churches consciously sought to divorce themselves from traditional styles of worship, preaching, and singing that were considered "heathen" or reminiscent of Africa and the plantation South (Levine 1977: 136–297; Murray 1976: 21–42; W. Jones 1927: 65–66; Higginbotham 1992: 44, 199–200).

Dancing was ubiquitous in Atlanta throughout black neighborhoods, in the city in dance halls, picnics, house parties and "in the churches, most of all," stated Bradford. "Every prayer meeting of the African Methodist Church ends in a sort of Black Bottom circle dance, with the dancers clap-ping their hands and crooning, and the preachers calling the steps," he explained further (Sampson 1980: 341–42). The circle dance Bradford described was probably very similar to the "ring shout," a reverent dance tradition that was a form of worshiping God and honoring ancestors.

Dancers formed a circle and shuffled in a counterclockwise direction; they swung their bodies, clapped their hands, and shouted for joy as they became possessed with the Holy Ghost (Stuckey 1987: 3–97; Levine 1977: 37–48, 141, 165–66; Hazzard-Gordon 1990: 81; Abrahams 1992: 44–45, 91–92, 141; Stearns and Stearns 1968: 3, 29–31, 32, 47, 123, 129; Stuckey 1995: 54–68). Some of the most fervent practitioners of the ring shout in Atlanta were members of the Sanctified Churches, derisively called the "Holy Rollers." They were held in nearly as much contempt by middle-class critics as the devotees of secular dance in the "dives." Neighbors and businesses in the vicinity of storefront houses of worship would call the police to arrest the "Holy Rollers" for disorderly conduct and disturbing the peace (Rouse 1989: 70, Jackson 1995: 73–76).[5]

The masses of black worshipers who continued to practice ecstatic religious expression disagreed with middle-class criticisms, though some may have opposed the sacrilegious uses of dance and music. The sacred shout, as musical sound and bodily movement, was a different variation of the "lowdown" blues that filled the airwaves of the night clubs and dance halls (Stuckey 1987: 11–98, 1995). But black worshipers objected less to the percussive beat of the music and the paroxysmic movements of vernacular dancers that generated merriment and exhilaration and more to the fact that secular performances paid homage to the Devil rather than to the Holy Ghost. In other words, the social context and intentions of dance mattered more than the physical movements per se.

Reconciling worldly pleasure and spiritual reverence, however, was not always as simple as choosing right over wrong, or God over the Devil, even for devout church people. In 1916, delegates at the annual Georgia Conference of the African Methodist Episcopal (A.M.E.) Church railed against the evils of the card table, the theater, and the modern dance (Dittmer 1977: 53). Yet individuals who engaged in popular amusements on Saturday night were among those who attended church on Sunday morning. Even as the gap between the sacred and the secular widened, the boundaries between these domains remained permeable and fluid. How else could one explain the pronouncements by the A.M.E. Church and the simultaneous practices of its congregants in Atlanta openly embracing popular amusements in their own sanctuaries? Henry McNeal Turner, himself an A.M.E. bishop, hosted vaudeville and minstrel shows in his well-regarded Tabernacle. Allen Temple A.M.E. sponsored Leon the Boy Magician, Ebenezer Baptist Church entertained Ulysses the Magician, and along with Olive Baptist Church and Philips M.E. Church, they also showed nightly motion pictures (see *Atlanta Independent*, 1903–10). Even Proctor's church sponsored an annual secular music festival, though he clearly intended Negro jubilee and European classical music to provide a moral alternative to those "places in this city that tend to drag down the colored servant" (*Atlanta Constitution*, 29 and 15 June 1913).

The black masses embraced dancing because it met needs not completely satisfied by the church or other institutions. Above all else, it was fun and exhilarating. In the context of a racist political economy, however, dancing also helped to counter the debilitating impact of wage labor. As free people, African Americans could pursue entertainment at will—an important distinction from slavery, in which masters largely, though not entirely, controlled and orchestrated both work and leisure. In unregulated and secluded dance halls, blacks could reclaim their bodies from appropriation as instruments of physical toil and redirect their energies toward other diversions (Gilroy 1990: 74).

Black women domestic workers were singled out in these attacks against dancing in public halls. The ubiquity of black female servants on the urban landscape, in the minds of most whites, made them metonyms for the black race. The black bourgeoisie understood and resented this "guilt" by association. It chose to deal with this tendency by lamenting the shame and disgrace that befell the entire race when workers failed to live up to the highest expectations of dutiful service. White employers opposed the violation of what they considered their rightful claim to restrict black women's exertions to manual work. Dance halls were a menace, declared Proctor, because "the servant class tried to work all day and dance all night" (*Atlanta Constitution*, 3 July 1903).[6] He warned employers that household laborers would not perform well if they used their leisure unproductively—dancing instead of resting in preparation for the next day of work (ibid., 19 February 1905). Not missing the lesson of subservience proposed in Proctor's counsel, the white newspaper seized the opportunity to offer a reform: "Let the dance halls and places of low resort for the negro give way to schools for the domestic training of the race—schools for cooking and housework." It continued, "instead of dancing and carousing the night away, he (and especially she) will learn to become proficient in the task [for which] he is employed" (ibid., 21 February).

White employers also objected to black domestic workers dancing because they feared that the dance halls bred social contagions that would infect their homes. Some child-nurses were accused of sneaking into the "dives" with white children during the day, exposing the little ones to immorality and vice (*Atlanta Journal*, 10 January 1900). The discourse of scientific racism was summoned to bolster fears of racial and sexual pollution. According to one clergyman: "The servants of the white people of the city were enticed into [dance halls] and corrupted by them. So the white people of the city were also affected by their presence" (*Atlanta Constitution*, 20 February 1905). Here again, the close affiliation between music and dance implicated both cultural expressions. Black music's non-material properties were difficult to contain, even within racial segregation—they could float through the air, permeate the floors and walls, and if unchecked, incite white bodies to be moved. Dancing was the embodiment of the music, the means by which the abstract, fleeting sounds were extended and articulated kinesthetically.

Some white employers also believed that dancing encouraged sexual promiscuity among black women, who would then taint their households through their illicit activity. The sexual connotations of black dance exacerbated these anxieties about women's behavior among the black and white middle classes. The combination of the racial threat and the sexual fears of black bodies contaminating white bodies created panic among the middle classes, especially given the realities of interracial commerce and conviviality on Decatur Street.

This panic was not limited to Atlanta but enjoyed wide circulation throughout the South. Anthony Binga, a black minister in Virginia, wrote a detailed treatise against dancing and other urban vices. He criticized the "unholy passions" provoked by dancing and the aggressive behavior of women: "Look at the young girl or some one's wife borne around the room in the arms of a man; his arms are drawn around her waist; her swelling bosom rests against his; her limbs are tangled with his; her head rests against his face; her bare neck reflecting the soft mellow light of the chandelier, while the passions are raging like a furnace of fire." Women, he noted, were careless and carefree in their dancing and choice of dance partners. "But who is the individual with whom she is brought into such close contact? She does not know; neither does she care. The most she cares to know just now is that he is a graceful dancer" (Binga n.d.: 10).

This image of women as socially dangerous and capable of arousing men's passions for evil purposes has a long legacy dating back to Adam and Eve. The particular association of black women dancing and illicit sex is evident in European perceptions of Africans and their descendants in the Americas dating back centuries (Rose 1989: 27, Abrahams and Szwed 1983: 290–91). Binga believed that women's corrupting power as demonstrated on the dance floor required measures to suppress and contain it, or society would face the consequence of mayhem. His critique of unrestrained female sexuality in the dance halls may have been encouraged by the perception that certain dances, with erotic overtones, were feminine and performed mostly by women. The "shake" and the "shimmy," also referred to as the "shimmy-she-wobble," were dances that were associated with women (Stearns and Stearns 1968: 112, 235; Leppert 1988: 73–74). These were dances that may have been transformed from solo to couple dances, however, with their eroticism intact. Another version of the "shimmy" was depicted as very similar to the "slow drag." As Thomas Dorsey described it: "You couldn't do no shimmy alone, by yourself. They danced all night. You look around and nobody be moving. They'd just be shimmying" (Harris 1992: 53).

Ironically, castigating remarks made by middle-class people shared something in common with the meaning conferred by the working class itself. Though working-class people did not have a voice in public discourse, as it was circulated through newspapers and pamphlets, they made their views known through their actions. Both sides understood that dancing interfered with wage work, though clearly from antithetical perspectives. The elite saw dancing as a hindrance to the creation of a chaste, disciplined, submissive, and hard-driving labor force—the hallmarks of the Protestant work ethic. Workers saw it as a respite from the deadening sensation of long hours of poorly compensated labor—critical to the task of claiming one's life as one's own.

Black dance itself embodied a resistance to the confinement of the body solely to wage work. The transformation of physical gestures in black dance from slavery to freedom demonstrates the rejection of wage work as the only outlet for physical exertion. Ex-slaves tended to abandon the references and gestures mimicking labor routines in their dances that they had practiced during slavery (such as "pitchin hay" or "shuckin' corn") as urban freedom gave more meaning to making a living beyond the needs of subsistence alone. Consumption, entertainment, and personal gratification were also vital to working-class livelihoods and essential to an emergent modern ethos or blues aesthetic (Hazzard-Gordon 1990: 87). In the world of urban poverty and segregation where enjoyments were limited, the affirmation of life embodied in dancing captivated working-class women and men and offered moments of symbolic and physical restoration of their subjugated bodies for joy, pleasure, and self-delight. Black workers sought to counteract the exploitative dimensions of labor through intensely social and kinetic experience.

Though dancing was seen as interfering with wage labor, the connotation of "work" in black culture had multiple meanings. Work not only meant physical labor, it also meant dancing. In addition, it meant engaging in sex. Dancing enabled a momentary escape from wage work, even as dance itself was considered work—of a different order. The ethics of drive, achievement, and perseverance took on a different meaning when removed from the context of wage relations. Dancers put a high value on mastery of technique and style, and they also competed with one another in jest and formal contests in which "working hard" became the criterion of a good performance. The proof could be found in the zeal and agility of body movements or in the perspiration that seeped through one's clothes. James P. Johnson, a pianist, suggested another way: "I saw many actually wear right through a pair of shoes in one night. They danced hard" (Stearns and Stearns 1968: 24, Gilroy 1987: 203).

The value placed on dancing as hard work resonated in particular with African-American women workers in a society in which the highest valorization of womanhood was largely defined by non-work. The ideal woman did not engage in wage work, and the ideal woman's vocation in the home was not considered work. Leola B. Wilson (Coot Grant) remembered her childhood in Birmingham, Alabama, at the turn of the century. Her aspirations to become an entertainer were nourished by her furtive glimpses through a peephole she drilled in a wall of her father's honky-tonk in order to observe adult entertainment. Wilson's recollections years later demonstrate how black women could reconstruct notions of womanhood through dance. "I remember a tall, powerful woman who worked in the mills pulling coke from a furnace—a man's job," she added. "It was Sue, and she loved men. When Sue arrived at my father's honky tonk, people would yell: 'Here come Big Sue! Do the Funky Butt, Baby!' As soon as she got high and happy, that's what she'd do, pulling up her skirts and grinding her rear end like an alligator crawling up a bank" (Stearns and Stearns 1968: 24). Sue worked hard, like a man, during the day, but she shed her industrial pants and worked hard as a woman at night, as she danced in a setting in which femininity was appreciated for its compatibility with work of several different orders.

African-American working-class people inscribed public dancing as a distinctive cultural form. It was a positive affirmation of their racial heritage and a way of enacting the meaning of community. Dancing itself was not new, but the forms of vibrant, public social dance among black workers and the interaction between dance and nascent musical forms reinvigorated its meaning and gave it new life. Vigorous dancing became transgressive in light of the criticisms and actions of middle-class reformers intent on exorcising it from public life. This transgression is best understood as an elaborate ethos that informed the ambitions, daily struggles, and consciousness of the black majority—a blues aesthetic. The major underlying principles that informed the blues aesthetic and embodied in vernacular dance were irreverence, transcendence, social realism, self-empowerment, and collective individualism.[7]

The blues and dance were developed with a fierce sense of irreverence—the will to be unencumbered by any artistic, moral, or social obligations, demands, or interests external to the community which the blues and dance were created to serve. While the blues and vernacular dance forms borrowed from traditions of both Euro-America and Afro-America, they ultimately paid homage only to their own interpretations. Despite protests by white authorities or black reformers, black workers persisted in their public dancing to "lowdown" music, continually reaffirming the value that they placed on sustaining a collective culture.

The feelings of self-empowerment and transcendence emanating from the blues and dance were evident in the power African-Americans invested in sound and bodily movement and in the particular ways in which they generated these forces, especially through the use of polyrhythms. In Euro-American music and dance, the basic pulse was dependent on an evenly partitioned beat. In contrast, the dancer and musician in Afro-American culture was challenged to play and move around the beat, to subvert linear notions of time by playing against it. The complex rhythmic structure and driving propulsive action endowed participants with the feeling of metaphysical transcendence, of being able to overcome or alter the obstacles of daily life. If the sung word was more powerful than the spoken or written word, then the danced song was even more mighty than singing alone (Andrews 1992: 52). It was the symbiotic relationship between music and dance that made their combination a complex and rich cultural form. Workers used them for personal gratification. They also used them to reclaim their bodies from drudgery and exploitation and actually changed, momentarily, their existential condition.

The blues and dance marked a new departure in the assertion of individualism, as well as a redefinition of the conventional Western meaning of that term. Slavery had largely denied this concept among African-Americans, but as free people they reclaimed the importance of the self without diminishing the imperatives of the collective. In slavery, blacks were denied ownership of their bodies. In freedom, they reclaimed their right to use their bodies beyond their needs for subsistence alone. But their assertion of their individual rights did not preclude the expression of a collective sensibility. Blues were personal music;

dance was a reclamation of one's individual body; yet both allowed and demanded an integral link between the person and the group. Some of the salient characteristics of the blues and of black music and dance in general, such as polyrhythm, improvisation, and antiphony, reinforced this notion of the simultaneity of the individual and the collective—of various elements going their own way but still being held together by their relationship to each other.[8]

Call and response were generated within the music, as well as executed at the level of performance—the blues were seldom performed without dance, at least not prior to the advent of the radio and records. The mimetic power of the music inspired the gestures of the dancers, and the dancers themselves were like musical instruments—stomping, clapping, shouting, and patting juba. And finally, the blues and dance were striking in their candor and social realism. The dancer, musician, and singer responded to what they saw and experienced in the material world and expressed the horror and the beauty of those feelings in terms uncensored by middle-class decorum and propriety. They openly flaunted and confronted the world of the flesh, of "body reality," and articulated joy and pain with emotional and kinetic intensity.[9]

The blues aesthetic is the key to understanding why African-American vernacular dance was such a contested terrain in Atlanta and the urban South and how it generated conflict over the black body. As an object of discipline and liberation, the body is a site where a society's ideas about race, class, gender, and sexuality are constructed to give the appearance of being mandates of nature while conforming to cultural ideologies. The body is the vehicle through which labor produces wealth, although the powerful usually resist acknowledging and rewarding the centrality of labor in the production of wealth. The importance of laboring bodies in the political economy is revealed, however, in the obsession of employers to repress and contain the autonomy of workers in order to reap the maximum benefits of their exertions. The mere sight of African-Americans, especially domestic workers, deriving pleasure and expressing symbolic liberation in dance halls by posing alternative meanings of bodily exertion seemed threatening to employers (Fiske 1989: 49–95).

The threat was real, since white employers were denied unmitigated control over black labor. Unlike other commercialized recreation, such as the new amusement parks, where one encountered replicas of industrial life in the mechanized, standardized forms of play,[10] dance halls still allowed for a great deal of creativity, imagination, improvisation, and thereby change. Dance halls contained a strong element of impulsiveness and unpredictability, as dancers and musicians inspired one another to enact infinite permutations of gestures and sounds. Reformers' efforts to regulate the dance halls or to introduce tame, patterned movements were designed to counteract the forms of free expression that were difficult to suppress when patrons were left to their own devices.

Yet despite the tirades of incensed critics, dancing did have the effect of renewal and recovery, even if on the workers' own terms. It reinvigorated them for the next day of work and enabled them to persevere. It helped to maintain the social order by providing an outlet for workers to release their tensions, to purge their bodies of their travails on the dance floor. Dancing hard, like laboring hard, was consistent with the work ethic of capitalism. Black working-class dance, like the blues, looked back to vernacular roots and forward to the modern world. Black women had played a pivotal role in asserting this expressive practice, replicating dimensions of the social order around them.

Much was at stake for the black middle class in this struggle to contain and eradicate vernacular dance. The controversy over dancing occurred as a modern black bourgeoisie asserted its claim to define and direct racial progress. The black elite sought to impose its own values and standards on the masses, to obliterate plebeian cultural expressions that, in its view, prolonged the degradation of the race. While the black elite asserted its paternalism through the language of morality, "civilization," law and order, and the Protestant work ethic, the white elite exercised its rhetorical and repressive will through mechanisms of state power, not just through language. White Southerners had even more at stake in controlling black leisure and dancing as they continued to make claims for reaping the benefits of the black labor power long after African-Americans had been divested as literal commodities. White fears of the bodily excesses perceived in dance were rooted in racial and class-coded constructions of bodily carriage, in their own obsessions with sex, and in their anxieties about interracial sex. Their fears were contradictory, however, since these same values, the so-called Anglo-Saxon values that were the measuring rod by which "racial" fitness was judged, were undergoing change. Increasingly, Victorianism wore thin; middle-class people felt shackled by their own inhibitions and began adopting the very same behaviors (such as passion, rough sport, and visceral amusements) that they so derisively associated with black and working-class people—sometimes unabashedly imitating the "primitive" (Bederman 1995: 168–69, 184–86). The racial paranoia was further nurtured by the context in which much of the dancing occurred, in the subterranean world of the red light district on Decatur Street, "the melting pot of Dixie," where urban dwellers crossed over the color line more freely than elsewhere in the city. The contest over the black body assumed profound proportions in the dance halls, yet it did not rest there alone.

NOTES

1. *Journal Magazine* (18 May 1913) in Garrett 1969, 2: 607–9; Atlanta City Directory, 1910; Atlanta City Council Minutes, 6 July 1910, 22: 438, Atlanta History Center.

2. For stories of police arrests of women and men for crime related to dance halls, see *Atlanta Constitution* (23 June 1900, 7 May 1904, 9 March 1905); *Atlanta Journal* (19 and 23 June, 12 September 1900).

3. For broader ideas about the importance of the image of music, see Leppert 1993.

4. Bailey also owned the Dixie Theater and the Arcade Theater. *New York Freeman* (12 December 1913) in TINF; Barlow 1989: 121, 192; Kuhn, Joye, and West 1990: 301; Waters [1951] 1959: 88–89.

5. See *Atlanta Constitution* (10 November 1908, 13 August, 14 August 1910). A group of white Holy Rollers was arrested on similar charges (see *Atlanta Constitution*, 13 October 1910).

6. Employers of domestics and other workers in the North also complained about "Blue Monday," the trouble getting workers to perform their duties after a weekend of festivities (Peiss 1986: 34).

7. My analysis of the blues aesthetic is informed by previously cited historical and cultural studies of the blues, but it has especially benefited from Dwight Andrews (1992) and Larry Neal (1972). For a theoretical analysis of blues and literature see Baker 1984.

8. On the relationship between the individual and the collective in music and feminist theory see Brown 1992 and Levine 1977: 133.

9. The term "body reality" is taken from Neal 1972: 38.

10. For insights into how amusement parks reinforced and challenged the social order of industrial life, see Kasson 1978.

REFERENCES

Abrahams, Roger D. 1992. *Singing the Master: The Emergence of African American Culture in the Plantation South.* New York: Pantheon.

Abrahams, Roger D., and John F. Szwed, eds. 1983. *After Africa: Extracts from British Travel Accounts and Journals of the Seventeenth, Eighteenth, and Nineteenth Centuries Concerning the Slaves, their Manners, and Customs, in the British West Indies.* New Haven, Conn.: Yale University Press.

Albertson, Chris. 1972. *Bessie.* New York: Stein and Day.

Andrews, Dwight. 1992. "From Blues to Black." In *Sacred Music of the Secular City: From Blues to Rap*, ed. Jon Michael Spencer, 47–54. Durham, N.C.: Duke University Press.

Baker, Houston. 1984. *Blues, Ideology, and Afro-American Literature*. Chicago: University of Chicago Press.

Barlow, William. 1989. *Looking Up at Down: The Emergence of Blues Culture*. Philadelphia: Temple University Press.

Bederman, Gail. 1995. *Manliness and Civilization: A Cultural History of Gender and Race in the United States, 1880–1917*. Chicago: University of Chicago Press.

Binga, Anthony. n.d. *Binga's Address on Several Occasions: Should Church Members be Disciplined for Attending Balls or Theaters*. Printed by Vote of the General Association of Virginia, 190?. [Held by Schomburg Center for Black Culture, New York Public Library.]

Brown, Elsa Barkley. 1992. "'What Has Happened Here': The Politics of Difference in Women's History and Feminist Politics." *Feminist Studies* 18: 295–311.

Dittmer, John. 1977. *Black Georgia in the Progressive Era, 1900–1920*. Urbana: University of Illinois Press.

Fiske, John. 1989. *Understanding Popular Culture*. Boston: Unwin Hyman.

Garrett, Franklin. 1969. *Atlanta and Environs: A Chronicle of Its People and Events*. 2 vols. Athens: University of Georgia Press.

Gilroy, Paul. 1987. *"There Ain't No Black in the Union Jack": The Cultural Politics of Race and Nation*. London: Hutchinson. Repr. Chicago: University of Chicago Press, 1991.

———. 1990. "One Nation Under a Groove: The Cultural Politics of 'Race' and Racism in Britain." In *Anatomy of Race*, ed. David Theo Goldberg, 262–83. Minneapolis: University of Minnesota Press.

Harris, Michael. 1992. *The Rise of Gospel Blues: The Music of Thomas Andrew Dorsey in the Urban Church*. New York: Oxford University Press.

Hazzard-Gordon, Katrina. 1990. *Jookin': The Rise of Social Dance Formations in African American Culture*. Philadelphia: Temple University Press.

Higginbotham, Evelyn Brooks. 1992. *Righteous Discontent: The Women's Movement in the Black Baptist Church, 1880–1920*. Cambridge: Harvard University Press.

Jackson, Jerma A. 1995. "Testifying at the Cross: Thomas Andrew Dorsey, Sister Rosetta Tharpe, and the Politics of African-American Sacred and Secular Music." Ph.D. diss., Rutgers University.

Jones, Leroi. 1963. *The Blues People: Negro Music in White America*. New York: Morrow.

Jones, William H. 1927. *Recreation and Amusement among Negroes in Washington, D.C.* Washington, D.C.: Howard University. Repr. Westport, Conn.: Negro Universities Press, 1970.

Kasson, John. 1978. *Amusing the Million: Coney Island at the Turn of the Century*. New York: Hill and Wang.

Kuhn, Clifford M., Harlon E. Joye, and Bernard E. West. 1990. *Living Atlanta: An Oral History of the City, 1914–1918*. Athens: University of Georgia Press.

Leppert, Richard. 1988. *Music and Image*. Cambridge: Cambridge University Press.

———. 1993. *The Sight of Sound: Music, Representation, and the History of the Body.* Berkeley and Los Angeles: University of California Press.

Levine, Lawrence. 1977. *Black Culture and Black Consciousness: Afro-American Thought from Slavery to Freedom.* New York: Oxford University Press.

McClary, Susan. 1991. *Feminine Endings: Music, Gender, and Sexuality.* Minneapolis: University of Minnesota Press.

Murray, Albert. 1976. *Stomping the Blues.* New York: McGraw Hill.

Neal, Larry. 1972. "The Ethos of the Blues." In *Sacred Music of the Secular City: From Blues to Rap,* ed. Jon Michael Spencer, 36–46. Durham, N.C.: Duke University Press.

Oliver, Paul. 1960. *Blues Fell This Morning: Meaning in the Blues.* Cambridge: Cambridge University Press.

———. 1984. *Songsters and Saints: Vocal Traditions on Race Records.* Cambridge: Cambridge University Press.

Peiss, Kathy. 1986. *Cheap Amusements: Working Women and Leisure in Turn-of-the-Century New York.* Philadelphia: Temple University Press.

Rose, Phyllis. 1989. *Jazz Cleopatra: Josephine Baker in Her Time.* New York: Vintage.

Rouse, Jacqueline Anne. 1989. *Lugenia Burns Hope: Black Southern Reformer.* Athens: University of Georgia Press.

Rusch, Bob. 1978. Interview with Georgia Tom Dorsey. *Cadence* 9.

Sampson, Harry T. 1980. *Blacks in Blackface: A Source Book of Early Black Musical Shows.* Metuchen, N.J.: Scarecrow.

Stearns, Marshall, and Jean Stearns. 1968. *Jazz Dance: The Story of American Vernacular Dance.* New York: Macmillan. Repr. New York: Da Capo, 1994.

Stuckey, Sterling. 1987. *Slave Culture: Nationalist Thought and the Foundations of Black America.* New York: Oxford University Press.

———. 1995. "Christian Conversion and the Challenge of Dance." In *Choreographing History,* ed. Susan Leigh Foster, 54–68. Bloomington: Indiana University Press.

Waters, Ethel. 1951. *His Eye Is on the Sparrow.* New York: Doubleday. Repr. New York: Bantam, 1959.

PART II

Hybridity/Mix

5

Race Music: Bo Chatmon, "Corrine Corrina," and the Excluded Middle

CHRISTOPHER A. WATERMAN

onceptions of racial identity and difference vary from place to place and time to time.[1] It is for precisely this reason that an adequate understanding of the universalizing power of racism—that family of ideologies whose primary subject matter is the relationship between biological "destinies" and cultural "essences"—depends on comparative study of the myriad cultural practices through which it is instantiated.

In the field of popular music studies, the last decade has seen a critical reappraisal of the notion that particular musical genres, styles, forms, and practitioners can reasonably be taken to summarize or encapsulate the historical experience of human races.[2] This critique of "ethnic absolutism" (Gilroy 1993: 2) is particularly relevant in the case of the United States, where music has long played a privileged role in the naturalization of racial categories and where commonsense conceptualizations of musical "blackness" and "whiteness" have been manipulated by racial supremacists, politicians, academics, and—perhaps most efficaciously—the entertainment industry.[3] In music-historical discourses, the retrospective construction of well-bounded, organically unified race traditions—musicological corollary of the infamous one-drop rule[4]—has tended to confine the complexities and contradictions of people's lived experience (including their experience of racism) within the bounds of contemporary ideological categories. Performers, genres, texts, and practices not consonant with dominant conceptions of racial difference have as a result often been elided from academic, journalistic, and popular representations of the history of American music.

One effective way to analyze the logics of inclusion and exclusion that have informed the production of racialized music histories is to examine music that springs from, circulates around, and seeps through the interstices between racial categories. The analysis of such forms, and of the circumstances of their production and reception, can help us to understand musicians and audiences not as instances of idealized types, but as human beings working under particular historical conditions to produce, texture, and defend certain modes of social existence.

The substantive focus of this essay is a song, the venerable "Corrine Corrina." I have use "Corrina" as a chronotope (Bakhtin 1981), a unit of analysis that allows us to read particular musical events as "x-rays of the forces at work in the culture system from which they spring" (Emerson and Holquist in Bakhtin 1981: 425–26). My purpose is to understand broader cultural processes through the multiple lenses of particular expressive forms and acts. Close attention to the nuances of musical structure, style, and rhetoric is as central to this method as is the analysis of culture at large, for the traces of ideology and aesthetics, identity and memory are often inscribed in the finest grain of expressive detail.

First recorded in December 1928 by the Mississippi guitarist and singer Armenter 'Bo' Chatmon (1893–1964), "Corrina" is a blues, in the well-known 12-bar, AAB-texted form. It is also an "old-timey" country song, with roots in the southern common stock tradition[5] (Russell 1970: 28); and a pop tune, carefully crafted to appeal to a wide audience. Chatmon's recording was subsequently covered by musicians working in a variety of genres, including jazz (Red Nichols, Art Tatum), blues (Muddy Waters, Albert Ammons, Mississippi John Hurt, Jimmy Witherspoon, Albert King), country and western music (Bob Wills, Merle Haggard, Floyd Cramer, Asleep at the Wheel, Freddy Fender, the Tennessee Drifters), cajun music (Leo Soileau), rhythm & blues and rock 'n' roll (Big Joe Turner, Bill Haley, Jerry Lee Lewis), urban folk music (Bob Dylan, Taj Mahal), rock (Steppenwolf), various forms of mainstream pop (Bing Crosby, Lawrence Welk, Bobby Vinton, Phil Spector), and New Age music (George Winston).

This essay examines "Corrina"'s seventy-year trajectory, focusing on the song's shifting yet coherent relationship to conceptions of racial difference and commensurability. In the first section I locate Bo Chatmon's 1928 recording within a broader musical and social terrain, in an attempt to account for the marginal status to which both the song and the musicians who performed it have been relegated in subsequent accounts of the history of American music. I argue that Chatmon's "Corrina" can be understood as one outcome of a system of interracial musical circulation that originated in the paternalistic social relations of slavery and survived thoroughgoing institutionalization of the one-drop ideology in the decades following Reconstruction. By the late 1920s, when Chatmon's record was released, the song was positioned as a mass-mediated signifier of a vanishing rural past, "an echo of a displaced era" (Genovese 1976: 679 n.5) that traversed (but could not transcend) the boundaries between race-cultures in Mississippi between the World Wars.

In the second part of the essay, I analyze a series of cover versions of "Corrina" recorded between 1929 and the early 1990s. In the 1920s and 1930s, as the electronic mass media consolidated their hold on the leisure time of millions of Americans, "Corrina" was caught up in the production of mass-mediated images of cultural authenticity and of a putatively natural state of innocence grounded in the pre-industrial past and brought into focus by the twin lenses of rurality and blackness. In the 1940s and 1950s, "Corrina" played a role in the production of cross-over music, essentially African-American music promoted to a predominantly white youth audience. In the 1960s folk song revival, the song came to signify a utopian space beyond the reach of racial politics, in which notions of difference ultimately derived from the one-drop rule were simultaneously reproduced and ameliorated. A variant of this logic surfaces once again in the 1994 film *Corrina, Corrina* starring Whoopie Goldberg as an African-American woman involved in an interracial romance in 1950s Los Angeles. In this context, the utopian project of recovering a space prior to or outside of racial difference is embodied in the tropes of the nuclear family and the child (conceptualized in contemporary therapeutic discourses as "the child within" the alienated adult subject) (Ivy 1993).

BO CHATMON'S "CORRINE CORRINA" (1928)

Early in 1929, Brunswick Records—the label of Bing Crosby, Al Jolson, and Fred Astaire, seeking to make inroads into the then-thriving "race" and "hillbilly" music markets—released the first recording of "Corrine Corrina," performed by the singer and guitarist Bo Chatmon (a.k.a. Bo Chatman, Bo Carter).[6] Chatmon was accompanied by his brother Lonnie Chatmon on violin and by Charley McCoy on mandolin and supporting vocals. The trio, which had been recorded by Brunswick's mobile unit in New Orleans in December 1928, was a somewhat informal affair, drawn from a network of African-American musicians from the hill country of central Mississippi. These musicians worked together in various configurations, playing dance music for both white and colored audiences. During the same recording sessions that produced "Corrine Corrina," the Chatmons, McCoy, and the guitarist Walter Vinson recorded two so-called "coon songs" ("The Yellow Coon Has No Race" and "Good Old Turnip Greens"), several vaudevillian-style blues with the singer Mary Butler, and a country blues song ("East Jackson Blues") (Dixon and Godrich 1982: 131,150).

The copyright for "Corrine Corrina" was filed in 1932, in the names of Bo Chatmon, Mitchell Parish, and J. Mayo Williams. Williams worked as talent scout and assistant recording director for the race music departments of Paramount Records (1923–27), Brunswick Records (1928–34), and various other labels. He was the most powerful black figure in the race record business, identifying and grooming recording stars such as Ma Rainey, Blind Blake, Blind Lemon Jefferson, and Georgia Tom; overseeing recording sessions; and providing urban "jive talk" copy for advertisements in Negro newspapers (see Dixon and Godrich 1970). Williams's nickname, "Ink," was at least in part a reference to his skill at talking musicians into signing away the rights to songs they recorded. Thomas A. Dorsey (Georgia Tom), a pianist and singer who was later to become a central figure in gospel music, worked for Williams in the studio. "A guy'd come in with a song, and he'd sing it. He had nobody to arrange it or put it down on paper. So I put it down on paper and then the company could copyright it" (Barlow 1989: 131). Big Bill Broonzy recalled a 1927 Paramount recording session supervised by Ink Williams.

> They kept telling us to relax and giving us moonshine whiskey to drink, and I got drunk. I went to sleep after the recording and when I woke up, on my way home, [Broonzy's accompanist] John Thomas told me that I had signed some paper, signed in ink. "You've let them make you drunk" Thomas said, "and you've signed our rights away." (Barlow 1989: 132)

According to Samuel Charters, Williams "handled musical copyrights through a Paramount subsidiary, the Chicago Publishing Company, and made considerable money with some of the successful blues. He usually listed himself as a composer" (Charters 1975: 51). In 1927 Williams left Paramount for the race music division of Brunswick Records, working as assistant recording director under Jack Kapp (who later went on to head Decca Records).

Mitchell Parish (1990–1993), who is listed as a co-composer of "Corrine Corrina," was a white Tin Pan Alley lyricist who supplied the lyrics for "Stars Fell on Alabama," "Sweet Lorraine," Duke Ellington's

"Mood Indigo," and Hoagy Carmichael's "Stardust." It does not appear that Parish actually composed any part of the lyric of "Corrine Corrina"; rather, he was operating as an intermediary for Irving Mills, a music publisher and promoter who specialized in jazz and race music. During the early 1930s, Mills was hired as a talent scout for Brunswick Records. The fact that Mayo Williams and Irving Mills both worked at Brunswick may explain why "Corrine Corrina" was published with the Mills company in 1932, more than three years after the record's original release. In any case, it is interesting to note that publication of "Corrine Corrina" (and determination of its legal status as property) involved interaction across class, geographical, and racial lines, between a rural musician from the deep South, a successful African-American entrepreneur in the urban North, and a white intermediary for a Tin Pan Alley music publishing firm. These sorts of relationships were central to the emergence of the race and hillbilly music markets and, more broadly, to the American entertainment industry's ability to shape and exploit taste communities during the 1920s.

"Corrine Corrina" was advertised in Brunswick's race record catalog, among other items intended primarily for sale to African-American listeners, but it also sold well among southern whites, both in Mississippi and farther afield. For the listener whose model of the Mississippi blues may be the work of Robert Johnson (recorded eight years later), "Corrina" offers an alternative view of the musical landscape. The song follows the AAB text form and 12-bar musical structure which had already, via the mediation of professional musicians such as W. C. Handy, been established as the classic blues form:

> Corrine Corrina, where you been so long?
> Corrine Corrina, where you been so long?
> Ain' had no lovin' since you been gone
>
> Corrine Corrina, where'd ya stay last night?
> Corrine Corrina, where'd ya stay last night?
> Come in this mornin', sun was shinin' bright
>
> I met Corrina way across the sea
> I met Corrina way across the sea
> She wouldn't write no letter, she didn' care for me
>
> Corrine Corrina what you goin' a' do?
> Corrine Corrina what you goin' a' do?
> Just a little bit of lovin', let your heart be true

> I love Corrina, tell the world I do
> I love Corrina, tell the world I do
> Just a little bit a' lovin', let your heart be true
>
> Corrine Corrina, dear pal a' mine
> Corrine Corrina, dear pal a' mine
> Now she lef' me walkin', tears are rollin' and dryin'
>
> Corrine Corrina, what's the matter now?
> Corrine Corrina, what's the matter now?
> Ya wouldn' write me no letter, ya didn' love me no how
>
> Goodbye Corrina, it's fare ya well
> Goodbye Corrina, it's fare ya well
> When I come back here, cain' anyone tell

A search of the most comprehensive concordance of lyrics performed on race records (Taft 1984) reveals only a few references to a female character named Corrina. "Corrine Corrina" shares a number of textual and melodic elements with another staple of the songster repertoire, "Alberta"; the two are regarded by some scholars as variants of the same song (see Oster 1969: 421 n.5). Blind Lemon Jefferson, the first down-home blues singer to achieve substantial record sales, recorded a "Corina Blues" in 1926. However, apart from its title, that song bears little resemblance to "Corrine Corrina" and is in fact a variation on a blues song family more widely known as "See See Rider." The reference to meeting Corrina "way across the sea" may have been added during the First World War, when black soldiers serving in segregated platoons developed a topical song repertoire based on a combination of southern rural forms, rag-time, and Tin Pan Alley song (David Evans, pers. comm., 1995; see also Niles 1927, Levine 1977: 196–97). Although it is not possible to specify the precise origins of "Corrine Corrina," it is clear that Chatmon's song drew on textual and musical formulas already long in circulation.

The 1928 recording opens with Lonnie Chatmon's fiddle, playing the last four bars of the song's melody as an introduction (a foreshadowing strategy common in pop recordings of the time). Throughout the recording, Bo Chatmon's guitar maintains a steady "boom-chick" dance rhythm, and Charley McCoy's mandolin alternates between emphasizing the off-beats and doubling the vocal melody. The fiddle shifts from foreground to background, heterophonically ghosting the melody, playing descending pentatonic licks between sung phrases, and in a few places providing a delicate tremolo background.

After the four-bar introduction, Bo Chatmon begins to sing, with

McCoy harmonizing in thirds. The melody (in the key of A major) is basically heptatonic, and avoids the seventh degree.[7] The melody is structured mainly around a second inversion tonic triad (E–A–C$^\sharp$), with some use of blues notes (especially the flatted third). The first phrase of the song—a cleverly designed melodic hook—begins with a pitch sequence common in ragtime and jazz of the 1920s: half-step movement from the third to the fifth degree below the tonic, followed by a leap of a major sixth up to the third degree above the tonic (C$^\sharp$–D–D$^\sharp$–E–C$^{\sharp 2}$, the opening melodic gesture of Scott Joplin's rag "The Entertainer").[8] The final phrase of the tune ("since you been gone") descends stepwise from the fourth degree to the tonic in a somewhat flat-footed fashion, more like a contemporaneous pop or hillbilly song than a country blues. In harmonic terms the performance is fairly straightforward, sticking closely to the I, IV, and V chords and avoiding the cycle of fifths–derived chords (e.g. II and VI) used by Chatmon in other recordings.

The Chatmon-Chatmon-McCoy recording of "Corrine Corrina" draws on a vast and variegated stylistic terrain. The overall feel of the music—its four-square dance rhythm, texture, and tone color—is derived from the African-American string band tradition, a genre which had for at least a century existed in a relationship of continual cross-pollination with English, Celtic, and German-derived fiddle traditions and popular dance music.[9] The musical and textual form (12-bar, AAB blues) and blue notes link "Corrina" to the country blues tradition and the vaudevillian blues. The careful arrangement of the song—including its instrumental introduction and well-defined hook—suggests a firm grasp of mainstream pop aesthetics and the expressive possibilities of the three-minute recording span. Chatmon and McCoy's vocal technique is relaxed and slightly nasalized—a kind of cross between country twang and pop crooning—and the dialect employed is best characterized as Southern, i.e., not explicitly coded in racial terms. (His later work as a solo artist suggests that Bo was adept at dialectal code-switching.) It could, in fact, be argued that "Corrine Corrina" is a regional variant of a tradition that DeFord Bailey, African-American harmonica player on the Grand Ol' Opry, called "black hillbilly music" (Wolfe 1990: 32). At the very least, a comprehensive genealogy of the song would have to include minstrelsy and the medicine show, Tin Pan Alley, ragtime, jazz, rural blues, and a spectrum of country music ranging from jump-ups to reels.

Bo Chatmon

Armenter "Bo" Chatmon was born in the hill country of Hinds County, Mississippi, south-by-southeast of the Mississippi Delta, in 1893. The

Chatmon family, comprising several generations of musicians, lived on the Gaddis and McLaurin plantation just outside Bolton. The patriarch of the Chatmon clan, Henderson Chatmon (1850–1934), was the grandson of a female slave and a white planter named Sam Heron. According to Josephine Williams, one of Henderson's daughters, the old man claimed that his mother had been brought up in the master's house by Heron's wife "just like . . . one of her own" (Calt and Wardlow 1988: 49). Sam Chatmon, Henderson's youngest son, has described aspects of his father's early life: "My daddy, he was a slavery-time man, married and had children in slavery times. He went by Chatmon cause his master was Old Man Chatmon. . . . [He] worked in the field awhile, but he played music in slavery times" (Lomax 1993: 382). The Chatmons are described by contemporaries as being of "mixed blood" or "bright" (light) appearance, and a photograph of the family (Calt and Wardlow 1988) shows a range of appearances that would have confounded even the most discriminating census taker.

The scope of Henderson's musical repertoire appears to have been shaped by his long-standing interaction with whites in central Mississippi. He learned the core barn dance fiddle repertoire from a white planter named Bob Lacy, some time in the 1860s or 1870s. According to Sam, his father played for dances with a fiddler named Old Man Miller, and his repertoire included barn dance standards such as "Can't Get the Saddle on the Old Grey Mule," "Little Liza Jane," and "Granny Will Your Dog Bite" (Lomax 1993: 383). It is clear that music was not only a means of personal expression for Henderson Chatmon, but also an alternative mode of labor. The relative prosperity and stability of the Chatmon clan was in large part based on carefully husbanded musical skills, which allowed them to weave a set of socio-economic relationships that crossed the color line (echoing, though not reproducing exactly, their genealogical links to local white families).

Bo Chatmon started out around 1900 as an accompanist, playing bass viol, banjo, and guitar behind the fiddling of his father Henderson and brother Lonnie. Beginning in 1908, a gramophone purchased by a Bolton cafe owner exposed the young Chatmons to "contemporary pop material like *Wild Cherry Rag, Ballin' the Jack* and *Chicken Reel*" (Calt 1992: 3). The first blues that Bo's younger brother Sam remembered learning were published songs such as "St. Louis Blues," "Beale Street Blues," and "Sugar Blues," heard on gramophone records and at the minstrel shows that toured near Bolton, where the Chatmons heard vaudevillian blues singers such as Ma Rainey and Ida Cox. If any of the Chatmons liked a particular song, Lonnie would drive into town and buy the sheet music so that they could learn it (he was one of the few rural musicians in the area who could read musical notation).

From around World War I until 1928, the Chatmon family formed a septet, which played at dances in the hill country and the Delta. "We played for parties everywhere," Sam remembered.

> For colored and white, too. All we wanted was the money. If we would play two hours and a half, we'd get five dollars a man. When we'd get through with [our] crops, late on by June or July, we'd all get together and take a tour all up through Memphis, Chicago, and different places like that. We played *Donna, Somebody Stole My Gal, Sit Right Down and Write Myself a Letter*. See, we was playin' jus' jazz music. (Lomax 1993: 384)

On the road they often played with local musicians, usually a trumpet player and drummer (Javors 1977: 10), and Bo apparently sometimes played clarinet.

The Chatmons' circulation between white and colored communities enabled (and required) them to develop a broad repertoire of square dance music, waltzes, fox-trots, and one-steps, country blues, jazz, and current pop songs. The Chatmons made a strong impression on Delta bluesmen such as Charlie Patton, who began his career as a guitarist with them and later claimed to be Henderson's son,[10] and Muddy Waters, who said that as a young man in the Mississippi Delta he "walked ten miles to see them play" (Calt, Kent, and Stewart 1992: 2).

From around 1926 to 1935, Bo Chatmon worked with Lonnie and Sam, the guitarist Walter Vinson, members of the McCoy family (including brothers Charley, the mandolinist on "Corrina," and Joe, who recorded as The Hillbilly Plowboy [Garon and Garon 1992: 288 n. 47]) and various other musicians in a string band called the Mississippi Sheiks. The name of the band—actually more a booking agency, sending out several units on particularly busy nights—was inspired by the Tin Pan Alley song "The Sheik of Araby."[11] A sardonic reference to a long-standing Orientalist strain in American popular culture, epitomized by the films of Rudolph Valentino, the reference to popular images of Arabs (played by Latin American actors) also evoked an interstitial racial identity no longer officially recognized in the United States, where the category "mulatto" had a few years earlier been eliminated from the federal census.

The Sheiks, "probably Mississippi's most successful blues musicians" (Calt, Kent, and Stewart 1992: 2), expanded and contracted on demand for live engagements. Between 1930 and 1935, the group toured throughout the Deep South and as far afield as Illinois and New York, playing picnics, country dances, and parties. Their popularity brought them to the attention of Polk Brockman, a white talent scout for Okeh Records, and he signed them to the label in 1930. The group's records on the Okeh and Bluebird labels—especially their big hit "Sitting on Top of the World" (1930)—further expanded their opportunities for live engagements.

The Sheiks were widely heard in African-American households, where the gramophone was rapidly becoming a center of domestic social life.[12] They performed popular blues pieces, including a version of Tommy Johnson's "Big Road Blues" called "Stop and Listen Blues" (Evans 1982: 285), and frequently made use of Delta-style blues texts and melodies in their performances. According to Samuel Charters (1991: 136–37), some of their records sold well in the growing black communities of Chicago and other northern cities. The motivation to extend their appeal among whites—who, according to Sam Chatmon, formed the bulk of their audience in live performance situations—led the Sheiks to record songs such as "Yodelling, Fiddling Blues" (1930), an homage to hillbilly musician Jimmie Rodgers (F. Davis 1995: 88). On some recordings, including their rendition of "Jail Bird Love Song" (Okeh 8834, 1930), Bo Chatmon and Walter Vinson skillfully emulated the "high lonesome" vocal style popularized by the Carter Family and the Blue Sky Boys. Although racist promotional principles prevailed for the most part—the Sheiks' records generally being advertised in the race record catalogues—at least one of their recordings was cross-listed in the old-time hillbilly catalogue. This was a rare occurrence and an indication of the degree to which the Sheiks, and the Chatmon family as a whole, occupied an interstitial position between colored and white musical domains.

In a recent attempt to rescue Bo Chatmon from the neglect of historians, John Miller argues that he was "the most sophisticated of all country bluesmen from a harmonic viewpoint" (1992: 4) and that he possessed a "personal musical aesthetic unique in the country blues idiom" (1992: 5). Miller bases this claim in part on Bo's ability to play the same guitar licks in two or three different tuning systems. In the playing of most Mississippi blues guitarists, the tuning system employed—for example, standard (EADGBE), Spanish (DGDGBD), or Vastapol (DADF♯AD or EBEG♯BE)—determines which licks are used. Chatmon's ability to transpose these melodic-rhythmic patterns across multiple tunings and his use of diminished chords and cycle of fifths-derived progressions suggest that he possessed both a high degree of technical proficiency and a well-developed understanding of Tin Pan Alley songs, ragtime, and jazz. Bo Chatmon's hybrid musical idiolect stemmed from, and in turn helped to extend, a broader pattern of musical circulation across boundaries of class, race, and region. Certainly Chatmon—a light-skinned, somewhat finicky teetotaler who dressed in suits, owned a Model T Ford, and developed professional skills such as carpentry and gramophone repairing—does not fit the stereotypical mold of the foot-loose, hard-drinking (and, in the popular imagination, almost always dark-skinned) Mississippi bluesman. While Bo Chatmon's musical hy-bridity cannot be taken as an unmediated expression of his mixed racial identity—for such an argument would critique the conflation of race and culture, only to reinsert it on another level—detailed analysis of his work as a musician must, I would argue, rest on some understanding of the patterns of social and musical circulation that shaped his career. It seems that Chatmon's voraciously cosmopolitan sensibility—a struc-ture of feeling not easily apprehended through dichotomous distinc-tions such as black and white, urban and rural, or folk and popular—is in some measure responsible for the marginal position to which he has been relegated in most accounts of the history of American music.

Blues and the Excluded Middle

No genre has played a more prominent role in racial identity politics in the United States than the blues, continually invoked as a baseline or core of black experience. Blues music has been figured as a totem of Negro experience (Le. Jones 1963), a metaphor for black resistance throughout the Americas (Finn 1986), "a survival technique, aesthetic equipment for living" (Murray 1983: 58), a "way of life" (Guralnick 1982: 16), a noble and "essentially American" epic (Palmer 1982: 17), an em-bodiment of African-American theology (Spencer 1993), and a privileged source of vernacular literary theory (Baker 1984). Over the last thirty years, a powerful logic has shaped popular and scholarly discourse about the blues: Robert Johnson is in, the Chatmons are out; the guitar is in, the fiddle out; the deep Delta blues is in and the African-American string band, suspended between dominant conceptions of whiteness-as-performance and blackness-as-performance, is out. I am not simply com-plaining here about the exclusion of a particular song, style, performer, or repertoire from the historical record. This empirical gap is significant because it illuminates the limits of scholars' conceptualizations of the to-pography of American music during a crucial period in its development.

Charles Keil has suggested that the years 1928 and 1929 were piv-otal in the emergence of downhome blues as a mass-mediated genre, disseminated and to some degree shaped by the phonograph record industry. I would push Keil's argument a bit further and suggest that a broader view of the topography of American music in the years around the Great Depression reveals an even more complex set of interactions shaped not only by the double dialectics of class and race, but also by the record industry's production of nostalgia. By the late 1920s, the triumph of American industrial capitalism was essentially complete. As consumer capitalism penetrated and transformed agrarian and urban ethnic communities with a traffic in cosmopolitan images, it also produced images of its putative opposite, a state of naturalness or authenticity which, once lost, could only be reclaimed through the same mass-mediated forms responsible for its displacement.

Although "Corrina" bears many of the diagnostic traits most commonly used to identify authentic blues, its hybrid stylistic surface places it outside the tradition as such: a blues performed by rural Mississippians, but, strangely enough, not a rural Mississippi blues. This exclusionary logic can be seen at work in the analytical equivalent of a Freudian slip, in Stephen Calt's notes for the 1978 compilation *Roots of Rock* (Yazoo Records 1063), which includes Bo Chatmon's recording of "Corrine Corrina." Calt suggests that the 1928 recording "indicates a pre-blues origin by virtue of its *eight bar structure*, melodic structure, and conventional accenting" (emphasis added). The mixed sensibility of the performance apparently led his ears astray, for "Corrina," whatever its stylistic affinities, is in formal terms indisputably a twelve-bar blues. In this instance, the discursive necessity of situating "Corrina" outside of (prior to) the blues as such—quintessentially defined by the Delta solo vocalist and guitar tradition—apparently induced a kind of anachronistic hallucination on the part of this knowledgeable scholar of the blues.

Apart from Memphis Minnie (Lizzie Douglas), Bo Chatmon appeared on more pre-war gramophone recordings than any other Mississippi musician (Calt 1992: 2), yet his image scarcely registers on the radar screen of American music scholarship. Similarly, the Mississippi Sheiks are generally treated as less than wholly authentic supernumeraries of the blues tradition. The blues scholar Samuel Charters, for example, is somewhat dismissive of the central Mississippi string band style, represented by the Sheiks and Charlie McCoy's Mississippi Hot Footers:

> The rhythm was a heavy 4/4, steady, even monotonous, but clearly defined so that there would be no difficulty dancing to it. At times the rhythms—especially when Bo Chatmon was the guitarist—were so dull

that the bands were almost as bad as the white music that was being played in the area. (1991: 136)

"Almost as bad as the white music"—it is hard to imagine a more stark denial of racio-cultural *bona fides*. What claim is being advanced here? That the Chatmons, the McCoys, and their associates sold out, diluting black rhythm in order to make a profit? That they sought to "get over" by mimetically appropriating whiteness-as-performance? At the very least, Charters's comments suggest that something more than aesthetics per se is at stake in historical representations (and non-representations) of the musical and social matrix within which Bo Chatmon and many other Mississippi performers operated.

In his study of mulattos in the United States, Joel Williamson (1980) documents the incorporation during the post-Reconstruction era of people of mixed race into an expanding Negro identity. By 1920—when the category "mulatto" was eliminated from the federal census of the United States—most "had allied themselves rather totally with the black world" (62). In *Roll, Jordan, Roll*, Eugene Genovese asserts that "the two-caste system in the Old South drove the mulattos into the arms of the blacks, no matter how hard some tried to build a make-believe third world for themselves" (1976: 431). However, while Bo Chatmon might well have been regarded by many whites as "just another nigger" (414), I am not comfortable with interpretations which *a priori* regard cultures built around the fuzzy boundaries between normative racial categories as exemplars of false consciousness. While mulattos in early twentieth-century Mississippi were the target of color prejudice in both white and African-American communities—their hybridity being conceptually associated on the one hand with excess, and on the other with infertility and dilution—musicians such as the Chatmons had succeeded for several generations in constructing a way of life—and a way of making music—around their intermediate social position between communities defined, however arbitrarily, by "color" (actually a rather fuzzy conflation of phenotype and putative descent). What is striking here is the slippage between the codification of racist ideologies in social-institutional forms (private and public, formal and informal) and the symbolic representation of racial identity in music.

It might be argued that the lack of attention paid by historians to certain genres simply reflects shifts in African-American musical tastes, which began to coalesce during the Depression. Certainly, the generation that included Robert Johnson and his contemporaries, born in the early twentieth century and raised during a period that was arguably the apex of racial terrorism in the Deep South, appears to have had an even more fatalistic view of the color line and its consequences than their parents. This may in turn have catalyzed a move toward styles marked in more explicitly oppositional terms as black music (a process that, as Keil [1985] has suggested, involved the internalization and amplification of mass-mediated images of black difference). This hardening of conceptual boundaries between Negro and white traditions was correlated with the contraction and eventual collapse of the interstitial zone within which musicians such as Chatmon circulated.

There is, of course, no way to disentangle changes in popular taste from the spread of new technologies of mass dissemination and the workings of the recording industry, which played an important role in codifying and promoting selective aural images of blackness. There is evidence that agents for race record labels selected certain styles and performers as emblematic of Negro taste and rejected others. The decline of the African-American string band and ballad song traditions was in part determined by this process, which was in turn driven by white (and, to some degree, middle-class African-American) notions of black authenticity. Interviews with blues performers who recorded in the 1920s and 1930s suggest that gatekeepers such as producers and recording engineers frequently urged performers to narrow their repertoires in the interest of producing a saleable product. In the late 1920s, when fiddle-led bands were a mainstay of the hillbilly music business, African-American string bands were sometimes turned away from recording sessions (Charles Wolfe, pers. comm., 27 June 1996). Some popular musicians, like Lonnie Johnson, dropped the fiddle and concentrated on guitar. The biographies of southern bluesmen who grew up in the 1920s and 1930s suggest that their musical tastes were strongly shaped by the availability of certain styles and performers on gramophone records and by the application of modern advertising techniques to African-American communities.

While "Corrine Corrina"'s urban audience likely regarded it as a somewhat old-fashioned record, it is worth remembering that the process of urbanization itself involved the production of "the rural" as a category. The best-selling race records of the Depression era included not only the cool, urbane blues of Leroy Carr and Scrapper Blackwell, but also items explicitly promoted as "hokum" (country, cornball) music. Hokum records, which drew on aspects of the string band, jug band, and traveling medicine show traditions, offered migrants in Chicago and other northern cities "a reminiscence of their rural past combined with a sense of being above it" (Shaw 1978: 11). It is clear that such self-consciously archaic genres, disseminated by the rapidly expanding electronic mass media of the 1920s, played an important role in triangulating the shifting field of urban African-American identity.

From around 1930, Bo Chatmon developed a productive niche as a studio performer, a move necessitated by the gradual loss of his eyesight and the fact that he could make more money as a solo act. He still toured occasionally with the Mississippi Sheiks but made a lasting name for himself with dozens of party records featuring mildly bawdy songs such as "Ramrod Daddy" and "Banana in Your Fruit Basket." Although precise sales figures are not available, there is evidence that these recordings were also widely popular among both blacks and whites. In 1940 he made his last recordings and settled in Memphis, working outside of music (as he had periodically throughout his career) for another quarter century.

In the end, although he commanded an audience on both sides of the color line, Bo Chatmon was no more able than Robert Johnson or Bessie Smith to beat Jim Crow. He spent his declining years in poverty, blind and unable to play, living in "shabby wooden building on [a] rutted alleyway behind Beale Street" (Charters 1991: 139). Despite his ability to amalgamate aspects of European-American and African-American folk music styles within a pop music framework, and the steady demand for his recordings, Chatmon was never able to cash in on his early crossover success. It could be argued that he was simply a quarter of a century early. Elements of African-American folk and popular music, married to an insistent though flat-footed rhythm derived from Anglo-American traditions, with a text delivered in a dialect that does not admit of easy racial identification—it is not too much of a stretch to hear Chuck Berry's "Maybelline" (based on the country tune "Ida Red") or Elvis Presley's "Mystery Train" (a countrified version of an R&B song) as direct descendants of "Corrine Corrina."

Even if the 1928 recording of "Corrine Corrina" cannot with confidence be taken as the unmediated expression of a "culturally mulatto" identity (McKnight 1993), it is clear that the performance can be read as a refraction of the circulatory system of Bo Chatmon's musical world, a fluid network traversing white and colored cultures, the hill country and the Delta, the barn dance and the recording studio. Whatever the heuristic merits of W. E. B. Du Bois' famous formulation, "double consciousness" seems altogether too shallow a metaphoric vessel to contain such experience. In Raymond Williams's (1977) terms, "Corrine Corrina" is at once emergent and residual. It can be heard as a harbinger of things to come (the first rock 'n' roll record?), and as an echo of something very much like a Creole culture situated smack in the middle of early twentieth-century Mississippi, a structure of feeling elided by the inexorable anti-miscegenation logic of American law and custom.[13]

"Corrina"'s Covers

I have suggested that Bo Chatmon's recording of "Corrine Corrina" can be interpreted as both an outcome and an emblem of circulatory patterns that linked South and North, city and country, oral tradition and mass-mediation, agrarian and proletarian modes of subsistence, and cultures based, in increasingly oppositional fashion, on racial identity. In the pages that follow, I present a series of brief analytical snapshots of subsequent versions of the song, following its migration through numerous genres, repertoires, and markets, and across seven decades of American musical history.

Within a few years of the song's initial release, record labels specializing in the race music and hillbilly markets had released cover versions of "Corrine Corrina." In particular, Brunswick Records and its sister label Vocalion (both owned by the Brunswick-Balke-Collender conglomerate) quickly sought to capitalize on the success enjoyed by Bo Carter's 1928 recording. In 1929, two of the company's biggest race music stars, Tampa Red and Georgia Tom (Thomas A. Dorsey), recorded a version of the song, accompanying themselves on guitar and piano.[14] Mayo Williams oversaw the recording session, conducted at Brunswick's Chicago studio and released on the Vocalion label. This record represented an attempt to update "Corrine Corrina" for the race music market, nudging it toward the then-popular urban blues style of Leroy Carr and Scrapper Blackwell (also Vocalion artists).

That same year, Paramount Records released a version of "Corrine Corrina" by The Too Bad Boys, a white group that usually recorded under the name Westbrook Conservatory Entertainers.[15] (The group was named after its leader, the steel guitar player John Westbrook, who accompanied Jimmie Rodgers on several of his earliest recordings.) This rendition, recorded in New York City, is basically a straight cover of Chatmon's 1928 recording, with a lugubrious bottleneck slide guitar substituted for Lonnie Chatmon's fiddle. Although all the other items performed by Westbrook and his colleagues during this recording session were categorized and promoted by Paramount as "hillbilly" songs, company executives apparently decided to try a crossover gambit with "Corrine Corrina," creating a pseudonym for the band, and releasing the song in their race record series. It is worth noting that this attempt to cross white performers over to the race music market—or more to the point, to present white musicians *as* black musicians—was the converse of the strategy pursued by Okeh Records in releasing at least one of the Mississippi Sheiks's recordings as a hillbilly record. The fact that these instances of cross-promotion were relatively rare during the late 1920s makes them no less interesting in terms of the general thesis we are pursuing here.

In 1931, the white old-time Carolina group Ashley and Abernathy recorded yet another version of "Corrine Corrina," adding Appalachian dialect and four-part white gospel harmony to the mix.[16] They also altered the lyric slightly and instituted a change in the form of the song: Carter's fifth verse ("I love Corrina, tell the world I do. . . Just a little bit a' lovin', let your heart be true") became a refrain, more in keeping with Tin Pan Alley song forms and the Anglo-American ballad tradition. It is worth noting that Ashley and Abernathy also chose the only verse with the word "love" in it for this purpose, perhaps an attempt to amplify the romantic overtones of the song for an audience accustomed to sentimental songs.

This pattern of dual proliferation into the race and hillbilly music markets continued throughout the 1930s and 1940s. A 1934 recording by Leroy Carr and Scrapper Blackwell entitled "Hold Them Puppies" was a cover version of "Corrine Corrina" with new lyrics added.[17] The great boogie-woogie pianist Albert Ammons recorded an instrumental version of the song, entitled "Has Anybody Seen Corrine?" in 1939 (Storyville Records 670.184 [Dixon and Godrich 1982: 42]). In 1937, Cliff Bruner's Texas Wanderers, a white band comprised of fiddle, mandolin, banjo, two guitars, piano, and string bass, recorded a cover of the song in San Antonio, emphasizing its affinities with the Euroamerican string band tradition (Decca De 5350 [Ginell 1989: 143]). Later that year, Hal O'Halloran's Hooligans (led by a former announcer for Chicago radio station WLS's Barn Dance show) recorded the song with an old-timey jug band, including clarinet, fiddle, guitar, jug, washboard, and kazoos.[18] The great popularizer of cajun music, Leo Soileau, recorded the song in Chicago in 1935 (Decca De 5101 [Spottswood 1990: 90]).

The song's biggest success on the country music charts came in 1940, when Okeh Records released a version of "Corrine Corrina" performed by Bob Wills and his Texas Playboys.[19] Wills (1905–1975) was the most important popularizer of Western Swing, a dance-hall style that combined cowboy ballads, hillbilly music, blues, and the Kansas City big band jazz of Bennie Moten and Count Basie, with touches of Mexican and Cajun music. While maintaining the basic harmonic and melodic structure of "Corrine Corrina," Wills introduced extra beats, in the manner of a "crookedy" old-time fiddle tune (pers. comm., Hank Bradley, 19 February 1996), creating a 12-bar blues a total of 56 (rather than 48) beats in length:

Measures: 4 6 4 6   4   6   4 6 4   4   4 4
Harmonies: I I I I   IV IV I I V   V   I I

After a fiddle introduction by Wills—a parallel with the 1928 Chatmon version—the arrangement presents a series of vocal choruses alternating with instrumental solos. As is often the case with dance band arrangements featuring modifications of the blues form (for example, Glenn Miller's "In the Mood"), the improvised solos follow the straight 48-beat, 12-bar form most familiar to musicians and listeners. The tempo of Wills's arrangement is considerably faster than Bo Chatmon's version, in keeping with the norms of Western Swing dancing, a blend of African-American and European-American social dance styles popular in the ballrooms and roadhouses of the American southwest. The Texas Playboys' recording of "Corrina," made on the eve of America's entrance into World War II, reveals another dimension of the song's evolving role as a nexus within a complex web of stylistic interchange linking the blues, jazz, old-time fiddle music, and Tin Pan Alley pop song.

Bo Chatmon's version of "Corrine Corrina" soon became a staple of oral tradition. In 1935, Bascom Lamar Lunsford (1882–1973), a pioneering performer and scholar of Appalachian hill music, set down his "memory collection" of songs, classifying them under headings such as "popular" and "folk." He included the song "Corrina" under the latter heading (Lo. Jones 1984: 153). In 1942, John Work, a folklorist in the employ of Fisk University, recorded the song "Corrine" performed by the African-American banjoist Nathan Frazier.[20] Frazier had worked for many years in the Nashville area, playing a regional variant of the string band music that had been Bo Chatmon's training ground in Mississippi some thirty years earlier. In a letter to the president of Fisk, Work recommended that Frazier's "vast repertoire of secular folk songs should be placed in our archives, both on phonograph record and on paper" (Wolfe 1989). He did not mention that Frazier's vast repertoire was in fact partly derived from commercial phonograph records, including Bo Chatmon's "Corrine Corrina."

In July 1942, the enthnomusicologist Alan Lomax (1993: 413–14) conducted a survey of music-makers in Coahoma County, Mississippi, and interviewed a young fieldhand named McKinley Morganfield (a.k.a. Muddy Waters). Like other Delta bluesmen, Morganfield's repertoire included Tin Pan Alley hits ("Dinah," "I Ain't Got Nobody," "The House," "St. Louis Blues") and country-and-western songs ("Home on the Range," "Deep in the Heart of Texas," "Missouri Waltz") as well as country blues. When asked to name the most popular songs at local dances, where Muddy performed with a quartet led by a fiddle player, he listed "Chattanooga Choo-Choo," "Down by the Riverside," "Dark-town Strutters Ball," "Red Sales in the Sunset," and "Corrine Corrina."

The song also soon found its way into the repertoire of jazz musicians. In 1931, Red Nichols and the Five Pennies, with Wingy Manone on trumpet and vocals and Benny Goodman on clarinet, recorded the only version of "Corrine Corrina" to reach the pop charts before World War II (the record, Brunswick 6058 [Whitburn 1986: 336], peaked at number 18). In 1936, Bing Crosby recorded a bawdy version of the song that was never released commercially but apparently circulated as an underground party record. (Crosby's version describes Corrina as a naughty German girl who is spanked with a swastika by Adolf Hitler!)[21] Johnny Temple, a vocalist and harmonica player, recorded the song in New York in 1941, with Henry "Red" Allen on trumpet, Buster Bailey on clarinet, and Lil Armstrong on piano (Decca De 7825 [Dixon and Godrich 1982: 745]).

Later that year, a performance of "Corrine Corrina" by Art Tatum and his Band was released by Decca Records.[22] The recording featured Joe Turner (1911–1985), a blues shouter from Kansas City who had already scored several hits in the race record market. Turner's rendition of the song, supported by a medium-tempo shuffle rhythm, is made up of selected verses from the Bo Chatmon version. Although Tatum's brilliant work as a pianist is generally discussed in the context of jazz history—that is, as part of the evolution of an African-American art music—this record is clearly aimed at a broader market for popular music, a strategy which Decca was to perfect a few years later with the hit records of Louis Jordan and his Tympany five, which sold well among both blacks and whites. It is interesting to note that almost all the cover versions of Corrina cited in the last few paragraphs were released on Brunswick and Decca Records. The American branch of Decca was headed by Jack Kapp, who had previously directed the race record department at Brunswick. In 1934 Kapp hired J. Mayo Williams away from Brunswick, and it seems likely that this web of corporate and personal relationships—and the fact that Mayo Williams received partial composer's royalties—had something to do with the frequency with which the song "Corrine Corrina" appeared on Decca recordings of the 1930s and 1940.

By 1956, when Joe Turner recorded a second version of "Corrine Corrina" for Atlantic Records,[23] the term "rock 'n' roll" had emerged as a marketing label for rhythm & blues–inspired dance music promoted to a predominantly white teenage audience. Turner had recorded a string of hits for Atlantic Records, including the song "Shake, Rattle and Roll," which reached number 2 on the Rhythm & Blues (a new term for "race recordings") charts in 1954. Within a few months, Decca Records released a bowdlerized version of the song by Bill Haley and the Comets, a country-and-western band from Pennsylvania. Haley's version reached the *Billboard* Top Ten and made him a national star. Interviews with Jesse Stone, Jerry Wexler, and Ahmet Ertegun, producers at Atlantic Records, make it clear that they wanted to combat the covering of their artists' recordings by larger labels, in part by marketing African-American singers such as Big Joe Turner, Ray Charles, and Ruth Brown directly to a predominantly white teen audience. Of course, the very concept of crossover music presumes the existence of racially defined styles and repertories and depends on (as it helps to reproduce) the notion of racial difference as a form of cultural capital, an ideology reinforced in the post-war era by the circulation of images of "Negro" popular culture in the mass media.

Joe Turner's 1956 version of "Corrina" includes several important changes in structure and sensibility. Perhaps most strikingly, a 16-bar bridge or refrain was added to the song, creating a kind of compromise between the blues and typical Tin Pan Alley forms. This remodeling preserved the 12-bar blues form while at the same time incorporating it into the verse-and-refrain logic of mainstream popular song. This was not a particularly novel strategy—many of the blues songs produced for mass consumption by professional composers in the early twentieth century had similarly hybrid structures—but it does provide a clear musical indication of the producers' desire to cross "Corrina" (and Big Joe) over into the pop market.

In the 1941 recording session with Art Tatum, the rhythm section had played a two-beat feel at around 86 main pulses per minute, typical of 1940s couple-dancing; on the 1956 Atlantic record, the band—comprising some of the best R&B session players of the time—plays a four-beat feel at a brisk 156 beats per minute, in keeping with the aesthetic dictates of jump-blues–derived rock 'n' roll. The rolling barrelhouse piano of Turner's earlier recordings has been replaced with an electric guitar playing an insistent boogie-derived single-string riff. The syncopated horn parts are supplemented with subdued "ooh-aa" vocal pads performed by Wexler, Ertegun, and Stone and the female vocal trio the

Cookies (best known for their later work as the Raelettes). These textural devices distinguish the Atlantic recording of "Corrina" from Turner's previous work, which was largely in a stripped-down, hard-swinging, jump-blues mode.

"Corrine Corrina" represented the last serious attempt by Atlantic to market the 45-year-old singer as a teen idol. Although the data are somewhat contradictory, it appears that Atlantic released the song into the R&B market backed with the Leiber and Stoller song "Lipstick, Powder and Paint" and into the pop market backed with a song called "Boogie Woogie Country Girl" (a crossover gambit if ever there was one!). This was the last of Turner's four singles to register on the pop charts (peaking at number 41 pop, number 2 R&B [Whitburn 1988: 41]). "I made all those things before Haley and the others, but suddenly all the cats started jumping up, and I guess I got knocked down in the traffic," he later said. Ironically, subsequent attempts to promote "Corrina" in the expanding teen pop market of the late 1950s and early 1960s—including versions by crooner Bobby Vinton (complete with the 16-bar pop song refrain) and Bill Haley (who reverted to the 12-bar form and added a primitivist jungle drums-cum-Gene Krupa introduction)—were even less successful commercially than the Turner recording.

In December 1960, "Corrina" was covered by the teen singer Ray Peterson, best known for his renditions of morbid love songs (e.g. the car-crash epic "Tell Laura I Love Her").[24] In 1961, Peterson's version reached number 9 on the *Billboard* charts (Whitburn 1983) and number 7 in *Cashbox* (Hoffman 1983), the highest position ever attained by the song. The verse-and-refrain framework of the Joe Turner/Atlantic recording was preserved, but its sensibility and aural texture had mutated almost beyond recognition: a moderate bolero tempo, with plinky arpeggiated guitar chords (dripping with tremolo), angelic "aa-ooh" vocal pads, maracas and woodblock (sonic icons of Latin romance), and dramatic solo scoring for string orchestra, bathed in studio reverb.

Once again, we encounter "Corrina" at the crossroads of miscegenation and commerce, hovering over a charged (and profitable) space between evolving conceptions of musical whiteness and blackness. This was the first recording session overseen by the young producer Phil Spector, a prototypical example of his "wall of sound" recording technique, which linked the intensity of adolescent experience to the sonic splendor and class symbolism of western European orchestral music ("little symphonies for the kiddies," in Spector's words). Peterson's voice quivers with emotion, using the break between chest voice and falsetto to evoke the vulnerability of male teen-age sexuality. Recordings of this sort played an important role in naturalizing a particular conception of adolescence, thus facilitating the mass-mediated internalization of a marketing category, the teenager.

Spector's blend of teen angst and orchestral opulence was articulated with another syncretic gambit: the melding of black and white styles within a pop music framework. Spector's recordings of 'girl groups' such as the Chiffons and the Ronettes (whose lead singer, Ronnie Bennett, he eventually married) established a "racially unidentifiable" (Romanowski and George-Warren 1995: 849) crossover sensibility that linked African-American music with the prestige of European classical music and the professional song craftsmanship of the Brill Building composers. In a sense, Spector's work is both a descendant of the Mayo Williams–Bo Chatmon conjuncture and a direct predecessor of the Motown Sound. (This is a stylistic debt explicitly acknowledged by Berry Gordy.) The most radical transformation of "Corrina" was recorded by Bob Dylan in 1962 and released on the May 1963 album *The Freewheelin' Bob Dylan* (Columbia 8786). Dylan's singing and harmonica playing are accompanied by piano, two acoustic guitars, string bass, and drum set played with brushes, an intimate texture that simultaneously evokes the coffee-house folk music scene and the singer-with-band idiom of popular music (a fusion more fully developed in his later recordings with The Band).

> Corrina Corrina, gal where you been so long?
> Corrina Corrina, gal where you been so long?
> I been worr'in' 'bout you baby, baby please come home
>
> I got a bird that whistles, I got a bird that sings
> I got a bird that whistles, I got a bird that sings
> But I ain' a-got Corrina, life don't mean a thing
>
> Corrina, Corrina, gal, you're on my mind,
> Corrina, Corrina, gal, you're on my mind,
> I'm a-thinkin' 'bout you baby, I just can't keep from crying

Note that the bridge introduced in the 1956 Joe Turner recording has been unceremoniously discarded, returning the song to its original 12-bar blues form. The first line of Dylan's lyric echoes the opening stanza if previous versions, although the mood of the responsorial phrase changes from a complaint ("Ain' had no lovin' since you been gone") to a profession of anxiety ("I been worr'in' 'bout you baby, baby please come home"). The second stanza, however, is imported wholesale from "Stones in my Passway" (1937), one of the most frequently cited of Robert Johnson's songs. During the early 1960s the retrospective canonization of Johnson as an icon of the Delta tradition—a process initiated in 1938 when the jazz impresario John Hammond sought to sign Johnson up for the *Spirituals to Swing* concert at Carnegie Hall—was well under way. If a folk singer wanted to signal his knowledge of and sympathy for the blues—the baseline of black authenticity—there was simply no one better to cite than Robert Johnson. This process in turn reinforced Johnson's canonization and directed attention away from the breadth of his repertoire, which like those of Charley Patton and Muddy Waters had included Tin Pan Alley songs as well as deep blues (see Lipsitz 1998).

But this reworking of "Corrina" was more than the authentication of a white subject via the black other. The racial politics of the urban folk revival—centered on icons of rural American, Caribbean, or African negritude not threatening to white leftists (e.g. Harry Belafonte, Leadbelly, Odetta, Miriam Makeba, Olatunji)—militated that white performers not attempt to produce aural simulacra of the "American Negro folk music" preserved on Library of Congress field recordings: interracial mimesis (à la blackface minstrelsy) was not an option. In his liner notes for *The Freewheelin' Bob Dylan*, Nat Hentoff quoted Dylan: "I'm not one of those guys who goes around changing songs just for the sake of changing them. But I'd never heard 'Corrina, Corrina' exactly the way it first was, so that this version is the way it came out of me." The "way it came out" involved a canny double movement typical of Dylan's early work and reminiscent of the French surrealists' appropriation of ethnographic exotica (Clifford 1988): a signaling of commitment to the folkloric enterprise (mediated through the romantic image of Woody Guthrie), combined with a detached, ironic attitude toward the very notion of tradition. Dylan's ability to stand simultaneously inside and outside the space conventionally demarcated by the term "tradition" lies at the core of his projection of an iconoclastic modernist folk subjectivity. "All I'm doing is saying what's on my mind the best way I know how. And whatever else you say about me, everything I do and sing and write comes out of *me*" (Dylan in Hentoff 1962). An interpretation of Dylan's persona, presented in the liner notes for *Freewheelin'*, registers here as an astute analysis of his artistic modus operandi: "He's so goddammed real, it's unbelievable!" (Harry Jackson in Hentoff 1962).

One study of Dylan's recorded work identifies "Corrina" as "a rare Dylan cover of an old song *of mixed origin*" (Nogowski 1995: 25; emphasis added). Once again, the song's perduring indeterminacy with

regard to dominant notions of racial difference had economic consequences. An alternate take of "Corrina, Corrina" served as the B side of
Dylan's first 45 rpm single, "Mixed Up Confusion," and played a role in
Columbia Records' earliest attempt to nudge the young folksinger toward mainstream commercial success. While this single did not appear
on the pop charts, there was a pecuniary method to Dylan's madness:
the song credits on the single, as on the LP, are "Traditional/adapted
and arranged by Bob Dylan." This strategy put "Corrine Corrina" into
the public domain and allowed Dylan—rather than the estates of Bo
Chatmon or Mayo Williams—to claim composer's royalties.

Another twist in the trajectory of "Corrina" occurred in the late 1960s,
when Bob Dylan's version of the song was adapted by Taj Mahal (Henry
St. Claire Fredericks). Mahal, son of a jazz arranger and pianist from the
West Indies, was born in Brooklyn and began to play in coffeehouses
around 1964 while a student in animal husbandry at the University of
Massachusetts–Amherst. His eclectic style was shaped by an interest in
the academic disciplines of folklore and ethnomusicology and by his
own field research on a variety of African-American genres, including
the blues, ragtime, jazz, string bands, and brass band music. In developing a repertoire of material from the rural South, Mahal made use of instruments (the banjo and tuba), genres (fiddle music and ragtime), and
songs (including the truck drivers' anthem "Six Days upon the Road")
that few other young black musicians would even have considered
adopting in the late 1960s. As Mahal recalled later:

> The majority of Afro-Americans at the time had no idea, were not even
> interested in these musicians, or were embarrassed that they *existed*. My
> mind said that there was something here bigger than that kind of emo-
> tional response to years of mistreatment and second-class citizenship. It
> was a case of people throwing the baby out with the bathwater. (Liner
> notes to *Taj's Blues* [1992, Columbia AAD 5245])

The heterogeneity of Mahal's repertoire was also related to his early experience growing up in a West Indian household in Brooklyn:

> Jamaican music was inside my house. My stepfather's Jamaican. I spent a
> lot of time dancing to this music. When you're raised with Marcus Garvey
> and jazz and a different kind of political slant in your life that includes
> blues and all these other things that are in and around it, you have a dif-
> ferent kind of view of the whole diaspora, the African diaspora. To top that
> was growing up in a multi-ethnic neighborhood, and within your own
> ethnic group there are different people from different cultures. You see
> the blend and you see the differences. (Ibid.)

Mahal's arrangement of "Corrina [*sic*]" clearly reflects his insistence on performing material that did not fit neatly into contemporary canons of black authenticity. Mahal recorded the song several times, in the studio with country-rock accompaniment, and solo in a live performance at Big Sur, re-released as part of an American folk song collection produced by the Smithsonian Institution.[25] In Mahal's version, the substance of the Bo Chatmon song is completely melted away and replaced by an improvised performance evocative of the unpolished ambiance of a field recording. Mahal accompanies his rough-hewn voice with finger-picking on a National steel guitar, leaving out or adding a beat here and there and stretching the form to suit his purposes, much in the manner of early rural blues musicians such as Charley Patton or Blind Lemon Jefferson. The Robert Johnson blues stanza initially introduced by Bob Dylan becomes a new center of gravity, around which a series of floating textual formulas are assembled.

> Got a bird what whistle, baby got a bird, honey got a birdie
>   would sing
> Baby got a bird, honey got a birdie would sing
> Without m' Corinna, sure don't mean, sure don't mean a natural
>   thing
>
> I learned to love you, baby 'fore I call, honey 'fore I call your name
> Baby 'fore I call, honey 'fore I call your name
> I wouldn' trade your love for money, honey you're my warm heart,
>   baby you're my love light thing
>
> Have mercy, have mercy, baby on my hard luck, honey on my hard
>   luck soul
> Baby on my hard luck, honey on my hard luck soul
> I got a rainbow roun' my shoulder, look like silver, baby shine like
>   Klondike gold

Mahal has referred to his songs as "bluesscapes," and this topographic metaphor seems particularly apt in the case of "Corinna." The song text's panorama includes a range of historical references, including Mississippi Delta blues (via a Jewish folk singer from Minnesota), a reference to Klondike gold (redolent of the nineteenth-century American frontier), "a rainbow roun' my shoulder" (an old blues line, and the title of Howard Odum's pioneering study of African-American folk songs), and the contemporary phrase "love light" (evoking Otis Redding's soul recordings of the 1960s).

It could be argued that Bo Chatmon's and Taj Mahal's versions of

"Corrina"—separated by some forty years—both flow from an interstitial space between conventional definitions of black and white performance. However, when we focus on the reception of each recording, some notable differences appear. Chatmon's version on Brunswick was apparently purchased by an interracial audience and emulated by both white and black musicians, while Mahal's popularity has been concentrated among a predominantly white folk and roots music-oriented audience. In the Big Sur recording of "Corrina," the domain of the rural—iconically represented in Mahal's purposefully sloppy and slightly out-of-tune guitar accompaniment and rough-grained voice—evokes an imagined landscape beyond the reach of racial politics, a place where a largely white audience can sing, clap, and whoop along with a non-threatening version of the black authentic.[26] Here, the excluded middle exists mainly as a utopian possibility in the imagination of a predominantly white audience.

A final instantiation of the "Corrina complex" surfaces in the 1994 film *Corrina, Corrina*, starring Whoopie Goldberg and Ray Liotta. Liotta plays Manny Singer, a Jewish-American advertising jingle composer whose wife's funeral provides the film's opening scenario. His daughter's reaction to the death of her mother is to become mute. Enter Corrina Washington (Goldberg), a college-educated black woman forced by circumstances into domestic work, who captures the child's affections, teaches her to communicate by gesture, shares magical secrets, and eventually gives her back the power of speech. Corrina also introduces the girl to aspects of working-class African-American life in Los Angeles— a visit to the extended family's house, to a jazz club, a gospel service, even to a mansion where Corrina and the girl work side by side, stopping only to parody the pretensions of the mansion's owners.

The initially awkward relationship between Liotta and Goldberg's characters blossoms into genuine affection and soon runs up against the color line. Out with Corrina and his daughter at a Chinese restaurant, Manny is called a "nigger lover." Later in the film, Manny's elderly mother takes him aside and cautions him: "A fish and a bird can fall in love, but where will they build their nest?" When Corrina comes home late one night after working at Manny's house, her sister warns her: "You got to stop kiddin' yourself. Now you know these white folks gonna pretend you part a' they family, so they can work you all hours and not pay you for your time. Corrina, you workin' too hard to be givin' it away for free." To which Corrina bristles, "Givin' what away for free?!" This is by no means an irrelevant question, for the most striking aspect of Manny and Corrina's relationship—particularly given the long-standing association of race and eroticism in American popular culture—lies in its predominantly *asexual* character. The film's portrayal of an interracial relationship is closer to Walt Disney's *Jungle Book* than to Spike Lee's *Jungle Fever*, for at every important juncture in the plot the little girl initiates, channels, and mediates the adults' interaction. In the end, it is clear that the underlying impetus for the establishment of emotional intimacy between Corrina and Manny is domestic, not erotic.

While the character of Corrina seems initially to conform to standard Hollywood tropes of black difference—she is musical, religious, prefers spicy food, and has an uncanny ability to communicate with children and animals—she also undermines these stereotypes, speaking learnedly about poetic meter, the compositions of Erik Satie, and the jazz recordings of pianist Bill Evans. It turns out that Corrina holds a bachelor's degree in creative writing, and that her dream is to write the liner notes for jazz albums ("Basically they just let us play the music, they don't let us write about it," she tells Manny). Music is, in fact, a central source of the film's emotional impact. Throughout *Corrina, Corrina*, the music of Big Joe Turner, Billie Holiday, Louis Armstrong, Dinah Washington, Jackie Wilson, Duke Ellington, and Hank Ballard and the Midnighters serves as a constant reminder of the generative power of African-American tradition. Thus, another central argument of the film is revealed in its soundtrack—the therapeutic efficacy of black music, its ability to fill the emptiness of white middle-class life, configured, in accordance with dominant stereotypes, as a kind of cultural absence.

Although *Corrina, Corrina* appears at first viewing as a straightforward, even somewhat formulaic film, its portrayal of racial identity and difference is in fact remarkably complex and unstable. At one level *Corrina, Corrina*—based in part on the personal experience of its writer, director, and producer, Jessie Nelson—is explicitly anti-racist: it argues that African-American culture is a learned thing, that it's okay for little Jewish girls to sing, dance, eat, and play black, that Bill Evans was an authentic jazz musician. However, at another level it can be argued that *Corrina, Corrina* is a not atypical Hollywood fantasy about the ability of individualized relationships to transcend institutionalized racism, the romantic heterosexual corollary of interracial buddy movies like *White Men Can't Jump* or *Die Hard with a Vengeance*. Benjamin DeMott has analyzed the links between such mass-mediated images of racial harmony and an ideology he calls "do-nothingism," in which "acts of private piety substitute for public policy while the possibility of political action disappears into a sentimental haze" (DeMott 1995: 35).

In the film *Corrina, Corrina*, the utopian space beyond racial conflict is the nuclear family, ideological lynchpin of what Marilyn Ivy (1993: 247) has called the "privatized imaginary" of late twentieth-century America. At the core of this domestic space we find the child, icon of the pre-political, pre-racial, natural (and therefore innately musical) self. It is worth noting in this connection that the song "Somewhere over the Rainbow," from the film *The Wizard of Oz*, plays a pivotal role in the young girl's internalization of black expressive style and in her emotional recovery. Throughout the film, childhood is represented as the last stronghold of innocence (a contemporary analogue of the images of vanishing rurality alluded to earlier), a Yellow Brick Road back (or forward) to a landscape beyond the reach of "agents of racial discourse" (Gilroy 1993: 2). Infused with a wistful sentimentality, a feeling tone evoked by the carefully chosen soundtrack of post-war (i.e. pre-rap) black music, the film *Corrina, Corrina* discloses a complex articulation between music's role in destabilizing dominant conceptions of racial difference and its implication in contemporary celebrations of the putative triumph of individual enlightenment over systemic patterns of racial inequality.

CONCLUSION

The assumption that people of a given "race" ought to sound a certain way has been critiqued eloquently by Reginald McKnight, in his essay "Confessions of a Wannabe Negro":

> When whites "do blackface," people don't so much as blink. . . . I daresay they are looked upon by many with a kind of admiration. . . . As for blacks who are influenced by expression that is not, as some would say "preponderantly black," the response is rather more ambiguous. Charley Pride, for example, or Richie Havens, or Jimi Hendrix, or Tracy Chapman may be praised for their talents, their virtuosity in the "pure" sense, but I know of no one who lauds such artists for their mastery of art forms that could be referred to as decidedly "white." . . . Is blackness-as-performance somehow regarded as a free-floating entity, belonging to no one in particular, while whiteness-as-performance can, and should, only belong to whites? After all, it appears to me that black-influenced whites are very often thought to be deepened and ennobled by such processes, while white-influenced blacks are regarded as weakened, diluted, less black. (1993: 104)

In this essay, I have sought to describe the complex historical trajectory of a so-called common stock, black hillbilly song, the product of a network of musicians of mixed race, situated in the middle of a segregationist political order. I have also tried to ask what such a song might, over a period of some seventy years, reveal about music's ability to exceed the discursive force field of racial classification in American society.

Before summarizing my argument, I want to note a couple of omissions. My focus on "Corrine Corrina"'s relationship to what I have called the excluded middle of the American racial imagination has only obliquely addressed the ways in which other racist discourses—for example, those relating to Latin American, Arab-American, Jewish-American, Asian-American, and Native American peoples—have intersected with images of black–white difference. The adoption by Bo Chatmon and associates of the term "Sheik"—derived from Hollywood films that featured Latin American actors playing Arabs—and Phil Spector's use of stereotypical Latin features in his pop arrangement of "Corrina" suggests interactions that deserve further exploration.

In addition, although I have concentrated on "Corrina"'s relationship to discourses of racial difference, this is a story with other, equally compelling subtexts, including the role of rural imagery in the formation of urban cultures and the evolution of the American entertainment industry. Like many other popular songs whose origins lie in the traditions of the American South (or in romanticized images of the South as repository of the American past), the history of "Corrine Corrina" is intimately bound up with the entertainment industry's production and promotion of images of racial difference. While the roots of American racism obviously predate the rise of electronic mass media, public discourse about race—as realized in cultural forms ranging from television situation comedies to the political tracts of racial nationalists—has long been powerfully shaped by commercial interests. Despite the relentlessly liberal discourse generated by the publicity departments of American entertainment corporations, racial stereotypes generate more and more profit with every passing year.

What significance, if any, can we derive from "Corrine Corrina"'s multiple identity as a common stock fiddle-band song, a western swing standard, a would-be rock 'n' roll hit, a teenage torch song, a folkloricized deep blues, and the anthem of a 1990s film about interracial love? In more general terms, what can the comparative study of cover versions tell us about the relationship between popular music and evolving conceptions of racial identity and difference in twentieth-century America?

The 1928 version of "Corrine Corrina," by Armenter "Bo" Chatmon, Lonnie Chatmon, and Charlie McCoy, released on the eve of the Great Depression, was the product of a flexible network of skilled artisans of mixed race working out of the hill country of central Mississippi. I have argued that this was an interstitial social formation, whose very existence was denied by the logic of racial segregation and, eight years before the first recording of "Corrina," by the categorizing apparatus of the Federal Bureau of the Census. In retrospect, it is evident that the near-erasure of Bo Chatmon, his associates, and their music from the literature on American popular culture has a great deal to do with their habitation of this middle zone, and their retrospective lack of fit vis-à-vis long-standing and deep-rooted ideologies of racial difference. Where music functions as a talisman of the purity of "blood," stylistic hybridity is correlated with miscegenation and, by extension, with cultural dissolution.

In this connection, it is interesting to remember that the same session in New Orleans at which Chatmon, Chatmon, and McCoy recorded "Corrine Corrina" also yielded a performance entitled "The Yellow Coon Has No Race." This seriocomic reference to the plight of the "tragic mulatto" (Roach 1996: 182), a common theme of late nineteenth- and early twentieth-century American theater and literature, seems a fitting, if crude, allegory for the elision of Bo Chatmon from American musical history. It also indexes a long-standing popular ideology of racial purity that reaches at least as far back as the later stages of minstrelsy, when light-skinned African-American performers found themselves compelled to "black up" in order to fit white expectations.

In the second half of this article, I sought to map the circulation of "Corrina" across the landscape of American popular music, paying special attention to the song's positioning vis-à-vis racial discourses. By the early 1930s, Chatmon's version of the song was circulating widely among jazz, blues, and country musicians and had appeared in the race music, hillbilly music, and mainstream pop catalogues of record companies. When Bob Wills recorded it, in 1940, "Corrina" was firmly positioned as a generic country song, part of a common stock interracial oral tradition, redolent of the good ol' days.

By the mid-1950s—the so-called Golden Age of rock 'n' roll—the economic freight carried by the dichotomy between white and Negro music had increased a thousandfold. (The commercial importance of this distinction for the American music industry is reflected in the adoption around this time of the term "crossover," a spatial metaphor that presumes the existence of distinct and more-or-less fixed race-traditions.) The 1956 version of "Corrina Corrina," sung by Joe Turner and produced by Jerry Wexler and Ahmet Ertegun, crossed the song over into an explicitly cosmopolitan space—jump blues R&B cum rock 'n' roll—and exploited the song's multivocality in an attempt to extend

Turner's pull in the predominantly white teen music market. (Recall that the Atlantic single of "Corrina Corrina" was backed with one song in the R&B market—"Lipstick, Powder and Paint"—and another in the white market—"Boogie Woogie Country Girl.") Four years later, Phil Spector brought this commercial possibility to fruition, presenting "Corrina" as a lushly orchestrated 12-bar-blues-with-a-bridge tear-jerker underlain by a bolero rhythm (a signifier of the Creole, displaced south of the border). There is no evidence that the Spector/Peterson cover of "Corrina" made any impact at all on the R&B market, but it was the song's high-water mark of commercial success in the pop market.

During the urban folk revival of the 1950s and 1960s, the romanticization of black folk music involved another stage in the public triangulation of images of racial difference. In 1962 Bob Dylan recorded a radically altered version of "Corrine Corrina"—one of the few recordings he made during this period of a so-called traditional (i.e. public domain) song. Dylan had apparently never heard the 1928 recording of "Corrina" and started his version from scratch, inserting a stanza from Robert Johnson's song "Stones in My Passway." On the one hand, the reference to Johnson—avatar of the Mississippi Delta blues—might have been read by folk music fans as a gesture toward black authenticity. It could, however, be argued that Dylan's iconoclastic approach to the song had more to do with an emerging (though not yet named) postmodern sensibility—characterized by pastiche, irony, and a cut-and-paste approach to history—than to anything resembling an homage to folk tradition or black authenticity.

Taj Mahal's 1968 interpretation of "Corrina," loosely modeled on Dylan's version, is closely bound up with a vision of African-American musical tradition as an incorporative, dynamic, and open system. This is a vision that seems, at first glance, quite consonant with the hybridizing spirit of Bo Chatmon's 1928 recording of "Corrine Corrina." Yet we must recognize the historical specificity of each recording; forty years had elapsed, and the circumstances of their production and reception were very different. Bo Chatmon's aesthetic was formulated within a rural family-based socio-economic network that emphasized—in fact, demanded—musical versatility. Mahal, born almost half a century after Chatmon, was also shaped musically by his early experiences, but his approach to the song is more explicitly bound up with a consciously formulated artistic and cultural agenda. Despite Taj Mahal's great good cheer and sardonic sense of humor, his music is clearly a defense against cultural loss, a technology of memory:

Black artists, they always gotta do the new thing with the latest stuff, do the present and up-to-the-electric-last-minute nasty on video to even get recognized or noticed. I'm always amazed at how much music is good that people don't know about. It fascinates me. If they don't hear it on the radio then it can't be good. And now, if they don't see it on a video it can't exist! It's ridiculous! I just refuse to accept that that's the way things should be done. (Liner notes to *Taj's Blues*, Columbia AAD 5245 [1992])

It is clear from Mahal's phrasing that this should be read as a criticism of the music industry and not of the musicians. The drive of many contemporary African-American musicians to "do the new thing with the least stuff" is bound up with the perceived need to keep ahead of (and therefore at least obliquely profit from) the insatiable demand of the music industry and its predominantly white mass audience for a steady stream of new black material.

Finally, the song "Corrine Corrina" (and its central character) appeared as the anthem of a mid-1990s Hollywood movie about the post-racial/pre-racial utopian possibilities of childhood and personal relationships. In arguing that *Corrina, Corrina* is permeated by a kind of liberal romanticism, particularly in regard to the problem of racism, I do not mean to denigrate the motivations of the film's writer and director, Jessie Nelson. George Lipsitz has addressed this issue eloquently in his book *The Possessive Investment in Whiteness:*

If we are going to be honest about the words that we share—and the worlds we share—we have to face the harsh facts that divide us as well as the fond hopes that might one day unite us. Romanticism gives us a wishbone, but combating racism requires us to display some backbone. (Lipsitz 1998: 129)

If there is to be a Yellow Brick Road to a post-racist utopia, its materials will necessarily be forged in the struggle for public justice as well as in the hearts and minds of lovers of children.

Like a tongue insistently probing the socket of a missing tooth, "Corrina" has returned again and again to the excluded middle of the American racial imagination, the gap between blackness and whiteness. From the perspective of the *longue durée*, the song "Corrine Corrina" appears as a trace element caught up in the vascular system of American popular culture, channeled by the practical interests of institutions and actors, ideologically charged constructions of cultural authenticity, tenacious ontologies of racial difference, and the production, marketing, and consumption of utopian desire. In methodological terms, the example of "Corrine Corrina" points us toward a mode of interpretation that emphasizes musical circulation, movement, and traversal. In following the multiple pathways of a popular song, we transect history from various angles, each cut across the grain disclosing a unique pattern of relationships.

In focusing on "Corrina"'s heterogeneous origins and circulation, I have sought to question the conflation of race and culture, a habit of thought still deeply embedded in American culture(s). But this kind of critique brings responsibility as well as insight. Contemporary academic criticisms of essentialism are in fact loaded with political risk, for the argument that racial difference is a social fiction can easily be reinterpreted as a criticism of all cultural formations based, to some degree or another, on racial identity. If some forms of cultural essentialism continue to stoke the fires of genocide, others necessarily remain important tools in the struggle *against* oppression.

A comprehensive study of the crossover phenomenon in American popular music could easily yield hundreds of examples of music's implication in the production and circulation of racist imagery. But it is vital that this important subtext of American music history be counterpoised with another set of narratives—stories about circulation, traversal, and indeterminacy, about the slippage between musical forms and social ideologies, and the ability of popular cultural forms to hold open alternatives to the way we live now.

NOTES

The initial inspiration for this paper was a panel on the folk roots of American popular music at the 1986 Northwest Folklife Festival in Seattle. I thus owe a special debt of thanks to my co-panelists: Joseph Vinikow, Jack Cook, and Bruce Chapman (a.k.a. Bruce Chatmon). I am also indebted to Hank Bradley, Tom Diamant, Veit Erlmann, David Evans, Steven Feld, Aaron Fox, John Gibbs, Stuart Goosman, Eileen Hayes, Marilyn Ivy, George Lipsitz, Portia Maultsby, Peter Nabokov, John Pemberton, Ron Radano, Howard Rye, Laurel Sercombe, Richard Spottswood, Rob Walser, Miles White, and Charles Wolfe, all of whom read the paper or contributed to its substantive base.

1. It should be noted at the outset that this essay focused on discourses of black/white difference, since they are most immediately relevant to the cultural practices and products under consideration. In so doing, I do not mean to imply that other patterns of racial identity and classification—for example, American Indian, Latin American, and Asian-American identities—are irrelevant to the study of American popular culture. In future work, I hope to explore the complex relationship between these other discourses of difference and the "excluded middle" of black/white difference.

2. Much of this work has concerned itself with critiquing dominant representations of musical "blackness." Paul Gilroy (1993) focuses on the transnational circulation of musical forms and styles, and the local interpretations of black music by people differently situated within the Atlantic Diaspora. Ronald Radano (1995) argues that the topos of an undifferentiated black tradition is a product of language; that is, of discourses about folk authenticity that emerge in a powerful and coherent form around the middle of the nineteenth century. George Lipsitz's trenchant analyses of American popular music (1990, 1994) focus on the complex interpenetration of racial, class, gender, generational, and regional identities, while Charles Keil's groundbreaking comparison (1985) of the development of blues and polka music in the United States brings out previously unremarked parallels between these quintessentially "white" and "black" genres, especially in regard to the commercial circulation and internalization of mas-mediated stereotypes. Denis-Constant Martin (1991) and Ingrid Monson (1994) have theorized the "heterogeneity" of black musical practices, while Andrew Bartlett (1995), in a study of Cecil Taylor's music, urges us to consider the *intentions* of African-American cultural producers before rendering judgments about their relationship to "black tradition."

Not surprisingly, less has been written about the role of music in the construction of "whiteness." Eric Lott's pioneering *Love and Theft* (1993) links the rise of blackface minstrelsy in the 1830s to the emergence of white working-class identity and a specifically American variant of bohemianism, both triangulated vis-à-vis popular images of "blackness," while Ingrid Monson (1995) has critiqued an ideological formation that she calls "white hipness." George Lipsitz's essay "White Desire: Remembering Robert Johnson" (1998) is a penetrating analysis of white romanticism and paternalism vis-à-vis certain iconic black musicians.

3. V. Kofi Agawu has published a critique of the trope of "African rhythm" in studies of sub-Saharan African music (Agawu 1995). It should be noted in passing that published interviews with African-Americans who do not identify themselves as professional musicians or academics often do not emphasize music as a criterion of racial difference (see, e.g., Gwaltney 1993, Terkel 1992). Other elements of culture—especially culinary, child-rearing, and hygienic practices—are much more frequently cited than "musicality" as diagnostic traits of an oppositional (and generally superior) cultural "blackness." The notion that peoples of African descent are uniquely musical has not, of course, been an unalloyed blessing, given the ambivalent valorization of music-making in relation to other, more "serious" fields of human endeavor (say, science, mathematics, or literary criticism).

4. The "one-drop rule," also known as the "one black ancestor rule," the "traceable amount rule," and the "hypo-descent rule," specifies that any person who can be demonstrated to possess a single "drop" of "black blood" is ipso facto a black person. This bifurcating logic, peculiar to the United States—even apartheid South Africa legally recognized intermediate racial categories—emerged from the South during the period after the Civil War to become the

dominant mode of racial conceptualization in twentieth-century America (see F. J. Davis 1991).

5. The term "common stock" is sometimes used by folk song scholars to describe a musical repertoire shared by black and white performers in the American South.

6. The matrix number of the Brunswick/Vocalion disc is NOR-761-Br7080. The cut is anthologized on *Roots of Rock* (Yazoo L-1063) and *Bo Carter Volume 1* (Document Records DOCD-5078).

7. The major seventh degree or leading tone can be interpreted as an indication of the influence of mainstream pop harmony, while the lowered seventh is frequently associated with country blues. Of course, skipping the seventh degree circumvents the issue altogether.

8. By coincidence, this is also the opening contour of the core melody of early *jùjú* music, which developed in the Creole Afro-Christian culture of Lagos, Nigeria, around 1928, the year Bo Chatmon recorded "Corrine Corrina" (see Waterman 1990).

9. Interestingly, the violin, derived from European prototypes but sometimes played with techniques derived from the bowed lute traditions of the West African savannah, plays only a slight role in popular and scholarly accounts of African-American musical history. There is, for example, considerable evidence to suggest that the violin played a crucial role in early New Orleans jazz, a phenomenon given at most cursory attention in most authoritative accounts of the genre's development (however, see Gushee 1994). In the present context, it is interesting to note that the violin is by and large not consonant with late twentieth-century representations of musical "blackness." This may in part explain the mainstream press's incredulity at discovering Louis Farrakhan's aspirations as a classical violinist.

10. Like the Chatmons, Patton claimed Africa, European, and Amerindian ancestry. Despite his canonization as "Father of the Delta Blues," Patton recorded ballads, vaudevillian blues songs, Tin Pan Alley hits, and (under a pseudonym) gospel sermons. The diversity of Patton's repertoire can be traced to his early experience playing with the musically omnivorous Chatmons (Calt and Wardlow 1988).

11. The first successful recordings of "The Sheik (of Araby)" (composed by Ted Snyder, Harry B. Smith, and Francis Wheeler) were performed by white dance bands. In 1922, renditions of "The Sheik" by the Ray Miller Orchestra and the Club Royal Orchestra reached number 3 on the charts (Whitburn 1986).

12. Zora Neal Hurston, who conducted ethnographic research in southern African-American communities in 1927, reported that "the bulk of the population now spends its leisure in the motion picture theatres or with the phonograph" (Levine 1977: 227).

13. A similar conflation of musical syncretism and miscegenation was an important factor in colonialist discourses about race and popular culture in Anglophone West Africa during the 1920s (Waterman 1990).

14. Vocalion Vo-1450, recorded 23 December 1929 (Dixon and Godrich 1982: 723).

15. Paramount Pm 12861, recorded in New York City 23 October 1929 (Dixon and Godrich 1982: 758). Anthologized on *The Voice of the Blues: Bottleneck Guitar Masterpieces*, Yazoo Records L-1046.

16. Anthologized on *Going Down the Valley: Vocal and Instrumental Styles in Folk Music from the South*, New World Records NW 236 (1977).

17. Vocalion Vo 02751, recorded in St. Louis 21 February 1934 (Dixon and Godrich 1982: 143).

18. Decca De 5188, recorded in New York City (Ginell 1989: 226).

19. Okeh 06530, recorded 15 April 1940. Anthologized on *Bob Wills and His Texas Playboys: Anthology [1935–1973]*, Rhino Records R2 70744, disc 1, cut 5 (1991).

20. Anthologized on *Black Stringband Music from the Library of Congress*, Rounder Records 0238 (1989).

21. Thanks to Tom Diamant, a long-time scholar of "Corrine Corrina," for sharing this example.

22. Decca De 8563, recorded in New York City 13 June 1941 (Dixon and Godrich 1982: 765).

23. Atlantic 1088, recorded in New York City 21 April 1956. Reissued on *Atlantic Rhythm & Blues*, vol. 2, Atlantic 7 81392-2 (1985).

24. Dunes 2002, recorded 19 December 1960.

25. "Corrina," on *Folk Song America 4: A Twentieth Century Revival*, Smithsonian Collection of Recordings RD046-4 (1991). An earlier version of the song, recorded in 1968 and released on Columbia CS 9698, has been reissued on *Taj's Blues*, Columbia/Legacy CK 52465 (1992).

26. The link between "Corrina" and the bucolic—a recontextualization of the song's long-standing associations as an old time fiddle tune—is evident in more recent renditions of the song. In a 1991 recording on the Windham Hill label, George Winston, a New Age pianist, uses the outline of Chatmon's melody as the basis for a tone poem called "Summer." This is one of a series of pieces evoking the rural countryside, designed to aid his listeners' meditative exploration of their own interior landscapes.

REFERENCES

Adams, Samuel C., Jr. 1947. "The Acculturation of the Delta Negro." *Social Forces* 26: 202–5.

Agawu, V. Kofi. 1995. "The Invention of 'African rhythm.'" *Journal of the American Musicological Society* 48: 380–95.

Baker, Houston A., Jr. 1984. *Blues, Ideology, and Afro-American Literature: A Vernacular Theory*. Chicago: University of Chicago Press.

Bakhtin, Mikhail. 1981. *The Dialogic Imagination: Four Essays*. Trans. C. Emerson and M. Holquist. Ed. M. Holquist. Austin: University of Texas Press.

Barlow, William. 1989. *Looking Up at Down: The Emergence of Blues Culture*. Philadelphia: Temple University Press.

Bartlett, Andrew. 1995. "Cecil Taylor, Identity Energy, and the Avant Garde African American Body." *Perspectives of New Music* 33: 274–93.

Baudrillard, Jean. 1993. *The Transparency of Evil: Essays on Extreme Phenomena*. London: Verso.

Calt, Stephen. 1992. Liner notes for *Bo Carter 1931–1940*. Yazoo L-1034.

Calt, Stephen, Don Kent, and Michael Stewart. 1992. Liner notes for *Mississippi Sheiks: Stop and Listen*. Yazoo 2006.

Calt, Stephen, and Gayle Wardlow. 1988. *King of the Delta Blues: The Life and Music of Charlie Patton*. Newton, N.J.: Rock Chapel Press.

Charters, Samuel. 1975. *The Country Blues*. 2d ed. New York: Da Capo.

———. 1991. *The Bluesmakers*. New York: Da Capo.

Clifford, James. 1988. *The Predicament of Culture: Twentieth-century Ethnography, Literature, and Art*. Cambridge: Harvard University Press.

Davis, F. James. 1991. *Who is Black? One Nation's Definition*. University Park: Pennsylvania State University Press.

Davis, Francis. 1995. *The History of the Blues: The Roots, the Music, the People, from Charley Patton to Robert Cray*. New York: Hyperion.

DeMott, Benjamin. 1995. *The Trouble with Friendship: Why Americans Can't Think Straight about Race*. New York: Atlantic Monthly Press.

Dixon, Robert M. W., and John Godrich. 1970. *Recording the Blues*. New York: Stein and Day.

———. 1982. *Blues and Gospel Records 1902–1943*. Chigwell, Essex, England: Storyville Publications.

Epstein, Dena. 1977. *Sinful Tunes and Spirituals: Black Folk Music to the Civil War*. Urbana: University of Illinois Press.

Evans, David. 1982. *Big Road Blues: Tradition and Creativity in the Folk Blues*. New York: DaCapo.

Finn, Julio. 1986. *The Bluesman: The Musical Heritage of Black Men and Women in the Americas*. London: Quartet.

Fulmer, Douglas. 1995. "String Band Traditions." *American Visions* 10,2: 46 (April-May).

Garon, Paul, and Beth Garon. 1992. *Woman with Guitar: Memphis Minnie's Blues*. New York: DaCapo.

Genovese, Eugene. 1976. *Roll, Jordan, Roll: The World the Slaves Made*. New York: Vintage.

Gilroy, Paul. 1993. *The Black Atlantic: Modernity and Double Consciousness*. Cambridge: Harvard University Press.

Ginell, Cary. 1989. *The Decca Hillbilly Discography, 1927–1945*. Westport, Conn.: Greenwood.

Guralnick, Peter. 1982. *The Listener's Guide to The Blues*. New York: Facts on File; London: Quarto.

Gushee, Lawrence. 1994. "The Nineteenth-century Origins of Jazz." *Black Music Research Journal* 14: 1-24.

Gwaltney, John. 1993. *Drylongso: A Self-Portrait of Black America.* New York: The New Press.

Hentoff, Nat. 1962. Liner notes for *The Freewheelin' Bob Dylan.* Columbia Records 8786.

Hoffman, Frank. 1983. *The Cash Box Singles Charts, 1950–1981.* Metuchen, N.J.: Scarecrow.

Ivy, Marilyn. 1993. "Have You Seen Me? Recovering the Child in Late Twentieth-century America." *Social Text* 37: 227–52.

Javors, Robert. 1977. "Sam Chatmon: The Mississippi Sheik is Alive and Well." *Sing Out!* 26,1: 10–11.

Jones, Leroy [Amiri Baraka]. 1963. *Blues People.* New York: Morrow.

Jones, Loyal. 1984. *Minstrel of the Appalachians: The Story of Bascom Lamar Lunsford.* Boone, N.C.: Appalachian Consortium Press.

Keil, Charles. 1985. "People's Music Comparatively: Style and Stereotype, Class and Hegemony." In *Music Grooves,* by Steve Feld and Charles Keil, 197–217. Chicago: University of Chicago Press, 1994.

Levine, Lawrence W. 1977. *Black Culture and Black Consciousness: Afro-American Folk Thought from Slavery to Freedom.* New York: Oxford University Press.

Lipsitz, George. 1990. *Time Passages: Collective Memory and American Popular Culture.* Minneapolis: University of Minnesota Press.

———. 1994. *Dangerous Crossroads: Popular Music, Postmodernism and the Poetics of Place.* New York: Verso.

———. 1998. "White Desire: Remembering Robert Johnson." In *The Possessive Investment in Whiteness: How White People Profit from Identity Politics,* 118–38. Philadelphia: Temple University Press.

Lomax, Alan. 1993. *The Land Where the Blues Began.* New York: Pantheon.

Lott, Eric. 1993. *Love and Theft: Blackface Minstrelsy and the American Working Class.* New York: Oxford University Press.

Martin, Denis-Constant. 1991. "Filiation or Innovation? Some Hyphotheses to Overcome the Dilemma of Afro-American Music's Origins." *Black Music Research Journal* 11: 19–38.

McKnight, Reginald. 1993. "Confessions of a Wannabe Negro." In *Lure and Loathing: Essays on Race, Identity, and the Ambivalence of Assimilation,* ed. G. Early, 95–112. New York: Penguin.

Miller, John. 1992. Liner notes for *Bo Carter 1931–1940.* Yazoo L-1034.

Monson, Ingrid. 1994. "Doubleness and Jazz Improvisation: Irony, Parody, and Ethnomusicology." *Critical Inquiry* 20: 283–313.

———. 1995. "The Problem with White Hipness: Race, Gender and Cultural Conceptions in Jazz Historical Discourse." *Journal of the American Musicological Society* 49: 396–422.

Murray, Albert. 1983. *The Omni-Americans: Black Experience and American Culture.* New York: Vintage.

Niles, John Jacob. 1927. *Singing Soldiers.* New York: C. Scribner's Sons.

Negowski, John. 1995. *Bob Dylan: A Descriptive, Critical Discography and Filmography, 1961–1993.* Jefferson, N.C.: McFarland.

Oster, Harry. 1969. *Living Country Blues.* Detroit: Folklore Associates.

Palmer, Robert. 1981. *Deep Blues*. New York: Viking.

Randano, Ronald. 1995. "Soul Texts and the Blackness of Folk." *Modernism/Modernity* 2: 71–95.

Roach, Joseph. 1996. *Cities of the Dead: Circum-Atlantic Performance*. New York: Columbia University Press.

Romanowski, Patricia, and Holly George-Warren, eds. 1995. *The New Rolling Stone Encyclopedia of Rock & Roll*. New York: Fireside/Rolling Stone Press.

Russell, Tony. 1970. *Blacks, Whites and Blues*. New York: Stein & Day.

Shaw, Arnold. 1978. *Honkers and Shouters: The Golden Years of Rhythm and Blues*. New York: Macmillan.

Spencer, Jon Michael. 1993. *Blues and Evil*. Knoxville: University of Tennessee Press.

Spottswood, Richard K. 1990. *Ethnic Music on Records*, vol. 1, *Western Europe*. Urbana: University of Illinois Press.

Taft, Michael. 1984. *Blues Lyric Poetry: A Concordance*. 3 vols. New York: Garland.

Terkel, Studs. 1992. *Race: How Blacks and Whites Think and Feel about the American Obsession*. New York: The New Press.

Waterman, Christopher A. 1990. *Jùjú: A Social History and Ethnography of an African Popular Music*. Chicago: University of Chicago Press.

Whitburn, Joel. 1983. *Billboard Book of Top 40 Hits, 1955 to Present*. New York: Billboard Publications.

———. 1986. *Pop Memories 1890–1954: The History of American Popular Music*. Menomonee Falls, Wisc.: Record Research, Inc.

———. 1988. *Top R&B Singles, 1942–1988*. Menomonee Falls, Wisc.: Record Research, Inc.

Williams, Raymond. 1977. *Marxism and Literature*. New York: Oxford University Press.

Williamson, Joel. 1980. *New People: Miscegenation and Mulattoes in the United States*. New York: Free Press.

Winans, Robert B. 1990. "Black Instrumental Music Traditions in the Ex-Slave Narratives." *Black Music Research Journal* 19: 43–53.

Wolfe, Charles. 1989. Liner notes for *Black Stringband Music from the Library of Congress*. Rounder Records 0238.

———. 1990. "Rural Black String Band Music." *Black Music Research Journal* 10: 32–35.

Zwigoff, Terry. 1991. "Black Country String Bands." *American Visions* 6,1 (February): 50–52.

6

Mestizaje in the Mix: Chicano Identity, Cultural Politics, and Postmodern Music

RAFAEL PÉREZ-TORRES

Contemporary Chicano music represents an incongruity. It responds and corresponds to the musical landscape of postmodern North America and Latin America, yet it also moves toward an affirmation of a distinct Chicano cultural identity. It moves both with and against popular musical movements. So in 1978 a group called Los Lobos del Este de Los Angeles release their independent debut album titled *Just Another Band from East L.A.* Kid Frost's second album, *East Side Story*, emerges in 1992. In 1996 Delinquent Habits perform their rap single "Tres Delinquentes" on MTV and give a shout out to Norwalk, their neighborhood on the lower east side of Los Angeles. This emphasis on specificity of place and identity occurs through the production of a musical style of displacement, one that emphasizes hybridity, the synthesis of various forms: rap, soul, rock and roll, heavy metal, ska, hip hop, reggae, salsa, banda, cumbia.

Rap and hip hop, in particular, as postmodern forms evocative of simultaneous placement and displacement, would seem best to mesh with established patterns of Chicano cultural production as a process.[1] Much critical work on Chicano culture emphasizes the importance of hybridity and mestizaje to the creation of both a cultural and a racial Chicanismo. Similarly, the use in rap and hip hop of sampling, mixing, toasting, word play, punning, and personal affirmation—indeed, creation—of self are all characteristics that seem in synch with the direction of Chicano culture. Yet rather than simply appropriate rap, hip hop, or rock and roll as modes of expression, Chicano music transforms those genres as it synthesizes and hybridizes them in order to express a sense of mixture— mestizaje—in the music.

206

An impressionistic portrait of Chicano musical culture: Los Lobos record a Latinized version of the song "I Wanna Be Like You" from Disney's animated feature *The Jungle Book*. The ironic refrain, "O, o, o, I wanna be just like you, / I wanna walk like you, / talk like you too. / You'll see it's true, / it ain't like me, / 'cause I'm to be human too" is underscored by a heavy rumba rhythm. *Roqueros en español* Los Olvidados played heavy metal when living in Mexico, but since immigrating to the United States they play a melange of ska, punk, rai, and soukos.[2] Aztlan Records releases a compilation album titled *Raza Punk y Hardcore* that opens with a mispronounced bilingual remake of the Sex Pistols' "God Save the Queen" ("Dios salve la reina, / ella no es humana. / No hay abertura, / ni necesidad" [God save the queen, / she's not a human being. / There's no opening, / no need]). Given the incessant discussion of Latinos and their increasingly important demographic profile, the faux-English accent ironizes the original lyrics ("We're not the future / we don't understand. / We're not the future / we're not your birthday. / We're not the future/ join the machine. / We're the future / Your futura"). Mestizaje on a linguistic, rhetorical, and formal level seems central to the creation of contemporary Chicano music.

Given the political battles waged over language and culture in certain sectors of the United States, it should be no surprise that Chicano music forms a site where the mixture of language takes on great significance. The rapper Kid Frost busts rhymes on his song "La Raza" from *Hispanic Causing Panic* that rhyme and pun cross-linguistically:

> The form that I'm speaking is known as caló,
> ¿Y sabes qué, loco? Yo soy muy malo,
> Tu no sabes nada, you're brain is hollow,
> Been hit in the head too many times with a palo.
> Still you try to act cool, but you should know,
> You think you're so cool that I'm a call you a culo.[3]

The punning and dissing characteristic of the wordplay of African-American rap in this type of polyglot Chicano rap works only for those auditors capable of making the linguistic leaps between caló, Spanish, and English. This reference to code-switching has been a facet of popular Chicano musical production since even before the opening of "Wooly Bully" by Sam the Sham (the count-off commences: "One, two— Uno, dos, tres, cuatro"). Where the brief code-switching there is used to evoke a sense of play and celebration, Frost employs code-switching in order to establish a sense of imagined community between himself and his auditors. This represents one manifestation of the polyglossia characteristic of Chicano linguistic expression.[4] While the use of multilingual expression is not unique to Kid Frost, his work combines polyglossia, word play, and a thematic affirmation of Chicano racial and cultural identities. His work thus helps establish the tenor of contemporary Chicano music.

The conjoining of the personal and political, the individual and the social, is evident in his song "La Raza," which serves to affirm the self as well as the cultural and racial identities that presumably make up the imagined community to which the rapper speaks:

> It's in my blood to be an Aztec warrior
> Go to any extreme, we hold no barrier.
> Chicano, and I'm brown and proud.
> Want these chingazos? Simón, ese, let's get down
> Right now, in the dirt
> What's the matter? Afraid you're gonna get hurt?
> . . . .
> Yo soy chingón, ese.
> Like Al Capone, ese.
> Can throw a throw so don't ever try to sweat me.
> Some of you don't know what's happening
> ¿Qué pasa?
> It's not for you anyway
> 'Cause this is for the raza.[5]

Formally and thematically, the song works to bring together various disparate elements in order to affirm Chicano identity. The song is for "the raza," for a community whose cultural repertoire would allow it to comprehend the linguistic shifts and puns and rhymes. This construction of community highlights the mestizo quality of Chicano racial and cultural identities. The emphasis on an indigenous heritage (signaled by the iconic "Aztec warrior"), on a racial identity as "brown and proud," and on a polyglot form of expression all make of mestizaje a dominant key. Musically as well, the song asserts a type of mestizaje as it employs a xylophone for the fadeout, referencing both the marimba used in *musica veracruzana* and the Latin-jazz work of musicians like Willie Bobo. On numerous semantic levels, the work of Kid Frost signals an assertion of mestizaje in social, cultural, and racial terms.[6]

While mestizaje is celebrated, its significance oscillates between being a static identity—the mestizo—and a means of absolute transformation, the endless becoming of a Chicano community. These two polarities, of being and becoming, form the horizons between which Chicano musical expression employs notions of mestizaje. As a constructive strategy, mestizaje within Chicano culture proves a durable formulation because of its seemingly interminable dynamic quality. It allows for strategic movements among distinct racial or ethnic classes (indigenous, Hispanic, Caucasian, Latino) and strategic reconfigurations of cultural forms (mythic, postmodernist, nativist, Euro-American).[7] Unlike the typically binary notions of identity within a U.S. racial paradigm (choose black or white), a focus on mestizaje allows for other forms of self-identification, other types of cultural creation, other means of social struggle. At the same time, as a historical and social fact, mestizaje is one of the unifying factors that invaders, migrants, and immigrants from Mexico have shared across time—all are born from the violent encounter between European and Native peoples. From the earliest explorers of the present U.S. Southwest to the latest migrant workers braving the militarized border, a mestizo heritage has formed the predominant racial subjectivity of Spanish Americans, Mexicans, Chicanos.

Mestizaje forms both a strategy for agency and the name of a racialized subjectivity. The tension between the fluid and the fixed evident in these uses of the term "mestizaje" find their parallel within contemporary critical discourses that range from the poststructural to the postcolonial to the postmodern. These polarities of fluid and fixed partially form the horizon by which critical notions of mestizaje or hybridity can be understood.

Critics who employ mestizaje as a strategy of absolute transformation, a marker of discursive dislocation, a free-floating signifier represent one polarity. The French academic Jean-Luc Nancy, for one, warning against biological or cultural essentialism when deploying the term mestizo, highlights the deterritorializing quality of mestizaje:

> Like any proper name, *Chicano* does not appropriate any meaning: it exposes an event, a singular sense. As soon as such a name arises—cut—it exposes all of us to it, to the cut of sense that it is, that it makes, far beyond all signifying. "Chicano" breaks into my identity as a "gringo." It cuts into and re-composes it. It makes us all *mestizo*. (1994: 121)

For Nancy, mestizaje represents a means by which to undo—meaning, place, self—so that all of us as "mestizos" stand "on the very border of *meaning*" (123). The signifying process is restless, unsettled, transgressive. A dilemma arises in thus representing the mestizo as a perpetually new subject: as Norma Alarcón points out, this recasting leads to "a reobjectification of the 'new subject,' a reification or a denial of the historical meaning posited by the differential signifier" (1994: 131). The mestizo is no longer an agent in history, ceases being subject to discourses that invest brown bodies with meaning. Instead, the mestizo becomes pure signifier, endlessly subversive, free-floating, but detached from the historically bound practices that both form and delimit the mestizo self.

Critics who see in our contemporary emphasis on fluid identities a sense of stasis or calm as regards contemporary subjectivity mark the other polarity by which mestizaje is understood. Robert Young, for example, contrasts the contemporary celebration of fluid identities with the nineteenth century's profound anxiety about fixity of identity. Nineteenth-century English identity, he argues, was "estranged from itself, sick with desire for the other" (1995: 2). However: "Today's self-proclaimed mobile and multiple identities may be a marker not of contemporary social fluidity and dispossession but of a new stability, self-assurance and quietism" (4). Ours is an age, in other words, in which the affirmation of a border consciousness, a liminal state, an atomized subjectivity reveals at heart a sense of security as regards identity.

These positions are horizons, and Chicano cultural and critical production has typically been less concerned with what lies beyond horizons than with the passage between them. As Norma Alarcón's comments about Nancy indicate, the historical and social conditions of Chicanos and mestizos in the Americas is about transformation, yes, but also about the inscription of mestizaje within a racial code delimiting subjectivity and agency. The construction of Chicano subjectivity moves through contended territory, dynamically shaping something familiar and yet something other.

Chicano musical production emerges from such a shaping. The reliance on mestizaje as a critical cultural strategy helps us move from understanding mestizaje as a racial theory to understanding it as a form of cultural criticism as well. Incongruities remain, however. Within the conflicted and complex history of Chicanos in the United States, the issue of a cultural mestizaje sometimes is elided with assimilation. For example, it has been argued by scholars such as Manuel Peña that Chicano music oscillates between poles of "authenticity" and "assimilation." In his book *The Texas-Mexican Conjunto*, Peña attempts to draw distinctions between conjunto music as a resistant cultural product of the working class and orquesta music as an example of assimilationist desires expressed by the middle class. Thus conjunto music (comprising accordion with guitar and vocal) is more organic to the working class and working poor of Mexican descent, while orquesta music (more orchestrated, elaborate, and akin to American swing bands) represents a form of cultural disloyalty. This disloyalty stems from the contradictory position of an emergent Chicano middle class that does not identify with the working class but that is not accepted by an ethnically xenophobic American society.

Peña argues that the music reflects the complexities Mexicans in Texas have encountered in their quest to adapt to the difficult conditions of life in the United States:

> These conditions, often uncompromising, have forced Texas-Mexicans to yield to the stronger power, but not without resistance, not without a determined effort to counter American cultural hegemony by striving to maintain some of their antecedent symbols—or creating new ones as they reinterpreted newly introduced American cultural elements into more familiar symbolic structures. As a countercultural symbol forged by proletarian artists, *conjunto* falls under the former category; as a symbol of the middle class's doubly contradictory position vis-a-vis the working class and a formidable ethnic boundary, *orquesta* falls under the latter category. (1985: 13–14)

The orquesta with its incorporation of dominant Euro-American musical styles marks a cultural separation between the aspiring Chicano middle class who recognize their exclusion from dominant society and the Chicano/Mexicano working class rejected by their middle-class brethren. The mestizaje implied in the incorporation of American swing music and Mexican musical forms represents not the creation of a new, critical, empowered identity, Peña argues, but one of betrayal to working-class origins and the larger Chicano/Mexicano population.

The paradox of Peña's argument lies in the fact that Mexican music itself emerges from the very cultural melding he views with suspicion in relation to the orquesta. The *son jarocho*, for instance, originates in Veracruz and is "a stylistic amalgam of influences derived from the Spanish colonizers of Mexico, from Africans taken to New Spain as slaves, and from the indigenous population of the southeastern region of Mexico" (Loza 1992: 179) that developed during the seventeenth and eighteenth centuries. That is, musical form *per se* cannot easily be ascribed to a particular ideological position. This is especially evident in discussions about postmodern art such as that created by contemporary Chicano musicians.

George Lipsitz finds in Chicano music ingenious and evocative strategies that create for communities a historical consciousness. In terms of contemporary music, the reality of postmodernity—its commercialization and mass distribution of consumer culture—does not simply wipe out local forms of knowledge and resistance. Rather, it can enable moments of critical consciousness. Contemporary musicians can

> use the powers of electronic mass media to transcend time and space, connecting themselves to the pasts of others, pasts that bear moral and political lessons. Instead of serving as an instrument of division, commercial culture in these instances serves as a way for bridging barriers of time, class, race, region, ethnicity, gender, and even nationality. This 'return of the repressed' within the media creates one of its conditions of possibility. (Lipsitz 1991: 261)

Musical production becomes a form of resistance, a means by which subcultural groups resignify forms in order to voice historical memory and personal identity.

In ways ranging from Los Lobos's use of the *son jarocho* in their music, to the sampling of El Chicano's "Viva Tirado" (1970) by Kid Frost on his album *Hispanic Causing Panic* (1990), historical memory serves to identify ethnic and political subjectivities. Steven Loza notes, for instance,

> Los Lobos' conscious adoption of and stylistic adaptation to Mexican musical genres represented an affirmation of their ethnic origin and identity. The form of nationalism that evolved among mestizos in Mexico during the Nineteenth Century is not substantially different from the political spirit and awareness among twentieth-century Chicanos, mestizos of a particular sort themselves. (Loza 1992: 186)

The connections between contemporary musical production and historical moments of ethnic formation or political struggle evoke a cultural memory even within the very decentering and potentially destabilizing funhouse of postmodern mass culture. Kid Frost's use of the popular "Viva Tirado" evokes that moment of great political and social activism among Chicano populations in the late 1960s and early 1970s. From the affirmation of Brown Power to the Blowouts (the school walkouts in East Los Angeles), the Chicano Movement formed a high-water mark of the struggle by Chicanos for civil rights and political engagement. The musical incorporation of El Chicano suggests a recollection of subaltern resistance.

Evoking and transforming musical forms through mass cultural distribution represents a stake in the changing face of North American culture. Lipsitz argues that the "buried" narratives of Chicano music—

narratives about group identity, oppositional subcultures, and a desire for unity—amount to more than a 'political unconscious.' As Chicano musicians demonstrate in their comments about their work, their music reflects a quite conscious cultural politics that seeks inclusion in the American mainstream by transforming it. (1991: 159)

Unlike Peña's view, this inclusion does not signal a desire for acceptance through assimilation. Rather, the dynamic construction of new musical formations—via the reinterpretation and representation of traditional music or the incorporation of popular, even commercial forms—serves to deterritorialize the culture into which that music is being inserted.[8] A radical mestizaje of musical forms represents the active and impassioned assertion of a subcultural self into a larger national culture. This willful act seeks to transform the face and consciousness of the national culture.

The use of traditional or established musical styles stands as one of the incongruities that Chicano music manifests. How does one comprehend the complex insertion of pre-modern forms within postmodern music like that composed and performed by Los Lobos? In his study of subcultural music, Peter Manuel concludes that

the interdependence of postmodern and more traditional discursive realms can be seen to illustrate how subcultures communicate, compete, conflict and contrast with other cultures in the process of indigenising and resignifying transnational cultural forms. Postmodernism is at once an underlying condition and an aesthetic vehicle for this struggle. (1995: 238)

Chicano music melds multiple musical forms in a process of resignification.

Yet clearly the issue of cultural resistance is constantly being problematized within the actual production and distribution of Chicano music. Los Lobos, for example, gained huge national exposure through their hit record *La Bamba* in 1987. Rather than capitalize on their success with another album of rock songs, the following year they released *La Pistola y el Corazón*, a collection of traditional Mexican songs and original music echoing pre-modern music. Their decision emerged from a concern that their commercial success would lead the band away from its rootedness in Mexican and Chicano cultures. Rather than reassert, as they had on their previous albums, their musical mestizaje—an appealing and seamless combination of rhythm and blues, rock and roll, country western, and Mexican musical forms—Los Lobos evoked an earlier moment of cultural melding, but one strongly associated with Mexicanness and Mexican national culture. *La Pistola y el Corazón* represents an assertion of ethnic, national, and linguistic identity. But it moves away from the postmodern melding of divergent styles and forms a source of cultural affirmation and critique.

A group like Cypress Hill, by contrast, plunges headlong into the aural experimentation, quotation, and sampling characteristic of hip hop as a postmodern phenomenon. Their music, however, generally lacks the same type of cultural or social critique that characterizes such artists as Los Lobos or Kid Frost. Their 1993 album *Black Sunday*, for example, does occasionally drop lexical signals of Chicanismo like "let's kick it, ese," or "who you trying to get crazy with, ese? Don't you know I'm loco?" However with songs titled "I Wanna Get High," "Insane in the Brain," "Legalize it," and "Hits From the Bong," the general thematic thrust of their work should become clear. These ruminations on the power and purpose of marijuana alternate with meditations on the violent side of barrio life. From the 1991 album *Cypress Hill*, such songs as "How I Could Just Kill a Man" and "Hole in the Head" reflect the themes found in a good deal of gangster rap:

> Here's an example, just a little sample
> How I could just kill a man.
> One type tried to come in my home
> Take my chrome, I said you is zoned
> Take cover son, or you're ass out
> How you like my chrome?
> Then I watched the rookie pass out.
> Didn't have to blast out, but I did anyway [laughter]
> Yo, punk had to pay.
> So I just killed a man.
> Here is something you can't understand
> How I could just kill a man.

The celebration of personal bravery in the face of danger, the casual use of deadly violence, the propping up of self-esteem through physical control all resonate with other forms of gangster rap. Thematically, Cypress Hill—though a multiracial band comprised of Chicano and African-American members—does not overtly address notions of mestizaje, either racial or cultural.

Musically, their work is characterized by a heavy hip hop beat, clever sampling from a variety of sources ranging from De La Soul to "The Duke of Earl," and a whiny rap voice addressing the finer uses of cannabis and firearms. The beats are compelling and mesmerizing, and the sophisticated use of samples to create intricate rhythms distinguishes

Cypress Hill as a master hip hop combo. Yet on a formal level their re-liance on postmodern pastiche does not quite address the issue of mes-tizaje in the same critical manner as other Chicano and Latino musicians.

As the work of Kid Frost reveals, the role of contemporary Chicano music as a mestizo music does not rely solely on borrowing and reform-ing African-American musical art forms. In addition to the polyglot ex-pression, the mestizaje of Chicano music can be heard in the musical sources for the samples drawn by rap artists. These sources tend to in-vest the music with historical consciousness and cultural distinction. One interesting experiment from 1991 is the cooperative production of Latin Alliance, which brought together Latino rap artists from both the East and West Coasts, in order to create a multicultural, multiracial al-liance to—in the words of the liner notes to their album *Latin Alliance*— "uplift the minds of our Raza." In part this uplift is accomplished through the celebration of multi-ethnic unity, in part through the evocation of cultural distinction.

"Lowrider (On the Boulevard)" samples the 1975 hit "Lowrider" by War, a song supremely popular among the cruising populations of Los Angeles in the mid-1970s. Slipped in the mix is a brief sample of "Evil Ways" by Carlos Santana, another Chicano musician whose synthesis of Latino rhythms with rock guitar virtuosity has proven inspirational for numerous artists. These musical weavings serve to celebrate cultural dif-ference and affirm those elements of distinction by weaving and reweav-ing familiar melodies and rhythms in the hip hop styling of the early 1990s. This mestizaje on a musical level affirms the racial and linguistic mestizaje that characterizes Chicano and other Latino cultures in the United States. The sonic interaction is one of play and celebration as Kid Frost, ALT, and Mellow Man Ace take turns rapping about the joys of cruising along the boulevard ("Kicking back and yo I'm soaring like an eagle / Frost in a Jeep and Ralph ends in a Regal / We're looking at the fine ladies bumping the fresh tapes / Seeing the sparks from my car when the frame scrapes"). The reveling in heterosexual courtship, flir-tation, and car culture, backed by some quintessential mid-1970s Chi-cano music, sonically reconfigures a space of familiarity and celebration, asserting a recognition and affirmation of lived daily practices within a notably masculine Chicano/Latino community.

The aural mestizaje of sampling is used not just for the construc-tion of an identity-affirming music. "Runnin'" addresses the dilemma of undocumented immigrants maneuvering through the militarized bor-der zone. Over an energized beat, the song samples actual radio com-munication between border patrol agents as they track down Latinos

crossing into U.S. territory. The tape is chilling in its clearly militarized tones. A mechanized voice calls for assistance in apprehending suspects. In juxtaposition to these heated calls for help, the coldly officious
tone of the INS answering machine ("To find out how to report illegal
aliens, or employers of illegal aliens, dial 6 now") gets added to the mix.
Against these official government voices, Kid Frost offers a contrapun-
tal countermemory:

> Let's go back into history.
> It's not much of a mystery.
> The Indians run for the mountains and hills.
> As the white man hunts and kills.
> Murder in the first degree today
> But way back when it was okay.
> What they teach in school is the dumbest,
> And don't talk no shit about Christopher Columbus.

The melding of these voices highlights the contested position of the mestizo within contemporary society. The official governmental discourse
about illegal employment, the discourse of a militarized police state, the
countermemory linking today's violence against mestizos with historical genocide—all these combine in the mix to signal how the mestizo
body is incessantly inscribed with meaning. Certainly the mestizo does
not solely represent a free-floating agent of deterritorialization as Nancy
avers, nor do the mobile and multiple identities of mestizos represent
"a new stability, self-assurance and quietism" as Young suggests. Rather,
mestizaje becomes at once both a source of repression and a locus of
reclamation and resistance.

The sense of affirmation and resistance evident in the mix of Latin Alliance parallels the ways in which mestizaje is thematized as a racial reality and a source of personal pride. On "What is an American?" ALT raps
over samples from War's "Heartbeat" and from "On Your Face" by Earth
Wind and Fire, affirming the creolization that has led to Latino culture:

> Two, now it's three flowing together,
> It's Hispanic and French blood,
> Create a lyrical flood.
> Latin Alliance band together to speak out
> For those who are afraid, you should stand up and shriek out:
> "I'm proud!"

The miscegenation of French, Spanish, and Indian blood becomes the
locus for pride in mestizaje as well as the font for the "lyrical flood" that

ALT's rap best represents. (Later, on the track "Smooth Roughness," Lyrical Engineer raps: "They can't handle this smooth roughness. / Taking two words meaning totally opposite. / The Lyrical Engineer will take 'em and make 'em fit, / Create another definition out of the two." Again, another form of mestizaje, on a linguistic and semantic level, occurs.) The creation of language, meaning, and culture is tied intimately to the creation of a mixed-race people, and all this taken together represents the source of Latino pride. "What is an American?" continues:

> Call me a wetback then get back,
> Better yet open your mind and set back.
> And just think about it,
> Homeboy, what are you dumb?
> If you're not Indian then where did your family come from?

The reclamation of racial pride extends to the indigenous elements of Latino existence. The rejection of the term "wetback" sets up the didactic lesson to be learned:

> 'Cause I feel freedom is golden,
> No border patrollin'
> The land that you stand on is stolen.
> Word up, yo, I'm saying it loud
> Every Hispanic in the crowd stay proud.

The evocation of stolen land refers both to the European invasion of indigenous lands and the U.S. practice of nineteenth-century expansionism. In rejecting the militarization of the border and the military invasion of native lands, the rap offers both a well-worn critique common to Chicano critical discourses and a reason to take pride in the right of "every Hispanic in the crowd" to claim a place in United States society. The racial/cultural mestizaje that helps demarcate Latinidad works to dissolve and transgress national boundaries. Yet there remain some boundaries, and it is the political implications of these boundaries that the rap examines:

> And just be yourself at best.
> I trip when I see an African medallion on a Mexican's chest.
> For what I say you'd like to cut my throat.
> But what is an American quote unquote?

The "you" that wants to cut ALT's throat is rather ambiguous. But the message that one should claim one's own racial and cultural identity—rather than latch onto another's—comes across clearly.

Indeed the issue of racial/cultural identity becomes more complex in the increasingly inmixed world that a multi-ethnic, multi-racial location like Los Angeles represents.[9] For this reason, three Los Angeles bands who released albums in mid-1996—Delinquent Habits, Rage Against the Machine, and Los Lobos—offer illuminating examples of how notions and strategies of mestizaje resonate through contemporary Chicano music.

In their two releases, *Delinquent Habits* (1996) and *Here Come the Horns* (1998), the multiracial rap group Delinquent Habits make it a point to highlight the hybrid nature of their cultural and racial identities. Employing caló, English, Spanish, and street slang, the rappers Ives, Kemo, and deejay O. G. Style employ code-switching and bilingualism as both their linguistic and personal identities are foregrounded. In the single "Tres Delinquentes" from their first CD, the rappers trade off busting rhymes, interweaving Spanish and caló, English and street slang:

> ¿Qué hondas muchacho? Hey vienes, te miro.
> Si me traes bronca me loco de atiro.
> Me paro, te tombo, no es tu rumbo.
> Y con el lingo talvez te confundo.[10]

> Shifts the attack with the five foot ten
> The blaxican once again with the cocktail pin
> As I emerge from the depths of the realm my son
> I got the black, yeah, black track coke and rum.

The linguistic mestizaje of the rap serves to distinguish and establish an audience. Thematically, the rhymes do little more than assert the supremacy of the rapper over an imagined adversary. However, there is an interesting elision between the linguistic and racial mestizaje addressed in the song:

> Otra vez ya lo ves en the crew somos tres[11]
> One blaxican on the squad you don't test
> Sitting hard like an Aztec, swift like a Zulu
> That's what it's like with the pump shot through you.

The multiracial background of the "blaxican" Kemo is thematized in the rhymes and romanticized through the iconic images of the hard Aztec and the swift Zulu. The rap represents an acknowledgment of the complicated interracial and multiracial relationships developing in an increasingly diverse society. In these passages the song addresses the ways mestizo cultures and societies are coming to terms with the cultural significance of these racial identities.

While the song offers a thematic engagement with a different aspect of contemporary racial and cultural mestizaje, formally "Tres Delinquentes" employs predictable sampling techniques that reflect the typical blank parody of postmodern pastiche.[12] Drawing on "The Lonely Bull," recorded by Herb Alpert & the Tijuana Brass, Delinquent Habits invokes a simulacrum of Latino music, a shadow of mariachi music, a sanitized version of pleasant melodies with a slight tinge of ethnic flavor. However popular Herb Alpert may once have been, among Latino communities his music does not typically enjoy the kind of sustained popularity and cultural identification as do War, Earth Wind and Fire, or Carlos Santana.[13] The sense of simulacra is carried over to the video Delinquent Habits produced for "Tres Delinquentes." To the trumpeting of "The Lonely Bull," the video opens on a setting that suggests an over-the-top Sergio Leone spaghetti western. Absurdly, the trip of rappers stroll through the dusty streets while mustachioed bandidos and menacing soldiers look on. This sense of endless quotation and dissociated images suggests some of the shortcomings an uncritical mestizaje can engender.

Rage Against the Machine—whose lead singer, Zack de la Rocha, asserts his Chicano identity and identifies with Third World struggles—offers another example of the mestizaje to be found in contemporary Chicano music.[14] The sound created by the band on its two albums, *Rage Against the Machine* (1993) and *Evil Empire* (1996), is a cross between rap and speed metal, a hybrid musical form over which de la Rocha spits anti-imperialist and anti-capitalist rants about resistance to repressive authority.[15] An intense mestizaje of influences and confluences, Rage Against the Machine, unlike many hip hop bands, does not use samples, keyboards, or synthesizers in creating the sonic bombardment that roils behind and through de la Rocha's defiant lyrics. Tom Morello creates all the complex scratching and wailing via effects on his guitar, a fact that hearkens back to the celebration of the rock and roll guitar hero embodied by such rock icons as Jimi Hendrix, Eric Clapton, and Jimmy Page. The influence of rock as performance melds with the influence of hip hop and its emphasis on heavy aural experimentation.

Against the funk bass and sonic distortion of electric guitar, de la Rocha articulates a sharp political critique:

> Since 1516 minds attacked and overseen
> Now crawl amidst the ruins of this empty dream
> With their borders and boots on top of us
> Pulling knobs on the floor of their toxic metropolis.

So how you gonna get what you need to get?
The gut eaters, blood drenched get offensive like Tet.
When the fifth sun sets get back reclaim
The spirit of Cuahtemoc alive and untamed.
Face the funk now blasting out ya speaker, one to one Maya, Mexica.
That vulture came to try and steal your name, but now you found a gun.
This is for the people of the sun,
It's coming back around again,
This is for the people of the sun.

Again, as we have seen with other Chicano musicians, a countermemory is offered by de la Rocha in "People of the Sun" from *Evil Empire*. Drawing on history as a source by which to critique and reflect on contemporary ills links the thematic issues of this song with other Chicano music. The rhetoric of rebellion, the critique of colonial dispossession, the claims for indigenous rights, the invocation of pre-Columbian imagery, the convergence of Third World struggles come together against a barrage of funk bass lines and industrial guitar whining.

As several critics have noted, there seems a discrepancy between such radical political commentary and the role the band plays as a part of the contemporary culture industry.[16] Guitarist Tom Morello, a Harvard University graduate with a political science major, does not avoid the contradictions inherent in the way the band's music gets distributed. Speaking on behalf of the band, he notes: "We feel that, given the injustices perpetrated by our economic system, we have no choice but to talk about them. . . . For the time being, just letting people know that confrontation is okay is a worthwhile exercise. That's something we do every night and on every record sold."[17] Through the mass marketing of their music, Rage Against the Machine can disseminate a political message that encourages action and involvement; the efficacy of such a move remains, of course, ambiguous. Nevertheless, such negotiations through the belly of the postmodern beast, in this case transnational entertainment corporations, represent how artists may articulate a complicitous critique of the systems they occupy.[18] Moreover, such negotiation reveals some of the contestatory strategies possible within a postmodern cultural context.

It would be too tedious to recount the various ways in which discussions about postmodernism and politics have played themselves out. As is well known, either postmodernism is the death of political action through the co-optation of all resistant impulses and actions, or it enables a more effective, decentered, and insidious form of political activism.

Rather than perform such well-rehearsed debates, what the study of contemporary Chicano music enables is an exploration of the way critical consciousness articulates itself through specific cultural forms. As Philip Bohlman notes, "The arguments for resistance, post-colonial discourse, and subaltern voices are already in the musics that surround us, and we ignore them only by not listening to them" (1993: 435).

The incessant sonic assault of Rage Against the Machine signals the urgency (and contradictory position) articulated by these voices. The convergence of rap, hip hop, speed metal, political commentary, and industrial noise driven by a funk beat represents another form of aural mestizaje than that offered by more conventional forms of Chicano rap. The difficulty in categorizing the music created by Rage suggests the ways in which Chicano music moves expansively into areas not visited previously by "ethnically identified" artists.

This move beyond cliché is undertaken with equal delight and equal innovation by that standard-bearer of mestizo music, Los Lobos. Either as a racial condition informing a sense of cultural and national identity, or as a strategy by which to meld disparate musical influences into a cohesive and seamless unity, mestizaje best characterizes the musical development of Los Lobos. Be it their 1978 independent release of acoustic Mexican music *Just Another Band from East L.A.* through their first three albums, the EP . . . *And a Time to Dance* (1983), *How Will the Wolf Survive?* (1984), and *By the Light of the Moon* (1987), which blend rhythm and blues, rock and roll, country and western, as well as rancheras, norteños, and conjunto music; or the 1987 soundtrack for the movie *La Bamba* about 1950s Chicano rocker Richie Valens; be it the recording of traditional Mexican songs in Spanish on *La Pistola y el Corazón* (1988) or the more sonically innovative *The Neighborhood* (1990) and *Kiko* (1992); the band has consistently fused different musical influences and styles to create a compelling and critically acclaimed musical art.

A significant shift occurred in 1994 as the main songwriting team of Los Lobos, guitarist David Hidalgo and percussionist Louie Pérez, undertook a side project. Working with Los Lobos's producers Mitchell Froom and Tchad Blake, they created an experimental and improvisatory music under the name Latin Playboys. Colored as much by mariachi music as by experimental jazz (Louie Pérez is a fan of the improvisational jazz of Roland Kirk and John Coltrane), their albums, *Latin Playboys* (1994) and *Dose* (1999), range widely in search of musical influences. The songs range from the Puerto Rican plena heard in the rhythm of "Same Brown Earth" to the bolero stylings of "Manifold De Amor." The move toward greater experimentation and location of influences proves a shift in relying on particular sources as the substance for mestizaje. The incorporation of so varied influences propels the notion of cultural mestizaje forward. Rather than mining familiar sources for an affirmation of identity, this move reflects a greater challenge to the substance of mestizaje. As Louie Pérez explained upon the release of their first album, "We don't even know what our own Chicano fans will think about it, because it really stretches the definition of what Chicanos should do" (Garcia 1994).

Over dissonant horns, clanging bells, an inverted Afro-Latin rhythm, and an indigenous drum beat, David Hidalgo sings on "Same Brown Earth": "When woman was a rock / On distant mountain top / When woman was like that / Reflecting like the moon." On the one hand, the sense of mysticism and pre-Columbian imagery connects the song to a well-established repertoire of Chicano cultural icons. On the other hand, the musical references are less expected, and the experimentation with electronic distortion, squawking guitar, and clanging and banging percussion presents a challenging aural experience. More to the point, it offers a cultural challenge as the boundaries of what counts as "Chicano music" expand exponentially. It is clear, however, where the band members stand in this regard. Louie Pérez regards the move as a logical progression in a culture that is based so profoundly on notions of mestizaje: "Chicanos are like antennas. . . . We have all this information. We pick up all these different stations, and it blurs into one thing, and that's the Chicano experience."

The 1996 release of Los Lobos's *Colossal Head* underscores the significance of this definition of Chicano experience. "Marisela" calls on the plena to provide the moving rhythm over which Cesar Rosas sings a paean to Puerto Rico ("Allí en la isla del encanto / Orgulloso yo les canto / Con sus sierras y sus santos / Y un placer a mí me ha dado").[19] By contrast, the mid-tempo blues jam absurdly called "Buddy Ebsen Loves the Night Time" swings through a traditional three-chord blues progression as David Hidalgo repeatedly plays and moves off a distorted guitar riff. The album weaves together sonic distortion, stuttering guitars, funk rhythms, references to traditional African-American, Latin American, and Latino musical traditions, and odd accidental or improvisational aural moments such as the inclusion of coughs, gurgling PVC tubes, police sirens, and random street noise.

Analogously, the song lyrics often emphasize the comic, the absurd, the surreal, the accidental. On the loose and bluesy "Manny's Bones," for example, David Hidalgo sings:

Manny's dead and didn't leave me nothing
Went off to heaven left his bed undone
Gone away, he didn't leave us sad
The dogs are all wondering where their daddy went, oh my.

"Don't go leave me here by myself
Won't hear me calling when you all done left
Guess I didn't make it out this time
But I'll be waiting on the other side, bye bye."

Way down in Manny's bones
The dry old river and a dusty soul
We'll take him to the fishing hole
And let the water take him to his home.

The use of blank and near rhymes creates a sense of unease juxtaposed against the relatively structured musical framework of honky-tonk pianos and honking baritone saxophones. The lyrics make allusion to traditional blues songs about death and mourning but shift the content enough to highlight the incommensurate. Mestizaje here represents less an affirmation of an established historical or racial identity and becomes instead the site of transformation, a borderlands with an emphasis on the what is to be, not the what already is at hand.

Throughout *Colossal Head* there is a mixture of the familiar with the defamiliarizing. This thematization of unease is struck in the first cut, "Revolution." The song is a meditation on the failed revolutionary practices that Rage Against the Machine, for instance, so staunchly affirms. The song proves finally to be a touching questioning of youthful illusion:

Where did it go?
Can't say that I know
Those times of revolution.
The burning burning burning
All so cool and gone
What was just was.

We try my brother
To hold on to our faith
But was it late for revolution
Too tired, too tired sister
To hold my fist so high
Now that it's gone.

Where the questioning of revolutionary change takes place on a thematic level, on a musical and cultural level there is an insistence on change, on transformation, on affirming the sense of revolution as a turn. Los Lobos help to make that turn, to invite their auditors into a space where the terms of mestizaje are re-examined on a political and (most potently) cultural level. If Chicano music is characterized by its deployment of mestizaje as an affirming and resistant strategy, as a way of giving meaning to Chicano racial identity, then Los Lobos amplify this strategy as their songs engage on a sonic and discursive level with what mestizaje— what meaning itself—means.

As a coda to this discussion, it is worth bearing in mind that the fluidity of musical—indeed all cultural—creation prohibits a cohesive understanding of Chicano music. The ground beneath one's feet shifts away at every step. To view music as a semiotic system informed by racial discourse leads one into the treacherous terrain of identity and identification. A group like the Los Angeles rap group Aztlan Underground in their album *Sub-Verses* highlights these difficulties as they meld indigenous instrumentation, rap rhythms and images ("This is a lyrical drive-by, / so hit the ground, / don't make a sound / and watch the truth fly. / I got the rage, / I got the rage, / I got the rage / to pump the twelve gauge"), statements recorded by EZLN's Commandante Marcos ("Ser Zapatista es buscar una nueva forma de vida y una nueva forma de relacionarse" [To be Zapatista is to look for a new way of living and relating]), and Nahuatl incantations ("Intonan / Intotah / Tlatecuhtli / Tonatiuh / For our mother / our father. / The earth / and the sun"). The numerous political and musical references suggest a movement across national, transnational, and international concerns.

Likewise the group Ozomatli reveals a concern for transnational issues both political and cultural. A multiracial group living in Los Angeles, their songs move among and mix North American hip hop, Central American cumbia, Puerto Rican salsa, Dominican merengue, Spanish flamenco, Argentine tango, and Mexican mariachi. Their song "Como Ves" on their eponymous album is a prime example of the musical mestizaje being produced in the cultural borderlands of Southern California. The song borrows South African guitar riffs, the feel of Brazilian samba complete with surdo drums and whistles, and lyrics that declare transnational connectivity: "Como ves, como ves / La historia no es como crees. / Como ves, como ves / Cuba y Africa, soy hermano / con todo mi corazón. / Cuba y Africa, soy hermano / y veo su dolor. / Quiero besar su espíritu / y su alma."[20] The face of Chicano music continues to undergo a profound transformation as the Latino population in the U.S.—and in traditionally Chicano communities—comes to be increasingly diverse. The great continued flows and fluxes of transnational movements signal an ever-shifting musical landscape.

With the huge success of Rock en Español, the greater exchange of musical commodities across national and natural borders, and the proliferation and diversification of music and music video programming in all countries and continents, there may not be any purpose in employing a term like "Chicano music" much longer. The 1999 Cinco de Mayo festivities in Los Angeles serve as an excellent example. The live entertainment comprised bands that mixed, matched, and melded tejano, cumbia, ranchera, norteño, banda, merengue, and salsa music. A programming director for a Latino radio station in Los Angeles, where Spanish-language radio has a greater market share than its English-language counterparts, commented on the diverse lineup: "There's a demand for different kinds of music. There's a lot of crossover in styles now that you didn't have before" (Valdes-Rodriguez 1999). This crossover, this mestizaje, may very well mark the end of Chicano music.

Or perhaps it marks the culmination of what Chicano music has, in all its myriad manifestations, always undertaken: a musical process of inclusion, transformation, critique, and affirmation. It is impossible to characterize inclusively the broad spectrum of Chicano musical expression. It is also impossible to miss the vitality and urgency infusing that expression. In part, this vitality emerges from mestizaje as a cultural concept that arises from the racialized imaginary of Chicano and Mexican populations. Simultaneously, there emerges in the music a recognition that mestizaje is both a liberating process and one inscribed by tremendous political, social, and cultural conflict. Mestizos and mestizas in North America move through a world in which their somatic, linguistic, cultural selves are often devalued. Simultaneously, these same mestizas and mestizos move through and create a culture that celebrates mestizaje as a strategy both affirming and resistant. The incongruities evident in Chicano music indicate the difficulties involved in this project. It is a difficult movement since the idea of a firm ground on which to stand melts away as Chicanos cross a diverse landscape in the construction of a cultural identity. This because racial identity for Chicanos has in the past and present crossed so many racial territories. Chicano music similarly finds itself in motion. It moves through the heavily patrolled borderlands between cultural affirmation, cultural dislocation, and cultural commodification. Finally, if nothing else, the music affirms that the passage between cultures, between nations, between communities is at once difficult, necessary, and inevitable.

NOTES

1. "Postmodern" here includes those stylistic features that Richard Shusterman lists (1991: 614): "recycling appropriation rather than unique originative creation, the eclectic mixing of styles, the enthusiastic embracing of the new technology and mass culture, the challenging of modernist notions of aesthetic autonomy and artistic purity, and an emphasis on the localized and temporal rather than the putatively universal and eternal." My research assistant at the University of California, Santa Barbara, Ruth Razo, helped me locate this and many of the articles here cited. Without her, the production of this essay would have been impossible and I thank her for her help.

2. For a brief discussion of Los Olvidados and their diverse musical styles, see Gonzalez (1996).

3. Caló: Sánchez (1983: 84–85) notes that the origins of caló "have been traced back to Spain where the gypsy language (of Indic origin) had become heavily hispanicized and mingled and greatly blended with *germanía*, the speech of Spanish delinquents. In Spain *caló* generally means 'language of the Gypsies' but is now used by the Gypsies to refer to themselves." Used in the El Paso underworld in the early part of this century, it has spread throughout the Chicano world as a form of linguistic demarcation. From its inception, the term "caló" has been associated with marginal constituencies. *Y sabes que, loco, yo soy muy malo:* And you know what, dude, I'm very bad; *Tú no sabes nada:* You don't know anything; *palo:* stick; *culo:* asshole.

4. Code-switching is the borrowing or substitution of a word in one language for the corresponding word in the other. Incorporated borrowing or lexicalization occurs where the dialect has borrowed the particular word from another language. This type of linguistic interpenetration on the sociodiscursive stage forms a type of bilingualism (more precisely polyglossia) in which speakers use code-switching to establish a social relation. Peñalosa (1980: 68) notes: "Chicano code switching can also be a verbal strategy for conveying social information, such as a sociopolitical identity marker or intimate relationship, for signalling social distance from an Anglo role, and for implying that one's own interlocutor will not be offended by language mixture."

5. *Chingazos:* blows; *simón:* yes; *ese:* dude, cuz, bro, guy, etc.; *Yo soy chingón:* I am the boss; *¿Qué pasa?:* what's happening?; *raza:* race, vernacular for Mexicano, Chicano, Latino.

6. For a brief discussion of Chicano musicians like Kid Frost drawing on African-American musical forms, see Watrous 1990.

7. See Rosaldo 1989: 216 for a discussion of Chicano subjectivity as being "crisscrossed by multiple identities." This is a type of transculturated identity of the borderlands. For a discussion of the ways in which border theory has

supplanted liminal studies as advocated by Victor Turner, see Weber 1995: 530–33.

8. The clumsy term "deterritorialization" implies not simply an alienation or estrangement, but also a dissolution of system, stratification, order. As Gilles Deleuze and Felix Guattari ([1975] 1986: 28) explain, deterritorialization is marked by an expression that "must break forms, encourage ruptures and new sproutings. When a form is broken, one must reconstruct the content that will necessarily be part of a rupture in the order of things." See also Bogue 1989, esp. 116–21, for a discussion of this sort of linguistic deterritorialization.

9. For a discussion of the development of Chicano music in Los Angeles, see Loza 1993. For a discussion of the development of rap music in Los Angeles, see Cross 1993.

10. "What's up, dude? You're coming, I see you / If you bring trouble I get mad crazy / I stand up, I hit you, this isn't your neighborhood / And with my lingo maybe I confuse you."

11. "Once again, now you see, in the crew we are three."

12. "Pastiche is, like parody, the imitation of a peculiar mask, speech in a dead language: but it is a neutral practice of such mimicry, without any of parody's ulterior motives, amputated of the satiric impulse, devoid of laughter and of any conviction that alongside the abnormal tongue you have momentarily borrowed, some healthy linguistic normality still exists. Pastiche is thus blank parody, a statue with blind eyeballs: it is to parody what that other interesting and historically original modern thing, the practice of a kind of blank irony, is to what Wayne Booth calls the 'stable ironies' of the 18th century" (Jameson 1984: 65). While I disagree with Jameson's blanket characterization of postmodernistic pastiche, in this case his discussion of blank parody seems apt.

13. Kemo says of the song: "It's straight-up hip-hop to us. We didn't try to do something special 'cause we're Latino. This is just our form of expression." Yet clearly the desire to strike a "Latin" note is evident, and Cheo Hodari Coker, who interviewed the band, notes that "the music juxtaposes the soothing, mariachi-tinged strains of Herb Alpert & the Tijuana Brass' 'Lonely Bull" with a hard-core rap aesthetic" (Coker 1996: 60).

14. I have been using the term "Chicano music" rather unproblematically throughout this discussion. Just because de la Rocha is Chicano—son of the troubled visual artist Roberto de la Rocha, who with Carlos Almaraz, Gilbert Luján, and Frank Romero formed the art group known as "Los Four" in 1974— does not unequivocally make Rage Against the Machine producers of Chicano music. Guitarist Tom Morello, drummer Brad Wilk, and bassist Tim Bob form a multiracial band with numerous musical influences and interests. However, without dwelling on biography or racial categorization, the political stances articulated by the lyrics penned by de la Rocha as well as the hybridization of musical forms and reliance on hip hop and rap as both an African-American and Latino art form compel me to classify the band as producers of Chicano music. By contrast, a band like Everclear—whose bassist, Craig Montoya, is a Latino from Seattle—does not produce music that forms a dialogue with the political

or formal interests characteristic of other Chicano music. These are random but not unconsidered distinctions.

15. In an interview, Zack de la Rocha cites as musical influences Minor Threat, Public Enemy, Led Zeppelin, Run DMC, The Clash, and Bad Brains, "from hardcore to hip hop to heavy rock" in a seamless combination (see Price 1993: 7). Culturally and politically, if the liner photo of over thirty books on *Evil Empire* is any indication, the band's influences range from *The Age of Reason* by Jean-Paul Sartre to *Guerilla Warfare* by Che Guevara, from *Play It As It Lays* by Joan Didion to *The Wretched of the Earth* by Frantz Fanon. A complete list of the books appears on the webpage www.RATM.com.

16. A review of the band's 1993 New York City concert is a prime example: "In classic rock-rebel style, the paradoxes of disseminating its ideas via the mass-media machinery of Epic Records and Sony Music, alongside Michael Jackson, go unexamined" (Pareles 1993).

17. Smith (1993: 10). This sense of confrontation informs such performances as the benefit concert Rage Against the Machine held in New Jersey on 28 January 1999 with proceeds donated to the International Concerned Family And Friends Of Mumia Abu-Jamal. Mumia is an African-American print and radio journalist who was sentenced to death for the murder of a Philadelphia policeman. His defenders claim that he is the victim of a miscarriage of justice.

18. Linda Hutcheon discusses this process as "inside yet outside, inscribing yet contesting, complicitous yet critical" (1989: 158).

19. "There in the land of enchantment / Proud I sing to you / With its mountains and its saints / And a pleasure it has given me." For an insightful review of the album, see Dibbell 1996.

20. "As you see, as you see / History is not what you believe / As you see, as you see. / Cuba and Africa, I am your brother / with all my heart / Cuba and Africa I am your brother / and I see your pain. / I want to kiss your spirit / and your soul."

References

Alarcón, Norma. 1994. "Conjugating Subjects: The Heteroglossia of Essence and Resistance." In *An Other Tongue: Nation and Ethnicity in the Linguistic Borderlands*, ed. Alfred Arteaga, 125–38. Durham: Duke University Press.

Bogue, Roland. 1989. *Deleuze and Guattari*. New York: Routledge.

Bohlman, Philip V. 1993. "Musicology as a Political Act." *The Journal of Musicology* 11: 411–36.

Coker, Cheo Hodari. 1996. "Stirring It Up With Latino Hip, Hip-Hop." *Los Angeles Times* (9 June): Calendar Section, 60+.

Cross, Brian. 1993. *It's Not About a Salary: Rap, Race, and Resistance in Los Angeles*. London: Verso.

Deleuze, Gilles, and Félix Guattari. 1975. *Kafka: For a Minor Literature*, Trans. Dana Polan. Foreword by Réda Bensmaïa. Minneapolis: University of Minnesota Press, 1986.

Dibbell, Carola. 1996. "Found in Translation." *Village Voice* (16 Apr): 57, 62.

Garcia, Guy. 1994. "Extending Chicano Roots into Polyglot Textures." *New York Times* (3 Apr), natl. ed.: H27.

Gonzalez, Carolina. 1996. "Rockeros Deluxe: Rock en Español Head North of the Border." *Spin Magazine* (March): 68–72.

Hutcheon, Linda. 1989. "The Post-modern Ex-centric: The Center That Will Not Hold." In *Feminism and Institutions: Dialogues on Feminist Theory*, ed. Linda Kaufman, 141–65. Oxford: Basil Blackwell.

Jameson, Fredric. 1984. "Postmodernism, or The Cultural Logic of Late Capitalism." *New Left Review* 146 (July/August): 53–93.

Lipsitz, George. 1991. *Time Passages: Collective Memory and American Popular Culture*. Minneapolis: University of Minnesota Press.

Loza, Steven. 1992. "From Veracruz to Los Angeles: The Reinterpretation of the *Son Jarocho*." *Latin American Music Review* 13: 179–94.

———. 1993. *Barrio Rhythm: Mexican American Music in Los Angeles*. Urbana: University of Illinois Press.

Manuel, Peter. 1995. "Music as Symbol, Music as Simulacrum: Postmodern, Pre-Modern, and Modern Aesthetics in Subcultural Popular Musics." *Popular Music* 14: 227–39.

Nancy, Jean-Luc. 1994. "Cut Throat Sun." Trans. Lydie Moudileno. In *An Other Tongue: Nation and Ethnicity in the Linguistic Borderlands*, ed. Alfred Arteaga, 113–23. Durham: Duke University Press.

Pareles, Jon. 1993. "Rage Against the Machine: Roseland." *New York Times* (8 Nov), natl. ed.: C14.

Peña, Manuel H. 1985. *The Texas-Mexican Conjunto: History of a Working-Class Music*. Austin: University of Texas Press.

Peñalosa, Fernando. 1980. *Chicano Sociolinguistics: A Brief Introduction*. Rowley, Mass.: Newbury House.

Price, Simon. 1993. "Rage Against the Machine." *Melody Maker* (28 Aug): 6–7.

Rosaldo, Renato. 1989. *Culture and Truth: The Remaking of Social Analysis*. Boston: Beacon.

Sánchez, Rosaura. 1983. *Chicano Discourse: Socio-Historic Perspectives*. Rowley, Mass.: Newbury House.

Shusterman, Richard. 1991. "The Fine Art of Rap." *New Literary History*. 22: 613–32.

Smith, Andrew. 1993. "Rage Against the Machine." *Melody Maker* (28 Aug): 10–11.

Valdes-Rodriguez, Alisa. 1999. "More Than a Single Voice." *Los Angeles Times* (4 May): F1+.

Watrous, Peter. 1990. "Bilingual Music is Breaking Down Cultural Barriers." *New York Times* (2 Sept), natl. ed.: H19.

Weber, Donald. 1995. "From Limen to Border: A Meditation on the Legacy of Victor Turner for American Cultural Studies." *American Quarterly* 47: 525–36.

Young, Robert J. C. 1995. *Colonial Desire: Hybridity in Theory, Culture and Race*. New York: Routledge.

DISCOGRAPHY

Aztlan Underground. *Sub-Verses*. Xican@ Records 40003-2, 1999.

Cypress Hill. *Cypress Hill*. Columbia 47889, 1991.

———. *Black Sunday*. Columbia 53931, 1993.

Delinquent Habits. *Delinquent Habits*. RCA 66929, 1996.

———. *Here Come the Horns*. 1998.

Kid Frost, *Hispanic Causing Panic*, Virgin Records 91377, 1990.

———. *East Side Story*. Virgin Records 92097, 1992.

Latin Alliance. *Latin Alliance*. Virgin Records 91625, 1991.

Latin Playboys. *Latin Playboys*. Slash/Warner Bros. 45543, 1994.

———. *Dose*. Atlantic Records 83173-2, 1999.

Los Lobos. *Just Another Band from East L.A.* Independent release, 1978. Reissued
    Slash/Warner Bros. 45367, 1993.

———. *. . . And a Time to Dance*. Slash/Warner Bros. 23963, 1983.

———. *How Will the Wolf Survive?* Slash/Warner Bros. 25177, 1984.

———. *La Bamba*. Slash/Warner Bros. 25605, 1987.

———. *By the Light of the Moon*. Slash/Warner Bros. 25523, 1987.

———. *La Pistola y el Corazón*. Slash/Warner Bros. 25790, 1988.

———. *The Neighborhood*. Slash/Warner Bros. 26131, 1990.

———. *Kiko*. Slash/Warner Bros. 26786, 1992.

———. *Colossal Head*. Slash/Warner Bros. 46172, 1996.

Los Punkeros. *Raza Punk y Hardcore*. Aztlan Records 08012, 1997.

Ozomatli. *Ozomatli*, Almo Sounds 80020, 1998.

Rage Against the Machine. *Rage Against the Machine*. Epic 52959, 1992.

Rage Against the Machine. *Evil Empire*. Epic 57523, 1996.

7

Performing Decency: Ethnicity and Race in Andean "Mestizo" Ritual Dance

ZOILA S. MENDOZA

omparsa performance is a vital and creative realm where Andean people explore and redefine their "ethnic/racial" distinctions and identities. Comparsas are ritual dance associations whose members sponsor the annual festivity of a particular Catholic "saint" and perform masked and costume dances in his or her honor.[1] In San Jerónimo, Cusco, the focus of this study, the relevance of comparsas extends beyond their ritual performance. They have a central role in everyday life, shaping social relations and categories. The purpose of the analysis of comparsas that I carry out here is twofold. First, I join recent efforts with other Andeanist scholars to re-assess assumptions about Andean "ethnicity," assumptions that neglect the study of "race" as a central category of social differentiation (Poole 1994). The study of comparsas in San Jerónimo demonstrates that race is a constant referent for the local construction of identities. Second, by showing how comparsa performance mediates between ideologies about ethnicity and race and the everyday practice through which these ethnic/racial relations take place, I seek to contribute to studies that focus on the key role of performance in creating and giving expression to human and social experience (cf. Cowan 1990, Erlmann 1992, Fabian 1990, Waterman 1990).[2]

In Cusco, comparsa members, through both ritual performance of dances and their associations, redefine and give form to disputed local distinctions and identities. They comment and act on key sociocultural categories that shape the relations among local groups as well as between these local groups and the larger context of Cusco-region and Peruvian society.[3] These categories draw on and comment on regional, national, and transnational hierarchies and dichotomies (i.e. rural/urban, "white"/"Indian," highland/coastal, center/periphery) that are central to *cusqueños'* (Cusco people's) understanding and practice of ethnic/racial relations.

Here I focus my attention on two of these categories: *decencia* (decency or propriety) and *elegancia* (elegance) and how the members of a comparsa called the Majeños in the town of San Jerónimo have given form to and impersonated these categories.[4] Placing ritual performance at the center of their group activity, members of this comparsa have used their cultural, economic, and social resources to establish a superior position in local power relations, thereby replacing the old elites. I regard the members of the Majeños comparsa in San Jerónimo as successful "bricoleurs" who have used the signifying capacity of ritual symbolism to generate new meanings for their dance (Hebdige 1985). By incorporating into their performances a series of iconic symbols (costumes, masks, music, body movements), and through metaphoric comparisons (to muleteers, *hacendados*, and city dwellers), the Majeños of San Jerónimo have creatively brought together different domains of society (defined by ethnicity, race, class, and gender) and specific situational contexts (their strategic position close to the city of Cusco, the demise of the hacienda system, and the promotion of "folklore") to make convincing "arguments" through ritual performance (Fernandez 1986, Munn 1974). Through this performance, the Majeños have mediated between the conceptual and material aspects of those domains and specific situational contexts, shaping local categories that are the basis on which to redefine local distinctions and identities.

INDIOS, *CHOLOS*, AND MESTIZOS: CLASS, RACE, AND ETHNICITY IN PERU AND CUSCO

As a Peruvian anthropologist I chose to study comparsas among people who would be considered "mestizos" by most contemporary students of Andean society and by Cusqueños. I was interested in learning about the processes of identity creation and redefinition of a sector of Peruvian highland society that, broadly labeled as "mestizo," had often been neglected by anthropologists and ethnomusicologists seeking the "authentic Indian."[5] "Mestizo" is in Cusco and Peru an "ethnic/racial" category, and my own use of the category (as an analytical one) has drawn on its regional and national meanings.

To use the concept of either "ethnicity" or "race" alone to analyze the category of mestizo, as well as those of *cholo*, Indian, and white, would only limit such analysis. Generally, the concept of race privileges somatic indices of status distinction, while that of ethnicity emphasizes those of style-of-life such as language, dress, or occupation (Alonso 1994: 391). While it is true that Indian, white, mestizo, and *cholo* were categories that formed part of the legally established racial hierarchies during colonial times, and extra-legally reinforced during the Republic, it is equally true that at least since the eighteenth century, phenotype has had less to do with these categories than has, for example, occupation and clothing (Abercrombie 1992). Therefore, because of the importance of both kinds of referents for establishing social distinctions, the biological or somatic and those derived from the style-of-life of the individual, I have decided to use the compound concept "ethnic/racial" to refer to the above mentioned categories.

In order to analyze the dynamics of contemporary ethnic/racial relations in Cusco and Peru, two important issues need to be addressed. First, to study these relations, "class" relations should be understood. Second, both class and ethnic/racial relations in Peru, separate only in abstraction, are today very clearly marked by the differences between city and countryside or rural and urban culture. Classes, according to Bourdieu (1987), are relational and shaped by various forms of power relations. Classes are not groups that are ready-made in reality; they are defined historically by their members' possession of similar not only economic capital but also cultural (or informational) capital, social capital ("which consists of resources based on connections and group membership"), and symbolic capital ("which is the form the different types of capital take once they are perceived and recognized as legitimate") (Bourdieu 1987).[6]

Class and ethnic/racial relations in contemporary Cusco are clearly marked by the differences established by the urban–rural dichotomy and the "chain" of power relations that connect the two realms (De la Cadena 1991). From the 1940s on, and more clearly after the reconstruction of the capital city following the 1950 earthquake, the entire region underwent a series of socioeconomic, cultural, and political transformations that led to the destruction of the hacienda (large estate) system with the agrarian reform during the 1970s. Eclipsing the countryside, the city has gradually become pivotal in the regional economy. In this process the relationship *hacendado*–peasant (servant) on which the regional definitions of ethnicity and race drew was altered.[7] This led to a redefinition of inter-ethnic/racial relations, with the former axis of identity differentiation—ownership of land—being replaced by the city and the culture which derives from it (De la Cadena 1991). This has been clear in the case of the members of the Majeños comparsa who, in order to become less indigenous, incorporated elements of urban culture into their dance.

In terms of the poles that define ethnic/racial identities in Peru, one should always remember the contrast that has been historically established between the coast and the highlands and more specifically between the coastal metropolis, Lima, and the rural and urban centers of the highlands. With the Spanish Conquest and the political and spatial reorganization of what had been the Inca empire, Cusco and the highlands in general entered a process by which they gradually moved from the center to the periphery of the new coastal political and administrative center, Lima. What happened to the official language of the Inca empire, Quechua, under Spanish colonial rule was characteristic of the process of subjugation and standardization of the Andean population. Quechua became the "stigmatized language of peasants, herders and rural proletarians" (Mannheim 1991: 1).

Ethnic/racial identities bind together ideological and material aspects that transform each other historically (De la Cadena 1991). The importance of making an analytical distinction between the two aspects, the ideological and the material, is that it allows the exploration of how different ethnic/racial identities are acquired or lost by people in a very dynamic, albeit conflictual, way. Particularly relevant for the present analysis is that it permits an understanding of the key role that comparsa performance plays in this process precisely because in this performance, as we will see in the case of the Majeños, the actors explore and rework the relationship between the material and ideological aspects of such identities.

In Cusco, the discourses in which mestizos and Indians are distinguished are omnipresent. According to regional hegemonic ideology, the status of Indian and mestizo "are fixed and the barriers that separate them are insurmountable" (De la Cadena 1991: 9).[8] However, through everyday practice and, as I argue here, through comparsa performance, Cusco people explore their ethnic/racial identity and place themselves within and/or between the indigenous and the mestizo past and present. As part of the redefinition of ethnic/racial and class relations associated with the demise of the hacienda system in Cusco, new material elements have emerged as markers of difference and status. To become part of the urban world through formal education, occupation, language use, clothing, music, and dance style has become a strategy used by Cusqueños to leave behind their "Indian" identity and to become more powerful in local society.[9] For *jeronimianos* (people of San Jerónimo) to become more mestizo, which is the equivalent of being less Indian, has meant at least since the 1940s to leave behind elements associated with rural life and to incorporate those associated with urban life. In this process they have tried to blur the differences between themselves and the higher-status inhabitants of Cusco city and other towns considered "mestizo."

Here I intend to unravel some of the connotations of "mestizo" (literally "mixed blood," Spanish and Indian) identity in the context of San Jerónimo and Cusco, especially as expressed in performance. As a general statement, it can be said that the contemporary meanings of "mestizo" are associated with ownership of the means of production (i.e. a factory, store, or motor vehicle), advantageous position in labor relations (i.e. being a *patrón* or boss as opposed to servant or worker), and/or identification with urban/national culture (i.e. through fluent Spanish and formal education).[10]

Cholo, like mestizo, was a "mixed blood" (Indian and Spanish) category established during the colony. However, *cholo*, in contrast to mestizo, has become a pejorative term associated with low social and ethnic/racial status. At the national level and largely linked to the massive migration of highlanders to cities (mainly to the coastal capital of the nation) since the 1940s, the term has come to imply a more or less incomplete transition from rural to urban culture and a marginal position within the economic structure. As in most of Peru, people of San Jerónimo use the term *cholo* for a person they consider lower in status than themselves. While the material indicators of *cholo*-ness have varied through time, and vary also according to the context in which the term is used, these indicators tend to cluster around preferences in language, clothing, economic activity, and music and dance style.[11]

Through the Majeños' performance I explore some of the particular connotations of *cholo* in San Jerónimo. The members of this comparsa have collapsed the categories of Indian and *cholo* into one personage, the Maqt'a. Through the contrast between the characteristics of the Majeño and the Maqt'a, the comparsa members enact the exaggerated alternatives—the polarities of the marking system—and situate themselves in an unambiguously dominant position. Through their performance and their association, the members of the Majeños comparsa have tried to blur the differences between themselves and the urban elites. In practice this has been a very conflictual and dynamic process in which these Jeronimianos have had to manipulate the mechanisms that mark boundaries between rural and urban culture and between Indian and mestizo identity. In Cusco, some of these mechanisms, relevant in giving shape to comparsa performance, have been established by the so-called *instituciones culturales* (cultural institutions). These institutions, through their promotional activities such as contests and "folkloric" presentations, have since the first decades of this century become active agents in the separation of what they consider "indigenous" and "mestizo."

The first *instituciones culturales* were formed in the 1920s by representatives of the intellectual movement called *Indigenismo.*[12] Members of these institutions—artists, intellectuals, and other sectors of the mestizo middle class in the city of Cusco—have since devoted their efforts to configuring a regional identity based on their idea of "folklore" and their created repertory of Cusqueño traditions (Mendoza-Walker 1993a: chap. 2). The members of this provincial urban class were the first to re-create and "invent" a music and dance repertoire, staging presentations and thus initiating the process of "folklorization" of Andean music and dance (Mendoza-Walker 1993a, Turino 1991).[13] By the 1960s, the first state-sponsored *instituciones* were founded. These institutions became widespread in the 1970s as an integral part of the military regime's attempt to create a national identity based on tradition and folklore.

For "folkloric" contests and staged presentations, the members of *instituciones culturales* distinguish between indigenous and mestizo dances. The difference between the two is often of degree and theme. Indigenous dances are supposed to be less elaborate, and they are not supposed to display traces of industrialized (i.e. synthetic) materials in their costumes and paraphernalia. Preferably, they should represent scenes that correspond to the "authentic" ethos of Andean peasantry elaborated by the *indigenista* members of the *instituciones:* the warrior and aggressive spirit (conceived of as deriving from the Inca past), the bucolic and peaceful communal existence, and finally the festive and lustful spirit in celebrations. By contrast, mestizo dances display elaborate and synthetic costumes as well as obviously fabricated and stylized "choreographies."[14] They may evoke themes that might have become Cusqueño through Spanish influence (i.e. colonial themes) or that represent aspects of urban life in the past.

One interesting phenomenon that these contests and folkloric festivals started was the gradual consolidation of a regional repertoire of folkloric dances, some classified as indigenous and some as mestizo, shared by peasant and urban populations. Urban and rural populations have drawn from this repertoire according to their own purposes. Peasants perform "mestizo" dances in their local festivities and regional pilgrimage sites in order to gain popularity and prestige, making themselves less indigenous. Mestizos perform "indigenous" dances in urban settings such as schools, universities, and patriotic celebrations in order to promote and "preserve" this indigenous identity as a source of regional identity.

The people of San Jerónimo have made an effort since the 1940s at least to incorporate into their local repertoire those dances that are regionally considered "mestizo," and through performing them in their main public ritual the participants have gradually become mestizos. The members of the first Majeños comparsa in San Jerónimo took a pioneering step in this process, incorporating their dance into local tradition. Through the performance of the Majeños dance, the members of this comparssa have since the 1940s redefined and given local meaning to categories such as *decencia* and *elegancia*. Through their performance and later through the formation of an organized "folkloric" association, they have defined themselves as the local *decentes* and become a local mestizo elite.

THE MAJEÑOS DANCE: A PERFORMANCE OF *DECENTES*

The Majeños is a dance-drama that has become part of the regional repertoire of mestizo folklore. It first emerged in the town of Paucartambo in the 1920s and became popularized in the entire region through the contests initiated in 1967.[15] The performers of this dance agree that they impersonate a particular group of *arrieros* (muleteers) from the valley of Majes in Arequipa (thus the name Majeño, a person from Majes) who traded in liquors. A less overt though explicit meaning of the dance, as we will see below, is that it also represents the *hacendados* of the colonial and Republican periods.

The two comparsas that have gained regional recognition as the best performers and that have given shape to the contemporary form of the dance are the Majeños of San Jerónimo and the Majeños of Paucartambo. These two competing comparsas have made a particular effort to incorporate the characters of their dance into the reconstruction of their local past. The local meanings that the San Jerónimo comparsa has generated among Jeronimianos have been linked to those created by *Paucartambinos* (people of Paucartambo) since the 1920s. Here I limit my analysis to the San Jerónimo comparsa, referring only occasionally to that of Paucartambo.[16]

The study of the Majeños comparsa permits the analysis of some of the specific meanings of the concept of *decencia* in San Jerónimo and how a particular group of Jeronimianos has constructed and appropriated them through ritual performance. It also allows the exploration of how the members of this particular group have made an effort to define themselves as *decentes* outside ritual. The highly condensed and elaborated symbolism present in the ritual performance of the dance, such as the emphasis placed on certain aspects of the costumes, music, choreography, and paraphernalia, is crucial for disentangling those meanings.

Several key ethnic/racial and class differences in San Jerónimo, Cusco, and Peru are defined around the concept of *decencia*. Almost any study of Andean towns has found that local elites are often defined as the *gente decente* or *los decentes* (decent people) (cf. van den Berghe and Primov 1977). This implies that members of local elites are the ones who are able to conduct themselves in the most decent or proper way within society. *Decencia* is then a concept through which one can explore aspects of the hegemonic or "common sense" level of sociohistorical constructions that are labeled as "propriety" or "decency." In contemporary San Jerónimo, the concept of *decencia* is also defined in terms of ethnic/racial and class hierarchies. In this town a person is *decente* if she or he looks, dresses, and behaves like historical or contemporary local or regional elites. For comparsa members, their dance is *decente* if it is acknowledged as representative of a high-status group. *Decencia* has become a central concept that powerful social sectors have tried to shape and appropriate in an effort to assert hegemony. The moral judgment of clean, upright, and good behavior implied by the term legitimizes the status of those who control the signs of "decency."

During my research in San Jerónimo, the Majeños dance was performed on two occasions. One was for the Octave of Corpus Christi (a one-day celebration in June), and the other was during the patron saint festivity of the town. This four-day celebration is the main public ritual of this town. The dance was performed by about nineteen men and one woman, all fully costumed and masked. The music for these performances was played by a *banda*, a brass band composed of wind instruments such as tubas, trumpets, and trombones and percussion instruments such as drums (among them one bass drum) and cymbals. Three personages were physically distinct in the dance: the Majeño, performed by the majority of the men; the *Dama* (lady), performed by the woman; and the Maqt'as or Cholos, performed by two men noticeably smaller than the rest. All the Majeños wore matching costumes: brown leather boots with spurs, jodhpurs, wide brown leather belts *(cinchos)*, long-sleeved buttondown shirts, hip-length brown leather jackets, and wide-brimmed straw hats (Mexican *charro*-like).[17] Their masks had big, rosy cheeks, most of them had blue eyes, and the noses were extremely long (up to ten inches) and phallic, with a bulky black birthmark almost at the end (fig. 7.1).

Figure 7.1. Majeño donning his costume at the beginning of the four-day celebration. The San Jerónimo Majeño's masks are characterized by extremely
long, phallic noses with birthmarks near the end. San Jerónimo, Cusco, 1990.
(Photo by Fritz Vilasante)

Coming out of their nostrils they had long (approximately seven inches) mustaches made of horsehair. All the masks had extremely wide smiles (almost across the whole face) showing their shiny white teeth and a gold one, and their bright red lips.[18] Each Majeño carried a bottle of beer that he switched from hand to hand as he performed the dance.

The Dama wore a very stylized San Jerónimo market-woman-like outfit. This Dama wore high-heeled ankle boots, transparent hose, a knee-length *pollera* (flared skirt) with various *centros* (petticoats) underneath, a long-sleeved embroidered blouse, a long silky shawl, and a tall white stovepipe hat. Her mask resembled the face of a light-complexioned white woman, with blue eyes, a medium-sized perfectly shaped nose, and rosy cheeks with a small birthmark on one of them. She had a very discreet smile showing perfect teeth, one of which was gold (fig. 7.2).[19]

The two Maqt'as, often also called Cholos, were dressed very similarly to the way that Indians or peasants are portrayed in folkloric staged presentations. They wore *ojotas* (rubber sandals made of tires worn by peasants to work in the fields) without socks, black knickers made of *bayeta* (coarse wool material), hand-woven colorful wool sashes, long-sleeved

Figure 7.2. The Machu, the leader of the dance, and the Dama character, his wife, dancing on his arm. The Dama usually plays the role of a beautiful, passive adornment to the dance. Cusco City, 1990. (Author's photo)

Figure 7.3. Simulating the arrival of the muleteers in the past, the Maqt'as pull the mules that carry the purported kegs of sugarcane brandy. Cusco City, 1990. (Author's photo)

shirts, bayeta-embroidered vests, colorful *chullos* (hand-knitted hat), and *warak'as* (hand-woven wool whips) tied around their waists and across their chests. While the colors on their masks were not too different from those of the Majeños' masks, the complexion of the Maqt'a face differed greatly. The Maqt'a face exaggerated two main features considered characteristic of the "Indian" phenotype: the hooked nose and the prominent cheekbones. Their noses contrasted with the long, straight, phallic noses of the Majeños. Their faces were smiling but their mouths were smaller than the Majeños' and they did not show any teeth. They did not have any facial hair (fig. 7.3).

The complete ritual performance of the comparsa was designed for the different sequences of the patron-saint festivity. For the initial part of the fiesta, the *entrada* (entrance), every Majeño and the Dama rode a horse and the Maqt'as went on foot, each pulling a mule that carried two big kegs. The Majeños showed their equestrian prowess by swaying from side to side on their horses as if they were dancing while riding (fig. 7.4). The basic dance step used in the dance was a swaying, gentle body movement accompanied by long and firm steps. This kind of movement and steps have been defined by the Majeños as *elegantes*, as we will see below. The Majeño dancer veered his body right and left following the

Figure 7.4. Majeños showing their equestrian prowess by swaying from side to side while riding during the *entrada* (entrance) on the eve of the patron saint festivity. San Jerónimo, Cusco, 1990. (Photo by Fritz Vilasante)

call-and-response structure of the accompanying melody. This march-like melody of the dance is the one locally and regionally known as the characteristic Majeños melody.[20] This dance also includes *wayno* melodies and *marineras*.

Wayno (also *wayño* or *huayno*) is a situationally defined term that "refers to the most ubiquitous mestizo song-dance genre of the highlands as well as to specific musical genres and dances as defined by indigenous communities" (Turino 1993: 293). The basic dance structure of mestizo Cusqueño wayno consists of a *paseo* (slower dance) followed by a *zapateo* (foot-stomping) performed by couples (as opposed to group dancing).[21] Wayno music is "characterized by: duple meter, sung stanzas in Spanish, Quechua or Aymara, or Spanish mixed with an indigenous language" (ibid.).

Various sections of the Majeños dance resembled a very stylized mestizo wayno but without singing. In one section, for example, the two lines of Majeños faced each other and in a coordinated way combined very soft, almost imperceptible stompings, 180-degree body turns in place with a swaying movement, and front and back repeated slow foot movement (about eight times each foot). In another, one line approached the other, with the dancers again almost dragging their feet, until they met. This kind of flattened out movement of the feet is supposed to give an impression of refinement. Their stompings were always very soft and gentle, and they moved in a very slow, controlled motion.

The marinera, another section of the dance, is a genre that originated in the coastal tradition known as *criollo* (therefore coastal mestizo) around the end of the nineteenth century (Romero 1988: 215–64). It is like a mestizo wayno, a couple dance, whose music has typically a 6/8 meter. The two genres, the marinera and the wayno, have been gradually fused by Andeans into various combinations, the most typical of which is now the marinera with wayno *fuga*.

During all the Majeños performances, the Maqt'as played a marginal, servant, or buffoon-like role. They pulled the mules, they cleared the space in the crowd for the performances, and they teased members of the audience to make them laugh. They moved their bodies in a contrasting way to the Majeños: they made quick, sudden, and uncontrolled movements such as jumping up and down, pushing and shoving each other, as well as exaggerating their stomping when performing wayno sections of the dance. Always hunched over in a sign of subservience, the Maqt'as' posture also contrasted with that of the Majeños. In every respect, they marked out differences and acted as foils to Majeños dignity.

THE FIRST MAJEÑOS IN SAN JERÓNIMO:
THE RE-CREATION OF THE CONCEPT OF *DECENCIA*
IN THE EMERGENT MESTIZO IDENTITY

The "invention" and "re-invention" of the Majeños "traditions" in Paucartambo and San Jerónimo should be understood in the context of change and innovation that has taken place in Cusco since the first decades of this century.[22] By the 1920s the Cusco region was undergoing many transformations that accelerated after the 1950 earthquake and developed further in the 1970s. Three interrelated processes had started to affect the whole region: the gradual shift of the axis of the region's economy toward the capital city, the demise of the hacienda system, and the emergence of new socioeconomic sectors linked to the growth of state infrastructure (i.e. roads, schools, and bureaucracy). As explained above, since the 1920s regional traditions have been "invented" and the "folklorization" of dances has been promoted by the *instituciones culturales*.

In the 1940s, a small group of truck-owners/drivers who traded in cattle, in local terms a group of *transportistas-ganaderos*, emerged in the town of San Jerónimo. In an attempt to gain social recognition as a distinct local group, this petit bourgeois sector took a prestigious symbolic element from the main ritual of the town of Paucartambo (with which they had contact through their commercial activity) and introduced it as a local tradition in their own patron-saint festivity. It was a dance that impersonated a particular group of *arrieros* (muleteers) from Majes, a dance that in Paucartambo was only performed by the *hacendados*. This was the Majeños dance, which this group of Jeronimianos considered *decente*. Besides being performed by prestigious members of Paucartambo society (the *hacendados*), the dance was itself an impersonation of another regionally prestigious and economically important group of the near past with which these Jeronimianos identified: the muleteers from Majes.

By the 1920s the *hacendados* of Paucartambo had appropriated the memory of this merchant group that had gained regional recognition. It is difficult to know if the landowners had participated in comparsas before, but by then they had an important presence through the presentation of the Majeños dance.[23] These *hacendados* succeeded in establishing a continuity between their ritual performance and the reconstruction of local history, a characteristic of invented traditions. The landowners were able to blur the line between the memories of what the "actual" muleteers did in the fiesta and what they themselves, through their comparsa, started to re-create when the muleteers did not come anymore.

With nostalgia, the *hacendados* invented the Majeños dance glorifying the memory of these muleteers, choosing an appropriate image of beneficent travelers.

While by the end of the 1940s San Jerónimo had begun to undergo important transformations and a petite bourgeoisie had started to emerge, the *hacendados* still existed as a local elite, the local *decentes*. Local hierarchies were apparent in the patron saint festivity of the town, of which the *decentes* had most of the privileges of sponsorship. One main element, however, differentiated this festivity from the other two important ones in honor of local saints. The patron saint festivity did not have dances. In San Jerónimo, the performance of dances was not a tradition of local *decentes* but rather of those who were largely excluded from the privileged sponsorship roles of the *decentes*. In fact, the performance of dances was excluded from the central festivity of the town.

The leaders of the first group of Majeños in San Jerónimo, the transportistas-ganaderos, told me that they selected the dance from Paucartambo because it was *decente*. Moreover, for their first performance toward the end of the 1940s they chose the arena where the *decentes* of the town had the preeminent place, the patron saint festivity. For the leaders of this first comparsa, the elements that made the dance *decente*, one that only *decentes* performed, were its brass band music, horseback riding, riding clothes (i.e. jodhpurs, boots), wide-brimmed hats, and above all that it was performed by the Paucartambo *decentes*, the *hacendados*, and impersonated prestigious personages of the recent past, the muleteers. These entrepreneurs found a dance whose central symbols were, in and outside ritual, associated with two regionally prestigious male groups, the *hacendados* and the muleteers from Majes. Also, the fact that the dance had as one of its central choreographic elements the consumption of liquor made it even more attractive in the eyes of these Jeronimianos. The Majeños always had a bottle of sugarcane brandy in their hands, and their mules carried this liquor in kegs that they then offered the fiesta participants. Also, their patterned movements simulated drunkenness. This aspect of the dance added an element of masculinity to it because male public behavior was, and continues to be, associated with drinking.

The Majeños dance in Paucartambo, as was the one performed by the first comparsa in San Jerónimo, was much more of a dance-drama than it is today. The fiesta participants were also more directly involved in the performance. The Majeños used to dance and play "with" the fiesta participants, much more than "for" them. Most of the performance replicated the activities and personality of the muleteers as they were remembered. The performers simulated the arrival, the unloading of the mules, and the camaraderie of the muleteers with the townspeople. In this reconstruction, the generosity and the liveliness of these personages were emphasized. This was clearly an idealized impersonation in which these muleteers were presented as local benefactors.

Another central symbolic element of the Majeños dance that made it *decente* in the eyes of the transportistas-ganaderos was the place of origin of the muleteers. This is particularly important because it highlights an element of racism in this construction of local distinctions and identities. As mentioned above, the muleteers were supposed to be from Arequipa. This Peruvian department has been known by Peruvians and social scientists not only as one of the centers of regional economic power throughout the colonial and republican periods, but also as one of the "whitest" and most "aristocratic" centers of the country (Flores Galindo 1977). The phenotypic characteristics associated with "whiteness" are for most Peruvians signs of superiority. Many Peruvian popular jokes refer to Arequipa as a foreign country and to the purported haughtiness of Arequipeños. Being a foreigner in Peru is often a course of social prestige, especially if white features are characteristics of this foreigner.

The appropriation of the Majeños dance (one with *decente* characteristics and impersonated by the *decentes* of Paucartambo) and their ritual performance in the patron saint festivity (one dominated by local *decentes*) was one of the main vehicles for the members of the emerging local petite bourgeoisie to become gradually acknowledged as local *decentes*. Through the ritual metaphoric association of their group with the muleteers and the *hacendados*, the members of this comparsa redefined their local identity as *decentes*. This performance had a particularly strong impact in the town because the patron saint festivity was a privileged arena where local hierarchies were annually re-created and where the former elite groups asserted their predominance. The first Majeños opened a space for performance in this exclusive realm. All this was aided by shifting notions of national identity that fetishized folklore and its artistic performance.

Besides the muleteer/*hacendado*-like costuming and paraphernalia, one feature of the dance that attracted many townspeople was the brass band. Up to that point, all the other comparsas in San Jerónimo were accompanied with instruments such as *pitu* and *tambor*, which were, and continue to be, associated with the indigenous peasantry and which by then had been sanctioned by *instituciones culturales* as "authentic" and characteristic of "Indians."[24] As is still true today, brass band music was a status symbol because it was associated with economic power and European bourgeois and Peruvian urban/coastal culture. It made the dance even more *decente*.

The first Majeños comparsa members initiated the participation of the town's emerging socioeconomic groups in the sponsorship and ritual performance in honor of the patron saint. They took the first and crucial step for the comparsas of San Jerónimo to gain little by little the central sponsorship role that they now have in the main ritual of the town. This pioneering performance has since then awarded the members of this comparsa a preeminent place in local ritual performance.[25] Because of its unprecedented ritual action, this group has been able to obtain a series of privileges within the patron saint festivity and for the Octava (eighth-day celebration) of Corpus Christi that other comparsas have not been able to take away from them. By bringing closer to the majority of the townspeople various privileges previously held by the former elite, the Majeños established supremacy over other local groups.[26]

The Majeños dance seems to have appealed to a new local mestizo identity emerging in the town and in the whole region. This new mestizo identity which idealized elements of the rural past would increasingly incorporate status markers from the emergent regional urban culture. This identity was given form in San Jerónimo by the first members of the Majeños comparsa, converting them into the "new mestizos," the new *decentes* of the town. The elements that the dance introduced in the ritual performance were seen as innovative and as less indigenous than those that characterized old dances.

The members of the first Majeños comparsa had started to perform their dance when they were already middle-aged (most were around forty years old) and economically stable. They were part of an emerging regional social group that was leaving behind an indigenous identity marked by rural life. In San Jerónimo, this group was still small. These transportistas-ganaderos, economic and cultural intermediaries between the rural and the urban Cusco poles, took the lead in the exploration of new local identities. They gave local form to powerful symbols that they appropriated from former elites and that they re-created through ritual performance in their town. Nevertheless, when in the mid 1950s new Majeños performers were needed, there were not many other townspeople from the same social group who could take their post. It remains unclear why other townspeople did not continue the performance. But the fact that only the relatives of the old Majeños and other successful transportistas could in the 1970s re-create the dance reveals that already in the 1950s this dance was seen as exclusive of a new local elite. The disappearance of the San Jerónimo comparsa and that of Paucartambo around the same time coincided with the demise of the hacienda system in the region and with the *hacendados'* new focus of interest in the emerging areas of economic investment in the city of Cusco.

THE "MODERN" MAJEÑOS IN SAN JERÓNIMO

In both Paucartambo and San Jerónimo, the Majeños tradition was "reinvented" after the mid 1970s by members of the growing regional petite bourgeoisie (i.e. merchants, transportistas, state employees), a sector that greatly expanded in Cusco from the 1950s on.[27] As mentioned above, many ongoing transformations of the region had been accelerated during the period of reconstruction of Cusco city and the promotion of the regional economy following the 1950 earthquake. Migration to Cusco city and the new areas of colonization in the jungle (within the department), peasant pressure over hacienda lands, pauperization of the countryside, and peasant syndicalization increased during this period. Also between the 1950s and the 1970s, the new character of the city of Cusco as a tourist resort and as the new axis of the economy crystalized, enhancing the performative spaces for enacting local identities before an audience.

The agrarian reform carried out during General Velasco's government (1968–75) marked the end of the hacienda system in the region, symbolically underscoring the end of the domination of the landowning elite over the peasant majority.[28] During Velasco's regime, the growth of the state bureaucracy and public education, the development of new areas of commerce, and the increase in public and private transportation enlarged the middle class in Cusco. The number of petty merchants, schoolteachers, bureaucrats, and transportistas increased greatly during this period in other provinces and districts outside Cusco city. By the mid 1970s, the private and state promotion of "folklore" had become widespread in the region. The state had taken a particular interest, sponsoring local, regional, and national "folkloric" contests and festivals. The schools had also become a channel through which "folklore" was taught as a way to construct national identity. In this context, the preoccupation of the state and private *instituciones culturales* with the construction of regional and national identity merged with those of the emergent social groups in the towns of San Jerónimo and Paucartambo, concerned with the redefinition of their own local and regional identity. Fusing the memories about an idealized group that had already been gone for some time (the muleteers from Majes) with that of another prestigious sector that was waning at the time (the *hacendados*) allowed the two new groups of Majeños to re-create their local identity.

In San Jerónimo, the reinvention of the Majeños tradition by a group of transportistas displayed a continuity in the social sector that originally performed the dance in the town. This new group of wealthy truck owners, however, stood out from other transportistas and from the rest of the townspeople not only in economic terms but also in social, cultural, and symbolic terms. They were all members of well-known San Jerónimo families, they had high-school educations, they spoke fluent Spanish, and they were relatives or close friends of the members of the town's first Majeños comparsa.[29] By the end of the 1970s, the transportistas of San Jerónimo had sponsored on many occasions the local patron saint festivity, and some of them had formed comparsas. Other local fiestas that used to have dances waned during this period, and the patron saint festivity became the focus of comparsa performance. In this context, in 1978, the relatives and close friends of the old Majeños, surely encouraged by their identification with the dance and the memory of the successful performance of their predecessors, decided to re-create the local Majeños.

As mentioned, since its re-creation the new Majeños comparsa tended to include Jeronimianos who stood out at various levels. For example, all the transportistas who formed the first group were owners of motor vehicles (truck, bus, or automobile). This comparsa became known from that time on as that of *dueños de carro* (vehicle owners), one of the distinctive features of its leaders. This has continued despite the fact that subsequently, as explained below, this group started to incorporate the town's professionals. When this comparsa was officially made into a "Folkloric Association" in the 1980s, it became clear that this organization had become for these Jeronimianos one of the main channels toward constituting themselves as a distinct local class, a new elite.

The new group of Majeños identified with the dance because, as they said, "it was in them" *(les nacía)*. This expression "it's in me" *(me nace*, literally "born in me") was often used by members of other comparsas in Cusco to explain why they identified with the dance they performed. In the case of the Majeños, however, this identification was often explained as if "they had it in their blood," as if they had inherited it as a privilege from their relatives. Two of the wealthiest and most powerful members within the new comparsa are children of one of the leaders of the first comparsa of the 1940s. The members of this new comparsa have contin-ued to feel since the reinvention that this dance is the one that goes best with their personalities and that of Saint Jerome, their patron saint, be-cause it is *decente*. According to the re-creators of the Majeños in San Jerónimo, none of the dances that had begun to be performed by other transportistas was adequate or *decente* enough to honor their patron saint.[30]

When the new group of Majeños re-created the dance, they wanted to do it *a la moderna* (the modern way). This statement had various im-plications. First, it meant to implement a "choreography." The incorpo-ration of this requisite for the Majeños dance may be seen as a result of the development of the models of folklore and regional traditions in Cusco. This new comparsa re-created many of the old features of the former, such as the simulation of the arrival of the *arrieros* and the offer of liquor to the townspeople. However, two other aspects of "modernity" were very important for the San Jerónimo comparsa. First, Jeronimianos introduced new symbols of mestizo power and prestige, several of which represented urban culture. Two elements were particularly important: the introduction of bottled beer as one of the central symbols of the dance and the innovation of the costumes.

The second aspect of modernity for the new comparsa members was to develop a long-lasting, strictly organized institution which would allow them to establish a continuity between their ritual performance and their social life outside of ritual: the Asociación De Comparsa Los Majeños. Although it took them approximately five years to consolidate the Asociación, this institution has become an essential mechanism to maintain the power and social prestige that the comparsa has gained in the town. At the same time that the Asociación serves to control tightly the group membership, it gives them respectability because it is the only officially acknowledged "folkloric" institution of the town.[31]

The Performance of an "Elegant" Style

Since the invention of the Majeños tradition, alcoholic beverages have been one of the central symbols of the dance. By metonymic association, this element had made the Majeños an even more masculine dance. Be-sides carrying mules loaded with *aguardiente* (sugarcane brandy), the members of the original comparsas in Paucartambo and San Jerónimo also carried a bottle filled with this liquor in their hands. Aguardiente was the liquor that the muleteers from Majes sold. Nevertheless, the

Majeños of San Jerónimo decided to replace it with bottled beer. Aguardiente was not, according to them, an alcoholic beverage characteristic of *caballeros* (gentlemen). Instead, it was a liquor commonly consumed among peasants, for example during agricultural work. Bottled beer, an expensive industrial product originally from urban Cusco, as opposed to aguardiente or *chicha* (corn beer, another drink associated with rural culture that is produced locally), had already become the most expensive and prestigious drink consumed in private and public celebrations in Cusco towns. In San Jerónimo, both the bottle and the beer itself have become important in the performance of the dance. One of the most garish and awaited parts of the Majeños choreography in this town was the *jaleo*.

In the jaleo, the two lines that form the basic structure of the dance form a circle. While turning clockwise and counterclockwise, they spray the beer upward and outward, in a coordinated way, giving the impression of an erupting geyser.[32] The body movement of the Majeños while performing the jaleo is controlled and slow, as they shift their bodies from one place to another by dragging or sliding their feet on the floor, barely lifting them. In that section of the dance, unique to the performance in San Jerónimo, the Majeños make a show of their ability to manipulate the bottle of beer.[33] During my research, most of the fiesta participants and the Majeños were aware that the jaleo was a controversial part of the dance because it could be taken as proof of both the aggressiveness and the haughtiness of the Majeños. In their organizational meetings before their performances, the ambivalence of the Majeños toward the jaleo became evident. While they were all aware that the spraying of the beer could make some people uncomfortable or angry, they were also aware that it would earn them the attention of most townspeople.

The attitudes of the other fiesta participants about the jaleo are equally ambivalent. While they often criticized the Majeños for splashing beer all over people, they enjoyed this part of the performance and admired the ability of the Majeños. Whatever the reaction of the crowd about the jaleo, it became clear during all the public and private performances of the Majeños that bottled beer had become a central symbol of their economic power and their masculine abilities.

As mentioned above, since the re-creation of the dance, the new Majeños in San Jerónimo have also emphasized the innovation of the costume. Three central prototypic figures of prestigious males have had a central role: the *hacendado*, the urban male, and the Image of their patron saint. All three have served as the source of inspiration to re-create the old and to introduce the new elements of the Majeños costume, and, in general, the meanings of the dance. Here I only analyze the first two. The Majeños of San Jerónimo called their dance *tipo hacendado* (*hacendado*-like) when they referred to their costumes. They wanted to impersonate the *hacendados* but *a la moderna*, meaning that their costumes should make them look like contemporary prestigious mestizos. Therefore, they had to display some markers to make them appear elegant according to contemporary urban culture.

The former Majeños dancers had worn wool ponchos, which the new Majeños replaced with hip-length leather jackets. In their different qualities and shapes, ponchos have been worn in the Andes by peasants, urban people, and *hacendados*. Gradually, however, because of its association with highland and rural culture, the poncho had nationally become a marker of Indianness and a symbolic icon associated with the peasantry (i.e., it had started to be used as a symbol for political and folkloric events organized by the state). A leather jacket, on the other hand, was an expensive piece of clothing not commonly worn by peasants. It was seen by the Majeños as a sign of elegance because it was distinctive of urban people. Leather, itself a non-indigenous material (cattle were originally European), was also seen as characteristic of the clothing of Arequipeños (considered in regional dominant ideology as the "whites" and "aristocrats" of the southern Andes). Jeronimianos said that replacing the wool poncho with the leather jacket would make the dance even more historically accurate because what the muleteers "actually" wore were leather jackets. They said they had also seen that the local *hacendados* used to wear leather jackets. Whether or not the muleteers from Arequipa or the *hacendados* "actually" wore leather jackets (which is likely), this piece of clothing had ethnic/racial and class connotations of which the new Majeños were very aware. Even for the contemporary comparsa members, the hip-length high-quality leather jacket necessary to perform the dance is expensive and difficult to find. It is definitely one of the most precious pieces of the costume.

San Jerónimo Majeños have also innovated their costumes by introducing elements of urban culture that would make them look like "elegant" mestizos outside of ritual. But these new markers of social status and "modernity" introduced by the Majeños of San Jerónimo, as part of an elaborated ritual costume, took a more exaggerated form. For example, they have been changing the colors, the patterns, and the materials of their jodhpurs and shirts. During my research their jodhpurs were not made of natural-color wool as were those worn by their predecessors and the Paucartambo comparsa. Instead, they were made of bright mustard-color, expensive corduroy.[34] Their shirts, also different from the plain white cotton shirts worn by the Paucartambo comparsa, were made of shiny, colorful, patterned polyester.

The Majeños of San Jerónimo have also modified some of the characteristics of the hat. The hat that had been worn before was a wide-brimmed straw hat still worn today in Paucartambo. Nevertheless, in San Jerónimo the brim has been extended to the point of making the hat look like those of the Mexican charros. From the beginning, the wide-brimmed hat has been seen as a sign of elegance. For those who first brought the dance to the town, it made the dance *decente* and *elegante* because this kind of hat was distinctive of *hacendados* and in general urban mestizos. For the re-creators of the dance in the town, the exaggeration of the brim made the hat even more elegant and masculine. Thus, to make the hat resemble the hat of the Mexican charro made the dance a more elegant and masculine one.[35]

In order to incorporate a new member into the comparsa, the Majeños verify the ability of the dancer to keep a correct posture and to make what they considered "elegant movements," both essential to performing the dance. Always keeping a very upright posture, with an air of haughtiness, the dancer has to be able to take long, firm steps while swaying his body in an very unhurried, controlled, almost stiff manner. This kind of body control is another element that differentiated the performance of San Jerónimo Majeños from that of Paucartambinos. From the beginning, Paucartambo dancers have staggered and emulated drunkenness with their dance. This imitation of intoxication through body movement was eliminated by the Jeronimianos because, according to their codes of *conducta etólica* explained below, it took away the air of superiority and seigneurialty that they wanted to give to the dance.[36]

The Majeños believed that their gentle, unhurried, and controlled movements distinguished them from the characteristic peasant ways of dancing. While performing the wayno melodies, for example, they minimized the zapateo. In the most widespread traditional peasant/indigenous style of performing the wayno, as portrayed in the regional repertoire of "authentic" folklore, the zapateo consists of very quick foot movement, raising the feet high (one at a time) and letting them stomp very heavily on the ground. When the Majeños performed the zapateo, they barely lifted their feet from the ground and put them down very softly in a slow motion. In the rehearsals, the older members of the comparsa corrected the new dancers when they stomped too hard or made quick and jumpy movements. They taught them how to control their bodies to make slow, swaying movements and take gentle steps. They taught them how to move from one position to the other almost dragging their feet. The new dancers were not the only ones corrected. Other comparsa members who were caught making the wrong movements were sometimes criticized by being told that they were dancing like "cholos." Following their Indian/cholo identity, the Maqt'as exaggerated the indigenous-style wayno, making funny jumps and shaking their bodies and buttocks.[37]

An upright posture and an air of arrogance are both very important elements that the Majeños emphasized during their performances. This posture and attitude differentiated them from the Maqt'as, their servants, who were always portrayed hunched over as a sign of subservience. The Majeños' arrogance and haughtiness is highlighted by several elements during their performance of the dance. One, already mentioned, is showing their control of the bottled beer during the jaleo, always holding this symbol of economic power in their hands. Another is that while dancing, they pushed back their jackets and put one hand at the waist, imitating a male posture of defiance. Most of the time during the performance of the dance, the Majeños keep making a particular body movement. They turn to one side and stop briefly before turning to the other. While doing this they raise the opposite arm holding the bottle of beer, and when they stop the bottle is held with the arm straight up. At the same time, they put their opposite hands on their waists and push back their jackets. While the dancers bent their bodies slightly as they turned, they constantly tried to keep a very upright posture. The swagger in all these gestures gave the dance a distinct air of arrogance.

THE IDEAL *MAJEÑO* OF SAN JERÓNIMO

San Jerónimo Majeños considered their comparsa exemplary not only in the matter of local "folklore" but also in terms of local *decencia* and urbanity. The members of this comparsa were always very careful to guard their public image not only during the ritual and other group public performances but also during their everyday lives. They considered themselves members of an exclusive "family," a closed elite that had to set an example for the rest of the town. They were obliged to help and support each other in any case of need. Each member was made responsible for behaving according to their institutional rules, as a respectable, proper social being who would not dishonor the name of the institution. This responsible behavior in all circumstances was one of the main criteria given by the members of the comparsa when asked about their strict process of selection of new comparsa members. Each new member had to be carefully chosen, tested, and endorsed by two senior members of the comparsa. These two members had to ensure that the candidate fit the characteristics of the "ideal" Majeño in and outside ritual performance.[38]

An important characteristic of the Majeño performer (not of the Maqt'a) necessary to become part of the comparsa was that he had to prove a very secure economic base—a good income—that would allow him to cover all the expenses required not only for the ritual performances but also for all the social activities held by the comparsa throughout the year. The Majeño had to be able to afford the expensive costume, the large amounts of beer drunk during the dance performances, the quotas for hiring the brass band, and, when his turn arrived, a sumptuous *cargo* (sponsorship role).

As mentioned, several of the re-creators of the comparsa were prosperous truck owners. By that year, 1978, although the group of Jeronimianos whose main economic activity was transportation (bus, automobile, pickup, or truck owners or drivers) had grown, owners of motor vehicles continued to be an economic elite within the town. The most prosperous of them had been able to combine this activity with other wholesale and retail commerce (i.e. commerce with lumber and hardware stores). Like the first group of Majeños in the town, transportista members of the comparsa today see themselves as having the same role as that of the old muleteers. They say that owning the means of transportation, working in commerce, and being wealthy make them counterparts of the muleteers. Their control over space through constant movement between commercial points and in general their key role as intermediaries between the city and the countryside, as well as between the jungle, the highlands, and the coast, give them a privileged role in the society. Like the muleteers, they are intermediaries in economic as well as cultural affairs. In a conversation I had with two Majeños transportistas, they referred to the pickup truck in which we were riding as "the horse."

After the first few initial years, the comparsa started to incorporate members of a new emerging elite in the town, the professionals, a sector that in San Jerónimo continues to be very small.[39] As mentioned above, despite the incorporation of these professionals and other successful employees of state or private institutions, the comparsa continues to be known as that of the *dueños de carro*. Another main criterion for admission into the Majeños was membership in a "traditional" San Jerónimo family (families who have resided in the town for several generations). This criterion has become central in the context of a strong migration into the district of people mainly from other provinces of the department and in some cases from other departments.[40] During my research, the few non-Jeronimianos who were members of the comparsa were close relatives of one of the local families (i.e., one was married to a Jeronimiana and another was the cousin of a senior member). Kinship played an important role in membership. Among the members of the comparsa there were sets of brothers, cousins, and some in-laws. Also, as mentioned above, two of the main current leaders are sons of one of the founders of the comparsa in the 1940s.

Another important characteristic of the ideal Majeño was showing the capacity to behave like a *patrón* or *jefe* (master or boss) in all given situations. A Majeño, in and outside ritual performance, had to maintain an authoritarian but at the same time patronizing posture. During ritual preparations and performances, and with respect to other comparsas and local authorities, the members of this comparsa often took a condescending attitude. With a paternalistic stance, they have designated themselves the defenders of "traditional" San Jerónimo and Cusqueño folklore, drastically opposing the introduction of "Altiplano" dances by the comparsas of young Jeronimianos. These dances are originally from the Altiplano region (Puno-Bolivia) and two of them were performed for the patron saint festivity by the two comparsas formed by the younger generation.[41]

The authoritarian attitude of the Majeños was often criticized by other comparsas, local authorities, and townspeople. Nevertheless, most of the privileges that they have obtained in the main rituals of the town have been conceded to them because of the local recognition they have gained through their organization. This comparsa is clearly the most organized, strict, and therefore respected of the town. Their ability to construct and maintain a solid *Asociación* is acknowledged as proof of their economic, social, and cultural resources that convert them into a local elite. Their *Asociación* has clearly consolidated the local power of the Majeños as the main comparsa of San Jerónimo.

Within the dance performance and as part of their patronizing attitude, the Majeños show an institutionalized generosity by offering *cambray* (a sweet, wine-like liquor made of sugarcane) to the fiesta participants.[42] On the main day of the patron saint festival, the Majeños go to the main plaza of the town carrying huge bottles filled with cambray, and after performing part of their choreography, they offer it to those who watch their performance. With this act, they reconstruct the idealized memories of the muleteers and at the same time show their fellow towns-people that they, the contemporary Majeños, also know how to share their wealth. The invitation of the cambray was not a simple "represen-tation" or "emulation" of what the muleteers did. It was an act that clearly showed that, thanks to their comfortable economic situation, the mem-bers of this comparsa could afford to put on this kind of expensive per-formance. In other words, by means of iconic symbolism and metaphoric comparison the members of the Majeños comparsa became, through rit-ual performance, a local beneficent elite.

During the four days of the fiesta, the Majeños performed a series of condescending public acts to establish their superiority and chivalry, in their own terms their *caballerosidad* (gentility). The main target of these performances was the other comparsa of adult men in the town, the one that has also become a "traditional" San Jerónimo comparsa, the Qollas. This comparsa (composed mostly of truck drivers and butchers), through its carnivalesque and grotesque dance performance, emphasized many of the opposite characteristics of the Majeños comparsa, eschewing char-acteristics such as *elegante, decente,* and *caballero.* Every time these two comparsas crossed paths during ritual performance, they teased each other. The Qollas called the Majeños "*patrón*" and "*hacendado,*" and the Majeños called the Qollas derogatory names such as "cholo," "servant," or "Indian." During the ritual, these comparsas treated each other as ab-solutely opposite social and ethnic/racial "others."[43]

There were several moments in which the Majeños tried to show the Qollas and the whole town that they were "*caballeros*" and that they were able to share with another group that was not as wealthy or powerful as they. In these opportunities, the tension between the groups was evi-dent, particularly on the side of the Qollas, who were bothered by the Majeños' condescending and authoritarian attitudes during the fiesta.

The asymmetrical relationship and the contrasting characteristics between a master/*hacendado* and an indigenous servant/peon is also man-ifested within the Majeños dance through the relationship Majeño–Maqt'a and in particular Machu–Maqt'a. As pointed out in the de-scription of the dance, the masks, costumes, and postures (white facial features/indigenous facial features, expensive urban clothing/cheap handmade or coarse peasant clothing, upright, arrogant posture/hunched-over, subservient attitude) emphasized the ethnic differences between the Majeño and the Maqt'a. During the *entrada* in the patron saint festivity and on the way back from the city of Cusco in the Octava, the Maqt'as were in charge of loading, unloading, and pulling the mules, while the Majeños purportedly carried the aguardiente (fig. 7.3). The

Maqt'as also cleared the way for the Majeños to ride their horses, to march along the streets, and to perform their choreography in the plaza. The Maqt'as did not ride horses or form part of the coordinated group movement. Most of the time they remained marginal, either clearing the way or marking the borders during the performance of the choreography (sometimes going inside the figure made but most of the time keeping out). They also often acted like buffoons, making the public laugh while always keeping a marginal position within the performance.

The Maqt'a personage should be analyzed in a wider regional context. Many dances all over the Andes, and certainly most Cusqueño dances today, have Maqt'as or personages with aspects or functions similar to those of the Maqt'a in the Majeños (among the more peasant-like dances are the Ukukus). These characters usually play the role of figures who are at the borderline between domesticated and undomesticated and who at the same time have humorous and subversive features. In Peru, there are entire comparsas with these characteristics. Among them is the Qollas in Cusco, briefly explained above, and the Avelinos which I have analyzed elsewhere (Mendoza 1989).

Within the Majeños comparsa, the Maqt'as' performance emphasized the domesticated, harmless, funny, and servant-like side of this personage. The Maqt'as are also often called "cholos" by the Majeños. As mentioned, this national ethnic/racial term has been conflated in the Majeños performance with that of "Indian." While through their clothes, masks, and postures the Maqt'as are portrayed as the prototypic "Indian-peasant" of folkloric presentations and school textbooks, because of their subordinate relationship with a *decente* personage they are called "cholos." As explained, "cholo" has become a pejorative ethnic/racial term that implies low social status and cultural incompleteness (in Peruvian dominant ideology, incomplete assimilation to urban coastal culture). The Majeños often called the Maqt'as "cholos" when giving them orders. When Majeños described the role of the Maqt'as within the dance they often said, "They are our servants, our cholos."[44]

While Maqt'as or Maqt'a-like personages in other dances of the region harassed the main leader of the dance (the Machu or Caporal), pinching, punching, and attempting to outsmart him, Maqt'as in the Majeños comparsa minimized this role. Most of the slapstick play that took place to make people laugh was between the two Maqt'as and not between the Maqt'a and the Machu. Although some playful harassment took place, the respect that the Maqt'a owed to the Machu was emphasized. The attempt to minimize the grotesque and subversive characteristics of this personage was evident during their rehearsals, in which the Maqt'a performers were advised to be funny but not disrespectful.

In ritual performance and during the year, the members of the Majeños comparsa tried to exercise and talk about their power over other social and ethnic/racial sectors of society, including women. During their institutional meetings (once a month and, during the months of the central performances, two or three times a week) and informal ones (i.e. a private party or a conversation in a bar), the Majeños often recounted situations in which they were able to exercise their superiority using their economic power or their connections. In these meetings, the more powerful position of some members over others was also exercised. This was more clearly done with the members who impersonated the Maqt'as. They were ordered around, sent to do the hard work and to serve the rest (i.e., they carried the cases of beer and served the food and drinks). They were considered second-class members of the comparsa and treated like servants. The Maqt'as of San Jerónimo admitted that for them it was difficult to be "promoted" to become a Majeño because they lacked the qualities required to perform in that role within the dance and in the *Asociación*.

The Majeños' configuration of gender distinction, within and outside the dance, may also be understood as part of their attitude as "everyone's masters." In their private meetings, the Majeños often commented about the importance of being "the man of the house" *(el hombre de la casa)*— the boss—and of remaining independent of their wives. They made fun of members (absent or present) who had appeared to be in any way under the dominance of their wives. While these women were included in a few of the activities of the comparsa, mostly to be in charge of the food and to attend to the guests, they were excluded from association meetings, rehearsals, and decisions. During my research the only woman who participated in the performance of the dance, the Dama, was also excluded from those realms. She only participated in a couple of rehearsals.

According to the Majeños, the Dama dancer did not need to practice much. She only had to follow the movements of the Machu. Obviously, her role within the dance, as in the *Asociación*, was very passive. The Majeños said that her main task was to dress like an elegant mestiza and to behave and dance like a "dama" (a respectable lady), as the name of her dance role implied. What that meant was, first, that she was never free from her husband (she was supposed to be the Machu's wife): the Machu always took her by the arm and all she had to do was follow him and be gracious. Second, it meant that, as a *patrona*, the wife of the *patrón*, she was always protected and served by the Maqt'as, her servants. She acted most of the time like a beautiful, passive adornment to the dance. Her status as an elite woman, the wife of the Majeño, was bolstered by the leisure she incarnated. Her dependent, passive role in relation to the Machu, and the effortless personality shown by the way she was served by the Maqt'as, made the Dama, like the Majeño, a very idealized personage compared to the vast majority of women in San Jerónimo.

The members of the San Jerónimo Majeños have condensed many symbols of masculinity in their dance. A particularly graphic one was the most salient feature of their masks: their long, straight, phallic noses. The regionally known artist who makes most of the masks for the Majeños of both San Jerónimo and Paucartambo has explained the particular intentionality of this feature for Jeronimianos.[45] He recalled that the dancers of San Jerónimo always demanded that he make their noses particularly long and phallic, like that characteristic of the Machu personage appearing in various dances from the region. This nose style then became the "San Jerónimo style," according to the artist, together with the long, drooping horsehair mustaches. While the *Caporal* of Paucartambo had a mask similar to that of the San Jerónimo Majeños, the rest of the dancers in Paucartambo had smaller noses, not as phallic, and their facial hair (shorter mustaches and some goatee beards) was drawn on the mask itself. A regular-shaped big nose, together with facial hair, rosy cheeks, and light eyes were considered in Paucartambo characteristics of the "white" *arrieros* and *hacendados*. In both Paucartambo and San Jerónimo, it was obvious that in the elaboration of the masks for the dance, the purported "white" phenotypic characteristics of both the people from Arequipa and the local *hacendados* were emphasized.

In the case of the Machu (sometimes called *Caporal*) personage of Cusqueño dances, the long, phallic nose clearly symbolized his status as the oldest, most fully accomplished male of the dance group. The underlying concept was that, as a man gets older, he becomes more accomplished socially, economically, and sexually. In other words, the Machu nose was a central symbol of the maturity of this personage, a symbol that emphasized the sexual connotations of his fully realized social features. The Majeños of San Jerónimo appropriated this particular symbol, making their own performance of the dance a more condensed symbol of masculinity. This symbol reasserted their sexual and social superiority.

The reference to their long noses as phallic representations was made overt by the Majeños of San Jerónimo on many occasions. They joked among themselves about their different sizes. During the fiesta they approached women, trying to scare them with their noses or asking them while touching their long noses, "Do you like it?" One of the characteristics of the nose is that it had a big, lumpy birthmark almost at the end. Once a Majeño said to me while pointing to the birthmark, "This is what gets in the way," an obvious sexual allusion.[46] Long noses represent "symbols of the whole proud ethos of the males" in ritual performance in other areas as well (Bateson 1958: 164). In the case of the Majeños, the exaggeration of this particular male feature may be seen as an effort to highlight, through ritual play, their reproductive capabilities. These capabilities, by means of metonym and synecdoche, are made symbolic of the Majeños' social superiority.

Another important characteristic of the ideal Majeños comparsa member was that he should be tall. Height is seen in Cusco and Peru as one of the desirable characteristics of Europeans and North Americans, or people of that descent. According to local views, the characteristics that marked the "whiteness" of *hacendados* was their height and their physical strength. As recreated in local imagery, the prototype of *hacendado* or *patrón* was that of a tall, strong male. On the other hand, the prototypic Indian or servant was small and weak. This was obviously impersonated in the dance by the Maqt'a.

In San Jerónimo, height as a marker of ethnic/racial superiority has taken a particular symbolic dimension through the Majeños comparsa. During my research it was not only that a tall dancer was aesthetically preferred to a short one but that, since the *Asociación* became officially institutionalized, to be tall has become a prerequisite for entering the comparsa. As the president of the *Asociación* explained, all the members who have been incorporated into the comparsa in the last few years are tall. The short dancers in the group were those who had reinitiated the dance (at that time the requirement had not been strictly enforced) or the ones who performed as Maqt'as. The two Maqt'as were noticeably shorter than the average Majeño. The Maqt'a performers mentioned their height as one of the main reasons why it was almost impossible to be "promoted" to perform the Majeño personage.

The height of the Majeños performer was also one of the main criteria for determining his position in the two-line structure of the dance. This criterion was supposed to be combined with that of seniority. Therefore, the senior members were supposed to have been able to attain a closer position to the front as the years passed. Nevertheless, at the time of structuring the lines, height was the aspect most emphasized. There were some senior members who, because they were short, remained in a position almost at the end of the line. To put the tallest dancers in front was a deliberate strategy to give the visual impression that they were all tall, a strategy that worked. Jeronimianos often commented that the Majeños were all *grandazos, altotes* (huge, tall). This aesthetic element, based on the purported superiority of the white male, is zealously guarded by the *Asociación*.

Another comment that San Jerónimo townspeople repeated about the physical aspect of the Majeños was that they had huge bellies because they drank too much beer. This was another characteristic that, through ritual performance, associated the muleteer, the *hacendado*, and the Majeños comparsa member: the three were purportedly heavy drinkers. This characteristic highlighted both the socioeconomic superiority of the group (their capacity to consume) and their masculinity. Drinking is associated with male public behavior. Nevertheless, in San Jerónimo the *Asociación* has tried to regulate this potentially disruptive element, demanding that its members display in and outside ritual a good *conducta etílica* (behavior under the influence of alcohol).

While drinking, the Majeños had to be careful not to make public disturbances, get into fights, or pass out, commonplace behavior in San Jerónimo, particularly during the fiesta. The Majeños considered these acts to be indicative of bad taste and characteristic of indigenous people. Their good behavior while drinking had to be displayed during the days of the fiesta and particularly while wearing their costumes. While they were having their public banquets in the plaza or other public gatherings that involved drinking, they were not allowed to break away from the group and drink with other friends. They were all controlled by their comparsa fellows.[47] When they went to their private gathering places they were able to drink more and relax, although many of them were later sanctioned and criticized if they had gone beyond the acceptable behavior. The *conducta etílica* of a potential member of the comparsa is always carefully tested and observed before he is officially accepted among the Majeños.

Not all the members of the Majeños comparsa had equal wealth, family connections, authoritarian and patronizing attitude, physical characteristics, *conducta etílica*, or dancing skills. Nevertheless, there were some ideal attributes that these performers consciously guarded, highlighted, or tried to attain if they did not have them. Some of the comparsa members were in fact considered by the rest of the group as incarnations of all these ideal qualities. These particular Majeños tended to have more power over the other members and became leaders of the comparsa, imposing their views on organizational and performative aspects of the comparsa. All the Majeños, however, were, for the rest of the townspeople, members of a powerful, prestigious, and closed male elite in the town.

With the example of the Majeños comparsa, I have shown how, through ritual performance, Jeronimianos have been able to give shape to local distinctions and identities. The Majeños have redefined and given local meaning to central categories such as *decencia* and *elegancia*, drawing on regional and national ethnic/racial, class, and gender distinctions. They have done this by reinventing a dance based on the idealized memory of the muleteers from Majes and the *hacendados* and associating it with an emergent regional mestizo identity. Through ritual performance, in other words through the Majeños dance performance in the fiestas, Jeronimianos have experienced physically and conceptually the redefinition and negotiation of local identities around the categories of *decencia* and *elegancia*. These two categories, which the Majeños performers have re-created and appropriated, have strongly drawn on and given local reinterpretation to the reality of "whiteness" in contrast to that of the "Indianness" and "cholo-ness."

In San Jerónimo, the successful performance as well as the strict and organized *Asociación* have enabled the Majeños to become a distinct local elite, a group of "new mestizos." This mestizo identity has meant leaving behind an indigenous/rural identity and acquiring a more advantageous position in local and regional class relations. The Majeños have accomplished their superior local status not only through ritual performance but also through group and individual behavior outside ritual. Establishing a connection between the features of the Majeños characters impersonated and those of the performer outside ritual facilitated the process by which through metaphoric ritual performance the comparsa members could become their own alias outside ritual as well. That is, the comparsa members became acknowledged as local *decente* and *elegante* males. Their performance of the dance in the ritual is what actually makes these principles or values, *decencia* and *elegancia*, visible and tangible (masks with white features, horse-riding, bodily stiffness, swaying movements, bottled beer, brass band music, among other features), making them real and part of the performers' personality.

NOTES

I would like to thank Philip Bohlman, Bernard Cohn, Jean Comaroff, and James Fernandez for their insightful comments and constant support for this and other projects. I would also like to acknowledge Charles Walker for his editorial guidance. This chapter derives from my doctoral dissertation, which focuses on the study of comparsas (Mendoza-Walker 1993a). The research for the dissertation was carried out in 1989 and 1990 with support from a Fulbright-Hays fellowship. Research during the summers of 1991, 1993, and 1995 has supplemented the information presented here.

1. Although this kind of dance performance has been a central component of Andean Catholic ritual since the sixteenth century, this performative aspect of Andean ritual has been insufficiently studied. Of the studies that exist about contemporary comparsas, none has made the dance associations its focus of interest (Salomon 1981; van Kessel 1981; Poole 1990, 1991). Some historical data suggests that during Spanish colonialism in the Andes (1532–1821) the dances performed in Catholic festivals became an arena of confrontation and negotiation of symbolic practices and identity (Poole 1990, Ares 1984, Abercrombie 1992). The Andean people consider "saints" to be not only the martyrs or other salient personages of Christian history canonized by the Catholic Church, but also different representations of Jesus Christ and the Virgin Mary (Marzal 1977).

2. As Erlmann has argued, "Performance assumes a key role in the dialectic between structure, as the givenness of the world, and practice. [Practice understood as] more than the mere reproduction of unspoken, unexamined commonsense ways . . . involves the need and requires the power to make one's own meaning" (1992: 691).

3. Peru is divided into twenty-four departments. Each department has a number of provinces, and every province is organized into districts. As is the case of most of the literature dealing with Cusco, I refer to "Cusco region" as a synonym for the department of Cusco unless I indicate otherwise. This highland department, the third largest of Peru, is located in the southeastern section of the country.

4. San Jerónimo is a district of the province of Cusco located twelve kilometers southeast of the capital city on the main paved commercial road and railroad line connecting Cusco with the other major trade centers of the southern Peruvian Andes. The town of San Jerónimo, the site of my intensive field research, is the capital of the district and home to about 8,000 people.

5. The tendency of these two disciplines to study the "other," the one who is the least "western," the most "different," played an important role in this tendency. As I explain below "mestizo" is by definition "mixed."

6. For Bourdieu, "constructed classes" or "theoretical classes" may be characterized as "sets of agents who, by virtue of the fact that they occupy similar positions in social space (that is the distribution of powers), are subject to similar conditions of existence and conditioning factors and, as a result, are endowed with similar dispositions which prompt them to develop similar practices" (1987: 6).

7. The land-owning class in Cusco had grown since the end of the nineteenth century. The members of this social group, who developed innovative cultural and economic mechanisms to consolidate their local power, had expanded their estates, usually at the expense of the local peasantry (Poole 1988).

During this period, although a variety of labor relations existed on the states, the notion of a clear division between the powerful *hacendado* and the subservient peasant developed.

8. To define the concepts of ideology and hegemony I have drawn on Comaroff and Comaroff's (1991) use of the concepts and their discussion of the relationship between the two. Quoting Raymond Williams, they use the term "ideology" "to describe 'an articulated system of meanings, values, and beliefs of a kind that can be abstracted as [the] "world view"' of any social grouping. . . . This worldview may be more or less internally systematic, more or less assertively coherent in its outward form. . . . The regnant ideology of any period or place will be that of the dominant group. And while the nature and degree of its pre-eminence may vary a good deal, it is likely to be protected, even enforced, to the full extent of the power of those who claim it for their own" (1991: 24). Drawing on Gramsci's notion of hegemony and Bourdieu's development of it, Comaroff and Comaroff define it as "that order of signs and practices, relations and distinctions, images and epistemologies—drawn from a historically situated cultural field—that come to be taken-for-granted as the natural and received shape of the world and everything that inhabits it. It consists, to paraphrase Bourdieu . . . of things that go without saying because, being axiomatic, they come without saying; things that, being presumptively shared, are not normally the subject of explication or argument" (23). Comaroff and Comaroff suggest that hegemony "exists in reciprocal interdependence with ideology: it is that part of a dominant worldview which has been naturalized and, having hidden itself in orthodoxy, no more appears as ideology at all. . . . The hegemonic proportion of any dominant ideology may be greater or lesser. It will never be total" (25).

9. Because of the long history of subordination and violence to which the population defined as "Indian" has been subject, this category has taken on pejorative meanings indicating inferiority in regional and national hierarchies.

10. The use of Quechua, the indigenous language, or a Quechua accent, are clear indicators of Indian identity. Illiteracy is also associated with Indian-ness, since the rural population of the country has had the least access to formal education.

11. For example, in most Peruvian cities, the *chicha* dance-music style is associated with *cholo* identity. This style, developed by the offspring of highland migrants in Lima, fuses elements of highland music with elements of the Colombian Caribbean style called *cumbia*.

12. Dating from the 1850s in Lima and in the provinces, *Indigenismo* was a series of intellectual movements on the part of the non-Indians from different social and political perspectives that sought to make the "Indian" a central focus of study, identity construction, and sometimes political action. The bibliography on *Indigenismo* is large; for the case of Cusco see for example Rénique 1991. For an expanded analysis of the attempt of members of *instituciones culturales* at identity construction between the 1920s and 1980s, see Mendoza-Walker 1993a: chap. 2.

13. As Eric Hobsbawm has defined it, "'Invented tradition' is taken to mean

a set of practices, normally governed by overtly or tacitly accepted rules and of a ritual or symbolic nature, which seek to inculcate certain values and norms of behavior by repetition, which automatically implies continuity. In fact, where possible, they normally attempt to establish continuity with a suitable historic past. . . . The peculiarity of 'invented' traditions is that the continuity with it [historic past] is largely factitious" (Hobsbawm and Ranger 1986: 1–2). I find the Hobsbawmian concept of "invented traditions" particularly helpful to explain how members of such *instituciones culturales* have established a continuity between a suitable past and the repertoire of music, dances, and rituals they have created and promoted. The members of these institutions have devoted their efforts to link contemporary highland-rural society with an Inca ancestry.

14. A "choreography" is a requirement to make a dance an attractive one locally and regionally. Choreography is understood locally as a sequence of group-coordinated figures over space, such as circles or crossing lines and/or a drama-like representation.

15. Paucartambo is a district capital of the province of the same name located in the department of Cusco. Today this district is known, as is San Jerónimo, as mestizo.

16. For a complete analysis of both comparsas see Mendoza-Walker 1993a, 1993b.

17. In my 1995 visit I found that they had introduced a new piece to the costume, a small leather bag hanging across the body called *alforja*. There they carried candy to throw to the public at the end of their performance (a new part of the dance since my previous research). They said that the bag is supposed to be where the Majeños kept their money.

18. Most of the masks were made of a sort of papier-mâché and painted with bright-colored, shiny varnish. A few were made of plaster.

19. Gold teeth are a status symbol among Andean people. Birthmarks are considered characteristic of white people. In other parts of Peru, masks that resemble white people's faces have birthmarks on them.

20. This melody has a triple meter. Thomas Turino, who has observed the dance in Paucartambo, has characterized it as "staggering," having a relationship of iconicity with the drunken-like movement that the dancers of Paucartambo try to imitate in their performance (pers. comm.). The Majeños of San Jerónimo, however, have replaced that staggering movement of the body with a more controlled, swaying one. I analyze the meaning of this below.

21. See Roel Pineda 1959: 129–246 for a thorough description and analysis of the wayno genre in Cusco with an emphasis on the difference in the performative aspects. This author explains the differences between "mestizo" and "indigenous" wayno styles. Roel Pineda also traces the pre-Hispanic origins of the wayno.

22. Hobsbawm has argued that invented traditions are "responses to novel situations which take the form of reference to old situations, or which establish their own past by quasi-obligatory repetition" (Hobsbawm and Ranger 1986: 2).

23. Villasante 1989 provides a list of Majeños dancers since 1920 and of sponsors of the dance since 1925.

24. *Pitu* is a transverse cane flute. In Cusco, *tambor* (which literally means drum) refers to a medium-sized drum made of wood and animal skin tied with ropes. In Paucartambo the Majeños were also the only comparsa that had a brass band.

25. With respect to the patron saint festivity, the Majeños have assumed the lead in various preparatory events and a privileged position during the central performance of the ritual. For example, they have been able to establish the local tradition of being the first comparsa to perform in front of the Image after the processions.

26. One of these privileges was the fact that before the Majeños only the elite that sponsored the patron saint festivity could dance with a *banda*.

27. See Mendoza-Walker 1993a: chaps. 2 and 3 for further explanation of this process.

28. I say symbolically because this agrarian reform was not as drastic or efficient as desired and in many ways only officially sanctioned what the peasants had accomplished through long-term struggle. Symbolic also because the emphasis in ideological discourse against the traditional national elites and their representative culture was strongly propagated through the mass media. Moreover, there was a self-conscious effort to re-valorize symbols of highland society and rural culture.

29. In Paucartambo there was a change. The *hacendados* no longer performed. Schoolteachers, state employees, and petty merchants took the place and the ritual symbol of this landowning elite. These petit bourgeois members of the Paucartambo comparsa, however, did not represent a local elite. They were members of a local middle class that had been participating in other comparsas for at least a decade. The new local elite was constituted by professionals and by people who worked and lived in Cusco city and who still participated very actively in local affairs, mainly in the patron saint festivity.

30. Saint Jerome's fame as a Doctor of the Church (in reference to his scholastic accomplishments as the translator of biblical writings) and as an acknowledged figure in the Church hierarchy (because he became a cardinal) has made this particular *Imagen* a highly condensed symbol of *decencia* and power.

31. They were acknowledged as such in the Registro de Asociaciones of the city of Cusco around 1985.

32. They made this effect by making a little hole on the lid of the container and shaking the bottle.

33. In Paucartambo, the dancers splashed some of the aguardiente on the surrounding crowd at certain moments of their performances, but this was not part of a coordinated section of the dance and it was not nearly as showy as the performance in San Jerónimo.

34. Corduroy pants are, like leather jackets, considered elegant pieces of clothing in Cusco today.

35. The figure of the "macho," elegant Mexican charro has been disseminated in Peru for a few decades through television. The association with the personality of the charros was also evident when the band was playing the melody of the *Jarabe tapatío* (known in the United States as the Mexican hat dance) at

the moment that the Majeños were practicing with their horses before the *entrada*. The Majeños of San Jerónimo have also added to the hat some embroidered material that makes it look more like the Mexican hats. In Paucartambo, only the hat of the *caporal* looks similar to those of the San Jerónimo Majeños.

36. The Majeños of Paucartambo often criticized those of San Jerónimo for dancing "too straight" and not keeping the air of drunkenness that is supposed to characterize the dance.

37. Roel Pineda (1959) pointed out that among the rural popular classes in Cusco there was more body movement while performing the wayno than among the elites and the middle classes in the city. There were other elements that differentiated the choreography of the Majeños dance from those of other Cusqueño ones and from the more peasant-like wayno style of dancing. For example, with the exception of the Machu and the Dama, the Majeños did not hold hands or hook each other with their neckerchiefs, whips, or *varas*, and they did not perform a zig-zag pattern or the Yawar Mayu, typical of more peasant-style comparsa performances (cf. Roel Pineda 1959; Poole 1990, 1991).

38. I use "ideal" as deriving from "idealism," that is, as derived from the attitude that lays emphasis on perfection. I do not use "ideal" in the sense of "ideal types" as defined by Max Weber, although I refer to the construction of archetypes.

39. A professional in San Jerónimo is one who has completed a college education or has acquired some technical training. In my 1995 visit I noted that the group of professionals in the comparsa had continued to grow, now equaling the number of transportistas.

40. At least thirty percent of the population of the district is not originally from San Jerónimo and has arrived there in the last twenty years.

41. As of 1994, a third comparsa that performs an Altiplano dance has formed in the town. It was initiated by a faction that split from one of them. For details about the local and regional controversies around the performance of these dances in Cusco, see Mendoza-Walker 1994.

42. Outside ritual performance, they also carried out public activities to show their institutionalized generosity to the townspeople. In these events they tried to demonstrate that they were a beneficent local elite.

43. This asymmetrical relationship, which is also carried out outside ritual, is analyzed in Mendoza-Walker 1993a.

44. In San Jerónimo, as in the rest of Cusco and Peru, transportistas always have two or three *ayudantes* (helpers) whom they order around, mistreat, and make carry out the hard work. These ayudantes are often called cholos or *chulillos* (servants). In addition, middle and upper middle class Cusqueños always have lower status servants and sometimes *pongos* (serf-like servants) whom they also call derogatory names. The mistreatment of personal servants and other people considered of lower status because of their class or ethnic identity is common in Cusco and throughout Peru.

45. Santiago Rojas, a sculptor and maskmaker originally from Paucartambo, is a famous Cusqueño artist who lives in Cusco city. His statues and masks form part of national and international museums. The Majeños from San Jerónimo

buy their masks from him because it is a symbol of prestige to be able to afford one of his expensive masks.

46. Because I performed for the comparsa as the Dama for an Octava performance, I gained the confidence of the members. This factor, added to the fact that they considered me closer to their male personalities than any other Cusqueña and even Peruvian female (i.e., my education, my traveling experience, my way of dressing and behaving) allowed them to make sexual jokes in front of me or directed to me.

47. They had the rule that if one member had to go to the bathroom or do any important errand while these public gatherings were taking place, he should be accompanied by one or two other members of the comparsa who would be held responsible for his behavior.

REFERENCES

Abercrombie, Thomas. 1992. "La fiesta del carnaval postcolonial en Oruro: Clase, etnicidad, y nacionalismo en la danza folkórica." *Revista Andina* 20: 279–325.

Alonso, Ana. 1994. "The Politics of Space, Time and Substance: State Formation, Nationalism, and Ethnicity." *Annual Review of Anthropology* 23: 379–405.

Ares Queija, Berta. 1984. "Las danzas de los Indios: Un camino para la evangelización del Virreynato del Perú." *Revista de Indias* 44, 174: 445–63.

Bateson, Gregory. 1958. *Naven.* Stanford, Calif.: Stanford University Press.

Bourdieu, Pierre. 1987. "What Makes a Social Class? On the Theoretical and Practical Existence of Groups." *Berkeley Journal of Sociology* 32: 1–17.

Comaroff, Jean, and John Comaroff. 1991. *Of Revelation and Revolution: Christianity, Colonialism, and Consciousness in South Africa.* Chicago: University of Chicago Press.

Cowan, Jane. 1990. *Dance and the Body Politic in Northern Greece.* Princeton, N.J.: Princeton University Press.

De la Cadena, Marisol. 1991. "'La mujeres son más indias': Etnicidad y género en una comunidad del Cusco." *Revista Andina* 19: 7–29.

Erlmann, Veit. 1992. "'The Past is Far and the Future is Far': Power and Performance among Zulu Migrant Workers." *American Ethnologist* 19: 688–709.

Fabian, Johannes. 1990. *Power and Performance: Ethnographic Explorations through Proverbial Wisdom and Theater in Shaba, Zaire.* Madison: University of Wisconsin Press.

Fernandez, James. 1986. *Persuasions and Performances.* Bloomington: Indiana University Press.

Flores Glaindo. 1977. *Arequipa y el surandino.* Lima: Editorial Horizonte.

Hebdige, Dick. 1985. *Subculture: The Meaning of Style.* London: Methuen.

Hobsbawm, Eric, and Terence Ranger, eds. 1986. *The Invention of Tradition.* Cambridge: Cambridge University Press.

Kessel, Juan van. 1981. *Danzas y estructuras sociales de los Andes.* Cusco: Instituto de Pastoral Andina.

Mannheim, Bruce. 1991. *The Language of the Inka since the European Invasion.* Austin: University of Texas Press.

Marzal, Manuel. 1977. *Estudios sobre religión campesina.* Lima: Pontificia Universidad Católica.

Mendoza, Zoila. 1989. "La danza de 'Los Avelinos,' sus orígenes y sus múltiples significados." *Revista Andina* 7: 501–21.

Mendoza-Walker, Zoila. 1993a. "Shaping Society Through Dance: Mestizo Ritual Performance in the Southern Peruvian Highlands," Ph.D. diss., University of Chicago.

———. 1993b. "La comparsa Los Majeños: Poder, prestigio y masculinidad entro los mestizos cusqueños." In *Musica, danzas y máscaras en los Andes,* ed. Raúl Romero, 97–137. Lima: Pontificia Universidad Católica.

———. 1994. "Contesting Identities through Dance: Mestizo Performance in the Southern Andes of Peru." *Repercussions* 2, 3: 50–80.

Munn, Nancy. 1974. "Symbolism in a Ritual Context: Aspect of Symbolic Action." In *Handbook of Social and Cultural Anthropology,* ed. J. J. Honigmann, 579–612. New York: Rand McNally.

Poole, Deborah. 1988. "Landscapes of Power in a Cattle-Rustling Culture of Southern Andean Peru." *Dialectical Anthropology* 12: 367–98.

———. 1990. "Accommodation and Resistance in Andean Ritual Dance." *The Drama Review* 34: 981–26.

———. 1991. "Rituals of Movement, Rites of Transformation: Pilgrimage and Dance in the Highlands of Cuzco." In *Pilgrimage in Latin America,* ed. Ross Crumrine and Alan Morinis, 305–38. New York: Greenwood.

Poole, Deborah, ed. 1994. *Unruly Order: Violence, Power, and Cultural Identity in the High Provinces of Southern Peru.* Boulder: Westview.

Rénique, Jose Luis. 1991. *Los Sueños de la Sierra: Cusco en el siglo XX.* Lima: CEPES.

Roel Pineda, Josafat. 1959. "El wayno del Cuzco." *Folklore Americano* (Lima) 6–7: 129–246.

Romero, Raúl. 1988. "La música tradicional y popular." In *La Musica en el Perú,* ed. Patronato Popular y Porvenir Pro Música Clásica, 215–83. Lima: Patronato Popular y Pouvenir.

Salomon, Frank. 1981. "Killing the Yumbo: A Ritual Drama of Northern Quito." In *Cultural Transformations and Ethnicity in Modern Ecuador,* ed. Norman Whitten Jr., 162–208. Urbana: University of Illinois Press.

Turino, Thomas. 1993. *Moving Away from Silence: Music of the Peruvian Altiplano and the Experience of Urban Migration.* Chicago: University of Chicago Press.

Van den Berghe, Pierre, and Geroge Primov. 1977. *Inequality in the Peruvian Andes: Class and Ethnicity in Cuzco.* Columbia: University of Missouri Press.

Villasante, Segundo. 1989. *Mamacha Carmen: Paucartambo Provincia Folklorica.* Lima: Concytec.

Waterman, Christopher. 1990. *Jùjú A Social History and Ethnography of an African Popular Music.* Chicago: University of Chicago Press.

8

Indonesian-Chinese Oppression and the Musical Outcomes in the Netherlands East Indies

MARGARET J. KARTOMI

To appreciate the musical genres, styles, activities, and achievements of the Indonesian-Chinese who have lived in the archipelago over the past two millennia, we need to investigate how changing social conditions influenced, indeed paralleled, the ups and downs of their musical lives. In this article we shall restrict our discussion to the era of Dutch colonial power (1602–1945), leaving the musical and racial dilemmas of the Indonesian-Chinese in independent Indonesia to a sequel article.

The social conditions under which the Indonesian-Chinese lived (fig. 8.1) were largely determined by the racial imagination of the Dutch colonists, who from the seventeenth century had invented three main categories of citizenship among its subjects: "Europeans," "Foreign Orientals" *(Vreemde Oosterlingen)*, and "Natives" *(Inlanders)*, the last of whom are now called the *pribumi*, lit. "sons of the earth." Racial classification was the cornerstone of the colonial administration (Fasseur 1994: 32). Access to power and education was largely restricted to Europeans. Many privileges given to the Dutch were denied to the "Natives," though they were allowed to own land and, in the late colonial era, some were able to become middle to lower rung civil servants and were a little better off than the majority who were poor peasant workers or coolies. In contrast, except along the east coast of Sumatra, Bangka, Belitung, parts of West and South Kalimantan, and the greater Jakarta area, the "Foreign Orientals"—mainly Indonesian-Chinese—were prohibited from owning rural land. The Dutch pattern of settlement in the Netherlands East India company town of Batavia designated enclaves (Dutch *wijk*, "quarters," modern Indonesian *pecinan*) for the Chinese as well as other

Figure 8.1. Western Indonesia: Some places of Indonesian-Chinese settlement

racially distinguished groups,[1] and this practice spread to other towns. The business-entrepreneurial section of the "Foreign Orientals" category was useful to the Dutch because of its members' financial knowhow and willingness to take commercial risks as they plied their international or local trade. Like the Jews, Hanseatic Germans, and Lombards in Europe during its capitalist transformation, the Indonesian-Chinese entrepreneurial class was required to serve the interests of the dominant class, which naturally overrode theirs. The Dutch strove to develop, exploit, and dominate the lucrative international trade emanating from the

Indies, first via the quasi-sovereign power of the United East India Company (Vereenigde Oostandische Compagnie) between 1602 and 1799, and thereafter via the Dutch colonial government, always with their capital in Batavia (now Jakarta).

However, the great majority of Indonesian-Chinese in the seventeenth and eighteenth centuries were descendants of illiterate, landless farmers and workers who had become poor plantation workers or miners in the Indies, having emigrated there to escape poverty, famine, a call-up, war, or other disaster in China or in the region now called Southeast Asia. By giving them unpopular jobs, such as tax farming, money-lending, and running pawnshops, the Dutch allowed a pariah image of the Indonesian-Chinese to emerge among the pribumi population. Thus, all those who "looked Chinese" were perceived as being members of that pariah community, even if they had intermarried and lived in Indonesia for generations (i.e. were *peranakan*, lit. "of mixed blood"),[2] spoke nothing but the Indonesian language or languages, and had integrated into pribumi culture. By creating the "Foreign Orientals" category, the Dutch had in effect lumped rich and poor Indonesian-Chinese together, taking advantage of "the Natives'" growing resentment of the wealth and penny-pinching of some Indonesian-Chinese, but labeling them all—rich and poor—as "the Jews of the East" in terms which stressed commercial ability, greed, and subservience to those in power. Though pribumi communities in some areas and periods have maintained cordial relationships with the local Indonesian-Chinese, especially if they were Muslims,[3] the local pribumi population mostly came in time to accept the invented Indonesian-Chinese racial stereotypes, in so doing giving coherence to their resentment of the privileges they were allowed. This in turn deepened the dilemmas, increasing the danger for the pariah minority, and progressively forcing them into greater isolation. Unlike non-pariah citizens, theirs was a vicious cycle based on the chronic need to accumulate and save assets to buy their protection from members of the other racially designated categories of the population.

Thus the conflict between Dutch and Indonesian-Chinese commercial interests was the root of the racist oppression of the Indonesian-Chinese in the archipelago from the mid-seventeenth century. The racial imagination of the colonizer merged early on with that of the colonized and resulted in centuries of racial fear and persecution of the Indonesian-Chinese financiers, entrepreneurial traders, small businessmen, peasants, workers, and their families.

This oppression was the largest single factor determining the course of the Indonesian-Chinese musical experience during the colonial era. Indonesian-Chinese families promoted and practiced either local Indonesian music-culture or a combination of Indonesian and Chinese music-cultures. Sometimes new, creative, syncretic musical genres or styles developed as a result. Rich Chinese *tauke* (entrepreneur-bosses) frequently sponsored performances of both Indonesian and Chinese musical arts. In times of racial unrest, however, the Indonesian-Chinese tended to retreat into Chinese music-culture and religion, especially if interracial tensions had come to a head and exploded, whereupon they would once again become scapegoats for pribumi discontent with conditions in colonial society. At such times they unwittingly served Dutch interests in that they were deflecting some of the antagonisms felt by the pribumi against the colonial power itself.

What could they do to improve their lot? Only some of the rich totok had any wish to return to China, and the great majority could not have afforded to return even if they had wished to, after they and some of their ancestors had lived for generations in the archipelago. The poor miners, plantation workers, and shopkeepers were tarred with the same racist brush as the rich. Always a small minority, the Indonesian-Chinese as a group could acquire only limited political influence and ultimately no protection. All they could do was learn to live with being treated as a perpetual pariah-diaspora group, as will become evident as we piece together the outlines of the history of their music-culture.

A much less important determining factor in the Indonesian-Chinese musical experience was the diverse ethnic origins of the original totok Chinese who migrated to the archipelago. Most came from the southeast provinces of China (see fig. 8.2) or other parts of Southeast Asia. The majority were the Hokkienese from Fujian province, the Hakka from Guandong, the Teochew from Shantou city, the Cantonese from Guandong, the Hainanese from Hainan, and the Fuzhow from northern Fujian, some of whom migrated to Indonesia via present-day Malaysia and other neighboring countries. Different ethnic groups settled in different areas; for example, Hokkienese descendants have always been dominant in Java, whereas the Hokkienese have been second to the Hakka in Bangka, and the community in the Singkawang hinterland is predominantly Hakka. Until the end of the nineteenth century, virtually all the men married pribumi women, but if they married a Chinese woman it was virtually always from within their ethno-linguistic group. Thus Hakka communities and their performing arts remained Hakka and Hokkienese communities and arts remained Hokkienese over the centuries, even though their members' knowledge of the language was

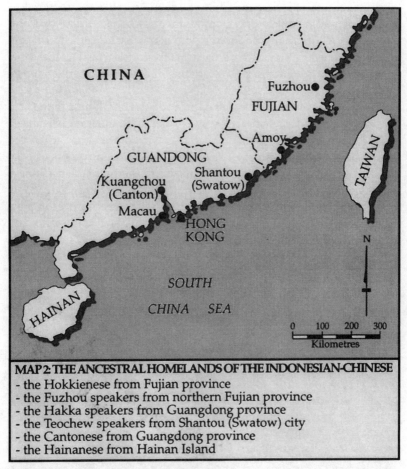

Figure 8.2. The ancestral homelands of the Indonesian Chinese. (Based in part on the map in Salmon and Lombard 1985: xi)

often minimal or nonexistent. All the colonial sources mentioning these communities were highly male-centric; peranakan women hardly ever rated a mention.[4]

Until recently, most scholars have neglected to research the story of the Indonesian-Chinese musical experience. This is presumably because it is an uncomfortable area of inquiry which is rife with popular misconceptions based on centuries of perpetrated racist thinking. Since 1965, the official government policy has stated that Indonesian-Chinese cultural expressions must be "totally assimilated" into Indonesian culture. Despite being mestizos, the Indonesian-Chinese are still treated as a permanent pariah-diaspora Chinese group; yet they are required to become totally assimilated by adopting Indonesian names and forsaking Indonesian-Chinese artistic and religious activities, except where a permit is obtained. These factors have made it embarrassing for some scholars even to contemplate researching Indonesian-Chinese culture and its history.[5]

Details of the musical practices of the Indonesian-Chinese in the precolonial era have largely been lost over time. The situation becomes a little clearer, however, from the early seventeenth century when the Dutch began to establish their suzerainty and to keep records as they did so. In this article I consider the impact of the Indonesian-Chinese racial stereotype on the output of Indonesian-Chinese musicians, composers, and commentators in colonial times, restricting my inquiry mainly to Java, Bangka (an outpost of Palembang, South Sumatra), and the Singkawang hinterland in Kalimantan.[6] To this day, Indonesian-Chinese musicians have practiced their art not as an autonomous musical entity but as part of religious ritual (see fig. 8.3), music theater, or commercial song and dance entertainment or music theater. Thus we shall discuss their music-culture largely in terms of these composite artforms.

Figure 8.3. Figurines in a shrine in Pangkal Pinang on Belitung Island, used to this day in religious rituals by people of Chinese descent. (Photo by H. Kartomi, 1992)

Indonesia's recorded history begins with accounts in Chinese annals dating back to the early centuries of the Christian era. A body of archaeological and literary sources show that musical and other artistic contact between Chinese and Indonesians dates back at least two millennia. Remains of bronze "drums" (i.e. with bronze, not skin heads) originating in the Dóng-son culture of southern China and northern Vietnam from 300 B.C. to A.D. 200 have been found in many parts of Indonesia, suggesting the existence of more or less direct contacts with China in the second or first centuries B.C. (Heine-Geldern 1945: 147). Stone megaliths found in the Pasemah area of southern Sumatra depict figures with the bronze Dóng-son "drums" strapped to their backs (see illustration in Kartomi 1996: 3).

In the first and early second millennia, Indonesian kingdoms such as Srivijaya and Majapahit sent tributes and ambassadors to the Chinese Emperor (de Graaf and Pigeaud 1984: 66–67, 157–58). Chinese men sailed to Indonesia as pilgrims, travelers, military men, refugees from war or famine, merchants, itinerant traders, or emigrant workers. Some Chinese travelers and their chroniclers wrote about the music they heard in Java.[7]

References in Old Javanese treatises to Chinese ceramics dating from the first millennium A.D. to the fourteenth century, remains of which have been found inter alia in the Palembang-Jambi area, suggest that a major Majapahit-Chinese city existed in or near the present site of Palembang in the thirteenth and fourteenth centuries (McKinnon 1985: 20). Legends and literary sources also underline the prominent role of China and Chinese in early Indonesian state affairs. By the fourteenth century, communities of Chinese merchants had become established in various coastal towns; and Indonesian élites had become accustomed to imported Chinese luxuries. A fourteenth-century Javanese manuscript refers to the Mongol invasion of Java by Kubla Khan and the sacking of the royal courts at Singosari and Kadhiri in 1293, leading to the founding of the Majapahit empire with its center in East Java (Pigeaud 1960, 1: 359) and links with kingdoms in Sumatra and elsewhere. The same source mentions that metal coins and ceramics were imported in bulk from China (ibid. 500). Chinese and Javanese manuscripts and legends mention the political marriages of Chinese princesses to Indonesian rulers in colonial times (ibid. 706, 3: 211), for example in Deli, Siak, Cirebon, Surakarta, and Ternate. The extant palaces, museums, and other historic buildings associated with these sites still contain many Chinese artifacts and items of furniture and costumes which were royal wedding or ambassadorial gifts.

Chinese traders also visited or settled along coastal areas of the archipelago, especially in north coastal Java, where they were highly influential and showed interest in both Chinese and local music-culture. It is widely believed that Chinese saints and traders played a major role in spreading Islam in Java in the fifteenth century, and that several of the Nine Saints *(Wali Sanga)* were included among them.[8] "It seems probable that the [Muslim] Mongol-Chinese invasion and subsequent penetration (far into the countryside) were important factors in the further development of Javanese economy and culture" (Pigeaud 1967: 120). By that time, numerous Chinese-Muslim merchant communities had been established along Java's north coast. Chinese immigrants who had married pribumi women and were living in rural and semi-rural areas often adopted Muslim names. Thus Chinese financial, commercial, and artistic skills complemented Indonesian agricultural, cloth-making, artistic, and other skills and practices. The eighteenth-century Javanese source *Serat Kandha* mentions a Chinese merchant whose ship foundered at Jepara and who settled there and was converted to Islam.[9] There is no evidence to suggest that Indonesians and Chinese were not on good terms with each other at the time.

On the contrary, there is evidence that by the sixteenth century the Chinese population at Banten in northeast Java practiced a lively artistic life, with pribumi participation, in and around the Chinese temple; and that while some had become Muslim and adopted pribumi rituals and associated performing arts as their own, others had retained their Chinese religious beliefs and practices. Those who did so naturally maintained the temple-associated arts, for Confucian teaching exhorts its followers to take part in many kinds of art—dance, music, theater, and fine art—as a form of worship and as a method of learning the eight virtues and the fifteen human relationships that facilitate social life (Lasiyo 1992: 1–92). Temple processions presenting dances such as the *barongsai* (lion dance) had long been organized by temple leaders for religious purposes and to collect money for the benefit of poor peranakan families. Edmund Scott's account of a voyage to Banten between 1602 and 1605 includes mention of the fact that a sung theater performance, which was probably a form of Chinese opera, was given in Banten on platforms in the streets whenever ships arrived from or departed for China (Salmon and Lombard 1985: 104). It is highly probable that many totok and peranakan as well as pribumi attended these colorful events. The absence of Chinese tombs, which might indicate the contrary, is explainable by the fact that the Chinese embalmed their dead and sent them back to China, as a seventeenth-century French observer noted (ibid. 103–4).

A form of folk Chinese glove puppet theater called *wayang potehi* accompanied by a Chinese orchestra *(pa tim)* was performed in Chinese temples in Java from at least as early as 1770. A two-month season of *"wajang pow-tee-hie"* performances was presented as part of the celebrations to mark the opening of the new *klenteng* (temple) in Semarang in 1770 (Liem 1931–33: 50). The puppeteer and musicians were brought from Jakarta for the occasion as there were no local performers in Semarang at the time. Members of the pribumi and the Dutch communities also attended the celebrations. It became common for Chinese tauke to sponsor performances of Chinese music, ritual, and theater in or near the klenteng in the towns where they had established their businesses, or in rural areas where they were allowed to own and work the land, such as in the surroundings of Batavia. The town of Batavia had been founded in 1619 as a trading post of the Dutch East India Company, before which it had been a port controlled by the Sultan of Banten.

Meanwhile, in east-coast Sumatra until at least as late as the second half of the eighteenth century, the Sultans of Palembang and Jambi were placing great importance on kinship links, legendary or otherwise, with China. This reflected the economic reality that Palembang was a major trading port for Chinese ships, being only twenty sailing days from China (Andaya 1993: 53–54). Many Chinese men were allowed to fill important commercial positions, having married local women and converted to Islam. This practice was encouraged by the Sultans of Jambi and Palembang, who could then accept them as their subjects. Indonesian-Chinese who lived in south and central east-coast Sumatra and the offshore island of Bangka included expert traders, miners, and businessmen who were brought there by Palembang royalty and the Dutch to exploit the local gold and tin (Wolters 1967: 355); and they and their descendants eventually bought land and were accepted into the surrounding pribumi communities. As the Sultans and the Dutch developed their cash crop plantations, large numbers of poor Chinese laborers were brought in; and some of the musically inclined took part in the artistic activities being developed among slave musicians and professional dancers for entertainments in and around the plantations.

Some of the music-cultural outcomes of this pribumi–Chinese contact in Bangka and elsewhere are discussed below. We shall now focus our attention on the social and musical situation and outcomes in Java, in comparison to which Bangka was but a backwater.

When the United East India Company began its operations in Java under Governor-General Coen, it did so on excellent terms with the local people of Chinese descent, who provided it with large quantities of sorely needed skilled labor and financial knowhow. They also provided individuals whom the Dutch used to collect rent, customs, and taxes. They were a highly visible community, constructing colorful temples and celebrating their festivals with spectacular performances and feasting. The Dutch issued them with licenses and taxed them on their every public function, festival, and industry. Indeed in the four centuries of Dutch colonial rule, "Chinese merchants were leading residents in all Javanese towns. . . . In Chinese communities in the archipelago, Malay, the interinsular medium of trade, was the dominant language. . . . Moreover, some members of Chinese families of long standing in Java developed into connoisseurs and patrons of Javanese art and literature" (Pigeaud 1967: 258).

Between its founding in 1619 and the Dutch massacre of the Chinese in 1740, Batavia was basically a Chinese totok-peranakan colonial town under Dutch protection (Blusse 1981: 60). There were also many slaves, some of whom originated in the eastern islands, especially Bali and south Sulawesi, and others in India's Malabar or Coromandel coasts and Malacca on the Malay peninsula. The Dutch opened up sugar estates in rural areas to the southwest, south, and southeast of Batavia in the seventeenth century, thus giving Batavia "its only original export" (Abeyasekere 1987: 25). Slave musicians on the plantations were directed to play European music in various *slavenorksten* (slave orchestras) which entertained their owners at plantation dinners and the like and eventually developed into the so-called *kroncong* string bands and *tanjidor* brass and percussion bands. These slave orchestras were also employed by Chinese tauke. They are still played in various parts of western Indonesia to this day in rural areas such as greater Jakarta, the area south of Palembang, West Kalimantan, and Bangka and Belitung islands.

As the Company opened up its plantation estates and gained the monopoly over the large-scale import and export of goods, it increasingly used the Indonesian-Chinese, with their international trading links, as middlemen. As the plantation era began, a large number of Chinese coolie immigrants rushed in to work in the plantations in Batavia's surrounding regions of Tangerang (modern spelling Tanggerang) and Bekasi, and they married pribumi women. From then on, Dutch relations with the Indonesian-Chinese community deteriorated. Successive Dutch governments took restrictive measures against the Indonesian-Chinese, using a policy of divide and rule among pribumi and peranakan (Carey 1984). In 1740, tensions between the Dutch and the Chinese over rival agricultural developments erupted into open warfare. Ten thousand Chinese were massacred in the city of Batavia while Chinese from the hinterland were attacking the city and burning the southern suburbs (Blussé 1981: 177). In the aftermath of the massacre, measures were taken to keep the peranakan alienated from the rest of the Indonesians (A. R. Kemasang, pers. comm.). Despite this, their descendants stayed and developed creole communities which succeeded from the eighteenth century in developing a syncretic musical form called *gambang* (or, as it was later known, *gambang kromong*) to accompany local *wayang cokek* performances which were of Chinese origin and in which female singer-dancers danced with male customers.

Dutch colonial sources in the mid-eighteenth century mention that these very same peranakan plantation laborer communities enjoyed *tandhak* [the Javanese name for dancing similar to wayang cokek] and *wayang* (theater) performances. In an attempt to control their "ruinous gambling" and "irresponsible" expenditure on Javanese tandhak dancing girls, the colonial government made the condition that a large entrance fee be charged for each show, as was documented in an account of 1751 by a certain J. Mossel, who was responsible for the Chinese in a certain settlement area (Seltmann 1976: 51). A paternalistic attitude to the recreational needs of the "Chinese" laborers can be detected behind Mossel's recommendation, which was announced by the then Governor of the VOC. Clearly the "Chinese" and the pribumi were treated as separate communities, despite much intermarriage. Yet major creative developments of the wayang or *cokek-gambang* music and dance tradition occurred within those local peranakan communities in the nineteenth and twentieth centuries. Moreover, these working-class performing arts activities intersected with the eclectic genres developing among middle-class mestizo or Eurasian (Dutch *Indische*, Indonesian *Indo*) sections of the community. Musically inclined members of the slave orchestras had been trained in Western music in the sixteenth century by the Portuguese colonists and later at the behest of the Dutch plantation owners. They were given Western musical instruments to play in bands in order to provide entertainment at the lavish dinners thrown by land and plantation owners, a practice which was prevalent until the nineteenth century (slavery was formally abolished in 1860). The Indonesian-Chinese tauke also sponsored the bands; and Indonesian-Chinese musicians joined Indo-European and pribumi musicians to play at these entertainments. Thus *kroncong*, *tanjidor*, and—from the late nineteenth century—*komedie stambul* and other associated music theater forms continued to develop wherever Eurasian and Indo-Chinese communities were actively engaged in the arts.

Meanwhile, throughout the eighteenth century, undifferentiated racist feelings against the "Chinese" as a whole were growing, unbridled.

Indeed anti-"Chinese" revolts and massacres in Java set the pattern for later centuries. The colonial government is documented as having failed to protect the "Chinese"—whether poor laborers or rich middlemen— when they needed it. In Batavia, for example,

> Jealousy of Chinese commercial success simmered among many . . . citizens, who took advantage of a breakdown in law and order to attack the Chinese and loot their property. Little protection of the Chinese has been offered by Jakarta's governments, who have often seemed prepared to allow the Chinese to be treated as scapegoats for the inadequacy of their own administration. (Abeyasekere 1987: 25)

Pribumi–peranakan relations appear to have been further eroded in the early to mid-nineteenth century. Bitter attitudes of distrust and fear of

> the Chinese communities in Central Java have only crystallised over the past 150 years. . . . Before that period (i.e. prior to the ill-fated Java War of 1825–30), in court circles at least, a very different relationship seems to have prevailed between the two communities. This was one based not on mutual suspicion, but on a marked degree of reciprocity, common interest, and intercommunal cooperation. The Chinese were needed at the courts as money-lenders and commercial experts. They could supply financial skills which were simply not available in Javanese society. . . . The Chinese, for their part, found that their links with the courts were often a *sine qua non* for their commercial success in the hinterland. . . . Well-acculturated Chinese mixed-blood communities appear to have grown up which had adopted, without ostensible difficulty, the mannerisms and language of their Javanese neighbours. (Carey 1984: 3–4)

As we have noted, the migrants from China were mainly men, and their Indonesian wives provided them with immediate access to the lifestyle, arts, and culture of the local pribumi population. In the early nineteenth century, rich peranakan began to serve as patrons and artists in local performances of the Indonesian arts, such as Javanese gamelan music and *wayang kulit* (shadow puppet) shows; nor was it by coincidence that this practice continued even as racial tensions against the Indonesian-Chinese grew to the boiling point at that time.

To our knowledge, the first Indonesian-Chinese patron documented to have shown a substantial interest in the *"Kunst Priboemi"* (indigenous art) of Javanese gamelan music was a wealthy *kapitein* (captain) in Semarang named Tan Tiang Tjhing, who sponsored the celebrations for the founding of the klenteng in Semarang in 1814 (see the description of this event in figure 8.4). He is mentioned in the description as being a "pranakan," not a "Tionghua totok" (Chinese totok) (Liem 1931–33:

Berdirinja klenteng Tan Sing Ong. — Awalnja ada seboetan gang di Semarang. — Moentjoelnja passen dan wijkenstelsel. — Kedatengannja njonja Tionghoa toelen dari Tiongkok. — Pembrontakan Diponegoro. — Kampoeng Tionghoa dipasang ampat pintoe. — Warta-warta jang membikin riboet publiek Tionghoa dan Kodja. — Majoor Tionghoa jang pertama.

Pada taon 1814 toean Tan Tiang Tjhing bikin klenteng Tjiang Sing Ong di koelon djalanan Sebandaran. Siapa adanja itoe Tjiang Sing Ong ada ditjeritaken pandjang lebar di satoe pay jang terdapet dalem itoe klenteng, jang ringkesnja menoetoerken djasanja Tan Goan Kong (陳元光), saorang jang hidoep di djaman Song Tiauw, siapa telah bikin pendoedoek di Tjiangtjioe jang itoe masa masih belon kenal kasopanan sahingga djadi beribadat, serta bikin Tjiangtjioe djadi satoe daerah jang mahmoer. Lantaran itoe djasa ia laloe dinamaken *Khay Tjiang Sing Ong* (開漳聖王). Itoe klenteng jalah jang sekarang terkenal dengen seboetan klenteng *Tan Sing Ong*, kerna ada boeat kaoem Tan dan kapoenja'annja kaoem Tan . . . .

Itoe waktoe di bagian wetannja itoe bio masih beroepa tegalan, maka oleh toean Tan Tiang Tjhing laloe didiriken satoe taman jang indah, dengen paseban dan goenoeng-goenoengan dari batoe karang; diatasnja itoe goenoeng-goenoengan ada dipasang bangkoe-bangkoe boeat orang berdoedoek, sedeng di bawahnja ini goenoeng-goenoengan ada dibikin sebagi gowa-gowa dan empang-empang dimana ada dipiara ikan-ikan goerami dan sebaginja. Di saben pintoe gowa ada dipasang lian jang maksoednja bagoes sekali. Pandjangnja ini taman adalah dari pinggiran kali sebelah Lor, sampe di djalanan sebelah Kidoel jang menoedjoe ka Broemboengan. Djalanan Lengkong Se'ong itoe tempo belon berada di sitoe, hanja sedikit mengidoel lagi. Djika di waktoe terang boelan toean Tan Tiang Tjhing bersama ia poenja sanak familie sering tjari hiboeran diatas paseban sembari dengerken sindèn atawa klonengan, kerna itoe Kapitein ada poenjaken wijogo sendiri, compléet berikoet gamelan pelok dan slendro jang indah! Atawa kadang-kadang bersama ia poenja sobat-sobat ia orang tjari kasenengan dengen mainken tetaboean Tionghoa, sembari minoem arak dan bikin sairan Tionghoa (Sie).

Ia ada tertjatei sebagi orang Tionghoa jang taro perhatian atas kunst Priboemi atawa gamelan, kerna pada itoe tempo gamelan belon populair diantara orang Tionghoa. Sedari toean Tan Tiang Tjhing kemarihin, baroelah gamelan banjak ambil bagian dalem berbagi-bagi perajahan jang dilakoeken oleh orang Tionghoa. Sementara dari lain fihak lagi kita dapetken katerangan, bahwea toean Tan Tiang Tjhing boekan satoe Tionghoa totok, tetapi ada satoe pranakan jang sedari ketjil dikirim ka

Figure 8.4. Account of the official launch of the Chinese temple in Semarang, 1814. The donor, Tan Tiang Tjhing, organized a complete gamelan pelog-slendro as well as a Chinese orchestra to be played, although, as the author wrote, "gamelan was not yet popular among the Chinese"

85). After building a pavilion in a park, he provided a performance in it by a *sindhen* (singer) accompanied by a group of *klonengan* (soft gamelan music) players, as well as performances of Chinese instrumental ensemble music. The group of gamelan players and the complete slendro-pelog gamelan which they played were his own (ibid. 50). However, sometimes such patrons provided Chinese music only, for gamelan was not yet very popular among the Chinese (ibid. 85).

In the early nineteenth century, tensions between the "Natives" and the "Foreign Orientals" were allowed to intensify to a frightening degree. In the trading port of Ngawi, for example, the local Indonesian-Chinese community was reported to consist of rice-brokers, petty traders, coolies, and refugees from the surrounding countryside. At the outbreak of the Java War in 1825, Ngawi's entire Indonesian-Chinese community was put to the sword (Carey 1984: 1). Following such a massacre, one might expect the Indonesian-Chinese community to lie low and retreat into its own Chineseness, practicing the Chinese temple arts rather than Indonesian ones. If they did so, it was not for long. In the mid-nineteenth century, open-air comic theater "wayang" troupes are again reported to have presented traditional Chinese stories about battles between the Chinese and the Tartars, with spoken or sung dialogue "in the Chinese language, amidst a clangour of Gongs, and other musical instruments," including wind instruments (one of which was probably a *sona* [Chinese shawm]) (Salmon 1981: 129, Weitzel 1860: 15). Moreover, the Indonesian-Chinese "greatly enjoyed *wajang* and *topeng* (mask dance), including *wajang goelit* with leather puppets, *wajang golloee* with masked wooden puppets, and most of all *wajang orang* (theater with human actors); and in the latter shows, only men were allowed to watch and only Chinese could be spoken" (Boachi 1855: 279). Chinese mask dances *("majin topeng")* and Chinese comic theater *(wajang Tjina)* were also very popular. In 1896, "wajang (po)tehi," with hand puppets whose heads and arms were said to be manipulated by the puppeteer's fingers, was performed (Serrurier 1896: 205).

At both Chinese and Indonesian celebrations in nineteenth-century Batavia, the Indonesian-Chinese élite mixed with the Dutch élite while "Chinese" workers and peasants mixed with "Indonesian" peasants and workers. That both pribumi and peranakan crowds participated in the Chinese religious festivals is evidenced by a report of the Capgomeh carnival in 1884.[10] Many members of the local pribumi population joined in the festivities, which included a range of entertainments: besides the usual Chinese processions, there were performances by a Eurasian *dangsu* (Old Portuguese–style dancer), twenty or thirty Malay *dendang* (singing) groups, an Arab *gambus* (six-string lute) band, and a kroncong band played by Eurasians. A European traveler reported in 1851 that Eurasians were very fond of Chinese wayang (Abeyasekere 1987: 79).

Throughout the nineteenth century, rich Chinese families frequently sponsored temple entertainments to celebrate the arrival of ships carrying new Chinese migrants or traders. Since the new arrivals were mostly southeast Chinese peasants and workers rather than members of the scholar class, their cultural expressions were based on southeast Chinese folk traditions, which were readily able to absorb local Indonesian artistic traits (Abeyasekere 1987: 62–63). Their three main annual celebrations were Chinese New Year—which ended in the opulent carnival and feast of Capgomeh, the Pecun and the Rebutan (also called Pu-du or Raja Jin).[11] Abeyasekere (1987: 62–63) described one such Rebutan festival in late nineteenth century Batavia as follows:

> Lavish offerings of food were made on a platform to the ghosts of the dead, after which the assembled poor were permitted to climb up and seize the food, resulting in a disorderly rush (hence the name Rebutan or Free-for-all). The Pecun festival, celebrated in the middle of the year, was of obscure origin but it always involved a boat race. Even though the canals in the old town were low during the east monsoon, the Chinese continued to stage these races until the end of the century. A Malay-language newspaper in 1891 described the gathering of four Pecun boats, accompanied by others full of musicians and dancers, in the canals of the Chinese camp before the race along the River Angke. The biggest festival was undoubtedly the Chinese New Year, which lasted for twelve days in January–February and culminated in the feast of Capgomeh. This involved enormous processions through the streets. One evening procession was described by a European newspaper in 1884 as wending its way from Kramat through to the lower part of town. Accompanied by torches and music, it featured various mythical creatures such as:

>> . . . a giant snake with protruding tongue on the end of which was seated a prettily clad child; also a colossal flower with a long stamen bearing a nymph; and a quaintly pointed crag on which sat one of the Chinese water-gods, and finally imitations of tigers and other animals ridden by neatly clad Chinese girls and boys. (*Java Bode*, 12 Feb. 1884)

> Indispensable at every Capgomeh was the *barongsai*, a dragon-like creature supported by a number of boys which visited households through the Chinese camp to the accompaniment of a barrage of fire-crackers intended to drive away devils.

In 1896 it was mentioned that shadow puppet theater of various kinds was common among the "Chinese" in the Batavia hinterland at Besuki (Serrurier 1896: 205). From the mid-nineteenth century there are references in the literature to Chinese leather puppet theater called *wajang thithi* (Seltmann 1976: 52). Wayang thithi was a syncretic Chinese-Javanese form of shadow theater using perforated Javanese-style leather puppets which depicted characters from *The White Monkey* and other Chinese tales, accompanied by a *pa tim* orchestra which—as in wayang potehi and Chinese opera ensembles—divides into a brass and percussion ensemble for military scenes and a string and percussion ensemble for civil scenes.

The literature refers to only one puppeteer who could perform both Javanese wayang kulit and wayang thithi. He was the profoundly talented "Chinese" puppeteer *(dhalang)* and puppet maker Gan Dhwan Sing, who was steeped in the Chinese and the Javanese performing arts and performed wayang kulit and wayang thithi from the early twentieth century until he died in 1967 (Seltmann 1976: 52–53). The elaborately carved puppets he made were based on a close knowledge of Chinese leather puppet models. He was a master exponent of both the military and the civilian scenes. He was clearly preceded by other—unnamed—wayang thithi puppet masters and makers in Java. His son served as his assistant in wayang thithi performances until the 1960s but did not, however, possess his father's interest or talent. Thus many of the leather puppets, as well as the paper puppets which his father had made during the Japanese occupation, when he could not afford to buy leather, fell into disrepair. The only surviving musical instruments in his collection are a pair of *cempala ageng*, a *cempala japitan* (wooden plates hanging from the puppet box), and a pair of *kepyak* (comprising four iron rattles, i.e. instruments to accompany military scenes) (Seltmann 1976: 59). It is unlikely that this list is complete, for it lacks the essential instruments such as the bowed strings and flute played in civilian scenes, which must have been lost. Figure 8.5 shows an example of the wayang thithi puppets that he made.

Chinese glove puppet theater, wayang (po)tehi, continued to be popular in the latter part of the nineteenth century (Serrurier 1896: 275, Moens 1949: 1–15). Chinese wedding celebrations at the time frequently included both Chinese and Javanese puppet theater, music, and dance. A nineteenth-century account of a Chinese wedding in Semarang mentions that *tandhak* (Javanese erotic female dancers) had been invited to travel from their home villages of Ambarawa and Sangklahan to perform

Figure 8.5. This *Wayang thithi* puppet, made by Gan Dhwan Sing, depicts the bearer of King Li Shi's sign, or the king himself. 56 × 20.5 cm. (Seltmann 1976: 70)

at a temple in Semarang and they sang *pantoenan* (songs in Malay quatrains) accompanied by a *gambang* (xylophone), *djie-hian*, a *soeling* (flute), and a *keprak* (clapper), their favorite song being *Dendang kija-lee* (Liem 1931–33: 130). This song may later have become known as "Jali-Jali," a very popular song occurring in many versions in Jakarta and environs to this day. Liem wrote that the pribumi liked the Chinese arts at that time, "strange as it may seem" (ibid.). Another source mentioned that when Chinese men sponsored a Javanese-style *tayuban* (in which male customers pay an erotic female dancer to serve as their dance partner) at a family celebration, those men could choose whether or not they would dance. Indonesian-Chinese tauke even invited tandhak dancers from as far away as Yogyakarta or Surakarta to join the performance (Lindsay 1985: 161).

By the late nineteenth century, many Indonesian-Chinese had become well versed in Javanese dance, music, and theater forms as well as Javanese script. The Dutch employed Indonesian-Chinese as pawnshop owners and tax collectors, as was immortalized in the title of a gamelan piece ("Cinonagih") which survived from the nineteenth into the twentieth century.[12] A newspaper in Semarang serialized some Chinese stories in the form of *tembang* (sung Javanese poetic meters) and printed them in Javanese script, while some Chinese literature was also translated into Javanese (Liem 1931–33: 144). From 1905, the Indonesian-Chinese communities in Java gave increased attention to the Chinese visual arts and literature, as is clear from newspaper and other sources (ibid. 188). They also continued to serve as patrons of Javanese music, dance, and drama. For example, when celebrating the opening of the Khing Tjiok Hwee temple in Semarang in 1911, hundreds of people present heard a great variety of music, including gamelan and a string orchestra (ibid. 202), the latter of which must have been the pa tim.

By the 1870s, wealthy Indonesian-Chinese had formed social clubs, sometimes in the form of music societies. The earliest social club in Semarang was the Boen Hian Tong, "organized in 1876 as a Chinese music society, with an exclusive membership of wealthy and prominent men" (Liem 1931–33: 130; see further on social aspects in Wilmott 1960 and Ong Eng Die 1973). Until the mid-1880s, wealthy peranakan, especially opium farmers who had been given the privilege of officer status by the Dutch, sponsored cultural festivals at Chinese New Year; and they endowed and maintained the temples, bringing out Chinese artists and craftsmen from China who performed or prepared ritual effigies and decorations at the temples. They also hired both Javanese gamelan and Chinese musicians to perform at their private family celebrations. They maintained links with China by sending money to relatives there. They had their children instructed in Chinese language and culture by sending them to private Chinese schools. However, their wives maintained a Javanese lifestyle in language, clothing, and customs (Rush 1991: 22).

Another cultural shift occurred in the mid-1880s, coinciding with the economic depression and the collapse of many Indonesian-Chinese opium farming establishments, together with their owners' fortunes. The economic downturn served to reduce the cultural authority of the leaders of peranakan society and forced them to redefine their own cultural identity, including their attitude to the Javanese arts. The leaders of peranakan society lost much of their wealth. Their authority and identity were further undermined by the large-scale immigration from China of large numbers of women as well as men, who strengthened the Chinese cultural orientation in their families and communities. Being culturally and linguistically oriented toward China, they gave increased emphasis to Chinese music-cultural practices and education for their children and helped revive Confucian/Buddhist/Taoist religious practices and musical forms. Though some members of the peranakan community were heavily involved in authoring and developing popular literature in the Malay language and sponsoring or performing music, dance, and theater, many of the pribumi continued to mistrust and reject them. At the time the peranakan became increasingly attracted by the trappings of Western modernity, which was evident in their shift to Western dress, their greater acquisition of Dutch and English language skills, and the move by some away from commerce to the professions (Rush 1991: 23–24). Some young peranakan became musicians and dancers, while some older tauke became owners of mixed kroncong and swing bands, or promoted pribumi and peranakan performers who joined the newly developing troupes of Malay-Indonesian stambul, bangsawan, and sandiwara commercial theater forms. Like the gambang bands which will be discussed below, these ensembles combined Western, pribumi, and in some cases Chinese musical instruments and dramatic plots (Manusuma 1919, 1922).

Despite their participation in Western and popular commercial culture at the time, the Dutch kept the Indonesian-Chinese strictly in their place on the second rung of the racial ladder. Nor were the Indonesian-Chinese able to regain access to the political power and influence that some had formerly enjoyed. Being "no longer close to power," they "now faced the state as outsiders" (Rush 1991: 24). The expression of another powerful wave of sinophobia was the gravest implication of the embryonic development of the Indonesian nationalist movement in the early twentieth century. The Indonesian nation-state was being devised by the pribumi for the pribumi, who wanted to wrest power from the Dutch, own their country, and control the means of production; and no clear place was reserved in this plan for the Indonesian-Chinese. Thus the turn of the century witnessed the fragmentation and diversification of the Indonesian-Chinese community and—once again—a heightening of racial tensions with indigenous Indonesians (ibid.).

The upper- and middle-class Indonesian-Chinese response to this was again to retreat into Chinese culture, to "reinvent" their Chineseness and to educate their children only in Chinese or Dutch-Chinese schools (Blusse 1981). However, many Indonesian-Chinese in Java were still attracted to Javanese culture and they remained patrons, collectors, and performers of the indigenous Javanese arts; the same applied in

other regions of the Indies. Such patronage also sometimes seemed to
buy them a measure of security. It was reported in 1919 that a Chinese
major in Cirebon, Tan Tjin Kie, had acquired a collection of beautiful
wayang topeng (masks) and puppets as well as many Javanese manuscripts, which must have gained him considerable prestige. Often the
largest wayang wong, stamboel, or kethoprak theater troupes were
owned by Indonesian-Chinese, who also sometimes performed in them
(Liem 1947). In the 1920s and 1930s, the owners of the best gamelan orchestras were the "ruling princes . . . , some members of the nobility,
some of the regents, a few *dhalangs*, and also . . . some wealthy Chinese
music lovers" (Kunst 1973, 1: 244). At the other end of the social scale,
poor "itinerant Chinese Shantung pedlars" in Java were reported to
being playing very small drums of Chinese origin called *klontong* (ibid.
219). Some folk genres of Chinese origin continued to be performed
and maintained. They were even discussed in accounts about local cultural life by Javanese authors, one of whom referred to the *tjembengan*
(Jav.), which derives from *tjembeng, tjeng-beng, tjing-bing*, or *Tsing Bing*,
the ceremony of the cleansing of offerings placed on Chinese graves in
the month of April (Pigeaud 1938: 175). That these and many other diverse Chinese cultural expressions had been absorbed into Javanese cultural life was documented in 1947 by Liem Thian Joe, who referred to
such syncretic Indonesian-Chinese forms as *gambang kromong* music,
popular commercial songs by Chinese composers, the adaptation of Chinese stories (with changed names) in Javanese *kethoprak* theater, and the
above-mentioned wayang thithi, which was described as being similar to
Javanese shadow puppet theater except that it presented Chinese stories
and used locally made Chinese-style shadow puppets depicting Chinese
characters (Liem 1947: 8–10).

We shall now resume the story of the development of the cokek
(tankhak)-gambang music and dance forms which were nurtured
in the rural towns and villages of the Batavia hinterland among the descendants of the China-born men and pribumi women who had been
massacred by the Dutch in 1740. Since that time, large numbers of poor
sugar plantation workers and farmers, mainly of Hokkienese descent,
had settled, intermarried, and integrated into the local pribumi population. Many were converted to Islam in the process (see further The Siaw
Giap 1965, 1990) but maintained some Chinese ritual and artistic elements in their religious observances. For example, some settled in the
village of Cengkareng (now an outer suburb of Jakarta), where mixed

ancestral Chinese and Muslim rites are still practiced at Indonesian-Chinese weddings (see Go Gien Tjwan 1966). Their weddings were led by a Muslim officiant, but the religious rituals and dance and musical performances given at them were syncretic Indonesian-Chinese.

Not surprisingly, the mestizo community living throughout the former plantation area succeeded in developing new syncretic styles of music, i.e. gambang music (later called gambang kromong), the associated cokek (tandhak) dancing and, from the 1920s, lenong theater. Indonesian-Chinese managers, shopkeepers, and farmers supported itinerant art troupes comprising both pribumi and peranakan artists. Due to the fact that generations of peranakan farmers had been allowed to own land and live in specified rural villages surrounding Batavia, where there were many privately owned estates, i.e. in east and northeast Tanggerang, north Bogor, and west Bekasi, conditions were ripe for the development of syncretic entertainments. Both peranakan and pribumi are reported to have enjoyed the festivities held regularly at the Chinese temples, including the barongsai (mythical lion) and liong (dragon) dance processions. Despite occasional racial outbursts, the peranakan were well integrated into the local communities and spoke local Indonesian languages, not Chinese (Go Gien Tjwan 1966).

Between the mid-eighteenth century and the 1880s, peranakan musicians and tauke-funded troupe managers living in and around Batavia developed the gambang, or orkest gambang (Indonesian; xylophone ensemble) as secular entertainment for hire. The repertoire they played was originally based on songs and dances transplanted from Fujian province. These lagu lama (old songs), as they were called in Malay, were originally accompanied by large, middling, and small Chinese bowed string instruments (called kongahyan [small], tehyan [middling], and sukong [large] respectively) and a side-blown flute (suling) plus a Sundanese xylophone (gambang) and a set of Sundanese drums (kendang) (Phoa 1949). Figure 8.6 shows two of these instruments, the kongahyan and the suling in a contemporary gambang kromnog ensemble. The songs were sung by a female pribumi singer-dancer-actor called cokek or wayang cokek, the equivalent term in Javanese tradition being tandhak or ronggeng (a female professional dancer-singer who performed with ronggeng ensemble music). Indeed, in Mossel's above-mentioned report of 1751 these cokek girls had been referred to under the name of tandhak. The cokek girls, who wore a baju kurung (long Indonesian blouse) and sarong and did their hair in a Chinese-style plait, were employed to sing and dance with male peranakan and pribumi guests at

Figure 8.6. A side-blown *suling* (flute) and a *kongahyan* (small bowed string instrument), part of a *gambang kromong* ensemble which accompanied a *lenong* theater perfornmance in Jakarta, December 1974. (Photo by H. Kartomi)

weddings and other family celebrations and for private entertainment, a practice that still continues in the Jabotabek (greater Jakarta) area today.[13] In prewar wayang cokek shows, only three or four cokek girls used to dance to the lagu lagu accompaniment provided, as opposed to many—up to fifty—at more recent Indonesian-Chinese weddings (e.g. in the 1980s and 1990s in the Tanggerang area), where each male guest present can choose a cokek partner if he wishes.

The economic depression in the 1870s and 1880s caused a major change in the gambang-cokek tradition. As peranakan managers, shopkeepers, and farmers adjusted to the depression, some became involved in establishing commercial entertainment venues, probably taverns, in Batavia from the 1870s (Yampolsky 1992). Gambang performances were given in these venues to attract drinking customers, forcing the musicians to adapt to the demands of their new business environment. They enlarged and enlivened the original ensemble by adding local Batavian or Sundanese instruments, including suspended gongs (Sundanese *goöng* and *kempul*) and a gong-chime (containing ten small gongs arranged in two rows on a frame) called *kromong*. The new ensemble was called gambang kromong and musicians played a separate musical repertoire on it as well as accompanying cokek dancing. Customers used to dance the so-called *ngibing* dance in pribumi style with a cokek girl, not only to the old songs (lagu lama or gambang Cina) but also to new Batavian gambang kromong songs, which were called *lagu sayur* (Indonesian vegetable songs) or *lagu dalem* (insider songs).

Lagu sayur were possibly named after the pribumi vegetable and fruit vendors who used to travel to market in Bandung or another town to sell their produce, stay at the market overnight before returning home, and pass the evenings by entertaining themselves with gambang kromong singing, dancing, and clowning of a kind that was later to form the basis of lenong theater, which developed in the 1930s.[14] In the late 1920s and 1930s, certain peranakan entrepreneurs who were conscious of the commercial opportunity offered by the theatrical sketches associated with wayang cokek and gambang kromong organized the business side of these shows, presented performances of widely appealing stories of both Chinese and Indonesian origin, as in stambul theater, and formalized the result under the name of *lenong* theater (Grijns 1976, 1981; see also Pasaribu 1954, Probonegoro 1974).

Lenong, then, is a Eurasian-Malay "opera" form. It is a synthesis of cokek dance, gambang kromong music, and stambul theater, which eventually absorbed Perso-Arabic, Chinese, Indian, and Indonesian components as it developed among traveling troupes of pribumi and peranakan players and musicians in Java from the early twentieth century.

These so-called new *sayur* songs performed by gambang troupes since the 1870s were clearly differentiated from the old Indonesian-Chinese gambang songs known as *lagu lama* (old songs). They included—and still include—two categories of instrumental music, which are called *phobin* (Batavian *pobin*) and *loban* respectively and are played either as separate pieces or—more often—as preludes and postludes to the basically pentatonic songs and are accompanied by the modern, enlarged gambang kromong ensemble (Dinas Kebudayaan Jakarta 1983: 6). Lagu phobin melodies, which were originally derived from Hokkien instrumental pieces, included song with corrupted Hokkien titles such as Phobin Matujin, Macutay, Lankinhwa, Cincoweke, Phebotan, Phepantauw, Citnosa, Kingkit, Cutaipan, and Kogjilek (ibid.).

In the late nineteenth century and the first half of the twentieth century, the Indonesian-Chinese were in the forefront of the development of the commercial music industry. For one thing, they were active in managing and performing in the traveling troupes which performed stambul and bangsawan theater in the Malay/Indonesian language with plots and musical repertoires derived from Malay, Chinese, Hindustani, and Perso-Arabic sources. Meanwhile, some Indonesian-Chinese families had opened up music businesses. They published records for sale and sold gramophones, music instruments, sheet music, and the like, advertising their wares in Indonesian-Chinese magazines, newspapers, and novels of the time. For example, in 1913 the author and publisher Lie Tek Long advertised in the back of his popular novel a series of records which he had made of his own poetry readings, adding that he had also made records of songs from Stambul, Krontjong, Pobin, and Wayang Tjiokek sources (Lie Tek Long 1913: 80).

In the early-to-mid twentieth century, rich peranakan families continued to serve as patrons of both local pribumi and Chinese arts. For example, in the Pariaman area of West Sumatra, the ten-day Shi'a Muslim *tabut* ceremony was richly sponsored by local peranakan residents and immortalized by the Chinese visual art designs on the tabut pageant tower (Lekkerkerker 1916: 171, Kartomi 1983: 153–55). In Java, peranakan leaders arranged for Chinese historical romances to be translated into Javanese verse forms (Pigeaud 1967: 258–59), in part so that their children—most of whom could speak only Malay-Indonesian—could be exposed to this literature and associated theatrical forms and songs. In recognition of their patronage and artistic contribution, peranakan leaders were frequently invited to official Indonesian court and Dutch state functions. Indonesian-Chinese musicians, actors, and managers continued to play a major role in performances by theatrical troupes of commercial komedie stamboel and other theater forms. Some Indonesian-Chinese actors, such as Hoogeven, upon whom Dutch nationality had been bestowed, became famous. The proceeds from amateur wayang potehi and other temple theater performances sponsored by rich peranakan leaders were frequently given to poor peranakan families. Thus peranakan art patrons and artists practiced both the Indonesian and Chinese arts and fulfilled thereby both Confucian and Muslim injunctions to perform charitable acts.

In Java, peranakan interest in Chinese music scholarship grew in the 1930s. In 1936 a group of mainly Dutch-educated Indonesian-Chinese and other Sinophiles from the European and Javanese communities founded a learned society which they called the China Instituut. The Institute adopted an active program to promote Chinese cultural expressions in the country. Its journal, called *Mededeelingen van het China Instituut* (Communications of the China Institute), dealt with aspects of both Chinese and Indonesian-Chinese culture. In 1937, for example, Sie Boen Lian published articles in it about gambang kromong music and Chinese zither playing; and in 1941, Shu Teo Ching wrote on Chinese opera. The journal ceased to exist during the war.

In march tempo, accompanied by Western brass and percussion band.

He·sa - ka·beh pe·mu·da In·do·ne·si·a Geus ni·tih ka·na·wan-

ci Ning·gang·ka·na·mang·sa Nga·be·la Nu·sajeung Bang·sa Na·donkeun ra·ga jeung pa-

ti Su·ci·tur mul·ya ka·wa·ji·ban la·la·ki

Example 8.1 The Sundanese-language revolutionary song "Durma," from sandiwara stambul (Indonesian-language folk theater), in which Indonesian-Chinese singer-actors and Western-style band musicians joined with pro-revolutionary pribumi and Indo (Indonesian-European) artists during the Japanese Occupation

When the Japanese invaded the Dutch East Indies in 1941, many peranakan artists and others became members of the Indonesian resistance against the Japanese and the ensuing revolutionary movement against the Dutch and their British allies (1945–49). For example, Indonesian-Chinese singer-actors and Western-style band musicians joined pribumi and *Indo* (mixed-blood, Indonesian-European) artists to perform *sandiwara stambul* (Indonesian-language folk theater), giving shows in liberated areas on such themes as Indonesian revolutionaries sabotaging the British military action in Surabaya, or the courageous response by the revolutionaries to Dutch massacres of Indonesian revolutionary patriots. Some of the songs were accompanied at times by local gamelan instruments and at others by a small Western brass and percussion band, as in the song "Durma" (ex. 8.1). (The title is the name of a hero, a demi-god [Th. Pigeaud, pers. comm.]). The text is written in the seven-line Durma verse form in the Sundanese language and translates as follows:

> Hey, all young people of Indonesia
> Now is the time
> Now is the moment
> To defend your country and people
> Surrender your bodies and souls
> A holy and noble aim
> The duty of all men.

Others were accompanied by a small Western band only, as in the song "Brontak" (Attack). These songs were sung in Banjar (West Java) in May

Figure 8.7. Cast of a *sandiwara* (theater) production, in Indonesian, of the Chinese love story "Tiauw Sian Lang Tang Toh." The director, Bp. L. Soema, is seated front right. Two actors doubled as musicians playing *gong, pan, kecrek*, and woodblock in war scenes. (Reproduced with permission of Marcus Soema)

1946 by Bp. Tjung Han Koen, the peranakan lead singer of a revolutionary sandiwara theater troupe which traveled around parts of West Java and western Central Java during the resistance against the Dutch.[15]

In the late colonial and early independent periods, not only Chinese glove puppet theater but also sandiwara performances of Chinese classical stories were given in Batavia/Jakarta in the Indonesian language for the benefit of non-Chinese speaking peranakan as well as a large pribumi audience. Figure 8.7 shows a sandiwara cast of sixteen actors posing in southeast Chinese opera–style costumes (which are somewhat Indonesianized, including some Pekalongan batik), after playing a Chinese love story in a theater in Batavia in May 1945. Three of the actors on the occasion doubled as servants and musicians who played military ensemble–style gongs, drums, clappers, and cymbals for martial occasions, duels, and journeys. The troupe frequently performed in Jakarta from the late 1930s until the death of the director, L. Soema, in 1947. President Soekarno saw a performance in 1946. The troupe raised money through their performances to help the Chinese resist the Japanese invaders in China during the early 1940s. They also gave frequent performances during the Japanese occupation of Indonesia and gave the proceeds to the Ati Suci Orphanage, run by Ibu Wee Tjan Tjun for the care of pribumi and peranakan war victims.[16]

The following section contains brief field-based accounts of late and colonial peranakan music-cultural life in four selected areas: Wangon in Central Java, Malang in East Java, the island of Bangka, and Singkawang in West Kalimantan. I found that elderly members of peranakan communities in these areas between the 1970s and the 1990s had selective but vivid memories of the distinctive aspects of the music-culture of their area in late colonial times. Wangon and Malang are typical of Javanese towns in which peranakan families lived in ghetto-like quarters. Bangka and Singkawang, on the other hand, like the hinterland of Jakarta (discussed above), are typical of areas in which peranakan families were allowed to own rural land and settle relatively freely in small villages.

Wangon

One of my informants[17] in Wangon, Banyumas, told me that in the last decades of colonial rule, local peranakan families were mostly shopkeepers, importer-exporters, construction bosses, hotel owners, and poor workers. Except for a few high-ranking public servants chosen by the Dutch, they all lived in one street, not being allowed to own rural land. Like most surrounding towns, Wangon had a klenteng which, until it was abolished in the 1960s, served as the home base of many performances of peranakan musical processions, including the barongsai and liong. The barongsai procession was frequently held on festival days, such as at Chinese New Year, with one or two men moving in unison underneath the cloth body and tail of the barongsai, who seemed to chase a big fireball along the street. The barongsai's movements were accompanied by three or four musicians playing martial-style music on drums, gongs, and cymbals outside each family's home as they moved along a street. Householders handed red envelopes containing money to the barongsai performers as a donation to the temple or as charity for the poor, as well as to cover the group's expenses. The richest families always gave the biggest donations.

On other occasions, the amusing and impressive liong figure appeared in the streets, accompanied by one or two clowns and a group of percussion musicians, who played gongs and drums very loudly. A group of ten to fifteen men supported the liong's long body and tail from underneath, with its head, body, and tail curving along and swooping up and down unpredictably, sometimes seeming to attack the crowds of children and adults—both pribumi and peranakan. Meanwhile, the clowns collected donations from the onlookers and wayside houses for charity. However, the dragon and lion dances were even more popular, my informant said, in the north coastal town of Tegal, where the tauke sponsored and local fishermen performed in the local troupes or watched the procession, thereby seeking good luck and protection while at sea.

Other performances held in or near the temple yard included *wayang klithik Cina* (clinking Chinese wayang), with a puppeteer *(dhalang)* telling Chinese legends in the Malay language while manipulating scores of small three-dimensional wooden puppets. Also popular was the *wayang gambar* (picture wayang), in which a dhalang told a Chinese legend while slowly unfolding a scroll containing paintings of scenes to illustrate the characters and events in that legend. There were also frequent wayang potehi performances in the temple courtyard. All three forms of wayang were accompanied by a pa tim orchestra, which consisted minimally of Chinese percussion instruments and sona for the military scenes, plus strings, flute, and soft percussion for the civilian scenes.

Malang

At least from early in this century until 1945, the most popular form of peranakan music-culture in Malang, East Java, was the glove puppet theater form called wayang potehi, being relatively cheap and easy for a temple or family to present at its celebrations.[18] The Javanese-speaking peranakan in Malang were so integrated into the local Javanese community that for the past three generations or longer the potehi puppeteers have presented their performances mainly in the Indonesian language, using Hokkien language only for some initial introductions to characters (followed by translations in Indonesian) and for the songs (Brandon 1967: 3). The Chinese monologues and song texts were not widely understood by the audience but contributed to the atmosphere, I was told.[19]

Po te hi is the Hokkienese pronunciation of the Chinese *budaixi*, which has been translated as "linen-bag theater" (Hazeu 1897: 93, van Groenendael 1993: 14). It was so called either because the puppets were brought out of a linen bag at the time of performance, or because the puppeteer hid himself in such a bag in a one-man show, or even perhaps because of the bag-shaped underdress (van Groenendael 1993: 14). Potehi may have originated in Chuan-chou city, Fujian province, about 300 years ago (Tan 1984: 40). However, some forms of puppet and shadow theater were already practiced under the T'ang dynasty (van Groenendael 1993: 16).

In the nineteenth and early-to-mid twentieth centuries, potehi was mainly performed as a religious observance, which could range from the exorcistic[20] to the redemption of a vow, or to celebrate the birthday of a Confucian, Buddhist, or Taoist deity to whom a temple was dedicated. In the late colonial and early independent periods, it also served as a form of entertainment at markets and at annual fairs (pasar malam) in Yogyakarta (Moens 1949) and elsewhere. It was enjoyed from the mid nineteenth century by Chinese emigrants and their guests living in many towns, including Surakarta, Yogyakarta, Semarang, Kediri, Jombang, Tulungagung, Blitar, Malang, Surabaya, Bandung, and Jakarta. Performances were mainly located in or just outside the temples or in a village square and were sponsored by the tauke or a family for a celebration. Sometimes a series of performances was given, lasting up to three months. Troupes were normally privately owned and managed, consisting of a puppeteer (dhalang [Javanese]), an assistant, and five or six musicians, who were normally paid only a small amount for their performances and necessarily had another job or two. The dhalang and musicians sat behind a stage "wall" on the front of a covered bamboo and wooden open-air theater-stage construction resting on four stilts, with the name of the relevant potehi company displayed in front. With his forefinger reaching into the puppet's head and his thumb in one arm, the puppeteer held the body under its gown with his hand, moving its head and arms with his fingers.

The miniature stage properties and musical components of a potehi performance resembled those of Chinese opera. The puppets, which stood about 20–24 cm tall, had wooden heads. They were dressed for a part by putting a gown over their cloth bodies and adding a headdress, beard, or other item as appropriate (see fig. 8.8a). Thus, as we have seen, potehi performances were often referred to by nineteenth-century Dutch writers by the name of wayang golek (Sundanese three-dimensional puppet) theater.

A set consisted of between twenty-five and thirty or up to a hundred puppets which were kept in a box, from which a number of puppets were selected for a particular play. They consisted of gods, goddesses, priests, kings, noble warriors, noble women, femal e generals, soldiers, robbers, clowns, servants and workers, animals, weapons, and clouds. In fact, as in Chinese opera, there were four types of characters, including the clowns (chou; fig. 8.8b), male characters (sheng, e.g. fig. 8.6c), female characters (dan), and painted faces (jing), with the latter incorporating several subtypes.

In the absence of recordings to describe the music in wayang potehi

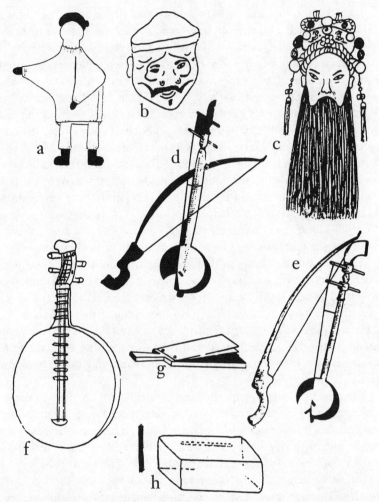

Figure 8.8. Wayang potehi: selected puppets and musical instruments used in a performance in the klenteng in Malang. *(a)* Undressed glove puppet. The puppeteer's hand manipulates the puppet under its skirt, with his forefinger reaching into the outstretched arm (reproduced with permission from van Groenendael 1993). *(b)* Face of a civilian clown, with mustache (reproduced with permission from Tan Sooi Beng 1984). *(c)* Face and beard of a powerful, high-ranking character (reproduced with permission from Tan Sooi Beng 1984). *(d) Cin hu* or *rebab batok besar. (e) Ol hu* or *rebab batok kecil. (f) Kecapi* (moon guitar). *(g) Pan* (a set of wooden clappers). *(h) Piak ku* (woodblock). (Figs. 8.8*d–h* are reproduced with permission from Muhadjir et al., 1968: 10–11)

Example 8.2 Example of (soft) civilian scene ensemble and music from a performance of wayang potehi, recorded by M. J. and H. Kartomi in the main temple in Malang, 1974. (Transcription by Aline Scott-Maxwell)

in colonial times, we can only examine the music played in recent times, which, we were told by elderly informants, does not substantially differ from that of the colonial-era shows. In a performance which we recorded in Malang (see exx. 8.2 and 8.3), a relatively soft ensemble played the accompaniment to the civilian scenes and a loud ensemble to the military scenes. The local people have long used a combination of Indonesian and Hokkien names for the instruments. The civilian scene ensemble comprised the *cin hu* (large bowed string instrument, fig. 8.8d), the *ol hu* (small bowed string instrument, fig. 8.8e), the *kecapi* (Indonesian, moon

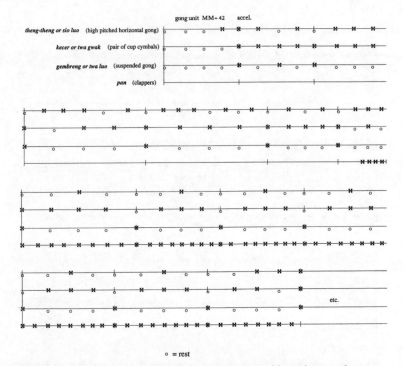

○ = rest

Example 8.3 Example of (loud) military scene ensemble and music from a performance of wayang potehi, recorded by M. J. and H. Kartomi in the main temple in Malang, 1974. (Transcription by Aline Scott-Maxwell)

guitar, fig. 8.8f), the pan (Hokkien, a pair of wood clappers, fig. 8.8g), and the *dongko* or *tambur* (Javanese, a two-headed suspended drum with a padded hammer). The bow of the long-necked string instruments moved between a pair of strings wound around pegs attached at the back. Each had a small wooden bridge on top of its sounding body which consisted of a half coconut shell covered with a thin wooden sound board and a rosette of small holes perforated into its back. The kecapi had a cylindrical, disc-shaped body to which a very short neck was attached; its four strings were wound around pegs fixed to each side of the neck, two by two.

The military *luogu* (lit. "gong and drum") ensemble, on the other hand, consisted of a high-pitched, horizontal gong called *sio luo* (lit. "small gong") or *theng-theng* (Javanese), a vertical gong called *twa luo* or *gembreng* (Javanese), a suspended barrel drum called *dong gu* or *tambur*, a wood-block called *piak ku* (fig. 8.8h), wooden clappers called *pan*, two pairs of cup cymbals (in a frame) called *twa gwak* or *kecer* (Javanese) and a shawm called *sona* or *slompret* (Javanese). Sometimes the melody played on the shawm was doubled at the lower octave by the larger of the two bowed string instruments *(cin hu)*. The barrel drum was prominent in many military scenes, either dominating certain percussive sections or played to balance the melody instruments, sona and cin hu. The puppeteer, or sometimes another musician in the troupe, sang vocal parts in the Hokkien language to string accompaniment, with melodies having five, six or seven tones in the octave. Sometimes he chanted on a few pitches. Clown comments were called out by the dhalang, his assistant, or another musician. The dhalang gave verbal cues or hand signs to his musicians via the leader/drummer to start or stop playing, increase or decrease their dynamic level, and hasten or slow down the tempo. The musicians played musical interludes on the civilian ensemble between scenes; and they accompanied happy or sad and contemplative dances and songs, narratives, monologues, dialogues, and battle scenes with either the civilian or the military ensemble instruments, as appropriate. Since many musicians used to belong to a travelling potehi troupe, they used only portable instruments, playing two or three instruments each. The lead musician in this "clapper opera," as Hokkien opera is often called, played the drum, woodblock, and clappers and sometimes also a frame-drum. He watched the dhalang closely for his musical cues, which he passed on to the others by playing rhythmic messages: for example, a series of accelerating rolls culminating in an accented stroke on the tambur, which attracted their immediate attention for a command to be given. The other musicians then recognized and acted upon the command. Another musician alternatively played both shawm and the cup cymbals with the high-pitched gong, while yet another alternated between playing the cymbals and the ol hu or cin hu, and sometimes the kecapi.

One of the most distinguishing features of the ensemble sound was produced by the gembreng (gong). Convex, narrow-shouldered, and about 30 cm in diameter, it was struck on its flat central striking area with an attached padded beater, thus producing a sudden descent in pitch. Like the high-pitched theng-theng (about 21 cm in diameter), it was made of an alloy of copper, tin, and zinc. The instruments which punctuated (subdivided) the periods between successive large gong strokes or highlighted the drama included the gong, the clappers, and the large drum (tambur).

The Singkawang Area, West Kalimantan District

Very little is known about the colonial-era performing arts in this area of "Chinese" dominance, but the story can be pieced together in part from accounts by elderly musicians.

The main port for export of goods from the northwest Kalimantan hinterland ever since the peranakan population settled there was Singkawang (derived from Sang Keu Yong, lit. "town at the foot of the hill"). From the seventeenth century or earlier, many landless, Hakka-speaking men migrated spontaneously to west and central Kalimantan to mine gold and later settled as farmers on the free land there, while some became fishermen and lived along the coast. Many married local Dayak or Chinese women and tilled the land, building and maintaining hundreds of klenteng[21] and enjoying a rich musical life at Chinese festival times. They performed the usual liong and barongsai processional dances and large-scale temple rituals, including rebutan or Raja Jin, which resembled rebutan in Bangka, as described below.

My peranakan informants in the Singkawang area said that until the 1960s they and their ancestors had enjoyed "clapper opera" performed in Hakka dialect by visiting or local troupes. However, the most popular form of entertainment had always—in living memory—been the *wayang gantung* (suspended puppet theater), accompanied by the pa tim orchestra.

In this form of theater, a separate puppeteer was needed to manipulate each puppet. Thus in plays involving thirty characters, up to thirty puppeteers took part. They stood behind a raised stage wall in a full-size temporary theater, manipulating between them scores of marionette puppets with Chinese faces and headdresses and wearing either Malay or southern Chinese–style opera costumes. Each puppet had about twelve strings attached to its arms, hands, feet, and other parts. The barrel drum was prominent in the music accompanying the military scenes, especially in purely percussive sections or when the *sona* (Javanese *slompret*) doubled the melody on the large bowed string instrument, with rhythmic punctuation on the cymbals and clappers.

Troupes were hired for the three main annual temple celebrations and for family and other occasions. The stories performed were episodes from the Chinese classic literature such as the Story of the Three Kingdoms and the journey of the Buddhist monk Xuanzang to obtain the holy scriptures, as in wayang potehi in Java (as discussed above).

According to 67-year-old Bp. Fa Chong Siang Ng of the klenteng in Desa Sembangkan, Kecamatan Pemangkat, instruments used in the former wayang gantung troupe there (until it was banned in 1965) comprised a double-headed drum called *ta ku*, a pair of large cymbals (30 cm in diameter) called *cem*, two small flat gongs called *po*, a wood scraper called *tahar*, a shawm called *tak*, a three-string, long-necked lute called *sanhian*, a two-string bowed instrument called *nanhu* or *niufu*, and a flute called *hsiao* or *tiaowa*. This band was also used to accompany funeral processions. Wayang gantung performances were given in or just outside the grounds of a temple, always in Hakka dialect, but with a few words in Indonesian now and then. At New Year, performances of one chosen story lasted up to eight nights in a row.[22] In the colonial period, many wayang gantung performers passed on their skills to the younger generation, and there was a lively Chinese temple theater life.[23]

In the early to mid-twentieth century, some Muslim peranakan families and communities also used to sponsor performances of Muslim *dhikir* (choral, solo vocal, and framedrum music-making), Malay *jepin* dancing, and Malay *mendu* and *bangsawan* theater at their weddings and other celebrations, and they were also partial to kroncong and tanjidor band music.

The Island of Bangka

The achievements of Bangka's peranakan performing artists throughout the colonial era remain undocumented, but I have been able to reconstruct part of their story by assembling word-of-mouth accounts of elderly Hokkienese musicians in the south, especially in and around Toboali, and of Hakka musicians in the north, especially in and around Muntok and Berinyu. As leaders of both communities recount, the development of their two music-cultures was closely tied to the hegemonic politics of tin mining and pepper plantations from the early eighteenth century. Since the Hakkas and Hokkienese did not intermarry, the northern and southern communities remained linguistically and musically distinct, though a few southern artistic influences in northern Bangka communities are observable from the late colonial period.

Tin began to be exploited in Bangka, which was then part of the southern Sumatran sultanate of Palembang, from the late seventeenth century. The Sultan controlled the commerce in tin via a network of peranakan traders who were related to his peranakan first wife, having allied themselves with both Palembang's and Jambi's royal families. Especially in the late 1740s, these traders brought in an influx of skilled Hakka tin miners from Yunnan, West Borneo, and other parts of Southeast Asia. Malays, Bugis, and others also mined the tin, but most of the miners were Indonesian-Chinese. The peranakan clients and relatives of the Sultan of Palembang supervised the migration of Chinese workers, who had the reputation of being skilled and diligent, to work in the tin mines as well as the pepper plantations. When the peranakan traders threatened to grow too powerful, the Sultan was able to restrict their activities (Andaya 1993: 219). By the middle of the century, large quantities of tin and pepper were being exported to China and beyond. In 1753, for example, Sultan Mahmud sent five ships carrying loads of tin and pepper to China and twelve ships loaded with tin to Batavia (ibid. 1993: 191). The Dutch then intervened aggressively, shifting the balance of power into their hands, and large numbers of Hakka tin workers from Siantan, Malacca, and Johore were allowed to settle and work in the mines in the early and mid-eighteenth century. Hokkienese pepper plantation workers were also encouraged to settle in southern Bangka to expand the output of the pepper plantations from the island.

Thus, the overwhelming majority of the 4,000 people of Chinese descent on Bangka in the mid-1750s were Hakka miners and Hokkien plantation workers. Evidence of slave orchestras on the plantations still needs to be discovered, but tanjidor bands became a prominent feature of Bangkas peranakan music-culture at least as early as the 1920s. As in the Batavia hinterland, the miners and plantation workers mostly married pribumi women and were allowed to own some land; and a remarkable social integration between peranakan and pribumi occurred over time. Many Chinese temples were built and kept in good condition by the large peranakan community.[24] From the late nineteenth century, many peranakan families were engaged in farming, mainly producing sweet potatoes, vegetables, and pigs. Most were regular worshipers in the temples, while a few became Muslim, and others attended both temples and mosques on feast days. The different religious and artistic communities were reportedly marked by a high degree of tolerance for each other.

In the south, Hokkien pepper plantation workers developed a unique music-culture associated with mass weddings. At such functions, fifty or more couples dressed in red wedding costumes were entertained by a variety of secular peranakan and pribumi musical and dance forms, including South Sumatran–Malay welcome dances performed by girls in bridal costumes and accompanied by musicians playing Malay drums, a pair of bronze gongs, and a melody instrument such as a *sarunai* (shawm) or *suling* (flute); agile male Malay or Chinese self-defense dances; Chinese marionette puppet theater, wayang gantung; and Chinese opera, performed by visiting troupes. The southern area produced more artists and a greater variety of presentations than in the north, which was known primarily for its wayang gantung and tanjidor band music performed at weddings and tanjidor or Chinese percussion ensembles played at funerals.

It was from the early 1920s, as noted above, that peranakan and

Eurasian musicians combined forces to play popular music in tanjidor bands. When touring the streets of prosperous Dutch and peranakan neighborhoods, their performances also earned them tips from the local householders. Since they played popular Chinese as well as American, Dutch, and Malay songs, including songs popularized by commercial touring bangsawan and komedie stambul theater troupes, it became fashionable for working-class peranakan families to employ tanjidor bands at their weddings and funerals. Thus, many towns spawned tanjidor bands from that time. The Dutch encouraged these bands by offering their all-male members small payments to play at government functions; and they even offered them the opportunity to take part in *korps Musik* competitions. Playing trumpets, saxophones, trombones, tubas, clarinets, Western bass and kettle drums, and cymbals, tanjidor bands often served as the main providers of music at poor peranakan families' weddings and funerals, being cheaper and more festive and modern than the more traditional pa tim.[25] At weddings they were requested to accompany the bridegroom's procession to the bride's house, playing old Malay songs such as "Sapu Tangan" (Indonesian, Handkerchief), Chinese favorites such as "Ai Cinde Kus Eu" (Mandarin, Story of love, a song from Hong Kong), and Western songs such as "Maria Waltz" and "La Paloma" (also called *Lagu Barat*, Western song). During the procession to the graveyard at a peranakan funeral, tanjidor bands played such songs as "Janji Tua" (Old promise, otherwise known as "Auld Lang Syne").

In both north and south Bangka, peranakan communities celebrated the same temple festivals, especially at Chinese New Year, rebutan and pudu. In fact the most uniquely Bangka-style Chinese festival in the late colonial and independent periods was the rebutan, which was normally called Raja Jin. Held during the seventh month of the Chinese calendar *(Cit Gwee)* in honor of the deity and princess Kwan Yim, protectress at sea, it took place in or outside a temple yard. Artists and crowds of onlookers and participants attended every year. For months, members of a local community would work to construct a nine-meter-high bamboo construction depicting a seated giant called Raja Jin or Raja Setan in Indonesian (lit. "King Satan")[26] or *Bong Fi, Bong Fehi,* or *Bong Fai* in Hokkien dialects. (In standard Hokkien, his name is actually *Tai Su Ya*). By voluntary cooperative work, the local villagers covered the giant's immense body, including his black trousers, with red, gold, and green shiny paper. During the festivities, a group of so-called *barong* musicians (who also played in the barongsai dragon dance) played percussion music on a flat Chinese gong, a *tambur* (local two-headed drum), a shawm,

and other percussion instruments. Formerly, Chinese string instruments
(rebab batok besar and rebab batok kecil) were added to play the main
melodic part. At the Raja Jin ceremony, each worshipper was expected
to bring an offering to appease this potentially wicked deity. These were
objects such as candles, *kukus menyan* (incense), *ubi rebus* (boiled sweet
potato), and fresh vegetables. Worshipers brought or sent temple offerings of large red candles which, when lit, could last for a whole year. The
aim during rebutan was for all present to take part in a free-for-all, by
trying to crawl up to the face of the effigy of the Raja Jin and to grab part
of a paper drawing of the princess-goddess Ibu Dewi Kwan Yim; for
to succeed in obtaining part of it was believed to bring luck. Around
rebutan time, local Chinese bands were often hired to play or accompany
dancing on a portable stage constructed outside a temple. Indonesian-
Chinese music and theater performances and barongsai processions also
took place, and tanjidor and kroncong and other popular band music
was played. The present generation of peranakan musicians report that
Bangka's peranakan musical forms in the late colonial era were vibrant,
strong, and diverse.

CONCLUSION

Throughout the three centuries of colonial rule, the Dutch treated the
Indonesian-Chinese mestizos who made up the bulk of the "Foreign
Oriental" section of the population as a diaspora-pariah group, and the
pribumi followed suit. As a result, the peranakan population of the
Netherlands East Indies involved itself in three categories of performing arts activity. One was the practice of the Chinese temple arts, including street processions, temple rituals, and puppet theater or opera,
which tended to be performed with minimal changes in what was believed to be the authentic Chinese musical style and which served as a
point of psychological refuge and retreat for peranakan communities
when under siege. Another was the secular, professional music, dance,
and theater which represented a new, syncretic, creative impulse and
style as the result of sustained contact between peranakan and pribumi
artists and their communities, each of whom contributed elements from
their own cultural traditions. The last category was the secular commercial music, dance, and theater genres which developed out of sustained
contact between pribumi, peranakan, and Dutch, or artists performing
syncretic Western band or popular music. Examples of the first category
are wayang potehi and the pa tim orchestra. Gambang kromong music
and lenong theater are instances of the second. And tanjidor, stambul

kroncong, and popular songs that exhibit a combination of Malay, Western, and/or Chinese (and even Indian-Muslim) elements are examples of the third.

Unlike other oppressed minority communities, such as European Jews, African-Americans, or Malaysian-Chinese, the Indonesian-Chinese do not possess a substantial body of protest music. Some evidence, however, survives to suggest that Indonesian-Chinese artists and communities sometimes used the performing arts to express their resistance to or protest against the conditions under which they lived. Given the exigencies of colonial government control, this mainly occurred within the insider anonymity of Chinese-language potehi, wayang gantung, and other Chinese theater performances. After the Dutch temporarily left the archipelago in the early part of World War II, the Indonesian-Chinese helped create and perform anti-Japanese protest songs and theater in mixed pribumi-peranakan theatrical and musical troupes in the countryside; and they continued to perform anti-Dutch songs and theater as members of such troupes in the resistance against the Dutch when they returned in force in 1945–49, after which they left Indonesia. The Indonesian-Chinese, however, who were ever conscious of their attributed diaspora-pariah status, mostly tried to minimize the public expression of their cultural differences from mainstream pribumi society. In times of racial stress and danger, they needed to find strategies for by-passing oppression, which included retreating into the haven of Chinese culture and religion and educating their children to boot, while temporarily minimizing their contribution to the pribumi performing arts. Where relative racial harmony prevailed, however, most of them renewed their efforts to integrate into the local community and sponsored, performed, or attended performances of both pribumi and peranakan music, dance, and theater.

Thus the story of the Indonesian-Chinese musical experience in the Netherlands East Indies was one of constant creative adaptation to changing social and artistic conditions and the search for workable musical solutions to the racial and socio-economic dilemmas which they encountered.

NOTES

This article is based in part on fieldwork by H. Kartomi and me among many Indonesian-Chinese communities throughout western Indonesia in the towns and areas shown in figure 8.1 between 1974 and 1995. I am grateful to the central and regional officers of the Department of Education and Culture in all these places, and especially its Director-General, Ibu Professor Dr. Edi Sedyawati for their support; to many musicians and cultural leaders in Malang, Jakarta, north Bogor, Belitung, Bangka, Singkawang, and elsewhere for their time and expertise; to the Australian Research Grants committee, which funded my research; to Sue Blackburn (Abeyasekere), Charles Coppel, Lee Han Koen, Andrew Gunawan, Basoeki Koesasi, Marcus Soema, Philip Yampolsky, and others for valuable critical comment; to my research assistant Aline Scott-Maxwell for transcribing some of our *potehi* recordings; and to my husband Mas Dris, who accompanied me on all fieldtrips and helped in many ways, including taking photos and making recordings. Gary Swinton of the Department of Geography, Monash University, prepared the maps. Dr. M. J. Volke drew the undressed glove puppet. "Bp." and "Ibu" are the Indonesian equivalents of "Mr." and "Mrs."

1. In 1624, the population included Dutch, Chinese, Japanese, and "especially Indonesian natives," Balinese and Makassarese, the latter two categories being transplanted slaves.

2. Indonesian-Chinese and pribumi alike distinguish the terms *peranakan*, *pribumi* ("native"), and *totok* (Chinese-born, or people of Chinese descent whose first language and culture is Chinese). The fact that many pribumi have some Chinese blood and the peranakan some Indonesian blood makes these racial labels—like most racial terms—rather slippery, but since they are in constant use in Indonesia, we shall need to use them here too.

3. In south Kalimantan, for example, whole Indonesian-Chinese communities living in the Banjarmasin and Amungtai areas have been devout Muslims for centuries.

4. Indonesian-Chinese women are rarely mentioned in the literature by colonial authors or peranakan and pribumi writers, nor in the secondary sources Lasiyo 1992, and Salmon and Lombard 1975, 1977, 1985, or others.

5. Part of the reason for past neglect of research into the topic is the low priority placed on it by most Indonesian scholars (a notable exception being Giok-Lan Tan 1963) and the appropriate Indonesian government authorities, who believe it is more important to study the cultures of the many "pure" Indonesian ethnic groups. Although the many pribumi ethnic groups in Indonesia are still under-researched, the low priority given to the Indonesian-Chinese is not, however, the main reason for the dearth of interest in their music-culture. Unlike in Malaysia, which adheres to an integrationist policy, Indonesia's official policy (Department of Education and Culture 1994: 1–15) excludes the Indonesian-Chinese from the list of "ethnic groups" whose culture is to be promoted because it is based on an official assimilationist policy, whereby "Chinese" culture must be assimilated (not integrated), i.e. must disappear into, mainstream Indonesian culture. Thus, the multicultural policy excludes the Indonesian-Chinese. The *pembauran total* (total assimilation) policy formally took effect in Indonesia from mid-1965 (see further Coppel 1977, 1983).

6. Areas of substantial peranakan settlement not discussed in this article include Bagan Siapi-api in coastal mainland Riau (Sumatra), the island of Belitung, and Amungtai in south Kalimantan.

7. Groeneveldt and Kunst interpret some of the evidence for such reports in

twelfth- and fifteenth-century sources. For example, the 489th Book of Chronicles of the second Sung dynasty, a colorful account of life at the East Javanese court of King Jayabhaya ca. 1150, mentioned music being made on transverse flutes, drums, and wooden slabs (Kunst 1968: 24). The Muslim priest Ma Huan, reporting on Cheng Ho's travels in Java in the Ming period (ca. 1405), wrote that the gamelan consisted of a set of copper drums (i.e. *bonang*, according to Kunst) and a large brass gong, while the wind instruments were made of coconut shells (i.e. ocarinas, according to Kunst) and that tournaments took place to the sound of rolls on the drums (Ma Huan 1937: 164, 167, 168; Groeneveldt 1880: 21, Kunst 1968: 89). In the *Ying-yai Shêng-lan*, dated 1416 (see Groeneveldt 1880: 21, 45–51), there is mention of brass "drums" and gongs, the blowing of coconut shells, and the beating of bamboo drums (possibly bamboo idiochord tube zithers, Kunst 1968: 89).

8. Evidence that several of the Wali Sanga had Chinese blood has been presented by Slametmuljana (1976: 126–29, 217, 230) and Sie Hok Tjwan (1990: 79–82).

9. The *Serat Kandha* is a series of historical texts belonging to the Javanese *pasisir* (north coastal) literature of the eighteenth century (Pigeaud 1967: 141).

10. *Capgomeh* (Hokkien, otherwise spelled *Tjap Goe Mei* in the Indies literature) is the carnival held between the fourteenth and fifteenth nights after the beginning of the Chinese New Year celebrations.

11. The *Pecun* is a mid-year water festival. *Rebutan* celebrates the birthday of a deity in the seventh month of the Chinese year (see description in section on Bangka below).

12. I am grateful to Sumarsam for this information (pers. comm.).

13. Jabotabek is a modern acronym for Jakarta, Bogor, Tanggerang, and Bekasi.

14. This is according to Pak Ining (Koesasi 1992: 1–47).

15. This is according to a personal communication from H. Kartomi, who saw several such performances in Banjar (West Java) in 1945–47 and remembers the Chinese and Dutch names of some of the Indonesian-Chinese and Indo (Indonesian-Dutch) performers, as well as some of the songs.

16. The information in this paragraph and the photograph reproduced as figure 8.7 were kindly supplied by Bp. Marcus Soema, son of L. Soema, who was director of the troupe and of the performance shown.

17. I have not included this and some other informants' names, because of the confidentiality they requested of me.

18. The discussion of potehi is based on an evening performance which we recorded and our interviews with a dhalang and musicians who did not want to be named. The dhalang chose to present an episode from *Sam Kok* (The Story of the Three Kingdoms, ca. A.D. 200), performing on a makeshift covered stage in the klenteng grounds in Malang in 1974 to mark a family celebration.

Other stories performed in the late colonial and early independent periods in Java include classic Chinese stories about gods (e.g. *Fung Sen Pang*), myths about the origin of Chinese civilization which had been adapted as popular novels in the late Ming dynasty, episodes from Chinese history such as the tale of *Si Kong*, accounts of self-defense groups, the *Swie Hu* story about a band of noble bandits, and the story about the journey of the Buddhist monk Xuanzang with his disciples and party, including the White Monkey (Su Wukong) to obtain the holy books in India for the Emperor (see van Groenendael 1993: 29).

19. For more detailed descriptions of potehi theater in Java, see Hazeu 1897: 92–93, Moens 1949, and van Groenendael 1993: 11–33.

20. According to Poensen (1873: 163–64), in 1869 the temple in Kediri organized a series of potehi performances lasting a whole month in order to get rid of a smallpox epidemic.

21. In Kabupaten Pontianak alone, there are still over four hundred well-maintained klenteng today.

22. We were able to witness only one wayang gantung performance during a visit to Singkawang in December 1992. Organized by the Department of Social and Political Affairs official Bp. M. Hasan, the main performers were Bp. Tai Suk Jan, Bp. Tschin Hon Chiung, Bp. Tschin Wen Sin, and Ibu Tai Suk Lien from Dusun Lirang, Desa Sedan, Kecamatan Singkawang. The performance by the thirty-member Wayang Tri Dharma troupe was led by a local peranakan member of parliament, Bp. Gong Wui Kong. They presented a modern story about family planning which had been devised for performances in the three-week long *bupati*-led tours of the countryside for election campaigns. The *bupati* is the administrative head of a Region. The puppeteers did not speak at all in the performance but manipulated their puppets to the accompaniment of a prepared tape in the Indonesian language. Not being fluent in Indonesian, the only way they could comply with the government requirement that they perform in Indonesian—in part so that all present could understand the story-telling and dialogues—was to use a pre-recorded tape. According to local government officials, this process of the Indonesianization of wayang gantung is officially called *assimilasi* or *akulturasi*.

According to a local artist whose family had lived in the rural hinterland east of Singkawang for seven generations, peranakan artists and their communities have lived under conditions of heavy censorship since 1965. In the aftermath of the 1965 "coup" in Indonesia and the subsequent delayed massacre of the local peranakan community in October–November 1967, over 50,000 Indonesian-Chinese fled from the interior of central-north Kalimantan to live in the coastal region as farmers, traders, etc. However, others fought a guerilla war in the interior until the Indonesian Army defeated their organization (Pasukan Sukarela Kalimantan Utara, North Kalimantan Volunteer Troops) in 1974. Wayang gantung and other performances which were formerly frequently given are now rare, because of difficulties in obtaining police permits for them in this special military area. This is because its guerilla movement propagated its political line through wayang gantung performances and has carried out suspected fifth column activities since then. A few villages (e.g. Kali Asin, just outside Singkawang) still have wayang gantung puppeteers who can perform in the Hakka language, but they rarely do perform. Our trips in the Singkawang hinterland were always accompanied by Department of Education and Culture and police officials.

When security relaxes a little, detailed fieldwork needs to be carried out in this area.

23. Today only eight wayang gantung musicians remain in Kecamatan Jauwe, formerly a major wayang gantung center, to train young musicians.

24. According to my informants in *kecamatan* (government district) offices during a recent visit to Bangka, some villages registered between forty and sixty percent of the population as being of Chinese descent.

25. In mid-1994, a tanjidor band which we recorded in northern Bangka, i.e. Desa Puput, Susun Puput Bawah, Kecamatan Debus, comprised the following musicians: Bp. Rusdi (leader, on *bas tiup* or trombone), Bp. Liu Jun Po (trumpet), Bp. Husli (saxophone), Bp. Liu Kon Sew (saxophone), Bp. Tjhin A. Djin (clarinet), Bp. Bong Tjong Khiong (kettledrum), and Bp. Tjung Tai Kong (bass drum and cymbals). Bp. Rusdi's teacher was Lioe Djuen Fo, who led the band till his death in 1943. Bp. Rusdi still plays the main alto line on Bp. Lioe's own bas tiup, which was made locally in 1929. All the members of the band are middle-aged; and they say their tanjidor music will die with them because no young men want to join their band.

26. The King of all Raja Jin is called *Panglima Perang* (War commander).

REFERENCES

Abeyasekere, S. 1987. *Jakarta. A History*. Oxford: Oxford University Press.

Andaya, Barbara Watson. 1993. *To Live as Brothers. Southeast Sumatra in the Seventeenth and Eighteenth Centuries*. Honolulu: University of Hawaii Press.

Blussé, L. 1981. "Batavia, 1619–1740: The Rise and Fall of a Chinese Colonial Town." *Journal of Southeast Asian Studies* 12: 159–78.

Boachi, A. 1855. "Mededeelingen over de Chinese op het Eiland Java" [Notes on the Chinese of the Island of Java]. *Bijdragen tot de Taal-, Land- en Volkenkunde van Neêlandsch Indië* 4: 278–301.

Brandon, James R. 1967. *Theater in Southeast Asia*. Cambridge: Harvard University Press.

Carey, P. 1984. "Changing Javanese Perceptions of the Chinese Communities in Central Java, 1755–1825." *Indonesia* 37: 1–47.

Coppel, C. A. 1977. "Studying the Chinese Minorities: A Review." *Indonesia* 24 (Oct.): 175–183.

———. 1983. *Indonesian Chinese in Crisis*. Kuala Lumpur: Oxford University Press.

Dahm, B. 1969. *Sukarno and the Struggle for Indonesian Independence*. Ithaca: Cornell University Press.

de Graaf, H. J., and T. G. T. Pigeuad. 1984. *Chinese Muslims in Java in the 15th and 16th Centuries*, ed. M. C. Ricklefs. Clayton, Victoria: Monash University.

Department of Education and Culture. 1994. *Indonesian Policy Guidelines of Cultural Development*. Typescript. Jakarta.

Dinas Kebudayaan Jakarta [Jakarta Cultural Team]. 1983. *Proyek Konservasi Kesenian Tradisional Betawi: Serial Informasi Kesenian Tradisional Betawi*

[Batavian traditional art conservation project: Series of information about Batavian traditional art], 1–15. Jakarta: Jakarta City Council.

Fasseur, C. 1994. "Cornerstone and Stumbling Block: Racial Classification and the Late Colonial State of Indonesia." In *The Late Colonial State in Indonesia*, ed. R. Cribb, 31–56. Leiden: Koninklijk Instituut voor Taal-, Land- en Volkenkunde.

Giok-Lan Tan. 1963. *The Chinese of Sukabumi: A Study in Social and Cultural Accommodation*. Ithaca, N.Y.: Modern Indonesia Project, Cornell University.

Go Gien Tjwan. 1966. "Eenheid in Verscheidenheid in een Indonesisch Dorp" [Unity in diversity in an Indonesian village]. *Sociologisch-Historisch Seminarium voor Zuidoost Asia*. Amsterdam: University of Amsterdam.

Grijns, C. D. 1976. "Lenong in the Environs of Jakarta: A Report." *Archipel* 12: 175–202.

———. 1981. "Distributional Aspects of Folk Performances in the Jakarta-Malay Area." *Masyarakat Indonesia* 8: 187–226.

Groeneveldt, W. P. 1880. "Notes on the Malay Archipelago Compiled from Chinese Sources." *Verhandelingen van het Bataviaasch Genootschap van Kunsten en Wetenschappen* 39: 1–44.

Hazeu, G. A. J. 1897. *Bijdrage tot de Kennis von het Javaansche Toneel* [Contribution to the Knowledge of Javanese Music]. Leiden: Brill.

Heine-Geldern, R. von. 1945. "Prehistoric Research in the Netherlands East Indies." In *Science and Scientists in the Netherlands Indies*, ed. Peter Honig and Franz Verdoorn, 129–67. New York: Board for the Netherlands Indies, Surinam and Curacao.

Kartomi, M. J. 1983. "Tabut: A Shi'a Ritual Transplanted from India to Sumatra." In *Nineteenth and Twentieth Century Indonesia: Essays in Honour of Professor J. D. Legge*, ed. David P. Chandler and M. C. Ricklefs, 141–62. Clayton, Victoria: Centre for Southeast Asian Studies, Monash University.

———. 1996. "Contact and Synthesis in the Development of the Music of South Sumatra." In *Festschrift für Professor Andrew McCredie*, ed. D. Swale, 15–41. Wilhelmshafen: Heinrichshofen.

Koesasi, B. 1992. *Lenong and Si Pitung*. Clayton, Victoria: Centre for Southeast Asian Studies, Monash University.

Kunst, J. 1968. *Hindu-Javanese Musical Instruments*, 2d ed. The Hague: Nijhoff. 1st ed., 1927.

———. 1973. *Music in Java: Its History, Its Theory and Its Technique*, 3d ed. 2 vols. The Hague: Nijhoff. 1st ed., 1949.

Lasiyo. 1992. "Agama Khonghucu: An Emerging Form of Religious Life among the Indonesian Chinese." Ph.D. thesis, School of Oriental and African Studies, University of London.

Lekkerkerker, C. 1916. *Land en Volk van Sumatra* [Land and people of Sumatra]. Leiden: Brill.

Liem Thian Joe. 1931–33. *Riwayat Semarang (Dari Djamannya Sam Poo Sampe Terhapoesnya Kongkoan)* [History of Semarang (From the period of Sam Poo Sampe until the end of the "Backscratching" period)]. Semarang, Batavia: Boekhandel Ko Him Yoe.

————. 1947. "Pengaroeh Tionghoa di Java" [Chinese Influence in Java]. *Jade. Tijdschrift tevens Orgaan van het China-Instituut en de Unievan Federaties van Chineesche Studiekringen* [Journal of the Society of the China Institute and the Union of the Federation of Chinese Study Circles] 12/2: 7–15.

Lindsay, J. 1985. "Klasik, Kitsch or Contemporary: A Study of the Javanese Performing Arts." Ph.D. diss., University of Sydney.

Ma Huan. 1937. "Reisbeschrijving over de buitenlandsche reizen van Cheng Ho, gedurende de Ming-Dynastie (ca. 1405 AD)" [Description of the journey abroad of Cheng Ho during the Ming dynasty]. *Mededeelingen van het China-Instituut* 1: 164.

Manusama, A. T. 1919. *Krontjong als muziek instrument, als melodie, en als gesang* [Krontjong as musical instrument, melody, and song]. Batavia: Kolff.

————. 1922. *Komedie Stambul of de Oost-Indische Opera* [Komedie Stambul or East Indian opera]. Weltevreden: Kolff.

McKinnon, E. E. 1985. "Early Politics in South Sumatra: Some Preliminary Observations Based on Archaeological Evidence." *Indonesia* 40, 20.

Moens, J. L. 1949. "Een Chineesche Poppenkast en het Spel van den Linnen Zak" [A Chinese puppet show and play from the linen sack]. *Jade* (Batavia) 12, 3: 1–15.

Muhadjir, Multami R. M. T., Rahmat Ali, and Rachmat Ruchiat. 1968. *Peta Seni Budaya Betawi* [Map of art and culture of Batavia]. Jakarta: Dinas Kebudayan.

Ong Eng Die. 1973. *Chineezen en Nederlandsch-Indie: Sociografie van een Indonesische Bevolkingsgroep* [Chinese in the Netherlands Indies: Sociography of an Indonesian population group]. Assen: Van Gorcum.

Pasaribu, Amir. 1954. "Lenong Observasi MSDRD di Lenteng-Agung" [Observation of Lenong in Lenteng-Agung]. *Indonesia, Majalah Kebudayaan* 5, 10: 550–54.

Phoa Kian Sioe. 1949. "Orkest Gambang: Hasil Kesenian Tionghua Peranakan di Djakarta" [Gambang ensemble: Outcome of the art of the Indonesian-Chinese in Jakarta]. *Pantja Warna* 1, 9: 37–39.

Pigeaud, T. G. T. 1938. *Javanese Volksvertonigen: Bijdrage tot de Beschrijving van Land en Volk* [Javanese folk-theater: Contribution to the description of land and people]. Batavia: Volkslectuur.

————. 1960. *Java in the Fourteenth Century: A Study in Cultural History.* 3d ed. 5 vols. The Hague: Nijhoff.

————. 1967. *Literature of Java*, vol. 1. The Hague: Nijhoff.

Poensen, C. 1873. "De Wajang" [Wayang]. *Mededeelingen vanwegan het Nederlandsche Zendelingenootschap* 17: 138–64.

Probonegoro, Ninuh Irawati. 1974. "Kesenian Lenong, Suatu Analisa Antropologis" [The art of Lenong, an anthropological analysis]. Doctoral thesis, Arts Faculty, University of Indonesia.

Rush, J. 1977. "Opium Farms in Nineteenth-century Java: Institutional Continuity and Change in a Colonial Society, 1860–1910." Ph.D. diss., Yale University.

Salmon, C. 1981. *Literature in Malay by the Chinese of Indonesia: A Provisional*

Annotated Bibliography. Insulindiennes 129. Paris: Éditions de la Maison des Sciences de l'Homme.

Salmon, Claudine, and Denys Lombard. 1975. "A propos de quelques stèles chinoises recemment retrouvées à Banten (Java ouest)." *Archipel* 9: 104.

———. 1977. *Les Chinois de Jakarta: Temples et vie collective.* Cahier d'Archipel, no. 6. Paris: Societé pour l'Etude de la connaissance du Monde Insulinadien, Guéret.

———. 1985. *Klenteng-klenteng masyarakat Tionghoa di Jakarta* [Chinese temples in Jakarta]. Jakarta: Yayasam Cipta Loka Caraka (translated from the French 1977).

Seltmann, F. 1976. "Wajang Thithi: Chinesisches Schattenspiel in Jogjakarta" [Chinese shadowplay in Jogjakarta]. *Review of Indonesian and Malayan Affairs* 10: 51–75.

Serrurier, L. 1896. *De Wajang Poerwa, Eene ethnologische Studie* [Wajang Poerwa: An ethnological study]. Leiden: Brill.

Sie Boen Lian. 1938. "Gambang kromong musiek" [Gambang kromong music]. *Mededeelingen van het China Instituut* 2 (Dec.): 78–88.

Sie Hok Tjwan. 1990. *The 6th Overseas Chinese State.* Townsville: James Cook University of North Queensland.

Slametmuljana. 1976. *A Story of Majapahit.* Singapore: Singapore University Press.

Soema, M. 1993. "Soema Tjoe Sing (1902–47): Profile of an Indonesian 'Peranakan' Chinese Novelist, Journalist, Nationalist." M.A. thesis, Monash University.

Sulaiman, Satyawati. 1980. *The Art of Srivijaya,* ed. M. C. Subhadradis Diskul. Kuala Lumpur: Oxford University Press.

Suryadinata, L. 1971. *The Pre–World War II Peranakan Chinese Press: A Preliminary Paper.* Athens: Ohio University.

Tan Sooi Beng. 1984. "An Introduction to the Chinese Glove Puppet Theater in Malaysia." *Journal of the Malaysian Branch of the Royal Asiatic Society* 57, 246: 40–55.

The Siaw Giap. 1965. "Religion and Overseas Chinese Assimilation in Southeast Asia." *Revue du Sud-Est Asiatique* 2: 67–84.

———. 1990. "Cina Muslim di Indonesia" [Chinese Muslims of Indonesia]. *Jurnal Antropologi dan Sosiologi* 18: 23–39.

Van Groenendael, Victoria M. Clara. 1993. "*Po-té-hi:* The Chinese Glovepuppet Theater in East Java." In *Performance in Java and Bali: Studies of Narrative, Theater, Music and Dance,* ed. Bernard Arps. 1–33. London: School of Oriental and African Studies, University of London.

Weitzel, A. W. P. 1860. *Batavia in 1858.* Gorinchem.

Willmott, D. E. 1960. *The Chinese of Semarang: A Changing Minority Community in Indonesia.* Ithaca, N.Y.: Cornell University Press.

———. 1961. *The National Status of the Chinese in Indonesia 1900–1958.* Ithaca, N.Y.: Cornell University Press.

Wolters, O. W. 1967. *Early Indonesian Commerce.* Ithaca, N.Y.: Cornell University Press.

Yampolsky, P. 1992. Liner notes for *Music of Indonesia 3: Music from the Outskirts of Jakarta, Gambang Kromong.* Smithsonian Folkways CD SF 40057.

———. 1994. Liner notes for *Music of Indonesia 5: Betawi and Sundanese Music of the North Coast of Java: Topeng, Betawi, Tanjidor, Ajeng.* Smithsonian Folkways CD SF 40421.

9

Ethnic Identity, National Identity, and Music in Indo-Trinidadian Culture

PETER MANUEL

Much of the literature regarding race and culture in the Americas, including the English-speaking West Indies, has focused on the struggles of Afro-American peoples to establish cultural identity in the face of white discrimination. While this theme is not irrelevant to Trinidad, Guyana, and Suriname, race relations in these countries have a distinct dynamic due to the presence of substantial East Indian communities seeking to legitimize their own identity within traditionally black-dominated political and socio-cultural frameworks. As these East Indian populations grow in size, self-awareness, affluence, and political power, they find themselves engaged in complex processes of cultural reorientation. These processes involve, first, reformulating their own senses of culture and identity in relation to mainstream West Indian contexts; and, second, pressing for a multicultural framework that would accommodate both their East Indian ethnic identity and their West Indian national identity. Both processes have been the subject of intense negotiation and controversy, on national levels as well as within the East Indian communities themselves.

In Trinidad and Guyana, while a sense of distinct ethnic identity remains important to most East Indians, changing conditions have eroded some of the most important traditional emblems of Indianness, such as caste consciousness and, more importantly, the Hindi language (or its Bhojpuri Form), which is now known only to a few elders, pandits, and other learned persons. In such circumstances, music has acquired an unprecedented significance as a symbol of ethnic identity (La Guerre [1974] 1985: xiv), as reflected in the extraordinary amount of musical activity in Trinidad, among East Indians as well as others. Music's importance is also

318

manifested in the series of ongoing and spirited socio-musical polemics, waged in private and, more overtly, in public forums like newspapers, Parliament sessions, and calypsos. These controversies, aside from their inherent interest, often serve as remarkably concrete articulations of broader, more abstract socio-cultural processes.

Aside from studies of calypso, such socio-musical issues have received only passing reference in the otherwise considerable body of scholarly literature devoted to race relations in Trinidad, which, indeed, has been described as a "social science laboratory" for the academic attention it has received (Yelvington 1993: 15). Despite the value of this literature, dramatic developments within recent years have substantially altered the cultural and political situation in Trinidad, calling for an updating and revising of prior paradigms. This article explores aspects of the most prominent music-related ethnic controversies in Trinidad, with passing reference to Guyana. In particular, it aims to illustrate how these issues can be seen as key texts in the complex negotiations involved in the legitimization of new socio-cultural paradigms based on pluralism rather than assimilation. Given the fratricidal ethnic conflicts currently raging elsewhere in the world, and the lingering possibility of real violence in the Caribbean, the study of West Indian progress toward multiculturalism may be of more than academic interest.

EAST INDIANS IN THE WEST INDIES

After the emancipation of West Indian slaves in 1834–40, British colonists sought to replenish the supply of cheap plantation labor by importing indentured workers, especially from India. Under this program, between 1845 and 1917 some 143,000 East Indians came to Trinidad, 240,000 to British Guiana, and lesser numbers to other parts of the West Indies. While some of these workers returned to India, most stayed; their descendants now constitute a majority of the population of Guyana and the largest ethnic groups in Suriname and Trinidad, where they surpass the "creole" (black and mixed-race) population; together, East Indians account for around twenty percent of the English-speaking West Indian population.[1]

While most free blacks in colonial Trinidad and British Guiana spurned the arduous life of the sugar plantations, in many cases moving to the towns and cities, the first generations of East Indian laborers tended to remain concentrated in agricultural regions even after indentureship. Living in their insular, rural communities and shunning schools for fear of proselytization, most colonial-era Indo-Trinidadians took little part in the mainstream of their country's social and political life. Gradually, however, increasing numbers urbanized and established footholds in commerce. Aided by traditional values of thrift, industriousness, and family cohesion, East Indians have now come to dominate business sectors in both countries, surpassing the formerly entrenched creole populations. Accompanying this process has been a revival of cultural awareness, pride, and assertiveness, stimulated by such developments as the import of Indian films from the 1930s, the Black Power Movement erupting around 1970, and the spread of modern concepts of pluralism and cultural revivalism (see Vertovec 1992: chap. 4).

As Indians grow in power and self-assurance, they have come to be increasingly resentful of perceived sorts of discrimination. In Trinidad, from the mid-1950s until 1986, political life was dominated by the creole-oriented People's National Movement (PNM), with the predominantly East Indian opposition parties being marginalized through gerrymandering, electoral fraud, occasional persecution of political leaders, and their own internal difficulties (see, e.g., Mahabir 1995: 88–89, Hintzen 1989). The charismatic Eric Williams, who led the PNM until his death in 1981, was at best indifferent to the East Indians, whom he once characterized as a "recalcitrant and hostile minority." PNM economic policies since independence in 1962 largely favored the party's constituency—urban working-class and bourgeois creoles—at the expense of the East Indians, who have arguably constituted the country's most economically productive social sector (see Vertovec 1992: 132ff., Lowenthal 1972: 162, Hintzen 1989). Accordingly, as we shall discuss below, Indians have felt that state cultural policies have also tended to favor creole culture.

Since 1985, however, changes in Trinidad's political landscape and public culture have disrupted the comfortable hegemony previously enjoyed by the PNM and its constituency. In 1986, the increasingly discredited PNM government was ousted by a coalition which included an invigorated Indian-based party led by Basdeo Panday. While the fragmenting of this coalition enabled the PNM to regain power in 1991, the new prime minister, Patrick Manning, made concerted efforts to win over sectors of the now assertive, affluent, and organized East Indian population. Snap elections called in 1995 led to a triumph of Panday and his Indian-based United National Congress (UNC). In the same year, the East Indian presence was recognized by the declaration of May 30 as a national holiday, "Indian Arrival Day"; by the unprecedented prominence and recognition of Indians in the subsequent Carnival activities, including calypso; and, as we shall discuss, by a de facto collapse of creole cultural as well as political hegemony.

ETHNICITY AND CREOLIZATION

Trinidad and Guyana have been characterized as "plural" societies in the model described by M. G. Smith (1965), in which ethnic groups coexist without mixing or sharing basic institutions or values (see also Despres 1967, La Guerre 1982). Many Trinidadians continue to live in ethnically homogeneous communities where there is little exposure to other groups. Religion and family life still tend to be segregated, and politics and black consciousness movements have further polarized the races since Independence. However, urbanization and the greater participation of East Indians in mainstream society have made the situation more complex than Smith's model might suggest. Increasingly, and especially in towns, Indians and blacks interact and socialize amicably, and there is a gradual increase in racial intermarriage, producing a growing population of "douglas," or black–Indian mulattos. But as Lowenthal observes (1972: 165), increased contact has also generated increased tension, and many blacks have come to feel threatened by the greater Indian presence and assertiveness in society. In a 1951 calypso, Killer voiced the subsequently familiar sentiment that the Indians are "taking over":

> As for the men and dem I must relate
> Long time all dey work was in cane estate
> But now dey own every theater
> Yes, hotel, rumshop, and hired car. (Constance 1991: 8)

Ethnic tension is heightened by the different mainstream values of each community and the tendency to stereotype the other community in terms of these values. Daniel Miller (1994) describes Trinidadian society as being characterized by a fundamental dualism between, on the one hand, a "bacchanal" culture of partying, hanging out ("liming"), and informal and transient male–female relations; and on the other hand, values of frugality, hard work, and responsibility to the extended family. In popular discourse and to a considerable extent in reality, such polarized lifestyles are associated with blacks and Indians, respectively (see also B. Williams 1991).

Compounding the asymmetries between the two groups are the distinct cultural orientations toward their respective ancestral homelands. On the whole, Indo-Caribbeans have been able to maintain much closer links to India than have West Indian blacks to Africa, in terms of both cultural retentions as well as ongoing engagement with the Old World. Most of the Indians arrived later than did the blacks, and they were spared the deculturating effects of the slave plantation. Their traditionally strong, multi-generational family structure and geographic isolation also facilitated cultural retention (Despres 1967: 45ff., Vertovec 1992: 14). While Hindi as a spoken language has essentially died out, imported Hindi films (usually with subtitles) and film music recordings have promoted knowledge of and identification with India since the 1930s. Trinidad has also hosted a small but influential trickle of visitors from India, including Hindu pandits and figures like Hari Shankar Adesh, who taught Indian music classes in the 1960s and 1970s. Identification with India has been further facilitated by the existence of a pan-regional North Indian cultural "Great Tradition" and by the fact that most immigrants came from the same Bhojpuri-speaking region of India, thus sharing a language and a set of relatively uniform cultural practices.

By contrast, one can generalize that Trinidadian and Guyanese blacks are far more alienated from their African cultural roots, instead fashioning their own creole expressive arts like calypso and tending to serve as brokers for Euro-American, Afro-American, and Jamaican popular music and culture (see Lowenthal 1972: chap. 4, Deosaran 1987a: 7). Neo-traditional musics associated, for example, with orisha/Shango worship remain marginal phenomena, and most creoles, at least before the 1970s, have traditionally been largely indifferent to their African ancestry (see Herskovits and Herskovits 1947: 23). Some Indians regard this condition as the "tragic fate" of a rootless people who gave up their identity for secondhand Euro-American culture. As a letter in a Guyanese newspaper stated, "The Hindus in Guyana have a vibrant culture with its background much bigger than Guyana, they have not severed itself from its roots," unlike the blacks, who were "bought by cheap sermons to shed their religion for a watered-down Christianity which the white planters use as a tool and weapon even today." [2]

Countering this perspective is the recurrent theme in creole discourse that the Afro-Trinidadians' alienation from African culture, far from being an outright loss, inspired the dynamic creation of syncretic new cultural forms—especially calypso, Carnival, and steel band. As one Afro-Trinidadian told me, "I'm *glad* that the British banned our African skin drums, because that led us to invent steel band and calypso." It is this sense of having *created* a new culture (along with the prior arrival of most blacks in the Caribbean) that justifies for creoles the feeling that they, unlike Indians, are, in common parlance, the "indigenous" West Indians.

From this perspective, calypso and steel band, unlike Indian *bhajan* singing and *tassa* drumming, are similarly "indigenous" forms.[3] While creoles have thus reconciled themselves to their new homeland, Indians are seen as still looking back to the ancestral homeland and merely perpetuating or imitating Indian music and culture rather than creating. Trinidad is thus "the land of steel band and calypso," and of the people who created them.

This Trinidadian "creole" culture—English-based, syncretic, and "Afro-Saxon"—is traditionally upheld as the national mainstream culture. "Creole" culture thus largely excludes, on the one hand, neo-African forms like Shango worship and, on the other, Indo-Caribbean music, which again is seen as the foreign import of a particular ethnic minority, whose increased presence in public culture represents an essentially divisive "special interest." By contrast, the mainstream creole culture, although largely the province of Afro-Trinidadians and mulattos, has traditionally been celebrated as a national, cosmopolitan, and essentially universal idiom to which other groups have been expected to integrate (see, e.g., Lowenthal 1972: 175); such "melting-pot" ideals were explicitly articulated by Eric Williams and can be seen to have underlain state cultural policies and even the oft-heard slogan, "All o' we is one."[4]

Letters from creoles to local newspapers occasionally voice such sentiments with particular clarity, such as the following, addressed to the Indo-Trinidadian columnist and cultural activist Ravi-ji (Ravindranath Maraj), who had publicly lamented the low visibility of Indo-Trinidadian culture:

> Indo-Trinis [are] a minority outside the Pan-African mainstream to which our true national culture and our Afro-Caribbean culture belongs. We cannot regard dub, rap, reggae, soul, township jive, highlife and zouk as foreign—they are all the products of our people. In sharp contrast, Indo-Trini "culture", including chutney [an Indo-Trinidadian folk-pop style discussed below] and other forms not found in India, can be regarded as foreign—foreign to us. It's a black thing—Ravi-ji wouldn't understand.
> (*Trinidad Guardian*, 30 May 1993)

Indo-Trinidadian attitudes toward such ideologies have not been monolithic. Until relatively recently, many Indians remained largely indifferent to national political and cultural activities, and Indian sports fans have not helped the situation by cheering for the visiting Pakistani or Indian cricket teams rather than local ones.[5] Increasingly, however, Indians have come to acutely resent being regarded as immigrants, and they insist on their right to be accepted as Trinis while at the same time maintaining their distinctive ethnicity (see, e.g., Lowenthal 1972: 175, Dev 1993).

The accompanying Indian cultural activism can be seen as implicitly animated by demands for two complementary reforms. The first is that the concept of "creole" culture be broadened to include certain Indo-Trini syncretic forms—especially, hybrid entities like chutney-soca. The second is that the hegemonic notion of a creole mainstream itself be replaced or supplemented by a paradigm of multiculturalism—that the "melting pot" be traded for a "salad bowl." In the last decade, both these processes have in fact been occurring, amidst an ongoing din of intra- and inter-ethnic polemics and controversies that, however often acrimonious, can be seen as the relatively healthy negotiations accompanying the emergence of a genuine cultural pluralism in a civil society. While scholarly literature has tended to discuss these issues in the abstract, in popular discourse they are more typically articulated in terms of specific cultural and above all musical controversies, to which we may now turn.

STATE CULTURAL POLICIES AND INDIAN MUSIC

Trinidadian cultural policy, in however ad hoc a manner, has traditionally exhibited a marked favoritism toward creole culture and music at the expense of Indo-Trinidadian counterparts. The largely creole Carnival festival, with its core activities of calypso and steel band competitions, is heavily subsidized by the state, unlike Indo-Trinidadian events like the vernal Phagwa (Holi) festival. Until 1995, Indian music and dance were generally excluded from state performance ensembles at Carifesta, a pan-Caribbean performing arts festival; in an oft-cited remark, one politician (Ronnie Williams) explained this anomaly by stating that Indian culture was alien and not part of Trinidadian culture. Indo-Trinidadian culture is similarly marginalized at the state-funded "Best Village" (formerly "Better Village") folkloric contests; one Indian academic told me, "We are made to feel unwelcome there, and the orientation is mostly Afro-Trinidadian, but then we are criticized as clannish for not participating" (see also S. Maraj 1994a, 1994b). An offer by the government of India in 1966 to set up an Indian Culture Center was spurned by the PNM government, with Afro-Trinidadian critics denouncing the proposal as "Indian imperialism" (e.g. Ifill 1987). On the whole, Indian critics have accused the Trinidadian Ministry of Culture of trying to "douglarize" Indians by promoting assimilation and "integration" rather than multiculturalism, and they dismiss (whether fairly or not) its occasional Indian-oriented projects and hirings as tokenism.

Much of the debate regarding the role of Indian music in public culture has focused on the perceived under-representation of Indian music and culture on the broadcast media (Mahabir 1984).[6] In both Trinidad and Guyana until recently, radio and television were exclusively state-run, in accordance with British norms. While a few weekly radio programs of Indian music—primarily Hindi film music—had been established in the 1940s, these accounted for only a tiny percent of air time. Ravi-ji observed in 1993 that the two Trinidad public FM stations each broadcast only one hour of Indian music per week (and also, he noted, favor American pop over calypso); more Indian music was heard on the AM station (610), but its reception is poor throughout much of the island (R. Maraj 1993b). Shopping malls playing radio broadcasts would routinely change stations when Indian shows came on, leading journalist Ravi-ji to feel that he and his culture were being personally "switched off" (R. Maraj 1992). It was not until the mid-1990s that the situation changed, when new policies allowed the founding of private Indian-owned and Indian-oriented radio stations, and the state-owned stations increased their Indian programming in order to attract sponsors from the increasingly influential East Indian business community.

The achievement of such increased Indian media presence in Trinidad and Guyana provoked considerable backlash from creoles who regarded the trend as divisive.[7] Letters from creoles to newspapers in both countries reiterated, in various ways, the belief in the universality of the normal radio fare—primarily Afro-American and Afro-Caribbean popular music—and the perceived foreignness of the favored Indian genre, Hindi film music, with its unintelligible language and exclusively Indian audience. Indians, nevertheless, have insisted on the legitimacy of its presence, and that of Indian culture in general, in a national polity to be based on pluralism rather than an exclusionist creolism. To creole protests that the media largely excluded African music as well as Indian music, Indians have countered that "creole" musics are predominantly Afro-Caribbean and Afro-American, and further, that Indians would accept a presence of African music in a spirit of multiculturalism (see Deosaran 1987a: 6).

While Indo-Caribbeans have been demanding greater representation from state Ministries of Culture, they have also been increasingly able to bypass such institutions by sponsoring their own cultural activities. Such, indeed, had always been the norm, although the Indo-Trinidadians' dramatically increased affluence has greatly expanded the scope of their private-sector cultural patronage. Thus, for example, in 1994, the Trinidadian impresario Moean Mohammed could state: "Getting represented on state radio was an uphill struggle all the way. But now we have all the air time we want, and we don't need any help from the government" (pers. comm.). Aside from the new radio stations, such activities would include the massive Mastana Bahar amateur performance competitions, the similarly annual Indian Cultural Pageant (both dating from the 1970s), and the privately sponsored Chutney-Soca Monarch Competition inaugurated in 1996 as a new fixture in the Carnival season. Also largely funded by private Indian donors are the festivities surrounding the newly inaugurated Indian Arrival Day (unlike the state-subsidized, Afro-Trinidadian-oriented Emancipation Day). Pluralism in public culture, whether becoming an official state policy or not, has thus become a de facto reality via private-sector Indian sponsorship. Accordingly, for many Indians, creole acceptance of the Indian presence in national culture may be becoming both irrelevant as well as inevitable.

PAN VERSUS HARMONIUM

Despite the increasing ability of Indian cultural promoters to bypass the state, the perceivedly discriminatory policies of the Ministry of Culture continued to provoke controversies in the 1990s, including one polemic which exposed in a particularly dramatic way some of the paradoxes and complexities of the problematic relationship of Indo-Trinidadian identity to national culture. The focus in this case was the steel drum—a seemingly innocent instrument, but one which is of prodigious symbolic importance in the country. The steel drum, or "pan," was invented in depressed black neighborhoods like Laventille in the late 1930s and early 1940s for use in Carnival street processions. The steel bands were associated from the start with lumpen black youth gangs, whose violent rivalries provoked heavy-handed police repression and stigmatized the instrument among Indians and the middle classes. Since the 1970s, however, the steel drum has largely shed its negative associations, becoming a focus of Carnival festivities and one of the most cherished symbols of creole national identity, played by many dozens of amateur ensembles throughout the country and elsewhere in the West Indies. The steel drum, indeed, is an icon for creole culture in general, as a truly Caribbean entity created, as one correspondent put it, "out of a long history of common struggle of the people against Massa's brutal attempts to suppress their cultural expressions" (Clyde Weatherhead, letter to the *Trinidad Guardian*, 23 September 1992).

In 1992, the Trinidad government formally recognized the pan's uniqueness in local culture by declaring it to be the "national instrument." Proposals were made to fund the introduction of pan in schools and to construct a US $1.5 million theater for pan performances. While most Trinidadians, including Indians, presumably regarded such proposals as harmless, a small but vocal sector of the Indian populace vigorously opposed them. Most prominent among the latter was Satnarayan "Sat" Maraj, secretary general of the Sanatan Dharma Maha Sabha (SDMS), a conservative—and increasingly isolated—Hindu organization (see Vertovec 1992: 123–25, 183–84; La Guerre [1974] 1985: 181).

In two extensive paid advertisements in the *Trinidad Express* (S. Maraj 1994a, 1994b), Maraj vigorously denounced the proposal, arguing that if the Ministry of Culture were to support steel drums in schools, then equal funding should be given to the harmonium, which is the most popular instrument used to play Indian music. In the first manifesto, Maraj reiterated the patriotism of Indo-Trinidadians and its compatibility with their distinct sense of ethnicity. He further noted that although the pan is associated with the black experience, it is used primarily to play Western music, including calypso. Moreover, as advised by a local musician, he argued that the pan is inherently unsuited to Indian music, since its "discordant" timbre renders it unable to render the twenty-two *shrutis*, or microtonal intervals, allegedly essential to all forms of Indian music. The steel drum, he claimed, is an inherently "imperfect" instrument, unlike, say, the sitar or harmonium; indeed, in the pan, "Trinidad has given the world [merely] an Idea . . . which is being perfected but not here," rather in Japan, Sweden, and other countries. By contrast, the ideal instrument to render Indo-Caribbean music is the harmonium; "only the musically illiterate" would argue that the harmonium "is a Western instrument introduced into India," it having undergone various "adaptive changes" rendering it suitable for Indian music. The government's proposal of "pushing pan down everyone's throat" thus constitutes yet another instance of "afro-Trinidadian [sic] cultural arrogance," like the creole-oriented Best Village competitions.

Express columnist Kim Johnson reported the response of a Ministry of Culture official, who observed, among other things, that the harmonium, with its piano-like keyboard, is no more able than the pan to play microtonal *shrutis*. Johnson went on to (correctly) note that the legendary twenty-two *shrutis* have never been systematically used in the folk and popular music patronized by Indo-Trinidadians; even in ancient Indian treatises, their alleged use is confined to Indian classical music, giving that music, as he somewhat injudiciously put it, its "characteristic whining sound" (Johnson 1994). Maraj responded with another indignant advertisement, accusing Johnson of "contempt and ignorance" for calling Indian music "whining," and deriding Johnson's inability to hear the twenty-two *shrutis* which, Maraj insisted, pervade even Indian film songs and chutney. "Every Indian singer," Maraj claimed, "has an intuitive knowledge of *shruti*."

It is easy to see how this polemic could spin off into esoteric debates regarding the use of microtones in diverse African, Indian, and Caribbean musics, as happened in my own conversations with Indo-Trinidadians on the subject. One could opine that Maraj could have based his case for equal funding for the harmonium on three solid arguments: (1) the harmonium is a cheap, portable, and versatile instrument—suitable, indeed, for learning keyboard and harmonic skills applicable to all sorts of music, including calypso; (2) the harmonium is better suited to Indian music than the pan because of its ability to play sustained pitches and thus to better approximate vocal styles; and (3) the harmonium, quite simply, is the most popular instrument of the Indo-Trinidadian community. Maraj was perhaps ill-advised to rest his argument on the problematic issue of *shrutis*, whose systematic usage in modern Indian classical music, not to mention genres like chutney, has been thoroughly disproven.[8]

Aside from Maraj's factually questionable statements, the aggressive tenor of his manifestos no doubt offended many creole readers. While dismissing the pan as merely "an Idea," Maraj gratuitously belittled the originality of creole music as a whole, deriding blacks for "[giving] up their culture to satisfy the whims and fancies of the European and American." Kim Johnson's inability to hear the twenty-two *shrutis* in Indo-Trinidadian music, Maraj opined, was a case of "pearls before swine." (I would be inclined to compare the *shrutis* to the legendary emperor's clothing.) Indeed, the provocative and insulting tone of Maraj's articles clearly alienated many even in the East Indian community. While no systematic opinion polls have been taken, my own Indian acquaintances included some who trusted Maraj's discourse regarding *shrutis* and appreciated his righteous militancy, and others who dismissed him as a divisive fool increasingly out of touch with his constituency and unnecessarily provoking ethnic animosity.

In this chapter it is perhaps inappropriate to belabor the musicological esoterica involved in Maraj's arguments, and one might well sympathize with the succinct headline of an essay in the *Guardian*: "Pan versus harmonium is foolish" (letter to the editor, 6 July 1994). Nevertheless, the debate raged on, with leading politicians being asked to voice their opinions (e.g., letter to the editor, *Trinidad Express*, 13 July 1994), until 1995, when the state agreed to purchase harmoniums for some schools, and a conciliatory PNM Prime Minister Patrick Manning embraced Sat, saying, "I'll pump the bellows, and you play the keyboard." Clearly, the issue had touched a national nerve, no doubt because of the broader questions it involved regarding the relations between ethnicity/ race and cultural entities like music. Is the steel drum primarily an Afro-Trinidadian instrument, or a national and universal one? How do Indians and their music relate to the pan's "creole" status? What factors determine the ethnic character of a musical entity like steel band—the instrument's historical origin, the nature of the music played on it, or the ethnicity its performers and audiences?

In this case, the origin of the instrument in the urban Afro-Trinidadian community is a non-negotiable historical fact, but the ethnic associations of the pan's repertoire and personnel are inherently flexible, open to contestation, and arguably more important.[9] As we have seen, Sat Maraj argued that pan is essentially an Afro-Trinidadian instrument; even after the pan outgrew its lumpen black hooligan associations, Indians have often been made to feel unwelcome in pan bands by what one informant called the "proprietary air" displayed by many creoles toward the instrument.[10] As the calypsonian Chalkdust (Hollis Liverpool) sang in a 1982 calypso (or "kaiso"),

> Some still laugh at the Indian man
> When he sing kaiso or beat pan. (in Constance 1991: 35)

It is under these circumstances that Maraj and others regarded the official declaration of pan to be the national instrument as adding insult to injury.

For their part, supporters of the Ministry of Culture position argued that the steel drum, notwithstanding its Afro-Trindadian origins, is the patrimony of all Trinidadians.[11] They pointed out that one of the country's leading pan arrangers is an East Indian (Jit Samaroo of the Amoco Renegades) and that, further, the instrument is quite compatible with Indo-Trinidadian music. Indeed, among the flurry of contemporary crossover fads (pan-parang, rap-calypso, soca-reggae, etc.), there have been several local fusions of pan and Indian music, including some hybrid recordings by Moean Mohammad, a "pan chutney" competition started in 1995, and innovative "pan-tar" collaborations of the sitarist Mangal Patasar with leading black pannists. Patasar's group performs in a wide variety of locales, including calypso tents—otherwise strongholds of creole culture; in the new official spirit of ethnic inclusivity, he and a pannist were featured on the cover of the country's 1996 telephone directory. As the Indian soca singer Drupatee Ramgoonai sang in her "Hotter than a Chulha [stove]" (1989),

> From the hills of Lord way up in Laventille
> Pan man skills must spill into Caroni
> For we goin' an' cause a fusion with the culture
> To widen we scope and vision for the future.

(Caroni is a predominantly Indian region of central Trinidad). Steel drum, indeed, is not strictly associated with any one kind of music; although most pan ensembles play current soca tunes, many play everything from European classics to the national anthem. A fortuitous dramatization of this point was provided at the peak of the controversy when the national television network broadcast an Indian film, Bekhudi, featuring a dance sequence accompanied by a steel drum band. The *Trinidad Guardian* pithily noted, "There was a noticeable absence of . . . harmoniums (or is it 'harmonia'?) from the procession and none of the actors looked any the worse for the omission" (7 July 1994). As the *Bekhudi* scene illustrated, the pan is increasingly able to be re-signified or appropriated by other ethnic groups—indeed, just as the harmonium itself has gone from being an instrument of European colonial proselytization to being an icon of Indian culture. Such re-significations, indeed, are typical of a postmodern world where cultural artifacts are uprooted from their original meanings, and musical entities from the global style pool are freely borrowed, mixed, and scrambled. However, such musical re-significations do not occur without friction. Some blacks are said to resent Jit Samaroo's presence in the pan world, and Mangal Patasar himself has come under criticism from purist Indians who feel he has "degraded" the sitar by mixing it with pan. Nevertheless, the pan controversy, while a tempest in a teapot from one perspective, has also illustrated the inexorable redefining of Trinidadian national culture. The fusions of pan with Indian music have epitomized the broadening of the instrument's "creole" character, while the state's agreement to purchase harmoniums for schools reflects a simultaneous and self-conscious shift toward multiculturalism.

CALYPSO AND INDO-TRINIDADIAN IDENTITY

Calypso is justifiably the most renowned Trinidadian art form, perhaps occupying a greater prominence in national public culture than does any musical genre elsewhere in the world. At the same time, in Trinidad's multi-ethnic society, calypso's status as a "national" genre is inherently problematic in much the same sense as that of steel drum, in that its origin, content, and performers have always been overwhelmingly creole. Traditionally oriented toward the urban black lower-class male culture from which it emerged, calypso has only in recent years come to accommodate a few women and East Indians. As with steel drum, the complexities of calypso's relationship to the East Indian community are the subject of ongoing negotiation and controversy, which serve as indicators of changing concepts of ethnic and national identity.

One important aspect of this subject involves the representations of Indians in creole calypsos themselves. Here I will deal only in passing with this topic, partly because of my intent to focus on Indo-Trinidadian musical culture per se, and also because this subject has already been insightfully discussed in a number of publications (especially Constance 1991, Rohlehr 1990: 493–508, Warner 1993, Trotman 1989). The decades reflect changing creole perceptions and attitudes. On the whole, colonial-era calypsos tended to depict Indians condescendingly as exotic or laughable—much, indeed, as calypsonians portrayed Shango worshippers, Spiritual Baptists, and others on the margins of their rather narrow experience. In the 1950s, the increased participation of Indians in the social, economic, and political mainstream led to greater racial tension, greater mutual familiarity, and, correspondingly, to more varied representations in song. While a few calypsos appealed for racial harmony, others mocked Indians or portrayed them as a threat, often in the most unenlightened terms. As today, polemics raged in the media and in Parliament as indignant Indian leaders protested perceivedly racist songs.

By the 1970s, the crudely derogatory tone of earlier calypsos was passing out of vogue. Instead, the norm was represented by songs like Mighty Sparrow's "Marajin" (1982), depicting Indian women as desirable, or by calypsos whimsically exploiting bilingual puns, such as Crazy's "Nani Wine"—"nani" meaning "grandmother" in Hindi, and short for "punanny" or vagina in local slang. Calypsos continued to provoke ethnic controversy, as in the debate over Black Stalin's 1979 "Caribbean Unity," whose refrain asserted:

> Dem is one race—de Caribbean man
> From the same place—de Caribbean man
> That make the same trip—de Caribbean man
> On the same ship—de Caribbean man.

For obvious reasons, this song drew angry protests from Indians who were no longer willing to be written out of their country's history (see Deosaran 1987b). In the mid 1990s, songs by CroCro and others lewdly insulting a female politician, Hulsie Bhaggan, and Prime Minister Panday provoked protests, especially from Indians who felt that their tax dollars should not be used to subsidize calypso as a forum for their own vilification.

More directly relevant to the renegotiations of Indian culture in Trinidad has been the participation of Indians themselves in the calypso world. Indo-Trinidadian music itself played an indirect role in the evolution of modern calypso when in the late 1970s the black calypsonian Lord Shorty based his infectious soca (or, as he spelled it, "sokah") rhythm partly on Indian tassa drumming (Constance 1991: 64). Tassa drums were also used in some early steel bands and continue to appear in a few soca/calypso bands.

Direct participation by Indians as performers, however, has been relatively infrequent and occasionally controversial. As with steel band, some interested Indians have been made to feel unwelcome in the predominantly creole milieu.[12] On the whole, however, as one creole told me, "Most Trinis are happy to jump up to any song they like, regardless of who sings it." Accordingly, since the 1980s a few Indians have entered the calypso/soca field and been well received by creole audiences (see Constance 1991: 68–82).

Indeed, the controversy regarding Indian participation in calypso has come largely from within the Indian community itself and thus involves questions of self-image and the desirability of creolization rather than creole hegemony per se. The most heated polemic erupted over the lively entrance of a young Indian woman, Drupatee Ramgoonai, into the soca scene in 1987. Drupatee, although neither a lyricist nor a composer, gained some popularity among creole and Indian audiences with her bouncy fusions of soca, tassa drumming, and chutney, with lyrics celebrating the cultural mix (as in the "Chutney Soca" quoted above). While such songs were in themselves innocuous enough, other aspects of Drupatee's image provoked the ire of quite a few Indians. Particularly controversial was her song "Lick down me nani," which invoked the grandmother/vagina pun in a way that was either violent ("knock down my granny") or lewd ("lick my 'nanny'"). For some Indians, the spectacle of her performing this song while provocatively "wining" (dancing erotically) for a crowd full of lusty black men was too much to tolerate. As the local academic Ken Parmasad noted, the song insulted the revered domestic personality of the grandmother, inspired a subsequent barrage of "nani" calypsos exploiting the same pun, and exacerbated the sensitivities of Indians during a period of several well-publicized rapes of Indian women by black men (pers. comm.).

Once again, newspapers and radio talk shows came alive with sound and fury, as controversy erupted around Drupatee and the broader issues of Indian participation in calypso, and creolization in general. Letters by Indians to newspapers denounced Drupatee as "immoral and disgusting" and "a thorn among East Indian women"; one critic wrote:

> For an Indian girl to throw her high upbringing and culture to mix with vulgar music, sex, and alcohol in Carnival tents tells me that something is radically wrong with her psyche. Drupatee Ramgoonai has chosen to worship the Gods of sex, wine and easy money. (in Constance 1991: 51)

To those who argued that Drupatee was revitalizing Indo-Trinidadian music, one columnist asked, "Why is such extreme vulgarity necessary to maintain and perpetuate our Trinidadian culture?" (D. Maharaj 1993).

By the mid-1990s, the furor had dissipated somewhat as Drupatee became accepted as a minor fixture on the soca scene, and she continued to highlight Indian heritage in her music. In her "Hotter than a Chulha," she reflected on the controversy she had provoked:

> They give me blows, O Lord, last year for doing soca
> But it shows how much they know about the culture
> The music of the steel drum of Laventille
> Cannot help but mix with rhythms from Caroni.
> For it's a symbol of how much we come of age
> It's a brand new stage.

Drupatee's injection of Indianisms into the otherwise creole soca world has elicited a wide range of emotional responses among Indians, including both pride and shame (as well as indifference and, perhaps most commonly, casual bemusement).[13] Most pointedly, it has led concerned Indians to question whether participation in mainstream, "national" culture is desirable if it entails creolization and a sacrifice of traditional values. Sat Maraj, again represents a purist point of view, conflating calypso culture with broken families and "bacchanal," and denouncing racial mixing in general:

> Why must all girls want to be flag women [Carnival revelers] and our primary schools be Carnival? . . . We do not want to give your children the culture of "wine and jam" [creole dancing and partying] and single teenage parents . . . [nor do we want to] mix up everybody, as if we do not have enough child criminals and teenage mothers. (*Sunday Guardian*, 2 October 1994)

Musical syncretism is thus seen as linked—not entirely without justification—to a broader socio-cultural creolization, with its attendant weakening of traditional Indian values of hard work and family cohesion. Such concerns intensify the desires voiced by Indian spokespersons to be able to creolize on their own terms without eroding the values that have enabled them to progress, and to be able to maintain their own distinct cultural practices within a pluralistic conception of national identity.

MUSIC AND CREOLIZATION

In Trinidad, the phenomenon of creolization is as complex as it is controversial. Some Indian cultural activists have celebrated the syncretic musics of Drupatee, Mangal Patasar, and others as indications that Indians, rather than merely perpetuating or mimicking the culture of India, are creating distinctively local forms of culture. However, it could also be pointed out that local creation need not involve creolization, as in the case of the neo-traditional "tan-singing" or "local classical music" sung by semi-professional specialists at weddings and other functions. Although originally derived from North Indian folk and semi-classical music, tan-singing has developed into a unique song style, evolving along more or less Indian aesthetic lines without any significant creole stylistic influence.

Creolization itself has been used as a means of sustaining Indo-Trinidadian music culture, albeit in somewhat syncretic and accordingly controversial forms. The conservative SDMS and institutional Trinidadian Hinduism in general have survived partly by incorporating features of Christian practice, such as the custom of holding Sunday morning services (see, e.g., Lowenthal 1972: 152–53, Vertovec 1992: 120–21). Similarly, tan-singing competitions at once imitated calypso competitions, while serving as celebrations of traditional Indian music and lore. As Myers (1983) has observed, creole Carnival has served as a model for some aspects of the springtime Phagwa (Holi) festival—especially the chowtal (a Bhojpuri folksong genre) competitions organized by the Hindu Prachar Kendra (HPK).

In Indo-Trinidadian music itself, creolization is perhaps most overt in the form of language. While Indians in Trinidad and Guyana enjoy hearing Hindi-language songs and cherish the language as an icon of Indianness, very few are conversant in Hindi. Thus, as cultural activists like Ravi-ji have noted, Indo-Trinidadians have been unable to perpetuate the rich poetic heritage of India and, in the absence of an English-language Indo-Caribbean lyric tradition, they have contributed little to the realm of West Indian verse, which has instead been created mostly by creoles, from Derek Walcott to Mighty Sparrow. Ravi-ji observed, "We have failed to contemporise our music and lyrics . . . we have to make our music speak for us" (R. Maraj 1993a).

In hopes of ameliorating this perceived crisis of lyric self-representation, in 1993 Ravi-ji, director of the HPK, decided to establish a category of chowtal competition for so-called "pichakaaree" songs in English or mixed Hindi and English.[14] Anticipating objections by purists, he noted how Tulsidas' sixteenth-century rendering of the *Ramayana* in colloquial Avadhi (rather than in esoteric Sanskrit) helped popularize the epic and became one of the classics of Indian literature (R. Maraj 1993a). (Similarly, the SDMS itself had earlier instructed pandits to improve their English in order to better impart Hinduism; La Guerre 1985: 179.) When competing chowtal groups and amateur solo singers avidly rose to the occasion, purists did indeed protest the move as one more example of cultural erosion and creolization. Sat Maraj denounced the experiment as "seducing chowtals into calypso singing" (*Trinidad Express*, 11 March 1993), while another critic wrote, "if this practice . . . is not stopped, the age of soca, dub, and calypso tunes will obliterate all traces of Holiness in Holi" (letter to the editor, *Trinidad Guardian*, 8 April 1993). A pandit denounced the songs as "unnecessary concessions that are made to non-Hindus" and claimed that Tulsidas' translation was accepted only after it was sanctioned by God.[15]

God not having spoken on the subject of chowtal, it has been up to mere mortals to resolve the issue. Moderate reservations were raised by Mangal Patasar, who, while recognizing and even composing pichakaarees as a parallel development to Hindi chowtals, feared that the former might obliterate the latter and questioned whether such efforts would ever match calypsos in quality (pers. comm.). Ravi-ji and his supporters, however, see pichakaaree songs as illustrating how creolization—here in the form of using English—can promote Indian identity by revitalizing and contemporizing a music genre which remains Indian in style and orientation. Further, the pichakaaree songs, however amateurish, are seen as constituting yet another form of syncretic cultural *creation*, strengthening the Indo-Trinidadian stake to genuine citizenhood in the Caribbean.

The contradictions in the use of creolized practices to promote Indian music are even more evident in the Mastana Bahar phenomenon. Mastana Bahar is an Indo-Trinidadian amateur song and dance competition network founded in 1970 by Sham and Moean Mohammed, two energetic entrepreneurs also prominent as radio deejays, record producers, and concert impresarios. The primary Mastana Bahar activities are the weekly variety-show auditions held in various parts of the island throughout most of the year, leading to final competitions held in stadiums. Television broadcasts of the auditions are avidly watched by Indians, and some 80,000 people are estimated to have competed in the show since its inception (R. Maraj 1992). As such, Mastana Bahar has evolved into an institution in Trinidadian culture.

As Moean Mohammed readily acknowledges (pers. comm.), many aspects of the program have been modeled on the calypso competitions, with significant differences including the reliance on private commercial sponsorship and, of course, the show's orientation toward Indian art forms. Thus Mastana Bahar again illustrates how creolized sociomusical institutions can be used to promote Indian culture, serving as a bulwark against the "raging flood of Afro-Saxon and Afro-American cultural forces" (Shamoon Mohammed 1976: 29). The Mohammeds are quite justified in boasting that they have played a significant role in the Indo-Trinidadian cultural revival occurring since the early 1970s, not only spreading awareness of Indian music and dance but, more importantly, inspiring a prodigious amount of amateur performance. At the same time, they repeatedly proclaim their fierce Trinidadian nationalism and insist that Indian arts not be seen as foreign (e.g. Sham Mohammed 1979: 13).

Aside from the general goal of promoting Indian culture, the Mohammeds stress how Mastana Bahar is intended to inspire the creation of a uniquely Indo-Trinidadian musical culture, rather than mere imitation of India. The main vehicle for such attempts has been the encouragement of "local songs," which combine Hindi and English (see Sham Mohammed 1979: 17). The Mohammeds note with pride how a few traditional Indo-Caribbean local songs have even become popular in India, as rendered by Babla and Kanchan, a singer-producer duo from Bombay (e.g. Sham Mohammed 1983).

However, at least ninety percent of the Mastana Bahar fare consists of amateur (and decidedly amateurish) renditions of Indian film songs and dances. Indeed, critics allege that Mastana Bahar, rather than promoting local creation, has in fact served to stifle it with an inundation of film music. Ironically, much of modern Indian film music is itself heavily Westernized, incorporating disco rhythms and synthesizers, and often consisting of Hindi-language cover versions of Western pop hits. Thus Hindi film music, via Mastana Bahar, serves both as a celebration of Indian identity and a conduit for Western pop culture.

As Mastana Bahar uses calypso-influenced competition formats and Westernized Indian pop music to promote Indian culture in Trinidad, the dichotomies between "Indian" and "creole" musics in many respects dissolve, as does the utility of the concept of "creolization" itself. At the same time, one of the basic features of modern global culture is the uneasy coexistence of such inexorable trends toward syncretism and hybridity with tendencies toward ethnic essentialism. Such contradictory processes are particularly evident in the chutney boom, which we may consider as a final text in the (de)construction of Trinidadian national identity.

CHUTNEY

In the late 1980s, a dramatic new development occurred in Indo-Trinidadian music culture which threw the ranks of Indian critics and commentators into yet another round of polemics. The subject in this case was the phenomenon of "chutney"—a term which in Indo-Caribbean culture had long denoted not only a spicy condiment, but a loose category of lively, up-tempo Hindi-language folk songs and accompanying dance. Chutney was typically performed at Hindu weddings, wherein groups of women would indulge in animated and often whimsically lewd dances in secluded settings with no men present. By the 1970s, most Trinidadian Hindu weddings had come to include lively chutney dancing, in settings that were no longer sexually segregated, with music being provided by an ensemble of singer with harmonium, dholak (barrel drum), and dantal, a metal idiophone. In the mid-1980s, chutney enthusiasts spontaneously cast off most remaining social inhibitions, as public chutney dances started to be held in large entertainment halls. Since then, every weekend in two or three locales, several hundred Indians—male and female, young and old—gather to listen to chutney groups, to socialize, and, as the beer takes effect and the music quickens, to push aside the folding chairs and dance.[16]

Chutney is a mixture of old and new. On the one hand, most of the songs, although often original, are sung in Hindi and in standard Bhojpuri-derived Indo-Caribbean folk style. The dance style, although often flamboyant, is also largely traditional, combining graceful Indian-style hand gestures with sensuous pelvic "wining," whether performed solo or with a partner of either gender. On the other hand, the practice of men and women performing such dances together and in public is recent (except, paradoxically, insofar as it has been inspired by dance scenes in Indian films). Further, the chutney groups often add Western dance-band instruments and soca rhythms, producing a hybrid called "chutney-soca," as performed by Drupatee Ramgoonai and others.

The chutney vogue, in accordance with its merry flouting of conventions, provoked a barrage of vitriol from outraged Indian critics and community leaders (self-appointed and otherwise). The SDMS fulminated against it, letters to newspapers denounced it, and a women's organization called on the police to arrest lewd dancers. The controversy came to involve a complex range of issues, which can only be mentioned here. At one level, the debate concerned religion, with critics denouncing the dancing to devotional songs as blasphemous, and defenders pointing to the tradition of sensuality in Hinduism. Issues of gender were also involved, as moralists focus their wrath on women dancers, while proponents celebrate chutney as a vehicle for female liberation. Thirdly, class has played an important, if under-acknowledged, role in the debate, as chutney fêtes are predominantly working-class affairs, and the critics are mostly bourgeois.

Of greater direct relevance in this article are the ways in which the chutney controversy involves questions of local creativity and creolization. Much of the outrage over chutney has focused on the manner in which it allegedly reflects the negative aspects of creolization. Critics charge that chutney is a vehicle for the adoption of the worst features of Carnival and creole culture—drinking, vulgar dancing, and, allegedly, illicit sex and the subsequent breakdown of the family (e.g. in Danny 1990, 1992; see also Rampersad 1990). As one columnist wrote, using what might be interpreted as a euphemistic reference to black society, "Why do we have to follow the decaying sector of our society and destroy such an integral part of our Trinidadian heritage?" (D. Maharaj 1993).

For their part, chutney's defenders have stressed the ways in which it is an original and distinctly Trinidadian phenomenon, whose creole aspects (soca beat, public performance, etc.) strengthen the Indian claim of being West Indians rather than immigrants (e.g. M. Mohammed in Elcock 1987). Chutney supporters further argue that for all its hybridity, chutney-soca nevertheless serves to keep Indian culture alive and dynamic. As the columnist Kamal Persad (1990) wrote,

> Chutney occasions represent Indian cultural continuity and persistence. Such is the strength of this Indian cultural expression that it is holding its own against competition from other musical forms emanating from other cultural streams like African calypso, reggae and dub, and even rock 'n' roll and pop music from the US.

Another columnist hypothesized, in reference to the "bombardment" of Western pop music:

Could it be that the Chutney phenomenon, the wining, is a subconscious emulation by the Indian people, their response to that bombardment? That out of a fear of cultural annihilation, they have begun to respond? That attack—wining—is the best form of defence? That rather than be swallowed up whole by the omnivorous reach of the cultural imperialism of the West, the Chutney singers and dancers are now fighting fire with fire . . . that via the Chutney . . . Indians who might have strayed away in the past might once again return prodigally to the fold? (L. Siddhartha Orie, letter to the *Trinidad Express*, 30 December 1990)

Chutney is thus seen as constituting a bulwark against commercial Western and creole culture partially by incorporating some of its features. While this situation is paradoxical, it is also a common and oft-noted feature of syncretic musics throughout the developing world. Music genres that remain frozen and "pure" are often marginalized, while those that evolve and syncretize remain vital and are able to preserve at least some aspects of traditional culture.

Perhaps more immediately visible and relevant to Trinidadians has been the dramatic entrance of chutney-soca into "mainstream" national culture since 1995. That year saw the election of the country's first Indian prime minister, the establishment of Indian Arrival Day as a national holiday, and, on a more grassroots level, a lively fad of Indian-oriented calypsos and soca songs, as performed and enjoyed by creoles and Indians alike. In February/March, the Calypso Monarch prize went to (Afro-Trinidadian) Black Stalin's song entitled "Sundar Popo," dedicated to the veteran Indian chutney and "local song" crooner. In the subsequent Carnival season commencing in the latter part of the year, creole calypso singers released a veritable torrent of self-titled "chutney-socas" which, whether stylistically Indian or not, nevertheless foregrounded Indian themes in one way or another in an unprecedentedly appreciative spirit. One of these songs, Brother Marvin's "Jihaji Bhai" (Shipmate), won the 1996 runner-up award.[17] Meanwhile, a genuine chutney ("Lutela") by the Indian singer Sonny Mann became one of the season's smash hits and carried Mann to the Soca Monarch festival—where, however, he was pelted with missiles by creoles shouting "We eh [ain't] want de coolie." Such incidents notwithstanding, the Indian presence in Carnival was formalized the following year with the institutionalization of a Chutney-Soca Monarch Competition. Significantly, around half the competitors in this event were creole. At the same time, chutney seemed to be syncretizing out of existence, as Indianisms virtually disappeared from the new chutney-soca, with its English lyrics and soca style. Nevertheless,

Prime Minister Panday publicly hailed chutney-soca as "a symbol of the type of complete harmonization that must characterize our society in years to come." Indeed, chutney-soca has enabled Indians to finally enter the mainstream of Trinidadian culture, and on their own terms rather than on the traditional creole turf of pan and calypso. With chutney-soca entrenched on radio, in Carnival, in creole dance clubs, and even on BWIA's in-flight soundtracks, Trinidad is already being referred to—however belatedly—as "the land of calypso, steel band, and chutney."

CONCLUSION

In 1991 a *Trinidad Express* editorial described the ongoing debate about African, Indian, and Trinidadian identity as "tired old rumshop talk" ("Indians Flavour Cultural Callaloo," 11 August, 8). The vehemence of the ongoing socio-musical polemics, however, reveals that when provoked by concrete issues, the nature of Indian and Trinidadian identity continues to be a matter of prodigious import and animated negotiation. Indeed, what is at stake is no less than the forging of a workable cultural consensus in a country otherwise in danger of fragmenting along racial lines.

Trinidadian national identity was stunted from the start by the lack of any history of pan-ethnic independence struggle (see Trotman 1989: 184). While the labor movement of the 1930s (like Cheddi Jagan's Marxist mobilizations in Guyana) sought to foster a sense of proletarian solidarity, its goal of ethnic collaboration was premature, due to mutual ignorance between the two communities and the existence of too many problematic issues which remained to be worked out. The establishment of a creole "mainstream" under PNM leadership provided only a partial and temporary solution, as it largely excluded Indian as well as neo-African culture under a shallow integrationism, which was itself to occur largely on Afro-Saxon terms.

The Black Power Movement of 1970 forced a new and necessary confrontation of these issues. While celebrating Afrocentricity, it also re-ignited East Indian racial consciousness, leading to a cultural revival which came "perilously close to mimicry" (La Guerre 1985: 177), as dashikis and Afros on one side were matched by chutney and Mastana Bahar on the other. For the Indian historian John La Guerre, the frenetic cultural revivalism of the 1970s and 1980s constituted yet another stage which the East Indians were to undergo and eventually surpass. In fact, however, the revival appears to be intensifying rather than subsiding, and it is clear that whatever national consensus emerges will have to be based on new paradigms of multiculturalism and an expanded, or perhaps exploded, sense of "creole" culture. Accordingly, as Earl Lovelace's novel *The Dragon Can't Dance* dramatizes, the challenge facing Trinidad may involve starting from one's own cultural base in a way that opens up to others, relinquishing traditional clannishness but not cultural difference, to place culture in the service of a broader struggle for human dignity (see, e.g., Taylor 1993: 272). Accordingly, cultural activists have emphasized how Indian culture can at once sustain Indo-Trinidadians while enriching national culture as a whole (e.g. Parmasad 1973: 290). In the evolution of such a pluralistic rather than "plural" society, all ethnic communities would ideally transcend neo-colonial inferiority complexes and bigotries by achieving both self-respect and mutual respect.

At the same time, the self-conscious celebration of Indian identity and multiculturalism—with its dangers of ethnic fragmentation—has been offset by the trend toward various forms of syncretism. One aspect of this development is the increased East Indian participation in creole musical activities like steel band and calypso. As this process continues, such musics may become genuinely "mainstream" in the sense of being national and multi-ethnic rather than overwhelmingly Afro-Trinidadian. The symmetrical process of creole interest and participation in Indian arts, which had earlier commenced with tassa drumming, has now intensified dramatically with chutney-soca. A related form of syncretism involves the creolization of Indian musical culture itself, whether inspired by calypso or by Westernized Hindi film music. One ramification of these developments is that "the Trinidadian creole mainstream," in the words of one columnist, "is in a state of collapse . . . [and] is being replaced by a radically different understanding of society based on ethnicity" (Sankeralli 1996). Centrifugal ethnic revivals and centripetal syncretic hybridity thus emerge as the twin bases of Trinidadian culture, as of the postmodern global scene in general. Ironically, both trends serve to undermine the nation-state as a foundation for identity. The spirited sociomusical polemics in Trinidad illustrate how the transitions involved in such processes can be successfully negotiated in the public sphere, at once sustaining national polity and making it increasingly irrelevant.

NOTES

Research for this article was conducted in several field trips to Trinidad, Guyana, and Suriname in 1993–98 (two of which were funded by a PSC-CUNY grant), shorter excursions to Holland and Toronto, and in ongoing interaction with Indo-Caribbeans in New York City. While assuming full responsibility for the content of this article, I must acknowledge my debt to the friends and acquaintances who assisted me in my work, especially Mangal Patasar, Narsaloo Ramaya, Moean Mohammed, Praim Singh, the late Gora Singh, and other informants and musicians too numerous to cite.

1. The country of Trinidad and Tobago is referred to here simply as Trinidad; few Indians live on Tobago itself. In Guyana, Indians constitute 51% of the population; in Suriname, 37%; and in Trinidad, around 45%. The Indian population growth rate is roughly twice that of blacks, although their emigration rate may also be somewhat higher.

2. Letter to the *Stabroek* (Guyana), 1 December 1992. Several letters expressed such opinions in Guyanese newspapers in 1992–93, in the debate over the Indian demand for more media presence. See also S. Maharaj 1992.

3. One commentator wrote articulately of the Afro-Trinidadian experience: "Much had to be reinvented and even improvised on the spot, be it music, religion, or family organization. Such a challenge must indeed have been a creative one to the extent that it has had to be faced up to without many of the disciplines ordinarily exercised by the ancestral legacy. What the latecomers for their part more easily discern are the risks and the dangers of an uncharted journey, as it were, and the spectre of drift into a mongrel condition" (Best 1993).

4. In a much-quoted speech, Williams stated, "There must be no Mother India, no Mother Africa" (see E. Williams 1962: 281).

5. As the Indo-Trinidadian scholar John La Guerre stated, "It was only fairly recently that the Indian community formally decided that it would be part and parcel of Trinidad and Tobago" (*Trinidad Guardian*, 1 June 1990).

6. Mahabir calculated that in 1980 only 1.25% of Trinidadian television (TTT) programs had Indian content (1984: 2). In both countries, newspapers have for several years given expanded coverage to Indian affairs (see Centre for Ethnic Studies 1995).

7. A contemporary cartoon in the *Guyana Chronicle* parodied the situation by showing members of each of the country's six ethnic communities, and finally a dougla, seated around a table demanding their own radio programs.

8. Despite the discussions (themselves ambiguous and self-contradictory) of the *shrutis* in ancient Indian musicological treatises, empirical research has revealed that they are not used in any systematic fashion in modern North Indian classical music, not to mention folk or popular music, most forms of which instead use a flexible system of twelve semitones compatible with that of Western music (Levy 1982, Jairazbhoy and Stone 1963). Hence, for example, the relative compatibility of the harmonium with many forms of Indian music, despite the fact that the harmonium is indeed an instrument of European origin. (Maraj does not specify what structural "adaptive changes" the instrument underwent in India.) Maraj may correctly sense that Indian singing—including film music and chutney—sounds quite distinct from Western singing, but these differences are due more to nuances of style rather than intonation per se.

9. For example, the Venezuelan-derived genre *parang*, despite its obvious "foreign" character (including Spanish texts), is regarded as "indigenous" partly because it is cultivated primarily by creoles (see R. Maraj 1992); accordingly, it

is to some extent seen as a stronghold of Afro-Trinidadian musical culture. When an Indian girl sang parang at a 1993 concert, a creole acquaintance of mine laughingly quipped to his friend, "Now we really losin' it!"

10. The columnist Morgan Job commented on this sentiment in an article in the *Trinidad Guardian*, 11 February 1991. An Indian musician similarly commented, "Indians do not get too much involved in pan-playing because they probably were made to feel it belongs to the Afro-Trinidadians" (in Danny 1991).

11. The Afro-Trinidadian scholar Gordon Rohlehr (in criticizing the novelist V. S. Naipaul's disdain for pan) described pan music as "the single common ground where Trinidadians of all races meet on a basis of equality" (in Lowenthal 1972: 175).

12. Ken Parmasad related to me how his daughter's entrance in the calypso competition was greeted with heckles and calls of "What dat coolie girl doin' dere?"

13. The Syrian-Trinidadian singer "Mighty Trini" had earlier faced similar, if less vehement, opposition from his own, predominantly bourgeois community.

14. *Pichkari* is the syringe-like squirt-gun traditionally used in Indian Phagwa merrymaking. See articles in the *Sunday Guardian*, 23 March and 4 April 1997.

15. "Pundit: No Cause for English in Chowtal Songs," *Trinidad Guardian*, 29 March 1993.

16. For more expansive discussion of chutney, see Manuel 1998.

17. To the disappointment of many, the first prize went to a clannish song by CroCro denouncing blacks for letting Indians win the elections.

REFERENCES

Best, Lloyd. 1993. "I Am a Dougla." *Daily Express* (Trinidad) (7 June).

Centre for Ethnic Studies. 1995. *Ethnicity and the Media in Trinidad and Tobago: A Research Report.* University of the West Indies, St. Augustine, Trinidad.

Constance, Zeno Obi. 1991. *Tassa, Chutney and Soca: The East Indian Contribution to the Calypso.* San Fernando, Trinidad: By the author.

Danny, Phoolo. 1990. "UWI Student: Chutney Shows a Licence for Illicit Sex." *Trinidad Express* (14 December): 41.

———. 1991. "Bhajan on Pan: Sound of the Future." *Trinidad Express* (14 July): 16, 33.

———. 1992. "Indian Women Urged to Clean Up Chutney Act." *Trinidad Express* (17 August): 7.

Deosaran, Ramesh. 1987a. "The Social Psychology of Cultural Pluralism: Updating the Old." *Caribbean Quarterly* 33: 1–18.

———. 1987b. "The 'Caribbean Man': A Study of the Psychology of Perception and the Media." In *India in the Caribbean*, ed. David Dabydeen and Brinsley Samaroo, 81–118. London: Hansib/University of Warwick.

Despres, Leo. 1967. *Cultural Pluralism and Nationalist Politics in British Guiana.* Chicago: Rand McNally.

Dev, Ravi. 1993. "Nation and Integration in Guyana." In *East Indians in the New*

World: 155th Anniversary, ed. Somdat Mahabir and Isardat Ramdehal, 36–37. New York: Indo-Caribbean Foundation.

Elcock, Dave. 1987. Interview with Moean Mohammed. *Trinidad Express* (15 November): 13.

Herskovits, Melville, and Frances Herskovits. 1947. *Trinidad Village*. New York: Knopf.

Hintzen, Percy. 1989. *The Costs of Regime Survival: Racial Mobilization, Elite Domination, and Control of the State in Guyana and Trinidad*. Cambridge: Cambridge University Press.

Ifill, Max. 1987. *We Do Not Want Indian Imperialism in the Caribbean*. Port of Spain: author.

Jairazbhoy, Nazir, and W. A. Stone. 1963. "Intonation in Present-day North Indian Classical Music." *Bulletin of the School of Oriental and African Studies* 26: 119–32.

Johnson, Kim. 1994. "Experts Query Sabha Sruti Claim." *Trinidad Express* (10 July): 48–49.

La Guerre, John. 1982. *The Politics of Communalism*, 2d ed. Port of Spain: Pan-Caribbean Publications.

———. [1974] 1985. *Calcutta to Caroni: The East Indians of Trinidad*, 2d ed. Port of Spain: Longman Caribbean.

Levy, Mark. 1982. *Intonation in North Indian Music*. New Delhi: Biblia Impex.

Lowenthal, David. 1972. *West Indian Societies*. New York: Oxford University Press.

Mahabir, Noor Kumar. 1984. *Indian Culture in the Media, with Special Reference to Television*. Trinidad.

———. "The Politics of Love and Hate in a Plural Society." In *The Legacy of Indian Indenture: 150 Years of East Indians in Trinidad*, ed. Mahine Gosine, 86–100. New York: Windsor Press.

Maharaj, Drupatee. 1993. "Need to Become Aware as to Where We Are Headed." *Indo-Caribbean World* (Toronto) (9 June): 6.

Maharaj, Shastri. 1992. "A True Reflection of Our Culture." *Trinidad Guardian* (30 April).

Manuel, Peter. 1998. "Chutney and Indo-Trinidadian Cultural Identity." *Popular Music* 17: 21–43.

Maraj, Ravindranath [Ravi-ji]. 1992. "Mastana Syndrome: Neither Singer nor Song." *Trinidad Guardian* (26 January): 11.

———. 1993a. "Indo-Caribbean Images Must Be Recorded in Poetry and Song." *Trinidad Guardian* (31 January).

———. 1993b. "Begin National Debate on Cultural Policy." *Trinidad Guardian* (16 May).

Maraj, Satnarayan. 1994a. "Music in Schools: Statement No. 1" *Trinidad Express* (8 September).

———. 1994b. "Music in Schools: Reply to Kim Johnson." *Trinidad Express* (15 July).

Miller, Daniel. 1994. *Modernity: An Ethnographic Approach: Dualism and Mass Consumption in Trinidad*. Oxford: Berg.

Mohammed, Sham. 1979. "Indian Culture in Trinidad and Tobago?" In *Indian Cultural Pageant.* Trinidad.

———. 1983. *Mastana Bahar Cultural Pageant.* Trinidad.

Mohammed, Shamoon. 1976. "Mastana Bahar and Indian Culture in Trinidad and Tobago." M.A. thesis, University of the West Indies, St. Augustine, Trinidad.

Myers, Helen. 1983. "The Process of Change in Trinidad East Indian Music." In *Essays in Musicology,* ed. R. C. Mehta, 139–44. Bombay: Indian Musicological Society.

Parmasad, Ken. 1973. "By the Light of a Deya." In *The Aftermath of Sovereignty: West Indian Perspectives,* ed. David Lowenthal and Lambros Comitas, 283–91. Garden City, N.Y.: Doubleday/Anchor.

Persad, Kamal. 1990. "Fun Loving Dance in Tune with Hindu Values." *Trinidad Express* (16 December): 43–44.

Rampersad, Indrani. 1990. "The Hindu Voice in Chutney." *Trinidad Guardian* (25 December): 7, 10.

Rohlehr, Gordon. 1990. *Calypso and Society in Pre-Independence Trinidad.* Port of Spain: By the author.

Sankeralli, Burton. 1996. "Creole Culture on the Retreat." *Sunday Express* (4 February): 10.

Smith, Michael G. 1965. *The Plural Society in the British West Indies.* Berkeley and Los Angeles: University of California Press.

Taylor, Patrick. 1993. "Ethnicity and Social Change in Trinidadian Literature." In *Trinidad Ethnicity,* ed. K. Yelvington, 254–74. London: Macmillan.

Trotman, D. V. 1989. "The Image of Indians in Calypso: Trinidad 1946–86." In *Indenture and Exile: The Indo-Caribbean Experience,* ed. Frank Birbalsingh, 176–90. Toronto: TSAR.

Vertovec, Steven. 1992. *Hindu Trinidad: Religion, Ethnicity and Socio-Economic Change.* London: Macmillan; Warwick University Press.

Warner, Keith. 1993. "Ethnicity and the Contemporary Calypso." In *Trinidad Ethnicity,* ed. K. Yelvington, 275–91. London: Macmillan.

Williams, Brackette. 1991. *Stains on my Name, War in my Veins: Guyana and the Politics of Cultural Struggle.* Durham, N.C.: Duke University Press.

Williams, Eric. 1962. *History of the People of Trinidad and Tobago.* Port of Spain: PNM Publishing Co.

Yelvington, Kevin. 1993. "Introduction: Trinidad Ethnicity," in *Trinidad Ethnicity,* ed. K. Yelvington, 1–32. London: Macmillan.

PART III

Representing/Disciplining

10

Presencing the Past and Remembering the Present: Social Features of Popular Music in Kenya

D. A. MASOLO

And sweep out all the obscures, all the inventors of sub-
terfuges, the charlatans and tricksters, the dealers in gobbledy-
gook. And do not seek to know whether personally these
gentlemen are in good or bad faith, . . .
   From Gourou . . .
   From the Rev. Tempels, missionary and Belgian, his "Bantu
Philosophy," as slimy and fetid as one could wish, but discovered
very opportunely, as Hinduism was discovered by others . . .
(Aimé Césaire, Discourse on Colonialism, 34)

INTRODUCTION: THE "PRIMITIVE"
AS RATIONALIZED EXOTIC

Césaire was suspicious of the liberational capacity of Western discourse. Because of what he called "the objective social implications" of the radical genre of colonial discourse, he argued that
it marginalized even as it pretended to liberate; it recreates the same dichotomies embedded in the framework of its very other self. In the final
analysis, it does not matter whether the radical colonial theorists personally have good faith or not, "because the essential thing is that their highly
problematical subjective good faith is entirely irrelevant to the objective
social implications of the work they perform as watchdogs of colonialism" (1972: 34).
   How do the idea, the claims, and the practice of ethnomusicology
differ from those of the works held suspect by Césaire? Does ethnomusicology escape the tainting of "self-serving generalizations, . . .

349

tendentious speculations, [and] insistence on the marginal, 'separate' character of the non-whites" (ibid. 35), and if so, how? Do its results—its methodological and discursive practices—compromise, perhaps inadvertently, the good faith of its proponents? My worries are prompted by my understanding of ethnomusicology as part of critical theory, a movement whose underpinning character is its unrelenting impatience with essentialism. So, as such, ethnomusicology should be at least suspicious of an attempt to replace one dominant perspective with another. Yet its very idea, discursive location and manner of engaging with and drawing from non-Western, popular cultures, raise fundamental questions which have been asked several times before.

LESSONS FROM "ETHNOPHILOSOPHY"

The study of musical traditions of Africa, of peoples of African descent, and of other non-Western cultures under the rubric of ethnomusicology threatens to regenerate at least some of the polemics already encountered in regard to African philosophy over the past half century. The difference, and I am not sure how big it is, is that ethnomusicology appears to accept from the very beginning that it is an offshoot of cultural anthropology, where the prefix *ethno-* is at home, while it is not in philosophy. To this extent, unlike ethnophilosophy, ethnomusicology does not claim or try to make adjustments to the core of an intellectual history and tradition already deemed privileged in order to be assimilated. What is not clear is whether those who practice within the discipline of musicology are, like those who gave birth to ethnophilosophy, also aware that indeed what they are up to is the creation of a marginal space at the periphery of the discipline (of musicology) to take care of vocally and instrumentally produced sounds among, in reference to Europe and Eurogenic America, peripheral societies. The term *ethnomusicology* appears to echo the now familiar sentiments of *ethnophilosophy*.

Ethnophilosophy, and one would say ethnic studies in general, is made possible first by the imagination of the "savagery" of the Other, followed, after subjecting his "strange" behavior to "careful" scrutiny, by the suspicion that there might after all be something human even in the rawness of savagery. Both Placide Tempels (1945) and Joseph Conrad ([1902] 1971) have narrated how the embrace of the "Savage" Other begins with a strange suspicion of his being and representation of that which they—the civilized Europeans—refuse to recognize as their own distant past. This distant past seems so unreal and "unearthly," in Conrad's words, that it must be an essential characteristic of the "Savage" as opposed to those of the "Savantes." Conrad (1971: 36–37), describing the inhabitants of the then Congo Free State in what has been called a "work of art," says the following:

> The earth seemed unearthly. We are accustomed to look upon the shack-
> led form of a conquered monster, but there—there you could look at a
> thing monstrous and free. It was unearthly, and the men were——No,
> they were not inhuman. Well, you know, that was the worst of it—this
> suspicion of their not being inhuman. It would come slowly to one. They
> howled and leaped, and spun, and made horrid faces; but what thrilled
> you was just the thought of their humanity—like yours—the thought of
> your remote kinship with this wild and passionate uproar. Ugly. Yes, it was
> ugly enough; but if you were man enough you would admit to yourself
> that there was in you just the faintest trace of a response to the terrible
> frankness of that noise, a dim suspicion of there being a meaning in it
> which you—you so remote from the night of first ages—could compre-
> hend. And why not? The mind of man is capable of anything—because
> everything is in it, all the past as well as all the future.

Despite the large gulf of time separating them from the "Savages" "as sane men would be [from those in] a madhouse" (36), these special emis-saries—one an imperial emissary, the other a missionary—were coura-geous enough to notice that some trace of humanity could not be denied the Savage. According to Tempels ([1945] 1959: 167–68),

> This "discovery" of [a humanity in the form of] Bantu philosophy is so
> disconcerting a revelation that we are tempted at first sight to believe that
> we are looking at a mirage. In fact, the universally accepted picture of prim-
> itive man, of the savage, of the proto-man living before the full blossoming
> of intelligence, vanishes beyond hope of recovery before this testimony....
> It is as if, all at once, a light of intelligence illumines, radiates from and
> glitters in these animal countenances that have been thus [meaning by
> Tempels' own discovery] humanly transformed.

What transforms the "Savage" into a "sort of human," and his expressions from folklore and from "certain undefinable beliefs and influences" (36), or from "illogical lucubrations of 'gloomy Niggers'" (30), or still from "simple instinct or an irrational fear" (22), from Conrad's "shackled form of a conquered monster," into sound sense which is partially philo-sophical—what effects this transformation is the work of the "civilizer" who lends the "Savage" the humanizing and superior forms of his intel-lectual culture. He thus reformulates the "savage" expressions by giving them logical form and disciplinary ordering.

Tempels saw this humanizing project on a wider evangelical scale. His *Notre recontre* of 1962 prefigured what was later to find official ecclesiastical statement in the documents of the Second Vatican Council: "to explain Catholic teaching in a way that avoids giving unnecessary offence to persons accustomed to other modes of thought and speech" (Dulles 1966: 12). In an effort to define a new process of renewal, the decree document *Ad Gentes* sets, like Tempels earlier, the ways to assimilate "pagan" expressions into Christian revelation. But at the height of its implementation, it was African drums, the *kayamba* rattle shaker, and occasionally the cowbell, that were being incorporated into the Christian liturgy as the reconciliatory signs of renewal. This selective inclusiveness not only marginalized the real core of African expressions of the sacred, it also carefully left out the major African musical instruments. To date, neither *nyatiti, litungu, orutu,* nor animal horn have been incorporated into any African celebration of mainstream Christian liturgy (Catholic, Anglican, or Methodist)—for the "obvious" reason that such instruments are still very much part of what Conrad imagined as "the heart of darkness." By contrast, these instruments play a central role in the liturgies of the independent churches which are often viewed as rebellious and perpetuators of the past in the form of "traditional" values.

This oppositional separation of the distant and unaffected image of the Other as "savage" from its Western representation as a taming and civilizing act allows Erlmann (1991) to divide the *isicathamiya* music of South Africa into two distinct historical forms mediated by the newly acquired and affecting transformative processes of the European cultures of the urban settings. He contrasts (172–73) the earlier "male-dominated and robust or forceful" movements of *ingoma* with the later "gentle" and "civilized" steps of *isicathamiya* movements. The former, according to him, reflect the residual presence of the rough edges of traditional warrior-like values whose focus was the depiction of the fierce and virile fighting movements of young warriors. They symbolized the pastoral "bullness" of *ingoma* performers whose dance raised much dust with the thrust of their feet, in sharp contrast to the "slick city behavior" of mostly working middle-class *isicathamiya* performers. The urban and "tamed" *isicathamiya* is radically different. In Erlmann's eyes, it has aesthetic form in the regulated and polished motions of the feet, the gentleness of the step—in which the raising of dust is explicitly despised as crude. The vocal composition of their singing can also be reordered in the familiar terms which organize European pitch formation and musical knowledge as bass, tenor, alto, and soprano (Erlmann 1996: 31). The question is: what is the *a priori* value of such a formational order to other

African singing styles? What, for example, would such a reordering do to the singing of Owiti Origo and the Kajulu Boys (a Luo guitar group popular in the late 1960s and early 1970s and distinctive for their sharp voices and guitar style informed by the Kajulu inflections of Dholuo)? Do the South Nyanza Luo modify their use of European notation to enable them to sing some tunes sung differently from their counterparts from other parts of Nyanza? Or must they be all lumped together as "crude," "rural," and "formless" on account of their irreducibility to some conventional staff notation? And when the pitch patterns differ so audibly even within the same speech/song community, how do we define what constitutes the presumably characteristic rhythm of the Luo as a wider group?

Fortunately, Erlmann is both cautious about and cautioning against seeing the evolution of the urban *isicathamiya* from the rural *ingoma* solely in terms of a progression of form from "crude" to "polished" or "better." The separating images of (the urban) "here" and (the rural) "home," he says (1991: 158), are not absolute dichotomies. What seems hidden behind this claim of continuity, however, is the effort, made possible by the questionable claim of the universality of urbanization, to narrow the gap between the two spaces as merely the function of the recent and current scholarship of the new radicalism in the West that aspires to reach out with an embrace of that which is exotic, distant, and different. There is no favor done to African populations in claiming that their own indigenous socio-economic processes would have led to some sort of urbanization anyway. The question is not about the processes that lead to urbanization. It is about the implications of a specific historical process of urbanization. And there is no need for favor or sympathetic outreach in analytic and explanatory undertakings.

Erlmann (1991: 156–74) gives a fascinating history of modern *isicathamiya*. He asserts that (despite the glaring differences between the rural *ingoma* and urban *isicathamiya* styles which we referred to above) "what seems to emerge as the logical result of the 'prehistory' of *isicathamiya* is the fact that it can by no means simply be construed as a case of transformation of a 'traditional,' rural performance tradition through rural–urban migration." The fascination of this historical account is due partly to the comparative approximation of South African cultural politics, especially black South Africans' trajectory in and of it, to its African-American correspondence. It is an interesting painting of cultural dynamics disenveloping themselves on a racial *pista* or stage, itself built on the surface of a ground controlled by a supremacist white culture.

Erlmann's historical account of Zulu-based musical performance in South Africa stands between two other forms which the insights drawn from the South African scenario help to explain as simultaneously both similar to and different from it. On the one hand, Erlmann's account provides some general and relevant sociological insights for understanding the evolution of African-American musical tradition(s) in the context of struggles toward self-definition and articulation by social groups who are socially, physically, and culturally displaced and economically and politically controlled. While doing this, he almost convinces me—against my intuitively strong perception of the evolution of traditions under such circumstances as purely accidental in their origins, as opposed to being the function of a logical and deliberate pattern like the one he provides for the Zulu-based *isicathamiya*. In particular, I have usually remained skeptical of the imposition of a logical explanatory pattern for the evolution of the now-powerful tradition of jazz. My skepticism leads to the question as to whether the same logical pattern provided for the Zulu-based *isicathamiya* and its local historical correlates and affines can then be applied equally to other specific ethnic fields in South Africa. It is, finally, interesting that Erlmann gives little or no attention to the nature and outcome of the interethnic cultural influences through the mediation of the capitalist economy which so radically transforms the Zulu musical tradition according to his analysis.

LESSONS FROM VISUAL ART

The scholarly attention and general interest accorded African music are fairly recent in comparison with African visual art. For a long time, the anthropological imagination of static cultures retired African musical instruments from active performance and reduced them to silent inhabitants of private and museum collections under the category of "material culture." As in ethnophilosophy, the history of the study of African visual art also charts its course in terms of a gradual shift from perspectives of "primitivism" to those which view art as endowed with its own "ethnic" formal and value characteristics. The reason for this is partly to be found in the old tendency of Western scholarship to marginalize any tradition whose definitory characteristics neither resembled nor could be assimilated into Western categories. Obsessed with form and style as defined by Western aesthetic perspectives, Western scholars got used to uncritically studying and describing non-Western products of art under the guidance of Western formalistic criteria and standards. In the context of classification of such productions, an object's "artistic" value was determined by its comparative approximation to the criteria in Western art.

But because the criteria of Western art were considered to be rational, that is, as deliberate and definitive form(s) transferred to an object by an agent in the course of its willful and skillful reproduction, "primitive" art was essentially what Western art was not. In Aristotelian terms, an object of art is both abstract and concrete at the same time; it encapsulates all four causal modalities, the pivotal ones of which are the formal and the material. It bears the fusion of the abstract ideal (*causa formalis*) with concrete matter (*causa materialis*) through the mediation of appropriate means and agency (*causa efficiens*) of the artist. In "The Question Concerning Technology" (1977), Heidegger makes a powerful analysis of this process by which an artist—a smith in his example—transfers a specific form to matter in the act of "creating" a piece of art—a chalice in his example. Art, then, is a conscious and rational product. By contrast, "primitive" art was seen as lacking a rational basis. It was not "a product" in the strict sense of the term. And the idea of its distance from "standard" works of art was like Tempels' idea of the distance between "Bantu philosophy" and "real" philosophy.

The characterization of "proper" art as a conscious and rational product finds its possibility and justification in the history of Western Enlightenment and its culmination in Hegel's phenomenology. Its product is the ideological framework—well articulated by Hegel and Marx alike—in which all the different cultures and races of people are chained together in a hierarchical order reflecting their respective material and intellectual conditions in their advance toward perfection. But at the same time as this Enlightenment ideology arbitrarily places European cultures at the top of the evolutionary scale, it also becomes responsible for "the colonial primitivization of the non-European world," a practice that continues today in the form of ethnicization of non-European cultures globally as well as within Western societies. Today, primitivism refers almost exclusively to African and Oceanic cultures because their world, in contrast to the Western and salvaged Asian worlds, is the only one still considered

> a pagan or primitive entity that has been trapped in the irrationality of its past history, in its primeval or pre-rational existence. In fact this entity does not even possess consciousness of itself, its own past, present, and future. It is the victim of its own timelessness, a static condition characterized and contained by ethnic, tribal, communal, irrational, unconscious, traditional . . . modes of existence. (Araeen 1991: 160)

But today, thanks to the category of Western scholars who consider themselves to belong to the radical liberal left, or radical theorists as they are also called, the "primitive" can be accorded some voice to be heard, and some visibility for what he is, *à la* Tempels, provided he does not take control of history, which must remain the sole prerogative of the modern West. To make room for the "primitive" at the fringes of the disciplinary discourse, we shall erect a grass-thatched shrine on the fringes of the *boma* (main dwelling compound or homestead, in kiSwahili) and call it "Ethnic Arts." Just as ethnophilosophy was the product of one who thought himself radical and liberal, so we find the invention of "Ethnic Arts," including ethnomusicology, to be primarily an expression of an ideological stand within the Western academy. But while this is so, what does not change is precisely what is in the expression *ethnic*. It is not hard to see that it stands for "not quite," "non-mainstream," "not proper," and "marginal." In other words, just as with ethnophilosophy—which was used by many people in the Western academy as interchangeable with "African philosophy" when defined as a collection of myths and other "peculiar beliefs." (Prior to its coinage by Nkrumah in the early 1940s, presumably earlier than Possoz's use of the term in 1944–45,[1] terms such as "primitive philosophy" and "philosophy of the savage" were frequent in ethnographic or anthropological texts.) In its post-Nkrumah usage, especially in Possoz's and Hountondji's texts, the term ethnophilosophy came to stand for what "real" philosophy was not and was opposed to (as its perfect negation and rational reorganization). Similarly, ethnic arts, such as the content or subject matter of ethnomusicology, stand on the threshold between rejection and exotic admiration.

In his now infamous (because wrongly worded and unpopularized by an uprising) article, Philip Curtin (1995) warned that applying the preferential hiring policy of Affirmative Action to recruiting faculty for the already marginalized disciplines within the Western academy such as African history—and one need not work too hard to imagine that Curtin would include in this repertoire the rest of the marginalized disciplines that "traditionally" make up African Studies such as African Art, African Literature, African Politics (this is usually taught under the double coverage of comparative politics and African Studies), African Anthropology, etc.—would only worsen the already endangered status of such disciplines.

Curtin's idea of the endangerment—which he ill-advisedly referred to as "ghettoizing"—of "ethnic studies" is the function of the notion, perhaps even a growing conviction of the post-detente West, of the need to get rid of what Barry Schwabsky (1985: 120) called "the emblem[s] of a false exoticism: [in which] that which is foreign is reduced to the decorative exterior of a completely domestic mechanism." According to Schwabsky, the otherness of art holds a paradoxical relationship with the familiar: "The otherness of art challenges the self-evidence and self-sufficiency of the everyday, of the given world. [But] it is also part of that world" (ibid.). Evidently, Schwabsky has visual art in mind, as his observations have parallels in the critiques of Picasso's and Gaugin's co-option and appropriation of primitivism. But the practice spreads across all disciplines, "for, recently, artists have increasingly come to interest themselves in the belief systems of non-western and prehistoric societies as much as in the material artefacts produced by those cultures" (Cooke 1991: 137).

Several scholars have argued that Western fascination with the "tribal" cultures of the so-called "simple societies" is not a novelty of the nineteenth century. In one of his more recent works, *The Idea of Africa* (1994), Mudimbe traces its historical roots back to the Greco-Roman thematization of otherness and traces its articulation in such concepts as barbarism and savagery and the complex process that has shaped the idea of Africa as understood by Europeans. Dore Ashton (1984) identifies the sixteenth-century French philosopher Michel de Montaigne as an important link in the history of the identification and discrimination of the non-European Other as a significant representation of what Europe was no longer. Montaigne's assertion (in "Of Cannibals") that "each man calls barbarism whatever is not his own practice; for indeed, it seems that we have no other test of truth and reason than the example and pattern of the opinions and customs of the country we live in" (1957: 152) set the tone for the primitivization of the non-European in later centuries, even making it possible to claim the right to colonize.

If the Enlightenment turn started by people like Montaigne led to the perfect disdain for and distrust of sensuality in the subsequent rationalist movement, the particular assertion above certainly softens but nonetheless alludes to and foregrounds what was to become a familiar practice. Through colonial anthropology and history, Europe could look and see in the Other what it was not. The colonial disciplines created a sense of distance between the familiar home and the lands and cultures far away, mediated in the wide seas of cultural difference by anthropological representations and historians' notebooks. According to Ashton (1984: 76),

> There seem to be two projects here. One is to rectify and expand intellectual history. The other is to muse on the meeting, in art history, of stylistic change, traditional art historical method and originality. By juxtaposing works of art from radically differing cultures the Museum attempts to do for art history what anthropology has done for Western philosophy: it offers materials for vital critique.

Indeed, ethnophilosophy performs this juxtapositional and paradoxical contrast of radical opposites precisely by trying to bring together the stylistically and methodologically different. The ethnophilosophical text primitivizes the local while, or even as, it expresses admiration for it. It brings to a head-on collision the Hegelian *logos* on the one hand with what Ashton calls "a sense of the natural" on the other, in which the inequalities between logic and the poetic representations of savage thinking remain unmaskedly bare but somehow structurally natural, as claimed by Lévi-Strauss.

In a clear allusion to the Hegelian outline of the phenomenology of the Spirit, the idea of "simple societies" was indeed invented by anthropologists to refer to their objects as lacking in the abstract models of reality that allow for the emergence and development of complex structuralization of the social and physical worlds. To be simple meant to base the practices of economic production and social organization on what was merely and instinctively necessary, including the use of simple and unsophisticated tools. It also meant lacking in variation, whether horizontally among different groups, or vertically in historical mobility within any single group. Societies regarded as "simple" are then seen to be at par; their traditions and customs, beliefs and practices are all alike, having been stripped down to their imaginary essential characteristics. The idea of "simple societies" coincides with the idea of the colonial Other as a group of racial stereotypes, with their equivalent cultural stereotypes, in the development of primitivism in colonial discourse. Jack Goody (especially 1977, 1992) believes that orality, the sole medium of "simple" societies, is responsible for this lack of both variation and originality. A similar view allowed Placide Tempels to imagine a large group of Africans called the "Bantu" whom he believed to have an identical "philosophy." In fact, according to him, the basic "philosophy" embedded in the traditions and customs of the "Bantu" was the same for all "primitives." Yet, at the same time, Tempels believed that what he called "philosophy" in the Bantu modes of thought was not really philosophy. His reasons for believing so were obvious: the Bantu mode of thinking lacked the individualistic, critical and auto-critical, logical and systematic characteristics and grids of real philosophy—that is, philosophy as Western thinkers have defined and practiced it.

What is invoked here is the dialectic idea of the *Doppelgänger* or mutual mirroring, between Same and Other, in which what is present and knowable in each becomes absent and strange through the other and vice versa. It is this idea, according to Agawu (1995), that makes possible the imagination of "an African rhythm" as topologically different, *unheimlich*, unhomely, from that which the Western scholar knows as familiar, *heimlich*, homely. Marcus and Fischer (1986) already illustrated how the *Doppelgänger* works in ethnography. The reduction of African ethnic musics—in which I include even contemporary electronic equipment—to a schemata of "staff notations, bar lines, time signatures, clefs, and phrase marks" (Agawu 1995: 392), as a way of making them "rationally comprehensible" is to do precisely what Tempels, with "ethnophilosophy," considered a "generous" act of missionizing. This self-proclaimed project to "rationalize" is done on account of forgetting or deliberately choosing to ignore the wider and varied (non-unified) social contexts which define specific cultural forms, styles, and discourses. Like Conrad, Tempels believed his project would anthropomorphize his beasts. And so his project only draws the political boundaries of hermeneutic interpretation by which aesthetic hierarchies are laid out unmasked. In ethnic studies, the earthly and unearthly do not become one. What these ethnicists do not seem to notice is that their working tools, whether they are specific logical structures, metaphysical categories, disciplinary categorizations, or staff notation and bar lines, are already conceptualizations, and hence "formalizations" of the world, and that these are themselves historical products or artefacts.

This separation of the "rational" and the "savage" reaches its paradoxical irony in Tempels and Curtin. For Tempels, the "true savage" is not the local awaiting assimilation and transformation by the "rationally systematic." This local is the "noble savage" because it is endowed with the humility of realizing its limitations and thus gives itself up for assimilation and dependence. The "true savage," according to Tempels, is the one that resists, the proud and ungrateful who wishes to take control of his own destiny in vain. Similarly, for Curtin, "ghettoization" is not the function of the presence of non-Western materials for Western gaze and discourse. Rather, it is created when the subject matter takes control of itself, subjectivizes itself, and appropriates its own discourse as a gesture of resistance within the precincts of Western academic cathedrals. Their search became inevitably fixed on finding their "noble savage," the phantasmagoric embodiment of the essential properties of "africanity" (Maquet 1972, Serequeberhan 1995). Does a hermeneutic practice actually produce such beings as alluded to (see for example Serequeberhan 1995)?

THE IMAGINARY *NOBLESSE*

Senghor, pushing the essentialist thesis, had earlier argued that the characteristic difference between European and African modes of thought as separate genres was to be found in their separate and distinctive *uni*-forms, meaning that while the hellenic mode is analytic, that is, logical, critical, autocritical, and systematic, the African mode of thought is governed by participatory emotion. It is not clear whether Senghor's view meant that Africans are either incapable of or have a strong disregard for formally organized and deliberate discourse, but his idea of negritude spells the claim of race-based essential differences between peoples. In response to critics, Senghor evoked the Teilhardian balance of opposites—as in emotion against reason—as one in which, for different races, one characteristic co-exists with, even as it predominates over, the other and provides it definitory character. Africans, he contended, were the "people of rhythm."

Senghor's essentialist claim, in conjunction with Tempels' idea of a "Bantu philosophy," provided an avenue for constructing ideas of difference and sameness along racial lines. Ethnophilosophy was part of this new wave which culminated, in the context of academic disciplines, in the invention of many things deemed to be "specifically and uniquely African." Since then, it has been easy, although glaringly misleading, to imagine that uniqueness empowers. Besides ethnophilosophy, other examples include "African traditional religions" (see for example Shaw 1990), ethnolinguistics, and ethnomusicology. Concept-specific idioms such as "African rhythm" (see for example Agawu 1995), "African democracy," and so on have been added to the list. In other words, the adjective "African" appears in these instances to have become the huge dumpster for things not quite acceptable within mainstream definitions. Mudimbe (1988) has shown how this trend of trying to define and practice academic disciplines or identifying some areas of popular culture as uniquely African is actually only another side of the same colonial discourse that the trend endeavors to liberate itself from. Shaw (1990) and Agawu (1995) are part of the wide and still growing influence of Mudimbe's (1988) critique of ethnic studies. From them one gets the message that exoticizing the Other by ascribing to it uniqueness has become the hidden hand of subtle marginalization.

The invention of the "African" as a race with supposedly objectively unique and distinctive qualities has been criticized as both politically disabling (Fanon 1967, 1978 against Senghor's ideas of negritude and rhythm respectively; Césaire 1972 against Tempels) and scientifically flawed in its claims (Appiah 1992). Appiah's analytically meticulous argument contends that other than the physical continental block itself together with its physical features, the term "African" has no specific referent in the customs and traditions of the people who inhabit it, and so there cannot be anything such as an "African identity," "African dance," "African philosophy" in the Tempelsian sense, "African dress," "African view," or "African rhythm." But he also joins Fanon in criticizing the racial and cultural stereotypes regarded as a natural source of certain values to be passive and disabling to Africans as moral, cognitive, and political agents. According to Appiah (1992: 176),

"Race" disables us because it proposes as a basis for common action the illusion that black (and white and yellow) people are fundamentally allied by nature and, thus, without effort; it leaves us unprepared, therefore, to handle the "intraracial" conflicts that arise from the very different situations of black (and white and yellow) people in different parts of the economy and of the world.

The issue is not only about the hopelessly unitarian view of Africa as opposed to its cultural and ideological pluralism and diversity. It is, and has been, in epistemological terms, also about the possibility and political nature of cross-cultural conceptual transfers which, in the case of Mudimbe's view of an invented "Africa" as an ideological *significatum*, has resulted in what he (1988: 43) calls "a failed will to transcendence, now expressing its desire towards an ambiguous new beginning" that traps several texts of African philosophers within the same epistemic order while they simultaneously seek to transcend it. Identifying the texts in this "ambiguous new beginning" as constituted at least partly by the philosophical critiques of ethnophilosophy, Mudimbe says of them that

[they are] not the reverse of Tempels' and Kagame's school. It is a policy discourse on philosophy aimed at examining methods and requirements for practicing philosophy in Africa. As a trend, it derives its conviction from its status as a discourse which is firmly linked to both the Western tradition of philosophy as a discipline and the academic structures which guarantee institutionally accepted philosophical practices. As such, the critique of ethnophilosophy can be understood as subsuming two main genres: on the one hand, a reflection on the methodological limits of Tempels' and Kagame's school and, on the other hand (at the other pole of what ethnophilosophical exercises represent), African practices and works bearing on Western subjects and topics in the most classical tradition of philosophy. (154)

The debate that Mudimbe's passage sets up has been both interesting and complex and also has bearings on the claims of ethnomusicology at the epistemological level. Mudimbe is decrying the lack of an indigenous African episteme that would inform an African order of philosophy. But rather than be part of the invented essentialist program, Mudimbe sees the emergence of such an order in the conjunction between history and anthropology. He calls for a reconnection—after the rupture occasioned by the influence of the colonial power discourse—with the anthropological field(s) even as attention is crucially paid to the demands of history. As if in response to the challenge defined by Mudimbe, Kwasi Wiredu has argued (1992: 1–12) that the current philosophical practice in Ghana is both a function and continuation of the long-standing tradition in Ghanaian culture of critical thinking that stretches back to solid foundations in the traditional forms. Wiredu's reference finds easy support in an impressive list of Ghana's recent (that is, nineteenth- and twentieth-century) Western-educated intellectual and political elites who have not only kept the old debates alive through their new reformulations and re-visitations, but have also sometimes carried on some interesting debates among themselves regarding the interpretation and understanding of some key concepts in their traditional renditions and uses. A good example of this is Wiredu's own interesting debates, first with Beddu Addo regarding Akan concepts of truth, and then with Kwame Gyekye on the concept of the person. (Some of these interesting discussions can be found in Wiredu and Gyekye 1992, Gyekye 1995, and Safro Kwame 1995.)

In Wiredu's armory are the views which not only defend the cross-cultural translatability and commensurability of concepts and propositions, but also advocate conceptual exchanges, borrowings, adaptations, and other means of conceptual and general cultural growth. We have learned from Wiredu's good and persistent lessons (1980) that while this is so, cross-cultural translations and critiques should be carried out carefully, for example without the fallacious comparisons and contrasts of ordinary, everyday expressions and beliefs with technical expressions and theories of professionals.

Wiredu does not and has not explicitly addressed issues related to ethnomusicology, but his lesson in "How not to compare African traditional thought with Western thought" (1980: 37–50) allows us to ask, as Agawu (1995: 381) does in reference to W. E. F. Ward, whether African rhythm can be represented on the bar lines of staff notation and then be appraised in terms of those compositional forms. Like the cases already noted in philosophy, also in music, I see Agawu to be saying, there is a long genealogy of scholars, both African and European or American, whose studies of African music primarily use the formal grids analytically extracted from Western music for contrast with the latter. From these contrasts emerge theories of formal (aesthetic) similarities and essential differences. An example of the latter, Agawu argues, is the view that African music is essentially characterized by rhythm in a way that Western music is not—that its rhythmic tempo and other musical structural grids are so radically different from their European counterparts they stand distinctively and essentially on their own.

Such a view, as identified by Agawu, runs like a perfect musical reproduction of Tempels: "where we sing with a d sharp, they sing with a . . . whatever" as substitution for Tempels' own "where we speak of being, they speak of force." If, on the other hand, we were to take all those musical staves, bars, motifs, and other chartable forms to be the graphically reproducible abstract or conceptual representations of movements and voice pitches—just as the laws of logic are the abstract or conceptual representations of the relational nature of propositions and ideas (that is, some sort of "cultural universals" as Wiredu calls them)—as well as know that such musicologists believe that music, any music, is a mix of an orderly pattern of sound and a matching orderly pattern of movements whose pitch and movement forms respectively can be analyzed and represented on bar charts and understood by use of certain criteria, then why can African music not be so analyzable and notated on the European musical staff? What this suggests is an encore (re)formulation of the same old oppositional views encountered in philosophy that—*mutatis mutandis*—African music is so unique (by which is often meant strange and lacking decipherable order) it cannot be understood by means of the conventionally (meaning Western) established canonical grids of the discipline. Hence, in order to flag its exemption from judgments imposed by such disciplinary canons, one must refer to its disciplinary ordering as ethnomusicology. This view is then countered by the universalist position championed by Hountondji and especially by Wiredu (1990). But while one could argue for such universals, what remains unclear is the extent or degree of their usefulness in understanding the composition, production, performance, and consumption of African music. In the subsequent parts of this essay, I move away from both the critique of ethnomusicology and the reductionist structuralist approach to the study of African music. Rather, I attempt to give a descriptive/phenomenological account of the socio-historical conditions and contexts of cultural discourse through music as text. While I regard the studies and discussions of the structural form (what musicians refer to as tempo or rhythm, pitch levels measurable with notes on lines and spaces, etc.) as didactically interesting and informative, I consider them overemphasized to the point of being diversionary from other issues—the social and cultural issues—which African musicians equally, if not primarily, tackle in their compositions and performances.

Now if we continue to draw parallels between the particular endeavors in ethnomusicology with what has happened earlier in ethnophilosophy, one cannot avoid wondering why the experience in philosophy has not been sufficient in warning us of the impending marginalization of the scholarship on ethnic musical traditions. As in the areas of ethnophilosophy and African traditional religions or (African) theology, Agawu argues that the study of African ethnomusicology has led to the invention of something exotic but nonexistent called "African rhythm." Its correlate is "African dance," another exotic but nonexistent assumption. Again, as with ethnophilosophy, the tide of "African rhythm" has also met with resistance, at least for now.

Given the influence of Hountondji (1983), Wiredu (1980), Mudimbe (1988), Eboussi-Boulaga (1977), and more recently Appiah (1992), one can only hope that the idea of a passive, subjectless, and unanimous Africa has been dealt a death blow. In this essay I wish to show, first, that while many contemporary African musical artists draw significantly from the styles and tunes of their respective traditions, they constantly also borrow from and in turn contribute to various other styles and traditions outside their own. The anti-essentialist musical map thus drawn is of a multiplicity of traditions that preserve some local bases, but which at the same time also frequently and constantly burst into new musical configurations, mixing, unmixing, and remixing or, sometimes, as in David Fanshawe's now popular *African Sanctus*, merely juxtaposing the unmixable different forms and styles, old and new, local and distant.

Fanshawe's fascinating but odd collection almost violently suppresses every African singing sound by imposing on the songs and funeral wailings (what the Luo call *dengo*) the well-structured chants of the Gregorian Latin High Mass performed by the Bournemouth Symphony Chorus and the Choristers of St. George's Chapel, Windsor Castle. The following text explains the front cover picture, which depicts a ritualistically adorned Luo elder who took part in the making of the *African Sanctus:*

> The "Hippo Man" (Mayinda Orawo, A Luo elder of Kenya) is the symbolic figurehead of African Sanctus. He embraces the Bournemouth Symphony Chorus and the Choristers of St George's Chapel, Windsor Castle; we Europeans are his shoulders and the Choristers are his heart.

In the picture, as also in the arrangements of the songs, the holy and the pagan, the classic and the "primitive" are brought together in an exotic yet hierarchized reading of their contemporaneity. What could significantly remain of the "selfhood" of a person whose heart and shoulders are someone else's? Fanshawe makes music a unique example and model of the process of dominating and domesticating foreign symbols. They become juxtaposed side by side, but not mixed. Thus, like the "noble savage," the traditional songs, prayers, and funeral wailings in Fanshawe's composition can find cover under the shoulders of the polished note-based Gregorian chant, and solace in its heart. The superimposition of the Gregorian chant has a drowning effect on the local voices and styles. At the same time, Fanshawe succeeds in showing the multiple diversity of African musical styles, often defined by the diversity of the social contexts from which they emerge.

THE FRAGILITY OF TRADITIONS AND STYLES

Different African musical traditions, on the other hand, have moved and influenced each other both significantly and differently. A good example is the exchange of influence between the Zairean and East African genres. Certainly, similar exchanges could be cited with little effort for other regions of the continent. This dynamism allows historians of music as well as any careful casual observer like myself to identify a genealogy of various styles, to classify them in periods, and to identify their various hybridic components. Historians of music in Africa indicate a far-flung radius of exchange, suggesting that exchange has not taken place only within a limited area in Africa itself; rather it extends as far as Europe and the Americas and the Caribbean. From south to north, east to west, Africa is dotted with numerous varieties of musical styles from both within and without Africa. Some names—such as Cuban *marimba, taarabu*—or suffixes to names—such as "Jazz Band" or "Orchestre"—clearly suggest the influence of either specific foreign guitar styles or newly incorporated foreign instruments. All of these were effectively adapted, some slower than others, to the familiar local environments and tastes. Owino Misiani, a popular guitar musician and band leader from western Kenya, explains his own experience with this adaptive process as he introduced a faster variety of "Benga" in the mid-1970s (Paterson 1994). This latter variety clearly differs from the "Rhumba" style and beat he played in the 1960s and which, curiously, he identifies as "Swahili" (probably due to its urban origin and partner-holding dance style). His single "Akeyo nyar Kadem" (Pretty Akeyo the daughter of the Kadem clan) epitomizes his brief experience with "Rumba." His faster "Benga" also differs from the earlier and slower "Benga" of the 1960s, which was identified mostly with Gabriel Omolo, Ochieng' Nelly, and Ajwang' Ogara before it too was overlapped and briefly overshadowed by the "Sweko" style of Owiti Origo and the Kajulu Boys Band in the late 1960s and early 1970s.

Even a brief historical outline of the movements of musical traditions and styles in Africa throughout the twentieth century and earlier will show the resulting and complex hybrid formations which illustrate how several styles often co-exist and replace one another with such great rapidity. And the styles themselves, together with the rapidity with which new ones replace them, do in turn reflect corresponding rapid changes in the tastes of the major consumers of public culture as a symptom of the dynamics of social, political, and cultural transformations under which music is produced.

Thus, to argue against the reduction of the characteristics of African musical traditions to notation or formal structure is not the same as defending or claiming an oral base for its composition. What is claimed is that the representation of song in rhythmic and pitch notation is not what engages the crucial attention of most African composers. Nor do they explicitly regard it as a significant determining factor in their composition. Although African music is representable in these structural forms (and many composers now employ it), discussing African music as if its significance depended solely or significantly on structural forms amounts to ignoring or totally missing the other aspects that may matter most to African musicians, especially to traditional composers and performers. Most of them will know how melodies and pitch ranges fit their compositions. But they might not know or even care what notated music means in its graphic forms. And while many traditional composers read and write, these practices almost never reveal their usefulness in musical composition. And whether their compositions would be rendered better in whatever way(s) if they were first transcribed into and then learned and revised appropriately from notation is highly doubtful. Furthermore, as we shall see later, the multi-biographical nature of traditional compositions, the expressive uses of music, as well as the cultural language games and other uses that go along with musical composition and performance clearly speak against Goody's (1992) thesis of the critical limitations of orality.

In addition, judgments of the aesthetic form of a song imply much room for the recognized personal creativity of performers even as they are determined beforehand by the specific features of the languages they speak and sing in. Every speech community has its own specific indices that signify and transmit specific meanings as well as evoke specific reactions and responses in their listeners in the vast worlds of culture. The "goodness" of a performance may be judged in relation to one or more of these expectations in the uses and manipulations of speech forms as they are reorganized into songs. Certainly, these practical features and expectations of musical performance suggest that redundancy does not necessarily follow from a dominant use of orality.

BEYOND FORM AND STRUCTURE: MUSIC AS A SOCIAL TOOL

Despite their rapid change and transformation over the past several decades, African musical traditions continue to enjoy an important place as an integral part of the everyday production of knowledge, especially in the form of a genre of social, cultural, and political commentaries. Undeniably, the greater public forum provided by the transistor radio makes music the single most important means of cross-cultural and transnational interaction among Africans. Since the onset of colonialism, followed or accompanied by the availability of the radio, television, and other forms of electronic media, African traditions in music have influenced each other, and together they have been influenced by, as much as they too have influenced, Western musical traditions in both rhythm and dance. But despite the widespread adoption of European-type stringed and other instruments, African musicians remain both entertainers and "the eyes" or popular conscience in the articulation and interrogation of the changes taking place at the various levels of public life and the problems they pose to society.

For the above reasons, the social and political standing of African musicians remains fairly ambivalent—often used by politicians, but frequently also reviled and persecuted by them. In 1983, for example, Kenya's president Daniel Arap Moi ordered the arrest and subsequent incarceration of the musician Ochieng' Kabeselleh after accusing him of traveling to public performances in rural centers with "guns" hidden in acoustic drums "meant for use to topple his government," alleging that music was used as cover-up for political subversion. But in 1988, Moi himself, given another occasion and opportunity for a different political game, ordered the then Minister for Culture and Social Services in his government to invite the later popular Congolese musician Luambo Luanzo Makiadi (alias Franco) to give government-sponsored public performances in major cities in Kenya as part of the lavish self-glorifying celebrations of his first decade in office.

That music enjoys such high-profile political visibility in the modern state system, however uncertain the ways, is not surprising. At the traditional level, music and dance enjoyed a central role in the articulation of social events, both sacred and secular, happy and sad alike. Dancing, accompanied by either drumming or some other kind of instrumental performance, was frequently part of important ceremonies ranging from marriage celebrations to spirit possession rituals. These traditional roles for African music continue today, where it has been incorporated not only into regular school curricula in some countries, but also into the retinue of official performances at high-level political gatherings.

In these senses, African music enjoys a quasi-formal political recognition and occupies a central position in several national cultural policies. In several instances, it enjoys state sponsorship, at different levels, as an important medium of its popular expression, representation, and legitimization. At the formal scholastic level, traditional music and dance have been made part of school curricula in several African countries, with annual national performance competitions among schools and performing groups. In these courses, pupils of different school levels are trained to acquire and develop different performative singing and dancing skills. But even more importantly for the nationalist political discourse, the courses and performances are aimed at forging attitudes of national integration in the young citizens as they learn about and learn to appreciate and perform in the languages, tunes, and movements together with colleagues of ethnic communities other than their own. Apart from the instrumental, song, and dance styles from different local traditions, the spectacular musical competitions usually include (a cappella) choir groups which reflect the strong presence of missionary education and influence.

At the popular political level, music and dance have become an inseparable part of political visibility and dignitarism. In the guise of entertainment, it often serves as a form of social and political discourse, a performed statement of popular acceptance, enhancement, and legitimation of socially and politically coveted statuses and roles. In these senses, music and dance become signifiers of social and political hierarchizations.

But even within this modern-state arena, there is an almost perfect continuity with the traditional multifunctional importance of music. As biographers, musicians in the traditional settings were the indispensable sources of social knowledge. Through their biographical songs and lore, they became popular educators of the practical possibility of idealized social and moral virtues. Through the biographies of others and their own autobiographies, they sang to demonstrate the everyday embodiment of desirable qualities of social and moral integrity and leadership qualities. The *nyatiti* (an eight-stringed harp played by plucking the strings with all the fingers of both hands, usually played to a predominantly listening audience with an occasional two or three women getting up to *goyo otenga* (rhythmic shaking of the shoulders while making vigorous steps with the feet) in approval of the praises being attributed by the player/singer to someone they know and love. Sometimes the praises are recited by someone from the audience who stops the music to recite the praises of a loved friend or relative. The latter is called *pakruok* (virtue-boasting) and defines the peak of Luo performance. It is an incantation of one's own or another person's praises by members of the audience in turns and between songs. Often, incantations of one person's praises can lead to those of other people to whom they are related by kinship, friendship, or both. *Pakruok* is part of *chamo nyadhi* (display of self virtues), a poetic form of self-identification usually framed in idioms punctuated by proverbial irony. Parkin (1978) argues that in the early 1960s *pakruok* provided a unique forum for the Luo to define their political response to the rivalry between modernism and traditionalism in the context of Kenyan politics. This rivalry, embodied in the public and political rivalry between the modernist Tom Mboya and the traditionalist Oginga Odinga, their foremost leaders at the time, was their way of defining their identity, terms, and interests in the national politics of neo-independent Kenya.

The self-glorification in *pakruok* reaches its peak when the performer of *pakruok* gives prize money to the musician as a way of buying his time, and as a way of provoking rivalry and competition. Sometimes, depending on the amount of the prize, the *nyatiti* player would play on his harp and sing a short praise song for the one performing *pakruok* at the time; and this would trigger others in the audience to want to outdo the previous performer and each other depending on whose side one chooses to be; or, in consonance with the *nyadhi* that the show evokes, one could dismiss all others in preference for oneself. This is typical *chamo nyadhi* as part of the complex *pakruok* and involves display of linguistic artistry, virtue names,[2] and financial ability. Sometimes, a pretty wealthy individual would pay a high prize to the harpist to stop performing until someone else paid a higher prize set by her or him. This way, *nyatiti* scenes, and later other types of musical scenes as well, became prime means of fundraising for community programs.

But the complex and multibiographical approach to the politics of social performance in traditional cultural contexts is obviously and powerfully abused in the contemporary political instrumentalization of music. For example, while the *mouvement d'animation* that became ubiquitous in Mobutu's Zaire in the early 1970s, or the massed choirs in Kenya between 1978 and 1992, or even Kamuzu Banda's Women's Voices in Malawi in the 1980s, were all as biographical as in the traditional setting; they differed from the latter in their politically driven mass formations, which gave focus solely to their political settings and to the political biographee in disproportionate relation to the absence of the composer's self-reference and to the total disregard for the artistic aspect of the creation.

Other differences in today's political misuses and abuses of music include the performer's loss of control and self-focus. The singing and dancing youth of the *mouvement d'animation* in Mobutu's Zaire performed a deification of Mobutu by enacting the descent of his image onto the dancing field in front of a large audience through a screen of cloud-like smoke separating the up-above origins of the image from the world of cheering and adoring mortal humans below.

Ironically, these were also the times when there was strong popular suspicion of Mobutu's involvement in the murder of the popular Patrice Lumumba. But by using this self-deification under the thin veil of revolutionary anti-imperialist slogans of *authenticité*, Mobutu self-legitimated what was to be his deadly reign of terror over Zairean (now Congolese) citizens for decades. In Kenya, following Moi's initially shaky ascent to power after Jomo Kenyatta's death in 1978, massed choirs of schoolchildren, college students, and employees of public institutions were formed nationwide under government orders and invariably coerced into publicly reiterating, through song and dance, the eternity and invincibility of Moi's dictatorship as part of divine providence. Like his personal friend Mobutu's, Moi's power too was to be absolutely beyond human reach.

As in Mobutu's Zaire earlier, this mass musical culture in Kenya emerged at the time of widespread and popular doubt in Moi's leadership capabilities as well as suspicion of his complicity in several political deaths under Kenyatta. The number of these choir groups as well as the direct political evocations of their songs intensified greatly following the failed coup attempt on 2 August 1982. "Moi Tawala Kenya" ([President] Moi, rule Kenya), composed by the schoolteacher Thomas Wasonga of the then Mombasa Teachers' Mass Choir, and "Fimbo ya Nyayo" (Moi's [traditional] fighting club or stick), by Kenyatta University lecturer Arthur Kemoli, have served political ends of the latter type. Both Wasonga and Kemoli were personally and disproportionately rewarded with promotions and material gains by both the government and Moi himself for their "patriotic" songs. In local linguistic idioms, however, Kemoli's title could carry ironic and ambivalent moral connotations that could double as a severe but hidden critique of Moi's widely known and perceived excesses and abuses of political power.

At the same time as the above quasi-theatrical popular uses and abuses of music by politicians for self-legitimation take place, there have also been anti-establishment discourses through music. As argued by Erlmann (1996), performance and practice of power always meet or generate their opposition. As we saw above in reference to Parkin's (1978) analysis of *pakruok*, music, either in the content of its lyrics or by the political significance of the crowds it attracts and public forums it provides, can be part of a larger responsiveness to dominant political conditions. In some respects, the rise of *isicathamiya* can be seen as a response to the unhomeliness of the new (urban and peri-urban) centers of migrant labor settlements in apartheid South Africa. Erlmann's argument is that the rise and growth of *isicathamiya* can be read at least in part as a response to the social and cultural displacement occasioned by these rural–urban migrations, in which musical artists performed for members of their respective ethnic groups as a way of keeping their attention to cultural identity intact. In this sense, the groups, wherever and whenever they congregated for their respective musical performances, created a picture of multiple mobile power centers in defiance of the overarching power system of the apartheid regime. Erlmann's argument that this pluralism simultaneously and paradoxically served apartheid's divisive strategy and ideology of "one tribe, one culture, one homeland" helps to show the resistance quality of similar cultural performances in other colonial settings in the continent. The song by the Ashanti Boys, "Kam'ibetie k'ichiemo" (Wherever [and whenever] you sit enjoying modern urban material goods), whose first verse Cohen and Odhiambo use as an opening epigraph to their book *Burying S. M.* (1992), is—by its invocation of the primal role of home, represented as mother's location, in the construction of social, cultural, and political identity— partly anti-nationalist in the modern colonial sense, but also nationalist in the postmodern ethnic sense. While good in itself, the intensified fragmentation of specific ethnic consciousness checks the chances for the emergence of a united front against the dominant political conditions. Several African dictators have successfully used this colonial tactic of "divide and rule" to their personal gain against that of the nation.

LISTENING AS EXPERIENCE: THE EMOTIVE ROLE OF MUSIC

Erlmann's, Parkin's, and Cohen and Odhiambo's studies reaffirm Seeger's (1987) theme of the musical construction of space. According to Stokes (1994: 3), music plays a vital role in the definition of the several ways in which people constantly "relocate" themselves in society, whether this is the kind of society traditionally studied by anthropology, or the one defined by the industrial-capitalist order. The musical event, he says,

> from collective dances to the act of putting a cassette or CD into a machine, evokes and organizes collective memories and present experiences of place with an intensity, power and simplicity unmatched by any other activity. The "places" constructed through music involve notions of difference and social boundary [in complex ways]. They also organize hierarchies of a moral and political [as well as economic] order [as we saw in the case of *pakruok*].

Musical listening is thus a way of transcending the oppositions of time together with their respective social orders. It presences the past at the same time as it familiarizes the new present. And as we shall see later, Owino Misiani, Ogwang' k'Okoth, and Ochieng' Kabesseleh are good examples, in their respective ways, of presenting the consciousness of the local as past at the center of the national present. They do so by means of rhetorical inventions and definitions of the Luo as a separate but cohesive moral and political community that stands in contrast to the national political present in which it finds itself.

In these senses, music becomes a means for transcending one set of geographical, political, cultural, and social limitations and engaging with another by enabling the imagination and drawing of social and cultural connections. As we sit at this desk to write this paper while listening to the music of a distant community, for a few moments we imaginatively break the limitations of the physical distance of the location of this writing in order to reconnect with that distant community. We re-engage with and feel part of it as the words of the music reconstruct an imaginatively familiar world complete with its historical structures invoked by the meanings in the lyrics of the songs. Frequently, specific songs lead to conversations of specific reminiscences through which identities are then constructed or socially and historically significant decisions made. As the Dogon texts indicate (Griaule 1965), even the imaginary finds its order in anthropological structures. Thus the listening and writing, two absolutely different experiences, are placed side by side as simultaneous experiences in and of the same body. A good performance becomes thus, according to Stokes (1994: 5), "a patterned context within which other things happen." Stokes makes his own point with the support of C. A. Waterman's (1990) study of West African Jùjú music.

Most socially significant performers do not only entertain: they are also able, and frequently they aim, to raise the awareness level of their audience by arousing in them the imaginative and emotional experiences toward social re-engagement in the form of collective identity. They affect through performance (Kratz 1994). They provide the indices by which audiences generate their senses of specific group membership by participating in deciphering and internalizing the meanings generated by the performer. For performing these functions, *nyatiti* remains the music—*thum*—of the Luo. It remains the basic influence on Luo guitar-based musicians. In comparison to the guitar music, *nyatiti* has changed little in its own style and socio-cultural function and yet continues to be popular and at the center of what it means to be Luo in musical terms. Recently, some *nyatiti* performers have collaborated with guitarists in beautiful combined productions. The London-based *nyatiti* musician Ayub Ogada's compact disc collection *En mana Kuoyo* is an example of these attempts to modify *nyatiti* by aligning to it other instruments— sometimes *orutu* (a one-stringed instrument played with a bow like a violin) and drums, at other times the electric guitar as in the case of Ogwang' k'Okoth's collaboration with the guitar group Kawere Boys. Ogada uses both guitar and the electric keyboard to accompany his *nyatiti*.

But there is a problem. Because of his reliance on notation, several listeners of Ogada's music think it is far too "artificial," too "un-Luo," too "flat," or, as they say in Dholuo, too "straight." While these observations may only be indicative of the often familiar characteristics and critiques of a style in transition as it is contrasted to the familiar, Ogada's singing, his words, are often syllabically distorted or modified so as to fit the structural pre-formats of notes. Again, as observed by Erlmann, Ogada's and others' recent modifications of *nyatiti* and Dholuo might be better understood in the context of the process of its translocation and changing identity from being a strictly "rural" and mono-ethnic-based instrument and style to its assimilation as a new, "cosmopolitan," "urban," multi-ethnic, and multiculturally oriented instrument and style. These developments reveal something significant about how cultural change is coded and experienced: it is often multidirectional in its development, and it is certainly hybridic in its reflection of the operative and formative causal forces.

This symbiotic collaboration—between "traditional" and new instruments—might be a happy compromise for what started in the late 1950s and early 1960s as an open competition between *nyatiti* and other musical styles of the Luo, including the acoustic and later electric guitar styles. It might also be the best way to keep *nyatiti* within earshot of the younger generations who rarely or never attend and either lack or have different opinions about traditional musical performances. We know S. M. Otieno's children would call *nyatiti* and the social context of its performance "primitive." And there are several others like them who regard the world of their social, epistemological, economic, and political experiences as defined on the assumption of the discontinuous separation of so-called "modernity" from so-called "tradition."

The basis of the oppositional dichotomy is colonial in both its epistemological and economic expressions. They firmly believe the two to be not only precisely definable, but also to stand to each other in qualitative opposition: the former "good," the latter "bad" (because, they further believe, there is something necessarily good in and about what is designated "modern" and, vice versa, something necessarily bad in and about what is designated traditional), whatever the referents of these terms may be. Economically, they are, as a generation, the products of the consumer economy that reduced local economies to the production of "raw goods" and consumption of "technologically processed and advanced goods" from the West. Access to and consumption of Western goods becomes the sole index for measuring socio-economic and cultural "arrival" and sophistication. In local idioms, pen and notepad replace spear and hide-shield as the icons of the new warriorship and instruments of access to a new range and scale of consumer goods. Musically, for example, they identify the former with, say, Bach's or Mozart's or Beethoven's music, and at other times with Western popular music. It is to such a generation of people that the modification of *nyatiti* by artists like Ayub Ogada might relocate the "past" into contemporaneity more effectively and more significantly than the abstract persistence that there is some worth in the "traditional" for the "S. M. children's" generation to recognize and embrace.[3]

Music, both as a social performance and as a communicative medium, following Bourdieu (1977), Anderson (1983), de Certeau (1984), Kratz (1994), and Erlmann (1996), is more than a means for the reproduction of structural patterns of sound. According to Stokes (1994: 4), it is also "a practice in which meanings are generated, manipulated, even ironized, within certain limitations." Music generally, and *nyatiti* in particular, thus becomes a ritual process in itself, and as such constitutes, like what Kratz (1994: 39) observes of ceremonial processes related to initiation among the Okiek, a

> process of contextual re-creation [which] represents important cultural assumptions that are the background and context for the specific transformation. Re-created in ceremonial structure and performance, these

assumptions establish the frame of cultural understandings and social relations within which transformation takes place. At the same time, this process re-creates, continues, and often legitimates a sociopolitical organization based on those understandings.

Thus we come to understand the narratives of music only through interpretation, by paying careful attention to the contexts that shape their creation and to the worldviews that inform them. Sometimes the truths we see in them pull us away from our complacent security as interpreters outside the story and make us aware that our own place in the world plays a part in our interpretation and shapes the meanings we derive from them. That is why the ideas of S. M. Othieno's children, and of all those of their generation, on what they imagine as "tradition," are as legitimate as those to which they are opposed. And Ayub Ogada's transformation of *nyatiti* too is as valid as that of Ogwang' k'Okoth or of Kawere Boys Band.

Thum is a cultural practice, a ritual process, by which the Luo discursively and constantly invent themselves and their world, just as most other peoples do with their own musics too. As the Oxford-based Latvian philosopher Isaiah Berlin (1994: 2) put it in a critique of Charles Taylor, I too

> believe that it is human beings, their imagination, intellect and character that form the world in which they live, not, of course, in isolation but in communities . . . which cannot be causally predicted. It is not part of a determinist structure, it does not march inexorably towards some single predestined goal, as Christians, Hegelians, Marxists and other determinists and teleologists have, in varied and often conflicting ways, believed and still believe to the present day.

Yet, unlike Berlin, I do not believe that lack of essence and predictability in cultural representations of the world implies that such representations are therefore "unorganized." Rather, as I have tried to argue above, "organizing" is part of what people do and how they live their lives, including the political and ideological frameworks within and by which representations are formulated and sort of "objectified." And by "objectified" here I do not imply any sort of a metaphysical "real" at all, but rather the inexorable yet always also inexorably defeated tendency or "pull" toward objectivism. Again to argue like Berlin, I believe that ethnomusicology, like its similes, like ethnophilosophy for example, despite its apparently pluralistic and liberational self-image, is guilty of essentialism, however subtle it may be.

At the same time, I also believe, rather incompatibly with my opposition to ethnic studies as outlined above, in some sort of ethno-something as an indication of the non-cosmic and clearly open-ended socially responsive discursive process. The difference is that my version of the hyphenated *ethno-* applies to all epistemic positions. Its basis is similar to Wiredu's (1980) claim that "truth is opinion," while its aspiration is to capture what Mudimbe (1988) refers to as an independent and self-justifying epistemic order. And because it expresses itself in a universal order, this gnosis excludes relativism. But while I wish not to go farther into this, it is enough to say here that it is this sense of neo-ethnophilosophy that I aim at when I divide the history of African philosophy, for example, into three phases. In this tripartite interpretive organization, I reject the idea of ethnic studies, such as ethnophilosophy and its simile ethnomusicology, as part of colonial discourse. In their place I suggest a third tier interpretive format, also ethno-derived, but which I call, for lack of a better term, neo-ethnophilosophy and, by extension, neo-ethnomusicology. And the difference between them and their precedents is that in my new sense of them they reinstate the subject as the proprietor of her own discourse cast in the universal form. And because of the subject's control of her own discourse, the preposed "ethno-" will no longer be warranted as a prefix in the designation of her discourse. I am aware that this stage has been reached in philosophy, but I am not aware the same has happened with the study of musical traditions of Africa or most other non-Western genres for that matter.

The Moral Ambiguity of the "Modern": Music and the Politics of Spaces

Despite the consumer economy that helps to define the appropriation of new musical styles as a sign of new socio-cultural mobility, the new popular culture is still regarded with suspicion at the moral level. The history and development of musical styles in major African cities in the post–World War II period provides an excellent analogy for understanding the dynamics of both political and cultural discourse, change, and resistance in Africa. Erlmann (1991, 1996) has done a good job of depicting this picture, even if only for a section of South Africa.

The buoyant postwar economy made it possible for an increasing number of Africans to find employment in the growing industries, farms, service institutions, and bureaucratic system and to have access to the increasingly available Western musical paraphernalia, much of it initially brought back by war returnees but soon widely available through the importation of cheaper versions. The migratory nature of the labor force soon transported the new musical values and styles across the lands to the rural areas. As a result, the new music, its taste and ownership, came to be associated with the emergent urban elitism. This attitude has been made even stronger with the consumerist influence of electronic equipment. Possession of the latest models of electronic equipment firmly remains an index of social status.

But due to socio-geographical concentration, the new musical tastes and styles also came to be associated with the loose lures of urbanism. Even as the new guitar styles became popularly embraced, the conservative voice of tradition continued to regard them with moral contempt and suspicion. Widely associated with the moral permissiveness or decadence of the cities, the "modern" was in some ways seen as "corrupt" and "immoral" at the same time as it was admired as a "good" and "desirable" sign of the new elitism.

The fears associated with the negative socio-cultural impact of the new music and dance were particularly intense in the rural areas where the new music became a regular vacation-time visitor as a result of the coming of the portable phonograph and its later variations. Often, the intensity of these fears greatly depended on the social place and space from and in which such music was played to an audience. With the growing availability of local recordings, owners of musical equipment could play different types of music separately to their appropriate separate audiences. While this kept different age categories of audiences apart as several traditions require, it also made it hard for those in older ranks to apply strict cultural codes. Hence the persistence of the suspicion toward modern music. The Luo expression *jathum-a-thuma* (a mere musician) is a recent expression which does not apply to *nyatiti* performers but sums up the pervasive disdain with which modern music and its performers came to be regarded as icons of social and moral impropriety. It is then up to every performer to balance their social standing by using music in another way that will earn him or her some positive social standing within their communities. As we shall see a little later, the good ones turned to expressive music.

Due to the above conditions of performance, the modern guitar musician lives and performs under conditions that make the economics of musical production complex, uncertain, precarious, and often also politically and culturally polarized. First he has to be creative and able to respond to the tastes and styles of his time in order to impact his audience.

Second, because the marketing of his music can be done only through the sole, government-controlled, radio channel, these audiences remain firmly under the control of the disk jockeys at the broadcasting stations. Third, the artist also knows that his own social identity and success are not determined solely by how he participates in the production of the tunes and dance styles of his time. Often, African musicians are acutely aware of the political fragmentation of the public sphere in and to which they perform, and they cannot remain neutral. They know that in order to promote their own images and their music, they have to be good enough to impact the powerful d.j.'s at the broadcasting stations, and through them also audiences beyond their respective ethnic communities. But this carries its own risks for many musicians who constitute only one of the several interest groups competing for the attention of the d.j. at the station.

Apart from desiring to create and control his own social world of following among listeners in competition with his rivals at the station, the d.j. also competes for the control of and favors from the economic world of record producers, for the patronage and protection of the political worlds of government cultural policies and politicians' images, for the social world of the artists, and for that of the *japango*, the urban worker who is the prime target consumer and conduit to most others in rural settings to whom he or she is the domestic collector and host-entertainer. These urban and rural relatives and friends in the far-flung peripheries of the economy depend on him or her as derived consumers. All the people in these categories of society depend on the d.j.'s choices, biases, and whims as the meeting point and mediator between the private and the public, the ethnic and the national, the musical and the political.

Given this scenario, traditional performers literally do not record for economic gain, the reason being that due to the extremely ethno-specific nature of the style and language of their music, it is usually considered to be culturally too narrow for a wider national audience and market. Their recordings are enabled frequently through the sponsorship of their clients, who calculate social and/or political promotion through the songs composed in their praises, or through the sponsorship of a true philanthropist and lover of culture. Oluoch k'Anindo, a young but wealthy entrepreneur and Alego émigré to South Nyanza, rode to a national political platform on his relations to musicians from Luo Nyanza. He established a recording studio in Nairobi that produced most of the music by Luo artists in the 1970s and 1980s in Kenya. As payback, they sang his praises and the virtues of his wealth in almost every single recording. His social fame soared, and the returns were abundant for him and his lifestyle. Among other things, he was elected to parliament, was made a junior cabinet minister, and became a big polygynist as a result of adulation from teen-age girls. Onyango Ayoki, who also became a parliamentary representative for his Kisumu Rural constituency in 1974, was an even earlier political and social beneficiary of this kind of cultural philanthropy toward Owiti Origo and the Kajulu Boys band.

One way for artists to cross ethnic boundaries established along linguistic and musical traditions is to adopt the fashionable styles from Congo. But with original Congolese music available through the thriving record industry of East Africa, and enough resident Congolese groups on hand to provide original Congolese music, audiences tend to shun their own local imitations and adaptations. Only a few star performers like Ochieng' Kabeselleh have adapted Congolese style into their own ethnic languages and basic styles successfully enough to garner considerable acceptance and following. Others, like the late George Ramogi, had an overwhelming following when they performed only in the Luo vernacular and in the widely known *benga* style but lost nearly all their following when they tried to shift toward adaptation of the Congolese style. The tastes of the consumers are, as these data show, greatly unpredictable as well and appear to fluctuate with political and cultural sways of given times. Owino Misiani, perhaps cleverly, has managed to retain his huge following among his Luo people by sticking both to the local *benga* style and to the socio-political themes his audiences crave. Gabriel Omollo, one of the most talented Luo musicians, loved for his award-winning humorous and social text records like "Lunch Time," "Maro oketho Ugunja" (Mother in-law's tragedy at Ugunja), "Mr. Agoya" (Wife beater), "Jopango" (Townsmen), and "Jaluo asili" (Authentic Luo), has declined to some extent in recent years due to lack of philanthropic gifts.

A Phenomenology of a Post-Colonial Practice: Presencing the Past and Remembering the Present through Music

Obviously, music is not only about structural form, about "rhythms" and notes. Admittedly, while these factors provide interesting ways of analytically understanding the sonic form in music, sometimes it is not the dominant component in the imagination and composition of the vocal and/or instrumental constituents of music. Some music is not recognized by the precision with which its characteristic notes are struck. The complexities of music reveal and reproduce the complexities of society itself. I believe that due to these complexities, any observer of different musical traditions, even a casual one like myself, should find it easy to refute what has been called "the heresy of the separate experience" in music—which I have recently learned is, according to Aaron Ridley's (1995) discussion of Malcolm Budd (1985), "the heresy of representing 'a musical work as being related in a certain way to an experience which can be fully [and, supposedly, objectively] characterized [and valued] without reference to the nature of the work itself'" (my brackets). Ridley criticizes Peter Kivy (1989) for identifying the arousal affects of musical experience with private, idiosyncratic associations. The truth is, however, that there may be difficulties in regard to linking subjective psychological premises or experiences with objective ones à la Descartes, if that is what Kivy is guilty of. In that case, Ridley's critique, which, at least when levelled against Descartes, states that introspective conditions, or what could also be called subjective psychological states or experiences, are not absolutely reliable conditions for making objective propositions, is correct. In other words, one cannot assert a supposedly objective proposition about the outside world (such as music) based solely on subjective conditions. But that in itself does not establish that those experiences do not occur, nor does it establish the impossibility of such subjective arousals occurring to most if not all individuals under similar circumstances. Ridley's critique is based on the rejection of using introspective psychological conditions as criteria for claiming objective truths as Descartes did in *The Principles of Philosophy* and in the third *Meditation*. Rejecting introspective conditions as insufficient for grounding any claim to objective experience, Ridley challenges Kivy to match his claim of the arousal effects of music with a logically acceptable argument that demonstrates it. But this, like Descartes's own method, also amounts to reducing the criteria for the realism of the outside world and for the possibility of our experience of it to the logical patterns of thought. But to the extent that logical patterns are themselves things of the mind, there is a degree to which their implied subjectivism narrows down any read difference between Ridley and Kivy. Second, Ridley's critique of Kivy commits a categorical mistake, as it appears to treat "musical experience" at the same level as or to be equal to "perceptual experience."

This is simply not so at all. For while we assume some invariability in the manner in which an object presents itself to all subjects, any subject under similar conditions in perceptual "experience"—such as a hotplate kept at a specific temperature will feel to anyone who touches it under normal body temperature—in contrast to that invariability, music selects its listeners; it is intentionally crafted to be received or "experienced" in specific different ways by different audiences. Such an intention might not succeed with each individual member of the primary target audience, but it is not outside the range of their appropriation if they have the other "materials"—knowledge, technique, and so on—used to craft the music. In contrast to what occurs when we experience the sensation of burning when we place our unprotected hand on a hotplate, the "experience" of music requires that we have knowledge of at least some vital components that constitute it independently of their appearance in the music. The effects that music arouses in listeners are simply more varied and more complex than either Kivy or Ridley appears to recognize. For example, there is no limit to either the number or the nature of the psychological experiences that listening to specific music, say, the kiGanda evangelistic songs "Amazukira" and "Tukutendereza," by the Eschatos Brides of Kampala, can arouse. To some, the experiences may involve, as Kivy says, remembrances of some specific past, while in others the experiences could involve the evocation of an emotional experience of whatever other kind, such as dread, anxiety, fear, or even joy. The determination will depend on the event in the listener's memory with which they associate the music at any given listening experience. The act of listening becomes an independent experience to which single or multiple memories contribute. The point is that the act of listening to music is not always just an analytical and logical practice. It depends on, but is not co-terminous with, the act of hearing. It may be that too, depending on who is listening to what kind of music. But it also may, as people like Kivy claim it does, trigger a chain of associations with other circumstantial experiences related, as we just said, in either the past or present, with the subject's experience of that particular music, either in its entirety or only as a result of the meanings of its different specific parts or aspects. Remember, however, that if music has the capacity to arouse such effects in listeners, then it is also capable of failing to do so at all. I would be curious to know what kind of psychological experience(s), other than hearing sounds of a specific type in a specific order and combinations generally perceptible as musical, listening to a Mozart Adagio, or his Concerto in d minor, or Weber's clarinet concertos would arouse in my mother, and how they—her aroused psychological experiences, if any—would compare to those of a European or American listener to the same. Or should we try it the other way, play Oduor Nyagweno's "Ibrahim Ogutu" to an ordinary European or American

audience? But once heard, whatever their musical appeal or meaning-
fulness may be to the listener, their being experienced at subsequent
times can arouse memories associating them to other events in previous
experiences. They do not have to acquire additional meanings beyond
or other than these associations.

In the final analysis, however, Ridley himself agrees that expressive
music has arousal effects. But he argues that this characteristic of music is
to be found in the "melismatic" qualities of music. He defines these as
"timbre, dynamics, movement, phrase shape, harmony, and rhythm"
(1995: 49), and he certainly thinks that these are more "objective" features than Kivy's "private, idiosyncratic associations." The question,
however, is: What is objective about the "things" that these terms describe? And how objective is objectivity? Is there a "real" movement, for
example, objectively associable with a certain musical tune that would inform any listener, whoever and from wherever, to assert when they hear
it, "I am now listening to (or this tune now playing is) a *marche funèbre*,"
and that would elicit a specific form of reaction from them?

A more relaxed understanding of the ambiguities and selectivity of
audience responses to certain tunes and styles, or of their expectations
of certain performers, remains as wanting as ever. Furthermore, the criteria of selection are not constant; they shift as much as the very identities and occasions we purport them to represent do. Yet, simultaneously,
as Stokes (1994: 5) has argued,

> Music is socially meaningful . . . largely because it provides means by which
> people recognize identities and places, and the boundaries which separate
> them. . . . Musical performance, as well as the acts of listening, dancing,
> arguing, discussing, thinking and writing about music, provide the means
> by which ethnicities and identities are constructed and mobilized.

Musical language such as in the cases transcribed below, like most
forms of narrative language, is not merely descriptive. It does not just
try to tell people how things are. It tries to move people. There are three
analytically distinct but independent functions essential for the interpretation of meaning even in musical language. First, the ideational function expresses the referential meaning of what is said—that is, "content
in terms of the speaker's experience and that of the speech community"
(Burke 1950: 37). Second, the interpersonal function concerns the role
relationships between speakers, which allow for the expression of social
and personal relations through talk. This is what occurs in *pakruok*, in
the *gano* (narrations) by *nyatiti* performers, and in the biographical songs
framed in the personal second person. Third, the textual function refers

to structure, how parts of a text are connected syntactically and semantically. Meaning is conveyed at all three levels, although the ideational
functional—that is, informational content about people, situations, and
ideas that singers, as speakers and public intellectuals, mean their words
to convey—tends to dominate communication. Thus the meaning of
what someone says is not simply its ideational content; how something
is said (textual function) in the context of the shifting roles of singer/
speaker and listener (interpersonal function) is critical too. We shall see
how three songs operate and convey meaning at the three levels.

Daniel Owino Misiani and the Shirati Band:
Political Genealogies and the Modern State (recorded late 1979)

> I Owino the gentleman
> In my usual notoriety
> The descendant of the Owiti clan
> Of the ancestry of my fathers
> And of the Wagasi and Aloo clans
> Of the ancestry of my mothers
> Trace the historiography of my people
>
> To remind of the heroes and warriors
> For their leadership brought us forth
> For heroism is a virtue
> Heroes to be remembered even in good times
> Presently, a buffalo is grazing upstream
>
> Gor the son of Ogada son of Ogalo
> Was our spiritual leader and diviner
> With his medicines we conquered many lands
> And subdued many peoples
> Even as he becomes a legend
> We owe our knowledge and customs to him
>
> Obada son of Nyangile from the Ugenya clan
> Was a well-known hero and warrior
> He subdued many enemies
> Leaving nothing in his trails
> Oh it is virtuous to be hero
> It is virtuous to fight for your people
>
> Okore son of Ogonda of the Kisumu clan
> Was a great hero
> His expeditions are well known
> To all our people

And you know well too
Ogola son of Oyieke of ka Rateng' sub-clan of Kisumu
He too fought many battles

Ng'ong'a son of Odima
The great son of the Alego people
Man of justice and power
Was praised by the colonial whites

Magere the legendary son of Kano people
Was the undefeatable hero of all times
He wiped out the Kipsigis

Do not all the Luo remember
Omolo Mumbo's religious movement
How he saved the culture of our prole
By transforming Christianity into Luo divination

Ogot the son of Tawo of the Alego people
Was our warrior well into colonial times

Lala son of Obada of the Ugenya clan
Odera son of Akang'o of Gem
Major Owuor Ali
Are our warriors too
Crowned by the colonial whites
And recorded by colonial history.

Misiani almost redoes an old and famous text on Luo legends, *Thuond Luo* (Luo heroes). But he does so with significant and marked difference. He re-oralizes an originally oral text after it was committed to writing in the 1950s. Scripted for use in primary schools during colonial times, the legendary narratives constituted one of several vernacular texts adopted for teaching reading to children who attended school in their own speech community areas. Comparable vernacular texts were used for the same end in other speech communities in the colony, while kiSwahili texts were used in the multi-ethnic urban areas.

Misiani's reworking of this text reverses its use from colonial to post-colonial. Not only does he retell it as a lesson in the history and geography of the Luo people; he chooses to do so in musical form as the only way to reach the current school-going generation of Luo youth that is no longer taught nor cares to learn in the vernacular, but listens to his popular and influential music. He gives it a special idiom to signify its special importance in the context of Kenyan national politics. By listing heroes from all the major Luo clans, Misiani underlines the political invention of the Luo as a unified and historically homogeneous community whose social and geographical territory is due to the militant heroes of the past. In the second part of the song—which I have omitted here—Misiani adds to that list the more recent and current communal heroes. The latter, mainly the politicians who struggled for the independence of Kenya from the British in unison with others from other communities, are praised for their central roles in the creation of post-colonial Kenya. In light of the national politics which is hidden here as a subtext, Misiani cleverly intends to draw the attention of his audiences to the ironic contrast between the community's pivotal roles—through its leading representatives—in the struggle for independence on the one hand, and its marginalization from the benefits of post-colonial development on the other. He draws the social map of what Parkin (1978) identifies as the underlying political text in the practice of *pakruok* in Kaloleni (Nairobi). To get this powerful political statement, a listener must master Misiani's elegant and proverbial use of the Luo language as well as be familiar with Misiani's unique and easily recognizable textual tradition. This is indicated in a variety of ways in the first verse. By referring to himself as "the notorious one" *(Magunga)*, and by indicating that he is about to start on his usual themes *(ochako weche mage)*, he underlines a personal and established style. The proverbial phrase *Jowi oluwo aora* (There is a buffalo upstream) warns of as well as states the hidden social text and calls for keen listening to the oral text, thus giving emphasis to the informational function of the music. But the phrase is also a war cry; in the traditional rendering, it would be both an announcement that the community had been exposed to the threat of an invasion, and a call to the warriors of the community to take up arms in defense of the community. It exhorts a communal conscience and self-awareness which, in a curiously Hegelian sense, is elicited by means of identifying oppositions between self as a collective, and Other. The song, then, might also be seen as a critique of the current communal leadership for not doing enough, and so it is also a call on the leaders to take action with courage as they remember the achievements of the departed heroes—"Oh it is virtuous to be hero." The song is an evocation and provocation to political action.

Misiani's notoriety was built and defined through a sustained sense of courage to say things many Kenyans never dared say in other public ways in the days of Charles Mugane Njonjo's reign as Attorney General under

Kenyatta. Yet it was widely believed that Njonjo steered the anti-Luo crusade of Kenyatta's regime; and the strategies of dealing with the situation pitted the nationalist Mboya faction against the anti-establishment one led by Oginga Odinga. Misiani's cultural definition of a political response has always been swift, eloquent, and biting in its metaphorical representations. For example, soon after Njonjo resigned as Attorney General to become Minister for Constitutional Affairs in 1980, Owino composed and produced a single piece, "Kwach Rakido" (The spotted leopard), a masterpiece of rhetoric and oral performance in which he warned of and predicted Njonjo's canny and deadly ambitions.

Reference to Njonjo as "a spotted leopard" had a double habitual sense. Not only is Njonjo known to the public for and by his habitual pin-striped garb, he was, in his political heyday, also known for his political habit of punishing anyone who tried to come between him and his insatiable ambitions. During the proceedings of the judicial commission of inquiry into allegations of Njonjo's sabotage of Moi's presidency in 1983, several people, including prominent politicians, gave evidence about Njonjo's politically canny, vengeful, and destabilizing acts. Using the metaphor of the calculating and unrelenting habits of a leopard preying on expectant herds, Misiani's representation of Njonjo as a political leopard warned of his ability to sabotage the expectant future of the state unless he was immediately stopped. Indeed, two years after Misiani's rather predictive song (in 1983), President Moi saw the need to stop Njonjo, accusing him of possible treasonable and other types of politically corruptive acts.

Misiani enjoys the convenience of coming from the Luo of the northern Mara district in Tanzania, to which he runs after releasing politically sensitive musical pieces. The beauty of Misiani's music is attributable particularly to his brilliance in the use of proverbs and other types of cultural idioms to define and frame responses to the political experiences of the day.

Ogwang' k'Okoth (nyatiti player): Post-S. M. as
Post-modernity in Luo Cultural Politics (recorded June 1987)

Spoken introduction:

> *I wish to pay homage*
> *To Kager Umira Clan*
> *Which fought for S. M. Othieno*
> *Until we buried him*
> *May twenty three [1987]*

Oh how I keep wondering
Oh the slender one I wonder
I wonder about the Umira people
Oh how I keep wondering
I wonder about the Umira people
They begot Ywaya
The son of Angoro
The son of Onyango
And they begot Orunga
The son of Onyango
Who were the founders
Of Kager Umira [Welfare] Organization

Oh how I keep wondering
Ogwang' Lelo I keep wondering
I wonder about the Umira people
They begot Ywaya
The son of Angoro
The son of Onyango
And they begot Orunga
The son of Onyango
Who were the founders
Of Kager Umira Organization

And then Umira begot another son
They named him Mr. Othieno
And this son read his way to Europe
And there he read law
So they called him Attorney
Attorney for the elite of society

And then Othieno returned to Kenya
And he started his own business

But Othieno had misfortune
When he returned to Kenya
For he met a girl
A girl from Nairobi
And he married and lived with her

Othieno lived with the girl many years
They begot several offspring
Then Othieno dies
Othieno goes with the wind

The Kager Umira people assert
Othieno is the son of Umira
He must return to Umira
To be buried in Umira

Oh Othieno must return to Umira
To be buried in Umira

But Othieno's wife retorts
Othieno is a Kenyan
He can be buried in Kenya

But the Umira people stand firm
Othieno is from Umira
Othieno was never from Kenya
Othieno is from Kager Umira
Cannot be buried in Nairobi
Othieno must return to Umira
He must return to Nyalgunga
Then Othieno's wife responds
Othieno is Kenyan
She can bury him in Kenya
She can bury him in Ngong'
She can even bury him in Langata

So Othieno's wife goes to court
She got herself an Attorney
So the courts discussed Othieno's body
They discussed Othieno in his sleep
They discussed Othieno after death took him
They discussed Othieno in his sleep

In Anger
The Umira people got themselves an Attorney
His name was Kwach [the Leopard]
Kwach from Ugenya
The son of KaNyamuot clan

So they fought over Othieno's body
They fought over Othieno in his sleep
They fought over Othieno for six months

For six months
They discussed Othieno in his sleep
Oh how I keep wondering
Oh how I keep wondering
Oh I wonder about the Umira people
Who begot Othieno
This Othieno who was discussed
By the courts
For six months in his sleep
Oh the son of Kager Umira
Oh Siranga
Oh Siranga and Ougo
The sons of Umira

They got themselves an Attorney
To defend Othieno in his sleep
To return Othieno to Umira
So they defeated Othieno's wife
The girl from Nairobi
They defeated her
The girl from Nairobi

So Othieno son of Ugenya
Was returned to Umira
Was buried in Siaya
Was buried in Nyalgunga
We buried Othieno on May twenty three
We buried Othieno
The son of Umira
In Umira
We buried Othieno in Nyalgunga

Oh how I keep wondering
I wonder about the people of Umira
They begot Othieno
Othieno the great hero
Who was discussed for six months
Who was discussed in his sleep
Who was discussed for six months

Spoken conclusion:

> *This has been*
> *An homage to S. M. Othieno*
> *The son of Umira*
> *Whom we buried*
> *May twenty three*
> *Escorted by Luo dignitaries*

Clear and plain, but also dramatic words about "things ancestral," about cities and their new economies, about living and dying, about "home," and about the threats imposed on it by migrations and distances into the unhomeliness and amorphousness of the unstructured space *(thim)*. Ogwang' contrasts the imaginations of yesterday's "home" with the realities of today's modernity by defining the latter as the locus of the new hunting space, new struggles and encounters, and the new genre of social status that come with it. While talking cognizantly of the reality—almost inevitability—of change, Ogwang' at the same time poses the epistemological question regarding the conceptual cohabitability between the imaginations of yesterday and today's representations. And his response to the question seems appropriate: the dialectic of the relations is determined by political discourse and process rather than by conceptual incongruence. As a popular cultural performer, his response to the other questions he raises—for example the question of interethnic marriages and their role in the socio-cultural creation of nationalism and national identities—find strongly uncritical and culturally biased but genuine positionings. But what else would one expect, and why?

Despite the eight years between them, in this song, Ogwang' appears strikingly to take up and continue the theme of setting ethnic unity and separateness against national integration that was so characteristic of Misiani's song above. In some senses, Ogwang' makes a more poignant point about this opposition by referring to Kenya and Nairobi as "foreign" spaces—wilderness—to which Othieno, as a Luo, does not belong—and so should not (and cannot) be buried in. The subtext is in the meaning of burial and its relation to the cultural definitions of "home" and belonging. The Luo define an interment as "burial" only if it is done at one's appropriately—that is, strictly in accordance with culturally defined procedures—constituted "home," *dala,* either his own or that of his father. The Luo have, at least from the evidence of recent history, always buried their dead, and adults, especially those considered heroes in the eyes of the community, must particularly be buried at "home." Their bodies may fail to return "home" only in special circumstances, such as when the community or clan is routed by the enemy in battle, or if a person's body is for other reasons unrecoverable for appropriate burial. Once more, we see the same theme from Misiani, of culturally representing the processes of "nationalization" as acts of warfare in which groups participate under the leadership of their respective warrior heroes.

Ogwang' situates Othieno among Misiani's heroes and defines his communal role as that of representing the Luo image—rather than their communal interests—within the modern national politics of Kenya. Communal visibility at the contested national level was embodied in the personae and roles of individuals placed in high positions of public institutions. Yet the locus for the display of such personae and roles remained a foreign space, and its politics a sort of battle fought by the heroes of various ethnic communities, for their own personal gains at the material and intellectual levels, but on behalf of their communities for visibility and perceived control. This warfare is both against the new "state" and against competitors from other communities for the exploits and control of the "state." By incorporating Othieno into the ranks of Misiani's category of heroes, Ogwang' draws his audiences' attention not to the contradiction between past and present, rural and urban, village and city, home and wilderness, but to their socio-geographical contiguity and competition for control of public and private lives. They are separate but they coexist.

According to Fabian (1996: 198), in popular artistic representations of historical experiences, " 'Things ancestral' point to a rural past that is distinct from life in the cities but nonetheless present or coexistent, much as the dead are experienced as coexistent with the living. The village and the bush, hunting and fishing, political structures and ritual life are not just remembered nostalgically; they are invoked as the foundations on which present life and consciousness grow, or should grow." In light of this wisdom, interring Othieno's body in "Kenya" would not only equal discard the body of a communal hero in the wilderness, but it would also signify the community's defeat since, in this context, the wilderness is also a battlefield, made even more real by the fact that Othieno's body was being claimed by a widow from that wilderness—"the girl from Nairobi." Indeed, the case over S. M. Othieno's body provided the most open revelation of the ethnically polarized nature of Kenyan national politics since the assassination in 1969 of Tom Mboya, one of the frontline Luo leaders and a pivotal campaigner for Kenya's independence from Britain.

Mboya was assassinated at a time when he was considered, both locally and internationally, astute and politically mature enough to challenge Kenyatta for the leadership of Kenya (Goldsworthy 1982). The
Luo saw Mboya's assassination as a Kikuyu plot to shut them out of the
center of Kenya's political leadership, the same year that their other
erstwhile leader, Oginga Odinga, had his opposition party banned and
himself thrown into detention by Kenyatta. Since then the Luo have
consistently considered themselves "outsiders" to the center of Kenyan
politics and have taken every opportunity to rally together in opposition
to what may appear as a threat to them as a group. Or: some of those
cases, such as Othieno's death and subsequent court wrangle over his
body, have provided an opportunity for the Luo to assert and demonstrate their political unity and opposition to the Kenya nationalist ideology which they helped build in the first place but from which they became alienated soon after independence.

Ogwang"s song must be understood, at least partly, in this context of
Kenyan politics and how the Luo, doing what they are now notorious
for, perceived the claims of Othieno's widow within it by invoking the
socio-political knowledge from their own past. In the historical process
of their social and political constitution, the Luo intermarried with
and absorbed significant portions of the communities from whom they
wrestled territory. Cross-ethnic marriages were always a major means of
securing peace with new neighbors after long wars. And once a "foreign" woman was married into the community, she was expected to bond,
remain within, and accept the ways of her new place. This was particularly important in those cases where a "foreign" woman's marriage into
the Luo community was perceived as an explicitly peacemaking event. If
such a woman were later to declare a return to her community of birth,
especially following the death of her husband, her action was always perceived as a breach of the peace and a declaration of renewed interethnic suspicion or even enmity. She was a betrayer, and a battle with her
people was to be expected, because her marriage now came to be regarded as a masked intelligence-gathering scheme. And the community's heroes were sounded to prepare for a possible battle or war. In
the song, Ogwang' depicts Kwach—the attorney for the Kager Umira
clan—as the battlefield general who leads other heroes from Kager
Umira in this battle over Othieno's body. Wambūi, Othieno's widow
from the Agīkūyū, was situated squarely in the role of "a foreign
woman" who had instigated a battle through her act of betrayal. Her
claim to want to bury Othieno in Gikuyuland exposed the fragility of

her absorption and was perceived as a declaration of war on the Luo community, indeed a war the Luo would not want to lose hands down.

Significant, of course, are the details (see for example Ocholla-Ayayo 1989), which a public cultural performer like Ogwang' may either not have had the time and space to articulate or have chosen to omit in order to craft the cultural text he both wished his audience to have and knew they would like to hear. The latter may have been affected further by a careful choice of what becomes singable to the performer. As a public cultural performer, he plays mostly to uncritical audiences who are also the direct consumers of ideas and sentiments of ethnocultural integrity. (But even people who are severely critical by profession or just by good and habitual inclination rarely apply those skills to the entertainment-oriented listening to music as such.) Both his art and his ideational content are part of this cultural reality or what Sartre would have called "situation." By itself the performance is not a critical or intellectual activity. It is a cultural performance, laden, as Cohen and Odhiambo (1992: 116) point out, with hints of "semiotics of social status, of the social implications of mode of death, of the redistribution of the social relations of a deceased person, of linkages to other rites and the social units that perform them, of cosmological transitions of the deceased into an ancestor. These elements [of local knowledge] expose and map out a social, cultural, and psychological terrain, one that is neither simple, nor traditional, nor confined to the Luo conceived apart from other Kenyans." Against Bourdieu somewhat, local everyday discourse, of which music is part, is theoretically important without being importantly theoretical. The cultural performer's public text is just one—cultural and partisan—way of "how the story should be told" (ibid. 100–19). It differs significantly from a specialist's "way." And being oral, it stands sadly and beautifully incomplete, awaiting an indefinite number of styles and directions of future modifications.

At the same time, the role and effect of the artist in whipping up a certain kind of popular sentiment in his audience cannot be underestimated. In fact, they aim at it. At least in Africa, these sentiments often either lend themselves to manipulations by, or directly influence, specific political decisions and actions and reactions. The S. M. Othieno case was not exempt from this. In the light of the history of Luo–Gikuyu political rivalry, and of their respective importance as significant factors in national politics, the ethnic sentiments which surrounded the case unavoidably drew and involved presidential politics. "Performers," says Erlmann (1996: xix), "like diviners and healers, by virtue of their ability to direct the flow of power through special channels of words, music, and bodily movement, are privileged in handling power. This is why performance, unlike ethnographic description, potentially transforms individuals into persons in control of their own destiny." For instance, in 1969, following Mboya's assassination, George Ramogi, a talented mourner-musician, released the single "Why Tom?" which was quickly banned by Kenyatta's government. Sung in a sad mourning tone of a mixture of kiSwahili and dhoLuo with an emotionally charged and politically powerful spoken part, the song frequently pushed listeners over the edge into violent anti-government protests. Playing off Mboya's career in the labor movements in Kenya, Ramogi openly called for protest marches by workers in protest of their leader's killing. Earlier the same year, Ramogi had released another successful single to mourn Argwings K'Odhek, another independence-struggle Luo politician, leader, and lawyer, also widely perceived among the Luo as a victim of the Kenyatta government's moves against the community. In other words, music presents itself here as a mode—of a group representing itself as oppressed and subordinated—of expressing a countervailing power structure to that of another, rival group perceived in a hegemonic role (Erlmann 1996: xxii, Scott 1990). Performance becomes a hidden transcript of resistance, a variant realm of power and interests in opposition to the hegemonic force.

What is conspicuously missing in this essay is the view of the cultural present as it affects images of self-identity from the perspectives of those used as the beacons of collective identity by the artists. What do the heroes like S. M. Othieno, Mboya, Richard Kwach, and others in positions like theirs think themselves to be culturally? Although the silence of the dead cannot be awakened, that of the living becomes a meaningful act, almost a statement of public approval of the artist's inventions.

As we said earlier, performative art not only entertains. Nor is it only informational. It also creates action-oriented consciousness in its audience. In the aftermath of the "S. M." case, for instance, public performance and other genres of public discourse among the Luo called on the largely urbanized—and, by that measure, presupposedly also Westernized—Luo elite to carry out a re-examination of identity. While revealing interesting assumptions in certain sections of the Kenyan society that abandonment of one's own ethnic customary traditions equates with "doing well" or "being progressive," the "S. M." case became in the eyes of many a litmus test of the depth and extent of modernization among the Luo. Even in Western media coverage, the case was frequently represented as a confrontation between "modern laws of civil society" on the one hand and "primitive customs" on the other. In fact, Wambūi Othieno, S. M. Othieno's widow, played this card in her legal claim on her dead husband's body, thus raising the anger of those who thought she was playing the colonial card and to the tastes of the Western media which, in the traditions of Conrad and Tempels discussed earlier, are always eager to identify in African modes of thought and practice the "primitive" opposites of themselves. By means of journalistic ploys, her position was presented as arguing that he was a "modernized" S. M. who read Shakespeare and listened to Beethoven, had excised himself from primitive beliefs and practices, and that it would be "unjust," indeed "inhuman" and "countercivilization," to subject his dead body to them. Above all, as a modern legal practitioner, he had left behind a legally valid and binding will spelling out his choice of a burial site for his body.

The charges of "primitivism" rallied the Luo elite behind the Kager Umira clan's claim to Othieno's body. The court setting became a symbolic and literal battle ground for a showdown between so-called modernity and so-called traditionalism. The epistemological peak of this showdown came in the testimony of the late Henry Odera Oruka, a Western-educated University of Nairobi professor and leading African analytic philosopher. Asked by the presiding judge of the Court of Appeal whether he, as an analytic philosopher, believed in the existence and vengeful capacity of spirits as claimed by the Kager Umira people, Oruka responded: "From an analytic point of view . . . I have no ground for either affirming or negating such a claim." By his position, Oruka was for the ordinary Luo person the symbol of the highest possible form of "Westernization." But his argument, seen through all levels as indicating that there was no contradiction between being "modern" and believing or practicing one's ethnic customary traditions, became a popular reference for what the performers of public culture had been saying and singing for as long as the danger of the badly reasoned rupture between the new and the old was perceived as a real possibility.

In other words, while the people of the Kager Umira clan and the Luo community in general "defended Othieno in his sleep" as an inalienable one of their own, he was also an example of what many in social statuses like his own must avoid. Thus, in the aftermath of the case, many Luo elites struggled to "be unlike Othieno" by building houses and homes in their birthplace villages. Returning to the rural homes with greater frequency also became one of the post–S. M. practices among several Luo elites. For many, re-traditionalization became a norm of which they, like everyone else, were to be constantly and practically conscious. Besides, they were also constantly reminded of it by the likes of Ogwang', Owino Misiani, and Ochieng' Kabaselleh. Of the imagined ideals of separateness and continuity of ethnic identities and the dangers which modern migratory economy imposed on them, Ochieng' Kabaselleh and the Luna Kidi Band had the following to say as early as 1969:

> *Ochieng' Kabaselleh and the Luna Kidi Band:*
> *The Continuities of Self in the Discontinuities of Modernity*

> Oh you fellow Luo people
> You must beware of the changing times
> Beware of today's dangers
> Otherwise you face perishing

> Oh our young men
> Who migrated to towns
> In search of jobs
> At least marry Luo women
> We might be able to identify you
> To be Luo men

> On my part
> I know my clan home in Gem
> Where I return frequently
> So I must marry a Luo woman

> Oh our young women
> You must show
> Your symbols of identity
> Your dental work
> We might be able to identify you
> To be Luo women

> Oh our young men
> You must marry Luo women
> We might be able to identify you
> To be Luo men

> Oh our young women
> You must show
> Your symbols of identity
> Your dental work
> We might be able to identify you
> To be Luo women

Oh our young men
You must marry Luo women
We might be able to identify you
To be Luo men

Oh in accordance to the wishes
Of my Ujimbe clan
I will marry a Luo woman
With my maternal clan's approval
I will marry a Luo woman

All our leaders have approved
I will marry a Luo woman
All our ordinary people have approved
I will marry a Luo woman
All my relatives have approved
I will marry a Luo woman
All concerned Luo people have approved
I will marry a Luo woman

Super pretty Angela too approves
I will marry a Luo woman
Even to God's eternity
I will marry a Luo woman
Even to Hell's furnace
I will marry a Luo woman
In Luo homeland
I will marry a Luo woman

My eldest son
Has abandoned our traditions
The one after him too
Has abandoned our traditions
The following one too
Has abandoned our traditions
All my seven sons
Have abandoned our traditions

One of them recently returned
And brought home a strange woman
Who cannot respond to my greetings
Who cannot speak our language

These young men
Need to marry
Luo women
Like Anyango
My other daughter-in-law
Anyango my child
Make an ululation
To proudly demonstrate
Your cultural roots

Ah hi hi hi hi hi hi hi
Every young woman
Looks for a brother-in-law
To make her culturally proud

Oh my Luo people
Onyango my son
You have gone to the whiteman's town
You can speak this Oswayo [a demeaning Luo reference to kiSwahili]
Speak to this brother of yours
Ask him what he has brought back into my home

A dialogue between brothers

How are you brother?
I am fine brother
Are you from Orobi [a Luonized form for Nairobi]
Yes I come from Orobi
What have you brought back with you?
I have brought a wife with me
What is the identity of your wife?
My wife is Okuyu [a Luonized form for kiKuyu]
Does she speak dhoLuo? [in dhoLuo]
Oh no, she does not

[attribution rather ambiguous]

Oh what a messy situation!

This is a complex and multistructured piece. It is presented as a unified musical piece, but also as a multiform structure of different dialogues depicting multi-vocal, multi-generational, and multi-social levels. It is also rife with critical references to other languages and identities—not because they are necessarily bad in themselves, but because of the political fiat and economic displacements that have translated them into sources of potential threat and corruption to other identities. Finally, Ochieng''s sense of a tragic end is a statement on the nature of history, a kind of nostalgic lamentation for the inevitable loss and fluidity of essentialism. Our futures, even in the form of our very offspring, take undetermined and unpredictable turns, the functions of the complex processes of their own times. The present is the rupturous point between yesterday and tomorrow. The self, as the vehicle for transgressing the boundaries of time and identities, is the embodiment of contradictions; it is where the past and present, rural and urban, and village and city are made to coexist in a complex truce of plurality and contemporaneity. The poetics of music separate and keep them close, just enough for selves to migrate back and forth between them.

Notes

1. Nkrumah (1957) makes reference to his use of the term in his uncompleted Ph.D. dissertation at the University of Pennsylvania between 1943 and 1945.

2. Virtue names, or pak, nyinge mag pak, are often a complex mixture of proper names and descriptive phrases that one gives to oneself or are given to one by others in a game-like practice of virtue-boasting. These games are often played along with (during) musical performances and define cultural mechanisms of public self-fashioning by individuals and groups. Such self-characterizations may be real or invented, and their veracity as claimed is never the issue.

"S. M. Children" refers both to the real children of S. M. Othieno of the famed Kenyan government legal trial of tradition, and to the generation of young urbanized Africans whose ideas of and attitudes toward traditions find representation in the views of S. M. Othieno's children.

References

Agawu, Kofi. 1995. "The Invention of 'African Rhythm.'" *Journal of the American Musicological Society* 48: 380–95.

Anderson, Benedict. 1983. *Imagined Communities: Reflections on the Origin and Spread of Nationalism.* London: Verso.

Appiah, Kwame A. 1992. *In My Father's House: Africa in the Philosophies of Culture.* Oxford: Oxford University Press.

Araeen, Rasheed. 1991. "From Primitivism to Ethnic Arts." In *The Myth of Primitivism: Perspectives on Art*, ed. Susan Hiller, 158–82. London: Routledge.

Ashton, Dore. 1984. "On an Epoch of Paradox: 'Primitivism' at the Museum of Modern Art." *Arts Magazine* 59, 3: 76–79.

Berlin, Isaiah. 1994. Introduction. In *Philosophy in an Age of Pluralism: The Philosophy of Charles Taylor in Question*, ed. James Tully, 1–3. Cambridge: Cambridge University Press.

Bourdieu, Pierre. 1977. *Outline of a Theory of Practice*. Trans. Richard Nice. Cambridge: Cambridge University Press.

Budd, Malcolm. 1985. *Music and the Emotions*. London: Routledge and Kegan Paul.

Burke, Kenneth. 1950. *A Rhetoric of Motives*. New York: Prentice-Hall.

Certeau, Michel de. 1984. *The Practice of Everyday Life*. Berkeley and Los Angeles: University of California Press.

Césaire, Aimé. 1972. *Discourse on Colonialism*. New York: Monthly Review Press.

Cohen, David W., and E. S. Atieno Odhiambo. 1992. *Burying S. M.: The Politics of Knowledge and the Sociology of Power in Africa*. Portsmouth, N.H.: Heinemann; London: James Currey.

Conrad, Joseph. 1971. *Heart of Darkness* [1902]. New York: W. W. Norton.

Cooke, Lynne. 1991. "The Resurgence of the Night-mind: Primitivist Revivals in Recent Art." In *The Myth of Primitivism: Perspectives on Art*, ed. Susan Hiller, 137–57. London: Routledge.

Curtin, Philip. 1995. "Ghettoizing African History." In *The Chronicle of Higher Education*. (3 March): A44.

Dulles, Avery, S. J. 1966. "The Church." In *The Documents of Vatican II*, ed. Walter M. Abbot, S.J., 9–13. London: Geoffrey Chapman.

Eboussi-Boulaga, Fabien. 1977. *La crise du Muntu: Anthenticité africaine et philosophie*. Paris: Présence Africaine.

Erlmann, Veit. 1991. *African Stars: Studies in Black South African Performance*. Chicago: University of Chicago Press.

———. 1996. *Nightsong: Performance, Power, and Practice in South Africa*. Chicago: University of Chicago Press.

Fabian, Johannes. 1996. *Remembering the Present: Painting and Popular History in Zaire*. Berkeley and Los Angeles: University of California press.

Fanon, Frantz. 1967. *Black Skin, White Masks*. New York: Grove Press.

———. 1978. *The Wretched of the Earth*. London: Penguin.

Gates, Henry Louis, Jr., and Cornel West. 1996. *The Future of the Race*. New York: Knopf.

Goldsworthy, David. 1982. *Tom Mboya: The Man Kenya Wanted to Forget*. Nairobi: Heinemann.

Goody, Jack. 1977. *The Domestication of the Savage Mind*. Cambridge: Cambridge University Press.

———. 1992. "Oral Culture." In *Folklore, Cultural Performance, and Popular Entertainments*, ed. Richard Bauman, 5–20. New York: Oxford University Press.

Griaule, Marcel. 1965. *Conversations with Ogotemmêli*. Oxford: Oxford University Press.

Gyekye, Kwame. 1995. *An Essay on African Philosophical Thought: The Akan Conceptual Scheme*. 2d ed., rev. Philadelphia: Temple University Press; 1st ed., Cambridge: Cambridge University Press, 1987.

Heidegger, Martin. 1977. "The Question Concerning Technology." In his *The Question Concerning Technology*, 3–35. New York: Harper Colophon.

Hountondji, Paulin J. 1983. *African Philosophy: Myth and Reality*. Bloomington: Indiana University Press. 2d ed., 1996.

Kivy, Peter. 1989. *The Corded Shell*. Philadelphia: Temple University Press.

Kratz, Corinne A. 1994. *Affecting Performance: Meaning, Movement, and Experience in Okiek Women's Initiation*. Washington, D.C.: Smithsonian Institution Press.

Kwame, Safro. 1995. *Readings in African Philosophy: An Akan Collection*. Lanham, Md.: University Press of America.

Maquet, Jacques. 1972. *Africanity: The Cultural Unity of Black Africa*. Trans. Joan R. Rayfield. New York: Oxford University Press. French original: *Africanité traditionelle et moderne*. Paris: Présence Africaine, 1967.

Marcus, George E., and Michael M. J. Fischer. 1986. *Anthropology as Cultural Critique: An Experimental Moment in the Human Sciences*. Chicago: University of Chicago Press.

Montaigne. 1957. *The Complete Essays of Montaigne*. Trans. Donald M. Frame. Stanford, Calif.: Stanford University Press.

Mudimbe, V. Y. 1988. *The Invention of Africa*. Bloomington: Indiana University Press.

———. 1994. *The Idea of Africa*. Bloomington: Indiana University Press.

Nkrumah, Kwame. 1957. *Ghana: Autobiography of Kwame Nkrumah*. London: Nelson.

Ocholla-Ayayo, A. B. C. 1989. "Death and Burial: An Anthropological Perspective." In *The S. M. Otieno Case: Death and Burial in Modern Kenya*, ed. J. B. Ojwang' and J. N. K. Mugambi, 30–51. Nairobi: Nairobi University Press.

Parkin, David. 1978. *The Cultural Definition of Political Response: Lineal Destiny among the Luo*. London: Academic Press.

Paterson, Douglas. 1994. "Until Morning: The Life and Times of Kenyan Pop." In *World Music: The Rough Guide*, ed. Simon Broughton, Mark Ellingham, David Muddyman, and Richard Trillo. London: Rough Guides.

Possoz, Emile. 1945. Preface to Tempels 1945. English translation in *Bantu Philosophy*. Paris: Présence Africaine, 1959.

Ridley, Aaron. 1995. "Musical Sympathies: The Experience of Expressive Music." *The Journal of Aesthetics and Art Criticism* 53, 1: 49–57.

Schwabsky, Barry. 1985. "Exotica: A Different World." In *Arts Magazine* 59, 7: 120–21.

Scott, James. 1990. *Domination and the Arts of Resistance: Hidden Transcripts*. New Haven: Yale University Press.

Seeger, Anthony. 1987. *Why Suyá Sing: A Musical Anthropology of an Amazonian People*. Cambridge: Cambridge University Press.

Serequeberhan, Tsenay. 1995. *The Hermeneutics of African Philosophy: Horizon and Discourse*. New York: Routledge.

Shaw, Rosalind. 1990. "The Invention of African Traditional Religions." *Religion* 20: 339–53.

Stokes, Martin. 1994. "Introduction: Ethnicity, Identity and Music." In *Ethnicity, Identity and Music: The Musical Construction of Place*, ed. Martin Stokes, 1–27. Oxford: Berg.

Tempels, Placide. 1945. *La Philosophie bantoue*. Elizabethville, Belgian Congo: Lovania. English translation: *Bantu Philosophy*. Paris: Présence Africaine, 1959.

————. 1962. *Notre rencontre*. Limete-Léopoldville: Editions du Centre d'Etudes Pastorales.

Tully, James, ed. 1994. *Philosophy in an Age of Pluralism: The Philosophy of Charles Taylor in Question*. Cambridge: Cambridge University Press.

Vansina, Jan. 1964. *The Oral Tradition*. Chicago: Aldine.

————. 1985. *Oral Tradition as History*. Madison: University of Wisconsin Press.

————. 1990. *Paths in the Rainforests: Toward a History of Political Tradition in Equatorial Africa*. Madison: University of Wisconsin Press.

Wallis, Roger, and Krister Malm. 1984. *Big Sounds from Small People: The Music Industry in Small Countries*. London: Constable.

Waterman, Christopher Alan. 1990. *Jùjú: A Social History and Ethnography of an African Popular Music*. Chicago: University of Chicago Press.

White, Luise. 1990. *The Comforts of Home: Prostitution in Colonial Nairobi*. Chicago: University of Chicago Press.

Wiredu, Kwasi. 1980. *Philosophy and an African Culture*. Cambridge: Cambridge University Press.

————. 1990. "Are There Cultural Universals?" *Quest* 4, 2: 4–19.

————. 1992. The Ghanaian Tradition in Philosophy. In *Person and Community: Ghanaian Philosophical Studies I*, ed. Kwasi Wiredu and Kwame Gyekye. Washington, D.C.: Council for Research in Values and Philosophy.

————. 1996. *Cultural Universals and Particulars: An African Perspective*. Bloomington: Indiana University Press.

Wiredu, Kwasi, and K. Gyekye, eds. 1992. *Person and Community: Ghanaian Philosophical Studies I*. Washington, D.C.: Council for Research in Values and Philosophy.

11

Béla Bartók and the Rise of Comparative Ethnomusicology: Nationalism, Race Purity, and the Legacy of the Austro-Hungarian Empire

KATIE TRUMPENER

On the five-thousand acre Batáry estate the girls worked for
thirty krajcárs a day. They hoed the beet and sang, for it was
May. . . . Jusztina busied herself at the head of the girls. It was
she who broke into a new song whenever with a sigh or two,
they had finished the old. . . . Further in the back hoed the two
gypsy girls, Petyka and Juliska. But unlike the others, they did
not sing. The other girls would have nothing to do with them,
even though they all worked for just thirty krajcárs a day. . . .
Petyka and Juliska nearly perished from thirst. . . . They were
Tom Batáry's hired hands, same as the others. They were girls,
too, and young, just like them. The other girls concealed their
jug in a nearby grove, and as they sang, they laughed at the
misery of the two gypsy girls.
Endre Ady, "Hoeing the Beet" (1906)

[The musicians in the provincial orchestra] had no way of
knowing that their misfortune was to have arrived in Hungary
in the latter half of the nineteenth century—a time of provin-
cialism and poverty, when no one was in the mood to bother
over music, nor had time to. . . . They never knew they'd been
victimized by an uncultivated Hungary, ruined by a nation that
could appreciate only gypsy music. They'd been deprived of
music's pleasure, which they had a right to, despite their medi-
ocrity. They'd been robbed of their ambition, and driven to
drink, forced to lead lives of misery, and die disillusioned and
poor.
Géza Csáth, "Musicians" (1913)

THE NURSE'S AND THE GYPSIES' SONGS

Born in the Banat in 1881, Béla Bartók spent his formative years in various provinces of the Kingdom of Hungary, in multiethnic and multilingual towns which now belong to Romania, Ukraine, and Slovakia.[1] In early childhood, according to his mother, he responded eagerly to various forms of local music, from the songs of his nurse to the popular dance music played by traveling Gypsy musicians. "His nanny sang to him a lot, and he always listened to her with delight. . . . When from time to time gipsy music was played in our town (on some special occasion), he urged us to take him there and then listened to the music with amazing concentration" (Gillies 1982: 6). From childhood onward, however, Bartók's own formal musical training was primarily classical in nature, and in 1899, at the age of 18, he moved permanently to Budapest, to study piano at the Budapest Academy of Music.

Five years later, while vacationing in a Slovakian resort, Bartók chanced to overhear a woman singing in an adjacent hotel room: Lidi Dósa, a nursemaid originally from Transylvania, was singing a Székely folk song to her young charge (ibid. 50–52). This accidental encounter was to prove a musical (re)awakening for Bartók, altering the course of his career as a composer and musician, and initiating a parallel, pioneering career as an ethnomusicologist. A year after he stumbled on the sound of "real folksong, on the voice of a young girl" (Griffiths 1984: 15), Bartók embarked with Zoltán Kodály on the first of many folk song–collecting expeditions across the hinterlands of Hungary (and eventually across other parts of Europe and North Africa as well). At first, as a committed nationalist, Bartók's primary interest was in collecting Hungarian village music, which he saw as an ancient national patrimony, a potentially revitalizing cultural force, and a site of resistance to the cosmopolitanizing force of the Austro-Hungarian Empire. Yet he soon became interested as well in the songs of the other national groups within the Kingdom of Hungary and the Dual Monarchy, beginning to collect Slovak songs in 1906 and Romanian songs in 1908. In turn, this new research on the interplay and diffusion of national cultural traditions led Bartók to develop his own version of a comparative ethnomusicological method. It resulted in a series of essays on comparative musical history and finally in his 1934 book *The Folk Music of Hungary and of the Neighbouring Peoples* (Elschek 1993: 92).

In retrospect, then, Bartók's 1904 encounter in Slovakia with the Transylvanian nursemaid seems decisive. As an inadvertent re-enactment of a forgotten yet vital scene from Bartók's own childhood (Platthy 1988: 22), the nurse's singing seems to have moved the young composer to an emotional and aesthetic reconnection with his earliest musical influences. Bartók at first understood this newly recovered patrimony in narrowly nationalist terms, as the recovery of a primal relationship to a primal and primary Hungarian music. His subsequent investigations, however, pushed him to investigate the interplay of national cultural traditions within and beyond the borders of the Dual Monarchy and to understand Hungarian music in relationship to Slovak and Romanian music, shaped by their influence and helping to shape them in turn.

Bartók's career as an ethnomusicologist, then, is marked by a steady broadening of perspectives—and the recognition of cross-cultural influences and interdependencies remains at the core of his life's work as a scholar and composer. In crucial respects, however, his conceptual framework remains oddly static, caught in the historical paradoxes of Hungarian nationalism and circumscribed by the racialized world-view of 1900. Ever since the *Ausgleich* of 1870, Hungarian nationalism had been notoriously Janus-faced, agitating for full national sovereignty within or beyond the Dual Monarchy, even while it worked within the Kingdom of Hungary itself for the forcible assimilation or "Magyarization" of the half of its inhabitants who were not ethnically Hungarian (Hoensch 1988, Jászi 1929, Trumpener 1996). Bartók's rediscovery of folk music in 1904 replicates both aspects of Hungarian nationalism. His discovery of a music that is deeply, indigenously, unmistakably Hungarian helps to stake a broad nationalist claim for the antiquity, magnificence, and innate distinctiveness of Hungarian culture, against the cosmopolitanism of imperial musical life. At the same time, the specifics of the discovery—as Bartók recovers Hungarian folk music during a sojourn in Slovakia, from the mouth of an ethnic Hungarian from Transylvania—feed a version of nationalism which presupposes a "greater Hungary" and a history of Hungarian cultural presence (and dominance) in large parts of southeastern Europe.

Bartók's interest in folk music also begins at a moment when all of Europe is openly preoccupied with questions of race and eugenics and when a crumbling Austro-Hungarian empire, obsessed with the threat of nationalism, has begun to think about its own constituent ethnic groups in consciously racializing (and often demonizing) terms. Bartók's reinvestment in folk music presents a striking asymmetry. For if he is captivated by the strains of the nurse's song, to such a degree that he subsequently consecrates much of his life to the recovery of (and musical elaboration on) similar songs, he decisively fails to develop any sentimental reattachment to the other form of music which delighted him as a small child: the music played by Gypsy musicians. Bartók's initial nationalist interest in folklore-collecting and his initial criticism of musical cosmopolitanism are, as we will see, fueled partly by racism, specifically by a fear of both Gypsy and Jewish influences on Hungarian cultural life. Already from the outset, then, the question of a national cultural heritage is framed by the question of racial alterity as much as by the political hierarchies of the Austro-Hungarian empire.

So too, at the other end of his career, Bartók's famous denunciation of the racial and cultural policies of the Axis powers continued to depend on unspoken racialist principles of his own. Despite the importance and relative internationalism of Bartók's work during the interwar period, as he attempted to develop a supra-national, comparative study of ethnomusicology in the teeth of post-Versailles and post-Trianon national hatreds, his ethnomusicological career as a whole nonetheless remained framed, in problematic ways, by early twentieth-century understandings of race. Indeed, it remained consecrated to the attempt to describe the relationship between nation and race, between cultural influence and cultural essence.

BUDAPEST 1900: THE RECLAMATION OF NATIONAL CULTURE FROM THE FORCES OF COSMOPOLITANISM

Stirred like many of his generation to patriotic consciousness by the 1896 Millennium Celebration (commemorating a thousand years of Magyar settlement in Hungary), Bartók spent the early years of the twentieth century as a dedicated nationalist. His first critical success, the symphonic poem *Kossuth* (composed 1903, premiered 1904) glorified the life and political struggles of the Hungarian nationalist leader Lajos Kossuth, who led the unsuccessful 1848 Hungarian uprising against the Habsburg empire and died in Italian exile in 1894. As Bartók announces in a 1903 letter to his mother, he himself intends to carry on the nationalist struggle against Habsburg domination in present-day Budapest by scrupulously avoiding the German language and speaking only Hungarian, whatever the occasion. The letter is striking for its peremptory tone and its latent misogyny, as its zealous young writer (writing self-consciously as the male head of his family) denounces the attempts of his mother and sister to assist the linguistic integration of non-Hungarian friends and exhorts them instead to protect and extend the use of the Hungarian language.

> I have no news at the moment. The most I can send you is a social-political dissertation to the effect that the ruin of the Hungarians will . . . be

caused . . . by the fact that the individual members of the Hungarian nation, with insignificant exceptions, are so distressingly indifferent to everything Hungarian. Not in high politics, where there is plenty of enthusiasm for national ideals, but in everyday life where we incessantly commit wrongs against the Hungarian nation in all sorts of seemingly unimportant trifles. "It's all the same to us whether and how anybody speaks our unique and peerless language, instead we ourselves speak everybody else's language; we deride people who speak only Hungarian as uneducated, no matter how much they know; our girls, the mothers of future generations, we ruin at a tender age with foreign education." This is what Jeno Rákoski says in one of his fine speeches. He is right! This is how Hungarians act when really they ought to do all they can to foster the use of their own mother tongue. But of course we don't mind, Hungarian speech or German (we even take pride in this), Hungarian goods or Austrian. . . . For my own part, all my life, in every sphere, always and in every way, I shall have one objective: the good of Hungary and the Hungarian nation. I think I have already given some proof of this intention in the minor ways which have so far been possible to me. Unfortunately there are in this respect many things in my own home which need correcting. The last time we were together, I noticed with sorrow that both you and Böske [Bartók's sister Elza], whether from negligence or forgetfulness, committed the very errors I have mentioned. . . . [Ordinary people] should work quietly and unobtrusively in their everyday life for everything that is Hungarian. Spread and propagate the Hungarian language, with word and deed, and with *speech!* Speak Hungarian between yourselves!!! How ashamed of myself I should be if for instance in Pozsony or perhaps later in Budapest an acquaintance who knows my way of thinking visited me and by chance heard that you speak German between yourselves and perhaps even to me. He would think me a hypocrite. . . . Why didn't you get used to speaking Hungarian when you were young? . . .

Hear now the thesis addressed to every Hungarian.

Speak a foreign language only when absolutely necessary! . . . If "it's difficult to get used to it," then one must take pains; the Hungarian language deserves it.

As for you addressing me in German—well, not even as a joke do I want this. You know how I am in the shops, and when anybody in the street asks me the way in a foreign language. I wish you to follow my example. If "it's difficult," well, you must get over the first difficulties; it will be quite easy later. I have got used to it completely. It would be sad if those closest to me did not co-operate with me for a common goal. . . . How often I have noticed, when the conversation is going on in Hungarian, that suddenly *you* are the one who switches over to German, out of sheer for-getfulness, because it is "all the same" to you. (Bartók 1971: 29–30)

Significantly, Bartók's letter echoes a nationalist critique of "foreign" (i.e. higher) education for women, which envisions feminist emancipation negatively, as a form of cosmopolitanism threatening the traditional transmission of cultural values from mother to child. His own mother, Bartók insists, betrays a comparable cosmopolitanism; her feckless bilingualism is a form of linguistic faithlessness, which sullies her honor as a Hungarian woman. A year later, Bartók will discover in Lidi Dósa, the Székély nursemaid, the prototype of true Hungarian womanhood: if his own mother heedlessly alternated between Hungarian and German as the social situation required it, the peasant woman (apparently untouched by the cosmopolitan influences of feminism, imperial culture, or urban popular music) continues to sing and perpetuate her country's ancient musical tradition, whether she finds herself in Transylvania or Slovakia.

In 1903, Bartók still postulates a linguistic basis to national identity: the proud use of a national vernacular is thus the most important badge of nationalist commitment and the most important defense against an imperialist cosmopolitanism.[2] A year later, when he discovers the existence (and the survival) of an ancient indigenous folk music tradition, he comes to see music itself as a comparable kind of national musical vernacular and as an even better carrier of nationalist values.[3] Thus in a letter of 15 August 1905 to Irmy Jurkovics, Bartók moves from a discussion of the current supremacy of German music (Bach, Beethoven, Schubert, and Wagner) to assess the likelihood that Hungarian music will someday hold its own against it.

For we're in a surprisingly favourable position, compared to other nations, in regard to our folk-music. From what I know of the folk-music of other nations, ours is vastly superior to theirs as regards force of expression and variety. If a peasant with the ability to compose tunes . . . had but emerged from his class during childhood and acquired an education, he would assuredly have created some outstanding works of great value. Unfortunately, it is rare for a Hungarian peasant to go in for a scholarly profession. Our intelligentsia comes, almost exclusively, from foreign stock (as shown by the excessively large number of Hungarians with foreign names); and it is only amongst intellectuals that we find people capable of dealing with art in the higher sense. And now our gentry lack the capacity; there may be the occasional exceptions, but such people are not in the least susceptible to our national art. A real Hungarian music can originate only if there is a real *Hungarian* gentry. This is why the Budapest public is so absolutely hopeless. The place has attracted a haphazardly heterogeneous, rootless group of Germans and Jews; they make up the majority of Budapest's population. It's a waste of time trying to educate them in a national spirit. Much better to educate the (Hungarian) provinces. (Bartók 1971: 50)

What holds back the emergence of a Hungarian national music, then, is less the persistence of a feudal social order in rural Hungary than the cosmopolitanism of the country's intellectuals, and particularly the influence of German and Jewish culture in Budapest itself. Throughout the nineteenth century, in fact, Hungarian Jews had identified themselves with the cause of Hungarian nationalism to an unusual degree (Hoensch 1988).[4] Yet what really preoccupies Bartók—and a long line of Hungarian and European anti-Semites before and after him—is the opposition between the rootedness of his own nation (settled in the same country for the last millennium) and the "haphazardly heterogeneous, rootless" character of Jewish culture.[5]

From 1904 onward, Bartók continually execrates the Gypsy influence on Hungarian musical life on similar grounds. First of all, the introduction of Gypsy music into rural Hungary was inseparable, historically, from imperial influences: in the eighteenth century, when the imperial government resolved to raise a standing army, it hired Gypsy musicians to accompany the military recruiters and to play alluring recruitment dances (or "verbunkos") in every village across Hungary (Sárosi 1971). The effects on rural musical idiom were very long-lasting. For one unforeseen result of the recruitment campaigns was the fashion for Gypsy music which swept rural Hungary, displacing or covering over older, very different indigenous musical traditions; throughout the nineteenth century, Gypsy musicians, their repertoire, and above all their style of performance continued to dominate rural musical life.

Thus when Franz Liszt traveled in rural Hungary in the mid-nineteenth century, he took Gypsy musicians to be the true bearers of Hungarian musical tradition; his 1859 treatise *The Gypsies and their Music in Hungary* not only perpetuated this mistake but began a fundamental chain of error in Hungarian ethnomusicological scholarship which persisted into the early twentieth century. Bartók's own ethnomusicological journeys across Hungary, then, are meant at once to undo Liszt's inordinate influence on Hungarian musical scholarship and, by recovering surviving indigenous traditions, to undo the Gypsy-imperial hold on

Hungarian musical life. Yet although he continues to regret Liszt's interest in the Gypsies and his fatal conflation of Gypsy and true Hungarian music, Bartók is quick to defend Liszt's own status as a great Hungarian composer. Liszt, he argues in a 1911 essay on "Liszt's Music and Today's Public," led a life of contradictions, yet his devotion to Hungary remained constant and passionate.

> He did not mind going into dirty Hungarian gipsy camps, but he was equally at home living the life of the highest society. He always thought of Hungary as his "beloved home," he made sacrifices for it, he worked enthusiastically at the music that he heard in Hungary—but he never learned Hungarian, although he had a great talent for languages. (Bartók 1911a: 451)

Unlike Bartók, then, Liszt had mastered neither the Hungarian language nor even the true Hungarian musical idiom, the ancient folk music of the Hungarian peasantry. Yet as Bartók argues in his 1936 "Liszt Problems," it would still not be right, in light of Liszt's conscious identification with Hungarian culture, to deny him his place as a major Hungarian composer.

> Obviously if one maintains, in spite of all this, that Liszt was not Hungarian, one is forced to call him a homeless cosmopolitan. . . . It is public knowledge that Liszt himself always maintained, whether Hungary's fortunes were good or bad, that he was a Hungarian. And it is the right of such a great artist as he that the whole world should take note of his wishes in this matter and not dispute them. . . . Liszt called himself Hungarian; everyone, Hungarian or not, should know of this and let the matter rest at that. (Bartók 1936a: 509–10).

What is perhaps most striking here is the double standard with which Bartók adjudicates national identity. Although Liszt does not speak Hungarian, and although he lives most of his life outside Hungary, his identification with the Hungarian idea saves him, despite his peregrinations, from homeless cosmopolitanism. Yet the Jews of Budapest, regardless of how long they have been resident in Hungary, and whatever their identification with Hungarian culture and Hungarian nationalist aspirations, remain a completely separate and extraneous population, whose inherent rootlessness poses a vital threat to Hungarian cultural traditions. Even more rootless and even more extraneous, Hungary's Gypsies live an openly parasitic existence. Without a music of their own, Gypsy musicians can offer the Hungarian public only "the melodic distortions of an immigrant nation," only a deformed and deforming version of Hungarian folk music (Bartók 1911b: 29). Gypsy performance destroys the "unity" of word and music which previously characterized the Hungarian song tradition (Bartók 1931: 221). And yet for the "half-educated multitude," and for "those whose artistic sensibilities" are "of a low order," this music appears as the true Hungarian national music. (ibid. 206–7).

In Liszt's case, Bartók argues, eclecticism is a sign of genius:

> Whatever Liszt touched . . . he so transformed and so stamped with his own individuality that it became like something of his own. What he created from these foreign elements became unmistakably Liszt's music. . . . We can say he was eclectic in the best sense of the word: one who took from all foreign sources, but gave still more from himself. (Bartók 1936a: 503)

The Hungarian peasantry manifest a similar assimilative capacity in their own music, borrowing the music of neighboring cultures and making it their own: this is why a comparative approach to folk music makes sense.

Yet Bartók's stance is very different where Gypsy music is concerned. Like Liszt and like the Hungarian peasants, Gypsy musicians developed their repertoire by adapting both new and old music until it bore the mark of their own unmistakable style. But if Liszt's composing involves a genial appropriation of diverse sources until the music becomes his own, and if peasant music-making involves the filtering and repurification of foreign materials, Gypsy music-making seems to involve theft, defilement, contamination, alienation (Trumpener 1995).

From the turn of the century onward, much of Bartók's ethnomusicological writing addressed what he saw as the urgent need to distinguish, within the heterogeneous body of music known popularly as Hungarian "folk song," between genuine peasant music on the one hand, and on the other the folkloristic art song of the Romantic period and the popular songs played and spread by the Gypsies. "Old Hungarian Style" songs represent a Hungarian peasant tradition in its purest, most undiluted forms, songs which Bartók believes were handed down from generation to generation. As he writes in his 1933 essay "Hungarian Peasant Music,"

> The melodies of the old Hungarian peasant music style were not derived from the peasant music of the neighbouring peoples. Their partiality for the pentatonic scale renders more plausible the conjecture that they are remnants of our primitive Asian musical culture. . . . They are quite free from any Western European influences. (Bartók 1933a: 92)

The "New Hungarian Style" melodies, in contrast, have their origins in the popular music of the eighteenth and nineteenth centuries. This music is not, then, inherently or indigenously rural: in fact, Bartók sees it as sophisticated and international both in its terms of appeal and in its mode of dissemination.

> These new melodies were taken up chiefly by the younger generation, who, in the course of time, depended wholly on them for the gratification of their craving of song. . . . Perhaps it is these very peculiarities of the new songs that explain the great attraction they possess for the young people among the neighbouring nations to the north. The young men of Slovak and Ruthenian ancestry had an opportunity during their army service to become intimately acquainted with these melodies. A similar opportunity was offered the Slovak harvest workers who were in the habit of working for the Hungarian landed proprietors during the summer season. It is likely that the gipsies, too, participated in the promulgation of the songs, theirs being the role of disseminator among all three peoples. . . . The Slovaks, however, were not content with a supine acceptance of the tunes: under the influence of the melodies taken over by them, new melodies arose, differing essentially in their construction from the forms which had served as patterns, although showing undeniable traces of their origin. (ibid. 101–3)

The Gypsies are culturally supine, perennially appropriating and disseminating other people's music without being able to create a true national music of their own; the Slovak peasantry (like the peasantry of Hungary itself) are culturally vital, actively reworking and assimilating all new influences. In Hungary and throughout Central Europe, it seems, ethnic and racial differences are reiterated by differences in work ethic and in modes of cultural production. Where peasant music is a "product of nature," Gypsy music is "foreign trash" and a "mass article" (Bartók 1931: 221, 206–7). "Of course, the gipsy musicians, as 'professionals,' place their art at the disposal of any one who engages them to sing" (Bartók 1933a: 81). The "gipsies always played what their clients asked for" (Bartók 1921: 70): by performing Hungarian music for profit rather than as an indigenous expression of cultural experience, Gypsy musicians alienate this music from its original context and purpose.

In an age of high nationalism, Bartók's anxieties about the ill effects of Gypsy music on national consciousness are not unique.[6] In his 1913 short story "Musicians," Bartók's friend Géza Csáth thus describes a group of provincial musicians driven to drink and to despair by the debased musical tastes of their audiences, as by a performance repertoire of music that is trivial rather than sublime; in Csáth's words, these men are "ruined by a nation that could appreciate only gypsy music" (1980: 136). Yet for other contemporaries like the radical poet Endre Ady (whose poetry the young Bartók admired and set to music [Dille 1981, Ingyesi 1998]) and Zoltán Kodály (Bartók's closest friend and collaborator throughout the 1910s and 1920s), the popularity of Gypsy music raises a very different kind of political issue: the disenfranchisement and ostracism of Hungary's Gypsy minority. In an article of 1907, Ady thus condemns the police persecution of Gypsies in Wallachia, comparing the situation of the Gypsies to that of Native Americans in the United States. In two stories of 1906, moreover, Ady invokes the question of Gypsy music in particular in order to condemn the feudalism and racism of Hungarian estate life. "Hoeing the Beet" (1994: 15–19) chronicles the petty cruelties which Hungarian day laborers visit on the Gypsy laborers working among them; disenfranchised and impoverished themselves, they wish to feel they are better than somebody—and therefore exclude their Gypsy counterparts even from their collective singing. "Joba the Stone-Breaker" (1994: 27–32), in contrast, links Gypsy music-making to an untapped revolutionary potential: hired to play at a village political rally, the Gypsy musicians play the Kossuth song (celebrating the glorious nationalist uprising of 1848) over and over, all day long, to frame the complacent speeches of the local land-owner. Their music serves as a constant reminder both that the revolutionary traditions of 1848 have been forgotten or misappropriated to buttress a domestic order of striking social injustice, and that a true nationalist revolution, a true social transformation, the true liberation of Hungary's peasants, is yet to come (Trumpener 1996).

For Ady, the Gypsies are at once those excluded from Hungarian national life and those, paradoxically, whose music continues to uphold the nationalist wish for freedom. For Kodály, Gypsy musicians appear at once as the mainstay of village musical life in Hungary and as figures of continuing social vulnerability. In a 1960 introduction to a reissue of his 1952 *The Folk Music of Hungary*, Kodály appears to follow Bartók both in seeing Gypsy music as a distortion of "true Hungarian folksong"— "Gipsies falsify the folksongs they play by introducing the augmented intervals of [the so-called 'gipsy scale'], which are rarely used by peasants"—and as innately inferior as well: "Gypsy composers at best are never more than second-rate imitators of the true Hungarian style" (1971: 6–7). Taken as a whole, however, his book actually refutes many of Bartók's arguments against Gypsy music. For it argues that fears of Gypsy cultural dominance have no reality—and neither does the fabled loss of musical self-sufficiency (whereby a vital, indigenous performance tradition is replaced by a joyless and alienated Gypsy professionalism). Instead, Kodály insists on viewing the Gypsies simply as part of the social fabric of Hungary, and their music simply as part of the nation's cultural landscape.

> Even in the song tradition, all do not have equal shares. There is a sharp distinction between active and passive types. . . . Where instrumental music is concerned, however, everyone is a listener; performance is the task of a few. Whether the musician is a gipsy or a peasant, he stands alone, or with a few companions, face to face with the listening masses. These are not entirely passive; they dance to the music and are quick to feel if it is not played to their liking. They are critical and discriminating and can distinguish what is good. In 1910, a young village gipsy in Transylvania said it was hardest of all to play to the old Székely—a young gipsy could never really do it as they wanted.
>
> Hence, in instrumental folk music, peasants have long since strayed away from the original lines of folk-culture—a state of self-sufficiency. . . . Peasants never pay for what they themselves produce (for them "bought bread" or "bought linen" are unthinkable). It is, however, an old and deeply-rooted custom to recompense the musical contribution to dance and wedding celebrations. Here the paid specialist is already in existence, the professional expert has been substituted for "home industry."
>
> Whether the musician is able to live off this payment is another question. Under more primitive conditions it seems to have been impossible. In 1921, I was present when a well-to-do Székely farmer engaged a gipsy to play at his son's wedding: he was the only musician in Kászonfeltiz, a place of some 10,000 inhabitants. This single fiddler had to play for twenty-four hours straight in return for food and drink, some kerchiefs and five forints. Naturally, he could not live on this. His main occupation was that of smith, so he was called away from his anvil into the bargain. Such unpretentiousness—on both sides—is perhaps surprising: popular fancy imagines sizable bands of gipsies in even the smallest village. It should be realized, however, that as long ago as the 1880s, they "made do" in quite a number of places . . . with a single bagpiper even for a well-to-do wedding. Gipsy musicians at that time preferred to confine themselves to the outskirts of provincial towns. (ibid. 126–27)

Kodály's attempt to reconstruct the perspectives both of Gypsy musicians and of their village audiences suggests that village musical life is much more complicated than it might first appear. From Liszt's day onward, Gypsy musicians had often been represented as all-powerful in their ability to shape village musical life. Yet as Kodály is also quick to point out, this formulation presupposes a complete passivity on the part of village listeners. Although the reception situation has a certain passivity built into it (if only some play, the others find themselves as listeners), the villagers are in fact quick to criticize, to request, and to differentiate between what they like and what they do not. The position of the Gypsy musicians is not always, or not only, one of unchallenged influence and power. Indeed, as Kodály's examples suggest, they often find themselves working under relatively unfavorable conditions, for relatively little pay; they may even see their playing as a kind of "service" or favor to their fellow villagers.

Kodály understands his own sociological study of Hungarian music as a complement and supplement to Bartók's more formally oriented approach to the same musical tradition. Yet Bartók's classificatory work leads, finally, to the reaffirmation of rigid national categories, while his belief in music as the essence or guarantor of national identity leads him toward a eugenically influenced notion of musical purity. Kodály, in contrast, understands identity as relational and defined by the social differences of age group, occupation, gender, and ethnicity. If Bartók and Kodály, who begin their lives as ethnomusicologists together, increasingly part ways politically as well as methodologically (Bartók collaborates with, then retroactively opposes the short-lived Communist government of Béla Kun, Kodály is persecuted for his continued support of it; Bartók reacts to the Horthy period by going into exile in New York, Kodály by remaining in Hungary and working in the resistance), it is in part because they understand the nature of musical scholarship and the stakes of culture in such different terms (Trumpener 1990, chap. 3). Indeed, if we are tempted to explain (and explain away) Bartók's racialism as a typical component of Hungarian nationalist thinking or as product of its period, the contemporaneous counterexample of Kodály should remind us what a more flexible, more democratic ethnomusicology might look like instead.[7]

COSMOPOLITANISM AND THE COMPARATIVE IDEA IN THE ERA OF THE LEAGUE OF NATIONS

During the final months of World War I, while the Austro-Hungarian empire was collapsing under the pressure of nationalist revolts and military mutinies, Béla Bartók collaborated with the imperial Ministry of War in planning a Budapest concert to showcase the military song traditions of the empire. As is clear from his January 1918 letter to his Romanian colleague Professor Ion (János) Busiţia, Bartók is at once defensively aware of the rights of the empire's smaller nationalities to have their songs represented and determined that Hungary receive full credit for all nationalities living within *its* national boundaries. In Vienna, he reports,

> the generals who organised [a similar] concert produced some very peculiar things. . . . [O]nly German and Hungarian was permitted (dualism); and so the Slovakian songs had to be sung in German, which is clearly a legal offense against us, as the Slovaks are living in Hungary and not in Austria, and therefore, if they had to be translated at all, the songs should have been given in Hungarian. Then in the programme they were only allowed to mention *oesterreichische* and *ungarische Lieder*. Thus the Slovakian songs (and it would have been the same with the Rumanian if there had been any) were listed as *ungarische Lieder*, and it was only at the end of the printed text that there was a note: *deutsche Übersetzung aus dem Slowakischen* [German translation from the Slovak]. In short, it was all very bureaucratic and typically brass hat. But what do we care! . . . The Ministry of War would like to repeat that Viennese concert in Budapest, but they've been given to understand by certain "official" circles that only Hungarian songs may be sung in Budapest. The War Ministry which had commissioned me to arrange the programme for the Budapest concert is furious. When I was in Vienna, I had said that it was indeed possible to have a few Austrian songs—a fair enough exchange—and that on the Hungarian side some Slovakian, Rumanian and possibly Croatian songs might be given alongside the Hungarian ones. If the Budapest people do not accept my proposed programme, I shall withdraw from the whole business. They can get on with it by themselves as best they can. Here it is supposed to be a performance of the soldiers' songs of the Army, and this is actually the title of the concert, so it would be quite insupportable and unjust to pass over the various nationalities in silence. Well, that's the way things are in Hungary! (Bartók 1971: 137–38)

If Bartók here continues to advance the claims of Hungarian nationalism, in part by insisting on Hungary's virtual ownership of Slovak, Romanian, and Croatian traditions, he is also willing to assist the imperial army in its efforts to present the army—and thus the empire itself—as a place of multinational cooperation. At a moment in which mass desertions and nationalist agitation within the army have severely threatened military morale, and in which the pressures of competing nationalism threaten the collapse of Austro-Hungary itself (Hašek 1922–24, Weiskopf 1931), Bartók emerges as an apologist at once for the imperial army, for Greater Hungary, and for the empire itself.

Less than a year later, both the war and the empire were irrevocably lost; the 1920 Treaty of Trianon would assign the "Hungarian" provinces or territories of Slovakia, Croatia, Bukovina, and Transylvania to the newly constituted republics of Czechoslovakia, Yugoslavia, and Romania. For Hungary, the dissolution of Austro-Hungary therefore meant not only new national autonomy but an enormous loss of prestige, power, and territory. Since 1867, when the *Ausgleich* had granted Hungary relative national autonomy within the empire and relative sovereignty over a number of other ethnic groups, the Kingdom of Hungary's resident "minorities" (who made up about half the population) had been subjected to continuous, coercive "Magyarization" campaigns and had therefore long been engaged in independence struggles of their own (Hoensch 1988, Jászi 1971). Most Slovaks, Croats, and ethnic Romanians, therefore, welcomed the provisions of Trianon, while most Hungarians remained completely unreconciled to them.[8]

Hungary's post-war relations with Romania remained particularly strained. Romania had fought against Austro-Hungary in World War I, and following the collapse of the Hungarian Soviet Republic in 1919, the Romanian army had actually occupied and looted Budapest. Even long after their withdrawal, a succession of ultra-nationalist and fascist governments in Hungary kept alive a popular bitterness toward Romania, a sentiment only deepened by the Romanian government's persistent mistreatment (right down to the present day) of *its* Hungarian and other minorities (Nagy-Talavera 1970, Jászi 1924, Schenk and Weber-Kellermann 1973, Welisch 1980, Muzsikás 1990, Thumann 1995).

In this political climate, Bartók's continuing insistence on the interconnection of Hungarian, Slovak, and Romanian musical traditions often faced embittered opposition both from his own countrymen and from Romanian nationalists as well. In most respects, indeed, Bartók's stance remains resolutely cosmopolitan. Throughout the 1910s and 1920s, despite growing political tensions (and lengthy interruptions in the postal service) between Hungary and Romania, Bartók maintains a close scholarly correspondence and collegial friendship with Busiţia. In 1912, Bartók sends Busiţia a book of poems by Ady, particularly recommending one pan-Slavic, anti-Habsburg poem which argues, in Bartók's words, that "Hungarians, Romanians and Slavs in this country should all be united, since they are kindred in misery" (Bartók 1971: 113). Both during and after the war, indeed, Bartók's letters to Busiţia continue to express a profound sense of connection to Romanian culture. In 1915, for instance, expressing his sense of depression at the way in which the war has separated those of different nations, Bartók writes Busiţia that "nothing matters, but to remain good friends with Rumania" (131). In a 1917 letter to Busiţia which reports how narrowly his wife and son escaped detention by an invading Romanian army, Bartók ends by reporting that "I long to hear some Romanian song or speech" (135).[9] And indeed, in August, 1919, when Romanian soldiers occupy Bartók's house near Budapest, Bartók uses the opportunity to collect folk melodies from them (Gillies 1990: xxi).

In the years after World War I, Bartók complained repeatedly to Busiţia and to colleagues in other parts of Eastern Europe about the now-insurmountable material and ideological barriers to collaborative fieldwork and research. It was now forbidden to transport phonographs across the Romanian–Hungarian border in either direction: "They wouldn't even let me bring my own notebooks through!" (Bartók 1971: 154). So, too, on the frontier to Yugoslavia, a border guard was able to impose an arbitrary "intellectual blockade," stamping "INTERDITE" on a booklet Bartók was attempting to forward to a colleague in Zombor and returning it to its sender (236).

Appointed in 1931 to the League of Nations' Commission for Intellectual Cooperation, Bartók drafted a motion condemning the growing politicization of culture and arguing for the protection of artistic and scientific freedom (Gillies 1990: 86). Bartók's own research had long since become a case in point, for throughout the 1920s and 1930s, over vociferous nationalist and then fascist protest, Bartók had continued to insist publicly that the study of Hungarian music could not take place in nationalist isolation. As he explains in a 1937 essay on "Folk Song Research and Nationalism," generalizing from his own experience, the "impulse to begin folk song research . . . is attributable to the awakening of national feeling," and the unrecorded folklore tradition of one's own nation represents a unique cultural treasure. Yet what comparative ethnomusicological work always reveals is that "the neighbouring nation was also in possession of the treasure which up to that point had been considered as an ancient, original national property." Ethnomusicologists thus find themselves, sooner or later, engaged by problems of cultural exchanges and overlaps, transformations and diffusions as much as by questions of cultural essence. And folk song research, in the end, is bound to disappoint ultranationalists, because it is bound to disprove their claims of cultural supremacy and priority.

As Bartók points out, he has frequently been held responsible for this kind of nationalist disappointment. When he published research demonstrating the strong musical influence of the Székely Hungarian minority in Transylvania upon the "Romanian" music of the region, Romanians of "pathological sensitivity" accused his work of political bias and political revisionism (Bartók 1937a: 25–27). Hungarian nationalists attack him on similar grounds: by claiming village music as the true musical heritage of Hungary, and by studying the multi-ethnic determinants of this music, he has betrayed the interests not only of his class but of his country. Yet in all of these attacks, Bartók argues, his accusers were unable to impugn either the scientific method or the scholarly integrity of his work. "Please believe me," he writes to the Croatian ethnomusicologist Vinko Žganec in a letter of 27 October 1934,

> when I say that in my studies I have not been, and never shall be, guided by any chauvinist bias; my sole aim is to search for the truth and to conduct my research with as much impartiality as is humanly possible. As the clearest proof of this I can point to my explicit statement... [in *Hungarian Folk Music and the Folk Music of Neighbouring Peoples*] that approximately 38 per cent of the Hungarian material [collected in Muraköz] is of foreign, chiefly of Slovak origin. . . . I should like to point out that there is nothing humiliating in the fact that one nation, or especially a small region such as the Muraköz, falls in one respect or the other under the influence of their neighbours on this side or that. The people of the Muraköz could still remain, and in fact have remained, Croatian, just as, for instance, the Slovenes have remained Slovenes, however much their folk music has been Germanized. My personal feelings in this matter can be summed up, broadly speaking, in this way: as a Hungarian, I'm tremendously interested that there has been in the Muraköz such a powerful infiltration of the old-style Hungarian melodies . . . but from the general human point of view I would naturally be more pleased if this were not so—if, in fact, the material from the Muraköz had proved to be unique. Just as I am, for example, very pleased—and this, I think, can be read between the lines of my booklet—that the Rumanians of the Bihar region have been able from their own resources to produce something so marvelously different, musically speaking; and so on. The most pleasing thing of all would be if each country, each region, each county, even each village, could produce something of its own, original and unique. But this is impossible, for people—whether they speak the same language or not—come into contact with one another, influence one another—It is these interactions that we, as research workers, must endeavour to unravel with the utmost impartiality. (Bartók 1971: 229–30)

Yet throughout the post-war period (and especially during the 1930s), Bartók will also argue that nationalist attacks on the comparative method are gratuitous, in that they overlook the ability of the comparative method to pinpoint as well as to relativize the national character of music. Indeed, as early as 1920, he defends the comparative study of Hungarian and Romanian music on the grounds that such work can actually strengthen Hungarian claims to national superiority on several levels.

> As to the charge that the publication of the article ["The Folk Music Dialect of the Hunedoàra Rumanians," 1914] "is now extremely untimely, nay unfortunate," I declare that my opinion is diametrically opposite. Its publication now is downright desirable, because it makes evident the cultural superiority of the Hungarians. I cite the following from my article: "From among the peoples of our country (that is, Hungary) the Rumanians are the ones who have conserved in a relatively intact form the ancient conditions of their folk music." Anyone who is not completely illiterate in the science of ethnography knows that the survival of such "ancient conditions" is possible only on a low cultural level. The article also makes it quite plain that not a single Rumanian has appeared who is suitable for the systematic study of the Rumanian folk music: a Hungarian had to undertake this scientific research which is extremely important from the Hungarian viewpoint.—Is this not proof of our cultural superiority?
>
> The publication of my article is also desirable in order to show those abroad in what high esteem we held our nationalities, the extent of our concern for their cultural questions, how little we oppressed them. Or does Hungary's interest possibly not require that we refute our enemies' charge that we oppress our nationalities? (Bartók 1920b: 201)

If Bartók's ethnographic work appears to colleagues and contemporaries outside Hungary as embodying a new spirit of internationalism, his own countrymen, according to his self-accounting here, ought to regard it as nationalist and patriotic instead: it deflects potential criticism of Hungary's historic intolerance toward its ethnic Slovak and Romanian populations, and it asserts Hungary's superiority over its neighbors both in standard of living and in intellectual initiative.

Yet when he describes his work as a composer in a 1931 letter to a Romanian colleague, Octavian Beu, he presents more idealistic principles.

> My creative work, just because it arises from 3 sources (Hungarian, Rumanian, Slovakian), might be regarded as the embodiment of the very concept of integration so much emphasized in Hungary today. . . . My own idea . . . of which I have been fully conscious since I found myself as a composer—is the brotherhood of peoples, brotherhood in spite of all wars and conflicts. I try—to the best of my ability—to serve this idea in

my music; therefore I don't reject any influence, be it Slovakian, Rumanian, Arabic or from any other source. The source must only be clean, fresh and healthy! ... Whether my style—notwithstanding its various sources—has a Hungarian character or not (and that is the point)—is for others to judge, not for me. For my own part, I certainly feel that it has. For character and milieu must somehow harmonize with each other. (Bartók 1971: 201)

In the 1920 piece, Bartók seemed to envision Central Europe as a region in which Hungarian culture—and Hungarian intellectuals—remain the dominant force. Here he declares his belief in the equality of cultures and the brotherhood of peoples. In the process, however, he enshrines a different sort of hierarchy, that of music that is "clean, fresh and healthy," true to the essence of its respective culture, over music that is impure. His own music, to be sure, like that of Liszt before him, shows the influence of a wide variety of sources, while somehow still remaining true to itself and retaining its "Hungarian character." Yet when a national folk music is subjected to a similar variety of influences, the result may be a fatal contamination. What Bartók's letter to Beu announces is a tension which will inform much of his ethnomusicological writing of the 1930s and 1940s: the persistence of the vocabulary of universal brotherhood, and the reemergence, at the same time, of the vocabulary of eugenics.

RACE PURITY IN MUSIC: NATIONAL ESSENCE IN THE ERA OF EUROPEAN FASCISM

Over a period of more than thirty years, Bartók's ethnomusicological researches were primarily concerned with broad questions of cultural exchange and with the musical consequences of particular cultural overlaps and borrowings. His first framework for investigation was the collapsing Austro-Hungarian empire, brought into crisis by its unresolved nationalities problems. Temporarily checked in his researches by the advent of World War I and then by the residual jingoisms it left in its wake, he undertook his most ambitious comparative studies in an era which saw the rise both of a new internationalism and a new, fascist ultra-nationalism. During the same interwar period the map of Central Europe was transformed almost beyond recognition, as the multi-national Austro-Hungarian Empire and the Kingdom of Hungary itself shrank into small, residual nation-states and as lands which had long been mere imperial provinces were bundled together to form the new multi-national states of Czechoslovakia and Yugoslavia.

At least indirectly, then, Bartók's work addressed problems and phenomena of central relevance to Central European political history and cultural self-understanding. Yet he remained profoundly uninterested in the actual mechanisms of cultural transfer. And his vision of rural life in Eastern Europe remains apparently unaltered by the social and political transformations of the early twentieth century. His 1936 essay "Why and How Do We Collect Folk Music" thus reiterates the ethnomusicological commonplaces of 1904, in cautioning that folk music should be collected only in isolated areas and only from informants who have remained rooted in their native community.

> The most promising villages are those in which less foreign or urban influence has been felt. A mining district, for instance, is an unsuitable area, because there is, so to speak, too much "tourist traffic." Village people who travel often or who are pedlars are not recommended as sources of folklore supply. The oldest settled villages are still the very best—especially those in which village life has been going on for centuries and still continues according to the unwritten laws of the locality. And that is still the very reason, for example, that one cannot collect absolutely satisfactory material in the settlements of landworkers on large estates: the inhabitants flock together from different regions, and the unifying compass of village life is missing. . . . It is not expedient to record village people who are found in foreign places, such as domestics in the city, pedlars, and prisoners of war. Those who have been torn away from their home may have lost contact with their village musical community to such an extent that their mode of performance changes. . . . It is not permitted to accept educated persons as informants. (Bartók 1936b: 13)

In Bartók's 1942 "Race Purity in Music," written six years later, we see the other side of this lack of interest in the dynamics of change: a stance of singular detachment at the prospect of absolutely cataclysmic transformation. With the exception of Russia, the Ukraine, and Poland, Bartók argues, Eastern Europe is a region of "small peoples" and

> there are no insurmountable geographical obstacles at the frontiers. Some districts have a completely mixed population, the result of war devastation which has been followed by colonization to fill the gaps. Continued contact between these peoples has been quite easy. (Bartók 1942: 30)

Invasion appears here quite simply as the prerequisite for cultural transfer.

Only a few years earlier Bartók had responded to the Nazi invasion of Czechoslovakia with surprising ambivalence. In 1936, Germany's so-called *Anschluß* with Austria had left him full of indignation at "this catastrophe," afraid that Hungary itself "will surrender to this regime of thieves and murderers," and ashamed at the widespread support for the Nazis among his own class of "'educated' Christians" of Hungary (Bartók 1971: 267). The Nazi threat to Czechoslovakia, in contrast, leaves him finally indifferent, for, as he argues in a letter of 9 October 1938 (the day before the German occupation of the Sudetenland), there is little to choose between the ultra-nationalism of Nazi Germany and the ultra-nationalism of the Czech Republic.

> As regards the Czechs—just to look at the other side of the coin for a moment—they are not much better either. They used every kind of trick to try to deprive my mother of her citizenship and thus of her pension; they robbed my mother-in-law of a considerable part of her pension; and, throughout these last 4 or 5 years *I have not had permission* to appear publicly in Slovakia. When so many injustices can be enumerated by one single person, you can easily imagine what an immense number of them have been perpetrated in the course of these 20 years—. (Bartók 1971: 272)

Bartók is deeply offended at the forms Czech nationalism took after the breakup of the Austro-Hungarian empire, and particularly at the Republic of Czechoslovakia's punitive treatment toward his mother. He seems to have forgotten his own youthful nationalist extremism, as well as his own nationalistically motivated efforts to police his mother himself. Despite his own early commitment to national self-determination, indeed, he is so incensed by the long-term political consequences of the collapse of Austro-Hungary (and of the Kingdom of Hungary as a miniature empire in itself) that he can contemplate the rapid expansion of a new empire, the Third Reich, with relative tranquillity.

In "Race Purity and Music" he appears to contemplate the Nazi racialization of culture with similar equanimity.

> There is much talk these days, mostly for political reasons, about the purity and impurity of the human race, the usual implication being that purity of race should be preserved, even by means of prohibitive laws. Those who champion this or that issue of the question have probably studied the subject thoroughly (at least, they should have done so) spending many years examining the available published material or gathering data by personal investigation. (Bartók 1942: 29)

Bartók himself, as he assures the reader, is not an expert on the subject of race. Yet at least where music—and language—are concerned, he opposes the notion of racial purity as an impracticable, and ultimately undesirable, ideal. Any "artificial erection of Chinese walls" in order "to separate peoples from each other" (31) is doomed to failure; if nationalists undertook such measures in the hope of safeguarding the purity of their beloved national culture, they would ensure only its eventual sterility.

"A complete separation from foreign influences means stagnation: well assimilated foreign impulses offer possibilities of enrichment" (31). The history of Eastern European music, for Bartók, is of "a continuous give and take of melodies, a constant crossing and recrossing which had persisted throughout centuries" (30), and it is this history of interchange which gives the region's musics their richness, ensuring a proliferation of melodies, rhythms, and modes, and at the same time forcing each music to explore, develop, and ultimately reconfirm, in every changing form, its own essential character. "A Hungarian melody is taken over, say, by the Slovakians and 'Slovakized'; this slovakized form may then be retaken by the Hungarians and so re-magyarized. But—and again I say fortunately—this re-magyarized form will be different from the original Hungarian. . . . The transformation of foreign melodies prevents the internalization of the music of these peoples" (30). Paradoxically, then, a process of musical "miscegenation" which might be expected to dilute a music's national essence ends up pointing up and strengthening the national character of music.

"Race Purity in Music" appears at a moment in which much of Central Europe was occupied by the Nazis, in which the Nuremberg Laws, prohibiting intermarriage between Aryans and non-Aryans, and mandating strict racial segregation within Germany itself, were matched by comparable legislation in Hungary, in which Hungary's Jews—labeled as "infiltrators" by the Horthy government—were dying in large numbers in domestic forced labor camps, and in which the Nazis had just begun to carry out their full-scale genocidal campaign against the Jews and the Gypsies of Europe. On one level, "Race Purity in Music" offers an important rebuttal to the racialist and anti-Semitic arguments propagated by the Nazis and by Hungary's own fascist Arrow-Cross Party (Nagy-Talavera 1970). Yet it does little to challenge the racialist assumptions underlying these arguments.

Already in the mid-1930s, when Bartók received an official German questionnaire asking him to situate himself in relation to Nazi taxonomies of race, his response was to declare proudly that he was a non-Aryan, since the Magyars were descendants instead of the Finno-Ugrian tribes. While this answer ridicules Nazi categories of race, it does nothing to dismantle their presupposition of an essential racial identity—or even to challenge their anti-Semitic stance. To all appearances, indeed, Bartók shares with his Nazi antagonists a belief both in racial essence and in the quantifiability of ethnic traits. The Nuremberg Laws, famously, drew up criteria whereby individual Germans might be adjudged 100% or 50% or 25% Aryan. For all his discussion of cultural exchange, Bartók's classificatory schemes enable similarly "precise" determinations: a particular body of Hungarian musical material is thus adjudged to be 38% Slovak in origin.

At the beginning of "Race Purity in Music," Bartók carefully qualifies his discussion of race in music by making clear that "I apply the word racial here to the music itself, and not to the individuals creating, preserving or performing the music" (Bartók 1942: 29). Already in 1920, in the period of right-wing reaction and persecution which followed the fall of the Béla Kun government, Bartók had publicly criticized the efforts of Hungarian ultra-nationalists to dismiss musicians either for their political beliefs or because they were Jewish (Bartók 1920c: 463). Here, too, he distances himself emphatically from Nazi polemics about the need to Aryanize German performance life. In the process, however, he concedes the innately racial nature of music.

Written two years after Bartók's own emigration to America and two years before the Nazi occupation of Hungary, "Race Purity in Music" might appear full of the pathos of an anti-fascist exile, as it pleads for cultural hybridity, charts the path of "'emigrated' melody" as it moves from location to location, and insists on its fundamental continuity of character even while in motion (Bartók 1942: 30). From another vantage point, however, Bartók's essay is oddly heartless: written at a moment when the Nazis have occupied Czechoslovakia, Poland, France, and much of the rest of Western, Eastern, and Southern Europe, "Race Purity in Music" describes the imperial conquest and colonization of the peoples of Europe as if stating a dynamic of historical inevitability, and as if describing a development of primarily musicological interest.

THE LEGEND OF BÉLA BARTÓK

To late twentieth-century commentators and biographers, Bartók's intellectual development appears an exemplary one, for his movement from a partisan, nationalist interest in traditional music toward a pluralist, comparative, internationalist understanding of musical influence encapsulates the development of modern ethnomusicology itself. In the culminating passages of his 1979 book *The Music of Man*, for instance, Yehudi Menuhin invokes the memory of Bartók as if summoning up the very spirit of music itself.

Bartók's heart and mind belong to all mankind; at the close of his self-imposed exiled life in the United States, unable to bear the fascist totalitarian regime that had taken over his native Hungary, he was about to embark on a study of the Indians of the American Northwest, which would have enriched North American music beyond belief. It would also have given the Indians a vivid sense of their own culture, the most valuable elements of which would have renewed their self-confidence and their sense of human dignity. . . .

We are told that Saint Francis of Assisi could attune his ear to the conversation of the birds, bringing to life the legend of Orpheus. To me, the same sense of communication with every living thing underlies all that Bartók wrote, linking our past with our future. (Menuhin 1979: 307)

Other commentators show similarly hagiographic tendencies. In an era and a region of Europe scarred by recurring ethnic conflict, Bartók seemed singular, even "saintly" (Gillies 1990: 100) in his resolutely cosmopolitan perspective as in his humanistic integrity, his "human conscience" (Gergely and Vigué 1990). Hans W. Heinsheimer insists that

one could never think of him as a Hungarian, or, for that matter, as belonging to any nation, group, or race. He was a human being, pure, strict . . . governed only by the laws of decency, integrity, and faith, which he applied uncompromisingly to his own conduct and whose breach by others he never forgave.

His angelic righteousness made him unfit for a world where everything has become a give-and-take. (Gillies 1990: 216)[10]

In a post–World War I climate of acute xenophobia and national hatreds, indeed, Bartók continued to promulgate a comparative musicological approach, undeterred by right-wing attacks, and he demonstrated an equally resolute anti-fascist stance during the 1930s, refusing to allow the performance of his music either in Nazi Germany or in Fascist Italy and resisting the blandishments of the fascist government in Hungary as well (Gillies 1990: 64, 78–80). His own emigration to the United States in 1940, writes Peter Csobádi, was thus "analogous to those of a Kurt Weill, Max Reinhardt, Thomas Mann or Albert Einstein: it saved the honor of a whole people" (1982: 23).

In an age of scientific specialization and intellectual alienation, furthermore, Bartók was at once composer, performer, and scholar, his work in each sphere enhancing that in the others. "His creative and performing work," writes Kodály in 1950, was accomplished with the precision and fastidious care of the scientist. His scientific work, apart from the necessary precision and thoroughness, is brought to life by artistic intuition. The folklorist offered the artist knowledge of a rich musical life from outside the ramparts of art music. On the other hand, the folklorist received from the artist superior musical knowledge and perception. . . . Thus it was possible, without any university studies, without scientific training, for someone who started out as a great artist to become a great scientist. (Gillies 1990: 219)

"His great legacy to the younger generation of composers," writes Edith Gerson-Kiwi in 1957, "is to have conveyed to them the definite possibility of a new alphabet, grammar and syntax for modern music, not contrived in a vacuum of speculation like the dodecaphonic system, but built up on the pre-alphabetical elements of a living folk language in song and dance" (Gillies 1990: 153). In an age in which much of the most interesting modern art defined itself in opposition to the art of the past, he found a way of forging a new music out of the region's most ancient musical traditions and thus of reconciling and reintegrating past and present. Indeed, in an age of technological innovation and escalating social alienation (in which, as Bartók himself argues in a 1937 essay on "Mechanical Music," the growing influence of the phonograph and the radio in rural areas heralds the demise of traditional, regionally specific music-making, and the advent instead of a homogenous, mechanically reproduced popular music and of newly passive modes of musical reception), his own use of the phonograph to record "endangered" music conserves regional tradition rather than erasing it (Bartók 1937b; Trumpener 1990, 1996). Above all, in an age (and a region) where nationalism often took on imperialist and racialist overtones, his scholarly vision transformed ethnomusicology into a supranational and internationalist discipline: if romantic antiquarians all over Europe had collected folk poetry and folk song as a means of stimulating nationalist consciousness and of furthering nationalist interests (Trumpener 1990, 1997; Wilson 1976; Herzfeld 1982; Harker 1985; Emmerich 1968, 1971), Bartók's mature ethnomusicological writings worked not to reinforce the cultural claims of his own nation but to emphasize instead the interconnection of cultures. "Bartók's nationalism," writes Jean Gergely, was

a popular nationalism (*Volksnationalismus*), which leads directly to an internationalism, also of a folkloric nature. Folklorism is the actually determining factor in Bartók's development: it makes him, the patriot, into a citizen of the world, through the pure sources of music, and it enables the rapprochement of both of his efforts at synthesis, that of the artist and that of the scholar. . . . His love of humanity was innate. (Gergely 1982: 44) "The Journey made by Bartók and Kodály contributed to the enrichment of ethnography, musical science, the art of music and ultimately to universal human culture," writes Gyula Ortutay. "In Bartók's life-work the scientist's service to his nation's culture, his passionate and pure internationalism and the creative method he adopted into his art are thus inseparable" (1972: 415, 418).

To all of these commentators, Bartók appears as a figure standing above his troubled age, unsullied by its contradictions, and ceaselessly insisting on higher ideals. This essay has placed Bartók, and the narrative of his career, rather differently. On the one hand, it has pointed out the extent to which his scholarship is shaped by its historical moment, especially by Hungary's history within and after the Austro-Hungarian empire. On the other hand, it has pointed out the essentially static and ahistorical nature of Bartók's thinking about national musical culture and the way his continuing belief in cultural essence parallels the ultranationalist, racialist, and fascist thinking he has usually been perceived (and clearly perceives himself) to be opposing. Bartók refuses to understand national character as historically contingent, insisting on the ability of national culture to assimilate all outside influences (and thus to transcend history itself). Throughout his writings, therefore, the notion of ethnicity (cultures constructed through human agency, through human history, and in relation to one another) continually yields to the notion of race (cultural differences as permanent, immutable, and anchored in biology itself).

This essay has tried to pose the question of music and race in two rather different but finally complementary ways. What the influential case of Bartók can help us to see is both the internal logic of a racialist approach to music and its historical context, its intellectual preconditions. In our own moment, essentialist and racialist thinking is on the rise again in many parts of the world. And in an area that once formed part of the Austro-Hungarian empire, a murderous rhetoric—and practice—of "ethnic cleansing" continues to defend a program of "eugenic" genocide on nationalist and historical grounds. The problem of Bartók is thus of more than retrospective interest.

NOTES

1. Bartók's schooling began in Nagyszentmiklós (now Sînnicolau Mare, Romania) and was continued in Nagyszöllös (now Vinogradov, Ukraine),

Nagyvárad (now Oradea, Romania), Pozsony (now Bratislava, Slovakia), and Beszterce (now Busitriţa, Romania). "Not one of the provincial towns in which Bartók lived during the 1880s and 1890s remained in Hungary [after the 1920 Treaty of Trianon], and all assumed new names—in three different countries" (Gillies 1990: xii). See also Gergely 1982: 42.

2. As late as his 1937 "Folk Song Research and Nationalism," an essay otherwise critical of the excesses of "today's ultra-nationalism," Bartók still sees nationalism as rooted, deeply and organically, in the mother tongue: "The sentiments connected with the maternal language, and the affairs of his country are just the most intuitive, the strongest" (Bartók 1937a: 28).

3. The analogies between music and language recur throughout Bartók's ethnomusicological writings. The music of folk songs is, in the first place, clearly linked to the words, so that "when a folk melody passes the language frontier of a people, sooner or later it will be subjected to certain changes . . . especially by the differences of language. The greater dissimilarity between the accents, inflections, metrical conditions, syllabic structure and so on, of two languages, the greater the changes that . . . may occur in the "emigrated" melody (Bartók 1942: 30). By the same token, "the declamatory attempts in vocal works of our predecessors were nothing else but imitations of Western European patterns which were inconsistent with the rhythm of the Hungarian language" (Bartók 1920a: 306). But beyond the influence of language *on* music, Bartók advocates a "comparative musical folklore" that "has a certain likeness to comparative linguistics" (Bartók 1912: 155). Indeed, "folk language and folk music have much similarity in their appearance, life and function. We cannot trace the origin of the single words and grammatical forms to their absolute source, to the very intention of these words and forms. And, in a similar way, we cannot indicate the very source of the single tunes of pure folk music" (Bartók 1933b: 173). Thus he speaks of the Hunedoara Rumanians as using a "musical dialect" (Bartók 1914: 103).

4. Thus in *Radetzkymarsch*, Joseph Roth's famous novelistic allegory of the nature and collapse of the Austro-Hungarian empire, the Hussar officer Baron Nagy Jenö, although "of undeniably Jewish origin . . . considered the Magyars the noblest race in the monarchy and, indeed, on earth, and took immense and successful pains to forget his Semitic ancestors by taking on all the defects of the Hungarian gentry. . . . He had come to the point of loving or loathing spontaneously all that seemed to further or retard the national policy of Hungary." When Archduke Franz Ferdinand is assassinated, the Baron shows his patriotism by publicly dismissing the news. And a fellow Hussar "of purer Magyar extraction than the Baron" becomes "suddenly worried by the thought that a Jew was exceeding him in Hungarian national feeling" (Roth [1932] 1983: 285).

5. Yet as the Hungarian composer and music critic Alexander Jemnitz points out, Bartók later reacts to Nazi anti-Semitism with unbridled hostility: "Although he was not a Jew he was so hugely incensed that he filled out the infamous questionnaire of the German Reich with 'Jew'! Just like the magnificent Hungarian singer, Mária von Basilides, who, when that decree had been passed was so outraged that she wore the yellow star" (cited in Gillies 1990: 97). See also Bartók's somewhat ambiguous 1935 letter to László Rásonyi, lecturer in the

Department of Hungarian Studies at Ankara University, who had invited Bartók to Turkey to organize the collecting of Turkish folk songs. Bartók replies by suggesting that other advisors travel to Turkey as well but points out that his "'unemployed'" colleagues who might be interested in settling permanently in Turkey "are for the most part Jewish; I do not know if this is a disadvantage there or not?!" (Bartók 1971: 242).

6. Judit Frigyesi's important new contextual account of Bartók (published after this essay was finished) argues that his condemnation of Gypsy music (while admittedly "extreme") represented an important break with a conservative Hungarian nationalism. By 1900, she argues, Gypsy music had become associated with "the gentry lifestyle" and a symbol of "gentry chauvinism" (1994: 270, 276). In this cultural climate, Bartók's insistence on privileging archaic peasant music as Hungary's true national music "seemed nothing less than high treason," for it "called into question important tenets of the official, gentry-centered nationalism." (274). In return, as she establishes, Bartók's critics mounted spirited defenses of Gypsy music and thus of their own brand of nationalism. Frigyesi's reconstructions of the political and social climate of prewar Hungary (Frigyesi 1994, 1998) are invariably nuanced and often extremely illuminating. What she does not discuss in detail, however, is Bartók's participation in the period's anti-Gypsy rhetoric, nor the way some aspects of Bartók's own youthful chauvinism continue to inform much later writings. Instead, she stresses the "incompatibility of the ideology of the young Bartók with the radical, avant-garde thinking of the mature composer"; Bartók's developmental trajectory, she argues, is "symptomatic of the development of many members of the Hungarian intelligentsia" (1994: 257).

7. See also the contemporaneous ethnomusicological work of Constantin Brăiloiu (1984) and John Meier (Meier 1905, 1906), both of which offer less rigidly class-bound approaches to the question of folk music than Bartók's work.

8. In *The Glance of Countess Hahn-Hahn (down the Danube)*, which recounts a journey through Central Europe in the wake of 1989, Péter Esterházy recapitulates the history of Hungarian revisionism with sardonic distance: the bitter poverty of Romania, where his journey ends, "confirmed the traveller in his suspicion that the self-image of his own country, as one treated cruelly by fate, was utterly mistaken, false, and no more than a form of self-pity. Offendedness and lamentation as Hungarian national characteristics. The endless whining. The terrible Turks, the awful Austrians, the trickery of Trianon, the indifference of the English, and, to cap it all: the Russians. Oh, outrageous fortune. But wasn't this really just an average European destiny? Now and again countries disappeared from the map, where shunted around like furniture and sooner or later along came the Russians. We have no special cause to feel sorry for ourselves" (Esterházy 1998: 217). Esterházy's journey down the Danube yields a very different sense of cultural relativism than Bartók's earlier journeys—and the stark contrast, perhaps, allows us to see how much Bartók's ostensible cultural pluralism still presupposes the cultural and historical primacy of Hungary as a nation.

9. Along with his next letter he sends three Hungarian books "as tokens of a

happier Hungarian–Romanian relationship in the future" (Bartók 1971: 131, 135). As late as January 1919, Bartók asks Busiţia for news of "how things work out for you in the new world; and how Romanian–Hungarian friendship develops generally. And our work of collecting Rumanian songs?!" (142)

10. Although see also the more ambivalent assessments by Kodály, the publisher Ernst Roth, and the music critic Cecil Gray. Analyzing Bartók's character in 1946 according to "scientific" schemes of characterology, Kodály characterizes him as "severe, withdrawn, . . . mistrustful, lonely" (Kodály 1974: 98). "Behind the unapproachable façade," Roth remembers in 1969, "lay an extreme intolerance in both artistic and human matters. I cannot agree with the romantic descriptions of him which insist that he was the kindliest of men but was ashamed of himself and took refuge behind a wall of reserve. His reticence and intolerance were no deliberate protection from a world which would not understand him. They were his very nature and only in his music could he escape from it" (Gillies 1990: 127). In 1948, Cecil Gray remembers him as "one of the saints and fanatics of music," with "a strain of harsh asceticism which in some of his works amounts to almost physical cruelty: whether to himself or his audience, whether masochistic or sadistic—or both . . . it is hard to determine" (Gillies 1990: 67). For a more sustained (and, it would seem, nationalistically motivated) attack on Bartók's character, see also Platthy 1988.

References

Works by Béla Bartók

All references to *Essays* are to Béla Bartók, *Essays*, ed. Benjamin Suchoff. London: Faber and Faber, 1976.

1911a. "Liszt's Music and Today's Public." *Essays*, 541–44.
1911b. "On Hungarian Music." *Essays*, 301–3.
1912. "Comparative Musical Folklore." *Essays*, 155–58.
1914. "The Folk Music Dialect of the Hunedoara Rumanians." *Essays*, 103–14.
1920a. "Hungarian Peasant Music." *Essays*, 304–15.
1920b. "Reply to Jenö Hubay." *Essays*, 201–3.
1920c. "Post-war Musical Life in Budapest to February 1920." *Essays*, 460–63.
1921. "Hungarian Folk Music." *Essays*, 58–70.
1931. "Gipsy Music or Hungarian Music." *Essays*, 206–23.
1933a. "Hungarian Peasant Music." *Essays*, 80–102.
1933b. "Some Problems of Folk Music Research in East Europe." *Essays*, 173–92.
1934. *Hungarian Folk Music and the Folk Music of Neighboring Peoples* [*Népzenénk és a szomszéd népk népzenéje*]. Repr. In András Szöllösy, *Bartók Béla Öszegyüjtött Írásai*. Budapest: Zenemökiadó Vállalat, 1966.
1936a. "Liszt Problems." *Essays*, 501–10.
1936b. "Why and How do We Collect Folk Music?" *Essays*, 9–24.
1937a. "Folk Song Research and Nationalism." *Essays*, 25–28.

1937b. "Mechanical Music." *Essays*, 289–98.

1942. "Race Purity in Music." *Essays*, 29–32.

1971. *Letters*, ed. Janos Demeny. London: Faber and Faber.

1981. *The Hungarian Folk Song*. Ed. Benjamin Suchoff. Albany: State University of New York Press.

General References

Ady, Endre. 1907. "Herrings etc. The Main Thing Is That There Should Be A Confession of Guilt." Repr. in his *The Explosive Country: A Selection of Articles and Studies 1898–1916*, ed. G. F. Cushing., 142–44. Budapest: Corvina, 1977.

———. 1994. *Neighbours of the Night: Selected Short Stories*. Trans. Judith Sollosy. Budapest: Corvina.

Brăiloiu, Constantin. 1984. *Problems of Ethnomusicology*, ed. and trans. A. L. Lloyd. Cambridge: Cambridge University Press.

Csáth, Géza. 1913. "Musicians." In *The Magician's Garden and Other Stories*. Trans. Jascha Kessler and Charlotte Rogers, 129–36. New York: Columbia University Press, 1980.

Csobádi, Peter. 1982. "Béla Bartók und das Ungarn seiner Zeit." In *Béla Bartók: Zu Leben und Werk*, ed. Friedrich Spangemacher, 9–23. Bonn: Boosey and Hawkes.

Dille, Denijs. 1981. "Bartók et Ade." *Studia Musicologica Academieae Scientiarum Hungaricae* 23: 124–33.

Elschek, Oskár. 1993. "Ideas, Principles, Motivations, and Results in Eastern European Folk-Music Research." In *Comparative Musicology and Anthropology of Music: Essays on the History of Ethnomusicology*, ed. Bruno Nettl and Philip V. Bohlman, 91–109. Chicago: University of Chicago Press.

Emmerich, Wolfgang. 1968. *Germanistische Volkstumsideologie: Genese und Kritik der Volksforschung im Dritten Reich*. Tübingen: Tübinger Verein für Volkskunde.

———. 1971. *Zur Kritik der Volkstumsideologie*. Frankfurt: Suhrkamp.

Esterházy, Péter. 1998. *The Glance of Countess Hahn-Hahn (down the Danube)*. Trans. Richard Aczel. Evanston: Northwestern University Press.

Frigyesi, Judit. 1994. "Béla Bartók and the Concept of Nation and Volk in Modern Hungary." *The Musical Quarterly* 78: 255–87.

———. 1998. *Béla Bartók and Turn-of-the-Century Budapest*. Berkeley and Los Angeles: University of California Press.

Gergely, Jean. 1982. "Zwischen Folklore und Expressionismus: Zur unaufgelösten Dialektik im Werk Béla Bartóks." In *Béla Bartók: Zu Leben und Werk*, ed. Friedrich Spangemacher, 39–49. Bonn: Boosey and Hawkes.

Gergely, Jean, and Jean Vigué. 1990. *Conscience Musicale ou Conscience Humaine? Vie, oeuvre et heritage spirtuel de Béla Bartók*. Paris: La Revue Musicale.

Gillies, Malcolm, ed. 1990. *Bartók Remembered*. London: Faber and Faber.

Griffiths, Paul. 1984. *Bartók*. London: Dent.

Harker, Dave. 1985. *Fakesong: The Manufacture of British "Folksong" 1700 to the Present Day*. Milton Keynes: Open University Press.

Hašek, Jaroslav. 1922–24. *The Good Soldier Svejk and His Fortunes in the World War*. Trans. Cecil Parrott. New York: Crowell, 1974.

Herzfeld, Michael. 1982. *Ours Once More: Folklore, Ideology and the Making of Modern Greece*. Austin: University of Texas Press.

Hobsbawn, Eric, and Terence Ranger, eds. 1983. *The Invention of Tradition*. Cambridge: Cambridge University Press.

Hoensch, Jörg K. 1988. *A History of Modern Hungary 1867–1986*. London: Longman.

Jászi, Oscar. 1924. *Revolution and Counter-Revolution in Hungary*. London: P. S. King and Son.

———. 1929. *The Dissolution of the Hapsburg Monarchy*. Repr. Chicago: University of Chicago Press, 1971.

Kodály, Zoltán. 1946. "Béla Bartók the Man." In *The Selected Writings of Zoltán Kodály*. Trans. Lili Halápy and Fred Macnicol, 97–98. London: Boosey and Hawkes, 1974.

———. 1971. *Folk Music of Hungary*. New York: Praeger.

Liszt, Franz. 1859. *The Gypsy in Music*. Trans. Edwin Evans. London: William Reeves, n.d.

Meier, John. 1905. *Kunstlieder im Volksmunde. Materialien und Untersuchungen*. Repr. Hildesheim: Olms, 1976.

———. 1906. *Kunstlied und Volkslied*. Halle: Niemeyer.

Menuhin, Yehudi. 1979. *The Music of Man*. Toronto: Methuen.

Muzsikás. 1990. *Blues for Transylvania*. Rykodisc.

Nagy-Talavera, Nicholas. 1970. *The Green Shirts and the Others: A History of Fascism in Hungary and Rumania*. Stanford, Calif.: Hoover Institution Press.

Ortutay, Gyula. 1972. *Hungarian Folklore: Essays*. Budapest: Akadémiai Kiadó.

Platthy, Jeno. 1988. *Bartók: A Critical Biography*. Santa Claus, Ind.: Federation of International Poetry Associations of Unesco.

Roth, Joseph. 1932. *The Radetzky March*. Trans. Eva Tucker. Woodstock, N.Y.: Overlook Press, 1983.

Sárosi, Bálint. 1971. *Gypsy Music*. Budapest: Corvina.

Schenk, Annemie, and Ingeborg Weber-Kellermann. 1973. *Interethnik und sozialer Wandel in einem mehrsprachigen Dorf des rumänischen Banats*. Marburg: Marburger Studienkreis für europäische Ethnologie.

Thumann, Michael. 1995. "Mit verschwitztem Pathos: Haßtiraden gegen die ungarische Minderheit gafährden Rumäniens Reformen." *Die Zeit* 8 (24 Feb): 8.

Trumpener, Katie. 1990. "The Voice of the Past: Anxieties of Cultural Transmission in Post-Enlightenment Europe. Folklore, Tradition, Textuality, History." Ph.D. diss., Stanford University.

———. 1995. "The Time of the Gypsies: A 'People without History' in the Narratives of the West." In *Identities*, ed. Kwame Anthony Appiah and Henry Louis Gates, Jr. Chicago: University of Chicago Press.

———. 1996. "Imperial Marches and Mouse Singers: Nationalist Mythology in Central European Modernity." In *Text and Nation: Debates on Cultures in Conflict*, ed. Laura Garcia-Moreno and Peter C. Pfeiffer, 67–90. Camden House.

———. 1997. *Bardic Nationalism: The Romantic Novel and the British Empire.*
Princeton, N.J.: Princeton University Press.

Weiskopf, F. C. 1931. *Das Slawenlied: Roman aus den letzten Tagen Österreichs und den ersten Jahren der Tschechoslowakei.* Berlin: G. Kiepenheuer.

Welisch, Sophie A. 1980. "The Bukovina-Germans in the Interwar Period."
East European Quarterly 14, 423–37.

Wilson, William A. 1976. *Folklore and Nationalism in Modern Finland.* Bloomington: Indiana University Press.

12

Racial Projects and Musical Discourses in Trinidad, West Indies

JOCELYNE GUILBAULT

Music has historically played a vital role in the cultural life of West Indians. Stripped of political and economic power, slaves and indentured workers found solace in music, and from it they built moral strength, developed social networks, and gained prestige in their communities. In such a context, music was not simply entertainment: it served socially and emotionally to nurture and show one's sense of belonging. Used as a political strategy within the repressive colonial system, music, as described by Sara Cohen in her study of Liverpool's popular music but equally applicable here, came to exercise "territorializing power, framing public and private spaces or domains" (1994: 133) for both the colonized and the colonizer.

Music, then, has always been part of the "régime of truth" in West Indian politics.[1] Through musical discourses in particular—and here I mean not only lyrics but other ways of saying/writing which are also part of music as a cultural phenomenon (liner notes, newspaper editorials, articles, and commentaries; news releases and published interviews) —politicians as well as social activists, artists, and journalists, to name only some of the most prominent public voices, have identified, classified, and ghettoized population groups. Such musical discourses, it could thus be said, have not only reflected but effectively helped produce, sustain, and challenge relations of power. The statements[2] which they put forward, according to Allor and Gagnon, conceived as the "events" of discourses, can be understood as "accomplish[ing] the elaboration of positions," as being already "the traces of practices, the accomplishment of projects." The authors add, "Following Foucault, we consider that their effectivity is precisely located in their articulation of different orders of 'ideas, projects and possibilities' (O'Regan 1992) about the social world. Thus, as objects of inquiry they are already discursive and praxical in character" (Allor and Gagnon 1994: 35).

In practical terms, this means that, through the examination of statements, one can find the "traces" of a multitude of projects from various historical times and geographic spaces. For instance, one can observe through musical discourses in the West Indies the articulation of political projects as in Haiti's political revolution (Averill 1994), cultural projects as in the French Caribbean islands' cultural emancipation (Guilbault 1993: 20–46), economic projects as in Jamaica's development of its tourist industry (Fox 1990, *Sunday Punch* 1990),[3] and social projects as in feminist movements in many islands (Cooper 1993: 136–73). From this perspective, the goal of this paper is to look at how some discourses construct musical projects in racial terms and, by so doing, inscribe them as racial projects,[4] to use Omi and Winant's expression (1994). What must be stressed is that, within such a perspective, musical discourses are therefore conceived not as the mere reflection of racial projects, but rather as being actively engaged in their very production. A racial project, according to the aforementioned authors,

> is simultaneously an interpretation, representation, or explanation of racial dynamics, and an effort to reorganize and redistribute resources along particular racial lines. Racial projects connect with what race means in a particular discursive practice and the ways in which both social structures and everyday experiences are racially organized, based upon that meaning. (1994: 55)

What this implies is that there is "no racism in general and consequently there can be no general theory of race relations or race and politics. . . . It demands that the development of racist discourses must be periodized very carefully and that the fluidity and inherent instability of racial categories is constantly appreciated" (Gilroy 1990: 265).

Applied to the Caribbean region, this means that a study of discourses articulating musical projects in racial terms would yield different information depending on the choice of island—since the interactions among the various population groups of each island have been characterized by histories (political, economic, social, cultural, linguistic, and so on) which are unique to each of them. I chose to do this study in Trinidad because race has been a prominent and pervasive issue,[5] especially among the East Indian and African populations,[6] throughout the history of this island.

André Vincent-Henry in his article "Talking Race in Trinidad and Tobago" writes: "An observation of the media as well as the increasing and explicit salience of race in national politics . . . indicates that there is a heightened awareness of race as being important in the social processes in Trinidad and Tobago" (1993: 24). A few pages later, the author explains: "It is possible to detect a heightening of race as a political consideration since the start of the eighties. This can be traced back to the worsening of the economic conditions in Trinidad and Tobago, consequent on the rapid decrease in oil prices" (29). He adds, "Race has come explicitly onto the national agenda. Before this, while racial appeals were present, they tended to be not as obvious" (33).

Many studies on race and music have been done on Trinidad's dominant musical idiom, calypso, and most of them have been based almost exclusively on the examination of lyrics (e.g. Quevedo 1983, Regis 1993, Rohlehr 1990, Warner 1992). In this study, I want to focus on discourses on music practices through local newspaper articles—and not those exclusively concerned with calypso. As daily writings are easily accessible, circulate widely, and participate in defining public discourses on music, newspaper articles on music practices constitute in my view excellent material from which to examine the traces of projects articulated as racial projects. Moreover, they represent different points of view by being formulated from various political, social, cultural, and gender positions. Indeed, not only articles by full-time, regular journalists have been here examined. Letters to the Editor and special columns written by individuals and community representatives who have bought space in local newspapers to voice their opinions have also been included in this work. Unlike most previous studies on the issue of race in Trinidad, my aim is to look at these texts as participating in the local construction of the régime of truth, by inscribing race in Trinidad in particular ways (and not in others) and, by so doing, regularizing the production of certain statements on this issue.

Whether or not one agrees with Henry-Vincent that the heightened awareness of race in Trinidad and Tobago can be attributed solely to economic factors, his identification of the 1980s as the period during which the issue of race has become more prominent provides useful cues in establishing a timeframe within which to locate relevant newspaper articles. Since each type of discourse—political, social, cultural, or economic—has its own particular focus and does not therefore necessarily follow the same chronology (Foucault 1991: 55), I selected articles dealing with music from the main local newspapers, the *Trinidad Guardian*, the *Express* (Trinidad), and the *Mirror/Punch* (Trinidad), ranging mainly from the mid 1980s until 1999. (There are a few notable exceptions of pieces from the late 1970s on individual music events that drew wide media coverage and to which I will return below.) The period of the mid-1980s onward has indeed witnessed a proliferation in the form of newspaper articles of discourses on music articulating specific racial projects in connection, for instance, with the rise of specific artists and practices ethnically not usually associated with the musical milieus in which they have become prominent.[7]

This study is based on two levels of analysis. The first level involves looking at the selected articles as a whole and identifying the statements —that is, the elaboration of racial positions, the traces of racial practices, the accomplishment of racial projects—which emerge with some regularity and tension from the selected texts. The second level presents the particular mediations and agencies which have made these statements possible. I use the terms "mediations" and "agencies" to help focus our attention on what precisely orient worldviews, knowledges, and the formulation of statements (taken here as events) and what give them shape. The two terms, mediations and agencies, albeit conceptually interrelated, should not be confused. As I explained elsewhere, "whereas mediations point to the various forces which orient the ways in which experiences [read "projects"] are conceived and perceived, agency refers to the processes by and through which these experiences [projects] take place" (Guilbault 1997: 43 n. 21). Agents, it should be specified, should not be conceived as the exclusive province of human beings, as has often been proposed. What puts things into motion or what helps the materialization of a project may be as much a discourse, a physical location, as human beings.[8]

MUSIC CROSSOVER

The growing popularity of crossover and chutney music, plus the rapid increase of Indian music on the airwaves, and Indian cultural movies and programmes on television, can only be seen as progressive, positive moves.
(Peter Ray Blood, "In the Rainbow Land")

The album, a prime example of Rikki's unique versatility as an artist, contains a mixture of upbeat, crossover and laid-back soca.
(Kristine Seenath, "Rikki Shows His Motion!")

It is noted by all that this form [Chutney] of expression was an inevitable result, a fusion rising out of a coexistence of cultures. There is an awareness that any attempt to stifle such a trend will be like swimming against the tide.
(Atul Dev, "To Chutney . . . with Love and Devotion!")

Since the issue of race has been articulated historically to establish difference, to divide more than to unite, the widespread phenomenon of music crossover in Trinidad and Tobago has raised controversies. "Music crossover," a term commonly used locally, here implies the mixture of elements of various sorts, embodying long-time associations with what is taken for granted locally as identifiable "differences."[9] Accordingly, music crossover is articulated in terms of collaboration and fusion and in terms of diversity within the range of unity. It is articulated, I want to suggest, as a reaction against the monolithic view of identity, which is strategically nurtured in Trinidad and used by several people (including not only politicians but musicians also) for various interests at various times, depending on the contexts, as will be illustrated throughout this paper. As a counter-discourse to this monolithic view of identity, some authors thus argue that this mixture of elements today called "crossover" can be dated back to the beginning of the colonization period, though it seems to have acquired more prominence and new meanings since the acquisition of Trinidad's independence in 1962, the Black Power movements in the 1970s, and other significant events in the 1980s onward, such as the rapid increase of Indian music on the airwaves and Indian movies and programs on television, and the election of an East Indian prime minister in 1995. The various stands taken on this issue and their underlying rationales can be seen as the traces of what has been construed as racial projects, as the elaboration of positions of power relations enacted from specifically located mediations and agencies. In this section, I will look at the discursive productions of race through the various statements emerging from the selected articles on the issue of music crossover.

The statements that can be seen as the elaborations of racial projects, not only on the music crossover issue but on other music practice issues as well, it should be specified, concern almost exclusively the African and East Indian populations, the two most important cultural groups of Trinidad—a reality which could already be read as a particular articulation of race in Trinidad. The other cultural groups that also form a part of Trinidad's population—locally referred to as Spanish, Syrian, Lebanese, Chinese, French Creole, Europeans, and others—are not considered influential enough, politically or musically, and are therefore rarely addressed, with a few notable exceptions as indicated below.[10]

The remarkable number and frequency of published texts on Trinidadian music crossover during the latter part of the 1980s and in the 1990s can be related to a series of mediations among which three in particular, which are inextricably interrelated, seem to figure prominently: the change of political party from the People's National Movement (PNM) after thirty years in power from 1956 to 1986 to the National

Alliance for Reconstruction (NAR) in 1986 and the relatively prompt reelection of what has now been dubbed the "new" PNM in 1991; the attempted coup led by Abu Bakr in 1990;[11] and the resulting spate of publications on the contrasting positions of the various political parties and their respective stands on what constitutes "Trinidadianness" and what should be the official representation and rights of the various population groups—an issue which will be further developed below.

The simultaneous workings of several agencies contributed in their turn to making music crossover a headline issue. These included the arrival on the music scene (unusual at the time) of two celebrated stars: Denyse Plummer, a "white" Trinidadian known as a ballad singer,[12] who in 1987 entered the black male-dominated calypso scene[13] and earned the titles Calypso Queen of Trinidad and Tobago (1988, 1989, 1990, 1991) and Calypso Queen of the World (1989, 1990, 1991, 1992)— eight titles in five years, after which she retired from competition in 1992;[14] and Drupatee Ramgoonai, an East Indian woman who in 1988, through featuring chutney soca, a blend of calypso and East Indian musical traditions,[15] won the favor of the public. This is attested to by her award for Best Recording Artist in 1988, and for that honor she was granted the Gold Award by the National Carnival Commission as one of the top twenty stars of calypso in both 1988 and 1989.[16] Other agencies contributing significantly to the transformation of the music scene during this period included the progressively greater prominence of fusion musics (by the late 1980s), namely, soca[17] and chutney soca,[18] and new competitions, including the Chutney Monarch show and the Pan Chutney competition, which mix instruments and musics from different cultural sources (1995). One could argue that it is the specific conjunctural conditions, involving both the troubled political climate described above and the significant artistic achievements and innovations of recent years through music crossover, that have contributed in Trinidad to articulating the notion of nation in terms of crossover, revolving around questions of values, legitimacy, longevity, and continuity in time and space.

The first set of statements culled from the articles I reviewed on music crossover reveals indeed an almost consistent attempt to define "nation" as music crossover. Given that there have been various definitions of nation based on conflicting ideologies, depending on the position advocated, music crossover has been described differently, in relation to different times and spaces, people and musical ingredients, circumstances and events, and has received vastly divergent reactions.

In an attempt to establish its legitimacy, music crossover is described in these articles as a natural outcome, something seemingly given and unquestionable, explained in terms of historical circumstances, geographic proximity, and "natural" compatibility among East Indian and African musical cultures. Terry Joseph's piece "Drum Trinity in St. James" (1995) best illustrates this argument. He sees music crossover as something that has always been there and that can be traced as far back as colonial times, during which the collaboration of African and East Indian musicians during important celebrations was already documented. He explains this collaboration as a natural outcome of sharing the similar historical circumstances of slavery and plantation life and the same geographic space—living side by side in small communities.

> The three drums to whose rhythms this society vibrates—the African, Indian and steeldrums—harmonise in bustling St. James, where demographics easily accommodate the blend and the people defend the use of cultural bricks to build bridges instead of walls.

To show the longevity and continuity of such collaboration, today dubbed "crossover," Joseph focuses on St. James, a well-known community in today's Port-of-Spain famous for its "remarkable coming together of groups of people distinguished only by their obvious differences of skin colour, hair and ethnic origin." He refers to "the three drums to whose rhythms this society vibrates" (African, Indian, and steeldrums), the mixture of rhythms reflecting the combination of ethnic groups represented in bands, the mutual collaboration of people from different religious backgrounds (Orisha,[19] Muslim, Hindu, and Christian) in the celebration of various local festivals and the playing of instruments of various origins.

To further establish the "naturalness" of music crossover in Trinidad, Joseph notes the similarity and therefore the compatibility of some of the rhythms characteristic of the East Indian and African musical traditions. Based on this description highlighting the close relationships between members of the different population groups, he predicts: "Without an overt demonstration of presence, the steeldrum, African drum and tassa will again blend perfectly at this year's Hosay Festival." He then concludes: "So will the people from whom these rhythms originated." Throughout the article, the focus on harmonious musical exchange, collaboration, and mutual respect seems intended to prove how people of all races live together harmoniously in Trinidad. This could be read as demonstrating, while reifying, the official political project and rhetoric of the PNM from 1956 to 1986: "One Love," "*Unity* in Diversity" [emphasis added].

The "Unity in Diversity" definition of nation by the PNM is found in another series of statements on music crossover from articles which, this time, highlight *difference* and characterize it ideologically within a pluralist approach of race, expressed as "the healthy *diversity* within the range of unity" (Danny 1988, emphasis added). Here the articles discuss racial projects that explicitly strive to send a message of solidarity to the two main cultural groups. Music crossover is depicted in reference to collaborations that capitalize on bringing to the fore the respective contributions of Africans and East Indians in the Trinidad and Tobago music industry. Within this perspective, the article "King Stalin Plays One for Unity" (Ali 1995) acclaims the five-time Calypso Monarch Black Stalin who won the 1995 competition by singing a calypso in a chutney style to praise the contributions of Sundar Popo, the East Indian local artist who pioneered this style—which has become today one of the most thriving and commercially successful popular musics coming out of Trinidad. A few years earlier, in "Calypso—Indian Soca Mix is Here to Stay" (*Express* 1989), it is Sundar Popo, the respected East Indian chutney singer himself, who is used as an authority to endorse publicly any East Indian artist who tries to do music crossover. "I see nothing [wrong] with us singing calypsoes as long as we do not forget our Indian culture. We must appreciate our country is of mixed races and we must be able to make a contribution."

Following the same line of argument, another article featuring in a most positive light the East Indian singer Drupatee uses the singer's own words to present her as one of the best representatives of those who aim to use music crossover as a way of making a contribution to the two cultures:

> I think I have a contribution to make to calypso. If I choose to sing songs based on Indian culture then I think I am perfect because I will not mispronounce any Indian words . . . Calypso is a Trinidad "ting." . . . Is it wrong for an Indian to fit into calypso without losing his/her identity, providing the merger allows for a healthy diversity with the range of unity? (Danny 1988)

Another series of statements depicts music crossover from a perspective diametrically opposed to the preceding one. Here the concept of nation underlying the previous statements is replaced by an assimilationist approach of race which sees music crossover as a means of nation-building, the sign of the gradual disappearance of difference. Here the idea is to forget Mother India, Mother Africa, Mother Lebanon, Mother England, etc. "The only mother we can have is Mother Trinidad and Tobago" (Hollis 1988). The goal is "to transform this potential nation into a Rainbow Republic paradise."

Within this perspective, the East Indian singer Drupatee, who was presented in the earlier series of statements as someone promoting music crossover, is now depicted as a model of an artist who has beautifully assimilated: "What we need is a few more daring people like Drupatee who can identify with the assimilation theory as a means of nation building" (ibid.). Its underlying rationale here, "Let's put all differences aside and unite cultures for a better TnT" (Danny 1988),[20] is constructed through several other articles. The article on Rikki Jai, "Rikki Shows His Motion!" (Seenath 1992), is a case in point. Here the artist is introduced as "aim[ing] to break through limiting stereotypes pinning the 27-year-old singer as an 'Indian' Calypsonian rather than simply 'a Calypsonian.'" The article ends by reiterating that "the album, a prime example of Rikki's unique versatility as an artist, contains a mixture of upbeat, crossover and laid-back soca, destroying again, all stereotypes marking him as simply an 'Indian Calypsonian.'" According to this piece, here is an artist who should be better viewed as a Trinidadian calypsonian—creed and race apart—not only for his own sake but for a better, more integrated Trinidad.

It is precisely against this stance that another series of statements emerges as "anti–music crossover." In this case, music crossover is portrayed as the emblem of a sociocultural "callaloo," a stew of ingredients with the potential of bringing cultural oblivion. The concern about music crossover could be read here as a deployment of the fear of racial/ethnic assimilation and acculturation (Khan 1992: 190). The series of statements about music crossover highlights opposed conceptual pairs such as morality/desacralization, purity/prostitution, to emphasize what is seen as being dangerously at stake in music crossover practices. On the overt concern of some leaders for maintaining the purity of ancient ethnic forms, Vincent-Henry suggests that "a more dubious motive is possible to discern." He writes, "For many leaders the cultural purity argument is a means to mobilisation and to the maintenance of traditional particularistic patterns of communal power" (1993: 28). As illustrated by the series of statements aforementioned, for others, the cultural purity argument represents what could be described as their fight against both their feelings of alienation and their fear of assimilation.[21]

THE POLITICS OF REPRESENTATION

Maha Sabha Sounds Warning: Don't Deny Us Our Cultural Rights. Officials in the Ministry of Culture are blocking the introduction of the harmonium in Hindu schools, Sat Maharaj, secretary-general of the Maha Sabha, charged yesterday. (Kathleen Maharaj)

There is still a long way to go. Despite Indian leaders claiming alienation and discrimination on political, social, religious and cultural matters, the African continues to be ostracised from Indian cultural affairs. (Peter Ray Blood, "In the Rainbow Land")

The second group of statements brings forward the issue now commonly labeled the politics of representation. This issue is the product of at least two interrelated mediations. The first concerns "the efforts over the last 20 years by the Indian group to establish the validity of their culture and its claim on national resources" and the concomitant feeling of threat by some Afro-Trinidadians who perceive this demand "as an attempt at domination of the society" (Vincent-Henry 1993: 31). In this context, the politics of representation in musical discourses becomes a particularly sensitive and widely addressed issue since, on the one hand, "the argument is often made by Afro-Trinidadians that Indians already dominate in the economy and they are seeking now to extend that domination into all other aspects of life in Trinidad and Tobago" (ibid.);[22] on the other hand, Indians feel they have been denied proper recognition of their contributions in most Trinidadian activities and have therefore been alienated from official representation in national forums. The second mediation has to do with the changes of political parties in power over the past few years and the new opportunities for addressing the politics of representation this situation has offered for East Indians in particular. After a thirty-year period of complete monopoly by the PNM (from 1956 to 1986), which has been openly criticized for presenting Trinidad and Tobago almost exclusively in terms of a black nation (Taylor 1992: 257), the issue of the politics of representation has been more than ever the object of heated debate during the political developments of the last few years with the coming into office of the NAR[23] in 1986 and the re-election of the PNM in 1991, and the election of an East Indian prime minister in 1995.

During this period, the concurrent workings of agencies that have served to effect the gradual recognition of the East Indians' contributions have also inevitably fueled many debates over the politics of representation. These include the declaration of East Indian Arrival Day as a national holiday in 1995, the growing popularity nationwide since 1986 of artists of East Indian origin, and the proliferation over the past decade of publications documenting the contributions of East Indians to most aspects of Trinidadian life.

The first series of statements on this issue enacts what appear to be the struggles and conflicts among various population groups over power, as follows: How, for example, do explicit policy and political actions of the Trinidadian government over music practices favor inter- and intra-group domination of either the African or East Indian population groups? How do social activists, artists, journalists, and community representatives manipulate and reify musical icons, indices, or symbols to exclude or debase the "Other"? This first series of statements can be seen as elaborating positions in the construction of power relations by focusing on the population group which seemingly gets favored in particular racial projects. This way of positing music in terms of race and power is constitutive of the widespread belief (or regime of truth) that in Trinidad "cultural representation and political competition are often synonymous" (Khan 1992: 195–96).[24]

In the first series of statements, the issue of politics of representation is articulated more precisely in terms of demands for rights defined in legal terms. Based on the words of the Trinidad and Tobago national anthem, "Every creed and race shall find an equal place," the demands for rights that are to be (re)presented or given official recognition within music discursive practices are embodied in a rhetoric aiming to demonstrate how the projects under discussion either violate the rights of a given population group or are used to grant it long-overdue recognition. The projects discussed in terms of legal rights are all related to or directly under the aegis of the government's policy and political actions.

Over the past few years, one of these projects concerns national music education. In this case, the government's decision to introduce the steelpan instrument—the symbol par excellence of the African Trinidadian achievements—in all schools is challenged by the representatives of Hindu schools who want to claim their cultural right to promote the harmonium instead (Maharaj 1995).[25] Another project deals with the institutionalization of a new competition, namely, the National Chutney Monarch Competition. Held for the first time in Trinidad in 1995, this national event is described as a major achievement by finally granting East Indians the equal right to "[feel] a sense of national pride *just like* calypsonians and panmen" and also a way "to foster unity between the two major ethnic groups in Trinidad and Tobago" (*Sunday Punch* 1995, emphasis added). Yet another project involves the appointment in 1987 of the Carnival Advisory Council to the National Carnival Commission. The Minister's appointment of twenty-five members with, among them, representatives of some sections of the society which "do not normally get involved" in carnival (DeLeon 1987) raises suspicion, this time, about the motivations that prompted the government to then use this approach to deal with the issue of representation. Two other projects in 1995, both entailing a switch of programming to an exclusively East Indian format, involve Radio 730-AM and NBS Radio 610 (National Broadcasting Services), which is now dubbed NBS Radio ICN-610.[26] While some view such changes as the result of "the sheer force of economics and not cultural compassion which has been mainly responsible for the rapid increase in media coverage of East indian culture" (De La Bastide 1995), others associate it with the relationship between the Indian and African cultures in Trinidad and the Indian leaders' longtime claim of "alienation and discrimination on political, social, religious and cultural matters" (Blood 1995a).

In another series of statements, the issue of politics of representation is not discussed in relation to racial projects sanctioned by the government but rather in relation to those put into effect by agencies/agents functioning at a distance from it,[27] namely, social activists, artists, and East Indian and African elected or self-appointed community representatives.

Two such projects refer to two notorious calypso songs. By being featured in the press (as in all other public media of the time) almost exclusively in relation to the issue of the politics of representation, they received remarkable coverage. I am referring to the songs "Caribbean Unity" (1979) and "Sundar" (1995) by the calypsonian Leroy Calliste, called "Black Stalin."[28] The numerous articles on "Caribbean Unity" during the year it was first sung, and long after, all deal unmistakably with the issue of who (which population group) in this song represents the Caribbean. Dealt with in terms of ethnic representation, contributions, and pride in what constitutes "Caribbeanness," the interpretation in the press of the song along racial lines—more precisely, around the questions of African versus East Indian representation—was strategically appropriated by many individuals, as well as organizations, as an opportunity to make a stand on the issue of the racial politics pervading Trinidad and Tobago history. Whereas the song aiming to promote "Caribbean *Unity*" and called by that name ironically spurred great *dissension* in the written press and got headlines such as "Stalin Setting Unity 20 Years Back," the composition "Sundar," written sixteen years later by the same artist, was greeted unanimously as a contribution to racial harmony and unity. One article reads:

> ONE LOVE: Calypso Monarch Black Stalin is becoming a symbol of national unity even as some politicians maintain racial divisiveness. Stalin was warmly applauded after he performed at the sellout national chutney championship at Pointe-a-Pierre last weekend. He later locked arms with crossover music stars, Sundar Popo . . . and Anand Yankeran. The veteran bard won the exalted calypso title this year paying tribute to Popo. (*TnT Mirror*, 12 May 1995)

Headlines such as "Stalin Plays One for Unity" (Ali 1995) or "Victorious Calypso Monarch Stalin Hopes to Put an End to Race Talk" (Nicholson 1995) view "Sundar" as an effort and, in some instances, as the accomplishment, in itself, of a project toward racial solidarity.[29]

The preceding examples are seen as racial projects by being interpreted in the press as enacting power relations—that is, featuring (or not featuring) specific population groups. The next examples, which also left their traces in music discourses, are viewed as racial projects but this time in relation to the ways in which some musical genres, taken as indices of the population group to which they are associated, are used to depict that particular group in what is perceived by the group to be racist terms.

This is put into effect in an article on the complaint of an East Indian person about how some people confuse bhajan (a religious music) with chutney (a party-type music). This confusion, which in other times and places and for different people, could be read in many different ways, for example, as simply a misunderstanding or the result of a lack of knowledge of East Indian musical traditions, is here described as offensive by portraying Hindus as morally irresponsible, "[who could] play religious music for any festival" (Cardinez 1995). It is also being explained as the result of badly intentioned people who know better but choose not to clarify the matter in order to damage the reputation of East Indian people. The article reports the use of the following expressions to describe the implications of the (nurtured) confusion about bhajan and chutney music, "[it] presents a conflict of interest," "[it makes] people go away with the wrong idea," "we need to stop the racial conflict now." This (re)enacts, it could be argued, the fight over power through the construction/interpretation of musical indices.

The second group of statements on the politics of representation articulates what could be described as a rejection of any system of representation, classification, and ghettoization based on racial categories.

While it refers to population groups, its object does not concern population groups, but the strategies by which they are constructed, namely, as a political card to win votes.[30] The rejection of such strategies based on racial categories in this second group of statements is elaborated in many articles profiling artists acknowledged for their multicultural/multiethnic sense of belonging and for their achievements in several musical practices usually associated with an ethnic group different from their own.

One article on Jit Samaroo best illustrates how the rejection of any racial politics of representation is articulated. "Listen to the Music" (Brown 1995) describes Samaroo in the following sequence: as an East Trinidad saga boy; as a reputed steelband arranger; as a Christian (then, further, as a Presbyterian) living alongside Indian laborers, newly arrived "panyols" (people of Spanish/Latin American descent), and a few remnants of the colonial English. The artist's multiethnic/multicultural allegiance is simply depicted as the way one grew up, an outcome so natural in fact that any reference that could be construed as a conscious effort to adapt to another cultural practice would be misleading. Within this perspective, the author emphatically repeats in reference to the artist that "the racial line of enquiry [here] may illuminate less than it obscures." To confirm this, the article reports a reputed local musicologist Pat Bishop as saying: "They didn't even bother to get race conscious there. I mean, Jit didn't have to work for that sort of freedom—from racial self-consciousness—'he inherited it'" (ibid.). Samaroo himself is quoted, emphasizing that for him to be portrayed as someone who has easily adapted to the African culture because he comes from Lopino where there is "a mixture a people and the absence of conflict" is wrong—given "that 'adapt,' it seems to me now, implies too self-conscious a process" (ibid.). Before moving on to detail the talents of Samaroo as revealed in specific pieces of music, the author could be said to elaborate Samaroo's position in relation to the racial politics of representation in Trinidad and Tobago: "His music is a triumph over race, over Indianness and Blackness and Whiteness (though all are incorporated in it). The prime experience it conveys, to this listener at least, is that of a towering musical mind" (ibid.). The issue of race, we are told here, as in many other articles, is superseded by enculturation—that is, the way one grew up.[31]

REDISTRIBUTION OF RESOURCES

Sundar Popo created a whole industry of chutney songs, many, many years ago. Chutney sells more than calypso, especially abroad. Some of the biggest shows held

here in Trinidad are chutney-oriented. So many singers have paid tribute to other deserving Trinis, why can't I sing about Sundar Popo?
(Black Stalin, quoted by Denise Nicholson, "Victorious Calypso Monarch")

The third group of statements centers on the issue of economic contributions and the redistribution of resources. While this issue is less developed than the two preceding ones and is articulated in only a few articles, it seemed nevertheless important to include it here. The question is: which groups get what? This question in Trinidad and Tobago is certainly not new, but it has received new attention since the early 1980s in the context of economic hardships and a new political philosophy. Whereas in the 1960s and 1970s political campaigns hailed the sociocultural motto "One Love" for the construction of a nation, in the 1980s and 1990s they have promoted a new slogan, "Let's Share Its Richness and Beauty," to build up the economy of the country.

Some of the forces that have contributed to this new political direction include, of course, the economic crisis with the fall of oil prices in the 1980s and, along with the economic recession ever since, the noticeable increase of domestic violence. At another level, the growing emphasis worldwide on the need for cooperation, demonstrated by new trade accords (e.g. the Free Trade agreement between Canada and the United States, the North American Free Trade Agreement, the European Economic Community), has instilled, I would like to suggest, a desire for big and small countries alike—including Trinidad and Tobago—to unite forces to develop greater economic strength and better bargaining power. Some local agencies related most particularly to music practices have initiated action to help address economic issues: the setting up of the National Carnival Commission (1987) to oversee, among others, the carnival organization in relation to the tourist industry;[32] the creation in 1984 of the Copyright Organization of Trinidad and Tobago and the greater enforcement of music copyright laws over the past few years; and the organization of at least two symposia under the aegis of the NCC and the University of the West Indies to focus on, to use the title of the one held in May 1995, "Carnival—New Roads for Our Culture and Industry."

Examining the statements in music writings related to economic issues, one could interpret them to mean: "let's recognize everyone's music contributions and share the richness Trinidad and Tobago's cultural capital represents economically." The ultimate goal (or racial project) here is to recognize and promote, irrespective of creed and race, all the musical talent in Trinidad and Tobago to develop a stronger cultural and economic presence on both the local and the international music markets.[33] The focus is on collaboration, consolidation, and expansion. The numerous references to the interdependency of commercial success and cultural partnership (Blood 1995b) could be read in effect as a recommendation to everyone directly or indirectly related to the music business, to use common sense.

All the articles I reviewed in which such a stand is articulated focus unmistakably on the spectacular achievements of East Indian artists—at both the artistic and the economic levels—and celebrate the ongoing collaborations between African and East Indian artists or else plead that these continue and multiply. Wayne Bowman's article "Hot Chutney for Indian Arrival Day" (1995) best illustrates how the call for developing greater collaboration to ensure a stronger music industry and economy in general is presented as the outcome of the remarkable development of East Indian music in the public sphere. He writes:

> Over the past 15 years, local East Indian music has moved out of the "underground" to become part of the mainstream music scene. . . . East Indian music has steadily weaved its way into the very fibre of Trinidad's music industry, earning a place within almost every niche available.
>
> We all enjoy and appreciate Indian soca, Indian parang, Indian dancehall and even popular jingles advertising national newspapers.

Bowman then goes on to confirm the strong presence of East Indian music today by referring to its increased visibility in all local media, including radio and television, and its central position in the curricula of some schools of music in the country. To further "prove" that "chutney is a form that now enjoys a great degree of acceptance across the island," Bowman describes the careers of two East Indian stars who enjoy great popularity in dancehalls and at the same time praises the musical characteristics of chutney. His final conclusion is this: "The music has become part and parcel of Trinidad's heritage, let us all share in its richness and beauty." Several other articles endorse the same position and use the same terms of reference—namely, the great visibility of East Indian artists, the increasing commercial value of chutney music, and the subsequent expansion of Trinidad and Tobago's music market at home and abroad. This new market opening, the underlying rationale goes, can only be beneficial, in that it fosters greater respect and harmony between the African and East Indian population groups and, it is hoped, economic growth for all.

CONCLUSION

The examination of the production of racial projects through musical discourses in Trinidad and Tobago has been an attempt to show how the issue of race cannot be discussed in the abstract. As stated at the beginning, there can be no general theory of race since each project articulated as a racial project enacts the dynamics of a particular historical period and space; it involves specific circumstances and events, and people with varying interests, agendas, and possibilities. Not only must racial projects be carefully situated, but they must also be presented as inseparable from their inherent instability. The presentation of such projects in connection with their inherent instability and various faces allows us both to acknowledge agencies and to examine how these work to effect change—a power/knowledge (Foucault 1980) which, it is hoped, might be wisely used in future studies and practice. As Rex Nettleford has congently remarked: "We are not in the position to be racist, but not fool enough not to be race-conscious."[34]

The examination of the production of racial projects through musical discourses, I would like to argue, has demonstrated how particular social, political, economic, and gender positions on issues as sensitive as race are articulated in ways that are unique to musical discourses—whose singularity is characterized by the specific institutions to which they are connected and their distinctive traits as a social activity (Grenier 1990). Further, I would suggest, such a study shows how discourses articulating musical projects in racial terms can be best understood in light of the "politics of truth" which works to regularize the production of statements on race in Trinidad and hence accounts for their social and political efficacy.[35] Last, and perhaps most important, this study has hopefully allowed us to see how such inquiries about musical discourses can introduce possibilities and projects that are positively effective when others are not.

NOTES

I would like to acknowledge with gratitude the financial assistance of the Social Sciences and Humanities Research Council of Canada, without which this paper could not have been written. I also want to warmly thank Dennison Webster of the High Commission of Trinidad and Tobago in Ottawa and Alvin Daniell, President of the Copyright Organization of Trinidad and Tobago, for their gracious and helpful collaboration, and Line Grenier, Gordon Rohlehr, Junior E. Telfer, Thomas Turino, and Alexander Brown for their continued support and judicious advice on an earlier version of this paper.

1. Michel Foucault coined the expression "régime of truth" to explain how truth is "linked in a circular relation with systems of power which produce and sustain it, and to effects of power which it induces and which extend it" (1980: 133).

2. The term "statement" is borrowed from Foucault (1972:86–87) and is used here in the sense he describes as follows:

The statement is not the same kind of unit as the sentence, the proposition, or the speech act; it cannot be referred, therefore, to the same criteria; but neither is it the same kind of unit as a material object, with its limits and independence. In its way of being unique (neither entirely linguistic, nor exclusively material), it is indispensable if we want to say whether or not there is a sentence, proposition, or speech act; and whether the sentence is correct (or acceptable, or interpretable), whether the proposition is legitimate and well constructed, whether the speech act fulfills its requirements, and was in fact carried out. We must not seek in the statement a unit that is either long or short, strongly and weakly structured, but one that is caught up, like the others, in a logical, grammatical, locutory nexus. It is not so much one element among others, a division that can be located at a certain level of analysis, as a function that operates vertically in relation to these various units, and which enables one to say of a series of signs whether or not they are present in it. The statement is not therefore a structure (that is, a group of relations between variable elements, thus authorizing a possible infinite number of concrete models); it is a function of existence that properly belongs to signs and on the basis of which one many then decide, through analysis or intuition, whether or not they "make sense," according to what rule they follow one another or are juxtaposed, of what they are the sign, and what sort of act is carried out by their formulation (oral or written).

3. It should be noted that the economic project to which I am referring in relation to Jamaica's development of its tourist industry does not concern the music played in hotels to entertain tourists, but the systematic effort to promote soca (cf. n.17) music festivals in collaboration with the Board of Tourism and with the financial support of the government in order to improve the local economy.

4. Racial projects, it should be stressed, should not be taken as synonymous with "racist" projects. As Omi and Winant explain,

The two concepts should not be used interchangeably. We have argued that race has no fixed meaning, but is constructed and transformed sociohistorically through competing political projects, through the necessary and ineluctable link between the structural and cultural dimensions of race in the U.S. [read, in the particular context at stake]. This emphasis on projects allows us to refocus our understanding of racism as well, *for racism can now be seen as characterizing some, but not all, racial projects.* (1994: 71, emphasis added)

5. It should be noted that the terms *race* and *ethnicity* are often used interchangeably in popular parlance in Trinidad and Tobago and in academic writings

on racial issues in the country (see, for example, Vincent-Henry 1993: 29). In this case, as Omi and Winant explain, race is treated as a component of ethnicity (1994: 16).

6. On 11 October 1995, the statistics on Trinidad and Tobago's demographics concerning more specifically what is referred to as the "ethnic" profile read as follows: 40.8% African descent, 40.7% East Indian descent, 16.3% Mixed descent, 1% European descent, 1% Chinese descent and 0.2% other (from the website of TIDCO [Trinidad], at press time www.tidco.co.tt).

7. To articulate racial projects in connection with the emergence of specific stars, it should be noted, is in itself a very specific way of articulating race. In Trinidad, artists from particular musical genres as well as some specific musical practices represent privileged sites by and through which racial identity has been articulated. Any change in the ways the racial identity of these artists or these practices has usually been conceived becomes the object of public discourses.

8. For further information on the subject, see Guilbault (1997: 39–40).

9. As Thomas Turino cogently remarked, "the concept of crossover only functions in relation to a monolithic view of identity" (pers. comm., March 1995).

10. Even though their influence may not have been major in the country, it should be noted that, in spite of their relatively small number, the local white bands have had their own following in Trinidad, especially among the East Indian population. I thank Junior E. Telfer from Trinidad, a very well known figure in the music business for over forty years, for bringing this information to my attention.

11. The attempted coup led by Abu Bakr in 1990 had to do with a land claim by the Muslims in relation to a promise made more than ten years earlier by the government to grant the group a piece of land where they could erect their mosque and school—a promise that was not kept by the successor of Dr. Eric Williams, the first PNM leader, who initially made that promise, nor by the leader of the NAR, the party in power at the time of the coup.

12. It should be noted that even though she is known as "white" because of her skin color, Denyse Plummer comes in fact from mixed ancestry, from a black mother and a white father (interview, Port-of-Spain, 7 August 1993).

13. The issue of crossover in relation to Denyse Plummer, according to one author, has too often been articulated in relation to what she describes as "the petty and irrelevant concerns of race and colour" (Anyika 1991). The fact is that for Denyse Plummer the issues of race and color have been intertwined with the issue of gender. Any woman achieving some recognition in the calypso scene has been indeed seen as "crossing over" a gender-based boundary by entering a scene traditionally dominated, over the past fifty years, by male calypsonians.

14. For further information on Denyse Plummer, see Ottley 1992: 84–93. It should be noted that it was after Ottley's book went to press that Denyse Plummer won her fourth title of Calypso Queen of the World in 1992.

15. The term "chutney" is a Hindi word for "a spicy sauce that one takes with one's meals, in small quantities, to add the right taste or flavour. It is made up of small proportions of many herbs and spices ground together to form a

paste—one which adds an 'extra tinge' to the routine meal" (Dev 1995: 23). This term was coined locally for a music that has emerged from the mixture of the musical traditions associated with East Indian weddings and childbirth celebrations, which is performed historically primarily by women. Traditionally, chutney songs were sung in Hindi and accompanied by the East Indian double-headed drum called *dholak* played with bare hands, a percussion instrument called *dhantal* made of a metal stick and beaten by another small piece of metal, and the harmonium or organ. Today, chutney songs can be accompanied by harmonium (which is now often replaced by a synthesizer reproducing the sound of a harmonium), dholak, dhantal, and occasionally a brass section. Whereas the label "chutney soca" refers to musical compositions which emphasize the calypso influence in terms of vocal and instrumental lines and the use of modern instruments such as electric bass guitar, guitar, drum machine, and synthesizers, the label "chutney music" refers to compositions in which the influence of the East Indian musical traditions—including the use of traditional instruments and distinctive vocal melodic lines with characteristic ornaments—predominate. The two terms connote fast-tempo music and dancing.

16. Drupatee's success has been widely commented on not solely because of her innovative music and ethnic origin, but also, as in the case of Denyse Plummer, because she is a woman, and what is more an East Indian woman—a category traditionally conceived by the majority of the African and East Indian population in terms hardly compatible with what is associated with "the calypso scene," as will be discussed below. I want to thank Gordon Rohlehr for reminding me about this important aspect of the way Drupatee has been positioned in the calypso scene. For further information on Drupatee Ramgoonai, see Ottley 1992: 90–93.

17. Soca refers to a mixture of influences, initially including the use of East Indian rhythms, sometimes the use of tassa drums (single-headed drums played with two sticks associated with the East Indian traditions) in juxtaposition with the typical vocal and melodic lines of calypso music accompanied by its traditional brass band (the traditional brass band here contains a five-piece horn section and the other usual instruments, namely, lead/accompanying guitar, synthesizer, electric bass, drum set, conga, and often a timbale equipped with a cowbell). It is important to make a distinction between what used to be called soca in the 1970s and what has been called soca since the 1980s. Whereas Lord Shorty (later named Ras Shorty I), who has been most consistently called the father of this music, featured East Indian elements in the compositions he dubbed soca in the 1970s, other artists later continued to use the label not necessarily to indicate that they use East Indian elements but rather to indicate that their compositions embody a wide variety of influences, feature a "new" sound, and are usually played in fast tempo often associated with party music. It should be noted that the paternity of soca is contested and the definitions of the music it encompasses are also objects of controversy. Even the term "soca" receives different etymological definitions: at times, it is said to refer to the "soul of calypso" by encapsulating the two words "soul" and "calypso" in the contraction so-ca, whereas at other times, it is said that Lord Shorty coined the term by using the last and first

syllables of "calypso" (interview with Alvin Daniel, 13 August 1994). More research is needed to clarify the many questions surrounding the name.

18. It should be noted that the musical genres of chutney soca, along with soca and chutney music, all clearly indicate that musical crossover in Trinidad has been happening among both population groups, African and East Indian.

19. The term "Orisha" refers to the deities in the African Yoruba pantheon. Note that one of the principal deities in Trinidad is Shango. For more information on the subject, see Pollak-Eltz 1993.

20. "TnT" is a common abbreviation for Trinidad and Tobago.

21. This is what Vincent Alexander would call "racial anxiety" (1993: 7–8).

22. A domination which, Vincent-Henry remarks, makes a complete abstraction of the fact that many Indians are dispossessed (1993: 31).

23. The NAR was formed as a coalition of three political parties: the United Labor Front (ULF), which is strongly associated with the East Indian population group; the Democratic Action Congress (DAC), which is associated with Tobago representatives; and the Organization for National Reconstruction (ONR), which is associated with the middle-class right of center.

24. For a similar position, see also Yelvington 1992a: 11 and Vincent-Henry 1993: 29.

25. It should be stressed that what is contested here is that one race, namely, the black race, should be given the privilege over all the other races also present in the country to represent the Trinidadian nation through the nationalization of its chief representative musical instrument, the steelpan.

26. "ICN" refers to the International Communication Network, which embraces a group of companies.

27. "At a distance from it" (the government) is an expression taken from Allor and Gagnon 1994: 28 which refers to "the organized and disorganized fields of government interventions; the formations of organic intellectuals." Their definition refers to the practices and projects which, even though they are polarized by the policies and actions of the state, are related to non-governmental organizations and to people acting in their own name.

28. Many calypso songs on the issue of racial politics have been written about in numerous newspaper articles and could have been selected here. My reference to these two songs is based on the fact that not only did they win for their author the Calypso Monarch competition in the years in which they were introduced, but they were also composed by the same artist and focused respectively on black people and an East Indian artist.

29. As Junior E. Telfer pointed out to me, it is in this sense that artists rather than politicians—encumbered as they are by previous rhetorics—are often said to be leading the way in Trinidad.

30. On this issue, see Alexander 1993: 6.

31. According to Allan Harris (1995), this position is underlined by a new rationale, which moved from being embodied in discourses on nationalism and protectionism in the 1970s to those on globalism and the question of ethnicity in the 1990s—issues which, according to the author, are seemingly superseding today those of class and race.

32. It should be noted that, while the National Carnival Commission was inaugurated by the NAR government in 1987 (DeLeon 1987), the Commission was legally established by Parliament only in 1991 (Act no. 9, assented to 5 August of that year).

33. I use the expression "the" international music market in keeping with current usage in Trinidad and Tobago and in most academic discourse so far. However, I believe that this notion of *only one* international market needs to be revised. For more information on this subject, see Grenier and Guilbault 1997.

34. This observation, transcribed from my conference notes, is from a speech Nettleford gave in a round-table discussion entitled "Integrative Studies 2," at the Symposium on Black Music organized by the Black Music Research Center (Chicago), held in New Orleans in 1993.

35. This argument has been developed by Line Grenier in an article on musical discourses in Quebec which articulates issues around Free Trade, and whose words are borrowed: "I argue that music trade people's discourse on free-trade and its underlying rationale of 'cultural exemptionalism' can best be understood in light of the 'politics of truth' which works to regularize the production of statements on popular music in Quebec . . . and hence, accounts for its social and political effectivity" (Grenier 1996).

REFERENCES

Alexander, Vincent. 1993. "Empowerment of the Races and Regionalism in the Caribbean." *Caribbean Affairs* 6,2: 1–10.

Ali, Ken. 1995. "King Stalin Plays One for Unity." *TnT Mirror*, 3 March: 16–17.

Allor, Martin, and Michelle Gagnon. 1994. *L'Etat de culture: Généalogie discursive des politiques culturelles québécoises.* Montréal: GRECC.

Anyika, Dara. 1991. "Commentary: Calypso Woman." *Express* (Trinidad), 5 February.

Averill, Gage. 1994. "'Se Kreyol Nou Ye' / 'We're Creole': Musical Discourse on Haitian Identities." In *Music and Black Ethnicity: The Caribbean and South America*, ed. G. Béhague, 175–86. New Brunswick, N.J.: Transaction Publishers.

Blood, Peter Ray. 1995a. "In the Rainbow Land." *Indian Arrival Supplement*, 28 May: 50.

———. 1995b. "Cultural Partnerships Foster Harmony." *Trinidad Guardian*, 30 May: 31.

Bowman, Wayne. 1995. "Hot Chutney for Indian Arrival Day." *Sunday Guardian* (Trinidad), 28 May: 23.

Brown, Wayne, 1995. "Listen to the Music." *Trinidad Guardian*, 30 May: 29.

Cardinez, Gary. 1995. "Bindra Maharaj: No Conflict with/Pan Chutney Contest." *Sunday Punch* (Trinidad), 14 May: 31.

Cohen, Sarah. 1994. "Identity, Place and the 'Liverpool Sound.'" In *Ethnicity and Music: The Musical Construction of Place*, ed. M. Stokes, 117–34. Oxford: Berg.

Cooper, Carolyn. 1993. *Noises in the Blood: Orality, Gender and the "Vulgar" Body of Jamaican Popular Culture.* London: Macmillan.

Danny, Phoolo. 1988. "No Culture Barrier for Drupatee." *Express* (Trinidad), 7 February: 10.

De La Bastide, Peter. 1995. "'Oh, How Radio Has Changed!'" *Sunday Guardian* (Trinidad), 4 June: 9.

DeLeon, Sherrie Ann. 1987. "National Confusion Commission?" *TnT Mirror*, 28 July: 3.

Dev, Atul. 1995. "To Chutney . . . With Love and Devotion!" *Trinidad Guardian*, 30 May: 23.

Express (Trinidad). 1989. "Calypso—Indian Soca Mix Is Here to Stay." 5 February.

Foucault, Michel. 1972. "Defining the Statement." In *The Archeology of Knowledge and The Discourse on Language.* Trans. Rupert Swyer, 79–87. New York: Pantheon.

———. 1980. *Power/Knowledge: Selected Interviews and Other Writings*, ed. Colin Gordon. New York: Pantheon.

———. 1991. "Politics and the Study of Discourse." In *The Foucault Effect: Studies in Governmentality*, ed. Graham Burchell, Colin Gordon, and Peter Miller, 53–72. Chicago: University of Chicago Press.

Fox, Angela. 1990. "Jamaica Can't Touch 'We Mas' . . . But They're Ahead in Marketing." *Sunday Punch* (Trinidad), 6 May: 28.

Gilroy, Paul. 1990. "Our Nation under a Groove: The Cultural Politics of 'Race' and Racism in Britain." In *Anatomy of Racism*, ed. David Theo Goldberg, 263–82. Minneapolis: University of Minnesota Press.

Grenier, Line. 1990. "The Construction of Music as a Social Phenomenon: Implications for Deconstruction." *Canadian University Music Review*, special issue *Alternative Musicologies*, ed. John Shepherd. 10, 2: 27–47.

———. 1996. "'Cultural Exemptionalism' Revisited: The Francophonization of Quebecois Popular Music." In *Media, Culture and Free Trade: NAFTA's Impact on Cultural Industries in Canada, Mexico and the United States*, ed. E. McAnamy and K. Wilkinson. Austin: University of Texas Press.

Grenier, Line, and Jocelyne Guilbault. 1995. "Créolité and Francophonie in Music: Socio-Musical Repositionings Where It Matters." *Cultural Studies* 11, 2: 207–34.

Guilbault, Jocelyne. 1993. *Zouk: World Music in the West Indies.* Chicago: University of Chicago Press.

———. 1997. "On Interpreting World Music: A Challenge in Theory and Practice." *Popular Music* 16, 1: 31–44.

Harris, Allan. 1995. "Failure of the February Revolution." *Sunday Guardian* (Trinidad), 26 February: 12.

Hollis, Clifton. 1988. "We Need More People Like Drupatee." *Express* (Trinidad), 31 March: 10.

Joseph, Terry. 1995. "Drum Trinity in St. James." *Sunday Express* (Trinidad), 21 May: 24.

Khan, Aisha. 1992. "What Is 'a Spanish'?" Ambiguity and 'Mixed' Ethnicity in Trinidad." In Yelvington 1992b: 181–208.

Maharaj, Kathleen. 1995. "Maha Sabha Sounds Warning: Don't Deny Us Our Cultural Rights." *Express* (Trinidad), 22 May: 3.

Nicholson, Denise. 1995. "Victorious Calypso Monarch Stalin Hopes to Put an End to Race Talk." *Sunday Punch* (Trinidad), 5 March: 29.

Omi, Michael, and Howard Winant. 1994. *Racial Formation in the United States: From the 1960s to the 1990s.* New York: Routledge.

Ottley, Rudolph. 1992. *Women in Calypso, Part I.* Arima, Trinidad: By the author.

Pollak-Eltz, Angelina. 1993. "The Shango Cult and Other African Rituals in Trinidad, Grenada and Carriacou and their Possible Influences on the Spiritual Baptist Faith." *Caribbean Quarterly* 39, 3–4: 12–25.

Quevedo, Raymond (Atilla the Hun). 1983. *Atilla's Kaiso: A Short History of Trinidad Calypso.* St. Augustine, Trinidad: University of the West Indies.

Regis, Louis. 1993. "Popular Music as Communication: The Political Calypso in Trinidad and Tobago 1962–1987." M.A. thesis, University of the West Indies.

Rohlehr, Gordon. 1990. *Calypso and Society in Pre-Independence Trinidad.* Port-of-Spain, Trinidad: By the author.

Seenath, Kristine. 1992. "Rikki Shows His Motion!" *Sunday Guardian Magazine* (Trinidad) 1 March: 4.

Shepherd, John. 1988. "Towards a Musicology of Society." *Echology* 2: 101–25.

Sunday Punch (Trinidad). 1990. "Jamaican Hits Jamaican Carnival; 'Back Reggae Sunsplash Too.'" 3 June: 5.

———. 1995. "Andrew Bickramshing: Indians Jealous of Stalin, Panorama." 14 May: 14–15.

Taylor, Patrick. 1992. "Ethnicity and Social Change in Trinidadian Literature." In Yelvington 1992b: 255–75.

TnT Mirror. 1995. "One Love." 12 May.

Vincent-Henry, Andre. 1993. "Talking Race in Trinidad and Tobago: A Practical Framework." *Caribbean Affairs* 6, 2: 23–38.

Warner, Keith Q. 1992. "Ethnicity and the Contemporary Calypso." In Yelvington 1992b: 276–92.

Yelvington, Kevin Al. 1992. "Introduction: Trinidad Ethnicity." In Yelvington 1992b: 1–31.

———, ed. 1992b. *Trinidad Ethnicity.* London: Macmillan.

13

Hot Fantasies: American Modernism and the Idea of Black Rhythm

RONALD RADANO

At the turn of the twentieth century, American public culture openly embraced a radically new conception of black music that gave special emphasis to qualities of rhythm. While rhythm had always been associated with African and African-American musical performances, it now seemed to overtake other aspects, identifying what many believed to be the music's vital essence. Black music's propulsive and seductive "hot" rhythm—a term linked etymologically to forms of excess—seemed at once underdetermined and saturated with context-specific meaning.[1] As a conflation of musical and racial discourses, it brought together two primary realms of otherness: those "unspeakable things unspoken" that consumed as they were denied by modern white America (Morrison 1988). Among African-Americans, moreover, hot rhythm frequently perpetuated the same racial myths while providing a means of affirming positive identities in an egregiously racist, national environment. The primitivist orthodoxy of "natural rhythm" afforded a new sense of racial pride that was ironically reinforced by white supremacist assumptions of a bestial Negro instinct. This exalted hotness in turn supplied the creative and economic basis of an emerging urban subculture of black professional musicians, whose traditional proclivities toward performance were soon marketed as expressions of a racially inherited rhythmic gift. For better *and* worse, then, hot rhythm, in its multiple varieties, traced the meanings of African-American music across the twentieth century, from the swing sensibility of early jazz to the funk and groove of hip hop. It is precisely this facility to convey a complexity of frequently paradoxical meaning that has made hot rhythm so vital to modern American culture and, in particular, to the ontology of "black-ness" itself.

In this essay, I will offer an interpretation of hot rhythm's sociocultu-ral formation as part of the overarching development of modern Amer-ican ideologies of race. I want to argue against the prevailing view of an African-derived rhythmic impulse, not to deny the significance of Afri-can retentions, but to reveal the peculiarly American historical frame-work on which this powerful notion is grounded. As a critique of nor-mative interpretations, then, this essay provides an elaboration on Kofi Agawu's seminal study "The Invention of 'African Rhythm',," while shift-ing focus here to specifically American musical circumstances (Agawu 1995). Unlike Agawu, however, whose outline of hegemonic Western representations (in the spirit of V. Y. Mudimbe's influential *The Inven-tion of Africa*) affirms dichotomies of colonialist fictions and inacces-sible African realities, I want to observe the black rhythmic construct not as an invention so much as something part and parcel of a cross-racial American cultural experience. The idea of hot rhythm depended on the material existence of traditional African-American performance practices that were ultimately commodified as "black form" through a transnational interplay of romantic and colonialist writing. More than a minor expression within a larger historical process, these texts provided a key means of both articulating and engendering social transformations that anticipated the modern age. Accordingly, black rhythm may be seen as a patently modern construct crucial to our historical understanding. As a key trope of twentieth-century discourse, it has enabled individuals and communities to negotiate the challenges of America's racial fan-tasies and to establish a sense of place within its contested and contra-dictory terrain.

My reading of the formation of hot rhythm relies on two overlapping analytical figures that speak directly to black music's "unspeakability." The first figure, the temporal concept of *descent*, refers to the evolution-ary myth of origins, which had cast black music as a primordial cure for the ills of a civilized and increasingly mechanized modern society (Lutz 1991, Sollors 1986).[2] The classical association of musical origins and rhythm takes on special significance around this time, building on a hy-brid of mid-century romantic and slave interpretations of African-American music as a pre-discursive, "spiritual" resonance. The second figure, the spatial concept of *displacement*, explains how primal black dif-ference emerges as a racial threat. It refers above all to the fear of a mi-gratory black population entering into social, economic, and discur-sive spaces previously controlled by whites. Cast as an elusive presence exceeding the norms of harmonically oriented European musics and figured in a hybrid rhetoric that reworked "descent" modes within the frames of blackface minstrelsy and the African travelogue, black rhythmic displacement provided a compelling metaphor for an African-American populace seemingly "out of place." The mediations of black music through print, recording, and public performance exacerbated this sense of threat, as a white populace contended with a newly constructed, African diasporic "origin" now based in and seemingly overtaking the United States (Gilroy 1991, 1993).

Through descent and displacement, then, African-American hot rhythm articulated a pairing of racialized extremes, one temporally preceding and the other spatially exceeding the plain view of white common sense. What had already challenged the limits of white comprehension now threatened to remake the everyday world through a process of mediation and exchange that paradoxically amplified the discernible sound of uncivilized black absence. As a result of these racial and musical mystifications, hot rhythmic music would command enormous social and cultural power, to the point of transcending the specifics of music as such. As modernity's grand, racially sounding other, the trope of a rhythmically "hot" black music would be written across American culture, informing everyday discourses with its infecting, dark resonance.

I

References to the bodily affecting power of hot rhythm consumed the attention of reporters and readers alike with the rise of the modern era. The depictions of "coon songs" in the 1890s, for example, already suggested an impetus engendering fears of a new racial menace (Dorman 1988, Linn 1991: 50). In this grotesque extension of the minstrel stage, the Sambo figure of the mid century gave way to a prefigurative version of Richard Wright's Bigger Thomas, a razor-wielding male beast whose violence was expressed musically as propulsive rhythm.[3] With the emergence of ragtime and ragtime song, moreover, popular cross-racial genres, public enthusiasm for the new "black" sound heightened concerns that a dark terror, figured in terms of a metric difference ("syncopated rhythm"), was seducing an unsuspecting white populace. If the white versions of ragtime song were taken as positive signs of urban progress— "the perfect expression of the American city with its restless, bustling motion"—so did they communicate the worst of modernity's consequences, commonly portrayed in a xenophobic rhetoric that linked immigration, disease, and race: "infection," "epidemic," "craze" (Leonard

1985: 103, Lutz 1991, Kraut 1994).[4] Such determinations would attain a grand scale in the 1910s and 1920s, to the point of defining an entire era as "The Jazz Age."

The double logic of white public responses to black music has a historical basis in the American construction of racial difference. Once blackness had been conceptualized as a quality exterior to whiteness (yet ironically deriving from the sameness of cross-racial social experience), it would outline an oppositional relation, expressing something both desirable and threatening to (because it was simultaneously reflective of and different from) the white, civilized self. In the modern era, this double logic becomes through the effects of mass mediation more visible, more real, amplifying a conceit that extends from nineteenth-century depictions of slave authenticity. As black music circulated within an emerging economy of global popular culture, its projections of racial and musical authenticities grew in direct proportion to its repetition. Constructed as an elusive and resistant "natural force," black music epitomized the outer limits of white common understanding to define the excesses to which both blackness and modernity, in all their uncertainty, were linked. The power and "truth" of hot rhythm related above all to these qualities of intangibility and difference. As a racialized "black essence," hot rhythm arose inexorably from modernity's primordial wellspring—the American market—to project an illusory folk authenticity, what Theodor Adorno named "second nature" (Paddison 1995). Through the socially constituted "naturalness" of hot rhythm, white Americans would dance around the unspoken truths of its racial condition to engage, however obliquely and indirectly, the other realms defining a hybridized national self.

Seen this way, the idea of black rhythmic music emerges from a peculiar historical circumstance bound up with the dialectics of racial ideology in an emerging modern era. This musical concept was profoundly and intimately connected to the idea of modernity itself: it not only reflected society but infiltrated the very texture of American social existence. When J. P. Wickersham Crawford, a University of Pennsylvania professor of Romance languages and literature decried the scourge of "jazz thinking," he ascribed a musical signature to a racially determined, irrational condition that was influencing the perception and behavior of urban whites (*New York Times* 1925). When Edmund Wilson spoke of "The Jazz Problem" in *The New Republic* (1926: 217–19), he involved a metonymic relation that conflated an insidious music with an enduring social condition, commonly characterized as "the Negro Problem." References to black rhythm's "infectious" nature in an era of epidemic diseases are particularly revealing, for they focus specifically on fears of material (human) transmission through the immateriality of sound. Entrancing and seductive, hot rhythm emerged as a version of the invisible "airborne menace"—a sonic simulation of Don DeLillo's "White Noise." As a metaphor of contamination, moreover, hot rhythm concretized fears of the "immigrant menace," whose ethnic habits, genetic makeup, and characteristically "hot blood" had purportedly caused a series of epidemics around the turn of the century (Kraut 1994).[5] When cast in the discourse of prohibition, finally, this hot musical menace threatened to intoxicate multiple generations of the American populace. As one writer observed, black music would "get into the blood of some of our young folks, and I might add older folks, too." It would make white America, like the "Negroes dancing in a Harlem cabaret . . . drunk with rhythm" (*New York Times* 1922, Nelson 1934: 13).

The modern figure of hotness seemed to conflate all these qualities of excess, from drunkenness to fever to sexual promiscuity and frenzy; together, they outlined a matrix of extremes that specified the dislocations of white physical and psychological certainty. Correlations between blackness, bodily violation, and aberrant "hot sound" had already appeared by mid century, when George G. Foster described a trumpeter at the New York watering hole, Dickens's Place, whose "red-hot knitting needles spirited out . . . [to] pierce through and through your brain without remorse" (1850: 72–73).[6] By the 1910s and 1920s, fears of racial transmission through sound had overtaken other dimensions of social life. For some, hot jazz marked the moral decline of civilization, as in the "fall of jazz"; for others, the popular "rhythm" tunes of the era expressed the pulse of the machine age, giving creative voice, as in the song by Fields/McHugh, in "Futuristic Rhythm" (1929) to an ethos of speed and "pep" that defined the modern era (Tichi 1987: 232, Crawford 1993).[7] From our late twentieth-century perspective, the first decades of the modern seemed consumed with a rhythmicized blackness whose dynamic properties provided a key, causal element in the constitution of modernity. Hot rhythm may very well be, in essence, a sonic articulation of what we are, bringing into relief the profound significance of Ralph Ellison's seemingly innocuous comment that "the real secret of the game is to make life swing" ([1970] 1986: 110).

II

If the power of rhythmic hotness develops from peculiarly modern determinations of racial difference, so does it relate to prior, pre-modern (and, in the United States, typically antebellum) constructions of blackness. Among Europeans, physical differences had long served as a way of determining the category of the outsider, from Medieval specifications of Orientalism to Colonialist references to African and Pacific "savages" (Said 1978, Appiah 1985, Bohlman 1987). With the emergence of modernity and the Enlightenment, these racial features had come to signify what Hayden White calls "the interiorization of the wilderness": qualities of intuition, emotional excess, irrationality, and naturalness repressed to the point of silence in the civilized self (1978: 154). Africans in particular were commonly determined by the "wild man" figure, which reinforced emerging European assumptions of Negro inferiority. By the eighteenth century, what had merely indicated the ignorance of a culturally undeveloped people now revealed an irreversible intellectual limitation. The African, according to Hegel, was "naturally inferior . . . no ingenious manufactures amongst them, no arts, no sciences" (Pieterse 1992: 41). White Americans, moreover, embraced similarly fixed determinations, particularly as a way of justifying white racial privilege and a southern slave economy. As David Roediger (1991) observes, antebellum racial categories provided an otherwise beleaguered northern, white working class with a semblance of social privilege, associating their superiority with the fact of whiteness itself. Yet such formations of difference came at a price, distinguishing a perceived white civility from parallel constructs of an authentic, natural world. In the romantic imagination of race, what blocked "the civilized" from its primal origins was the construct of civilization itself (Fredrickson 1971, Lott 1993).

Around 1830, the American idea of "black music" emerges as both a reflection of and an informing influence on white determinations of African-American behavior. As a concept, a discernible "black music" contradicted prior assumptions about Negro creative incapacity while also affirming romantic visions of a natural "folk." Whereas eighteenth-century observers credited an otherwise barbaric African sensibility—noise makers, or "*bruite* beasts"—with an uncanny ability to imitate European musical models,[8] nineteenth-century writers introduced a new idea that attributed to the slaves inimitable, racially determined qualities of expression (Pieterse 1992: 40, Radano 1996). African-American musical practices now revealed a natural creativity that stemmed from a pre-conscious, intuitive level. If the conception of black artistic genius had little to do with rational intelligence, it nonetheless ascribed to slaves special talents increasingly thought to surpass those of the "colder race" of Anglo-Saxons ("Songs of the Blacks" 1856: 51). Later in the nineteenth century, black musical expression would become admired particularly in intellectual, artistic, and religious contexts as the new height of a sublime, romantic expression. As a matter of course, it would grow correspondingly more familiar *and* different. Toward the end of the century, its increased visibility through public performance and mass media heightened its distance from the perceived normalcy of a civilized, unemotional, and hence inauthentic white populace.

Alongside antebellum depictions of a sublime slave music were the expressed fears of a "growing evil" sometimes attributed to black music's rhythmic character (Watson 1819: 62–63). These early commentaries may be seen as anticipations of the modern dynamic of hotness cast upon a trans-cultural topos equating music with bodily danger (Rouget 1985). Jean-Jacques Rousseau's neoclassical depictions of vocal stress and strain revived Platonic notions of physicality that were commonly associated with dark-skinned foreigners. A similar sentiment appears in Herder's *Kalligone*, in which he speculates on the bodily consequences of music's rhythmic effect: "Since the tones of music are *temporal* vibrations, they animate the body, the rhythm of their expression expresses itself through its rhythm. . . . Strongly moved, natural man can not abstain from it; he expresses what he hears through appearances of his countenance, through swings of his hand, through posture and flexing" (Lippman 1985: 36). For Hegel, moreover, such "temporal vibrations" merely revealed once again the baseness of the African sensibility. The musicality of blacks, he suggested, amounted to little more than "barbarisms of a uniform rhythm [that produced] sluggishness to the point of gloom and depression" (ibid. 117). If Hegel's comments represented the normative view of black moral and creative inferiority, they also affirmed a growing relation between rhythm and expressions of excess that would appear increasingly through the nineteenth century.

One of the most compelling anticipations of modern hot rhythm appears in the body of American literary expressions that responded to escalating fears of slave rebellion. Published in the wake of the emancipation of Haiti, the Nat Turner insurrection, and the rise of abolitionism, Edgar Allen Poe's "Tale of the Rugged Mountains" (1844), a parable of a slave uprising, begins with a direct reference to rhythmic threat: "very suddenly my attention was arrested by the loud beating of a drum" (Widmer 1993). In *Benito Cereno*, moreover, Herman Melville employs the clamour of hatchets as a leitmotif to foreshadow a slave mutiny (Melville 1854). Significantly, Melville's rhythmic depictions may have subsequently informed related images in Henry Didimus's (Henry Edward Durrell) biography of Louis Moreau Gottschalk, the New Orleans pianist and composer of *Bamboula!* (a Caribbean drum). As Edward

Widmer observes, the biography "included an enraptured description of Congo Square and its 'saturnalia', with particular praise for the drummer, [who] . . . 'beat with two sticks, to a strange measure incessantly, like mad, for Hours'" (Widmer 1993).

If the formation of black musical difference specified an increasingly tangible threat, however, it remained, prior to Emancipation at least, something accommodating to white public listeners. In fact, most mid nineteenth-century representations of black music-making cast its features in ways that affirmed the norms of European musical practice. In "black music," white antebellum observers heard familiar musical qualities: qualities of melody, lyric, and harmony that together transformed a prior construct of bestial "noise" into the work-oriented object, "Negro song." The slave spirituals epitomized the best of these black songs, expressing powers of glory and uplift that called to mind Rousseau's originary voice. When rhythmic features were mentioned, they appeared typically as oddities cast along the margins of singing practices that could only be comprehended within the frames of sacred melody. Even in the more sordid imaginations of blackface, rhythmic features remained far from the center of presentation. While minstrel groups employed non-harmonic instruments (fiddle, banjo, bones, and tambourine) and, judging from published sources, featured syncopated rhythms and rhythmic playing, these elements served mainly as sidelights to a more centrally located melodic emphasis. Compared with the hot fantasies that emerged fifty years later, the rhythmic character of "De Nigger's Banjo Hum" and "De Rattle of de Bones" referred above all to the disciplining of racial difference and the containment of African-American slaves, whose hopes of "Bobolashun" (abolition) were subjected to repeated stage parodies of black on white (Gumbo Chaff 1848).[9]

III

The slave song as site of wholes and origins becomes increasingly important after the Civil War as a way of aiding the larger social program of resolution. Of all the determinations that might explain the enormous appeal of the postwar "jubilees," none is more significant than aristocratic northern culture's belief in the healing properties of black "spiritual" sound (Radano 1996). Working against the background of a similarly constructed minstrel discourse and a legacy of ecstatic revivalism (Lott 1993, Bruce 1974, Hatch 1989), white listeners commonly heard in black sacred singing the key to a national revitalization of culture. They would enact through descent into this dark musical past what Nina Silber calls "the romance of reunion" (1993). In Europe, moreover, scholars had begun their own quest for a racial reunion of sorts, one that would link modern civilization to its evolutionary origins. Interestingly, this search for origins also involved a musical aspect that was articulated in a new version of the speech/music speculations of Enlightenment thought (Thomas 1995). Seminal discussions of rhythm by British evolutionists appear to have spawned an active investigation of "primitive music" in hopes of locating a living vestige of originary musical practices. By the 1870s and 1880s, the treatises of African colonization provided these theorists with a crucial source of ethnographic data. The data, of course, were hardly pure, unmediated presentations but rather were heavily informed by discourses stemming above all from American blackface parody. Accordingly, the musical imaginations of descent, while developing from well-intentioned scientific inquiries, had been inevitably pre-cast in a pervasive and infecting transnational, minstrel rhetoric. What finally emerges as the new expression of origins in hot rhythm would reinforce these stereotypes as they paradoxically inspired performer and audience enactments of racial crossing.

In his influential essay "The Origins of Music," which appeared as part of a larger study of *Illustrations of Universal Progress* (1854), Herbert Spencer paid tribute to the place of music in European philosophical thought. While best known for postulating music as an extension of heightened speech, Spencer also theorized primitive communication as a triune of integrated, dynamic expression: "Rhythm in speech, rhythm in sound, and rhythm in motion, were in the beginning parts of the same thing, and have only in process of time become separate things. Among various primitive tribes we find them still united" (Allen 1939: 115). Charles Darwin, in his turn, reversed Spencer's formula, proposing that primal sound preceded a more advanced speech practice. As did Spencer, however, Darwin also drew from a legacy of music/speech theory that magnified rhythm's significance. Evoking historical commentaries on the libidinous habits of birds, Darwin theorized that the origins of music could be found in the musical notes and rhythms of mating rituals: in "the drumming of the snipe's tail, the tapping of the woodpecker's beak, the harsh trumpet-like cry of certain water-fowl" (Darwin 1874, chap. 13; Van Orden 1995). Significantly, Darwin's ornithological references also betrayed sympathies for prevalent racialist views around the time. As Robert Lach observed, Darwin (ibid.) compared these primordial sexual utterances with the speech patterns of "excited Negroes," exercising a minstrel figuration that was already common to American discussions of slave singing (Allen 1939: 206–7).

By the 1870s and 1880s, the idea of a dynamic, native rhythm had emerged as the informing trope of black music, representing what Thomas Seward, the official transcriber of the Fisk Jubilees, called the "first peculiarity" of a previously melodic slave practice (Marsh 1880: 122). While American field researchers pursued transcription projects that sought to capture these "peculiarities" in song, European scholars increasingly focused their attention on a new scientific exploration of musical origin, working from Hans von Bülow's famous a priori claim, "in the beginning was rhythm." Frederick Rowbotham's theory of a primordial "drum stage" (1885, chap. 1) and Karl Bücher's Marxian reading of labor extending from musical play and work songs (1896) both conceived of rhythm as a marker of human beginnings. For Willy Pastor, moreover, who theorized the soporific and hypnotic effects of "primitive" rhythms, and Richard Wallaschek, who contended that "the origins of music must be sought in a rhythmical impulse in man," the ultimate source of this primordial impulse was the unchanging sound world of black Africans (Allen 1939: 197, 225n; Wallaschek 1893: 230). Wallaschek in particular underscored this connection by beginning his highly influential global survey, *Primitive Music*, with a discussion of the African propensity for rhythmic playing. The essence of sound, once associated with pure melodic affect, now traced backward to rhythmic impulses revealing a discernibly "colored" origin.[10]

Crucial to the hyperbolic character of this emerging discourse were the aforementioned colonialist literatures that narrated Europe's conquest of Africa. In the accounts of travellers, missionaries, and military expeditions, readers encountered vivid tales of jungle darkness and danger that helped to shape the modern concept of the primitive. While a systematic comparison has yet to be undertaken, a first look suggests that these colonialist texts, composed in the face of hostile conquest and against the background of a highly popular American minstrel commentary, tended to amplify the racial caricatures showing up already in eighteenth- and early nineteenth-century accounts. What was once a vivid, descriptive language had evolved into an exaggerated racist rhetoric that stressed in mock-tragic style images of savagery, cannibalism, and noise set against the superior intellectual powers of white, masculine reason (Bogdan 1988: 106, Pakenham 1991).

Musical discussions in these sources appeared in a variety of guises, from impressionistic accounts of performance practices to detailed reviews of instrument types. Most notable, however, were the projections of racial exoticism commonly associated with drumming practices. In *The Land of Fetish* (1883), for example, A. B. Ellis offers a portrait of a

West African world laced with vivid images of war, ritual, and cannibalism: "wattle racks . . . [of] innummerable human skulls . . . sacrificed to the Ju-ju, or fetish" (117). While his references to music are initially sporadic and diverse (they begin with an overview of common instruments), the most elaborate depictions draw relations between "death drums" and the gruesome violence of human sacrifice: "screams, the most horrible, the most blood-curdling . . . the most despairing—, it made my blood run cold, [and] was repeated; and then we heard the noise of the beating of drums . . . [as] night closed upon a wild scene of madness and intoxication" (170–71). Similar references to threat carry over into otherwise innocuous musical discussions. Complaining about the annoyances of Yoruba fifes, Ellis invokes images of violence: instruments "shreiking" (269) against a "diabolical rhythm"; the "torture rapidly grew worse and worse. . . . By 10 a.m. one of our number was down with fever" (270).

The famous adventures of Henry M. Stanley (1872), whose "search for Livingstone" was recounted in regular dispatches to the *New York Herald*, were central to the emerging hot fantasies about black music. While showing little interest in the daily lives of American-born blacks, a white readership zealously consumed Stanley's depictions of an exotic world of wild animals, native warriors, and spearchucking heathens, cast in the language of blackface. In Stanley's Africa, the threat of darkness is repeatedly overcome by the superiority of white mastery. It is a world in which Anglo-Saxon masculinity reigns, as if to mourn the passing of the American slave order. Stanley portrays himself in the image of the conqueror-hero, whose command over the jungle and its natives strangely parallels projections of white supremacy in many slave narratives.[11] When he turns to music, Stanley employs figures of rhythmic threat that anticipate late-century depictions yet without engaging the sense of anxious concern that commonly informs those same depictions. In a diary entry from 12 March 1872, for example, he recalls the ritual ceremony marking the end of his visit with Livingstone by juxtaposing tools of violence—axes, spears, guns—with images of "warlike music" and the "appalling energy and thunder of the drums" (Stanley 1872: 621). These are offset by patronizing, minstrel-based references to "my braves" and the "chorus-loving children of unyamwezi" (622).

The associations between "dark Africa" and blackface minstrelsy would become increasingly common in turn-of-the-century commentaries on black music. In this new phase, references to bestiality in minstrel songs of "Cannibal Love" (1909), presentations of Dahomey drummers at the World's Columbian Exposition in Chicago, and historical accounts of bans on slave drumming (in which the absence of drums paradoxically reveals the presence of a slave threat) all contributed to the rise of public displays of black music as a kind of "Negro oddity" or excess.[12] What had come to blacken the face of a minstrelized African and to Africanize depictions of African-America ultimately cycled back into the heart of darkness, creating an escalating tautology of transnational, primitive discourse that intensified fantasies of racial encounter. By the early 1910s, moreover, homologies of blackness had commonly informed popular depictions of African and African-American musics. Behind Du Bois's image of the "rhythmic cry of the black slave" lurked the cannibal savage; beneath the surface of Henry Krehbiel's engaging depictions of African song was the trope of pathetic slave suffering that traced from Frederick Douglass's autobiographies to Du Bois's own "sorrow songs" (Du Bois 1903, Krehbiel 1914, Douglass 1845). As a hybrid discourse of primitivism grew in direct proportion to black music's appeal, Americans became consumed with a hot fantasy of racialized sound that inspired enactments of simian-like "animal dances" and celebrations of a "savage" jazz animated by "jungle rhythms."

Serving, finally, as a kind of textual "missing link" between late nineteenth- and early twentieth-century depictions was Edgar Rice Burroughs's best-selling Tarzan series, which commenced with the publication of *Tarzan of the Apes* in 1912. As Marianna Torgovnick (1990) and Gail Bederman (1995) have shown, this novel played a crucial role in the formation of the modern primitive idea, as it affirmed newer "tribal" projections of white American manhood specific to a colonialist era. Musical references appearing at a crucial moment in the novel suggest ways in which these masculinist themes could reinforce hot rhythmic desire among a schoolboy readership. In chapter 7, "The Light of Knowledge," Tarzan appears at the center of an ape ritual, the dum dum, through which he is welcomed into the tribe. The dum dum becomes a pathway toward tribal belonging, the journey that enables Tarzan to descend from (white) civilization into the black wholeness of jungle Apes. Significantly, what triggers the transference is "the noise of the drums" (61). These black jungle rhythms accompany a "fierce, mad, intoxicating revel" that unites a civilized English boy with his primordial origins and enables his re-emergence as "King of the Apes" (88).[13]

IV

Descent alone, however, does not explain why rhythm would become so centrally located in black musical experience and command such fear among the white populace. For this, we need to turn to the tangible, real-life threats that give new significance to what might otherwise be dismissed as a kind of minstrel-based comic relief. In the figure of displacement, one may observe such a musical–social correspondence. Employed here, the term refers to the profound social and racial instabilities that were constituted rhythmically toward the end of the nineteenth century. As African-Americans began increasingly to leave their homes in search of jobs, to acquire an education, or simply out of hope for a better life, they inevitably challenged the codes of black behavior that had grown ever more precarious since Emancipation. Such transgressions could only further destabilize an already tenuous racial balance in which "blackness" variously signified threats to the social order, from foreign immigrations to infectious diseases to a broadscale economic failure. African-American music seemed particularly powerful in specifying these threats. Of course European concert music had also revealed its own kind of cultural power, accorded through romantic discourses of transcendence and an orchestral tradition of composer dominance over passive listeners. Yet black music translated absolute music's aesthetic violence into more palpable forms of terror, which were fueled by the "romantic racialisms" of primal descent (Fredrickson 1971). Assuming the form of hot rhythm, modern black music would be recast as a seductive yet diabolic force whose deformations of European musical mastery embodied both the white desire of difference and white fear of Negroes "out of place." For African-Americans, moreover, hot rhythm quickly emerged as an enabling force that combined local concepts of dynamic performance with these same racial fantasies. Soon the racialist myths challenged and ultimately complicated traditional black beliefs, particularly as a migratory population informed and embraced the urban sensibilities of modern America. Echoing forth from a ghostly, dark wholeness, these elusive hot rhythms articulated a new kind of black existence, a certainty in (white) uncertainty that has since been celebrated repeatedly in literary monuments from *The Souls of Black Folk* to *The Signifying Monkey* (Du Bois 1903, Gates 1987, Radano 1995).

Knowing one's place was a cardinal rule of survival among blacks in the post-Reconstruction "New South." "Place" referred to the severe constraints on black conduct that African-Americans were expected to honor, for fear of violent white reprisal. Yet so did "place" specify more overarching limits imposed on African-American life, determining opportunities of employment, forms of public speech and manners, places of residence, and modes and range of travel. The idea of place, as James

Grossman observes (1994), was where class and racial categories intersected. "Place" provided the means of extending the commodification of black labor beyond slavery, a practice justified on racial grounds.

In place and race, then, we locate two certainties of post–Civil War Southern public culture: together they articulated a social code whose import and influence reached far into northern locales. When these certainties appeared to be transgressed, whether in real terms or not, whites lashed back swiftly and through the most heinous forms of violence, epitomized in the increased incidence of lynchings across the South from the 1880s. Even indirect challenges were disciplined, as witnessed in the escalation of organized Klan terror, which sought to contain the perceived displacements of an increasingly mobile and threatening African-American population. As blacks moved steadily from towns and rural areas to urban locales, the perception of a "New Negro" on the loose began to consume the white imagination, contradicting earlier assumptions of Sambo docility in favor of a vivid, modern incarnation of "the Negro as Beast" (Fredrickson 1971). This intensification of the theme of African-American bestiality becomes part of a larger perception of tumultuous social displacement that would characterize the modern era. In the new social climate, racial, ethnic, and political others—blacks, Irish, Italian, and Chinese immigrants, and white labor radicals—were held responsible for a broad pattern of social and economic instability, for a new and uncertain future that left the United States "standing at Armageddon" (Painter 1987).

The modern American conception of black rhythmic difference, which finally emerges around 1890, powerfully communicated the threat of displacement. Whereas the jubilees had come to express a kind of benevolent spiritual and melodic ecstasy—songs of human perfection linking civilization and barbarism, reason and intuition—hot rhythm revealed blacks' "true," monstrous nature. In "The Bully Song" (ca. 1895) popularized by May Irwin, for example, the instability of elusive rhythm signified for many whites the dangerous behavior of the urban black male, who serves as both the perpetrator and victim of razor-inflicted violence. Ragtime in particular materialized the nightmare of new Negro licenses, as displacement and public access were committed to syncopated sound. The appropriation of ragtime by white composers such as Irving Berlin may have obscured somewhat the threat of black musical displacement. Yet in the end, this new repertory of "Nigger song" could only reinforce the reality of an encroaching darkness in an America "falling prey to the collective soul of the Negro" (Leonard 1985: 107,

Hamm 1994). For many Americans, indeed, coon and ragtime songs, whether composed by whites or blacks, were capable of vast, destructive potential. Likened variously to "menace," "poison," and "Black Death," they threatened to remake American civilization in black sound (Leonard 1985: 107). "A person innoculated with the ragtime-fever is like one addicted to strange drink," moralists claimed. "It poisons the very source of your musical growth [and] eventually stagnate[s] the brain cells and wreck[s] the nervous system" (ibid.). Elusive, displaced migratory black music, named variously according to its rhythmic character as ragtime, blues, syncopated music, jazz, and swing, revealed America to be displaced—a dissed place whose center had been re-sounded as dynamic and elusive black absence.

The absence of hot rhythm epitomized the white conception of racial difference: it articulated precisely what white presence was not. As Euro-America's blackened musical other, hot rhythm signified the antithesis of civilized artistic practice. It was a dimly lit soundworld of indiscernible dynamism set apart from the harmonic norms of civilized classes. Despite the appeal of hotness, most educated white Americans still believed harmony to represent the high point of Euro-Western civilization and to be the ultimate musical sign of colonial superiority. European harmonic music identified the pinnacle of a natural, evolutionary process, having developed according to the outlines of the overtone series.[14] From "the savage, who for the first time in our world's history knocked two pieces of wood together" (Rowbotham, 1: 2) to the grand orchestrations of Beethoven, Wagner, and Brahms, the evolution of music traced in its materiality the history of human development, positioning Europe over the rest. Africans and African-Americans, in their base inferiority, had simply failed to achieve such heights: "The wild music of these people is scarcely to be brought within the regular rules of harmony" (Thomas Edward Bowdich in Southern 1983: 12); "Hottentots and Negroes . . . have readily become excellent musicians, although they do not practise in their native countries anything that we should esteem as music" (Charles Darwin in Bujic 1988: 317).

Yet according to the same racial logic, the difference of hot rhythm also revealed in its baseness the impossibility of Western completion. As a vestige of human sound prior to civilization's development, it made audible an originary sound world that had existed prior to the emergence of "music" as such. Echoing forth from its pre-civilized and accordingly pre-musical origins, hot rhythm assumed an absence that also ironically destabilized the certainty of European-based presence. Constituted as a threat that formed the basis of white desire, it became recognized and named as it also resisted the assimilationist pull of common-time categories of reason and comprehension. Hot rhythm's absence, then, was also audible, heard; and in its incommensurability, it unhinged the West's cultural logic. As one observer put it, hot rhythm was "syncopation gone mad" (Lutz 1991: 149).

To be sure, the quality of black absence was something more than the mere silence that Frantz Fanon (1952) imagines for a pan-African humanity in *Black Skin, White Masks*. It placed into relief the "noise" that had confounded eighteenth-century white comprehensions of "Negro sound," turning up the volume to produce what Ralph Ellison calls in *Invisible Man* a "poetry out of [the] invisible." Having first been constituted in the ironic discourses of slave transcendence, spirit, and freedom, black music now revealed a second, supernatural power, a "second nature" specified by late-century discourses of descent and displacement. At once invisible and beguiling, its rhythm commanded a palpable form of terror, as if the swift and silent predatory apes of Tarzan's jungle— "intoxicated with wild rhythm"—had assumed their place in modern America (Burroughs 1912, chap. 7 [1990: 61]).

Such imagined instabilities of an infecting and affecting hot rhythm suggest that the figurations of contagion were to be taken quite literally. The vast repetition of references to black music as a fever, drug, disease, and intoxicant indicate that the threat of black music related above all to fears of miscegenation, through which hot rhythm becomes a metonym of the black male body and, specifically, Negro semen or blood. According to American racism's one-drop rule, the merest hint of blackness would disgrace the sanctity of white sameness (Fields 1982). Hot rhythm proved extremely dangerous since, as a sonic force, it could make racial transferences simply through audible recognition. Over time, these infecting capacities of modern black music would grow even more powerful, "louder," as the myth of folk authenticity circulated in a highly mediated modern public culture. Hotness gave to rhythm an elusive power directly related to its mass projections of racial difference. In its elusive dynamism, one could hear a kinship of "Body and Soul," to name a famous Harlem anthem, as the noise of a previously "uncreative" people now advanced the power of blackness across America: "the greatest music born this side of the seas" (Du Bois 1903). Accordingly, hot rhythm's most famous progenitors—James Reese Europe, the bandleader, who, like the character in "The Bully Song," fell victim to a rhythm master's blade; Bessie Smith, the raucous singer of tales of violence, intoxication, and womanly sexuality; Al Jolson, the ethnically and racially hybridized "Jazz Singer"—were certainly more than mere entertainers enlivening America's popular world. They may be likened quite correctly to conjure figures whose dynamic black magic effectively resounded the countenance of a nation.

NOTES

Versions of this essay were delivered to meetings of the Society for Ethnomusicology, the Modern Language Association (Chicago, December 1995), and to the Harvard/Sorbonne conference on black music (Paris, April 1996). For their help and advice, I would like to thank Kofi Agawu, Krin Gabbard, Brian Hyer, Cristina Ruotolo, Bill Van Deburg, and Chris Waterman.

1. In the eighteenth and nineteenth centuries, hotness was commonly equated with displays of anger, passion, and sexual desire. An angry person voiced "hot words"; the lustful were "red hot" or "in heat." By the 1890s, the term had also identified positive attributes ("hot art"), together with extremes of physical display and self indulgence: hotness evoked images of violence, suffering, danger, and intoxication. See definitions and exemplifications of "hot" in *The Oxford English Dictionary* and *Dictionary of American Regional English*, vol. 2. See also Dennison 1982: 409–10.

2. Sollors uses "descent" in a more conventional, anthropological way, referring to blood lines and generations. But this usage also shares important relationships with my own.

3. For a discussion of razor images, see Gaines 1993.

4. Such associations between black music and infection appear in the 1850s, as in John Sullivan Dwight's observation that Stephen Foster's "Old Folks at Home" "breaks out now and then, like a morbid irritation of the skin" (Leonard 1985: 106).

5. In *Afro-American Folk-Songs* (1914), Henry Edward Krehbiel reports that Lafcadio Hearn proposed a study of the effects of African physiology on African American music. Hearn speculated that the vocal cords of blacks were longer than those of whites and were "capable of longer vibrations." Hearn also believed "that the blood of the African black 'has the highest human temperature known'—equal to that of the swallow—though it loses that fire in America" (39).

6. Foster also noted a similar heat emanating from another rhythm maker, the "frightful mechanical distortions of the bass-drummer as he sweats and deals his blows on every side, in all violation of the laws of rhythm (72–73)."

7. Dorothy Fields and Jimmy McHugh published "Futuristic Rhythm" in 1929. George Gershwin's "rhythm" tunes included "Fascinating Rhythm" (1924) and "I Got Rhythm" (1930). The latter soon became standard in the jazz repertory and the basis for many other tunes. Duke Ellington, with Irving Mills, published among others, "Rockin' in Rhythm" (1930) and "It Don't Mean a Thing (If It Ain't Got that Swing)" (1932). In his poem, "Lenox Avenue," Langston Hughes claimed "The rhythm of life is a jazz rhythm."

8. A nineteenth-century observation provides insight into this lingering

rhetoric of "noise." In a review of the transcription project published as *The Slave Songs of the United States* (1867), an anonymous writer remarked: "We do not believe that the negro, in his native state, knows what music is. . . . He loves music dearly, however, when he hears it, and readily appropriates a portion of it when he has been brought within its sphere. But does he ever reach excellence in it? Have not all the colored musicians we have known been of mixed blood?" *Lippincott's* (March 1868): 342. Moreover, the negation of black music as "noise" may explain Colonialists' strange silence about slave performances, which, unlike parallel performances in the dense African populations of the Caribbean, went for the most part unrecorded. For a discussion of this absence, see Epstein 1977.

9. *The Ethiopian Glee Book*, by "Gumbo Chaff." The titles appear in book 3; the reference to abolitionism appears in book 1. In *Yesterdays* (1979: 116–17), Charles Hamm discusses the emphasis on melody in minstrel song particularly in the nineteenth century. Eric Lott, in contrast, argues for a more subversive reading of the rhythmic character of minstrelsy, focusing on its early expressions. Lott suggests that white musicians had already recognized black music as rhythmic form and proceeds with an imaginative analysis that links black rhythm with Adornian notions of repetition. While it is true that minstrels emphasized nonmelodic and percussive instrumentation associated with southern slaves, and occasionally involved rhythmic ideas in the songs themselves, it is also true that the main feature of emphasis was melodic form and song form. It seems more appropriate, therefore, to observe blackface as a step in the formation of the modern discourse of black rhythm rather than as its full-blown expression (see Lott 1993: 171–95).

10. An overview of the commentaries cited in this chapter appears in Allen 1939; see also Glyn 1913. It is noteworthy that Wallaschek's views of African musical significance did not carry over to the African-American slave songs. These New World practices, he argued in his lead chapter, were merely weak imitations of white singing.

11. One striking parallel is the drawing of Stanley aiming a pistol as an African crosses a river with Stanley's supplies. The caption reads: "Look out, you drop that box, I'll shoot you" (Stanley 1872: 643). The image recalls Frederick Douglass's tale of Covey shooting a slave in the water in chapter ten of *The Narrative of the Life of Frederick Douglass, an American Slave* (1845).

12. It is no coincidence that writers at this point began to reconceptualize the history of African-American music with increasing emphasis on the drum bans to suggest an uncontainability of black essence. Rhythm becomes certifiably constituted as a threat in scholarly discourse, signifying in sonic form the seeds of inexorable black rebellion. See, for example, Krehbiel 1914.

13. Tarzan is welcomed into the tribe after having killed the "bully" who attacked his surrogate mother. He was victorious through the help of his deceased father's knife, which he had found, without knowledge of its origins, in his parents' abandoned house. As such, Tarzan embodies a unity, combining primal strength and civilized cunning—"The Light of Knowledge" that names the chapter. Only then can he descend into his dark past, finding his way through the originary light of ape drumming. Rhythmicized civilization becomes the ultimate

agent of regression, the tool by which the rational-minded, when encountering the black (w)hole, gets hot.

14. The common perception of the overtone series as a metaphor for the development of harmonic complexity was already in place by the 1920s. In his *Harmonielehre* (1922), for example, Arnold Schoenberg writes: "What today is remote can tomorrow be close at hand; it is all a matter of whether one can get closer. And the evolution of music has followed this course: it has drawn into the stock of harmonic resources more and more of the harmonic possibilities inherent in the tone" (21). Two decades later, Schoenberg recalls, "In my *Harmonielehre* I presented a theory that dissonant tones appear [historically] later among the overtones, for which reason the ear is less intimately acquainted with them" (1941: 216). I thank Brian Hyer for calling these references to my attention.

REFERENCES

Agawu, V. Kofi. 1995. "The Invention of 'African Rhythm'." *Journal of the American Musicological Society* 48: 380–95.

Allen, Warren Dwight. 1939. *Philosophies of Music History*. New York: American Book Company.

Appiah, Anthony. 1985. "The Uncompleted Argument: Du Bois and the Illusion of Race." In *"Race," Writing and Difference*, ed. Henry Louis Gates, Jr., 21–37. Chicago: University of Chicago Press.

Bederman, Gail. 1995. *Manliness and Civilization: A Cultural History of Gender and Race in the United States, 1880–1917*. Chicago: University of Chicago Press.

Bogdan, Robert. 1988. *Freak Show: Presenting Human Oddities for Amusement and Profit*. Chicago: University of Chicago Press.

Bohlman, Philip. 1987. "The European Discovery of Music in the Islamic World and the 'Non-Western' in 19th-Century Music History." *The Journal of Musicology* 5: 147–63.

Bruce, Dickson D., Jr. 1974. *And They All Sang Hallelujah: Plain-Folk Camp-Meeting Religion, 1800–1845*. Knoxville: University of Tennessee Press.

Bücher, Karl. 1896. *Arbeit und Rhythmus*. Leipzig: Teubner.

Bujic, Bojan. 1988. *Music in European Thought, 1851–1912*. Cambridge: Cambridge University Press.

Burroughs, Edgar Rice. 1912. "The Light of Knowledge," *Tarzan of the Apes*. Repr. New York: Ballantine, 1990.

Crawford, Richard. 1993. "George Gershwin's 'I Got Rhythm' (1930)." In his *The American Musical Landscape*, 213–36. Berkeley and Los Angeles: University of California Press.

Darwin, Charles, 1874. *The Descent of Man and Selection in Relation to Sex*. Chicago: Rand, McNally.

Dennison, Sam. 1982. *Scandalize My Name: Black Imagery in American Popular Music*. New York: Garland.

Dorman, James H. 1988. "Shaping the Popular Image of Post-Reconstruction

American Blacks: The 'Coon Song' Phenomenon of the Gilded Age." *American Quarterly* 40, 4: 450–71.

Douglass, Frederick. 1845. *Narrative of the Life of Frederick Douglass, an American Slave*. Ed. Benjamin Quarles. Cambridge: The Belknap Press and Harvard University Press, 1960.

Du Bois, W. E. B. 1903. *The Souls of Black Folk*. Ed. Henry Luis Gates, Jr. New York: Bantam.

Ellis, A. B. 1883. *The Land of Fetish*. London: Chapman and Hall.

Ellison, Ralph. 1970. "What American Would Be Like Without Blacks." *Going to the Territory*. New York: Vintage, 1986.

Epstein, Dena. 1977. *Sinful Tunes and Spirituals*. Urbana: University of Illinois Press.

Fanon, Frantz. 1952. "The Fact of Blackness." In his *Black Skin, White Masks*. Trans. Charles Lam Markmann. New York: Grove Weidenfeld, 1967.

Fields, Barbara. 1982. "Ideology and Race in American History." In *Region, Race, and Reconstruction: Essays in Honor of C. Vann Woodward*, ed. J. Morgan Kousser and James M. McPherson, 143–77. New York: Oxford University Press.

Foster, George G. 1850. *New York By Gas-Light*. New York: Dewitt and Davenport.

Frederickson, George. 1971. *The Black Image in the White Mind: The Debate on Afro-American Character and Destiny, 1817–1914*. Rev. ed., Middletown, Conn.: Wesleyan University Press, 1987.

Gaines, Kevin. 1993. "Assimilated Minstrelsy as Racial Uplift Ideology: James D. Corrothers's Literary Quest for Black Leadership." *American Quarterly* 45: 341–69.

Gates, Henry Louis, Jr. 1988. *The Signifying Monkey*. New York: Oxford University Press.

Gilroy, Paul. 1991. "Sounds Authentic: Black Music, Ethnicity, and the Challenge of a Changing Same." *Black Music Research Journal* 11, 2: 111–36.

———. 1993. *The Black Atlantic: Modernity and Double Consciousness*. Cambridge: Harvard University Press.

Glyn, Margaret H. 1913. *The Rhythmic Conception of Music*, 2d ed. London: Bosworth.

Grossman, James. 1994. "'Social Burden' or 'Amiable Peasantry': Race, Class and Labor Relations in Early Twentieth-Century South." Paper presented to the Department of Afro-American Studies, University of Wisconsin–Madison, spring.

Gumbo, Chaff [pseud.]. 1848. *The Ethiopian Glee Book*. "By Gumbo Chaff, A.M.A. First Banjor Player to the King of Congo." Boston: Elias Howe.

Hamm, Charles. 1979. *Yesterdays: Popular Song in America*. New York: Norton.

———. ed. 1994. *Irving Berlin: Early Songs*, vol. 1, 1907–1911. Madison, Wisc. A-R Editions (published for the American Musicological Society).

Hatch, Nathan. 1989. *The Democratization of American Christianity*. New Haven, Conn.: Yale University Press.

Kraut, Alan M. 1994. *Silent Travelers: Germs, Genes, and the 'Immigrant Menace'*. Baltimore: Johns Hopkins University Press.

Krehbiel, Henry Edward. 1914. *Afro-American Folksongs: A Study in Racial and National Music*. New York: G. Schirmer.

Leonard, Neil, 1985. "The Reactions to Ragtime." In *Ragtime: Its History, Composers, and Music*, ed. John Edward Hasse, 102–16. New York: Schirmer Books.

Linn, Karen. 1991. *That Half Barbaric Twang: The Banjo in American Popular Culture*. Urbana: University of Illinois Press.

Lippman, Edward A. 1985. *Musical Aesthetics: A Historical Reader*. New York: Pendragon Press.

Lott, Eric. 1993. *Love and Theft: Blackface Minstrelsy and Working Class Culture*. New York: Oxford University Press.

Lutz, Tom. 1991. "Curing the Blues: W. E. B. Du Bois, Fashionable Diseases, and Degraded Music," *Black Music Research Journal* 11, 2: 137–56.

Marsh, J. B. T. 1875. *The Story of the Jubilee Singers; With Their Songs*. Boston: Houghton, Mifflin, 1880.

Morrison, Toni. 1988. "Unspeakable Things Unspoken: The Afro-American Presence in American Literature." *Michigan Quarterly Review* 28, 1: 1–34.

Mudimbe, V. Y. 1988. *The Invention of Africa: Gnosis, Philosophy, and the Order of Knowledge*. London: James Currey; Bloomington: Indiana University Press.

Nelson, Stanley R. 1934. *All About Jazz*. London: Heath Cranton.

New York Times. 1922. "Wants Legislation to Stop Jazz as an Intoxicant." 12 February: 1.

———. 1925. "Decries 'Jazz Thinking.'" 15 February: 17.

Pakenham, Thomas. 1991. *The Scramble for Africa*. New York: Random House.

Paddison, Max. 1995. *Adorno's Philosophy of Music*. Cambridge: Cambridge University Press.

Painter, Nell Irvin. 1987. *Standing at Armageddon: The United States, 1877–1919*. New York: Norton.

Pieterse, Jan Nederveen. 1992. *White on Black: Images of Africa and Blacks in Western Popular Culture*. New Haven, Conn.: Yale University Press.

Radano, Ronald. 1996. "Denoting Difference: The Writing of the Slave Songs." *Critical Inquiry* 22: 506–44.

———. 1995. "Soul Texts and the Blackness of Folk." *Modernism/Modernity* 2, 1: 71–95.

Roediger, David R. 1991. *The Wages of Whiteness: Race and the Making of the American Working Class*. New York: Verso.

Rouget, Gilbert. 1985. *Music and Trance: A Theory of the Relations Between Music and Possession*. Trans. Brunhilde Biebuyck. Chicago: University of Chicago Press. French original, 1980.

Rowbotham, John Frederick. 1885. *A History of Music*. 3 vols. London: Trübner.

Said, Edward. 1978. *Orientalism*. New York: Vintage.

Schoenberg, Arnold. 1922. *Harmonielehre*, 3d ed. Trans. Roy E. Carter. Berkeley and Los Angeles: University of California Press, 1978.

———. 1941. "Composition with Twelve Tones." In *Style and Idea*, ed. Leonard

Stein. Trans. Leo Black. Berkeley and Los Angeles: University of California Press, 1975.

Silber, Nina. 1993. *The Romance of Reunion: Northerners and the South, 1865–1900.* Chapel Hill: University of North Carolina Press.

Sollors, Werner. 1986. *Beyond Ethnicity: Consent and Descent in American Culture.* New York: Oxford University Press.

"Songs of the Blacks." 1856. In *The Negro and His Folklore,* ed. Bruce Jackson, 51–54. Austin: University of Texas Press, 1967.

Southern, Eileen, ed. 1983. *Readings in Black American Music,* 2d ed. New York: Norton.

Spencer, Herbert. 1862. "The Rhythm of Motion." In *First Principles* ("Synthetic Philosophy"), 4th ed., 259–81. New York: Appelton, 1898.

———. 1854. *Illustrations of Universal Progress: A Series of Discussions.* New York: Appleton.

Stanley, Henry M. 1872. *How I Found Livingstone: Travels, Adventures and Discoveries in Central Africa.* Repr. New York: Arno, 1970.

Thomas, Downing A. 1995. *Music and the Origins of Language: Theories from the French Enlightenment.* Cambridge: Cambridge University Press.

Tichi, Cecilia. 1987. *Shifting Gears: Technology, Literature, Culture in Modernist America.* Chapel Hill: University of North Carolina Press.

Torgovnick, Marianna. 1990. *Gone Primitive.* Chicago: University of Chicago Press.

Van Orden, Kate. 1995. "Sexual Discourse in the Parisian Chanson: A Libidinous Aviary." *Journal of the American Musicological Society* 48: 1–41.

Wallaschek, Richard. 1893. *Primitive Music: An Inquiry into the Origin and Development of the Music, Songs, Instruments, Dances, and Pantomimes of Savage Races.* London: Longman's.

Watson, John F. 1819. From *Methodist Error.* In *Readings in Black American Music,* 2d ed., ed. Eileen Southern, 62–64. New York: Norton, 1983.

White, Hayden. 1978. "The Forms of Wildness: Archeology of an Idea." In his *Tropics of Discourse,* 150–82. Baltimore: Johns Hopkins University Press.

Widmer, Edward, 1993. "African American Percussion in the Twentieth Century." Paper delivered at the annual meeting of the American Studies Association, Boston.

Wilson, Edmund. 1926. "The Jazz Problem." *The New Republic,* 13 January: 217–19.

PART IV

History/Modernism

14

Alban Berg, the Jews, and
the Anxiety of Genius

SANDER L. GILMAN

THEME: GEORG BÜCHNER

Are Jews truly "smarter" than everyone else? The problem of Vienna continues to haunt the representation of Jewish superior intelligence in high culture into the twentieth century. The negative ramifications of a Jewish superior creativity echo in complex ways through the culture of early twentieth-century modernism. In the most widely respected "modern" opera, Alban Berg's *Wozzeck*, we can examine the meaning of "intelligence" (and "virtue") and its opposite, "irrationality" (and "vice"), in light of the meanings attributed to them by nineteenth- and early twentieth-century German culture. Here I want to examine three intertwined problems in the representation of intelligence and the body in nineteenth- and early twentieth-century German culture: (1) the role of medicine in shaping the plot and ideology of Büchner's play *Woyzeck*, which was written in 1836, the year before Büchner's death; (2) how qualities associated with the idea of Jewish superior intelligence in the nineteenth century helped shape the Jewish writer and editor Karl Emil Franzos's interest in rescuing this play and publishing it for the first time in 1878; and (3) what Alban Berg made out of this aspect of the play and its reception, so central to its reading, when he set it to music between 1914 and 1925 in his opera *Wozzeck*.

I will begin, however, not at all with "smart Jews" but with "irrational Germans." My author, Georg Büchner (1813–1837), the author of the drama *Woyzeck*, was a German physician and a revolutionary. Now today, at least, this is a rather unusual pairing. Büchner was an active revolutionary, circulating broadsheets calling for a radical change in the government of his time, as well as being involved in the day-to-day reality of revolutionary culture in Hesse as the co-founder of the "League for Human Rights" in Giessen. For him the revolution concerned the need for oppressed peoples to be provided with the means to change their lives. A student of medicine in Giessen, and after his betrayal there as a revolutionary, in Strasbourg, he was also a figure caught between two models of understanding medicine: as a scientific undertaking rooted in research, and as a means of ameliorating suffering, a higher calling rooted in a complex romantic metaphysics.

Part of that rebellion is reflected in Büchner's very mode of argument in the original draft of his call for popular revolution, "The Hessian Reporter" (1834). This text employed detailed statistical argument to support the revolution.[1] Such argument was already part of the armament of early nineteenth-century German medical thought, not in terms of treatment but in terms of the beginnings of a German scientific medical thought. Following medical school, Büchner became an instructor at the University of Zurich, where he died in 1837. There is a link between Büchner's understanding of medicine and his revolutionary philosophy as inscribed in *Woyzeck*.[2] For the very roots of the drama lie in the question of the protagonist's diminished capacity.

Perhaps the place to begin is with the "real," i.e., historical, Woyzeck and his trial (with an eye on the other trials that may have contributed to the plot, such as those of Daniel Schmolling and Johann Dieß, whose corpse Büchner probably dissected as a medical student). Johann Christian Woyzeck, an unemployed wigmaker/barber and former soldier, killed his mistress, the widow of the surgeon Woost, on June 21, 1821. He was immediately arrested and admitted his guilt. Because of an appeal by his defense attorney, his mental status was examined, as the attorney hoped to document Woyzeck's diminished capacity and thereby to mitigate his sentence. This mental status examination was undertaken by the well-known physician Johann Christian August Clarus, whose published report formed the basis for Büchner's play. Büchner's version of Clarus's account of the crime virtually reversed Clarus's findings. For Büchner, Woyzeck's madness was the direct result of the power structures that deformed and destroyed Woyzeck's life. Central to these was the institution of the new scientific medicine.

In his published report, Clarus claimed that the new scientific medicine eliminated the impressionistic responses of coroner's juries and allowed the pure, objective truth of science to dominate.[3] Indeed, Clarus's report is representative of the high medical science of Büchner's day—and Büchner found it a source of true amusement. Clarus used every possible means of diagnosis from an analysis of the physiognomy of the murderer to his elevated pulse when asked questions (504). It is the physiognomy of the murderer that links Clarus's epistemology to that of the new science of seeing the insane.[4] It is an approach followed by his fellow physician Henke, whose evaluation of Woyzeck, undertaken on September 12, 1821, relies on virtually nothing but an analysis of the "normal" physiognomy of the murderer (546). In the play Büchner dismisses such an approach as "beastiognomy" (32). It is not the way a person appears that reflects his or her inner state. Such views had been a quiet but persistent result of Enlightenment skepticism since Lichtenberg's dismissal of physiognomy because of its links to irrationality and "subjective" modes of interpretation.

For the core of his mental status examination, however, Clarus relied on the standard notion of early nineteenth-century psychiatry that the patient's "speech and answers" revealed that he was "bad" rather than "mad" (491). Clarus used a form of what comes to be labeled the M'Naughten rule in Great Britain at mid-century—he claims that Woyzeck, even though he is morally ill, is sane as he can articulate the difference between "right" and "wrong." Woyzeck's admission of guilt showed that he could tell "right" from "wrong," and thus Clarus claimed that he was sane in medical terms. Later physicians who examined Woyzeck in prison, such as Carl Moritz Marc, argued that he was insane, as he began to have hallucinations in prison and claimed that he was the victim of a plot by Freemasons.[5] Büchner employed aspects of these later visions to place Woyzeck's sanity into question before and during the murder. For Büchner it is clear that Woyzeck had been driven mad by the social forces amassed against him. The real Johann Christian Woyzeck was executed by beheading on August 27, 1824, rather than committing suicide in his madness as he does at the conclusion of Büchner's play.

The question of Woyzeck's irrationality stands at the very center of Büchner's play and its claim for a revolutionary reading of society. Was Woyzeck mad, and if so, what drove him to madness? Certainly, one central aspect of the play is the social tension between the powers of the dominant classes in the drama, represented by the Drum Major, the Captain and the Doctor, and the underclasses. Woyzeck is exploited by all of them: the Drum Major, who seduces his mistress, Marie; the Captain, who uses him for menial tasks and mocks him; and the Doctor, who turns him into a human guinea pig. But the forces that are depicted most clearly as the most destructive are those of the institution of medicine, an area that Büchner knew so very well. Indeed, it is the essence "of Büchner in the scene between the Doctor and Woyzeck," as a reviewer of the first performance of the drama commented.[6] His brother, the philosopher Ludwig Büchner, had acknowledged that "it was only the study of medicine that had led Georg into such 'wayward paths'" of revolutionary activity.[7] And thus medicine and the idea of representing the person driven to irrationality colors the entire drama in very specific ways.

Büchner even portrayed the military life, with all its sexual exploitation, its abuse of power, and its betrayal of the individual, as relatively benign or at least somewhat human and self-questioning in comparison to the world of medicine. Büchner's Drum Major is the embodiment of an unselfconscious sexuality, and his Captain represents an odd, self-reflexive awareness of possessing power. Only the Doctor sees Woyzeck simply as a means to his scientific ends. Peter Gay agrees that "Georg Büchner's callous military physician in *Woyzeck* saw patients as interesting guinea pigs."[8] It seems to be true that Büchner used the figure of one of his former professors, the Giessen anatomist and physiologist Wilbrandt, to shape the figure of the Doctor. But Wilbrandt, whatever the reality of his attitude toward his craft, was part of a new revolution beginning to take shape at the University in Giessen. One must also remember that Justus Liebig was about to set up Germany's first chemical laboratory in Giessen when Büchner was a student.[9] The world of the new science of medicine was appearing in Germany, with some startling results over the next three-quarters of a century. It was a science that stressed materiality rather than spirit; it would become the basis for "scientific" medicine rather than "romantic" medicine.

The Doctor uses Woyzeck solely as a human guinea pig, testing his theories of diet on him. He has him eating peas for a year and measures the resulting increase in urea in his urine. There seems to be no reason to treat Woyzeck as a human being, given his position in society. The Doctor sees in him an intermediary stage between man and beast:

> Take note of this man [he says to his medical students]—for a quarter of a year he hasn't eaten anything but peas. Feel how uneven his pulse is. There—and the yes. . . . Apropos, Woyzeck, wiggle your ears for the gentlemen. I meant to show it to you before. He uses two muscles. . . . This, gentlemen, represents a transition to the donkey, frequently resulting from being brought up by women and from the use of the mother tongue. How much hair has your mother pulled out for a tender memory? It's gotten very thin in the last few days. Yes, the peas, gentlemen. (49)

For the Doctor, so it seems, Woyzeck is "degenerate half-human," which is Clarus's label in the published account of the case of Woyzeck for those who revel in public executions (488). Büchner picks up this oblique reference in his account, using the "prehensile" muscle of the human ear as a sign of the degeneracy of the working classes, a sign of physical degeneracy that Karl Marx will document in much greater detail decades later in *Das Kapital*. But according to Marx, such degeneration is the result not of inheritance, but of the exploitation of the working classes, especially children. It is important to note that here Büchner substantially antedates the first widely read accounts of degeneracy theory. The Doctor, too, sees the degeneracy of Woyzeck exacerbated by his context, but rooted in his biological inheritance. For him it is Woyzeck's feminization and his lack of *Bildung* (education), i.e., he can speak only German and not Latin, that proves his primitive state and the failing of virtue. But of interest as a marker of degeneration is also his loss of hair, a loss that the Doctor sees as one of the signs of the efficacy of his dietary experiment.

Woyzeck is little better than the animal show in the first draft of the play. The horse, like Clever Hans, responds to the questions of the announcer: "Show your talent! . . . Is there in the learned *société* an ass. (The horse shakes its head.) . . . That is beastiognomy. Yes, that is no dumb animal, that's a person! A human being, a beastly human being, but still an animal, *une bête*. (The horse behaves improperly). That's right, put *société* to shame" (59). The horse's improper act, one presumes his defecating on the stage, introduces us to another public act of shame, one which will serve to characterize the signs and symptoms resulting from the Doctor's experiment. For the signs of civic virtue, the signs of being truly civilized, are as lacking in Woyzeck as in the horse.

For Woyzeck is animal-like in not showing shame, or at least in committing acts that are shameful. "Behaving improperly" is one of the two further signs of the efficacy of the Doctor's experiment on Woyzeck. Woyzeck is unable to hold his urine:

> DOCTOR: I saw it, Woyzeck. You pissed on the street, you pissed on the wall like a dog. And you get two cents a day. Woyzeck, that's bad. The world's getting bad, very bad.
>
> WOYZECK: But Doctor, the call of nature . . .
>
> DOCTOR: The call of nature, the call of nature! Nature! Haven't I proved that the *musculus constrictor vesicae* is subject to the will? Nature! Woyzeck, man is free. In man alone is individuality exalted to freedom. Couldn't hold in it! *(Shakes his head, puts his hands behind his back, and paces back and forth.)* Did you eat your peas already, Woyzeck? I'm revolutionizing science, I'll blow it sky-high. Urea ten percent,

ammonium chloride, hyperoxidic. Woyzeck, try pissing again. Go in
there and try.

WOYZECK: I can't, Doctor.

DOCTOR *(with emotion):* But pissing on the wall! (38)

"Freedom," one of the concepts that marked the French Revolution, is
here given a purely biological context. Woyzeck is "free" to control his
bladder, but, of course, the intervention of science has made this impossible and has reduced him to below the level of the rational human
being. Woyzeck has reverted to type. Büchner's initial draft of this scene
makes the relationship between the act of urination and the Doctor's
science even more explicit:

DOCTOR: I saw it, Woyzeck. You pissed on the street like a dog. For that
I give you three cents and board every day? The world's getting bad,
very bad, bad I say. Oh! Woyzeck, that's bad.

WOYZECK: But Doctor, when you can't help it?

DOCTOR: Can't help it, can't help it. Superstition, horrible superstition!
Haven't I proved that the *musculus constrictor vesicae* is subject to the
will? Woyzeck, man is free. In man individuality is exalted to freedom.
Couldn't hold it in! That's cheating, Woyzeck. Did you eat your peas
already, nothing but legumes, *cruciferae*—remember that. Then next
week we'll start on the mutton. Don't you have to go to the toilet? Go
ahead, I'm telling you to. I'm revolutionizing science. A revolution!
According to yesterday's report: ten percent urea, and ammonium
chloride . . . But I saw how you pissed on the wall! . . . But pissing
against the wall! I saw it. (71)

The Doctor's experiment is not merely to feed Woyzeck peas and measure the contents of his urine, urine that Woyzeck cannot seem to hold,
but also to change his diet to add mutton within the week.

Before we go on to discuss the structure of the Doctor's experiment
with Woyzeck, the second sign and symptom of Woyzeck's reaction to
his monotonous diet of peas must be mentioned. It is Woyzeck's madness. Büchner introduces it in a discussion of the difficulty that Woyzeck
has in interpreting natural signs, through a comment by Woyzeck that
is taken by the Doctor as a sign of his deteriorating mental state. The
Doctor is delighted by this, as he seems to have expected it. Büchner has
Woyzeck comment on the hidden meaning of the circle of mushrooms,
the fairy circle, with all its folkloric associations as a sign of the derail-
ment of his thoughts:

WOYZECK (*puts his finger to his nose*): The toadstools, Doctor. There—
that's where it is. Have you seen how they grow in patterns? If someone could read that.

DOCTOR: Woyzeck, you've got a marvelous *aberratio mentalis partialis*,
second species, beautifully developed. Woyzeck, you're getting a raise.
Second species: fixed idea with a generally rational condition. You're
doing everything as usual? Shaving your captain?

WOYZECK: Yes, Sir.

DOCTOR: Eating your peas? (39)

A variant from the first draft makes the madness of the exchange (as seen
from the standpoints of both the audience and the Doctor) more evident:

WOYZECK (*stands rigidly*): Have you seen the rings of toadstools on the
ground yet? Long line, crooked circles, figures. That's where it is!
There! If only someone could read that. When the sun's standing high
and bright at noon and the world seems to be going up in flames. Don't
you hear anything? I think then when the world talks, you see, the long
lines, and it's like someone talking with a terrible voice.

DOCTOR: Woyzeck! You're going to the insane asylum. You've got a
beautiful fixed idea, a marvelous alienation *mentis*. Look at me. Now
what are you supposed to do? Eat your peas . . . (74)

Woyzeck suffers from a specific, localized madness, a madness limited to
one of his faculties. He can follow the Captain's orders as well as those
of the Doctor. He is mad, which is Büchner's if not Clarus's point, but
it is an induced madness that exacerbates his betrayal by his lover Marie.

For Büchner, Woyzeck has been driven made by the society in which
he dwells and the science by which he is controlled. But if Woyzeck is
mad in only one of his faculties or not mad at all, as the various doctors,
real and fictive, claim, there is a moment in Büchner's play that tests
Woyzeck's competence. It is the moment where Büchner illustrates the
difference between knowing right from wrong (i.e., sanity in the legal
sense) and his image of madness caused by societal forces. This comes in
the scene when he purchases the knife with which he will eventually kill
Marie. At that moment the murder is premeditated and Woyzeck's madness is not evident. He goes to the shop of the Jew who sells him a knife
for two pennies. Woyzeck cannot afford a gun, but is quite "rational" in
his choice of a knife: "That can cut more than just bread" (46). Now the
Jew's last line in this short scene is striking. Woyzeck has not haggled,
has paid the two cents asked for, and the Jew shakes his head in disbelief:

"There! Like it was nothing. But it's money! The dog" (46). Does this scene show conscious planned intent? Does Woyzeck know the difference between right and wrong? And what about the Jew? Is his love of money "natural" or is it "learned"? Is he "morally mad" because he defines the entire world in terms of its material value? Does this scene place the Jew among the victimizers who do likewise (such as the Doctor) or among the victims of such materialism (such as Woyzeck)? Is the Jew an analogous figure to Woyzeck or an example of the forces that exploit the working class? These questions cannot be answered in reference to this single scene. But there is a variant that is most revealing.

In a draft scene, Marie, Woyzeck's mistress in the drama, comments to her friend Margaret, who is quite aware that Marie's eyes are on the Drum Major: "Why don't you take your eyes to the Jew and have them polished—maybe they'll shine enough to sell as two buttons" (68). The Jew's materialism, in reducing the woman's eyes to a commodity, is indeed here paralleled to that of the Doctor who deals with humans as body parts. Never spelled out in Büchner's text, written during the first generation of the political emancipation of the Jews in Büchner's Hesse, it constitutes a commonplace of that era concerning Jews and the material world. Its most evident statement is in Karl Marx's notorious "On the Jewish Question" of 1844. But such a view of the Jew does leave us with a series of questions about what constitutes "free will" in Büchner's world. Here the forces that shape the definition of madness are the forces of the world. The Jew is amazed by Woyzeck's lack of response to the "natural" order of haggling (according to Marx the natural language of the Jew).[10] The Jew, like the Doctor, is part of the system and reflects the limitations that the system of exploitation imposes on all its members. For Büchner, Woyzeck's madness is evident in this scene only if the Jew's world view is taken as the baseline of the normal—and that would itself be mad.

One might note that Büchner does not free the Doctor from the madness that he attributes to Woyzeck's seeming mad desire to understand the meaning of the mushroom's magic circles. For the Doctor has found the visual pattern that makes sense of the world that eludes Woyzeck. The visual semiotics of medical science leads to the analysis of illness based on the visual association of signs and symptoms. This the Doctor does with Woyzeck's signs and symptoms and with many of the people he sees as he walks through the village. Büchner has his Doctor serve as a satire on the rampant use of physiognomy (or "beastiognomy") in contemporary medicine. The interpretation of what is seen, of the signs and symptoms of illness, as Clarus stated in his evaluation of Woyzeck, becomes a sign of the new scientific positivism. Büchner has his Doctor use this technique over and over again as a means of disqualifying him as a caring physician. He looks at the Captain and says: "Bloated, fat, thick neck, apoplectic constitution. Yes, Captain, you might be stricken by an *apoplexia cerebralis*" (40). On the street he sees a woman walking whom he immediately reduces to a classroom specimen: "She'll be dead in four weeks, via a *coronar congestionis*. She's in her seventh month—I've had twenty patients like that already. . . . In four weeks the stupid beast. She'll make an interesting preparation . . ." (75). Like Clarus's taking of Woyzeck's pulse, like the Doctor's experiment, the interpretation of signs and symptoms is not simply a sign of early nineteenth-century medical quackery. For the semiotics of disease, from Hippocrates to the present, play a real role in distinguishing the source and form of an illness in the Western tradition. And this is the central problem of Büchner's anger at "scientific" medicine—even though he dislikes it, it is and will become the most important contribution of German medicine to the improvement of the health and welfare of each individual member of society.

Now all the parodies of medicine and its world in Büchner's drama point to the destructive and divisive nature of the medical world view. Büchner's attack on the science of medicine is cast in a rather interesting light once one realizes that his parodied Doctor is seeking after the cause of one of the more recent disease entities to have been described, about the time Büchner's father, Ernst, would have been in medical school. It was first described in the medical literature by François Thiérry, who published an account of a new disease to be found in Spain in 1755. Its symptoms were marked as ugly alteration of the skin, a loss of hair, and, to quote a contemporary account, "a maniacal melancholia" or, to use our contemporary labels, "depression, irritability, anxiety, confusion, disorientation, delusions, and hallucinations." Another symptom was pronounced diarrhea. The disease received its popular name only when the first cases were found in Italy later in the eighteenth century: pellagra.[11] It is a niacin deficiency disease (or inability to convert tryptophan to niacin) and was understood as early as Thiérry as a disease of poverty. It was caused by the corn meal eaten as the staple food, with little meat or milk available to provide protein. Théophile Roussel writing in 1845 said the "predisposing cause" for the disease was too little animal substances. Indeed it is protein deficiency that is the basis for the disease. Büchner's Doctor attempts to evoke the disease with many of its attendant symptoms, such as loss of hair, madness, and persistent, constant urination (instead of diarrhea). However, Büchner has him feed Woyzeck on a diet of peas to cause this mock pellagra. But peas, as

Büchner could not have known, contain protein (if incomplete protein) as well as vitamins A and C. The mutton that was to be added to Woyzeck's diet would indeed have served as a "cure" for this phantom "pellagra," but the Doctor's regimen of peas would have not caused it. One can note that it was only in the 1920s that Joseph Goldberger induced scrotal dermatitis in convicts (rather than army volunteers) by having them eat only corn. With this experiment it was shown that pellagra was a vitamin deficiency disease and could be avoided and treated through adequate diet.[12]

Büchner's attack on the new scientific medicine is based on the charge that it is uncaring and destructive. Yet the type of experiment that Büchner's "mad" Doctor undertook was quite in line with the medical research practices of Büchner's day. One might add that the materialism of Büchner's medical world led to the laboratory science of the mid and late nineteenth century with its spectacular breakthrough in the treatment of a wide range of diseases, including the typhus from which Büchner was to die. Büchner was, if his scientific writing was any guide, firmly in the camp of the materialists. He wrote about the nervous systems of fish and of human beings. In his work he attempted to understand how the complex neurological structures of the individual determined the limitations of action and response. The "science" of the doctor's medicine is very much in line with the science of Büchner's own training and indeed, his own reading of the meaning of the body in his essays on nerves and their functions. Yet he dismisses this medicine as an exploitative social institution that was only concerned with self-aggrandizement. Büchner's Doctor is the antithesis of Francis Bacon's *buccinator novi temporis*—the trumpeter of the new era—he is rather a scientific buccaneer, living off the rewards of the revolution in science, a revolution that benefits him but not his "victims." The Doctor, in *Woyzeck*, does not care for his patients but rather sees them as subjects for scientific inquiry. It is this reduction of the complexity of the human being to the stuff of chemicals, fats, and drives that Büchner rejects; but also the clear improvements to the actual treatment of human beings for catastrophic ailments whose potential was evident even at the beginnings of the nineteenth century.

DEVELOPMENT: KARL EMIL FRANZOS

Büchner's *Woyzeck* was never published by its author. The young physician died in 1837 of typhus (and the doctors, specifically his colleagues at the medical school in Zurich, were of little help), and his few published texts give him the tiniest of footnotes in the emerging literary histories of the new Germany. Indeed, he comes to be known as the "most obscure of all German writers."[13] A volume of Georg Büchner's "posthumous works" was published by his brother Ludwig in 1850. And it is this brother who comes to be *the* Büchner for the rest of the century. This radical difference of the reputations of the two brothers maintained itself until at least 1915, when Rainier Maria Rilke wrote explaining that Georg was the "dead brother of the better known Ludwig Büchner."[14] Georg comes to be read through the lens of his brother's reputation and image.

Ludwig Büchner, like Georg a physician, became the icon of radical materialism at the close of the nineteenth century. His early work, especially his *Force and Matter* (1855), one of the flagship books of German materialism, had gotten him dismissed from the faculty of the University of Tübingen in 1852 as too radical and anti-religious. While he was also the executor of his brother's literary estate, his role in late nineteenth-century intellectual life was precisely as one whose radical rereading of social relationships was in the light of their material basis. One of the leading nineteenth-century monists, Büchner was also a political liberal. This can be seen especially in his reading of the meaning of anti-Semitism at the turn of the century. Ludwig Büchner's view was that Jews were neither better nor worse than other peoples, but that the system of capitalism had forced the Jews into exploitative professions. If they were not present, he states, non-Jews would (and often did) fill the gap. Yet he also condemns the Jews for maintaining their "odd and ancient ritual practices" as well as their self-imposed "separation from society." The Jews, however, do possess superior intelligence. Büchner saw the Jew's *Klugheit* as a learned response to their environment and claimed that they have always been a people with a desire for risky undertakings and the "drive for creativity."[15] Büchner's assimilationist model dominated German liberalism at the turn of the century. It argues that Jewish difference, especially Jews' preeminence in the realm of culture, was part of their nature yet was sharpened by their persecution. Such a view came to be strongly supported by the first editor of *Woyzeck*, Karl Emil Franzos (1848–1904).[16]

Georg Büchner's published work, specifically *Danton's Death*, had been discovered in 1867 by the young Eastern European Jewish intellectual Karl Emil Franzos, who was living in the outer reaches of the Austro-Hungarian Empire, in the Bukovina. Franzos published some forty essays on Büchner in his lifetime, but his initial publications came in the 1870s, at the very beginning of the expansion of German anti-Semitism. Franzos, himself the son of a German-speaking, highly acculturated

Jewish physician, was the author of *From Asia Minor* (1876) and most importantly, *The Jews of Barnow* (1877). These works were banned by the Austrian government, which saw them as revolutionary in their depiction of the poverty and ignorance of the Eastern Provinces. What Franzos advocated was the complete acculturation of the Eastern Jews into a German-speaking, Western society.

Central to Franzos's texts written about the Jews in the East during the period in which he was excavating Büchner's *Woyzeck* is his understanding of Jewish superior intelligence. Here we must add—his understanding of it within the perimeters of the Viennese belief in the intelligence of the Jews. For Franzos moved from the outer reaches of the Austro-Hungarian Empire to Vienna and Berlin. He brought with him the rather typical attitude of acculturated Jews in the East to the world of the *Ostjude*—an image, by the way, rather the antithesis of Zborowski and Herzog's some eighty years later. He was, as a contemporary critic notes, more a Jewish German than a German Jew.[17] Whether in Vienna, his first stop in the West, or in Berlin, he defined himself within the strict limits of German culture, in terms of the ideal of *Bildung*. It was an image of creativity that underlined the destructive and pernicious effects of Jewish culture on Jewish superior intelligence and its creation of a false intelligence marked on the body. His intelligent Jew was indeed *Woyzeck*—the individual whose potential, body, and mind is destroyed by the social institutions that have control over him.

Such arguments can be found throughout Franzos's writing. Let me use one text as a proof text for his attitude toward Jewish superior intelligence. In the continuation of the "ethnographic" writing *From Asia Minor* in the 1880s, Franzos presented a study of "Child prodigies in the Ghetto."[18] This literally undertakes to study a series of cases of child prodigies and presents them to us in mock-ethnographic form. One of these studies is more elaborate and serves as the centerpiece to his representation of Jewish superior intelligence. He begins with Moriz Frankel, a mathematical genius, who is able even as a small child to do complicated sums in his head. This gift is exploited and Frankel is turned into a sideshow attraction for the financial benefit of his parents. Once he outgrew his prodigy status he vanished from public interest. It is not trivial to note that Franzos begins this tale of the young Frankel, published in 1882, in 1879, at the time when he was working on Büchner. Franzos sees Frankel as typical of the difficult transition of a Jewish superior intelligence from the "orthodox, talmudic tradition" to the "denationalized Jew" of the West (29). The world of "mathematics" is at least secular, even if the mindset that exploits the child's gift is "talmudic."

The centerpiece of Franzos' account of Jewish superior intelligence is his visit with a number of local skeptics to the home of a not-quite-five-year-old prodigy, Ruben Grüner, in "Barnow," his pseudonymous town in Galicia. The child is "ugly and pale" (31). By two he knows all of his prayers in Hebrew and can even read the language. By five he is a wonder, at least in this little town. He is seen by the "educated" in the town as a "sad figure, the living proof of what horrible training (*Dressur*) can do to a gifted child at the costs of his health and length of life" (33). The child is produced for the skeptical visitors and shows off his abilities—he has memorized the Torah and the commentaries and can answer complicated questions, such as why God listened to Balaam's curse. His intelligence is indeed rote learning and his "rationality" is merely the repetition of existing knowledge. The child appears "deathly pale and tortured" to the narrator and looks like he will not survive to the next summer. In that winter the child dies of a high fever (47).

The result of the talmudic training of his mind is his physical death. But indeed, his spirit had been long dead, as Franzos had showed. Franzos speculates that the "incomparable material," the Jewish superior intelligence of these children, would have been otherwise better used in Berlin or Vienna—and to a greater reward (48)! Franzos's third child prodigy is a young man with "pale, sharply profiled face" who aspires to become a magician and watches the "miracle rabbis" and learns all their tricks by simply observing them. He does this through a "simple feat of memory" (57). Here the association between rote learning and the absence of virtue is made overtly. For the child-magician's stated intent is to dupe his victims and thus have power over them.

With these three cases, Franzos documents his view of the deforming power of Eastern European Jewish traditions on native high intelligence. He provides a summary of the reasons for the deformation and lack of true creativity on the part of these Jews. This begins with physical causes: the early marriages, which work against individual desire; "oriental physical laziness"; lack of exercise and physical work, which "allows the race to decay physically"; the "one-sided emphasis on the intellect" as a means of earning one's daily bread; the early physical development of the Jews; the use of educational traditions that stress memory ("With the messenger it is the musculature of the legs, with the wood cutter that of the arms that is overdeveloped, so too is it the brain of the Talmudist and the merchant" [59]). But this physical weakness is also the result of the centuries-long inheritance of mental gifts and dexterity. These prodigies are but the natural outgrowth of the complete living conditions of a people. They are neither intelligent in the Western sense nor can they be virtuous in the same way (59–60).

Franzos rereads Cesare Lombroso's idea that genius and madness are closely linked. For Franzos it is the internal and external conditions of the Eastern Jews—including their inheritance and their living conditions— that makes them brilliant but easily destroyed. Here the Jewish prodigy becomes Woyzeck *in nuce*. As Woyzeck's nature is deformed by the social institutions that alter his body and his psyche, so too are these Jewish children. They, like Woyzeck, are the victims of the greater society in which they are compelled to live. And this difference of the psyche is inscribed on their sickly bodies, bodies that will die because of the deplorable exploitation by the institutions in which they are trapped. Alter the institutions, writes Franzos, and you have at least a chance of redeeming the Jewish superior intelligence in the East. But this must be done through redeeming the physical body and loosing the intellect (denationalizing it in his terms) from the constraints of the educational system (the cheder) that destroys it.

Eastern Jews, such as a Dr. Lippe in Jassy, saw such arguments about Eastern Jewish difference as the first step to conversion, but Franzos stressed in his work the malleability of the Eastern Jews to become as "western" as their German and Austrian co-religionists.[19] In this light Franzos was a clear follower of Ludwig Büchner's view of the need for Jews to abandon their mental and physical difference and their ability to do so. Here the argument was that the basis for Jewish difference was the Jews' cultural context, rather than their race.

Franzos's early enthusiasm for Georg Büchner's revolutionary writing stemmed from a similar understanding of the revolutionary potential of human beings. It was in the context of his reading of German and Russian high culture (Heine, Goethe, Gogol, Turgenev) that he discovered Büchner and read *Danton's Death*. He saw Büchner as a "romantic realist" and read him as he wrote his early books on the redeemable state of Eastern Jewry. His story of Jewish prodigies is part of that tradition. But, according to Franzos, his advocacy of Büchner led people to comment that he wrote about "first crude people, then crude writers" (114). Franzos was asked in 1875 to edit Büchner's works and he undertook the first complete edition, one that included the unpublished *Woyzeck*. This was done while Franzos lived in Vienna from 1877 to 1886 as a journalist, freelance writer, and editor. The edition appeared in 1879 and formed the concrete basis for the editions used by scholars through World War I as well as the libretto of Alban Berg's opera.

But Büchner's *Woyzeck* came to be a major difficulty for Franzos. Not only was the edition difficult—the manuscript, written in the tiniest script, was faded and difficult to read, but it also consisted of a number of drafts of the play. His reconstruction has been challenged often since that initial reading. When Franzos finally sent the deciphered text to Ludwig Büchner, Georg's brother wanted to excise the "cynicism" and the "faulty expressions" (121). According to Franzos, Ludwig wanted to excise the "atheistic or excessively radical political" passages in the text for they could have caused offense to the reading public (and have negatively impacted on the reputations of the remaining siblings). But he also wanted to cut the already censored vulgarisms from Franzos's edition. (He had printed, for example, the Drum Major's explicit use of "asshole" as a "a—hole" while the brother wanted it reduced to "a——.") Ludwig Büchner was a liberal in the late nineteenth-century sense of the word. He is also someone who knew the proprieties of Wilhelminian literature. Dirty words, politics, and religion must be banned from serious "high" literature. Franzos quickly arranged for journal publication in *Mehr Licht* (Berlin) and the *Neue Freie Presse* (Vienna), and the relatively uncensored *Woyzeck* was out into the world.

Here, however, the link was made for the fin de siècle. The "radical" materialist Ludwig Büchner, the revolutionary Georg Büchner, and the assimilationist Jewish journalist and novelist Karl Emil Franzos became linked in the public image of the drama of Woyzeck and his madness. Woyzeck became part of "Jewish" culture in Germany. With the rediscovery of the drama as a staple of German-language expressionism with its first performance in Munich in 1913, this association came to include the modern, which defined itself as radical and revolutionary and was labeled by its detractors as Jewish. Büchner, in the words of Julius Bab in 1922, became the forerunner of German expressionism and Woyzeck his most contemporary drama.[20] He had, however, already been so labeled in an oblique manner by the proto-fascist critic Arthur Moeller van den Bruck in 1904. Moeller van den Bruck observed that Büchner was a psychopath whose physical and mental instability was clearly reflected in his literary work. Indeed, even his death, according to Moeller van den Bruck, was "a crisis of nerves." In other words, in the connection between his physical and psychological degeneracy and his corrupt writing, he was just like the sick Jews in German culture.[21] The fin-de-siècle critic Ottokar Stauf von der March observed, "Jewry today finds itself at the stage of a physical and psychic decadence."[22] And this decadence is most marked for him in the culture of decadence, modern high culture.

Thus Georg Büchner was linked to the image of the Jew as defined radically at the turn of the century. Here the meaning of Büchner's text undergoes a radical rereading. For his Jewish references, which could have been understood as examples of the influence of capital on the shaping of the image of the Jew in the 1830s, come to be read as a sign of the inherent racial difference of the Jew at the end of the century. Büchner's Jew and Büchner as a "Jew" (i.e., as a revolutionary and a materialist) come to set the stage for a subtle rereading of the text when it is transformed into a libretto by the Viennese composer Alban Berg.

RECAPITULATION: ALBAN BERG

On May 5, 1914, Alban Berg saw the visiting performance of Albert Steinrück as Woyzeck in a version of Franzos's reading of Büchner's play in Vienna. He was thunderstruck by the crudity *and* the beauty of the piece. Berg first experienced the drama on the stage and then read *Woyzeck* in light of its fin-de-siècle reception as a document of materialism and social criticism.[23] For revolutionary materialism and, specifically, Ludwig Büchner had come to represent the mindset of the Jew in turn-of-the-century Viennese culture. Otto Weininger had summarized the feeling about the Jewish materialistic science in 1903, and Viennese intellectuals, such as Ludwig Wittgenstein, were still very much under the thrall of his views in 1914. Weininger wrote:

> Because fear of God in the Jew has no relation with real religion, the Jew is of all persons the least perturbed by mechanical theories of the world; he is readily beguiled by Darwinism and the ridiculous notion that men are derived from monkeys; and now he is disposed to accept the view that the soul of man is an evolution that has taken place within the human race; formerly he was a mad devotee of [Ludwig] Büchner, now he is ready to follow [the chemist] [Wilhelm] Ostwald [1853–1932].[24]

Thus Weininger would have seen Berg's fascination with Woyzeck as merely a further example of the corruption of German culture by this materialism, "beguiled by Darwinism and the ridiculous notion that men are derived from monkeys." For Weininger, being Jewish was a mindset rather than a racial designation—and even non-Jews such as Berg (or, indeed, as Weininger noted, Wagner) could thus be "Jews."

Berg's sensitivity to this can be noted in an extraordinary letter to the direct of the Opera House in Brunswick prior to the premiere of *Wozzeck* there in 1931. Evidently the director had demanded (in 1931!) that Berg prove his Aryan heritage, and Berg sent him a stack of documents to do so. In the accompanying letter he observed that "it was a pleasure that he was given a chance to prove his Aryan heritage officially and thus to put to rest those newspaper lies that had been haunting him ever more loudly over the past years."[25] Those "newspaper lies" were that Berg (like his teacher Arnold Schoenberg) was a Jew. Given that any product of high modernism, no matter what its provenance, was dismissed as "Jew-trash" in Vienna, the question comes to be how Berg thought he could limit the reading of his music-drama as a "Jewish" opera.

I want to argue that Alban Berg cuts and trims Büchner's drama into a libretto for his opera with the notion of the Jewish associations of materialism, the modern, and the negative meaning of Jewish superior intelligence firmly in mind. He makes a series of overt alterations to the libretto to ameliorate the "Jewish" references. Alban Berg needed to ameliorate this potential reading of the Büchner text given the racial politics of early twentieth-century Vienna. And this racial politics implicated the very notion of the creativity of the composer—for could Jews really be creative? And are not all of the modern simply Jews in their imitative mode of thinking? Was Berg the modernist not merely imitative of Schoenberg the Jew? Schoenberg by definition could never be truly creative because of his "mechanical" approach to music. How could Berg use this arch-modernist text and still "put to rest those newspaper lies that had been haunting him ever more loudly"?

Berg does so by reworking the libretto so as to distinguish between himself and his work of art. Berg's alterations to the libretto reflect two overt cuts that lessen any potential racial reading of the drama. By eliminating any overt references to the Jews, Berg tries to remove this text from the discourse of anti-Semitism. The Jew's scene, which Büchner uses to document Woyzeck's madness, is cut completely, even though Berg had initially intended to set it and thought of the Jew as a role for a baritone.[26] Büchner had used this scene as the touchstone for the question of Woyzeck's mental status in light of Clarus's interpretation of Woyzeck's moral insanity. For Berg, it could only be read as a racial reference to the *Schacherjude*, the exploitative Jew, one of the stock characters of turn-of-the-century anti-Semitism. But in avoiding setting the Jew as a baritone, Berg also avoided associating the voice of the Jew with the other baritone role in the opera, that of the title character, Wozzeck. Wozzeck is therefore not to be vocally a "Jew" as he could have been read in light of Franzos's understanding of Jewish superior intelligence. Throughout the opera there is a careful placement of the "degenerate" characters beyond racial identification into the amorphous world of "modernism." And such placement obscures the association between the modernism of the "'racially' acceptable" Berg (to use Alexander L. Ringer's phrase) and the "Jewishness" of musical modernism and Arnold Schoenberg's twelve tone scale.[27]

The other reference to the Jews cut from the libretto is the final line in the mock sermon held by the apprentice ("Now let's piss crosswise so that a Jew will die") in act 2, scene 4 of the opera. (The aria now ends with the penultimate line of the text: "as for my soul, it stinks of brandy wine. . . .") For Berg, at a moment of intense anti-Semitism the cutting of these scenes means that he is excising the specific references to the racial difference of the Jews, a difference that, by the turn of the century, is placed in a very different relationship to material explanations than the state of the proletariat. For the body of the proletariat, so one can read Woyzeck at the turn of the century, is the product of the exploitation of the owners of capital (read: the Jews); the body of the Jew, however, is the marker of Jewish difference and is tied to the claim for uniqueness that the Jews themselves hold. This would be in line with Franzos's reading of Jewish superior intelligence.

The fantasy that is expressed in this scene is an anti-Semitic one rooted in a fantasy of omnipotence, especially one of a sadistic character. This is "associated with the jet of urine passed by the male." Karen Horney commented that "I can quote something I was told of a class in a boy's school: When two boys, they said, urinate to make a cross, the person of whom they think at the moment will die."[28] Thus the powerlessness of the apprentices is laid at the feet of the Jews, themselves only minor and marginal players in this world of the material. The diseased, malformed body of the proletariat is blamed on the Jew. Berg's editing of these references shows a conscious attempt to excise the overt Jewish references that could be read somehow or other as instances of special pleading on the part of the Jews. For they could be read as illustrative of the truly weak position of nineteenth-century marginal Jews in light of the German attitude toward them.

The most telling and subversive of Berg's cuts of the Büchner text is, however, tied to the role of the Doctor and to the image of the Jew and medicine of the turn of the century. He tries to refigure the Doctor in such a way as to deflect Weininger's accusation that it is the Jews who have converted medicine into biochemistry: "The present turn of medical science is largely due to the influence of the Jews, who in such numbers have embraced the medical profession. From the earliest times, until the dominance of the Jews, medicine was closely allied with religion. But now they make it a matter of drugs, a mere administration of chemicals. . . . The chemical interpretation of organisms sets these on a level with their own dead ashes" (315). Here the critique of "modern" scientific medicine, interpreted by Büchner as a sign of the power of the educated classes over the proletariat, comes to have a strongly anti-Semitic tinge. For the Jew in Büchner's play, in a Viennese reading of the turn of the century, is represented not only by the shopkeeper's materialism, but also by the "scientific" attitude of the Doctor. Berg alters the Doctor's central exchange with Wozzeck to maintain his materialism, but to separate this materialism from what comes, by the turn of the century, to be a specific sign of Jewish difference. This is undertaken in the opera through the creation of the Doctor's voice as that of the lowest register in the opera, separate from the tremulous, high-pitched "Jewish" voices of Wagner and Strauss and from the imagined Jewish "baritone" that Berg had finally not incorporated into the opera.

There is a verbal leitmotif that runs through the exchange between Wozzeck and the Doctor in the text that sounds—on its surface—as if Ludwig Büchner's anxiety about proper language had its impact on Alban Berg. Berg eliminates the word "piss" from the Doctor's speech to Wozzeck and replaces it throughout with "cough."[29] This change was read initially as an attempt on Berg's part to soften the "naturalistic roughness of expression" in the text.[30] Recently, and in a much more convincing manner, it has been read autobiographically as reflecting Berg's own asthma.[31] I would like to extend this argument, to tie into the "personal" reading the question of the materialism of medicine and science, the fin-de-siècle Jewish reading of coughing and urination, as well as the meaning of coughing in the opera at the turn of the century. For if Berg was indeed asthmatic, this personal sign could be read as a sign of his Aryan racial identity, or at least, as a sign of his not being Jewish.

Büchner's original reference to pissing was a red herring in his reconstruction of the mock pellagra that was to have been caused by the Doctor's prescribing a regime of peas to Woyzeck in the play. For people suffering from pellagra experience diarrhea, not polyuria, and that is why Büchner sets the stage by having the horse defecate on the stage early in the drama. Woyzeck's polyuria is linked to a set of ideas about medicine. First, the ancient notion of uroscopy, the physician's examination and tasting of the urine to find specific signs and symptoms of disease, is inscribed in the text. This practice was still in use, and the physician was the one able to look for the specific signs and symptoms of disease. This was very much in line with Büchner's representation of the Doctor's epistemology. Second, the question of the urination as the public act of exposure of the male genitalia—like that of the lower animals, as Büchner has his characters state in the drama. This is echoed in the now excised

scene where the apprentices go offstage to urinate and thus "kill a Jew."
Both of these make the act of urination a more highly symbolic one
within Büchner's construction of his image of Woyzeck's somatic suffering than would defecation.

But the reason physicians from the Greeks through to the early nineteenth century tasted their patients' urine was to examine for the sweet-
ness that marks diabetes. Thus the polyuria that is present in that disease becomes a further, public marker of diabetes. What is important by
the beginning of the twentieth century is that diabetes had come to be
understood as the essential "Jewish disease." Jean-Martin Charcot, the
famed Parisian neurologist, noted the predisposition of Jews for specific
forms of illness, such as diabetes, where "the exploration [of the cause of
the disease] is easy." For Charcot, the cause of such illness is the intramarriage of the Jews.[32] Charcot sees this intermarriage as exacerbating
the Jews' inherited racial predisposition for diabetes.[33] This dismissal of
Jewish ritual practices, such as endogenous marriage, was one of the
clarion calls of the liberals, such as Charcot and Ludwig Büchner at the
turn of the century. They believed in the inheritance of acquired characteristics and saw Jewish diabetes as a quality of the Jewish body that
reflected the Jewish character.

Diabetes is, for the physician of the fin de siècle, the Jewish disease
about which one can speak.[34] This disease, because of its evident association with the Jews, was seen as a sign of the Jews' racial degeneration.
William Osler, visiting Berlin in 1884, reported on the work of the famed
internist Friedrich Theodor Frerichs on diabetes: "With reference to
race, it is remarkable that 102 of the [400] patients were Jews, which he
attributes to hereditary excitability of the nervous system, the keen pursuit of business, and, above all, intramarriage."[35] Diabetes is thus a clear
sign of Jewish materialism, as clear a sign as the Jewish shopkeeper in
Büchner's *Woyzeck*. As late as the 1920s, this view remained quite alive
within German-language medicine. Diabetes is the "sole result" of "the
impact of the nervous excitement on the nervous system transmitted
from the time of the ghetto."[36] It is the physical parallel to Franzos's representation of Jewish superior intelligence. For the Jewish male, diabetes
provided an association of Jewishness and masculinity which not only
stressed the diseased nature of the Jew but also his physical and social
impotence. It is both the mind and the body of the Jew that are impaired
because of the very nature of the Jew, the "perverse" sexuality of his
"race," and his striving for the material aspects of life. This is the reason
he (and the Jew is always a male in this discourse) reads Ludwig Büchner.

Thus the male Jew would indeed be marked by his "pissing on the street," by the polyuria of diabetes, an illness that would also reflect his perverse sexuality and racial status.

If Jews did suffer from diabetes, they did not suffer from tuberculosis except in very specific cases. The myth of a Jewish immunity to the most operatic of illness, tuberculosis, frames the discussion of "coughing" in Berg's opera. Tuberculosis marked the operatic body as different, even in the seemingly attractive fantasy of the female tubercular in Dumas's *Lady of the Camellias* (set to music in Verdi's *Traviata*) or Murget's Mimi (set to music in Puccini's and Leoncavallo's *Bohème*). Woyzeck is suddenly put into the line of these coughing female protagonists. His madness is marked by his coughing. Jews, unlike operatic protagonists, were believed to have had a natural resistance to tuberculosis. While some critics, such as Leroy-Beaulieu, evoked the tubercular bodies of Sarah Bernhardt and Rahel Varnhagen to characterize the Jewish male body as ill and effeminate, the counter view also existed. Jews, according to much of the technical and popular literature of the time, were spared the ravages of this greatest of all killers. Thus in 1911, in his standard study of *The Jews: A Study of Race and Environment*, Maurice Fishberg stresses the view, expressed in this detailed study of the racial characteristics of the Jew, that all of the traditional hygienic virtues of Jewish law and family life enable Jews to have a lower incidence of tuberculosis through the inheritance of acquired characteristics.[37] Other views of the time stress the racial basis of this supposed resistance to tuberculosis. This racial argument was supported by anthropologists such as Georg Buschan, in the major popular geographic journal of the day, who saw increased predisposition or increased resistance as defining signs of racial identity.[38] For Buschan the "four to six times higher rate of mental illness" among the Jews must be the result of an inherited weakness of the central nervous system since Jews do not evidence any of the sociopathic etiologies, such as alcoholism, which, according to him, cause mental illness. But if Jews can be predisposed to acquire certain illnesses because of their racial identity, they can also be immune from certain diseases for the same reason. Thus, he also sees the relative immunity of the Jews from certain infectious diseases as a sign of their inherited biological nature.

Thus a coughing Wozzeck both undermines and continues the play of stereotypes in the opera. For it is not only Wozzeck but also the Captain who coughs in the libretto. In act 2, scene 2, the scene in which Büchner has the Doctor use his "scientific gaze" to diagnose both the Captain and a female passerby, the Captain is shown to be "quite out of breath." "He coughs with excitement and exertion, with the Doctor tapping him on the back to ease his cough. The Captain is moved almost to tears" (25–26). The tears come from considering his own demise. But both the Captain and Wozzeck cough in public. Berg can thus label the cough as both "Jewish" (and as such feminizing) and "universal" simultaneously. Wozzeck is the representative victim, but certainly not the Jew in any of his particulars, including his baritone voice. In the myth-making of the time, Jews don't cough; they piss.

The Doctor's materialism is removed from the contemporary discourse of Jewish difference. And Berg frees the libretto, he believes, from any potential rereading of Büchner's text as anti-Semitic, a rereading that is clearly in line with Berg's desire to not have the opera overtly associated in any way with this debate. Once *Wozzeck* is performed, however, Berg's detractors see him, the twelve-tone composer, as one more in the line of those diseased Jews, who like the stench of the canals spreads pestilence through the land. This quite literally is what the music critic in the *Deutsche Zeitung* (Berlin), Paul Zschorlich, wrote concerning the initial performance of the opera in 1925: "The work of a Chinese from Vienna. My name will be *Moses Kanalgeruch* (Canalstench) if this isn't a true swindle."[39] Zschorlich's use of the crypto-Jewish name in this "oriental" context places the opera firmly in the camp of the "Jewish modern." The image of the pestilence of the modern, associated with both Büchners, with Franzos, is now associated with Berg. While attempting to repress all references to the Jews, no matter how tangential, Berg remains caught in the web of an anti-Semitic rhetoric that sees the whole cultural production of the modern as corrupt and corrupting. This is the essence of Berg's own reading of the Doctor, who in the opera is the embodiment of the materialism of Wozzeck's world. Even the stripping of all of the "Jewish" references in the text does not free Berg or the Doctor from this association. Berg's Doctor remains the worse of all possible diagnosticians, captured as he is by his notion of "big science" and "big medicine." He comes in the drama to be the embodiment of the cruelties of medicine rather than its solace. But it is a label placed on "Jewish medicine" by "scientific" racists such as Otto Weininger, whose own claim is that their science is simply better than that of the Jews—not that it is kinder. Given the fact that the racial science of the fin de siècle provides the basis for the Shoah, this claim turns out to be parody.

The role of science in providing the vocabulary of images for the Jew that Berg desires himself not to be is echoed in Berg's opera. From the voice of the Jew to the very body of the degenerate, the stereotypical model of Jewish differences provides alternatives that Berg chooses or rejects. Behind all of it is Berg's anxiety of being seen (or heard) as a Jew. Certainly Jewish composers, even converts, such as Gustav Mahler, were anxious about their creativity and saw it in some way linked to their "Jewishness." For Berg, being associated with the "Jews" in terms of their "modernism" and their "illness" would have drawn his own creativity into question. All of this comes to be inscribed and projected onto the body of Wozzeck in the opera. Here the form of the rereading of a non-Jewish text (Büchner's play) through a Jewish anxiety about original genius (Franzos) that came to constitute the original text as a text of modernity leads Berg radically to reformat the libretto and rethink his setting of it. It is the anxiety of being seen as "Jewish" that frames the rethinking of the opera.

NOTES

I am grateful to Marc A. Weiner for his detailed comments on this chapter.

1. See Ian Hacking, *The Emergence of Probability: A Philosophical Study of Early Ideas about Probability, Induction and Statistical Inference* (London: Cambridge University Press, 1975) and Theodore M. Porter, *The Rise of Statistical Thinking, 1820–1900* (Princeton, N.J.: Princeton University Press, 1986).

2. All references to the historical character and to Büchner's figure are to "Woyzeck"; all references to Berg's opera and to his character are to "Wozzeck." The two best books on Büchner remain Hans Meyer, *Georg Büchner und seine Zeit* (Berlin: Aufbau, 1959) and Henri Poschmann, *Georg Büchner: Dichtung der Revolution und Revolution der Dichtung* (Weimar: Aufbau, 1983). See also Ludwig Fischer, ed., *Zeitgenosse Büchner* (Stuttgart: Klett-Cotta, 1979); Sabine Kubik, *Krankheit und Medizin im literarischen Werk Georg Büchners* (Stuttgart: M & P, 1991); Albert Meier, *Georg Büchner, "Woyzeck"* (Munich: W. Fink, 1980); David G. Richards, *Georg Büchners Woyzeck: Interpretation und Textgestaltung* (Bonn: Bouvier, 1975); Mario Regina, *Struttura e significato del Woyzeck di Georg Büchner* (Bari: Adriatica, 1976).

The citations from Büchner's play are to the translation by Henry J. Schmidt, *Georg Büchner: Woyzeck* (New York: Avon, 1969), which still remains the best English version. The question of the organization of the play and its various editorial levels is unimportant to this paper except for the historical context of the libretto. This is well examined in much detail in Peter Petersen, *Alban Berg, Wozzeck: Eine semantische Analyse unter Einbeziehung der Skizzen und Dokumente aus dem Nachlaß Bergs* (Munich: Text und Kritik, 1985). The references to the English libretto are to the standard translation by Eric A. Blackall and Vida Harford, *Georg Büchner's Wozzeck: Opera in 3 Acts (15 Scenes)* (New York: Associated Music Publishers, 1952).

3. This is reprinted in Werner R. Lehmann, ed., *Georg Büchner, Sämtliche Werke und Briefe* (Hamburg: Christian Wegner, n.d.), 2: 485–549, at 490.

4. See the discussion in Peter Uwe Hohendahl's chapter "Nachromantische Subjektivität," in his *Geschichte•Opposition•Subversion: Studien zur Literatur des 19. Jahrhunderts* (Cologne: Böhlau, 1993), 51–66.

5. Excerpted in Hans Mayer, ed., *Georg Büchner: Woyzeck. Vollständiger Text und Paralipomena. Dokumentation* (Frankfurt am Main: Ullstein, 1993), 138–40.

6. Cited from the review by Edgar Steiger of the November 8, 1913, production of *Woyzeck* from the excerpt in Dietmar Goltschnigg, ed., *Materialien zur Rezeptions- und Wirkungsgeschichte Georg Büchners* (Kronberg: Scriptor Verlag, 1974), 222.

7. Cited from Karl Emil Franzos, "Über Georg Büchner," *Deutsche Dichtung* 29 (1901): 195–6, 289–90 in the translation from Douglas Jarman, *Alban Berg: Wozzeck* (Cambridge: Cambridge University Press, 1989), 127.

8. Peter Gay, *The Cultivation of Hatred* (New York: Norton, 1993), 487.

9. See F. N. L. Ponyter, *Chemistry in the Service of Medicine* (Philadelphia: Lippincott, 1963).

10. See the discussion in my *Jewish Self-Hatred* (Baltimore: The Johns Hopkins University Press, 1986), 188–208.

11. The most striking contemporary account by a specialist in mental illnesses is Vincenzio Chiarugi, *Saggio di ricerche sulla pellagra* (Firenze: Presso Pietro Allegrini alla Croce Rossa, 1814). On the social history of the illness see Daphne A. Roe, *A Plague of Corn: The Social History Of Pellagra* (Ithaca, N.Y.: Cornell University Press, 1973), and on the medical history Kenneth J. Carpenter, ed., *Pellagra* (Stroudsburg, Pa.: Hutchinson Ross Pub. Co., 1981).

12. Milton Terris, ed., *Goldberger on Pellagra* (Baton Rouge: Louisiana State University Press, 1964).

13. Jarman, *Wozzeck*, 112.

14. Poschmann, *Büchner*, 333.

15. Ludwig Büchner, *Am Sterbelager des Jahrhunderts: Blicke eines freien Denkers aus der Zeit in die Zeit* (Giessen: Emil Roth, 1898), 347.

16. On Franzos see Fred Sommer, ed., *Karl Emil Franzos: Kritik und Dichtung* (New York: Peter Lang, 1992); Maria Klanska, "Drei deutschsprachige Schriftsteller im nationalen Spannungsfeld Galiziens," *Österreich in Geschichte und Literatur* 34 (1990): 26–39; Carl Steiner, *Karl Emil Franzos, 1848–1904: Emancipator and Assimilationist* (New York: Peter Lang, 1990); Carl Steiner, "Deutscher und Jude: Das Leben und Werk des Karl Emil Franzos (1848–1904)," in *Autoren damals und heute: Literaturgeschichtliche Beispiele veränderter Wirkungshorizonte*, ed. Gerhard Knapp, 367–87 (Amsterdam: Rodopi, 1991); Jörg Schönert, "Bilder vom 'Verbrechermenschen' in den rechtskulturellen Diskursen um 1900: Zum Erzählen über Kriminalität und zum Status kriminologischen Wissens," in his *Erzählte Kriminalität: Zur Typologie und Funktion von narrativen Darstellungen in Strafrechtspflege, Publizistik und Literatur zwischen 1770 und 1920*, 497–531 (Tübingen: Niemeyer, 1991); W. G. Sebald, "Westwarts–Ostwarts: Aporien deutschsprachiger Ghettogeschichten," *Literatur und Kritik* 233–34 (1989): 161–77; Margarita Pazi, "Karl Emil Franzos' Assimilations-

vorstellung und Assimilationserfahrung." in *Conditio Judaica: Judentum, Antisemitismus und deutschprachige Literatur vom 18. Jahrhundert bis zum Ersten Weltkrieg,* ed. Hans Otto Horch and Horst Denkler, 218–33 (Tübingen: Niemeyer, 1989); Ritchie Robertson, "Western Observers and Eastern Jews: Kafka, Buber, Franzos," *The Modern Language Review* 83 (1988): 87–105; Andrea Wodenegg, *Das Bild der Juden Osteuropas: Ein Beitrag zur komparatischen Imagologie an Textbeispielen von Karl Emil Franzos und Leopold von Sacher-Masosch* (Frankfurt am Main and New York: Peter Lang, 1987); Martha Bickel, "Zum Werk von Karl Emil Franzos," in *Juden in der deutschen Literatur: Ein deutsch–israelisches Symposion,* ed. Stéphane Moses and Albrecht Schöne, 152–61 (Frankfurt: Suhrkamp, 1986); Claudia Albert and Gregor Blum, "Des Sender Glatteis neue Kleider: Judentum und Assimilation bei Karl Emil Franzos (1848–1904)," *Die Horen* 30 (1985): 48–92; Frederick Sommer, "'Halb-Asien': German Nationalism and the Eastern European Works of Karl Emil Franzos," (Ph.D. diss., University of Wisconsin, 1983), published as *"Halb-Asien": German Nationalism and the Eastern European Works of Emil Franzos* (Stuttgart: H.-D. Heinz, 1984); Mark H. Gelber, "Ethnic Pluralism and Germanization in the Works of Karl Emil Franzos (1848–1904)," *The German Quarterly* 56 (1983): 376–85; Arno Will, "Karl Emil Franzos: Ein Beitrag zu den Gestalten der Polen in der österreichischen Literatur des 19. Jahrhunderts," *Lenau Forum* 1 (1969): 46–57; Alexander Malycky, "A Note on the Writings of Karl Emil Franzos on Heinrich Heine," *Studies in Bibliography and Booklore* 6 (1963): 73–74.

17. Dieter Kessler, "Die deutsche Literatur des Buchenlandes und die Juden," in *Juden in Ostmitteleuropa von der Emanzipation bis zum Ersten Weltkrieg,* ed. Gotthold Rhode, 295–309 (Marburg a.d. Lahn: J. G. Herder-Institut, 1989), 297.

18. All references are to Karl Emil Franzos, "Wunderkinder des Ghetto," in his *Aus der großen Ebene: Neue Kulturbilder aus Halb-Asien* 23–60 (Stuttgart: Adolf Bonz, 1888).

19. See the long autobiographical introduction, written in 1893, to his last and most important novel, *Der Pojaz* (Stuttgart: J. G. Cotta, 1912), 5–14, at p. 13.

20. Julius Bab, "Durch das Drama der Jüngsten und Georg Büchners" excerpted in Goltschnigg, *Materialen,* 153–58.

21. Arthur Moeller van den Bruck, "Über Georg Büchner" excerpted in ibid., 131–37.

22. Ottokar Stauf von der March, "Décadence," *Die Gesellschaft* (April 1894): 530.

23. On Berg see Siegfried Mauser, *Das expressionistische Musiktheater der Wiener Schule: Stilistische und entwicklungsgeschichtliche Untersuchungen zu Arnold Schönbergs "Erwartung", op. 17, "Die glückliche Hand", op. 18, und Alban Bergs "Wozzeck", op.* 7 (Regensburg: Bosse, 1982); Guido Hiss, *Korrespondenzen: Zeichenzusammenhänge im Sprech- und Musiktheater: Mit einer Analyse des "Wozzeck" von Alban Berg* (Tübingen: Niemeyer, 1988); Siglind Bruhn, *Die musikalische Darstellung psychologischer Wirklichkeit in Alban Bergs "Wozzeck"* (Frankfurt am Main and New York: Peter Lang, 1986); George Perle, *The Operas of Alban Berg.*

2 vols. (Berkeley and Los Angeles: University of California Press, 1980–85); Bo Ullman, *Die sozialkritische Thematik im Werk Georg Büchners und ihre Entfaltung im "Woyzeck"; mit einigen Bemerkungen zu der Oper Alban Bergs* (Stockholm: Almqvist & Wiksell, 1972); James Martin Harding, "Integrating Atomization: Adorno Reading Berg Reading Büchner," *Theatre Journal* 44 (1992): 1–13.

24. All quotations are from the English translation, Otto Weininger, *Sex & Character* (London: William Heinemann, 1906), here p. 315.

25. Ernst Hilmar, *Wozzeck von Alban Berg: Entstehung – erste Erfolge – Repressionen (1914–1935)* (Vienna: Universal, 1975), 66.

26. See Petersen, *Berg, Wozzeck*, 25.

27. Alexander L. Ringer, *Arnold Schoenberg: The Composer as Jew* (Oxford: Clarendon, 1990), 210.

28. Karen Horney, *Feminine Psychology*, ed. Harold Kelman (New York: Norton, 1967), 39.

29. There are at least four points in this exchange where Wozzeck's coughing is cited by the Doctor: "Ich habs gesehn, Wozzeck. Er hat wieder gehustet . . ." (110); "(Husten müssen)" (114); "Er hat wieder gehustet . . ." (120); "Er hätte doch nicht husten sollen . . ." (124). Not all of these appear in the English translation. All citations from the score: Alban Berg, *George Büchners Wozzeck* (Partitur) (Vienna: Universal Edition, 1955).

30. Rudolf Schäfke, "Alban Bergs Oper: Wozzeck," *Melos* 5 (1926): 267–83, at 268–69. Jarman, *Wozzeck*, 31, calls this change "dramatically meaningless."

31. Petersen, *Berg, Wozzeck*, 55–56.

32. Toby Gelfand, "'Mon Cher Docteur Freud': Charcot's Unpublished Correspondence to Freud, 1888–1893," *Bulletin of the History of Medicine* 62 (1988): 563–88, at 574.

33. Toby Gelfand, "Charcot's Response to Freud's Rebellion," *Journal of the History of Ideas* 50 (1989): 304.

34. There are references to diabetes as a Jewish disease in the standard textbook of internal medicine of the period, Adolf Strümpell, ed., *Lehrbuch der speciellen Pathologie und Therapie der inneren Krankheiten für Studirende und Ärzte.* 18 vols. (Leipzig: Vogel, 1883–1912), excerpted as *A Text-Book of Medicine*, trans. Herman F. Vickery and Philip Coombs Knapp (New York: Appelton, 1893), 967. The "Jewish" nature of this disease is discussed widely in the medical literature of the period. In addition to Strümpell, Buschan and Charcot wrote on this question. See the literature summarized in E. Morpurgo, *Sulle condizioni somatiche e psichiche degli Israeliti in Europa*, Bibliotece dell'idea Sionisa, 2 (Modena: Tip. Operai, 1903), 61–62. On the history of diabetes without covering this topic see Dietrich von Engelhardt, ed., *Diabetes: Its Medical and Cultural History* (Berlin: Springer, 1989).

35. W[illiam] O[sler], "Letters from Berlin," *Canada Medical and Surgical Journal* 12 (1884): 721–28, at 723.

36. Dr. med. A. Kühner, *Arterienverkalkung heilbar! Neue Mittel und Wege* (Leipzig: F. W. Gloeckner, n.d. [1920], 19.

37. Maurice Fishberg, *The Jews: A Study of Race and Environment* (New York: Walter Scott, 1911). German translation, 1913.

38. Georg Buschan, "Einfluß der Rasse auf die Form und Häufigkeit pathologischer Veränderungen," *Globus* 67 (1895): 21–24, 43–47, 60–63, 76–80, at 45–46, 60–61.

39. Konrad Vogelsang, *Dokumentation zur Oper "Wozzeck" von Alban Berg* (Laaber: Laaber Verlag, 1977), 20.

15

"Death is a Drum": Rhythm, Modernity, and the Negro Poet Laureate

LARRY SCANLON

LANGSTON LAUREATUS

Although more than three decades have passed since his death, the poetry of Langston Hughes still raises critical difficulties of the most elemental sort. The most prolific poet in the African-American tradition, he is also all but indisputably the most important and influential. Poems such as "The Negro Speaks of Rivers" and "The Weary Blues" were already widely anthologized before he was thirty, and his proverbial status as the "Poet Laureate of the Negro Race" suggests a centrality and stability in the notoriously protean modern American canon unmatched by any of his white counterparts.[1] Yet while their reputations have waxed and waned with shifts in critical fashion, poets such as Eliot, Pound, Stevens, Williams, Frost, and even H. D. and Marianne Moore have consistently received greater critical attention than Hughes. The same is true of other major figures in the African-American tradition (Mullen 1988: 46). Even among Hughes's supporters, there is little consensus regarding the contours of his career, the interrelations among the numerous strands of a widely variegated body of work.[2] Nor has there been much detailed examination of relations between his work and that of other modernists, black or white.

This essay will read the honorific *Negro poet laureate* to the letter. It seeks to understand how Hughes, as the public poetic voice of the black community, spoke at once both to that community and for it to other communities. The term itself neatly encapsulates the challenge Hughes poses to modern critical paradigms. Unmodern to the point of quaintness, the notion of a poet laureate takes art's primary purpose to be public, affirmative, and monumental—precisely those qualities, that is, that most modernists saw themselves as overthrowing. Yet Hughes's poetry is all of these things and thoroughly modernist as well. In contrast to many of his contemporaries, he took modernism to be both a public and a quintessentially popular phenomenon. Whenever he discussed the sources of his own poetic practice, he almost invariably located them in the traditions of the black vernacular, and above all in the blues.[3] This homage to the blues is more than a simple recognition of their value according to established aesthetic categories. It is an insistence on their authority as well, their power to call the categories themselves into question. In particular, Hughes challenges us to reexamine the distinction between music and poetry.

While this distinction is obviously a primarily philosophical and epistemological one, it is also culturally specific (that is, to the post-medieval West), albeit in a very broad sense.[4] Hughes characteristically conceptualizes his relation to the blues under the general rubric of *rhythm*. As a central formal constituent of both music and poetry, rhythm has also been a highly racialized category in relation to black musical traditions in North America from the moment of their inception.[5] Moreover, for all its centrality, rhythm has traditionally been understood as a subordinate feature of both media, subordinate in music to pitch, and in poetry to meaning. Hughes effects his affirmation of the blues in part by deconstructing this subordination, and this interest in form insures that the affirmation has ramifications well beyond the specificities of its immediate object. Indeed, the poetic authority Hughes draws from the blues enables him to redefine the very nature of cultural expression itself, both musical and poetic. This essay traces the contours of that redefinition. After sketching Hughes's notion of rhythm in general terms, its specific account of his actual poetic practice focuses on his longstanding interest in the elegy. For it is in his elegies, even more than in his blues poems, that we can see how the rhythmic consciousness he finds in the blues becomes the basis of a distinctively modern notion of temporality.

RACE AND THE POET'S CALLING

To define oneself as modern is to assert a particularly privileged relation to time, to claim an awareness of one's own temporality that eluded the past. Modernism's most characteristic polemic stance is that of the vanguardist, who extends the reach of this temporal privilege even further.[6] The authority the vanguardist claims is not only an authority over the past, but also an authority over everyone else in the present. The vanguardist is the one who knows where history is going and the one who will get there first. But precisely because of this complete dependence on temporality, the vanguardist stance can never achieve any lasting philosophical coherence. Its privilege is by definition evanescent and self-consuming. For vanguardism can justify its privilege only by convincing the rest of the culture to follow it, by bringing the culture up to its own "advanced" level, as it were, and thereby destroying the very basis of its privilege. Accordingly, as a historical phenomenon, modernism has always been driven, in spite of itself, by an evangelizing, democratizing impulse dependent on the very cultural and educational structures vanguardists characteristically disdain, such as universities, museums, and libraries. As the Negro poet laureate, Hughes both inhabits this contradiction and points a way beyond it. His message for modernism at large is that its fear of belatedness betrays a politics it cannot sustain. Modernism's reactionary strain viewed modernity as an irrevocable break, a wasteland dominated by the finality of loss and incoherence. But Hughes understands modernity as a dream deferred, an on-going confrontation with the contradictions of the past rather than a fallen alienation from its certainties. He anticipates the growing postmodern consensus which takes modernity's master trope to be repetition rather than rupture.[7] But postmodernism has its own anxieties about belatedness, as the very term indicates. Hughes's modernism offers an alternative to such anxieties within the modernist moment itself, and he does so through one of modernism's most favored forms, the lyric. Modernism took lyric to be the quintessential poetic mode, which it "mythologized as the purest and oldest of poetic genres" (Jeffreys 1995: 197). Hughes's interest in the blues made lyric an obvious generic choice. But the blues also enable him to expose and redefine the primitivism inherent in the reigning modernist notions of the form. Lyric's very name memorializes poetry's historic connection to music, a connection modernists held to be both registered and preserved in poetic meter. In the words of John Hollander, "Poetic form as we know it is an abstraction form, or residue of, musical form, from which it came to be divorced when writing replaced memory as a way of preserving poetic utterance" (1981: 4). Lyric's eponymous recollection of music is thus simultaneously a recollection of oral tradition. As Paul de Man has explained, this modernist notion of recollected loss has its source in the "primitivism" of "eighteenth-century speculations about the origins of language" (1983: 168), which viewed poetry as the original form of language and music as the original form of all human expression (cf. Tomlinson 1995, esp. 343–55).

Thus, "the music of poetry and the rationality of prose are opposed as the ancient is opposed to modern" (ibid.). As de Man points out, such primitivism should have made modern lyric poetry a logical impossibility, a contradiction in terms. Paradoxically, however, it was precisely the contradictory nature of this view that gave it its ideological power. The modern lyric poet, like the modern composer, became a vanguardist hero, a Nietzschean *Übermensch*. Only the vanguardist could recover the primitive unity which modern rationality recognized as irrevocably lost. These heroes stood alone, apart from both their own historical moment and their immediate past, in their recognition and partial transcendence of the loss that defined them as modern. Because what was lost was a primal unity, the heroism of the vanguardist was a singular one. In Sharon Cameron's memorable formulation, lyric poetry offered "a solitary voice that speaks out of a single moment in time" (1979: 23).

Hughes disrupts both the singularity and the neat temporality of this model. The music his poetry recalls is the blues, and the blues are not some lost ancient unity, but a mode of cultural expression contemporaneous with the poet. Whatever their roots in African folklore and African musical practice—and despite their orality,[8] their "primal" unification of words and music—the blues are very much a modern tradition. They emerge in the rural south at the end of the nineteenth century and move northward with the urban migrations of the early twentieth. They confront modernity head-on, both thematically in their concentration on such industrial innovations as the railroad, and formally in their use of factory-made Western instruments. Moreover, Hughes viewed the blues as an urban form even in their Southern origins, "*city* songs rising from the crowded streets of big towns" (original emphasis; Hughes 1941: 143, cf. Tracy 1988: 117). They were no less modern than his poetry, and in drawing on them, he was presenting himself as one modernist among many.

Where other modernist poets idealize solitude and the synchronic, Hughes's lyrics characteristically seek the multivocal and the diachronic. Thus in his very first published poem, "The Negro Speaks of Rivers," the narrating "I" successively locates itself at the Euphrates at the dawn of civilization, the Congo, the Nile during ancient Egypt, and the Mississippi "when Abe Lincoln went down to New Orleans" (Hughes 1995: 23). Even more striking are the many poems like "The Cat and the Saxophone (2 a.m.)," an early poem that bewildered Countee Cullen greatly. It begins:

EVERYBODY
Half-pint,—
Gin?
No, make it
LOVES MY BABY
corn . . .

(Hughes 1995: 89)

Here there are three voices, speaking simultaneously, the singer (EVERYBODY . . . LOVES MY BABY), the customer who orders the "Half-pint," and the bartender who serves him ("Gin?"). The poem will add a fourth voice, the customer's lover, and its point is to demonstrate the way the desire of these lovers is played out in the cacophony of other voices. Such self-conscious formal experimentalism bothered Countee Cullen sufficiently that in reviewing Hughes's first book, *The Weary Blues*, he was content to cast himself as Francis Jeffrey to Hughes's Wordsworth (Cullen [1926] 1993: 4). But for Hughes the issue of multivocality went beyond his interest in form, considerable though that was. What was at stake was nothing less than the source of his own poetic authority. The poem's title announces it as a single moment, yet the poem itself reveals the singularity of the moment to be constituted entirely by the multiple voices which contend across it. As the typography indicates, the dominant voice belongs to the singer, the voice which sounds above all the others. But this voice is itself multiple, since as a lyric performance it consists of the repetition of a musical composition constructed elsewhere. The poem's experimentalism inheres in Hughes's textual reproduction of this moment of repetition. Paradoxical as it may seem, Hughes's modernism lies not in the assertion of a new temporality, but in the recognition of the ruptures necessarily attendant upon a temporality of repetition.[9]

Hughes's commitment to notions of repetition was no less political than it was poetic. His 1940 autobiography *The Big Sea* tells the story of his poetic vocation, where it came from, and how it matured. Parodying the Grand Tour, Hughes frames the story as the chronicle of his travels between the ages of eighteen and thirty-two. The book begins with his first night on a freighter out of New York Harbor bound for Africa, which he celebrates by throwing all his books overboard. After visiting Africa, he works his way to Paris before returning to the United States. This narrative sequence suggests that Hughes brings a recuperated African identity to bear on European tradition. Hughes makes this suggestion with much greater precision as he recounts the various turning points of his early career. At these moments he recurs strikingly to the notion of rhythm.

Thus he offers an anecdote from the eighth grade as the moment he accepted the poet's calling.

> I was the Class Poet. It happened like this. They had elected all the class officers, but there was no one in our class who looked like a poet, or had ever written a poem. There were two Negro children in the class, myself and a girl. In America most white people think, of course that *all* Negroes can sing and dance, and have a sense of rhythm. So my classmates, knowing that a poem had to have rhythm, elected me unanimously—thinking, no doubt that I had some being a Negro.
>
> It had never occurred to me to be a poet before, or indeed a writer of any kind. (Hughes 1940: 14)

This account is ironic and self-deprecating almost to the point of parody. It turns out that the future laureate never even considered becoming a poet until it was suggested to him by his white schoolmates, and their suggestion was little more than the by-product of the widespread racist stereotype that blacks "have rhythm." Arnold Rampersad, Hughes's biographer, raises entirely plausible doubts about the literal accuracy of this account: "His election as class poet probably had less to do with rhythm and race than with his perceived merits and popularity" (1986b: 24). But if we accept these doubts, then that only makes the passage's interest in rhythm all the more telling. The episode is literally a calling, one with the originary quality of an Althusserian interpellation (Althusser 1971: 170–83): Hughes can achieve his poetic identity only by submitting to an entirely external and oppressive white ideology. Yet in contrast to Althusser, and indeed to most notions of ideology, for Hughes this moment of submission is simultaneously a powerful form of resistance. As he uses the stereotype of black rhythm to acknowledge that his poetic vocation arose within a dominant and hostile culture, he also deconstructs it. The notion that blacks have some kind of natural rhythm grows out of the racist fantasy of the black as wholly body (itself the product of a Christian–Platonic somatics that associates social subordination with carnality). This notion understands black expressive culture as a natural emanation rather than a conscious artistic construction. But precisely for that reason, the stereotype does not generally associate black rhythm with poetry. In the white imaginary, poetry as the most elite and privileged form of literary art is usually quite separate from the allegedly instinctual singing and dancing taken to illustrate black rhythm. Hughes's autobiographical fable conflates the two, exposing an incoherence within

the dominant notion of rhythm and claiming as a black poet a particularly privileged position for redefining it.

This episode fits neatly with a passage at the conclusion of *The Big Sea*
which constitutes a declaration of artistic independence. The autobiography ends in 1930, when Hughes broke with his wealthy white patron
(an elderly widow named Charlotte Mason, who also supported Alain
Locke and Zora Neale Hurston [Rampersad 1986b: 147–200]). As a result of this break, Hughes decided to become an entirely self-sufficient
professional writer, giving up both odd jobs and reliance on patrons. The
disagreement with Mason involved the direction of his work. Hughes
sums it up this way:

> She wanted me to be primitive and know and feel the intuitions of the
> primitive. But unfortunately, I did not feel the rhythms of the primitive
> surging through me, and so I could not live and write as though I did. I
> was only an American Negro—who had loved the surface of Africa and
> the rhythms of Africa—but I was not Africa. (Hughes 1940: 325)

At bottom, Charlotte Mason's vision of Hughes's career was only a more
sophisticated version of the natural rhythm stereotype offered by his old
classmates. Hughes not only disavows this vision but makes this disavowal
a crucial turning point in his poetic career. Yet the terms of the disavowal
are doubly paradoxical. Hughes proclaims the political integrity and historical specificity of his own position as "an American Negro" precisely
by denying any immediate connection with Africa: "I was not Africa." Yet
he also stays remarkably close to the view he is rejecting. He dismisses
Mason's primitivism, but not the notion of rhythm which accompanies it.
As he makes it clear he is "not Africa," he is also careful to make it equally
clear that he has "loved the surface of Africa and the rhythms of Africa."
When he explains, "unfortunately, I did not feel the rhythms of the primitive surging through me, and so I could not live and write as though I
did," his explanation seems a specifically political one. It leaves open the
possibility that he might still feel rhythms "surging through" him, even if
he cannot "feel the rhythms of the primitive." But these would be those
particular to the "American Negro," and not Africa: the political location has changed but the ideal of embodiment remains.

What are we to make of this ideal? What does it mean to ground black
rhythm in the black body? Even if we grant the political differences between Hughes's version of it and the stereotyped views of Charlotte
Mason, can such an ideal ever be anything more than a nostalgic, essentialist—and indeed, racialist—fantasy of an original unity forever lost?
I believe it can be, but only if we begin to think about rhythm in newer,

and larger, terms. Hughes offers a fuller, more nuanced statement of such a view in "Afro-American Fragment," a poem from *Dear Lovely Death*, the collection discussed in a later section. He will later use this poem as the opening to his *Selected Poems*.

> So long,
> So far away
> Is Africa.
> Not even memories alive
> Save those that history books create,
> Save those that songs
> Beat back into the blood—
> Beat out of blood with words sad-sung
> In strange un-Negro tongue—
>
> *(Hughes 1995: 129)*

While these lines are certainly nostalgic, Hughes crosscuts their nostalgia with a hard-edged political critique. He offers his desire for African origins as fundamentally mixed and impure, founded in a sense of loss that is irreducibly historical. The "songs / Beat back into the blood" provide the sole living memory of distant Africa. Hughes conceptualizes this memory as a sense of rhythm embodied in "the blood," but he also presents it as accessible only as the "words sad-sung / In strange un-Negro tongue," as if to concede that one can trace it no further back than the Jubilee movement of the 1870s and 1880s. ("Sad-sung" seems to be a direct quotation of Du Bois's formulation, "sorrow songs.") And even in this attenuated form, the memory is framed by the textuality of "history books." "Memory," then, is as much a self-conscious reconstruction in the present as the actual residue of an originary past. Motivated by an acute recognition of present loss, African-American culture returns to the past not out of a nostalgic desire to evade the present, but precisely as the most effective mode of confronting that present.

Hughes categorizes this entire process of cultural recovery as rhythmic, but he understands rhythm as a mode of constructing rather than preserving continuity, a mode paradoxically founded on discontinuity. Rhythm is a "beating back" that is also a "beating out." If the figure "Beat out of blood" suggests the violence and suffering of black captivity and enslavement, then "songs / Beat back into the blood" suggests the resilience of black musical tradition in the face of this violence and dislocation.[10] Yet as the adverbs "back" and "out" indicate, this rhythmic resilience is repetitive, a reinscription across a rupture, rather than a simple continuity or essence that persists unchanged over time.[11] Presenting this rhythm as embodied in blood is Hughes's way of insisting on the literal role it played in helping African-Americans to resist their bodily suffering. These songs resemble history books in that they recover the past by constantly recapitulating it. But they differ from history books in being not only oral, but also in crucial respects non-linguistic. That is, considered in their totality as a cultural practice, these songs contain elements that both precede and exceed the "strange un-Negro tongue" in which they are expressed.

Rhythm for Hughes is nothing less than an alternate mode of cultural articulation: material, embodied, oral, musical. This mode of articulation shadows language, neither fully distinct from it nor fully subordinate to it. Although originally African in its expression within African-American tradition, it is not identical with that origin. Moreover, rhythm's persistence within African-American culture as its ultimate source of continuity has as much to do with conditions of white oppression as with its African origins. White slave-owners successfully severed that culture's linguistic ties to Africa, displacing African languages with the "strange un-Negro tongue" of English. As that part of African culture not directly dependent on language, African musical traditions proved more durable. This durability exposes a blindness within the West's traditional privileging of the linguistic, a blindness which Hughes's broadened notion of rhythm attempts to illuminate. Clarifying this point will require a brief digression.

EXCURSUS: "RHYTHM IS . . . EVERYTHING"

When Hughes places rhythm at the intersection of the African and the Western (and of corresponding oppositions of oral and literate, musical and linguistic, and black and white), he crosses boundaries which are intellectual as well as racial. In so doing he anticipates a dialogue only now beginning between two discrete strands in current humanistic thought. These are musicology's current understanding of rhythm and post-structuralism's understanding of language. Current music theory has developed an expansive notion of rhythm that tends to confirm Hughes's, from which post-structuralism's expanded notion of language could benefit. Some musicologists have rightly complained that their field has for too long ignored poststructuralism (e.g., McClary 1991: 3–34). Yet, as others have pointed out, poststructuralism and related critical trends have also not taken sufficient notice of the specific problems raised by music (Abbate 1991: 14–19, Tomlinson 1995: 343–50).[12] In poststructuralism's desire to demonstrate that all cultural expression approaches the condition of language, it has too often left in place both the primitivist mystification that subordinates music to language and the vanguardist assumption of temporal privilege which underwrites that mystification. Hughes's politically engaged, anti-primitivist notion of rhythm anticipates the directions toward which both music theory and poststructuralist thought have been tending.

Western musicology has traditionally subordinated rhythm to pitch as the two fundamental constituents of a musical event. But this subordination is a complex one, involving its own metaphorics of embodiment. On the one hand, construed as "meter," rhythm is understood as a highly ratiocinative category, almost entirely formal and abstract. Its primary function is to measure, to serve as a transparent index of the complicated harmonic and melodic relations that constitute the tonal system of Western art music. On the other hand, rhythm is just as frequently grounded in the human body. To illustrate this tension one need look no further than *The New Grove Dictionary of Music and Musicians*. Walther Dürr and Walter Gerstenberg, the authors (with Jonathan Harvey) of its article on rhythm, begin section 1 this way: "The human mind seeks to interpret continuous time generally as a succession of durations; it assumes that a rhythmic principle operates in the whole of man's environment." This sentence seems straightforwardly idealist, treating rhythm as if it were a Kantian category. Yet in the next paragraph, the article seeks the source of this *a priori* category not in the mind, but in the body:

> The relationship between rhythm and the human organism is essential to an understanding of rhythm. Heartbeat, breathing, and walking order the passage of time in regular units, and have been used time and again to illustrate this relationship, despite their variability and complexity. (Dürr and Gerstenberg 1980: 805)

In some ways this conflation of mind and body is unremarkable. It does little more than illustrate a positivist nostalgia as prevalent in musicology as in any other modern humanistic discipline: the desire to ground cultural phenomena in some unshakable natural order. But there is also more to the matter than nostalgia. Because rhythm is the conceptual site where musicology is forced to encounter the problem of the body, we can also find there an implicit critique. For example, musicology commonly describes the "beat," the mechanism through which meter is effected, by means of an explicitly bodily metaphor, the "pulse." While this metaphor obviously relates musical expression to the body, the relation is not necessarily nostalgic or logocentric. The metaphor uses a bodily process to signify the production of musical order; it transforms the body into a signifier. Yet in this metaphor, "pulse" is not some pure source of vitality, but an entity which is already semiotic, which is regulatory as well as life-giving—life-giving *because* regulatory. Thus the metaphor draws together the ratiocinative and the sensuous. It does so not as a founding unity, but as interchangeable aspects of a repeatable tension, whereby the sensuous can enforce measure by reproducing itself, and measure can continually re-embody itself in the sensuous. For this reason Dürr and Gerstenberg are right to argue that such bodily phenomena as "heartbeat, breathing, and walking" are crucial to discussions of rhythm. They are right, however, not, as they seem to assume, on the idealist grounds that such processes provide the source for the "rhythmic principle" of the mind. On the contrary, such processes are important because they show that rhythmic measurement is no less a bodily activity than a mental one. Any dualistic account that erects a rigid boundary between these two aspects of rhythm will falsify the very complexity of the process it sets out to explain.

More exploratory treatments of rhythm within current music theory have not been specifically interested in deconstructing the metaphor of the pulse, but they have increasingly called into question rhythm's subordination to pitch and have emphasized its arbitrariness and heterogeneity. As the pioneering work of Cooper and Meyer makes clear, rhythm is inherently relational, even in its narrowest compass: "Rhythm may be defined as the way in which one or more unaccented beats are grouped in relation to an accented one" (1960: 6, cf. Lester 1986: 5). Subsequent discussions have steadily expanded this interest in the relational, context-dependent basis of rhythm. Thus Maury Yeston, in *The Stratification of Musical Rhythm*, attempting to do for rhythm what the great theorist Heinrich Schenker did for pitch, argues that the rhythm of a composition always consists of the interaction between or among at least two distinct structural levels or strata.[13]

Yeston's ultimate goal is to produce a systematic conceptual apparatus through which the rhythmic structure of a given piece might be unambiguously identified, and he remains confident that all tonal music consists of inherently hierarchical stratifications of pitch which will make this possible. Nevertheless, his work is informed throughout by a keen recognition of the essentially contingent and arbitrary nature of all such hierarchies, at the level of both their broad conceptual underpinnings and their actual articulation in specific musical contexts. Yeston sees nothing inevitable in tonality, showing, for example, that his analysis is much more difficult to apply to atonal music (1976: 148–50). But even more significantly, he demonstrates throughout that even in tonal compositions, tonality by itself is insufficient to account for rhythmic structures. Characterizing most previous analysis of rhythm as "pitch to rhythm," as seeking the source of rhythmic variation in variations of pitch, he offers many examples where the process can be analyzed the other way round, as "rhythm to pitch," where the source of pitch variation can be found in the variations of rhythm. Accordingly, the general subordination of rhythm to pitch that forms an essential part of the conceptual basis of tonal music often depends in specific cases on rhythmic management of pitch (85–118). These reversals occur through the interactions of what Yeston, following Schenkerian terminology, calls "middleground" strata, where the "foreground" is the "fastest articulated musical motion" occurring "at the absolute surface of a composition," and the background is the slowest, ultimately supported only by the structure underlying all tonal composition, "the tonic triad itself . . . a single event that is considered to be prolonged throughout the entire composition" (66–67). Within Yeston's analysis, the distance between foreground and background enacts the founding subordination of rhythm to pitch, making the articulations of the former the index of the harmonic variations of the latter. The middleground thus emerges as an inherently ambiguous space where this basic subordination must be continually renegotiated, driven by the complexities of rhythm no less than those of pitch.[14]

I should acknowledge two entirely plausible objections that could be made to my reading of Yeston. The first is that I have hijacked his theory for my own distinct purposes, ascribing to it deconstructive and political aspirations its author might well disavow. The second is a less charitable version of the first. It would point out that Yeston has taken as his model a harmonic theory (that is, Schenker's) which accepts without question the founding assumptions of Western tonality. To this extent, his account leaves in place the subordination of rhythm to pitch and counterpoint. I am happy to plead guilty on both counts in the name of my larger goal here, which is to suggest commonalities between musicology and poststructuralism, along with their relevance to the issue of race. Moreover, it should also be noted that in some shorter, more recent essays, other music theorists have taken the most exploratory aspects of Yeston's argument even further. Thus Wallace Berry declares, "Rhythm is: everything" (1985: 33). To understand music in the first instance as a construction of pitch is to remain too indebted to the specificities of Western tonality. The broadest, most neutral conception of music must begin with rhythm, the recurrence of sound through time (cf. Rowell 1985: 2–3; Berry 1976: 30; Lester 1986: 4–6).

This broadened conception of rhythm offers a specifically musical alternative to the current poststructuralist model of articulation, which is linguistic and textual. Poststructuralism's normative case is the written word, black on blank, the signifier standing alone on the page, separated by white space from other signifiers and separated from its referent by the materiality of the text. In this model, articulation is fundamentally a break, a fissure, a gap, a process of differentiation where difference is understood as equivalent to absence. But a specifically rhythmic model of articulation is less spatialized and more purely temporal. It involves differentiation alone. It imagines differentiation not as a matter of absence, but as a matter of repetition—that is, as a matter of that form of temporal continuity that is paradoxically founded on discontinuity. Poststructuralist thinkers have embraced textuality as a corrective to positivist models of language that assume that the oral is more immediate, more real, than the textual. They have rightly seen this belief in the immediacy of spoken language as symptomatic of the larger positivist and empirical modes of thought that have assumed language as a whole can be treated as a transparent vessel of the real. Building on the central insight of the linguist Ferdinand de Saussure that language is a system of differences without positive terms, they have offered another view which is not only more logically coherent, but is also increasingly coming to be recognized as more intuitively convincing as well. They have pointed out that language works not by preserving traces of the objects to which it refers,[15] but by differentiating itself from such objects. The word *tree*, for example, can refer to a tree precisely because it isn't a tree. Its entirely arbitrary relation to the reality of trees is precisely what enables us to refer to trees when there are none present. This point is best illustrated by the written signifier. With its obvious spatial and temporal disconnection from its referent, the written signifier demonstrates the condition of difference that must necessarily characterize all language, spoken and written alike. Paradoxically, however, when poststructuralists for this reason take the written signifier as the exemplar for all forms of human expression, they leave themselves beholden to the very model of linguistic transparency they have so cogently critiqued. For they retain its assumption that the purposes of the textual signifier are exhausted by its referential function. This assumption ignores, among other things, the alternative textuality of music.

Musical textuality is not just distinct from linguistic textuality, but it exists in unspoken opposition to it. In much the same way that it subordinates rhythm to pitch, Western thought also subordinates music to language. As we have already seen, the same Enlightenment ideal which takes spoken language to be more immediate than written language also takes music to be more immediate than language as a whole. Yet music is not for all that less inherently textual than language. As a number of recent theorists have observed (e.g., Randel 1992: 11–12), the development of modern European concert music would have been impossible without writing, and indeed printing. It is just that the musical tradition has expressed its textuality differently. Unlike linguistic textuality, musical textuality does not aspire to the condition of absence. A musical score is not designed to replace a performance. Instead it is designed to aid performance in a variety of ways: to enable the composer to project the form a performance will take, to enable a conductor to organize and regulate a performance as it occurs, to help the culture maintain essential features of past performance practice. In the first two of these functions, the textual is clearly no more than an extension of performance. The third may seem to be primarily referential, but in fact the score is never more than part of the mechanism whereby the musical tradition sustains itself. The necessity of performance is always written into it as a condition of its intelligibility, and indeed it always assumes the largely oral traditions of performance practice. For this reason, we might say musical textuality foregrounds repetition rather than reference; or, more precisely, that it conditions reference on recurrence rather than absence.

This foregrounding of repetition tells us as much about textuality as it does about music. It makes recurrence no less a defining feature of textuality than absence. We must therefore seek to understand not only how music is like language, but how language is like music. We must avoid mistakes of the sort Umberto Eco makes when he declares that music is "a semiotic system without a semantic level" (1976: 111, cited in Baker 1984: 7). Such observations do no more than dress up in poststructuralist jargon the traditional view that language is defined by reference and music by the lack of it. Indeed, in direct contradiction to this view, Susan McClary forcefully declares that "music signifies": it

> can sound happy, sad, sexy, funk, silly, "American," religious, or whatever. . . . Composers of music for movies and advertisements consistently stake their commercial success on the public's pragmatic knowledge of musical signification—the skill with which John Williams, for instance,

manipulates the semiotic codes of the late nineteenth-century symphony in *E.T.* or *Star Wars* is breathtaking. . . . It doesn't really matter that academic disciplines have tried to insist that music is only music, that it cannot mean anything else. In the social world, music achieves these effects all the time. (1991: 21)

But if we are to take full advantage of McClary's insight, it is crucial we recognize that music's capacity to signify does not make it identical to language after all. On the contrary, it means we must change the way we think of language as well. It requires that we recognize the a-referential level of language—the level I have been characterizing as rhythmic and repetitive—no less than the referential level of music. Thus the following rhetorical questions of Nattiez make an essential complement to McClary's comments:

Do not the rhymes at the end of a line of verse depend on symbolic functioning of a musical type? Is it truly for the sake of their meaning alone that one opposes the phrases "theory of practice and the practice of theory" (Bourdieu) or "the poetry of grammar and the grammar of poetry" (Jakobson)? It is interesting to look at the functioning of our so-called "associations of *ideas*," which are more often than not dictated by assonance or purely phonetic or rhythmic connections. If this is so, then cannot the formal aspect of the semiologic functioning of music serve as a model for other symbolic domains, at least preventing us from downplaying, within these other domains, dimensions that are utterly essential to them? (1990: 148)

Pursued to its logical conclusion, Nattiez's inquiries would considerably enhance our attention to sound in poetry, especially if we understand rhythm in the capacious sense envisioned by Berry. Poetic rhythm would no longer be merely a matter of rhyme and meter. It could instead account comprehensively for the particular durability associated with poetry— "What oft was thought but ne'er so well expressed." To the tags from Bourdieu and Jakobson we might add such poetic examples as Keats's "'Beauty is truth, truth beauty,'—that is all / Ye know on earth, and all ye need to know." The "musical" qualities of all these examples make them memorable by making them repeatable. In so doing they demonstrate that linguistic textuality is ultimately no more distinct from linguistic performance than the musical score is from musical performance. A linguistic text always projects a reading, and as these examples show, the reading it projects is also always at least partially a speaking. Unlike prose texts, the poetic text makes this condition explicit. Its disposition into lines serves as a rudimentary "score" by indicating the most prominent features of its rhythmic and sonic structure.

HUGHES'S MODERNISM:
A PULSE BEAT THAT KEEPS ON GOING

We may now return to Hughes. We might well say that rhythm is also everything to him. As the defining characteristic of the black vernacular, it is a single element of a specific musical tradition. But it simultaneously provides the broadest possible model for all forms of cultural continuity. Hughes uses it this way toward the end of *The Big Sea*, in the work's richest treatment of the issue. He is discussing his early career, during the days he was working as a waiter in Washington, D.C., before his "discovery" by the prominent white poet Vachel Lindsay.

> I tried to write poems like the songs they sang on Seventh Street [a neighborhood of working-class blacks]—gay songs, because you had to be gay or die; sad songs, because you couldn't help being sad sometimes. But gay or sad, you kept on living and you kept on going. Their songs—those of Seventh Street—had the pulse beat of the people who keep on going.
>
> Like the waves of the sea coming one after another, always one after another, like the earth moving around the sun, night, day—night, day—night, day—forever, so is the undertow of black music with its rhythm that never betrays you, its strength like the beat of the human heart, its humor, and its rooted power.

> *I'm goin' down to de railroad, baby,*
> *Lay ma head on de track—*
> *I'm goin' down to de railroad, babe,*
> *Lay ma head on de track—*
> *But if I see de train a-comin',*
> *I'm gonna jerk it back.*

> (Hughes 1945: 209)

This passage effects a grand conflation. As it connects Hughes's poetry to "the songs they sang on Seventh Street," the urban blues of the black working class, it also connects the blues to the vitality of natural processes like ocean waves, the motion of the earth, and the beating of the human heart. Hughes imagines this conflation in rhythmic terms. It is repetitive and periodic, but most important it is materially productive. As the "pulse beat of the people who keep on going," it is a grounding and an embodiment. The rhythms of the blues arise from and return to the bodies and material condition of the black working class. That process of return not only insures the continuity of the blues tradition, but through that tradition also helps insure, in entirely material terms, the continued survival of the black community. In arising from the "pulse beat," the blues become it. They are what keep "the people" going.[16] Yet despite this insistence on embodiment and materialization, this rhythmic ideal is also resolutely anti-essentialist. There is no unity here, as the multiple ironies of the lyrics Hughes appends make clear. These lyrics are not about unification, but about alienation. They assume a radical disparity between the human and the non-human, and they dramatize that disparity by imagining the singer's head lying on the railroad track. In their final, witty disavowal of suicide—"But if I see de train a-comin', / I'm gonna jerk it back,"—it is precisely the recognition of the disparity between the human and non-human that constitutes the principle of survival.

We can find the same dynamic throughout the passage, beginning with the abrupt shift into the second person in the opening sentence: "gay songs, because you had to be gay or die." The affirmations of the blues are constructed in the face of extinction. The colloquial generic suddenly puts the reader in this desperate position. But it also provides the reader with that position's discursive and cultural resources. That is, as the reader confronts the arbitrariness of his or her own cultural and political privilege, he or she also confronts the imperatives of continuity and survival provided the blues tradition: "You kept on living and you kept on going." As the next paragraph moves on to the natural world, the headlong energy of its single sentence leads us so insistently to its concluding image of "rooted power" that it is easy to forget that all the images that constitute that headlong rush—"the waves of the sea . . . the earth moving around the sun"—do not describe "rooted" states. On the contrary, they are entirely antithetical to rootedness and remind us that the characteristic state of the natural world is incessant motion and transformation. Even as Hughes moves through these metaphors to arrive at a notion of "rooted power," he also uses them to produce a much more fluid sense of what it means to be rooted. In a particularly nice reversal, Hughes identifies "the rhythm that never betrays you" as "the undertow of black music." An undertow, after all, working against the waves above it, is precisely what betrays and uproots you. Hughes may well have used this figure of the undertow to suggest the "crossrhythm," the conflict between "groundbeat" and melodic line which, William Barlow has recently suggested, defines the blues (1989: 3–4). But if so, this correspondence only reinforces the larger point: the grounding the blues offers the black working class is not some unchanging stability but an unending process of give and take, of rupture producing continuity, an abiding source of transformative energy.

For this reason, the blues can provide the source of Hughes's poetic authority even as they require the very nature of such authority to be re-examined. Hughes begins the passage by proclaiming his work to be an imitation of the blues tradition and ends it by letting that tradition speak in its own voice. And yet it is the essence of that voice not to speak but to sing. After defining the blues three times by reference to its rhythm, he represents it by its lyrics alone. This transposition is possible because Hughes has defined rhythm so broadly. But it also enables him to dem-onstrate the specifically poetic virtues of the blues. For the most promi-nent feature of the lyrics he chooses is their poeticness, their display of poetic wit of a fairly conventional sort, which exerts itself on the tradi-tionally poetic subject of frustrated desire.

This continuity between the blues and poetic convention does not make these lyrics less political. On the contrary, it displays the political potential of poetic convention. The figure of the railroad track provides the speaker's desire with a specific historical and political location. As Houston A. Baker, Jr., points out in his magisterial discussion of the blues tradition, the railroad symbolized both the great black migra-tions northward and the economic privation and political oppression that made them necessary. The trope summons the "image of the black blues singer at the railway junction lustily transforming experiences of a durative (unceasingly oppressive) landscape into the energies of rhythmic song" (1984: 7). Indeed, Baker's description admirably reca-pitulates the political point of Hughes's passage, on which it no doubt draws. The lyrics Hughes cites do enact a transformation, making the oppressive power of the railroad the occasion for a display of poetic wit. At the same time, Hughes's citation of these lyrics, with its complex interplay between the musical and the linguistic, the learned and the vernacular, foregrounds the diachronic aspect of this transformation in a way that Baker does not. Baker's model is synchronic. The singer's rhythmic song is a direct response to the oppressive landscape; its raw material is experiential rather than poetic. By contrast, Hughes accords artistic as well as political agency to the blues singer. While he aims at the same political end as Baker, he enables us to see how such an end is achieved by a detour through poetic convention.

The song transforms the oppressive landscape figured by the rail-road by drawing the figure of the railroad into a conventional drama of frustrated desire. There, as the mechanism whereby the singer will accomplish his threat to commit suicide, the railroad track signifies the absoluteness of his desire. The singer loves the "baby" he addresses so intensely that he literally cannot live without her, an entirely conventional claim. Indeed, the idea that to be in love is to be unable to survive without the beloved is probably one of the commonest conventions of erotic discourse in the West, as common in popular song as in the poetic canon. It can be traced all the way back to the trope of lovesickness that was central to Medieval romance. Appropriated by the Petrarchan tradition that dominated the European love lyric throughout the Renaissance, it no doubt passed into the domain of popular song thereafter, along with other Petrarchan conventions.[17] There are other Petrarchan traces in this blues as well. Petrarchan lyrics characteristically projected their speaker's internal erotic turmoil onto an external landscape, usually a battlefield or an ocean voyage, here updated as a railroad track. The wit of the final line, "I'm gonna jerk it back," arises from its deflation of the hyperbole built into these conventions. In point of fact, the singer *can* live without his beloved, as the actuality of a train bearing down forcibly reminds him. Yet even this deflation could be considered Petrarchan. Petrarchan poetry frequently satirized its own hyperbole (as in the particularly famous instance of Shakespeare's Sonnet 130, "My mistress' eyes are nothing like the sun"). Paradoxically, this Petrarchan deflation completes the singer's semiotic mastery of the oppressive landscape he figures in the railroad. Having reduced that landscape to a symbolic boundary within his own internal drama, he now definitively evades its menace by jerking his head back.

I am not suggesting that the author of these blues read Renaissance poetry, still less that his lyrics are a purely derivative, unconscious repetition of its conventions. What I am suggesting is that his lyrics constitute an engagement with that tradition nonetheless, an engagement which demonstrates the syncretic range of the black vernacular. While high culture defines its continuity through the canonical figure of the great master, that continuity actually depends on a massive process of reception, discrimination, and dissemination. The great masters become the great masters because their interventions pass into the quotidian structures of communal belief. Blues singers encountered Petrarch as a residue within oral culture rather than as the author of a discrete set of texts. But their encounter with that anonymous residue was an encounter with Petrarch nevertheless. Moreover, we must view this encounter as modernist, if that term is to have any consistency. For, no less than Eliot or Pound, Hughes's blues singer places himself in the center of a profusion of discursive structures, revaluing inherited forms according to the exigencies of modern experience. As with the high moderns, his modernism inheres neither in the inherited form nor in the sheer modernity of his experience alone, but in his lyrical conflation of the two. (We might note parenthetically that the same thing is true of the blues as a musical practice, which is why viewing them as derivative on the basis of their deployment of European tonal conventions badly misses the point.) That such conflations are oral in no way mitigates their modernism. On the contrary, the example of the blues singer exposes the orality inherent in all modernist artistic practice, no matter how self-consciously vanguardist. For the modern experience from which the vanguardist generates his authoritative break with the past is by definition a mass experience, one which the vanguardist experiences in exactly the same fashion as everyone else: anonymously, chaotically, unlearnedly.

Langston Hughes becomes the Negro poet laureate by recognizing this fact. His celebration of the blues names the cultural source of his modernism, gives his modern experience a specific political location. Yet paradoxically, the point of this specification is precisely its profusion. The cultural authority Hughes draws from the black vernacular was already syncretic and multiple. The blues expressed its political aspirations in a complex cultural practice that confounded traditional boundaries between the musical and poetic, and the oral and the literate. But even these dichotomies understate its multiplicity. It continually interleaved its oral retentions of African musical practice and folklore with more contemporary popular discourses, with Christian spirituality, with the conventions of elite poetic tradition and European tonality.

DEATH IS A DRUM: ELEGY AND THE BLUES

Hughes's popular notion of the modern gives his cultural nationalism an extraordinarily broad range. In the introduction to the radio anthology "12 Contemporary Negro Poets: USA," which he prepared for the BBC in the early 1960s, he remarks, "Even racial poetry can be universal—and local subjects like Little Rock may assume symbolic stature for everybody everywhere. The surface of a poem may be racial or regional, but if it is a good poem its core is universal" (Hughes 1964). Here we have Hughes speaking in his laureate role, both as a black poet and as an American to a British radio audience. Like many postmodern critics, I do not agree with the neo-Kantian perspective he expresses in the second sentence: I would argue that a poem's aesthetic appeal lies precisely in its cultural specificity, and that such specificity characterizes its core as well as its surface. But it seems equally essential to acknowledge that finding a satisfactory response to Hughes's universalist aspirations is

precisely the challenge which his laureateship poses. As I turn now to his
poetic practice, I offer as a partial response to that challenge his notion
of rhythm. One of Hughes's most characteristic poetic preoccupations
is death. In speaking to this most universal of human experiences, Hughes
also speaks to the center of modern poetic tradition. Coleridge declared
the elegy "the form of poetry natural to the reflective mind"; and modern poetry is relentlessly elegiac. Hughes draws his interest in the genre
both from Whitman and from his predecessors in the African-American
tradition. But he also recasts this traditional topic as the inevitable complement of his notion of rhythm. Death is the material, bodily rupture
against which the "pulse beat" of black song defines itself—as the metaphor literally requires. The rhythmic imperatives of the blues provide
Hughes with a material, atheological understanding of death, one which
he will locate convincingly in the materiality of poetic language itself.

Delineating this understanding will require us to rethink poetic
rhythm in the much broader terms Hughes advocates. When literary
critics address the question of poetic rhythm, they define it almost exclusively in terms of prosody. If rhythm really is everything, then an
adequate account of poetic rhythm must call into question any hard and
fast boundary between sound and meaning, examining all forms of
poetic repetition, from the rhetorical to the generic to the semantic. In
fact, Hughes's strictly prosodic debt to the blues is probably negligible,
consisting largely of a greater interest in rhyme than most of his white
counterparts. As many scholars have noted, Hughes's more obvious debts
to the blues are rhetorical and tropological: his frequent recourse to
blues refrains and other forms of line repetition, and to blues motifs and
metaphors. If these broader forms of repetition seem harder to place,
that is because they expose an important methodological problem.

Barbara Johnson has acutely noted that African-American poetry has
been put at a disadvantage by a "new Critical aesthetic . . . tied to the image of the mute, visible object ('the well-wrought urn')." Because this aesthetic virtually ignores "the oral dimension of poetry," it has no way of
accounting for the "extensive and effective use of repetition" so crucial
to the African-American poetic tradition (1989: 44–45). Nor is this a
difficulty for African-American poetry alone. Ironically, the very modernist poets from whom New Criticism draws its interest in the image
were equally interested in sound. When Ezra Pound and F. S. Flint published their manifesto for *Imagisme* in the March 1913 issue of *Poetry*,
they offered only three rules, one of which was, "As regarding rhythm:
to compose in the sequence of the musical phrase, not the metronome"
(Jones 1972: 129). While New Criticism developed a formidable array

of techniques for reading the poetic image, it ignored the problem of the phrase, and current practical criticism remains troubled by this lacuna. Learning to read the phrase will obviously involve questions of prosody, but it cannot restrict itself to prosody without reinstating the very subordination of poetic rhythm to poetic meaning that it should call into question. The phrase is a unit at once phonic and semantic; it points to the ultimate indissolubility of sound and meaning. Nor is the point purely methodological. It is hardly coincidental that the image Johnson justly cites (from the Cleanth Brooks volume of the same title) as an archetype, "the well-wrought urn," is an elegiac one. The image represses poetry's temporality by spatializing the quintessentially temporal relation between life and death and then investing the atemporal, ahistorical model that results with a death-like finality. Hughes's many versions of the elegy show us that this model misreads the temporality of death no less than that of poetry.

In his most widely anthologized and analyzed poem, "The Weary Blues," which first appeared in 1925, Hughes applies Imagist principles of prosody to the figure of the blues singer, but he does so in order to convey a larger blues vision of human mortality. In practice, Pound's notion of the musical phrase meant less abandoning traditional meters than juxtaposing different meters in the same poem and often the same line. In "The Weary Blues," Hughes continually alternates between duple and triple meters to suggest the cross-rhythms of the blues. Yet Hughes is less interested in demonstrating the capacity of poetic meter to capture blues rhythm than in articulating what we might legitimately call a blues sublime.

We hear the voice of the blues singer twice. The first time he proclaims the blues as catharsis: "I's gwine to quit ma frownin' / And put ma troubles on the shelf" (lines 21–22). Such cathartic, functionalist notions of black vernacular culture were fairly standard in African-American writing, and elsewhere Hughes is sometimes content with them himself. Here, however, the troubles won't stay put, and the next lyrics disavow all consolation.

> "I got the Weary Blues
> And I can't be satisfied.
> Got the Weary Blues
> And can't be satisfied—
> I ain't happy no mo'
> And I wish that I had died."

(Hughes 1995: 50, lines 25–30)

At once emotional state and expressive genre, the Weary Blues not only register the frustration of desire but perpetuate that frustration. As the death wish of the final line tersely indicates, they constitute a re-nunciation of mortality, a desire for transcendence that knows itself doomed from the start and so can do nothing but continually re-enact its own frustration. This is the stream of profound pessimism that Hughes found most central to the blues. As he explained in 1925 in a letter to Carl Van Vechten, which Van Vechten published in *Vanity Fair*: "The Blues always impressed me as being very sad, sadder even than the Spirituals, because their sadness is not softened with tears, but hardened with laughter, the absurd, incongruous laughter of a sadness without even a god to appeal to" (Van Vechten 1979: 46). In this godless laugh-ter, there is an unmistakable echo of Nietzsche, whom Hughes began reading in high school (Hughes 1945: 33). His reading of the blues effects a double revision. To the previous African-American tradition that, following Du Bois, located vernacular authority in the spirituals, Hughes speaks as a modernist and an atheist.[18] But to the political elit-ism endemic to Nietzschean pessimism, he offers the blues as a vernac-ular tradition every bit as rigorous in its rejection of religious forms of consolation.

The poem rewrites the sublime on the basis of this pessimism. As Arnold Rampersad has pointed out, it begins from a stance of anthro-pological detachment: "I heard a Negro play" (line 3; Rampersad 1986a: 147–48). Hughes marks his separation from the singer and his role of reporter for a primarily white audience. There is also an element of the *flaneur* here, the modern poet moving through an urban landscape finding aesthetic value in commodification and economic deprivation. Hughes insists on the geographic and material specificities of this scene, explicitly locating it on "Lenox Avenue" (line 4), and calling our atten-tion to the "old gas light" attached to the singer's piano (line 5), and the "rickety stool" on which he sits (line 12). However, the effect of the singer's own voice entering the poem will be to break down these modes of detachment. The poem ends:

> And far into the night he crooned that tune.
> The stars went out and so did the moon.
> The singer stopped playing and went to bed
> While the Weary Blues echoed through his head.
> He slept like a rock or a man that's dead.
>
> *(31–35)*

"Far into the night": the singer's "tune" spatializes time. The night becomes his only landscape and the modernist marks of urban deprivation vanish before an older, pastoral vocabulary that is itself the barest residue of a lost Romanticism: "the stars," "the moon," and "a rock." With this reduction the poem concentrates its politics entirely on the Weary Blues itself, which takes over the poem, directing the narratorial voice according to its own imperatives.[19] The singer goes off to bed, and still "the Weary Blues echoed through his head." The poems final line delivers the death that the song sought in its final line. Moreover, as the symbolic death of sleep, this ending maintains the indeterminacy driving the song's implacable pessimism. Is this sleep a cathartic renewal or simply the collapse of exhaustion? It is impossible to tell.

Yet in its very indeterminacy, this deathlike sleep is also a sublime transcendence. The singer "slept like a rock." Like the sleep it describes, this simile displaces the singer's immediate urban environment and registers a brief crossing over into the non-human, a momentary assumption of the transcendent durability of the natural landscape. An echo of the Weary Blues, this transcendence also echoes an earlier poet to whom Hughes was often compared, Wordsworth. The indeterminate, elegiac space in which this poem ends resembles that which Wordsworth (1984: 147) envisions in the Lucy poems:

> No motion has she now, no force;
> She neither hears nor sees,
> Rolled round in earth's diurnal course
> With rocks, and stones, and trees.

Hughes deploys this Wordsworthian projection of loss onto the natural landscape as a response to the singer's desire for death. Rampersad notes that this poem "honors both the tradition of Europe . . . and the tradition of black America. . . . The latter tradition, in fact, invades the former" (1986a: 147). Indeed, we might well read "The Weary Blues" as enacting the trope Harold Bloom describes as Apophrades, or the Return of the Dead (Bloom 1973: 139–55). It is as if Wordsworth came back as a blues singer, and the Romantic sublime was literally a belated echo of the blues "pulse beat."

Hughes achieves this reversal through a poetic logic that is repetitive through and through, and which he insistently marks as rhythmic. This final stanza begins: "Thump, thump, thump, went his foot on the floor. / He played a few chords then he sang some more—"(23–24). The three strong stresses of the onomatopoeic "Thump, thump, thump" signify the purely rhythmic, and the purely rhythmic is the pulse beat that keeps the poem going. Rhythm gives way to pitch, the "few chords," which gives way to lyrics: "then he sang some more." But this apparent progression from measure to meaning is belied by the words that ostensibly constitute its goal. As we have just seen, the song's extravagant desire to die issues only in an ambiguous sleep. The poem's closure is defined not by its achievement of some stable meaning, but precisely by the lack of it. We are literally left with no more than an echo, an empty repetition, a point definitively reinforced by the rhythmic structure of the last line. The stress pattern of its final three syllables, "man that's dead," echoes the purely rhythmic "Thump, thump, thump" that began the stanza. The Weary Blues' final significance is precisely this indeterminate echo, whose power of self-perpetuation depends on its semantic emptiness, whose meaning can never be more than its own rhythmic rearticulation.

What the poem offers by way of consolation is an uncertain resolution which is not quite consolatory and not quite cathartic but still does work which is a little bit of both. Its blues sublime is spare and distilled, an insistent return to poetic language as material utterance, as the sheer act of speaking, which it imagines as the compulsion to repeat. As Ralph Ellison will comment two decades later,

> The blues is an impulse to keep the painful details and episodes of a brutal experience in one's aching consciousness, to finger its jagged grain and to transcend it, not by the consolation of philosophy, but by squeezing from it a near-tragic, near-comic lyricism. (Ellison 1966: 78; cf. Hansell 1978: 24)

For Hughes, no less than for Ellison, the lyricism of the blues is elegiac, and his redefinition of the sublime in a blues idiom is convincing because it simultaneously redefines the elegiac. "The Weary Blues" reminds us that the elegist's rhetorical stance is by definition a compulsion to repeat. As its own way of fingering the "jagged grain" of loss, the elegy takes for granted poetry's inadequacy in the face of death. What consolation it derives from this predicament comes as often from a self-reflexive return to the indeterminacies of poetic language as from "philosophy" or religion, even if the latter forms of consolation have traditionally been considered more important.

The break Hughes's redefinition effects was also a break with previous African-American poetic tradition, where elegy had been an important genre since the heyday of Paul Laurence Dunbar. It was particularly important for three poets whose work first appeared in the decade after Dunbar's untimely death in 1906: Fenton Johnson (1888–1958), Georgia Douglas Johnson (1877–1966), and James Weldon Johnson (1871–1938).[20] Though no less insistent on the materiality of death than Hughes was to be, these poets nevertheless draw more heavily on the redemptive rhetoric of Christianity, which they derive from the spirituals and the traditions of the black preacher. This break was no doubt part of Hughes's larger, self-consciously modern preoccupation with formal innovation which would issue a year later (1927) in *Fine Clothes to the Jew*, "his most radical achievement in language" (Rampersad 1986a: 151). But his next collection, *Dear Lovely Death*, the first after his break with Charlotte Mason, privately printed in 1931, employs more conventional poetic diction and, with some exceptions, a less racially marked lyric voice. While this may seem to be a retreat, in fact this partial return to convention enables Hughes to engage more explicitly with the African American elegy while still retaining his rhythmic commitment to the blues and "the standards of . . . the black masses" (Rampersad 1986a: 145). Paradoxical though it may seem, he accomplishes this synthesis precisely by probing more deeply within the larger Anglophone tradition of elegy. Radically rereading the genre from a blues perspective, he finds within it an explicit acknowledgment of its own compulsion to repeat. This tendency is the *memento mori*, less a subgenre than an allied tradition.

Originating as an important element of Roman stoicism, the *memento mori* re-emerges as a much wider discourse about the same time Renaissance poets transformed the elegy from a general mode of praise to a lament for the dead.[21] As the death's head, its central emblem, suggests, the *memento mori* is concerned first and foremost to insist on the materiality and banality of death; its interest in consolation or transcendence comes afterward. Where the elegy traditionally offers spiritual consolation at the moment of a particular death, the *memento mori* demonstrates the paradoxical ways in which the generality of death gives particular urgency to the business of living (Stein 1986: 178). *Dear Lovely Death* is less concerned with death as the ultimate form of loss than with death's mysterious banality and its inextricable enmeshment with living.[22] The volume contains a total of twelve poems. Only the first six are elegies. (Death also features somewhat less prominently in two of the last six, "Demand," and "Poem," retitled "Garden" for the *Selected Poems*.) Yet the volume as a whole is quite tightly unified by the repetition throughout of incidental imagery and subsidiary themes. Indeed, the movement from the opening explorations of death to the drive to "meet Life face to face" celebrated in the closing poem, "Aesthete in Harlem" (Hughes

1931: 12, line 3),[23] is one of the chief ways the volume fulfills the generic imperatives of the *memento mori*. It remembers death by "seeking /
Life" (4–5).

The volume begins with "Drum," one of the great undiscovered short
poems of the twentieth century. In setting the collection's theme and poetic program, it aims at nothing less than the redefinition of its genre. I
quote the poem in full.

> Bear in mind
> That death is a drum
> Beating for ever
> Till the last worms come
> To answer its call,
> Till the last stars fall,
> . Until the last atom
> Is no atom at all,
> Until time is lost
> And there is no air
> And space itself
> Is nothing nowhere.
> Death is a drum,
> A signal drum,
> Calling all life
> To Come!   Come!
> Come!

The first two lines recapitulate the command that constitutes the *memento mori:* remember death. But here what is to be remembered is not
just death as sheer phenomenological fact, but also a particular way of
understanding it. Moving from command to contemplation, this *memento mori* aspires to take over the work of the elegy, to redefine the elegy's traditional language of consolation as subordinate to its own imperative mood.

The poem consists of two sentences. The first is an imperative, but it
ends with a long subordinate clause in the indicative. The second is an
indicative but it ends with an imperative. Through the course of these
two sentences, death literally moves from the imperative to the indicative
and back. Whatever meaning we can make of death, we can never be divorced from death's status as imperative. The poem defines this imperative through its central metaphor: death is a drum. With this metaphor
the poem generates all the rest of its language, both syntactically and
conceptually. Death is a drum: as the measure of life, death is a signifier,

but a signifier of a particularly rhythmic sort. It cannot be separated from the reality it measures, even though by definition it is antithetical to that reality. The finite temporality which death signals gives life a goal and invests it with a drum-like urgency. Death is a counter-heartbeat, a counter-pulse, a palpable bodily reality that surrounds life and drives it forward. With this insistence on the complete interpenetration between life and death, the figure of the drum fulfills the traditional imperative of the *memento mori* by redefining it. Where the tradition teaches us to expect the death's head, a mute skull, Hughes offers instead the drum, which makes explicit a condition the skull can only imply. What is horrifying about death is not its stasis, but precisely its lack of stasis, its continual intercalation with the quotidian processes of living.

While primarily philosophical, this redefinition is also political. The figure of the drum looks forward to "Afro-American Fragment," the seventh poem in the collection, which appears immediately following the last of its elegies. As he does in many other poems, there Hughes uses the drum as a figural shorthand for the cultural resilience of the African diaspora. In "Drum" Hughes annexes death itself to that resilience, recasting the diaspora in the mode of the *memento mori*, a confrontation with extinction that delivered survival. The figure of the drum thus leaves a barely perceptible political trace on this aggressively abstract and universalizing poem in the most aggressively universalizing of genres. Hughes speaks to the universal problem of death and does so in universal terms, but as the Negro *poet laureate*, the poet speaking for his community to others. Nor can the universality of this poem be approached except through the specificities of its central figure.

Until this point I have been treating this figure in classic New Critical fashion, as an image. Yet even as an image, the figure offers up a quintessentially rhythmic logic which demands we attend to the actual conditions of its utterance within the poem. We must read it as a phrase rather than simply as an image, for its phrasal significance comprehends its logic as an image. Death is not only a signifier, but a signifier whose capacity for repetition is virtually inexhaustible: "Beating forever / Till the last worms come." As the poem's central phrase, *death is a drum* is articulated twice, once at the beginning of the poem and once near its end. In between is the poem's only other major element, the long clause which begins with "Beating" and modifies the central figure. As an explication of this figure, the clause extends its logic syntactically as well as semantically. Constructed of an intricate pattern of repetitions and negations, this clause literally enacts the perpetuity it asserts, beginning with Hughes's extraordinary management of the line endings. Lines 3, 4, 7, and 11 each end with enjambments, all of them complicated by rhyme or semantic completion, or both. The pattern is best illustrated by lines 4 and 5. The enjambment of line 4, "Till the last worms come / To answer its call," is almost completely unexpected, masked by the strong rhyme of *come* with *drum* and the ostensible completeness of the entire line. Both the sound and the sense of the first four lines strongly suggest the sentence should end at "come." Yet the next line is an extension no less logical. Thus, in the very movement of the poem's language from line 4 to line 5, the ostensible finality of "the last worms" coming gives way to a further finality. This end beyond the end turns out fittingly to be essentially a linguistic one: "To answer its call." Death prescribes its own apocalyptic end by virtue of the measure it imposes on life.

As the long clause moves to its end, it will define this apocalypse in an increasingly distilled form. The vocabulary of a vaguely religious cosmology—"worms," "call," and "stars fall"—gives way to a more scientific one—"atom," "air," and "space"—with negations playing an increasingly prominent role. As it displaces religion with science, this clause imagines moving beyond even the more limited epistemological support of scientific categories. Attempting to move beyond time, air, and "space itself," the sentence ends in a realm that can be defined only as a pure negation: "nothing nowhere." And yet this negation contains an odd, nearly impossible consolation. As the completion of the poem's drive to imagine what is beyond death, this negation cannot itself ever be completed. That is to say, in order to make itself as full, as emphatic, as it needs to be, this negation must repeat itself. It is not enough to say "nothing"; one must say "nothing nowhere," and this necessity leaves the very notion of negation dependent on the materiality of the signifier that expresses or, more precisely, re-enacts it. There is no stable signified here, just an imperative to repeat, to speak again what has already been spoken, when what is spoken is nothing more than the impossibility of getting beyond death by speaking. This formal conundrum casts an odd light on the apocalypse it is charged with conveying. It creates a simple disconnect; the attempt to speak death in the fullness of its horror issues in little more than an encounter with the empty materiality of linguistic signifiers. While one might argue that this semantic disconnection intensifies the horror, the fact remains that any such intensification will necessarily be framed by the very detachment from which it arises. The problem of death becomes the problem of language, but that problem imagined rhythmically, as a matter of articulation and repetition.

The poem ends by reiterating its central figure in the face of the dilemma. The opening expression of the figure stresses rhythm, death as a drum beating forever. The ending expression stresses signification, first with the repetition "A signal drum," then with the twice repeated command "Come! Come! / Come!" If this command is macabre to the point of ghoulishness, it is also oddly welcoming. Far from resolving this tension, the poem finds closure precisely in its irresolution, an irresolution embodied in the peculiar semiotics of this command and the rhythm of its articulation in this poem. The triple articulation forces us to focus as much on the sound of word as on its meaning. The three consecutive stresses recalls the "Thump, thump, thump" from "The Weary Blues," and the effect here is similar, drawing the listener into an expectation, even a desire, that the articulation continue. The sole difference is that here the repetition is a command that anticipates resistance. Yet the resistance also serves to define the power of the imperative and to that extent intensifies it. Moreover, the repetition of the command reinforces the generative impulse that characterizes its meaning. For the command *come* projects an addressor, an addressee, a spatial expanse, and a temporal duration in which the expanse can be crossed. Death becomes a performative, a command that summons a new actuality into the world by virtue of its own articulation. As the negation of meaning, death becomes the source of its production as well. It names both the emptiness out of which meaning emerges and the necessity which drives that emergence. This collapse of death into language may not produce a consolation in the traditional sense. Nevertheless, it does force a recognition of the necessity of this failure, a recognition which achieves a similar effect. For it enables the poem to demonstrate the philosophical necessity of death in the very movement of its own language. In thus confronting its own expressive inadequacies in relation to death, the poem also recognizes death as the source of what meaning it can achieve.

If the elegy can do nothing more than shore up largely empty signifiers against the ineffability of death, it can also never not do that. In refusing the traditional form of consolation, the modern elegy, like the blues, must always return to a semiotic logic that is rhythmic. And that necessity is not only philosophical and spiritual, but political and material. Properly understood, modernity's alienation from the spiritual certainties of the past does not render its present urgencies meaningless. On the contrary, this alienation makes an engagement with them that much more crucial. As Hughes explores the imperatives of *memento mori* in the remainder of the collection, he continually comes back to this recognition. "The Consumptive," the volume's second poem, insists on death as an inevitable but banal bodily event, an event whose ineffable terror lies precisely in the excruciating slowness of its unremitting diurnal pace. "Dear Lovely Death," the title poem, is an apostrophe to death in an extended single sentence. It concludes "Dear lovely Death, / Change is thy other name" (9–10). Ostentatiously anticlimactic, this ending uses the very banality of death as the avenue toward accepting its inevitability. To make it a synonym for change is to suggest that death is a necessary concomitant to the constant possibilities of renewal that for a modern consciousness form the most hopeful and liberating aspects of life. Moreover, by its very reductiveness, this redefinition justifies the startling paradox with which the poem opens:

> Dear lovely Death
> That taketh all things under wing—
> Never to kill—
> Only to change
> Into some other thing
> This suffering flesh,
> To make it either more or less,
> But not again the same—
>
> *(1–8)*

Apparently, this "Death" does not kill. It has ceased to be deadly, becoming change instead—a change, moreover, that isn't really a change. Death as change makes "This suffering flesh / . . . either more or less, / But again the same—." Both these paradoxes take the grammatical form of infinitives. The syntax extends this sentence as if simply to repeat what has gone before, while in fact contradicting it, a paradoxical form of repetition which finds continuity in death, the ultimate form of rupture.

The consolatory power the poem thus finds in the enactments of its own language can be traced back to the apostrophe itself. The apostrophe opens the poem, ends the poem, provides its title, and maps its entire signifying field. An important resource of English poetry from its beginnings, apostrophe was a particular hallmark of the Romantics.[24] As Jonathan Culler has argued, they exploited to the fullest its rhetorical power to confer human subjectivity on inanimate objects. This maneuver was an ironic one, meant to dramatize the problem of loss in a world where the natural world refuses to respond to human desires for transcendent meaning (Culler 1981). Hughes, clearly parodying the self-consciously archaic diction of the Romantics in this poem, ironizes the irony a step further. He abstracts the trope from any explicit confrontation with the natural world and presents it as a purely linguistic transformation. The power the trope gives him to name Death enables him to address it as a beloved, benevolent deity "That taketh all things under wing." Having named Death from the beginning also means he can convincingly claim the power to rename it at the end. The poem's redeployment of Romantic apostrophe largely empties it of its sublime pathos, suggesting a more detached but no less rigorous view of death.

In fact, Hughes arrives at this redefinition by drawing on previous African-American elegy and playing it off against white tradition. The phrase *dear lovely death* is a double citation, first of the elegy "They Are All Gone into the World of Light" by Henry Vaughan (1621–1695), which contains the line "Dear beauteous death! the jewel of the just"; and second of Whitman's elegy for Lincoln, "When Lilacs Last in the Dooryard Bloom'd." "*Come lovely and soothing death*" is the opening line of the song Whitman assigns to the thrush, whom he apostrophizes throughout the poem. Whitman's elegy is heavily indebted to the *memento mori*, its penultimate section devoted to a vision of the Civil War's "battle corpses, myriads of them / And the white skeletons of young men." In his grief for Lincoln, what consolation Whitman finds in the thrush's song is undercut by its joyous acceptance of death as an inevitable, all-encompassing natural process, a "floating ocean." Against the explicit presence of Vaughan and Whitman, Hughes counterpoises, more implicitly but more pervasively, the influence of Fenton Johnson. "Dear Lovely Death" rewrites a Johnson poem entitled simply "Death":

> When from Eden's land we stray
> In the morningtime of life
> God in pity kisses us
> And around us sheds His love—
> Men have named this wonder Death.

> (F. Johnson 1915: 67)

Johnson's poem follows an important topos from the spirituals, death as deliverance, death as homecoming. While this topos is obviously Christian and assumes a Christian soteriology, it is not for that reason any less political or materialist. Indeed, both in the Spirituals and in subsequent African-American poetry the topos is almost always implicitly or explicitly an expression of resistance to slavery or racial oppression. Moreover, the citation of Vaughan reminds us that the Romantic sublime was itself heavily indebted to the very Christian tradition it strived to displace. Thus, African-American Christianity offers a conception of death every bit as hard-headed and skeptical as those issuing from the Romantic sublime, its piety notwithstanding. This is the point Hughes quietly makes in "Dear Lovely Death," abstracting death as deliverance from its soteriological context and using it to reorient the rhetorical capacities of apostrophe. Reading Whitman through Johnson, the poem's anticlimactic ending takes it as a given that there are worse things than death, and this grim political wisdom lies behind its philosophical equanimity.

The next two elegies assume the same detached stance, redefining death in the paradoxical enactments of their own language. The epigrammatic "Tower" in just four lines pares the problem down to a single, impossible paradox:

> Death is a tower
> To which the soul ascends
> To spend a meditative hour—
> That never ends.

In the next poem, "Two Things," Hughes makes the ineffability of Death the most certain form of reference instead of the least. Death is one of "two things" that "possess the power" and "can reawaken / Perpetually the flame" (3–4). In contrast to Death, the other "thing" eludes designation:

> One is known by the name of Death.
> And the other has no name
> Except the name each gives it—
> In no single mouth the same.
>
> *(7–10)*

This other thing, presumably desire, is unnameable because it resides only in ungeneralizable specificities, "the name each gives it." Death is nameable but incomprehensible beyond its inevitable generality. With each "single mouth" giving it a different name, desire is precisely what eludes this condition of linguistic generality. Desire is even less knowable than death, but for that reason logically subordinate to it. In a manner reminiscent of Freud's *Beyond the Pleasure Principle*, this poem makes death the necessary condition for the possibility of desire.

The last of the elegies in this collection revisits this intersection between death and desire, with a gruesome twist which savagely returns to the foreground the political concerns that have framed its philosophical meditations from the beginning. "Flight" occurs at the volume's midpoint and concerns a young black fleeing a lynch mob.

> Plant your toes in the cool swamp mud.
> Step and leave no track.
> Hurry, sweating runner
> The hounds are at your back.
>
> "No I didn't touch her
> White flesh ain't for me."
>
> Hurry! Black boy, hurry!
> They'll swing you to a tree.

Although I have just called this poem an elegy, it actually locates itself on the boundary of the genre in a way which lends added force to Hughes's redefinition of the *memento mori*. Whether this poem is an elegy will depend on whether the young man escapes. The poem literally conflates the question of its genre with a particularly horrific form of judicial terror. In this way, Hughes makes the indeterminacies of death definitively political. His preceding elegies treated the intelligibility of death as a primarily linguistic problem. "Flight" forcibly reminds us that it is precisely because of this dependence on language that death's relation to human existence is always already social. Death's indeterminacy is precisely what enables it to be harnessed to the ends of political terror, to be continually structured and restructured as the ultimate form of human power. If "Two Things" makes death the origin of desire, then "Flight" offers lynching as an illustration of how such power of origination can produce a horrific political efficacy.

The boy in flight denies his guilt by identifying and disavowing the murderous fantasy that motivates his pursuers: "No I didn't touch her / White flesh ain't for me." The crudeness of this angry, desperate joke emphasizes the entirely fantasmatic nature of the anxiety that drives his white pursuers. The white racist imagines white women as supremely attractive to black men. Yet the entirely fantasmatic basis of this conviction does not diminish one whit the reality of the lynching it motivates. On the contrary, the fantasy builds a horrifying engine of social control out of precisely the ontological indeterminacy that unites death and desire. From the first, the poem returns us to the materiality of bodies, its opening image the youth's "toes in the cool swamp mud." His purpose is to "leave no track," to elude signification, while the hounds of his white pursuers provide the material means of making their murderous fantasy literal. "Flight" places the philosophical meditations which precede it in an urgent political perspective. But the poem casts its political concern in precisely the terms which the meditations produced. Confronting death means confronting the social mediations which Hughes's philosophical understandings expose as inevitable. The youth's resistance is in his speech as well as in his flight. Indeed, his desperate witticism is itself a form of flight, an elusion of the hegemonic significations of white racism and an insistence on the autonomy of his own desire, of his right to rename it. Hughes appends the matter of lynching to his meditations on death precisely as a politicization not merely accommodated but demanded by the logic of his eschatological program. Death returns the eschatologist to life in all its historical and social specificity.

The six poems in the second half of the volume formulate their response to this demand by modulating from the terror of "Flight" to the complexities of migration and travel. The first of these poems is "Afro-American Fragment," the programmatic statement on the African diaspora, which I have already discussed. As this poem would lead us to expect, travel operates mainly as a form of exile and alienation, from the homesick revery of "Sailor" to the resilient irony of "Florida Road Workers": *"Hey Buddy! / Look at me! / I'm making a road!"* The collection concludes with the gently self-parodic "Aesthete in Harlem."

> Strange,
> That in this nigger place,
> I should meet Life face to face
> When for years, I had been seeking
> Life in places gentler speaking
> Until I came to this near street
> And found Life—stepping on my feet!

As I have already suggested, this poem fulfills the imperatives of the *memento mori* by completing the movement from contemplation to an engagement with life. In addition, it makes clear one final time that the political necessities this movement reveals are also aesthetic. The poem's closing image is a commonplace which Hughes reinvigorates by using to convey precisely the combination of banality and propinquity that constitute the aesthete's surprise. With this reinvigoration, Hughes can also turn the poem's self-critical irony outward. The aesthete's problem in Harlem is also the problem Harlem poses for the aesthetic. The aesthetic at stake is a specifically modern one—the quest to "meet Life face to face," to produce art out of the very contemporaneity of the present— "direct treatment of the thing," as the Imagists put it (Jones 1972: 129). The body metaphor which Hughes deftly employs in the final line alerts us in retrospect to the paradoxical body language in this modernist commonplace. The phrase *face to face* is not modernist at all. It is scriptural and

Pauline, and its presence here strongly suggests that the modernist dream of an unmediated engagement with the present is a transcendent yearning entirely dependent on the very past against which it defines itself. Hughes literally brings us to the other end of the body. With ironic understatement he suggests that an authentic engagement with the present will be an awkward affair, better conveyed with the metaphor of stepping on each others' feet than in the language of revelation. Two decades later, Hughes will use a similar metaphor in a poem destined to be much better known: "I am the American heartbreak— / Rock on which Freedom / Stumps its toe—" (Hughes 1995: 385). But in both cases his understated wit returns the issue of race obliquely to the problem of the body, and the body not as essential ground but precisely the source of change and motion. In "Aesthete in Harlem" the metaphor preserves an eerie echo from "Flight," the young man's "toes in the cool swamp mud." More generally it provides a suitably somatic recapitulation of the collection's concern with migration and diaspora, and with the rhythmic temporalities they inhabit and provoke. The problem Harlem poses for the aesthetic is a problem of an unfinished past, a problem that can't be satisfied until we meet its losses face to face. This encounter will of necessity be awkward and prolonged. As *Dear Lovely Death* demonstrates throughout, its political urgencies inform the most philosophical problems even at their most abstract. Yet the very range of these urgencies yields a paradoxical corollary to which this volume is equally committed. If the aesthetic is always political, then poetic genres can always do political work, even in their most rarified, conventional, and self-referential form. This account of Hughes's engagement with the elegy is not meant to displace the more explicitly political Hughes of such works as *Fine Clothes to the Jew* with the Hughes of *Dear Lovely Death*. Rather, it is meant to stimulate much more attention to all of his poetry, by suggesting the range of what is still unexplored. And while this goal is obviously aesthetic and critical, it is also profoundly political as well.[25]

NOTES

I owe a particular debt to Ronald Radano and Cheryl A. Wall, whose advice and encouragement were crucial as I pursued the minor scholarly indiscretion of writing on a subject outside my period. They saved me from many larger ones. Of course, those indiscretions that remain are entirely my own. I would also like to thank the staff of the New York Public Library's Schomburg Center for Research in Black Culture.

    1. The ultimate source of this honorific is unclear. It was long ascribed to Carl Van Vechten, but direct documentary confirmation of this ascription

has yet to be found. Conorroe suggests the source was Hughes himself (1991: 228).

2. The crucial work of mapping the various aspects has been begun by Arnold Rampersad, to whose work I am heavily indebted in this essay.

3. Hughes's relation to the blues is perhaps the one issue where his work has received adequate scholarly attention. While I am indebted to all of this scholarship, I have benefited particularly from Beavers, Hansell, Rampersad, Spillers, Tracy, Wall, and Williams.

4. At the risk of belaboring the obvious, I would note that poetry began in the West as an oral form that was also musical. Moreover, as many ethnomusicologists have pointed out, non-Western cultures imagine the relation between music and other forms of expression in radically different ways.

5. The racialized association between African music and rhythm is surprisingly archaic, substantially predating the European institution of black slavery in North America. Agawu notes, "The eleventh-century Christian physician and theologian Ibn Butlan, in a tract entitled 'On How to Buy Black Slaves and How to Detect Bodily Defects,' claimed that 'if a black were to fall from the sky to the earth, he would fall in rhythm'" (1995: 380).

6. In the wake of Peter Bürger's influential work (1984), it has become increasingly fashionable to draw a sharp distinction between modernism and the avant-garde. I have followed the looser, more traditional usage and treated the two terms as roughly synonymous. I have done this for two reasons. First, while Bürger's distinction is justified in relation to the two movements with which he is specifically concerned, Dadaism and Surrealism, it cannot, as a matter of mere descriptive accuracy, be maintained across the board. The artistic avant-garde was in general more highly politicized in France and Germany than in Britain and the United States (see Bradbury and McFarlane 1976). Second, part of my point is that whatever its politics, vanguardism's appeal to temporal privilege as the basis of its self-definition constitutes an elitism that is ultimately self-defeating (and may well contribute to the political failures of the Dadaists and Surrealists which Bürger takes as axiomatic).

7. The theorist whose presentation of this point most influences my argument in this essay is Slavoj Žižek. See especially "You Only Die Twice" in Žižek 1989. It is worth noting that inspiration for both of these texts comes from Walter Benjamin's "Theses on Historical Method."

8. *Orality* is a term which we should apply advisedly to the blues. It is most accurate in describing their transmission as a musical tradition. Strictly speaking, the term functions in opposition to *literacy* only when the latter is understood in an etymological sense, as meaning "learned" rather than simply the ability to read and write. Many blues singers were literate in the broader sense and characteristically described their composing as "writing a blues." See Charters 1963: 11–14. I have felt justified in retaining the term *orality*, despite its shortcomings, precisely because one of my aims is to deconstruct the opposition between orality and literacy.

9. Henry Louis Gates, Jr., notes, "Repetition and revision are fundamental

to black artistic forms, from painting and sculpture to music and language use" (1988: xxiv).

10. Later in his career, Hughes will make similar observations about violence and black music at least twice. His essay "Songs Called the Blues" begins: "The blues are folk-songs born out of heartache. They are songs of the black South, particularly the city South. Songs of the poor streets and back alleys of Memphis and Birmingham, Atlanta and Galveston, out of black, beaten, but unbeatable throats, from the strings of pawn-shop guitars, and the chords of pianos with no ivory on the keys" (Hughes 1941: 143). Then in the fifties he makes the following comment about bebop through Jesse B. Semple: "Be-Bop is the real thing like the colored boys play. . . . From the police beating Negroes heads. . . . Every time a cop hits a Negro with his billy club, that old club says, 'BOP! BOP! . . . BEBOP! . . . MOP! . . . BOP! . . . That's where Be-Bop came from beaten right out of some Negro's head into them horns and saxophones and piano keys that plays it" (Hughes 1961: 117–18, cited in Spillers 1982: 63).

11. Such discontinuous notions of repetition were an explicit element of the blues tradition, which it summed up in the phrase *worrying the line*. As Sherley A. Williams explains, "Repetition in the blues is seldom word for word, and the definition of worrying the line includes changes in stress and pitch, the addition of exclamatory phrases within the line itself, and the wordless blues cries which often puncture the performance of the songs" (1979: 127).

12. Readers will note particular affinities between my argument and Tomlinson's. Unfortunately, his essay appeared after mine was substantially drafted, which has prevented me from engaging his nuanced, magisterial, and provocative argument as fully as I might have. The major difference between us is one of focus. Tomlinson is concerned with the inadequacies of Western logocentrism as they relate to the notation of non-Western musics, Aztec in particular. I am concerned with these inadequacies as they relate to the Western culture's understanding of its own expressive practices. I should add, however, that this difference in focus may imply a more substantive difference as well. In my view, Tomlinson is occasionally less critical than he should be in his use of Derrida, taking the notion of logocentrism as an adequate characterization of the totality of Western culture. Such totalizing inevitably leads back to the kind of Western/non-Western polarizing that Tomlinson sets out to avoid. In this case, it leads him to the particularly dubious conclusion that Aztec musical notation is metonymic, whereas Western notation is metaphoric. What Derridean deconstruction teaches us is that any global opposition like metaphor and metonymy is mutually constitutive; to assign one pole to one culture and one to another is by definition logocentric.

13. In the discussion that follows, I have chosen to concentrate on Yeston because, among the recent comprehensive treatments of rhythm, his seems the most suggestive regarding the issue of rhythm's subordination to pitch.

14. Lerdahl and Jackendoff make a similar point, albeit more briefly: "Schenkerian analysis is workable at all only because the analyst himself supplies (consciously or unconsciously) the requisite rhythmic intuitions" (1983: 119).

Moreover, throughout their study they stress the interplay between rhythm and pitch in the construction of the "grouping structures" that enforce tonal hierarchies. Nevertheless, their commitment to the model of Noam Chomsky's generative grammar, with their concomitant quest for "musical universals," prevents them from stressing the arbitrariness of pitch/rhythm relations as fully as they might.

15. For a classic statement of the positivist view, see Ogden and Richards (1923, esp. 48–76), who define a sign as follows:

> A sign is always a stimulus similar to some part of an original stimulus and sufficient to call up the engram [that is, mental event] formed by that stimulus.
>
>   An engram is the residual trace of an adaptation made by the organism to a stimulus. (1923: 53)

Ogden and Richards illustrate this somewhat obscure definition with the example of the striking of a match, where the scrape of the match becomes the sign of its flame. They do not argue that all of language is tied quite so directly to real objects, but they treat more abstract propositions as "second or third order" signs (82–83). But such signs depend on "initial" signs like the match scrape. In this way, all of language is eventually linked to these originary moments.

16. Derek Attridge's observations about the somatic effects of rhythm are extremely apposite in this context:

> Once established, a regular rhythm has a tendency to self-perpetuation, a momentum like that of motion in a straight line: the producer of a rhythm will be inclined to impose it on further material, and the perceiver will be inclined to go on hearing, if it is possible for him to do so, if, that is, the physical reality does not depart too far from the established norm. Rhythm thus projects itself strongly into the future, and the occurrence of one rhythmic event, while it satisfies a previous expectation, simultaneously generates a fresh one. (1982: 78)

17. For the dispersion of Petrarchan conventions within popular traditions, see Vickers 1988.

18. The question of Hughes's own religious belief is a complicated one, not least because he is also the author of a considerable body of religious poetry. In *The Big Sea* Hughes reports an early loss of faith after faking a conversion at a revival meeting (Hughes 1940: 19–21). He expresses similar sentiments in a letter to Carl Van Vechten in the late 1920s (Rampersad 1986b: 159), and during his involvement with the Communist Party in the 1930s he achieved wide notoriety for the stridently atheist "Goodbye Christ" (Hughes 1995: 166–167; see Rampersad 1986b: 252–60). On the other hand, he was a frequent, if not habitual, churchgoer, and by the end of the decade he was making serious efforts to disavow this poem (ibid. 305–9). In testimony after the war before the House Un-American Activities Committee, he not only disavowed the poem once more

but declared he was not, nor ever had been, an atheist (Rampersad 1988: 205). I do not necessarily take the tendency in his work I have called atheist or atheological to characterize any of his poems beyond those I analyze in this essay, and its application to them I offer strictly on the basis of the evidence they themselves provide.

19. I am skirting here the more vexed issue of the exact relation between the narratorial voice and the blues singer, whether they achieve some sort of union or remain estranged (see Tracy 1988: 222–23; Rampersad 1986a: 148, and Beavers 1992: 3–4).

20. Of the three, Fenton Johnson had the heaviest poetic influence on Hughes. He published three volumes of poetry between 1913 and 1916, *A Little Dreaming, Visions of the Dusk*, and *Songs of the Soil*. Johnson employs elegy widely in these collections, taking subjects that range from fictional black working-class characters to his mother to Dunbar and Swinburne. Georgia Douglas Johnson's recourse to the genre is less frequent, but many of her poems have an elegiac cast, particularly those in her first volume, *The Heart of a Woman* (1918). The sermons in James Weldon Johnson's *God's Trombones* (1927) are consistently eschatological and elegiac. In 1953, *United Asia*, a progressive, internationalist bimonthly edited in Bombay, asked Hughes to pick "Twelve Favourite Poems" for a special issue on the American Negro. The poems Hughes selected included the elegies "Aunt Jane Allen" by Fenton Johnson, "A Death Song" by Dunbar, the elegiac "My City" by James Weldon Johnson, the title and opening poem of *The Heart of a Woman*, in addition to Claude McKay's "If We Must Die" and Robert Hayden's "Frederick Douglass." Without placing undue emphasis on this single exercise, we might nevertheless say it gives a fair indication both of the importance Hughes placed on his immediate predecessors in the African-American tradition and of the extent to which he identified that tradition with the elegy.

21. In its re-emergent form, the *memento mori* comprehends a wide variety of visual objects and aids to meditation. It also became a mainstay of Protestant homiletic. For an overview and further bibliography, see Llewellyn 1991.

22. In his recent book *Poetry of Mourning: The Modern Elegy From Hardy to Heaney* (1994), Jahan Ramazani offers Hughes along with Hardy, Wilfred Owen, Stevens, and Auden as the leading elegists of the High Modern period. While my discussion obviously draws on this classification, I read Hughes's deployment of elegy differently, viewing it as at once more traditional and more political than Ramazani does. It seems to me symptomatic that Ramazani ignores both Hughes's specific affiliations to previous African-American elegy and the larger affiliation between traditional elegy and the *memento mori*. In my view, Ramazani's thesis that modern elegy is uniquely "anti-consolatory" (7) ignores the considerable anti-consolatory impulses within traditional elegy.

23. Subsequent citations of poems from this collection are from this edition. Line numbers will appear in the text.

24. Apostrophe was also an important trope in blues lyrics, see Charters 1963: 29–30.

REFERENCES

Abbate, Carolyn. 1991. *Unsung Voices: Opera and Narrative in the Nineteenth Century*. Princeton, N.J.: Princeton University Press.

Agawu, Kofi. 1995. "The Invention of 'African Rhythm'." *Journal of the American Musicological Society* 48: 380–95.

Althusser, Louis. 1971. *Lenin and Philosophy and Other Essays*. Trans. Ben Brewster. New York: Monthly Review Press.

Attridge, Derek. 1982. *Rhythms of English Poetry*. London: Longmans.

Baker, Houston A., Jr. 1984. *Blues, Ideology, and Afro-American Literature: A Vernacular Theory*. Chicago: University of Chicago Press.

Barlow, William. 1989. *"Looking Up At Down": The Emergence of Blues Culture*. Philadelphia: Temple University Press.

Beavers, Herman. 1992. "Dead Rocks and Sleeping Men: Aurality in the Aesthetic of Langston Hughes." *Langston Hughes Review* 11: 1–5.

Benjamin, Walter. 1969. "Theses on the Philosophy of History." In *Illuminations*, edited with an introduction by Hannah Arendt, trans. Harry Zohn, 253–64. New York: Shocken.

Berry, Wallace. 1976. *Structural Functions in Music*. Englewood Cliffs, N.J.: Prentice-Hall.

———. 1985. "Metric and Rhythmic Articulation in Music." *Music Theory Spectrum*, vol. 7: *Time and Rhythm in Music*, 7–33.

Bloom, Harold. 1973. *The Anxiety of Influence: A Theory of Poetry*. New York: Oxford University Press.

Bradbury, Malcom, and James McFarlane. 1976. "The Name and Nature of Modernism." In *Modernism 1890–1930*, ed. M. Bradbury and J. McFarlane, 19–55. Harmondsworth: Penguin.

Bürger, Peter. 1984. *Theory of the Avant-Garde*. Trans. Michael Shaw, with Foreword by Jochen Schulte-Sasse. Minneapolis: University of Minnesota Press.

Cameron, Sharon. 1979. *Lyric Time: Dickinson and the Limits of Genre*. Baltimore: The Johns Hopkins University Press.

Charters, Samuel. 1963. *The Poetry of the Blues*. New York: Oak Publishers.

Conorroe, Joel, ed. 1991. *Six Americans: An Anthology*. New York: Vintage.

Cooper, Grosvenor, and Leonard Meyer. 1960. *The Rhythmic Structure of Music*. Chicago: University of Chicago Press.

Cullen, Countee. 1926. "Poet on Poet." *Opportunity* 4 (March): 73. Repr. in *Langston Hughes: Critical Perspectives Past and Present*, ed. Henry Louis Gates, Jr., and K. A. Appiah, 3–5. New York: Amistad Press, 1993.

Culler, Jonathan. 1981. "Apostrophe." In *The Pursuit of Signs: Semiotics, Literature, Deconstruction, 135–54*. Ithaca, N.Y.: Cornell University Press.

de Man, Paul. 1983. "Lyric and Modernity." In *Blindness and Insight: Essays in the Rhetoric of Contemporary Criticism*, 2d ed., with an Introduction by Wlad Godzich, 166–86. Minneapolis: University of Minnesota Press.

Derrida, Jacques. 1994. *Specters of Marx: The State of the Debt, the Work of Mourning*

& the New International. Trans. Peggy Kamuf, with an Introduction by Bernd Magnus and Stephen Cullenberg. New York: Routledge.

Dürr, Walther, Walter Gerstenberg, and Jonathan Harvey. 1980. "Rhythm." In *The New Grove Dictionary of Music and Musicians*, ed. Stanley Sadie, 15: 804–25. London: Macmillan.

Eco, Umberto. 1976. *A Theory of Semiotics*. Bloomington: Indiana University Press.

Ellison, Ralph. 1966. *Shadow and Act*. New York: Hill and Wang.

Gates, Henry Louis, Jr. 1988. *The Signifying Monkey: A Theory of African-American Literary Criticism*. Oxford: Oxford University Press.

———. 1989. "Canon-Formation, Literary History, and the Afro-American Tradition: From the Seen to the Told." In *Afro-American Literary Study in the 1990's*, ed. Houston A. Baker, Jr., and Patricia Redmond, 14–39. Chicago: University of Chicago Press.

Hansell, William. 1978. "Black Music in the Poetry of Langston Hughes: Roots, Race, Release." *Obsidian: Black Literature in Review* 4: 16–38.

Hollander, John. 1981. *Rhyme's Reason*. New Haven, Conn.: Yale University Press.

Hughes, Langston. 1931. *Dear Lovely Death*. Amenia, N.Y.: Troutbeck Press.

———. 1940. *The Big Sea*. New York: Knopf.

———. 1941. "Songs Called the Blues." *Phylon* (Autumn): 143–45.

———. 1953. "Twelve Favourite Poems." *United Asia* 5, 3: 190–93.

———. 1961. *The Best of Simple*. New York: Hill and Wang.

———. 1964. "12 Contemporary Negro Poets: USA." Transcript for British Broadcasting Company Radio Anthology. Langston Hughes Papers, Arthur C. Shomburg Center for Research in Black Culture, New York Public Library.

———. 1995. *The Collected Poems of Langston Hughes*, ed. Arnold Rampersad and David Roessel. New York: Knopf.

Jeffreys, Mark. 1995. "Ideologies of Lyric: A Problem of Genre in Contemporary Anglophone Poetics." *PMLA* 110: 196–205.

Johnson, Barbara. 1989. "Response to Gates." In *Afro-American Literary Study in the 1990's*, ed. Houston A. Baker, Jr., and Patricia Redmond, 39–45. Chicago: University of Chicago Press.

Johnson, Fenton. 1913. *A Little Dreaming*. Chicago: Peterson Linotyping Co.

———. 1915. *Visions of the Dusk*. New York: Trachtenberg.

———. 1916. *Songs of the Soil*. New York: Trachtenberg.

Johnson, Georgia Douglas. 1918. *The Heart of a Woman and Other Poems*. With an introduction by William Stanley Braithwaite. Boston: Cornhill.

Johnson, James Weldon. 1927. *God's Trombones: Some Negro Sermons*. London: George Allen & Unwin.

Jones, Peter, ed. 1972. *Imagist Poetry*. Harmondsworth: Penguin.

Lerdahl, Fred, and Ray Jackendoff. 1983. *A Generative Theory of Tonal Music*. Cambridge: MIT Press.

Lester, Joel. 1986. *The Rhythms of Tonal Music*. Carbondale: Southern Illinois University Press.

Llewellyn, Nigel. 1991. *The Art of Death: Visual Culture in the English Death Ritual, 1500–1800*. London: Reaktion Books.

McClary, Susan. 1991. *Feminine Endings: Music, Gender, and Sexuality*. Minneapolis: University of Minnesota Press.

Mullen, Edward J. 1988. "The Dilemma in Selecting Representative Scholarship in Langston Hughes." *The Langston Hughes Review* 7: 43–48.

Nattiez, Jean-Jacques. 1990. *Music and Discourse: Toward a Semiology of Music*. Trans. Carolyn Abbate. Princeton, N.J.: Princeton University Press.

Ogden, C. K., and I. A. Richards. 1923. *The Meaning of Meaning: A Study of the Influence of Language Upon Thought and of the Science*. San Diego: Harcourt Brace Jovanovich. Repr. 1989.

Ramazani, Jahan. 1994. *Poetry of Mourning: The Modern Elegy from Hardy to Heaney*. Chicago: University of Chicago Press.

Rampersad, Arnold. 1986a. "Langston Hughes's *Fine Clothes to the Jew*." *Callaloo* 9: 144–58. Repr. as "Hughes's *Fine Clothes to the Jew*." In *Langston Hughes: Critical Perspectives Past and Present*, ed. Henry Louis Gates and K. A. Appiah, 53–68. New York: Amistad Press.

———. 1986b. *The Life of Langston Hughes*, vol. 1: *1902–1941: I, Too, Sing America*. New York: Oxford University Press.

———. 1988. *The Life of Langston Hughes*, vol. 2: *1941–1967: I Dream a World*. New York: Oxford University Press.

Randel, Don Michael. 1992. "The Canons in the Musicological Toolbox." In *Disciplining Music: Musicology and Its Canons*, ed. Katherine Bergeron and Philip V. Bohlman, 10–22. Chicago: University of Chicago Press.

Rowell, Lewis. 1985. "Editorial: The Temporal Spectrum." *Music Theory Spectrum*, vol. 8: *Time and Rhythm in Music*, 1–6.

Spillers, Hortense J. 1982. "Formalism Comes to Harlem." *Black American Literature Forum* 16: 58–63.

Stein, Arnold. 1986. *The House of Death: Messages from the English Renaissance*. Baltimore: The Johns Hopkins University Press.

Tomlinson, Gary. 1995. "Ideologies of Aztec Song." *Journal of the American Musicological Society* 48: 343–79.

Tracy, Steven C. 1988. *Langston Hughes and the Blues*. Urbana: University of Illinois Press.

Van Vechten, Carl. 1979. *"Keep A - Inchin' Along": Selected Writings of Carl Van Vechten about Black Art and Letters*, ed. Bruce Kellner. Westport, Conn.: Greenwood.

Vickers, Nancy J. 1988. "Vital Signs: Petrarch and Popular Culture." *Romanic Review* 79: 184–95.

Wall, Cheryl A. 1995. "Whose Sweet Angel Child?" Blues Women, Langston Hughes, and Writing During the Harlem Renaissance." In *Langston Hughes, the Man, His Art, and His Continuing Influence*, ed. C. James Trotman, 37–50. New York: Garland.

Williams, Sherley A. 1979. "The Blues Roots of Contemporary Afro-American Poetry." In *Chant of Saints: A Gathering of Afro-American Literature, Art and*

Scholarship, ed. Michael S. Harper and Robert B. Stepto, 123–35. Urbana: University of Illinois Press.

Wordsworth, William. 1984. *William Wordsworth*, ed. Stephen Gill. Oxford: Oxford University Press.

Yeston, Maury. 1976. *The Stratification of Musical Rhythm*. New Haven, Conn.: Yale University Press.

Žižek, Slavoj. 1989. *The Sublime Object of Ideology*. New York: Verso.

16

Race, Class, and Musical Nationalism in Zimbabwe

THOMAS TURINO

In summary form, this paper analyses the intersection of "race," class, and African nationalism and the ways they articulated with musical values, practices, and style in Harare and northeastern Zimbabwe after 1955. I am particularly interested in the ways discourses about race intersected with specific class interests at given points in time and how musical practices and styles articulated within these conjunctures. I show how the black middle class shifted from emphasizing their own *class* distinction from other Africans during the pre-nationalist (pre-1958) period, trying to diffuse an identification based on color and geographical [African] heritage, to an emphasis on color and shared heritage— African unity—in the context of political nationalism (1960–1980); only to slowly revert to *class*-based alliances and interests throughout the 1980s after the state was secured.

Especially during the 1970s, African nationalists played down class distinctions within the African population and emphasized "race" as it had formerly been constructed by whites (color, geographical heritage). Echoing nationalist discourse, scholars have also written Zimbabwean music history with an emphasis on race relations but little mention of class. In this paper I suggest that the class *habitus* of the nationalist leadership is as important as "race" for understanding central music trends in Zimbabwe, especially after majority rule was achieved in 1980.

Race as a Category

The social category "race" is nested within more general ideas about, and functions of, social difference, but the power of racial constructs is in part based on an ideology of "natural" or physical difference. As Gilroy (1987) and common sense suggest, "racial" categorization (by self and others) and discourses about race have, in fact, variably emphasized "biological" (phenotype) distinctions such as color, as well as geographical heritage and cultural distinctions (social style, religion, etc.). Insofar as cultural practices and social style become markers, racial constructs may blur with the concepts of "class" (Bourdieu 1984) or "ethnicity" (Royce 1982) or both. Insofar as "race" determines and is determined by one's life chances in relation to control over educational, cultural, political, and economic capital, it intersects fundamentally with class. Insofar as geographical heritage and ethnicity come into play, the idea of "race" may also become tangled with ideas about "nation" (Gilroy 1987) within post-1789 conceptions of nation-states.

Given their variability, complex constitution, and myriad effects, racisms and discourses about "race" can only be understood within specific historical conjunctures as these are related to more permanent structures and processes of structuration. That is, as a category, "race" emerges vis-à-vis relations between specific social groups in particular political and socioeconomic contexts and may be sustained, contested, and transformed across and within specific historical moments. It is thus worth underlining that "race" is not a conceptual tool for social analysis but is rather the fodder for such analysis. This distinction is crucial; to miss it is to take discourses of "race" at face value.

While "race" has no fixed objective parameters, the power of racist discourses that stress biological traits and propensities stem from the claim of "naturalness" and hence immutability. This state of affairs has distinct advantages in common cases where social differences are used to define hierarchy, to rationalize relations of domination, or to unify a movement to overturn the social order. Emphasis on a "biological" definition masks the socially constructed, variable nature of "race" as a category and therefore helps explain its use where clear physical differences are evident (blacks and whites) and even where obvious differences do not necessarily pertain (German Jews and gentiles). A key hypothesis here is that struggles over the construction and redefinition of social categories involving "race" will emphasize or de-emphasize criteria projected as *immutable* depending on the goals of particular groups within specific conjunctures.

Discourses of Race in Zimbabwe

In Zimbabwe, from the colonial period through the present, discourses about race and racism have been at the center of social-political life. Regardless of what else was said, *color* was used by the white settlers to determine a hierarchical order affecting almost all realms of life; distinct categories included blacks, coloureds, Asians, and whites. Distinctions of color were fused with differences based on geographical heritage; Zimbabweans still use the terms European, African, and Indian to construct these social categories (being born in Zimbabwe, coloreds were exempt from this criterion). Like the issue of color, one cannot change where one or where one's ancestors were born, and hence *geographical heritage* supported the image of immutability within the construction of race. The white settlers also invoked criteria of *cultural distinction* as components of their construction of race. As is typically the case in colonial situations involving Europeans in Africa, the social hierarchy was often legitimated by discourses about the superiority of the colonist culture; in Zimbabwe this was articulated in terms of degrees of "civilization."

In the white construction of race, *class* was a relatively minor issue at specific points in time; the tendency was basically to view "natives" as a single class.[1] Because of white discourse about "civilization" and the cultural components of "race," however, *culture* and *class distinctions* became important aspects of alternative black constructions of social categories. I would emphasize, however, that this was largely a matter among Africans, and the musical effects (e.g. the "concert" tradition discussed below), likewise largely reverberated primarily among Africans. Nonetheless, *class* and *cultural criteria* were particularly important to Africans' attempt to reconstruct social categories precisely because these criteria potentially allowed for mobility whereas *color* and *geographical heritage* apparently did not.

Class

My definition of class involves combined economic (in relation to the means of production) and cultural (the emergence of a common habitus) criteria. Using Bourdieu's framework, it involves the relative degree of control over economic, political, social, and cultural capital within different social fields. Because of the structuration of a given field (as in a corporation, a university department, a band), certain types of capital may have more consequence or may be more available. Within the social system as a whole, economic and political capital usually have the greatest importance, whereas more leeway may be granted to subordinate groups in regard to access to types of capital deemed less consequential (e.g. cultural capital) within the overall social system. Such was the case in Zimbabwe, although this can misfire because, as Bourdieu has shown, one type of capital can be used to secure another.[2]

Colonial Zimbabwe (Rhodesia) was characterized by a multisphered class system. The white working, middle, and elite class system was legally elevated above and separated from the multitiered class system of people of color. Based on an early statement by Cecil Rhodes—"Equal rights for all civilized men"—the black class system revolved around levels of "civilization" which were defined by levels of "education," i.e. inculcation and display of cosmopolitan values, skills, and social-cultural style (West 1990: 391; Shamuyarira 1965: 51). Rhodes's statement was supported by the messages of mission education that proselytized for "modernity" and "progress" [capitalist cosmopolitanism] as the keys to civilization and ultimately, it was suggested, equality.[3]

State legislation cemented color/geographical heritage ("race") as the criteria regulating land ownership, residence, political participation, and even the types of alcohol one could consume. These same criteria structured daily interactions between blacks and whites. Thus the African middle class could not escape the way "race," as constructed by Rhodesian whites, structured African lives and livelihoods. Nonetheless, before mass nationalism the African middle class attempted to contest and redefine racial discourse that lumped all "natives" into one legal and social category by emphasizing their own class/cultural distinction. Cultural practices, dress, music, dance, styles of weddings, and social style in general were key to this attempt.

THE AFRICAN MIDDLE CLASS IN THE PRE-NATIONALIST PHASE

The historian Michael West has written a detailed study of the rise of the African middle class in Zimbabwe between 1890 and 1965. He fundamentally links the rise of the middle class to mission school education and shows how it was primarily an urban-centered phenomenon (1990: 4–5).[4] European-style education itself became one of the strongest markers of class, not simply as a means to a better livelihood but as a basis of class habitus and a primary criterion of social standing among Africans in its own right (ibid. 71). The inculcation of cosmopolitan dispositions was the mark of an "educated African" and was the result of spending relatively more time in the colonial education system. T. T. Moyana shows that higher education for Africans was very restricted in Rhodesia— fewer schools and classrooms the higher you went—and that the system was "explicitly designed to create an African elite who could be enlisted to support the established order" (1988: 45).

West persuasively demonstrates that

> by the end of the period under review [1965], there had emerged a self-conscious and corporate African middle class consisting of the more highly-qualified and better-paid teachers, preachers, clerks and, in the post–World War II era especially, businessmen, salesmen, social workers, journalists, nurses, doctors, lawyers and other professionals. For the most part, the material basis of this class, especially in comparison to the white settlers . . . was not very considerable. Its members, however, were held together by a unity of purpose, that is, they had interests, aspirations and ideas that set them apart from the other major social strata in Southern Rhodesian society—namely, the dominant white settlers on the one hand and the African peasants and workers from among whom they emerged on the other. (1990: 2–3)

The emergent African middle class contested racial boundaries defined by color and tried to overcome them with the assertion of a distinct class identity and cultural style. Unlike the later mass-nationalist phase, during this period the African elite was a class *for* itself and was not overly concerned with the position of lower-class Africans. As the Reverend E. T. J. Nemapare put it in the *Bantu Mirror* of 1954: "The trouble is that in Southern Rhodesia the social bar, *which I fully support,* is being taken for the colour bar, which no decent European or African wants" (in West 1990: 391, emphasis added). Similarly, the protonationalist B. J. Mnyanda wrote in 1954:

> Today, the African people—particularly the educated and the civilised among them—can no longer be treated in this Colony [Southern Rhodesia] . . . on the old "voetsalk-you-bloody-Kaffir" [a racial slur] basis. They demand a place in the sun; and he who thwarts their legitimate aspirations will do so at his own peril. *By all means, let us have a "culture bar" in place of the present colour bar.* (in West 1990: 391, emphasis added)

West illustrates time and again how, in the period before the rise of mass nationalism (circa 1958), members of the middle class sought to differentiate themselves from African workers and peasants and resented the white settlers' tendency to lump all "natives" into one category. For example, before the Liquor Act was changed in 1957, the prohibition on European beer and liquor for Africans was just one of many laws that served as daily reminders that discrimination based on color/geographical heritage could not be surmounted in Southern Rhodesia regardless of one's educational level, occupation, or class. As Michael West notes: "While able to obtain all the 'European' alcohol they desired, many elite Africans resented the fact that the liquor law both criminalized their behavior and failed to make social distinctions between them and the masses" (1990: 190–91). By the 1950s, elite Africans began demanding ever more loudly "that better conditions be created by recognition of the City Council of the *middle class African*" (*Bantu Mirror* 2 June 1956, emphasis added); in this case they wanted "exclusive drinking facilities" for "*progressive Africans*" (West 1990: 190–91, emphasis added).

Since many members of the black middle class had only recently emerged from the lower strata, and since their own material position "was not considerable," cultural markers of distinction—dress, language, artistic tastes, "refined" social style—were all the more important to their corporate identity. The call for separate drinking places, the preference for European-styled weddings,[5] and concerts and ballroom dancing were among the many public arenas for articulating class distinctions.

Middle-Class Music in Harare

While indigenous Shona music and dance continued to be performed in both the rural areas and the urban townships (African areas) throughout the colonial period by peasants and members of the working class, different styles based on European and especially North American models began to emerge in Salisbury (now Harare) during the 1930s. It would be an overstatement to claim that the urban audiences for the indigenous and cosmopolitan styles fell strictly along class lines.[6] As we shall see, however, the two types of traditions came to have strong class associations within the African population, and locals distinguished them according to the "traditional–modern" dichotomy and the imagery of progress which are key to the cosmopolitan discourse of modernity itself.

African-American traditions, in particular, were considered progressive models. A 1954 article in *African Parade*, the most widely read magazine among middle-class Africans in Zimbabwe (Stopforth 1972: 86),[7] is illustrative:

> Since the early thirties Africans in Southern Rhodesia and in Salisbury in particular have made tremendous progress in all walks of life. Nowhere perhaps is that progress more manifest than in the field of entertainment. The existence of so many choirs modelled on the American Negro pattern in Harare [Mbare Township] *is eloquent testimony to that progress.* (1954: 14, emphasis added)

Many people who graduated from mission or government schools in the 1930s came to Salisbury to seek employment. Mbare Township still housed the majority of Africans in the capital at that time.[8] Having been trained in choir singing in school, the graduates at first simply formed choirs in Mbare. Soon after, however, an urban performance style I will call "concert" grew directly out of, and flourished in parallel to, the school choir tradition.

As "concert" emerged, the number of performers in an ensemble was often reduced as compared to the choirs. While some "concert" groups added instrumental "jazz" accompaniment—e.g. some combination of piano, guitar, bass, traps, and winds—the focal point was usually a vocal quartet or quintet (a parallel instrumental "jazz" tradition also existed). The style first emphasized smooth, straightforward triadic harmonies and clean vocal diction learned at school. As with the school choirs, the repertories of "concert" groups included church hymns, African-American spirituals, and similarly styled choir music composed by South Africans. The "concert" repertory, however, was expanded to feature vaudeville and Tin Pan Alley styled numbers either directly from America or as filtered through South African performers. By the 1940s the Mills Brothers and, to a lesser extent the Ink Spots, were *the* major models for Zimbabwean "concert" groups and remained so until rock 'n' roll (Elvis Presley, Jerry Lee Lewis) took over at the end of the 1950s.

The Bantu Actors led by Kenneth Mattaka emerged in 1937 as the first important "concert" ensemble in Mbare Township (*African Parade* 1954: 20). Mattaka and the original members of the group were trained in singing and reading music in the Domboshawa Government School Choir;[9] Mattaka had learned to read music earlier at a mission school and so was chosen for the first choir at Domboshawa. Many performers of the "concert" tradition came out of school choir backgrounds and, like the *African Parade* writer quoted above, stressed the "progressive," "refined," and "sophisticated" nature of their music as compared to indigenous performance. Musical literacy, tightly arranged vocal harmonies, and cosmopolitan repertory were the basis of their assessment.

In the late 1930s and early 1940s, the Bantu Actors performed South African and American songs, but Mattaka told me that they did not sing many Shona songs.[10] They were careful to gauge the popularity of songs by audience reaction:

> KENNETH MATTAKA: Each time after a concert we would sit down and assess everything and see which number, you know, did not appeal to the audience.
>
> THOMAS TURINO: Were the American songs and the English songs popular?
>
> KM: They were. And people liked that, because in those days, you know,

when they are from school, people used to feel very proud of you. You see? So when you sing and it shows something advanced and so on, well, people would really want to hear your voice again or hear the song again. (Zim93–65:5)

Mattaka's statement suggests a new type of shared aesthetic among Africans who had been to school, the performance of "advanced" music as an indication of the group's aspirations. He contrasted the advanced music of his group with indigenous music (often called "tribal music" at the time), and even the closely related syncretic *makwaya* (village choir) tradition:

KM: Now makwaya is what we found before I started, I brought in this change I'm talking about with the Bantu Actors. We found the makwaya type of singing. Yeah, where one person leads and the others keep repeating.

TT: Answering? Call and response?

KM: That's it. And they'll clap hands and, you know—

TT: So that was more traditional in a way?

KM: Eh, not quite, because it started from schools out in the rural areas. Teachers used to teach singing, and that, so it became common. So you'd find also grown-ups you know, organized themselves in this, in the same form. So they used to call that makwaya. . . . But then we brought in now better singing, where we could read notes, we could read staff notation. You see, then that became the difference. (Zim93–65:7)

KM: In those days, people used to appreciate if you sing good songs. You know, musical, and all the parts in, and all the harmony. Educated people used to appreciate that. The makwaya was just a sort of shouting sort of singing. Different, not well composed. (Zim93–65:17)

In his discussion of makwaya, Mattaka suggests that syncretic musical forms in themselves were not a basis of class distinction any more than school attendance necessarily made one an educated person. Makwaya emerged out of mission schools, but in this case the style was largely shaped by village aesthetics ("shouting sort of singing," clapping, call-and-response) rather than cosmopolitan musical style and aesthetics of the "concert" tradition. It was inculcation of the latter that was the mark of "educated people" and "a better class of Africans."

As entertainers, the Bantu Actors and other "concert" ensembles performed almost exclusively on stages for well-dressed sit-down audiences in municipal recreation halls on weekends, rather than in lower-class beerhalls. Mattaka singles out educated Africans as being particularly appreciative of the style, and elsewhere he specifically identified the audience as middle-class Africans (Zim93–65:7). In describing concerts in the 1940s and 1950s, William Saidi of another "concert" group, the Milton Brothers, stressed the importance of the stage, of dressing well, and the respectable atmosphere at concerts:

> I don't go out to these musical shows [nowadays] too much, they are different from what we had. . . . There was the stage, and you the singers, the entertainers, were on stage. The audience they sat quietly. They came dressed up in their best. People brought their wives! their mothers-in-law!! to a concert which went on from eight o'clock to half past eleven. And it was an evening that had a lot of class. (in Makwenda 1992a)

Mattaka and others have commented that during concerts, the hall would be silent, "you could hear a pin drop," suggesting the adoption of the European concert conventions of a silent, seated audience.[11] A more radically different modus operandi from typical indigenous Shona musical occasions couldn't be imagined, with its ethos of group participation and aesthetic preferences for densely overlapping, interlocking parts, buzzy timbres, spontaneous vocal interjections, and dancing. The "concert" tradition, by contrast, exhibits central aesthetic features of modernist-cosmopolitanism including the emphasis on rationalist control of both musical features (timbres, harmonies, textures, standardized form) and musical roles (heightened specialist distinctions between artists and audience); the emphasis on music as product for exhibition rather than as group process; the preference for cosmopolitan genres; and all of this backed by the idea of "progress" which is central to the ideology of modernity.

The "concert" tradition is just one of many examples supporting Michael West's contention that by the 1950s a distinctive habitus had emerged among a middle-class African elite who came out of the higher levels of the educational system. This was a relatively small group, however, and as Mattaka's discussion of makwaya indicates, a few years of mission schooling was not enough to radically change aesthetic sensibilities, any more than it would necessarily inspire a deep inculcation of cosmopolitan ethos and ideology. The majority of Zimbabweans were still involved with indigenous musical traditions and syncretic forms like makwaya. By the 1950s it was the members of the African elite—the "tea-sippers," or for our purposes the "concert-goers"—who became involved with politics and liberal multiracial political organizations within the discourse of 'racial partnership.' This discourse generated a class alliance among middle-class Africans and white liberals during the Federation Period (1953–63), and subsequently set the stage for mass nationalism.

THE FEDERATION PERIOD

In Southern Rhodesia, interest in amalgamating with Northern Rhodesia (subsequently Zambia) and Nyasaland (Malawi) was expressed by Prime Minister Huggins as early as 1935, after the discovery of copper in Northern Rhodesia and for other economic reasons such as expanded "internal" markets and labor pools (Utlete 1978: 52; Holderness 1985: 106). Economic advantages would clearly accrue to the more powerful Southern Rhodesians, while the small white minorities in the two other colonies wanted allies to the south. As early as the Bledisloe Commission of 1939, the British government had begun to emphasize Africans' rights; hence whites in Northern Rhodesia and Nyasaland began to feel increasingly vulnerable.

The creation of the Federation was blocked until the early 1950s because the British disapproved of Southern Rhodesia's highly discriminatory native policies and did not want them spread (Vambe 1976: 117). In response, Huggins reversed his former stance on racial superiority and in a statement on native policy in 1941 urged white settlers to aid the advancement of "their black fellow men bringing them to their level of civilization" (ibid. 119). This was the impetus for the discourse of "racial partnership" diffused by the Southern Rhodesian state and embraced by liberals in the colony; by 1953 the British were convinced that the racial situation had improved, and the Federation of the three colonies was established.

Many observers have commented that it was the crushed hopes over the failure of partnership during the Federation years (1953–63), especially among the African elite, that fueled the fires of nationalism and ultimately led the country to civil war. Yet Nathan Shamuyarira, an acute observer of the period, notes that the early 1950s was a time of optimism: "The new policy of partnership, which was to be inscribed in the federal constitution, would bring to a speedy end the segregation, humiliation and indignation which we had suffered for forty years." He goes on to say, "This wasn't such a pipe-dream. The newspapers which catered to white readers were full of this spirit" (1965: 15–16).

The dream was not long-lived. Shamuyarira writes that a "major blow to African hopes of racial co-operation came in 1954 when the motion to outlaw discrimination in public places . . . was rejected in the Federal Parliament," and the "decisive blow" came in 1958 when the relatively progressive Garfield Todd was dismissed from the Southern Rhodesian premiership (1965: 22). Yet during the Federation period, a space was opened for new activities and attitudes among white liberals working in state and church institutions.

White-initiated Musical Reformism

In spite of rather blanket statements among nationalists and music scholars about the oppression of African culture and music in the colonial period, during the 1950s and early 1960s state institutions and various white-directed churches began to take an interest in African arts, albeit in the spirit of reformism and for their own complex reasons. It is striking that while the discourse of African cultural nationalism of the 1960s–1980s was explicitly anti-colonial and anti-European, in its main points of emphasis it mirrored the cultural discourse initiated by white liberals during the Federation period. This situation raises difficult questions about the orthodox view of blanket white cultural oppression vis-à-vis an African nationalist-inspired cultural renaissance after 1958.

As an example of this orthodoxy, Fred Zindi, a Zimbabwean university lecturer and musician, quotes an interview with an African disk jockey of the 1950s who said, "Even if one wanted to play African music, there was very little of it around on record because the whites were unwilling to record." Zindi goes on to comment, "The European minority who ruled Rhodesia found itself permanently on the defensive. It was either their 'civilised' culture or the African's and each D.J. who wanted to keep his job was made to promote western music and culture" (Zindi 1985: 9).

While these statements may be emotionally satisfying because they fit the usual black-and-white "good guys versus bad guys" scenario that has characterized the telling of Zimbabwean music history, in fact they fly in the face of a good deal of evidence to the contrary. It is true that settlers typically used the motif of "western civilization opposing the uncivilized [Africans]" as part of their rationalization of domination (e.g. Godwin and Hancock 1993; Kinloch 1975: 108–9, 116), but it is not true that whites were unwilling to record African music and air it on the radio during the Federation years and afterward.

The African Radio Services (CABS, later FBC) broadcast to the Federation territories out of Lusaka, Northern Rhodesia, until 1963, when African broadcasting (RBC) was transferred to Mbare Township outside Harare (then Salisbury).[12] African Radio was affiliated with the Federation, and later Rhodesian, governments through the Department of Information of the Ministry of Information, Immigration and Tourism

(Gwata and Reader 1977: 13). Hence the CAB/FBC/RBC's activities had implicit government acceptance.

In the early days of African broadcasting, CABS emphasized news and education and a "civilizing," "modernizing" mission. African broadcasting was also designed to attract Africans so that they would not tune into other radio-information sources that might go against colonial state interests (see Fraenkel 1959). In addition to diffusing enlightenment and proper information, however, African radio also emphasized entertainment and a respect for African music, stories, and drama.

Under Michael Kittermaster, the Broadcasting Officer throughout the 1950s, the Lusaka station built up its own sound archives through weekly recording sessions with African artists both at the studio and with a mobile unit that traveled through the Federation territories (Fraenkel 1959: 56, 222). Peter Fraenkel, who worked at the station during the 1950s, states that because of Kittermaster, "colour-discrimination was completely unknown" among the black and white staff members at the radio, and Kittermaster also defied the norms of segregation in his private social life as well.[13] He also had a genuine interest and respect for African arts and culture but let an expert African singer, guitarist, and composer, Alick Nkhata, handle most of the musical auditions and recordings. Nkhata had previously trained and worked with Hugh Tracey (Fraenkel 1959: 56).

Between the mid-1950s and 1972, when commercial recordings of African music became more available, the African Broadcasting Service recorded thousands of 78 rpm sides of different types of music, including a wide range of indigenous dance-drumming ensembles; mbira, njari, and karimba players; African guitarists; African "jazz" and "concert" groups; and village, school, and church choirs (Fraenkel 1959). Approximately 6,800 recordings of Zimbabwean music from the impressive FBC/RBC collection were available to me for study in the National Archives of Zimbabwe during my stay in 1992–93. From conversations and interviews it is clear that this music was commonly heard on radio and was appreciated by black Zimbabweans during the 1950s and 1960s.

Several points are worth underlining about the African Broadcasting Service. First, while the state had its own reasons for subsidizing the recording of African music, Kittermaster, the white director, had and fostered a genuine respect for African art; this is but one example that problematizes blanket statements about white attitudes (see also Holderness 1985). Second, regardless of the state's agenda, African Broadcasting upsets the orthodox vision of monolithic colonial oppression of indigenous music during and following the Federation years. The state-affiliated radio was, in fact, a major source of recording and diffusion of African music, albeit in objectified form. Finally, the FBC/RBC collection is but one of many indications that indigenous performing arts were alive and well during the colonial period.

During the Federation years there were other parallel streams of attention to African performing arts within white-directed institutions. Of all the arms of colonialism in Zimbabwe, missionaries have received a lion's share of blame for the direct oppression of indigenous Shona music and dance, and apparently for good reason. Attention to "Africanized" church music, however, begins in the Federation region with A. M. Jones in the 1940s. The trend of creating church music based on local songs and models was furthered with the arrival of Dr. H. Weman from Sweden for the Evangelical Lutheran Church after 1954; the Swiss Catholic missionary priest and musicologist Joseph Lenherr, in 1960; and Robert Kauffman for the American Methodist Board of Missions in 1960. Axelsson characterizes the results of the activities undertaken by the different denominations as a new type of "acculturated African art music" (1973, 1981).

"Africanized" church music was reformist in character: while the stated goals stressed respect for, and the need to preserve, local music, the result was a new kind of fusion of various local traditions with European elements which, like the radio, diminished the localness of given pieces and traditions. Axelsson and other commentators suggest that once this process started, it was the converted, educated [read middle-class] Africans who resisted the infusion of "African elements" into their church music (Axelsson 1973: 93; see also Carrington 1954). Again, class rather than race was the more important determinant of attitudes toward village music at this juncture.

Around 1957 a policy was initiated that explicitly encouraged the use of "African music" in the school curriculum for black students. While this idea was in keeping with the notion of "partnership" specific to the Federation, it was also gaining currency in other parts of Africa around the same time (e.g. see Carrington 1954, Hyslop 1955) and was being encouraged by international organizations such as UNESCO. James McHarg, who was enlisted by the Southern Rhodesia Native Education Department to design the music curriculum, states that the new policy was a pragmatic answer to shortages of teachers qualified to teach European music in Rhodesian schools. McHarg advocated a program in which indigenous songs should be used to teach sol-fa singing, ultimately leading to skill with staff notation. He concludes: "It is too early yet to say whether the scheme will succeed, but first reactions would indicate that the subject of music is now moving in the right direction and that indigenous music is being encouraged" (McHarg 1958: 48).

In 1961, the Kwanongoma College of Music was founded as part of the settler-directed Rhodesian Academy of Music in Bulawayo. The college was initiated in part to respond to the needs created by the shift in the state's music educational policies. Following McHarg's line of thinking, the goals of the new institution, according to its director Leslie Williamson, included "training African musicians and, in particular, African music teachers. It is the first venture of its kind in Southern Rhodesia and, as will be seen from the Syllabus, the work done covers a wide field of studies in which indigenous music plays a large part" (1963: 48).

As directly stated by McHarg and Williamson, the goals of both the state-directed music curriculum and Kwanongoma College reflected the idea of "partnership" and a reformist attitude in which local music would be "preserved," "improved," and made intelligible to cosmopolitan audiences through the teaching of music literacy and a European approach to arranging and performing African music (Williamson 1963, McHarg 1958). It was through the efforts of Kwanongoma College that the marimba, an "invented tradition" in the Zimbabwe context (e.g. see Kauffman 1970: 198), and the karimba (15–key lamallaphone) were popularized and diffused in the country, and later abroad by Kwanongoma graduate Dumisani Maraire.

On the importance of preservation, Williamson writes: "The encouragement, too, of an informed study of the *worthwhile elements* of indigenous idioms is a very vital necessity, if these are not to be brushed aside by a community subjected to the indifferent noises of modern mechanical reproduction imported from elsewhere" (1963: 48, emphasis added). Of significance to the present essay, very similar sentiments and goals were later articulated by African nationalists and African state cultural workers after 1980. At Kwanongoma College, distinct localist traditions were consciously fused with European techniques and cosmopolitan performance contexts (stage, radio, television), and genres (e.g. opera) in order to create a "specifically Rhodesian art-form." Such an approach militates against localism and "tribalism," and this goal of the white-directed College was also directly echoed by contemporary and later African nationalists and state cultural workers.

The fundamental features of African cultural nationalism—emphasis on local village music, preservation, and reformist "improvement"—were thus paralleled or anticipated in white liberal discourse. This is not surprising given the class habitus of the nationalist leadership and their former alliance with white liberals in organizations such as the Interracial Association of Southern Rhodesia (1953) during the Federation period. The important point to recognize here is that while the discourse of "racial partnership" was ultimately structured by colonial constructions of "race," it involved a middle-class alliance across color/geographical heritage ("racial") lines.

THE NATIONALIST PHASE

Especially during the militant 1970s, African nationalist discourse played down class and projected *race* as the key variable for understanding political, social, and cultural history in Zimbabwe. In regard to music, and cultural practice more generally, nationalists asserted an orthodox vision of a unilinear sequence of events with racial conflict as the key variable: (1) local African music went into serious decline because of *white-European* colonial/missionary oppression; (2) beginning in the 1960s *black-African* nationalism led to a "renaissance" of indigenous music–dance. This orthodoxy has been echoed in various scholarly works on Zimbabwean music.[14] In this construction of history, the middle-class nationalist leadership reproduced the two main immutable criteria for constructing race that were used by whites: *color* and *geographical heritage*. As I suggested earlier, it is the guise of "immutability" or "naturalness" that make racial constructs useful both for rationalizing relations of domination and for organizing movements to overturn such relations.

The Beginnings of Cultural Nationalism, Early 1960s

A survey of the biographies of the African nationalist leadership in Zimbabwe confirms that they fit the typical description of a cosmopolitan "middle group" (between the ruling elite and the working classes) which usually gives rise to nationalist movements (e.g. Gellner 1983: 57, A. Smith 1971: 87–88, Hobsbawm 1990: 10, Seton-Watson 1977: 439, Anderson 1991, Chatterjee 1986). The Zimbabwean leadership had at least received mission education; a good number studied at institutions of higher education in South Africa, Great Britain, and the United States.[15]

The Youth City League (1955), which marks the beginning of the mass nationalist phase, was led by more "populist" individuals (Shamuyarira 1965: 28), but they had difficulty forming a national party. They themselves felt that "they did not have sufficient education to lead the people" (Nyagumbo 1980: 106). When a meeting was finally arranged in Salisbury to form a national party in 1957, it almost fell apart because the three League leaders wanted an "African graduate" to lead, and no one readily acceptable was on hand. They even asked the white liberal Guy Clutton-Brock to lead the meeting (ibid. 107). Mr. Joshua Nkomo, who was on hand, was chosen for the task and was elected president of the new Southern Rhodesia African National Congress (ANC, 1957; banned 1959). Nkomo then went on to lead the subsequent countrywide nationalist parties: National Democratic Party (NDP, formed 1 Jan 1960; banned 9 Dec 1961); and Zimbabwe African People's Union (ZAPU, formed 16 Dec 1961; banned 20 Sept 1962, but continued underground). Nkomo remained the leader of the main nationalist party until the Zimbabwe African National Union (ZANU) split off in August 1963 under the leadership of "African graduates" Ndabaningi Sithole as president, Leopold Takawira as vice-president, and Robert Mugabe as secretary-general. Mugabe, of course, was later to emerge as the leader of ZANU and ultimately of the new nation-state after 1980.

In 1957, ANC president Joshua Nkomo was still talking in terms of "true partnership regardless of race, colour or creed" (cited in Shamuyarira 1965: 46). At this point, then, he was still working within the earlier African middle-class position that attempted to play down *color* and "race" as criteria defining social relations. The shift to the idea that Africans should rule themselves came with the NDP in 1960, as did the rise of cultural nationalism as an important component of the movement, which it remained thereafter. Schooled in nationalist strategy in Ghana, the new publicity secretary of the NDP, Robert Mugabe,

> added one important factor that had been singularly missing in Rhodesian nationalism: emotion. From the position of publicity secretary, Mugabe proceeded to organize a semi-militant youth wing. . . . Youth [Wing] started influencing and controlling some party activities. Thudding drums, ululation by women dressed in national costumes and ancestral prayers began to feature at meetings more prominently than before. A public meeting became a massive rally of residents of a given township. The Youth Wing, with a small executive taking charge of units of fifty houses in each township, knocked at every door on Saturday evening to remind residents about meetings. Next Sunday morning, thudding drums, and singing groups again reminded the residents, until the meeting started. . . . At the hall, Youth Leaguers ordered attendants to remove their shoes, ties and jackets, as one of the first signs in rejection of European civilization. Water served in traditional water-pots replaced Coca-Cola kiosks. By the time the first speaker, a European in bare feet, took the platform, the whole

square was a sea of some 15,000 to 20,000 cheering and cheerful black faces. The emotional impact of such gatherings went far beyond claiming to rule the country—it was an ordinary man's participation in creating something new, a new nation. (Shamuyarira 1965: 67–68)

Shamuyarira, a first-hand observer writing close to the time he is describing, captures the way symbolic gestures were used successfully to create a sense of African identity and participation in the early rallies. In a speech given after returning from Ghana in 1960, Mugabe indicates his awareness of the class basis of the nationalist leadership but warns that to succeed, the movement will have to have support and even allow leadership "from all classes of men" (quoted in D. Smith and Simpson 1981: 27, 37). This was the beginning of the move to unite the African classes and to emphasize a separatist racial unity marked by a celebration of local African culture and a rejection of European culture (Bhebe 1989: 101).

When ZAPU was formed, Mugabe stayed on as "National Publicity Secretary for Information," and the party continued emphasizing cultural nationalism. A mass rally celebrated the foundation of ZAPU in March of 1962, and the *African Parade* reporter covering the event, Stephen Supiya, summarizes ZAPU's reformist cultural agenda under the headline "ZAPU Endeavours to Blend the Old and the New" (Supiya 1962). Given that this was an event launching the new nationalist party, it is striking that Supiya stressed "tribal" music and dance activities, suggesting their novelty. His article opens with the words "The most significant part of the whole celebration was the introduction of African tribal dances."

Interspersed with speeches and the introduction of party leaders were performances of a range of regional dance-drumming groups as well as an mbira ensemble. Supiya was careful to note that the dances were representative of different ethnolinguistic groups: "such as Mbira (Shona), Kotsore (Manyika), Mbakumba (Budya), Muchongoyo (Shangan), Shangara (Zezuru), and Gure (Makorekore)" (1962: 8), thus discouraging tribalism by including the various localist groups within the incipient construction of the party and "nation." Like most middle-class Africans who wrote about "tribal" music and dance in the 1950s and early 1960s in Zimbabwean journals, Supiya describes them as being of "old Africa" and as "weird" and exotic. He thus reproduces the traditional–modern dichotomy of cosmopolitan discourse and, like others of his class, suggests an unfamiliarity with village arts, as if many these same groups could not be seen dancing weekly in the market area of Mbare Township.[16] In addition to the "tribal dances," two of the country's most popular "concert" ensembles, De Black Evening Follies and the Cool Fours, performed, groups with special appeal to middle-class Africans and providing an image of "modernity." Thus, as the headline read, "ZAPU Endeavours to Blend the Old and the New."

Other similar political rallies and festivals celebrating and, in fact, explicitly fashioning "the national culture" followed. The chairman of the Zimbabwe Traditional and Cultural Club, the cultural arm of the nationalist party, called 1963 the "year of the renaissance of Zimbabwe." In that year the Cultural Club held the "Zimbabwe Festival of African Culture," which included a dress contest to determine what would become the national costume of the country; a cooking contest in which local dishes were judged/legitimated by "two [medical] doctors of great repute"; and an art show juxtaposing "both modern paintings and traditional arts [carved stools, axes, walking sticks]." But "Dances of the Zimbabwe of old and of today were the highlights of the day" (*African Parade* 1963: 9).

This festival included the same regional dance-drumming groups featured at the rally previously described, as well as the Culture Club's own resident band, The Hurricanes. Although the club was formed to champion "traditional culture," their own ensemble consisted of two electric guitars, bass guitar, and traps. The *Parade* reporter describes the Hurricanes' music in the following terms: "Theirs is a combination of modern jazz, the twist, the madison, rock 'n' roll together with the *music of the years of yore* which in the end come to one: The Gallop, the dance of Zimbabwe" (ibid. 8, emphasis added).

Like the search for a national costume, the gallop was a conscious attempt to create a uniquely Zimbabwean musical genre that fused "old" village elements with "modern" genres and instrumentation for nationalist purposes—to create the image of a distinctive yet newly emerging cosmopolitan nation. The gallop didn't take hold, but as a stylistic idea it is a clear forerunner to electric-guitar band performance of mbira music and other village genres that became prominent after 1973–74 with the work of artists such as Jackson Phiri, M. D. Rhythm Success, Thomas Mapfumo, and others.[17]

PARTY DISCOURSE AND CULTURAL NATIONALISM IN THE 1970s

During the period of severe state repression and censorship, 1964–79, statements and articles explicitly about or expressing African cultural nationalism largely disappear from the black popular press and media. In the few official statements on culture that were issued by ZANU and ZAPU, the two leading nationalist parties, a reformist approach to constructing a new national culture was still being articulated, thereby representing a major point of continuity with the discourse of cultural nationalism of the early 1960s.

In statements made before the 1960–63 period, people who would become nationalist leaders actually gave credit to missionaries and European-style education for inspiring nationalism and their own models for future development. In the 1970s, however, missionaries, European education, and everything else associated with colonialism were officially recast, in black-and-white terms, as the evil engines of cultural domination. For example, writing in 1969 (published in ZANU's official *Zimbabwe News*, 1978: 14), Lazarus Mpofu states: "Christianity has been used as the subtle instrument to destroy Zimbabwe culture." While this attitude is understandable in the context of the violent struggle for majority rule, it becomes contradictory to the basic tenets of cultural reformism that persisted, and to the cosmopolitan habitus of the nationalist leaders themselves.

A ZANU document, "MWENJE No. 2. ZANU's Political Programme," issued from Lusaka 1 Aug 1972, contains one of the party's few clear official statements on cultural nationalism. The eighth article, called "The New Zimbabwe Culture," states:

> Eighty years of colonization have warped the minds of our people and shaken their confidence in themselves by a process of cultural alienation. The settler stage, screen, mass media, literature, school and church, have combined to create a false impression that a foreign culture was good and our own was bad. Consequently, our rich cultural heritage has been lost and at times despised by the young generation which has been indoctrinated and intoxicated with western cultural values.
>
> In a free, democratic, independent and socialist Zimbabwe the people will be encouraged and assisted in building a new Zimbabwe culture, derived from the best in what our heritage and history has given, and developed to meet the needs of the new socialist society of the twentieth century. We are prepared to learn from the accumulated experience and refinement of mind, morals and tastes from other peoples and cultures in the world, especially those from other parts of Africa and use such knowledge to improve and enrich our own. But our culture must stem from our own creativeness and so remain African and indigenous.
>
> The emphasis of Zimbabwe's new culture will be on the community.

The new screen, stage, mass media, literature and schools will project the richness of our community life and the role of the individual in it. (Nyangoni and Nyandoro 1979: 261)

This statement is reformist at its core. Borrowing from the colonizer's culture is played down, although adapting elements from contemporary cosmopolitan culture, and especially African models, is encouraged; Ghana was a prime model for Mugabe's cultural nationalism. Cosmopolitan contexts for cultural practice such as the screen, the stage, mass media, literature, and schools are not questioned in and of themselves. Rather, they are portrayed as neutral channels—when used by colonial rulers they were bad, reformed by the nationalists they will become positive. The promised turn to socialism as the basis for social-political organization itself confirms the importance of European-initiated cosmopolitan models. But in the Zimbabwe context, socialism represented a clear oppositional stance vis-à-vis the capitalist settlers. It fit with the populist necessity of the nationalist movement; and, moreover, China was an important ally of ZANU, and the Soviets supported ZAPU. Thus among the cosmopolitan models available, socialism was an obvious choice.

The nationalist leadership came out of the educational background they are depicting as evil, but in ZANU's statement, by rhetorical turn, it is "the young generation which has been indoctrinated and intoxicated with western cultural values." The writers of this document state rather categorically that ideological domination was complete and that the rich cultural heritage of Zimbabwe *has been lost*. In the ZANU document, the assertion of total loss served to dramatize the evil of the enemy; but it does not stand up well to historical evidence for certain rural areas and among sectors of the urban working class. Nonetheless, for their own reasons, the nationalists of the 1970s supported and helped perpetuate the "decline of traditional culture" myth that had been previously stated from other cosmopolitan quarters—missionaries, radio people, *Parade* writers, ethnomusicologists, and black and white teachers.

THE POST-1980 PERIOD

In the post-1980 period, the intersection of racial and class identities is more complex. In part because of the Lancaster House Agreement (negotiations for majority rule) and in part to stave off white/capital flight, the black elite who took control of the government made an alliance with the white settlers who still controlled the economy (e.g. see Knight

1992: 220). An official policy of reconciliation with the whites was instituted and remained in place. The black elite also began to move
into formerly white-elite neighborhoods, send their children to the best
schools, drive expensive cars, wear expensive suits, and patronize upper-
class, formerly white, restaurants and clubs. That is, they returned to the
cosmopolitan cultural markers that the African middle class had favored
in the pre–mass-nationalist period; but now they could more fully adopt
the lifestyles of their former colonial rulers.

Although diminishing gradually throughout the 1980s, the state at
first established programs in line with their cultural-nationalist discourse
of the 1960s and 1970s. In 1981 the National Dance Company (NDC)
was established by the Ministry of Education and Culture under the guidance of the foreign expert Peggy Harper of Britain. It originally consisted
of master performers of the regionalized shangara, mbukumba, dhinhe,
muchongoyo, and jerusarema dances as well as an mbira player. Interestingly, these were the primary traditions performed at the early 1960s
rallies.

The master performers taught their specific music and dances to each
other and to younger members who auditioned for the full-time sala-
ried positions in the company. Whereas formerly most organized dance
groups (e.g. urban burial or dance associations) specialized in the one or
more dances specific to their own region, the NDC was explicitly pan–
regional–national. Their first major production was a nationalist dance-
drama "Mbuya Nehanda—The Spirit of Liberation," which was created
for the second anniversary of Zimbabwe's independence in 1982 by
Peggy Harper, the African-American choreographer Kariamu Welsh-
Asante, and the Zimbabwean folklorist Father Emmanuel Ribiero. More
typically, they performed their usual repertory of dances on stage, television, and for state occasions and represented Zimbabwe abroad. The
shift to cosmopolitan performance contexts, and the important role foreign and local experts had in shaping these village arts, are striking although certainly not surprising, given the reformist agenda of the state.

Father Ribiero, who worked with the company between 1982 and
1990, told me that his goal had been to have the dances performed so true
to the local traditions that if they performed a dance in its place of origin,
the local people would be accepting and would be able to join in (field-
notes 7 May 1993). He indicated, however, that the increasing emphasis on stagework, showmanship, and artistic development, as well as the
group not being rooted in a given locale, led to major changes in the
dances. He said that this continued to the point where local people began
to reject the NDC version, saying simply, "that's not it," a result reported

from other quarters as well (e.g., Nyandoro, pers. comm., Dec. 10, 1992; Mutasa, pers. comm., 7 Aug. 1993).

By the mid to late 1980s, the NDC had cemented a canon of Zimbabwean traditional dance, had created their own versions of local dances, and through their public performances and work in the schools had begun to diffuse their versions as the model for performance, especially among urban youth, a process that I observed repeatedly between 1991 and 1993. The NDC, then, is a clear example of how the black-controlled state pushed cosmopolitan aesthetics, practices, and contexts to reform village arts and to make localist traditions national.

The Deputy Minister of Culture, Stephan Chifunyise, emphasized to me that village dances should be developed and not restricted to a single locality. While I agree that art involves processes of development, the crucial question is, Who should direct such processes and for what ends? Workshops designed by the Ministry of Culture have been used to diffuse local dances to other regions. Through its district cultural officers and through workshops, the Ministry is involved in getting village performers to establish formalized ensemble structures, establish set choreography, learn stagecraft, and "professionalize" their arts to generate income.

Whatever the pros and cons of such an agenda, there is certainly not enough work to support even the existing professional "traditional" dance troupes (many of which are offshoots of the NDC). Moreover, like many aspects of the Ministry of Culture's programs, the advocated line of development certainly contradicts their stated goal of "preserving" village music and dance. The Ministry programs are aimed at fundamentally transforming the more ad hoc, non-staged, communal structure of village performance; its localist participatory ethos and aesthetic; and the conception of music-dance as a socially interactive process rather than a commodity or product. Judging from the number of new (post-1980) bureaucratized dance groups I encountered in rural Murehwa District, I would suggest that the Ministry's programs are working and that they represent a basic continuity with the colonial missionaries' work of spreading cosmopolitan ethos and aesthetics.

THE PASSIVE REVOLUTION OF CAPITAL IN THE 1990s

During the 1980s there was a slow transformation from the nationalist and Marxist rhetoric and ideals of the war years to a laissez-faire capitalist position. Making good on two of their three promises to "the people," the victorious ZANU party improved African education and health care tremendously. In regard to land redistribution, the center-piece of their popular appeals during the war, however, little progress was made—again the Lancaster House treaty and fear of white flight and economic collapse were cited as reasons.

The watershed of the movement to a capitalist-elitist position oc-curred in 1990 with the formal institution of the IMF/World Bank–designed Economic Structural Adjustment Program (ESAP). This pro-gram clearly benefits higher-class Zimbabweans and international capital at the great expense of peasants and lower working-class Zimbabweans (see MacGarry 1993). As but one example of this, with ESAP's pressure to trim government expenses, the choice was made to close down many rural marketing depots in small-scale farming areas so that they cannot get their cash produce to market. ESAP's opening to international trade has also hurt many local companies; tremendous numbers of workers have been laid off (ibid).

By the early 1990s, in striking parallel to the institution of ESAP, even symbolic use and support of local Shona and Ndebele village perform-ing arts diminished. For example, funding was completely withdrawn from the National Dance Company in the early 1990s, and the institu-tion closed down. As another example, while village music and dance had been a centerpiece of National Independence Day Celebrations for much of the 1980s, by the time of the event I attended in 1993 even this vestige of cultural nationalism had disappeared. Instead, the imagery presented was of a "modern" cosmopolitan nation. The performances included military bands playing an international fare of marches, police dog rou-tines, paratroopers, and schoolchildren doing flag routines reminiscent of state celebrations in China. In terms of both economic policy and cul-tural policy and imagery, Zimbabwe had firmly joined the cosmopolitan-capitalist world.

I do not wish to belittle the complexity of factors and pressures im-pinging on the Zimbabwean leadership's political and economic options. I simply point out that the class habitus of the leadership has been an im-portant factor in the way things have developed. Indeed, certain people predicted the outcome well before it came to full fruition, based on an analysis of the class position of the leadership (e.g., Kanyangarara 1978; Astrow 1983). The issue of class habitus is even more pronounced in the artistic field, however, because here there are fewer external pres-sures directing state policy and action. Judging from interviews and conversations with officials in the Ministry of Culture and the National Arts Council, I believe that the cultural policies and objectives I have outlined above are internally generated. I also believe that they stand in fundamental contrast to the values and goals held by many villagers whose interests these officials are supposed to represent and serve.[18]

CONCLUSION

The shifting class–race–class identity pattern among the African middle class has had important ramifications for musical taste and production both within this group and more broadly. In the pre–mass-nationalist phase, the middle class favored cosmopolitan popular forms as emblems of refinement, and they sometimes even disparaged village traditions because of their own cosmopolitan cultural position. In the mass-nationalist phase, they celebrated local African music and culture for the purposes of political unification, creating the image of a nation, perhaps for their own identity needs, and for distinction from the white "settlers." Many of the central facets of black-nationalist cultural discourse and policy, however, had been foreshadowed or paralleled in time by white-directed institutions during the Federation period. This raises questions about the standard depiction of colonial cultural oppression and suggests that white discourse about African culture may have even had an influence on middle-class African cultural nationalism; this connection is particularly salient in light of alliances between the black middle class and white liberals during the Federation period (see Turino 2000).

After the late 1950s, the nationalists were instrumental in connecting local indigenous arts with national sentiment more broadly, especially among the urban population. In the rallies of the early 1960s, they juxtaposed localist dance groups with "concert" ensembles to create an image of the emerging nation—imagery that "endeavored to blend the old and new." In the early 1960s there was also an attempt to create a full-fledged reformist genre, the gallop, blending local and cosmopolitan elements, a movement that came to fruition in the *chimurenga* music of the liberation choirs and the electric-band renditions of indigenous music after the late 1960s.

Like nationalist movements in many places, in the end the Zimbabwean "revolution" did not represent a populist liberatory break with colonial or cosmopolitan attitudes and policies in relation to capitalism and in relation to indigenous African artistic practices and worldview. In fact, nationalists and the leaderships of newly formed post-colonial states are typically involved in bringing cosmopolitan values and lifeways to the villages in their effort to incorporate formerly differentiated communities into the nation. Getting people with a localist purview and identity to "imagine the nation" (Anderson 1991) is a basic intermediary step to getting them to imagine themselves as part of the cosmopolitan world. It is for this reason that nationalism as a phenomenon is theoretically crucial to understanding the processes of cultural and economic globalization in post-colonial countries. We have focused on some of the musical processes and results of this in Zimbabwe. In that country, at least, I do not think that these moves are the product of cynical manipulation, but rather they are viewed as a means to positive progress because of the cosmopolitan worldview of the leadership itself. From a localist and lower-class perspective, however, the results are not always viewed as positive.

While musical developments in relation to colonialism and nationalism in Zimbabwe have largely been interpreted by scholars in terms of race—following colonial and later nationalist discourse—we have seen that elite Africans projected their own identities and attempted alliances first in terms of class, then race, then class for specific conjunctural reasons. In this chapter, however, I have argued that it is the class habitus of the black elite, rather than racial identity, that is the most important variable for understanding key features of recent Zimbabwean music history.

NOTES

1. Colonial attitudes and policy varied at different times, and among different individuals, regarding the desirability of creating an African middle class. Many settlers viewed "natives" as one unified class fit only for labor. At other times, however, educational policies were created that fostered the creation of a black middle class that could serve as mediators between whites and the African masses (e.g., see Moyana 1988).

2. For example, "cultural capital"—knowledge of and control over Zimbabwean village arts, cultural imagery, and discourses—can theoretically be used to unite village Africans behind a given leadership, hence bolstering its "political capital" in relation to negotiations with the colonial state. Such is the utility of cultural nationalism for political nationalism.

3. For our purposes, the cultural complex of *modernity* includes Weberian rationalism; scientific method; cosmopolitan technologies; cosmopolitan habitus including aesthetic dispositions; capitalist economic principles and modus operandi, e.g. exchange value over use value and individual accumulation; with "progress" being the key symbolic trope that holds the whole thing together. Of particular concern, because of the needs of rationalist control and capitalist production, the ideology of *modernity* underwrites the increasing objectification/commodification of many aspects of life—e.g. music increasingly reconceptualized as a product rather than an interactive social-spiritual process. The very use

of the "traditional–modern" dichotomy—so common in nationalist discourse, reformist programs, and academic writing—is itself a product of the ideology of *modernity*, which asserts its own features and modus operandi as the inevitable, logical present and future while relegating alternative lifeways ("the traditional") to an outmoded past. Although contemporary (modern) in their own right, Zimbabwean indigenous arts were typically conceived as "being of the past" by middle-class Africans, and this operates as a self-fulfilling social definition when these same individuals come to direct state cultural programs, as we shall see.

4. Because of the key role of mission education in forming middle-class aspirations, ideology, and economic position, religious orientation and class become strongly intertwined.

5. Members of the black middle class usually preferred European-style weddings which they felt were not just for the settlers but "for all educated and civilised people" (quote from the *Bantu Mirror*, 5 Jan 1957: 15, in West 1990: 122).

6. Especially in the earlier decades, all urban Africans, regardless of class, lived in a single township, then known as Harare (now Mbare), outside Salisbury. A number of indigenous dances from different rural areas have been performed each Sunday and at other times in the Harare market area since at least the 1930s (this continues today). People who lived in the township during the 1930s and 1940s told me that while the performers in these dance groups were primarily working class, middle-class people might stop to watch and enjoy the fun when passing through the area. Conversely, I spoke with working-class people who told me that they had been fans of the more cosmopolitan musical styles as well as of village music and dance. Yet other working-class people stressed that they had only been interested in the indigenous styles, just as many middle-class people expressed strict allegiance to cosmopolitan music and even demonstrated ignorance of indigenous styles. There is clearly a range of possibilities.

7. *African Parade*, later simply *Parade*, is a monthly magazine published in Salisbury and directed specifically to an African readership, most specifically a middle-class readership. Sometimes following the magazine's title were the words: "The only magazine in Southern Africa edited and printed by Africans for Africans" (e.g. on the cover of vol. 7, 1 [1995]). To my knowledge, all the writers for the journal were black Zimbabweans. I surveyed the journal from its first volume through the 1970s. By studying the advertisements, letters to the editor, editorials, and articles, much can be learned about the political and cultural positions and concerns of urban middle-class Africans in the townships during this period.

8. Since independence, many place names have been changed; Salisbury became Harare, Harare Township became Mbare. I will use present-day place names.

9. Domboshawa was the first government school for Africans in Zimbabwe; most African education remained in the hands of missionaries although the state oversaw the mission schools in various ways.

10. Mattaka's daughter Bertha Mattaka Msora, by contrast, indicated that her father occasionally composed songs and that he translated a few American

popular songs into Shona or put altered Shona texts to the American tunes (in Makwenda 1992a). She, however, was referring to the 1950s, whereas when stating that they did few songs in Shona, Mattaka was referring to the earlier 1930s–1940s period.

11. As another example, Jeremiah Kainga, a guitar player and dancer who joined the Bantu Actors in 1947, comments: "We did not have amplifiers but our voices were heard by people even at the back of the hall. The audience was so quiet that if you dropped a coin everyone in the hall would look at you" (quoted in Makwenda 1992b).

12. CABS is Central African Broadcasting Service, FBC refers to the Federation Broadcasting Corporation, and RBC, the Rhodesian Broadcasting Corporation.

13. Fraenkel notes that Kittermaster "entertained Africans at his house, and oblivious of the reactions of white passers-by and neighbors, showed them over his garden, and served them drinks on his open veranda. When my predecessor as 'programme assistant' proved unable to get on with Africans, Kittermaster curtly asked him to resign or he would be fired" (1959: 24).

14. This trajectory is sometimes explicitly stated, strongly implied, or simply assumed in the literature on Zimbabwean music, e.g. Bender 1991; Berliner 1978: 25–26, 240–42; Brown 1994: 105; Frederikse 1982; Kauffman 1980: 43; Lane 1993: 30–33; Zindi 1985. Bender provides a particularly bald statement of the position:

> The traditional music of Southern Rhodesia has disappeared to an alarming degree. Christian missionaries, recognizing the close relationship between heathen religion and music, ensured a fast decline in traditional culture. . . . Only emerging nationalism during the 1960s . . . and worldwide recognition of black culture, including the Black Power movement in the United States, led to a reconsideration of their own traditions. (1991: 154–55)

The degree and specifics of the "cultural decline" have never been demonstrated or analyzed in any depth. My research for rural Murehwa and among certain portions of the urban working class in Harare, as well as the work of others (e.g. Lan 1985; Ranger 1984, 1985; Kriger 1992), suggests that the effects of colonialism *and* nationalism on local cultural ethos and practices varied greatly by region, the amount of dependence on missionary land, involvement with missionary services, individual inclinations and dispositions, class, occupation, and age, among many other variables. Sweeping statements like Bender's cannot be sustained.

15. Prominent nationalists who studied abroad include Canaan Banana (United States), Gordon Chavunduka (U.S.), James Chikerema (South Africa), Josiah Chinamano (S.A.), Herbert Chitepo (S.A., United Kingdom), Elliot Gabellah (U.S.), Morton Malianga (S.A.), Joseph Msinkavanhu (S.A.), Robert Mugabe (S.A.), Abel Muzorewa (U.S.), Joshua Nkomo (S.A.), George Silunkika (S.A.), Ndabaningi Sithole (U.S.), Leopold Takawira (S.A.), Edson Zvobgo (S.A., U.S.) (see Nyangoni and Nyandoro 1979: 444–47). Others had received less

formal education but became "self-made men" through private study or enterprise. George Nyandoro, a founder member of the City Youth League in 1955 and secretary general of ZAPU, 1963–70, received only seven years' formal education at St. Mary's Mission in Salisbury but qualified as an accountant privately (ibid. 446).

16. This has always struck me as odd, since many of the "tribal" dance groups called to perform at nationalist rallies were migrant dance and burial associations located in urban townships. In the Salisbury area, such groups had typically performed in the Mbare Township market area on a weekly basis since the 1930s, a location frequented by all classes of Africans.

17. A difference lies in that the Hurricanes' goals were specifically nationalist, whereas the motivations of later artists were more complex, involving professional career aspirations and an appeal to the national sentiment of their urban audiences previously established by the nationalist movement. For reasons of space, this distinction cannot be demonstrated here, but it is the subject of another paper (Turino 1995).

18. The Zimbabwe case exemplifies what Partha Chatterjee (1986), following Antonio Gramsci, has called "the passive revolution of capital." My use of this concept involves the ways local cosmopolitan elites may become the vanguard of anti-colonial struggles, but also the very ground upon which national and international capitalist relations are maintained, and even furthered, within the country once independence is achieved. A parallel situation exists on the cultural terrain when the directors of state cultural and educational institutions transform alternative localist arts from the basis of their own cosmopolitan ideologies of art and artistic practice.

REFERENCES

African Parade. 1954. "Entertainment in the Early Thirties, by an Old Timer," *African Parade* (November): 14; (December): 20.

———. 1963. "Zimbabwe Festival of African Culture." *African Parade* (July): 8–9.

Anderson, Benedict. 1991. *Imagined Communities: Reflections on the Origin and Spread of Nationalism*. London: Verso.

Astrow, Andre. 1983. *Zimbabwe: A Revolution that Lost its Way?* London: Zed Books.

Axelsson, Olof E. 1973. "Historical Notes on Neo-African Church Music." *Zambezia* 3, 1: 89–100.

———. 1981. "The Development of African Church Music in Zimbabwe." In *Papers Presented at the Second Symposium on Ethnomusicology*, ed. Andrew Tracey, 2–7. Grahamstown, South Africa: International Library of African Music.

Bender, Wolfgang. 1991. *Sweet Mother: Modern African Music*. Chicago: University of Chicago Press.

Berliner, Paul. 1978. *The Soul of Mbira: Music and Traditions of the Shona People of Zimbabwe*. Berkeley and Los Angeles: University of California Press.

Bhebe, Ngwabi. 1989. "The Nationalist Struggle, 1957–1962." In *Turmoil and Tenacity: Zimbabwe 1890–1990*, ed. Canaan S. Banana, 50–114. Harare: The College Press.

Bourdieu, Pierre. 1984. *Distinction: A Social Critique of The Judgement of Taste.* Cambridge: Harvard University Press.

Brown, Ernest. 1994. "The Guitar and the *mbira:* Resilience, Assimilation, and Pan-Africanism in Zimbabwean Music." *The World of Music* 36, 2: 73–117.

Carrington, John T. 1954. Letter to the Editor. *African Music Society Journal* 1, 1: 83.

Chatterjee, Partha. 1986. *Nationalist Thought and the Colonial World.* Minneapolis: University of Minnesota Press.

Frederikse, Julie. 1982. *None but Ourselves: Masses vs. Media in the Making of Zimbabwe.* Harmondsworth: Penguin.

Fraenkel, Peter. 1959. *Wayaleshi.* London: Weidenfeld and Nicolson.

Gellner, Ernest. 1983. *Nations and Nationalism.* Oxford: Blackwell.

Gilroy, Paul. 1987. *"There Ain't No Black in the Union Jack": The Cultural Politics of Race and Nation.* Chicago: University of Chicago Press.

Godwin, Peter, and Ian Hancock. 1993. *"Rhodesians Never Die": The Impact of War and Political Change on White Rhodesia, c. 1970–1980.* Oxford: Oxford University Press.

Gwata, M. F., and D. H. Reader. 1977. "Rhodesian African Cultural and Leisure Needs." Unpublished paper, Department of Sociology, University of Rhodesia, commissioned by the National Arts Foundation of Rhodesia.

Hobsbawm, Eric J. 1990. *Nations and Nationalism Since 1780: Programme, Myth, Reality.* Cambridge: Cambridge University Press.

Holderness, Hardwicke. 1985. *Lost Chance: Southern Rhodesia 1945–58.* Harare: Zimbabwe Publishing House.

Hyslop, Graham H. 1955. "Brief Report of a Music Course Conducted at Siriba for the Nyanza Musical Society." *African Music Society Journal* 1, 2: 58–59.

Kanyangarara, Maclay. 1978. "Class Struggle in Zimbabwe." *Zimbabwe News* 10, 3: 13–15.

———. 1970. "Multi-part Relationships in the Shona Music of Rhodesia." Ph.D. dissertation, University of California, Los Angeles.

Kauffman, Robert. 1980. "Tradition and Innovation in the Urban Music of Zimbabwe." *African Urban Studies* 6: 41–48.

Kinloch, G. C. 1975. "Changing Intergroup Attitudes of Whites as Defined by the Press: The Process of Colonial Adaptation." *Zambezia* 4, 1: 105–17.

Knight, Virginia Curtin. 1992. "Zimbabwe: The Politics of Economic Reform." *Current History: A World Affairs Journal, Africa:* 219–23.

Kriger, Norma. 1992. *Zimbabwe's Guerrilla War: Peasant Voices.* Cambridge: Cambridge University Press.

Lan, David. 1985. *Guns and Rain: Guerrillas and Spirit Mediums in Zimbabwe.* London: James Currey.

Lane, Martha S. B. 1993. "'The Blood that Made the Body Go:' The Role of

Song, Poetry and Drama in Zimbabwe's War of Liberation, 1966–1980."
Ph.D. diss., Northwestern University, Evanston, Ill.

MacGarry, Brian, S.J. 1993. *Growth? Without Equity?* Gweru, Zimbabwe:
Mambo Press.

Makwenda, Joyce. 1992a. *Zimbabwe Township Music, 1930s to 1960s.* Film produced for ZBC.

———. 1992b. "Dancer, Guitarist of the 50s." Harare *Sunday Mail*, 18 October, 13.

Mattaka, Kenneth. 1993. Recorded Interview Transcription Zim93–65.

McHarg, James. 1958. "African Music in Rhodesian Native Education." *African
Music Society Journal* 2, 1: 46–50.

Mnyanda, B. J. 1954. *In Search of Truth: A Commentary on Certain Aspects of
Southern Rhodesia's Native Policy.* Bombay: Hind Kitabs Ltd.

Moyana, Toby Tafirenyika. 1988. *Education, Liberation, and the Creative Act.*
Harare: Zimbabwe Publishing House.

Mpofu, Lazarus. 1978. "Pan-African Symposium Zimbabwe Culture and the
Liberation Struggle." *Zimbabwe News* 10, 3: 13–15.

Nyagumbo, Maurice. 1980. *With the People: An Autobiography from the Zimbabwe
Struggle.* London: Allison & Busby.

Nyandoro, Patrick. 1992. Recorded Interview Transcription Zim92–32.

Nyangoni, Christopher, and Gideon Nyandoro. 1979. *Zimbabwe Independence
Movements: Select Documents.* London: Rex Collings.

Ranger, Terence. 1984. "Religions and Rural Protests in Makoni District, Zimbabwe, 1900–80." In *Religion and Rural Revolt*, ed. Janos M. Bak and Gerhard
Benecke, 315–35. Dover, N.H.: Manchester University Press.

———. 1985. *Peasant Consciousness and Guerrilla War in Zimbabwe: A Comparative Study.* London: James Currey; Berkeley and Los Angeles: University of
California Press.

Royce, Anya. 1982. *Ethnic Identity.* Bloomington: Indiana University Press.

Seton-Watson, Hugh. 1977. *Nations and States: An Enquiry into the Origins of Nations and the Politics of Nationalism.* Boulder, Colo.: Westview.

Shamuyarira, Nathan. 1965. *Crisis in Rhodesia.* London: Andre Deutsch.

Smith, Anthony. 1971. *Theories of Nationalism.* London: Camelot.

Smith, David, and Colin Simpson. 1981. *Mugabe.* London: Sphere.

Stopforth, P. 1971. *Survey of Highfield African Township.* Occasional Paper no. 6.
Department of Sociology, University of Rhodesia.

———. 1972. *Two Aspects of Social Change, Highfield African Township Salisbury.*
Occasional Paper no. 7. Salisbury: University of Rhodesia.

Supiya, Stephen T. 1962. "ZAPU Endeavours to Blend the Old and the New."
African Parade (May): 8, 53, 58.

Turino, Thomas. 1995. "Musical Nationalism and Professionalism in Zimbabwe." Paper presented at Annual Meeting of the Society for Ethnomusicology, UCLA.

———. 2000. *Nationalists, Cosmopolitans, and Popular Music in Zimbabwe.* Chicago: University of Chicago Press.

Utlete, C. Munhamu Botsio. 1978. *The Road to Zimbabwe: The Political Economy of Settler Colonialism, National Liberation and Foreign Intervention*. Montclair, N.J.: University Press of America.

Vambe, Lawrence. 1976. *From Rhodesia to Zimbabwe*. Pittsburgh: University of Pittsburgh Press.

West, Michael. 1990. "African Middle Class Formation in Colonial Zimbabwe, 1890–1965." Ph.D. diss., Harvard University, Cambridge, Mass.

Williamson, Leslie. 1963. "Kwanongomo [sic] College, Bulawayo," *African Music Society Journal* 3,2: 48–49.

———. 1964. The Kwanongoma College of African Music, Newsletter, June. *African Music Society Journal* 3,3: 117–18.

Zindi, Fred. 1985. *Roots Rocking in Zimbabwe*. Gweru, Zimbabwe: Mambo Press.

17

Duke Ellington, *Black, Brown, and Beige,* and the Cultural Politics of Race

KEVIN GAINES

"When people listened to [Duke] Ellington's music, they forgot that they were white; they became human beings listening to great music. It gave them a moment in which they could transcend themselves." The speaker, Howard "Stretch" Johnson, appearing the PBS documentary on Ellington "Reminiscing in Tempo," might as easily have been referring to African-Americans as well as whites, for there is no doubt that if Ellington's music and image in some instances promised to tame the savagery of white supremacy, these and other qualities, amplified by records, radio, and motion pictures, also offered hope and inspiration to black audiences. Consequently, for Johnson and other participants in the documentary, and for scholars and countless aficionados, Ellington's reputation remains unassailable. This essay joins them in taking for granted Ellington's achievements and importance. Beyond that, my intention is to discuss Ellington as a creative intellectual whose interventions resisted aesthetic considerations imposed both by detractors during his lifetime and, more recently, by even his present-day champions.

Ellington's challenge to racial conventions and musical categories and his fundamental engagement with African-American history as inspiration for his efforts are obscured by proponents of formalism. A consideration of Duke Ellington's experiments with extended-form compositions and the critical discourse on him and his music provides an opportunity to disentangle the racialized meanings so often present, yet seldom addressed, in jazz discourse. The formalism that characterizes much writing about jazz emphasizes aesthetics, particularly from a high canonical perspective, and imposes evaluative criteria having little to do with Ellington's working conditions, intentions, or sociopolitical context. It is no surprise, then, that Ellington's reputation would diminish when viewed from such rarefied heights, reduced to a bundle of scores. Ellington become a text that fails, in one critic's estimate, to measure up to the standards of European modernist composers.[1]

Such distortions bred of formalism are put forth by Ellington's defenders as well. They canonize Ellington (and, generally, "classic jazz") in respectful, but limited terms. To be sure, they rightly demand that jazz and its leading creative exponents receive the long overdue recognition that they deserve. And their objection to the racial essentialism all too common in writing about jazz is equally laudable. But in its most extreme form this celebratory aesthetic purism shies away from the notion of jazz as an outgrowth of African-Americans' legacy of struggle.[2] As amnesia overtakes the recent history of antiracist struggles, this vision of a transcendent jazz canon represents the triumph of marketing over memory. Such distortions are an inevitable result of publicity-driven claims of a jazz "renaissance" with their indifference to historical memory and the music's social complexity, past and present. Far less innocuous are those among the boosters of "classic jazz" who adopt an antagonistic stance toward those critics who question the exclusionary politics, formalism, and outright commercialism of recent canon-building enterprises.[3] This defensiveness among those sharing a canonical vision of jazz history all but suggests a neo-conservative black aesthetic for a post–civil rights, "color-blind" American in which race is pronounced irrelevant.

The formalism of market-driven portrayals of a jazz renaissance obscures the importance during Ellington's lifetime of conflicts over race and representation in music and criticism. Ellington's compositions subverted the aesthetic hierarchies, with their often unenunciated racial overtones, that prevented some critics from a more judicious appreciation of his extended-form works. A number of interrelated factors enabled Ellington to challenge attempts by some critics to circumscribe his image and creative output: his formative years in the black musical community in Washington, D.C., whose cosmopolitan mentors impressed Ellington as exemplars of black pride and musical excellence; the cultural nationalism of the New Negro movement in Harlem during the 1920s; the importance of travel and diverse experience; and the opportunities this mobility gave Ellington to observe his own reception in various locales, ranging from audiences throughout Europe to Harlem to Africa and numberless points in between. These factors contributed to

Ellington's persona as a storyteller who envisioned his compositions as "tone parallels," narratives of African-American life and history. Most importantly, they encouraged in him a healthy disregard for musical categories mediated by racial assumptions. Ellington availed himself of a multitude of genres to achieve his own creative ends.

I would argue, following the recent work of John Edward Hasse and Mark Tucker, that there are alternative readings of Ellington and his legacy that surpass a narrow concern with aesthetic issues.[4] Surely there is more to be said of Ellington's extended-form compositions—including *Reminiscing in Tempo* (1935), *Black, Brown, and Beige* (1943), *New World A Comin'* (1943), and *The Deep South Suite* (1946), than that offered by the disparaging—or even laudatory—assessments of critics and historians.

Through an exploration of the context and reception of some of Ellington's extended-form works, particularly his *Black, Brown, and Beige*, which the composer described as a "tone parallel to the history of the American Negro," I will discuss Ellington's general efforts to express black cultural and historical sensibilities through his compositions. Above all, I am concerned here with his self-conscious construction of historically situated narratives of African-American group consciousness as part of a progressive, antiracist agenda during World War II. Ellington's formal experimentations, his scorn for constraining, indeed, racialized, musical categories, and his own descriptions of the uniqueness of his creative project in this period were crucial to his participation in his era's struggles for racial and social justice. Ellington's activities within World War II Popular Front culture accompanied a broader movement that laid the foundation for black freedom struggles and interracial cooperation within the movement. Ellington's presence and image were central to a pre–Cold War black consciousness located in jazz and black popular culture of the sort notably sketched in Malcolm X's autobiography. Performed at Carnegie Hall in 1943, *Black, Brown, and Beige* was much more than an artistic milestone. The progressive cultural politics of race during the Second World War lent it additional force and meaning.

Ellington's significance for politics and culture is evident on several levels, all of which clashed with the restrictions imposed on African-Americans in a segregated society. Along with other jazz musicians, he and his band challenged the hegemony of Western classical music and its values by altering and manipulating the conventions of classical composition and instrumentation into vehicles for black expression. This strategy was perfectly in keeping with the musical background of Ellington's hometown of Washington, D.C., which, as Mark Tucker has demonstrated, offered, along with its pioneers in ragtime and stride piano, a community of conservatory-trained black musicians committed to expressing black cultural identity through classical forms.[5] In this context, with such classical models as the black British composer Samuel Coleridge-Taylor, Will Marion Cook, and others, it was natural that Ellington incorporated classical motifs into his compositions along with themes from Negro spirituals, the blues, and other sources. This eclecticism confounded the race-inflected standards of some classical music critics. By quoting Chopin's funeral march theme at the close of his *Black and Tan Fantasy* (1926), or by bestowing on the seamless call-and-response between soloist and orchestra the title *Concerto for Cootie* (c. 1940), Ellington created music that was "beyond category," to use a pet phrase of his. Above all, he served notice of the experimental boldness of his project through his appropriation of the classics into the popular realm, in the process rendering claims of the purity or integrity of either category illusory, and discrediting attempts by critics to sever art from social relations.

Ellington's disregard for musical categories that would deny African-American creativity was well in evidence in such early major works as *East St. Louis Toodle-O* (1927), which for a discerning few had marked him as the most original American composer working in any field. For Ellington, however, such favorable pronouncements were rare. Nevertheless, through his pursuit of a distinctive voice blending African-American, popular, and classical idioms, Ellington engaged the on-going debate on the origins and aesthetic merits of jazz. Participants in this debate either privileged European classical music over jazz altogether, or otherwise displaced and denied African-American authorship of the form. From this latter perspective, many critics, record executives, and listeners may have derived pleasure from the music but, unable to surrender their high modernist outlook, preferred to identify jazz with such non-black figures as George Gershwin, Igor Stravinsky, or Benny Goodman. Regardless of whatever the critics were saying, Ellington was busily appropriating classical music to the service of his distinctive creative project.

One of Ellington's earliest champions, R. D. Darrell, was acutely aware of the racial barriers to reception that inhibited some critics from hearing Ellington more objectively, let alone recognizing his avowed project of portraying black sensibilities in his compositions.[6] In a 1932 essay entitled "Black Beauty" after an Ellington song (his tribute to the musical comedy actress Florence Mills), Darrell praised the composer's "keenly developed craftmanship in composition and orchestration." At the same time, he noted, defensively (with an apparent awareness of the limitations of many listeners), that others would likely find in Ellington "ludicrous eccentricity where I find an expressive expansion of the tonal palette . . . 'nigger music' instead of 'black beauty.'" Darrell stressed Ellington's ground in black culture, distinguishing his own praise from that of Ellington's more earnest supporters whose classical predilections led them to place him in the same league as Stravinsky, Delius, and Ravel. Although flattered, Ellington insisted that European influences were at best raw materials for him, incidental within his chosen idiom: "Whatever they attempt to prove . . . jazz had its origin in Africa. It's something distinct and well worth the cultivation and development it is now receiving; and its reception by the entire world within the past few years proves it's something impossible to dismiss with a gesture of contempt."[7]

Through composition, performance, and published statements of his intentions, Ellington embarked on the on-going project of racial vindication through creativity and musical expression, countering the devalued designation of race with a proud black consciousness. As early as 1931, Ellington's thoughts on these matters appeared in a British jazz magazine, affirming the sociopolitical convictions that guided his artistic development. Here, Ellington publicly announced his commitment to the project that would culminate in *Black, Brown, and Beige*. Ellington, by now the self-confident and successful Harlemite, was deeply attentive to the cultural forces impinging on the reception of his work. He also revealed himself as an exponent of the cultural aesthetics of the New Negro, drawing on popular black historicism to affirm African-American social progress and the immortality of black music, an eventuality in which he himself would play no small part:

> Always I try to be original in my harmonies and rhythms. . . . Because I think that the music of my race is something which is going to live, something which posterity will honor in a higher sense than merely that of the music of the ballroom, I put my best musical thoughts forward into my tunes. . . . I am proud of that part my race is playing in the artistic life of the world. . . . The history of my people is one of great achievements over fearful odds; it is a history of a people hindered, handicapped and often sorely oppressed, and what is being done by Countee Cullen and others in literature is overdue in our music. I am therefore now engaged on a rhapsody unhampered by any musical form in which I intend to portray the experiences of the colored races in America in the syncopated idiom.

> This composition will consist of four or five movements, and I am putting
> all I have into it in the hope that I shall have achieved something really
> worth while in the literature of music, and that an authentic record of my
> race *written by a member of it* shall be placed on record.[8]

Following Du Bois and other commentators, Ellington perceived the
music of African Americans as the product of "our sorrows." Accordingly, he regarded his artistic efforts as integral to African-Americans'
cultural identity and their struggles for freedom.

Ellington's involvement in wartime antiracist politics was prefigured
in his statements quoted in the black press and elsewhere throughout
the 1930s. Having borne the constant burden of racial discrimination on
the road, North and South, it is thus not surprising to learn that according to John Edward Hasse, Ellington performed a benefit for the
defense of the Scottsboro defendants, nine young men imperiled by the
absence of the rule of law for African-Americans in the deep South, in
the early 1930s.[9]

With Ellington's popularity as a composer and bandleader, the New
Deal coalition and the war would provide further impetus for Ellington's
emergence as a spokesman for African-Americans. As we have seen, well
before that, Ellington grappled with the limitless ironies and contradictions inherent in his struggle for autonomy as a black artist, composer,
and bandleader, occasionally turning stereotyped constructions of his
music into creative advantage. Supervising his band amidst the plantation decor of the segregated Cotton Club in Harlem, the black cultural
capital, negotiating the band's dependency on its white mobster employers, and saddled with the latter's benighted vision of black exoticism and
sensuality, Ellington, like so many other struggling African-Americans,
was compelled to navigate his organization through a perilous fog of
white supremacy. Ellington contested the label "jungle music" that he
performed for Cotton Club tourists, and the romantic racialism of those
critics who perceived black musicians as noble savages endowed with
primitive improvisational élan and natural spontaneity. Ellington's imaginative use in the orchestrations from his "jungle music" period of the
growling, speechlike style of his brass players challenged the myth among
some critics that authentic jazz was marked by torrid improvisation.
Ellington's incorporation of bent notes and other so-called "hot" jazz
performance styles into his orchestrations enabled a distillation of original tonal effects and subject matter entirely removed from the trappings
of primitivism. For example, when the band simulated a train's whistle
and slowly accelerating motion in "Daybreak Express" (1935), Ellington

achieved an unmatched level of tonal impressionism reinforced by its evocation of the sociohistoric importance of trains as symbols of mobility and opportunity in African-American life.

Black, Brown, and Beige was prefigured by several experimental extended works: Creole Rhapsody (1931); the soundtrack for the film short Symphony in Black, A Rhapsody of Negro Life (1934); and Reminiscing in Tempo (1935), the latter issued on two ten-inch records, its four sides totaling about thirteen minutes.

Ellington's film image was a major source of his popularity. Part one of Symphony in Black, "The Laborers," contributed a rehabilitation of black images on film, exploding minstrel stereotypes through its portrayal of black social diversity and the presentation of jazz as high culture. The departure from minstrelsy and Hollywood's antiblack stereotypes was achieved in the film's alternating images of the formally attired Ellington organization (including shots of Ellington the composer at the piano revising his score) and the struggling, but no less dignified, black laborers. At the same time, however, the film's symbolic effect was a stylized harmonizing of intraracial class differences as the workers' pace and movements are synchronized with the film's soundtrack, in the black folk tradition of the work song. These elements would re-emerge in modified form later as the "Work" theme in Black, Brown, and Beige.

The dignified presentation of Ellington and his orchestra in a classical music context, evidently permissible as a cinematic fiction, did not provoke the controversy among critics that ensued with the release of Reminiscing in Tempo. Having made his name in the field of jazz, Ellington's recorded output had been largely restricted to dance music selections tailored to the three and a half minutes allotted on each 78 rpm side. With the death of his mother, a grieving Ellington was moved to attempt a longer, more meditative work. Explicitly not written for the dance hall, the ruminative Reminiscing elicited strongly unfavorable reviews, which are revealing for their insights into critics' perceptions of what to them constituted authentic racial expression. Perhaps the most extreme of such views was that of John Hammond, the record producer and social activist. For Hammond, Ellington's excursion into extended form constituted a "formless and shallow" betrayal of jazz, the work's vapidity and "pretension" an indication that Ellington "has purposely kept himself away from any contact with the troubles of his people or with mankind in general. . . . He shuts his eyes to the abuses being heaped on his race and his original class." From the perspective of

Hammond's crude left-wing aesthetics, *Reminiscing* was damning evidence of Ellington's lack of militancy and political engagement.[10]

Hammond and others dismissive of *Reminiscing* were faulting in Ellington the absence of what they believed was the authentic Negro voice. An outraged Spike Hughes, the British bandleader and erstwhile Ellington supporter since his first European tour in 1933, threatened not to review any more of his records "until Duke realizes it is not 'smart' to write this sort of music." Neither Hammond nor Hughes in their paternalism seemed aware that Ellington had intentions underlying *Reminiscing* altogether different from the ones they prescribed for him as a jazz bandleader and tunesmith of popular dance music.

If not necessarily afflicted with the presuppositions of Hughes and Hammond, other critics, particularly those reluctant to attribute artistic value to anything outside the realm of classical music, brought a disabling attraction to their listening that invariably clashed with Ellington's aims. Ellington had consistently warned against such a bloodless approach to his work; in his statements and in the more astute critical assessments of him, one finds numerous explanations of the centrality of meaning in his compositions. As Ellington's biographer John Hasse put it, "Ellington seems to have done his best work when inspired by a mood or an image."[11] This referentiality, or connectedness in Ellington's music to individual personalities, places, or social conditions, obtained simultaneously at several levels, embracing form and content. It is well known that Ellington composed with the styles of his instrumentalists in mind, capitalizing on their distinctive talents. At another level, Ellington revealed his subject matter, and the source of many of his song titles, to be "taken from, and naturally, principally from, the life of Harlem." As we have seen, Ellington's ultimate frame of reference, his paramount criterion of value, was what he described as "a rigid adherence to the traditions of our own people." For Ellington, both artistic and commercial success for black artists was incumbent on their realization that "we are children of the sun and our race has a definite tradition of beauty and glory and vitality. . . . These traditions are ours to express, and will enrich our careers in proportion to the sincerity and faithfulness with which we interpret them."[12]

Ellington's remarks about the commercial prospects and outlook of blacks in the field of entertainment responded to considerable speculation in the press that swing music would not last, and that the influence of black swing bands might be waning as white bands were reaping popular success in that idiom. Against a white-dominated jazz marketplace that routinely expropriated the most innovative arrangements by blacks and lavishly remunerated the derivative efforts of white bands and band-leaders, Ellington insisted on the originality of his own endeavors. As he told the Chicago *Defender* in 1937, his compositions sought to capture and reveal "the emotional spirit of the race." "That is why," he was quoted, "so many white musicians find them difficult to understand and in several cases, meaningless."[13] This should not be taken as an outburst of racial essentialism. To the contrary, it suggests the extent to which Ellington's work presupposed a connection between a historical vision of black spirituality, struggle, and urbanization (including several compositions praising trains, as in *Daybreak Express*, as symbolic of black aspiration, mobility, and freedom), and the articulation, through his band, of a distinctive sound and style. On top of all this, Ellington's sense of himself as a politically conscious artist could not but have been enhanced by his experience in touring Europe in the spring of 1939. This respite, though fleeting, from the peculiar institution of American racism, as well as the respect accorded by critics overseas to his stature as a composer, was encouraging, to say the least. More ominously for Ellington and the band, which had omitted Nazi Germany from their tour, traveling through Hamburg may have reinforced a sense of the similarities between Nazi fascism and U.S. racism first introduced to the American public by the well-publicized exploits of the black athletes Joe Louis and Jesse Owens.

In the 1930s, popular culture, in music, sports, and films, was deeply politicized, a fact that renders questionable the belief among some jazz historians that such musicians as Ellington or Billie Holiday were apolitical. For audiences as well as musicians, jazz was a vehicle for the politics of everyday life and experience. This was evident with the band's arrival by train in Los Angeles later in 1939, where during an extended nightclub engagement the musical comedy revue *Jump for Joy* was launched. This project was very much a product of the moment, articulating rising social expectations among blacks, and marking a growing unwillingness to accommodate with Jim Crow. The revue flourished in the progressive, interracial climate of Hollywood, with many white film celebrities attracted to Los Angeles' black section of nightclubs on Central Avenue. *Jump for Joy*, described as "a grand emancipation celebration in dance, sketch and song," was hailed by the black press for its aggressive antiracist stance and its repudiation of the minstrel stereotypes that had constrained black entertainers and portrayals of blackness in popular culture. The original verse of the song "Jump for Joy," heard in performance but curiously nowhere to be found on record, went:

We're so fed up with the Southland . . . for all these years we've been
bored to tears with the blues. There's certain songs that are getting tired;
they're sweet, they're beat and uninspired. It's time they were retired, we
got news. Fare thee well, land of cotton, cotton land is out of style, honey
child, Jump for Joy. . . .[14]

Ellington and company were bidding farewell to nostalgic popular depictions of the plantation legend (most recently revived in the 1939
Hollywood extravaganza *Gone With the Wind*), which had long regarded
African-American sharecroppers as a raw material in themselves, virtually inseparable from the cotton they produced. Created for black audiences that included, indeed welcomed, the hippest nonblacks, the revue
campaigned vociferously against Jim Crow and the submissive mass media images of blacks that upheld that system.

With *Black, Brown, and Beige*, Ellington was not only transcending mere entertainment and dance music; the cultural and aesthetic breakthrough represented by the orchestra's Carnegie Hall debut
was widely heralded as a social watershed. Such New Deal liberals as
Eleanor Roosevelt were associated with the event, joining it in social importance with Marian Anderson's 1939 recital at the Lincoln Memorial,
which was staged in the aftermath of the Daughters of the American
Revolution's refusal to open their hall to the African-American contralto
(Anderson and other luminaries from the classical music world were in
attendance at the Carnegie Hall concert). Ellington's *Black, Brown, and
Beige* was eagerly anticipated by jazz enthusiasts, black audiences, and
progressives of all colors as striking a cultural blow against Jim Crow.
On the eve of the premiere, the critic and Ellington publicist Leonard
Feather stressed the social and political significance of the event even as
he strategically lowered artistic expectations with the admission that
Ellington had not yet finished composing and scoring the piece.[15]

For such observers as Feather, the Carnegie Hall premiere of *Black,
Brown, and Beige* heralded a new legitimacy for both jazz and antiracist struggle in Harlem and New York as a whole. Indeed, *Black, Brown,
and Beige* represented a second chance for Ellington to break social and
artistic barriers after his recent disappointment at the failure of *Jump for
Joy* to open on Broadway. While Ellington had long identified his compositions, particularly in the black press, as emblematic of a historical
black consciousness, this impulse gathered further momentum from the
heyday of Popular Front wartime politics. While in Los Angeles during
the run of *Jump for Joy*, Ellington chose Langston Hughes's poem "We

Too Sing America" as the theme for his remarks to a black church gathering, which were later published in the black press. He condemned the rise of fascism and paid tribute to African-Americans' indispensable contributions to American culture and society.[16]

Black, Brown, and Beige, along with Ellington's other wartime projects, provided a cultural counterpart to A. Philip Randolph's March on Washington movement. Randolph's threatened mass protest in the nation's capital had pressured President Franklin D. Roosevelt into issuing in June of 1941 an executive order establishing the Fair Employment Practices Commission, which promised defense jobs for African-Americans in proportion to their numbers in the population. It is important to realize as well that Ellington was hardly alone among musicians in addressing social concerns, for the 1930s also witnessed Billie Holiday's recording and inclusion in her cabaret act of the powerful antilynching song "Strange Fruit." The period also saw several attempts at integration in jazz ensembles and big bands, some, such as Holiday's brief sojourn in Artie Shaw's band, aborted by the white South's intolerance.

Ellington's stage introductions for the movements of *Black, Brown, and Beige* joined Popular Front support for the war effort with a historical vision of black consciousness rooted in slavery and emancipation but embracing the wider diaspora as well, in acknowledging the "West Indian influence." Ellington's programmatic remarks characterized the work as a musical narrative of black social advancement. As a play on racial signifiers, *Black, Brown, and Beige* appears to have been Ellington's rebuttal to homogenizing racist slanders that justified segregation by raising the specter of unassimilable, undifferentiated blackness. From another angle, since the 1930s, Ellington had been part of a progressive trend among black intellectuals to reclaim, and thus affirm, the despised label "Black" as a sign of group identity. His "Black Beauty" and "Symphony in Black" were echoed by W. E. B. Du Bois's *Black Reconstruction* (1935) and C. L. R. James's *Black Jacobins* (1938), both of which placed blacks at the center of historical struggles to expand democracy. Ellington's allusions to color in his song titles included yet another work from this period, "Sepia Panorama," which served as the orchestra's radio theme until replaced by Billy Strayhorn's "Take the 'A' Train." "Sepia Panorama," a majestic march-tempo blues built on a repeated ascending arpeggiated figure scored for the entire orchestra, particularly when heard in conjunction with its title, evokes a spirit of group solidarity and advancement. Like *Black, Brown, and Beige,* "Sepia Panorama" conveyed Ellington's vision of African-Americans' social and cultural diversity while upholding ideals of unity, dignity, and social progress. Following Du Bois's proposed synthesis of Negro and American identities in *The Souls of Black Folk* (1903) and the cultural assertiveness of black writers and artists during the New Negro renaissance, Ellington issued an unapologetic statement of black identity and insisted on the symbiosis of black and American cultures.

Ellington revisited the dignified portrayal in "Symphony in Black" of African-American workers whose lives were depicted as equal parts unrequited toil and redemptive spirituality. While acknowledging emancipation as a joyous occasion, he also noted the tragic aspect of those too old to reap the full benefit of freedom, implying, in accordance with New Deal reform philosophy, a redistributive social obligation recognizing "their right to sit down and rest on somebody else's property." In linking the emergence of the blues as contemporaneous with the "great Negro heroes of the Spanish-American war," Ellington drew a parallel with black soldiers' participation in the current war, while at the same time invoking popular black counternarratives of African-American soldiers' military prowess and heroism against the majority culture's persistent erasure and nonrecognition of their contributions.

Many in the audience at Carnegie Hall on 23 January 1943 were doubtless as attentive to Ellington's onstage remarks as they were to the evening's musical offerings. After all, segregation in the armed forces and racist assaults against uniformed black soldiers had elicited opposition throughout black communities and in the black press. Roi Ottley had detailed such black opposition to the war based in Harlem, which he sought to cast in a positive light as an exception to the rule of African-Americans' loyalty to the war effort. Nevertheless, *de jure* segregation in the South and poverty, slum conditions, and police harassment in northern urban ghettoes threatened to undermine black support, eliciting official suspicion of draft dodgers and dissenters who raged at the hypocrisy that seemed to confine the battle for the "Four Freedoms" to overseas theaters. In 1942, racial violence erupted in Detroit, its defense industries a magnet for black migration, when armed whites and police prevented African-Americans from integrating public housing. Eventually, state troopers were required to escort black families into their new homes. Detroit would witness one of the bloodiest episodes in a wave of race riots during the summer of 1943. Despite Ottley's disclaimers, this volatile atmosphere raised the prospect that African-Americans' debilitating struggle for equal rights on the home front might erode their morale for the fight against fascism overseas.

Ellington thus played a strategic role, and the political tensions of the moment are apparent in his confident, yet carefully measured, remarks. In his introduction to the final movement, Ellington stressed the uneven nature of black progress, reminding the audience of the struggling but ambitious masses who "don't have enough to eat and a place to sleep, but work hard and see that their children are in school." Giving voice to the social ambitions of proscribed working-class blacks whose lot is to pass their unfulfilled aspirations on to their children, Ellington observed that "the Negro is rich in education." In the spirit of the "Double V" campaign championed within the black press, which made black support for the war against fascism in Europe and the Pacific contingent on the U.S. government's commitment to the domestic struggle for jobs and equal rights, Ellington assured his audience that although African-Americans were "struggling for solidarity," the emergency of war found "the Black, Brown, and Beige right in there for the Red, White, and Blue." With these carefully modulated remarks, which created a decidedly different form of tension and release for the audience, Ellington's allusions to inequality, racism, and political struggle found resolution in his synthesis of black pride and national unity.

If Ellington's remarks were calculated not to give offense, evidently the music did, at least in some quarters. *Black, Brown, and Beige* elicited mixed reviews. For critics less enthralled by the event's political significance, Ellington's composition, however ambitious, lacked formal continuity. Be that as it may, the most brilliant and indelible portions of it, such as "Come Sunday" and "The Blues," would become classics in the Ellington repertoire. Wounded by the criticism, and by the antiblack violence of the previous summer, a somber Ellington vowed during a return engagement at Carnegie Hall in December that the band would not play *Black, Brown, and Beige* in its entirety until audiences demonstrated a fuller comprehension of African-Americans' contribution to the nation's history.[17]

Despite the lukewarm reception, similar projects followed. Roi Ottley's account of rising black activism and demands for desegregation, *New World A Comin'*, was the inspiration for an Ellington composition of the same name that sought to capture the optimistic mood of Ottley's text. Ottley described a united front of black leadership, artists, and intellectuals that minimized the ideological conflicts dating back to the clash between the NAACP and the Communist Party over the Scottsboro case. Such black cultural exponents as Ellington and Paul Robeson were integral to the left's anti-racist campaign against "white chauvinism," on which Ottley bestowed evenhanded praise. Ellington's cultural activism was further seen in his 1946 collaboration with lyricist John Latouche, *Beggar's Holiday*, its Broadway premier a benefit for the anticolonial Council For African Affairs.[18]

Discussions of Ellington in the press accompanied the ongoing campaign waged by the composer himself and his publicists to reshape Ellington's image. Claims of the universality, the artistic genius, and Americanness of Ellington's music merged with statements acknowledging the music's specific roots in African-American life and history. Such publications by or about Ellington situated him within an amalgam of European conceptions of high art and the Popular Front's celebration of indigenous American folk music. These portraits of the artist as a "race man" defied purist assumptions of the incompatibility of art with politics and protest that would become fashionable during the Cold War. Moreover, the cosmopolitan persona cultivated by Ellington could hardly be contained by the obsession with rural folk authenticity of an Alan Lomax.

Such a self-conscious disregard for racial and aesthetic hierarchies and the paternalism of left-wing aesthetics was elaborated in a three-part *New Yorker* profile by Richard O. Boyer which appeared in 1944 entitled "The Hot Bach." Here, Ellington's achievements and stature as an American composer were more taken for granted than asserted. Throughout, Boyer challenged the popular misconceptions that described jazz musicians as underworld denizens and exotics. He held that the only "righteous jazz" was performed by small groups "whose music is as spontaneous, unpremeditated and unrehearsed as Shelley's skylark." Boyer accompanied the orchestra on its preferred mode of travel by Pullman cars, where it was relatively immune from racial indignities. Portraying himself as "a Boswellian friend of Duke's who .. took notes on the scene," Boyer provided vivid descriptions of Ellington, his collaborator Billy Strayhorn, and such virtuoso players as trombonist Lawrence Brown and trumpeter Cootie Williams as sophisticated and urbane men who answered to nobody's stereotypes. Boyer's series contained a great deal of intimate information about the Maestro's background and career. Along with his well-known qualities of charm, elegance, and some mention of his eccentricities, including his prodigious appetite, Boyer provided a glimpse of Ellington's serenity and concentration forged by the demands of constant work, travel, and rehearsal. There was much revealing material on his methods as composer and bandleader, but a recurrent, dissonant theme was the chilling impact of Jim Crow and antiblack prejudice on the band's working conditions.

Boyer quoted Ellington's explanation of his own moodiness: "A Negro can be too low to speak one minute and laughing fit to kill the next, and mean both." In addition to conveying Ellington's and the band's painful and frequent encounters with segregation, the series offered a sympathetic rendering of Ellington's black consciousness. Boyer noted Ellington's avid interest in black history and his musical commemorations of such figures as Crispus Attucks, Harriet Tubman, Nat Turner, Denmark Vesey, and other "fighters for Negro freedom." Reflecting an era when the term "Negro" was synonymous with militant race pride, and when jazz was increasingly popularized and consumed as a nonblack musical style, Ellington was quoted, "I don't write jazz. I write Negro folk music."[19]

Ellington reiterated his view of the symbiotic relation between black and American cultural and political identities in a 1944 article in which he again dissociated himself from "jazz" and the "confusion" stemming from wrongheaded attempts by critics to capture the essence of syncopated music. Instead, Ellington simply declared, "Swing is my beat." Swing, "as I like to make it and play it," Ellington wrote, "is an expression of... modern ideas." Ellington emphasized rhythm as its central component, whose appeal derived in part because "this rhythm hits home to the people who hear it. It speaks their language and tells their story. It's the musician and his audience talking things over." Bypassing critics, Ellington went on that "music for me is a language. It expresses more than just sound." Ellington's wartime efforts demanded recognition that his music was not mere escapist entertainment, and they sought to ensure that the language represented by his extended-form compositions resonated beyond the performance halls.

Ellington's contribution to struggles against domestic racism and international fascism and his advocacy of anticolonialism was hardly unique to jazz throughout the postwar years. In the late 1950s and into the next decade, jazz musicians articulated musical protests against domestic and international systems of racism and colonialism. In addition, Ellington's longtime social engagement suggest his affinity with such younger musician/composers as Charles Mingus, Max Roach, and Abbey Lincoln, whose protest music responded to racial crises at home and abroad. Indeed, the fact that Mingus and Roach recorded the album *Money Jungle* with Ellington in the early 1960s further reveals the shortsightedness of critics' formalist periodizations (from "Swing" to "Bebop") which mask continuities of style and substance, articulated across generations through a shared social awareness.[20]

Ellington's achievements as an African-American artist are instructive in light of present-day attempts to circumscribe his legacy. The posthumous canonization of a jazz pantheon of individual artists hardly does justice to Ellington, who, one is reminded, kept his orchestra together despite the 1930s Depression and indeed, until his death in 1974. In its durability, the Ellington band thus connected the heyday of those collective black organizations known as big bands with their sociopolitical realization in the black freedom movement of the 1960s. At the height of the struggle in 1963, Ellington continued as a spokesman despite the limitations, discontinuities, and amnesia imposed by the Cold War, leading his orchestra on a State Department–sponsored tour of South Asia and the Middle East. At one of his press conferences, Ellington bristled at the suggestion that black artists like himself were disengaged, contributing little to the cause. Not unlike Ellington's other uncomprehending critics, the questioner and other younger militants were slow to realize that art and politics, after all, had gone hand in hand for some time: "After I had cooled off a bit, [I] explained that we had been working on the Negro situation and his condition in the South since the '30s, that we had done shows, musical works, [and] benefits." Ellington advanced an antiracist agenda within his role as cultural ambassador, and his diplomatically worded remarks sometimes challenged the worldview of his official sponsors. Ellington maintained that "the Negro situation in America . . . is not an international issue but a national one" and cautioned that those in the United States who refused to grasp this did so at the nation's peril. For a foreign policy establishment prone to viewing racial upheavals in the U.S. as potential fodder for anti-American Soviet propaganda, Ellington stated that racial justice took precedence over Cold War geopolitics. This position was quite different from his and other African-Americans' linkage of desegregation and the global struggle against fascism during World War II.[21]

Undoubtedly, the postwar social climate which made the antiracist impact of Ellington's music a possibility for whites is long gone and virtually forgotten. This is a sober reminder that it is possible for all too many whites to champion Ellington today as a self-vindicating liberal gesture while opposing on-going struggles for social gesture. It would seem that for some contemporary writers, Ellington's memory is enlisted in an enduring culture war on the side of a dubious canon-worship which reasserts the very race-inflected aesthetic hierarchies the composer had resisted even as it disingenuously preaches color-blindness. Whatever their intentions, those who, in celebrating Ellington, would deny the relevance of the politics of race, are not just rewriting history.

Ironically, the moment that jazz writers abandon the extensive record of Ellington's own formulations of his antiracist creative project may well signal that the immortality of jazz, and of Ellington's legacy as an exponent of freedom and democracy, is far from assured.

NOTES

1. James Lincoln Collier, *Duke Ellington* (New York: Oxford University Press, 1987).

2. For an example of such formalism, see Wynton Marsalis, "What Jazz Is—and Isn't," *New York Times* (31 July 1988): H-21, 24.

3. Claiming that "the old order is giving way to the new" in jazz in a manner that confers a natural inevitability on the aggressive marketing of a handful of younger musicians, Frank Conroy goes on to say that "it will take a new generation of writers to write about a new generation of players and composers, and let us hope that the deconstructionists, politically correct busybodies and agenda-driven theorists will not be in their number." See his profile of Marsalis, "Stop Nitpicking a Genius," *New York Times Magazine* (25 June 1995): 28, 30.

4. John Edward Hasse, *Beyond Category: The Life and Genius of Duke Ellington* (New York: Simon and Schuster, 1993); Mark Tucker, *Ellington: The Early Years* (Urbana: University of Illinois Press, 1991).

5. Ibid., 16–62.

6. For a related discussion of the impact of race on American literary criticism and fiction writing, see Toni Morrison, *Playing in the Dark: Whiteness and the Literary Imagination* (New York: Vintage Books, 1993), 3–28.

7. R. D. Darrell, "Black Beauty," in *The Duke Ellington Reader*, ed. Mark Tucker (New York: Oxford University Press, 1993), 57, 59. An account of Ellington's response to the praise of the classical-oriented critic Constant Lambert is reprinted ibid., 112–14. Ellington is quoted ibid., 53–54.

8. Quoted ibid., 48–50.

9. Hasse, *Beyond Category*, 150–51.

10. Hammond is quoted in Tucker, *Reader*, 118–20.

11. Hasse, *Beyond Category*, 216.

12. Tucker, *Reader*, 88, 131.

13. Ellington is quoted in Hasse, *Beyond Category*, 209.

14. These unrecorded lyrics are recalled in the documentary "Reminiscing in Tempo" (PBS, *American Masters* series).

15. Leonard Feather, "Duke Ellington at Carnegie Hall," n.p., n.d., in Duke Ellington Clipping file, 1925–1974, Schomburg Center, New York Public Library.

16. Duke Ellington, "We Too Sing America," in Tucker, *Reader*, 146–48.

17. See Brian Priestly and Alan Cohen, "Black Brown and Beige," in Tucker, *Reader*, 185–204. Ellington's remarks from the stage at Carnegie Hall are heard on the recording of the band's concert, *Duke Ellington at Carnegie Hall, December 11, 1943* (Everest Records, FS 327).

18. For an extended discussion of the intersection of Popular Front culture

and anticolonial movements, see Penny Von Eschen, *The Rise and Fall of the Politics of the African Diaspora: African Americans and Anticolonialism* (Ithaca, N.Y.: Cornell University Press, 1997). Ottley's account of a united front in African American politics would be challenged by Harold Cruse's later sectarian discussion of Harlem leftwing politics in *The Crisis of the Negro Intellectual*, originally published in 1968 (repr. New York: Quill, 1984).

19. Richard O. Boyer, "The Hot Bach," in Tucker, *Reader*, 214–45; Ellington is quoted on pp. 217, 218.

20. Ronald Radano has described Ellington's work in the 1940s as a precedent for the explosion of jazz releases inspired by African independence movements in the 1950s and early 1960s. See his *New Musical Figurations: Anthony Braxton's Cultural Critique* (Chicago: University of Chicago Press, 1993), 64–65n.

21. Ellington is quoted in Stanley Dance, *The World of Duke Ellington* (New York: Da Capo, 1970), 20–22.

PART V

Power/Powerlessness

18

Naming the Illuminati

CHRISTOPHER HOLMES SMITH
AND JOHN FISKE

> Put on the whole armour of God, that ye may be able to stand
> against the wiles of the devil. For we wrestle not against flesh
> and blood, but against principalities, against powers, against the
> rulers of darkness of this world, against spiritual wickedness in
> high places. (Ephesians 6:11–12)

> In this central and centralized humanity, the effect and instru-
> ment of complex power relations, bodies and forces subjected by
> multiple mechanisms of "incarceration," objects for discourses
> that are in themselves elements for this strategy, we must hear
> the distant roar of battle. (Michel Foucault)

On August 30, 1996, agents from the Bureau of Alcohol, Tobacco, and Firearms arrested DaVaughan Roper, a 26-year-old
black man, in his home in Staten Island, New York, on illegal weapons charges. Authorities alleged at the time of Roper's arrest
that he obtained the money for his estimated $10,000 stockpile of guns
and ammunition from cocaine sales. Several dozen envelopes of a pow-
dered substance believed to be cocaine were found at the scene, as well
as $1,700 cash, yet Roper was never officially detained for drug posses-
sion. Though Roper's case may appear rather typical initially, the bizarre
rationale he offered to explain the variety of contraband discovered in
his residence distinguishes the seizure of his body and property from the
thousands of other drug-related arrests in New York City that year. In
fact, upon his arrest, Roper claimed an alibi based on an unorthodox
version of the self-defense plea, offering that he had initiated his illicit
business in order to protect himself and the United States government
from an organization called "Illuminati," a tight-lipped cabal of elites

who were hatching a secret conspiracy to rule the world. Predictably un-swayed, authorities shredded the credibility of Roper's conspiracy sug-gestion, contending that their perpetrator's rant had been culled from science fiction novels and dystopian literature on the "New World Or-der" found in his apartment, reflecting nothing more than the inner workings of a paranoid imagination.[1]

This case may appear to be a minor blip on the radar screen tracking "newsworthy" events in America. But, when minor blips are multiplied, they indicate not occasional reconnaissance, but full-fledged invasion. And that may be the case here. The spreading belief in the Illuminati and their operations to further the New World Order indicates and exacer-bates the ongoing dissolution of American democracy's fragile consensus over the benevolence and sincerity of "official knowledge." In short, the arrest of DeVaughan Roper may represent a small ripple in a groundswell of a dispersed and fragmented, but consistent, popular belief that there is a conspiracy of elites to consolidate national and international power into their own hands, and to further oppress and enslave the disempow-ered to the extent that popular resistance will become impossible. A, if not the, crucial strategy in disempowering and disenfranchising is "truth control," or the meticulous management of what is and what is not to be made publicly known, and thus of what is and what is not to become part of the official knowledge that aggregates into a regime of truth.

There may be little hard evidence of a cabalistic conspiracy, but, in a system of truth control, the absence of evidence carries no injunction to disbelieve: There is, however, widespread evidence of popular belief in the conspiracy. Naming the conspiracy is an attempt to counter the strategic management of official knowledge and to give a discursive ma-teriality to forms of power whose very existence is denied by knowledge control. The "Illuminati" and the "New World Order" are not so much signs of the "inner workings of a paranoid imagination" as of a tactical naming of the unspeakable, and of a deep-rooted distrust-verging-on-hatred of powerful elites that could be the harbinger of dire civic unrest in our nation's immediate future.

Michiko Kakutani of the *New York Times* recently coined a fashion-able monicker for this secession of popular opinion, christening it "the new paranoia."[2] This trend implies that significant numbers of people are more willing than ever to refuse belief in the existing power struc-ture's ability and willingness to produce a credible "truth" about the tur-moil of daily life. More broadly, significant and very different fractions of the American people just can't seem to square official discourse on the quality, that is to say "reality," of life in their nation with their own specific experiences. In the face of official denial of this intelligibility gap, and the neglect of the social problems which define it, the variously disempowered have devised their own way of explaining things and diverged quite radically from dominant opinion on prevalent social phenomena.

Naming the Illuminati, then, is a politico-discursive tactic whose ambitions will vary according to the social situation of the tacticians. And these social situations vary widely: the Christian talk show host, New World Order doomsayer, and former presidential candidate Pat Robertson believes in the Illuminati.[3] Louis Farrakhan, the charismatic leader of the Nation of Islam, used its numerology in his speech at the Million Man March. Racist paramilitary groups like the Sons of Liberty frequently use their reading of the Illuminati as the basis for their campaigns of hate. White college students in Middle America amuse themselves with computerized versions of the Illuminati scenario in their spare time. Simultaneously, impoverished black and Latino youth use rap's musical and lyrical citation of the Illuminati to help them contemplate and negotiate their relatively limited lot in life. The need to use the Illuminati as a means to grant discursive visibility and form to a regularity of oppressive forces that officially have no visibility, form, or even existence is spread more widely through our society than the specific belief in the Illuminati or distrust in the New World Order per se.

This chapter makes no attempt to analyze the use of the Illuminati in the knowledge systems of the likes of Pat Robertson or of white militia groups, necessary topics of analysis though they be: it focuses rather on the recent tactics of naming the Illuminati in contemporary rap. Many rappers have chosen to document the existence of a multidimensional array of power operating upon black bodies through the tenets of the Illuminati. As with all historical accounts, we should listen to these reports critically. But by no means should we summarily ignore the warnings they are giving us about the neo-Fascist nightmare lurking within our nation's attempts to literalize a phantasmagoric social order.

One of the conditions of postmodern oppression is a regularity of material effects whose originary source is so immaterial as to appear to be absent. Effects without a cause leave a black hole of uncertainty, a vacuum of not knowing, that makes it difficult to take an oppositional stance. That which cannot be seen all too readily becomes that which cannot be opposed. Naming the Illuminati may be seen as an oppressed group's attempt to provide a source of responsibility for the clandestine disruption of their most intimate sense of freedom and liberty.

Two of the phantasmatic, formless entities that are so diffused that they can be perceived only dimly if at all yet whose power effects constitute the imperative materiality of life in the ghetto are, to name them simply, whiteness and global capital. And maybe the two entities are, in the final analysis, one. The unreality of global capital is partly a function of its electronic mobility, its being everywhere and nowhere, always absent as it is inescapably present, and partly in its ever increasing distance from the pauperized pavements of the ghetto from where it appears like a shower of meteorites forever circling the globe, forever out of reach and growing more so—and yet, and yet—someone, somewhere, somehow can access it, control it, and milk it—the Illuminati. Pauperization is the process that widens the gap between the haves and the have-nots to the extent that it appears to put the haves and having out of reach, out of touch. The globalization of capital puts wealth into orbit and localizes poverty into anchored, grounded, immobile fixity. Gravity ties poverty down while wealth flies freely. The New World Order and the international banking conspiracy that funds it and benefits from it make sound sense from the ghetto. Like global capital, global whiteness is everywhere and nowhere. If you reach up to grab either, your fist will be always empty upon opening. Whiteness works always to be absent from its own operations: it was never there when the civil jury came to the right (white) verdict in the second O. J. Simpson trial; it was never there in the beating of Rodney King, for the truth was that it was his blackness that originated and orchestrated the breaking of his own flesh and bones.

Global capital and global whiteness may be always disembodied and absent from their local effects, but their effects are really embodied and really present. Naming some of them is necessary but insufficient: black males have the lowest life expectancy of any group in the United States. Their unemployment rate is more than twice that of white males, and the gap has increased steadily since the 1980s. The income of employed blacks is about 60% of that of whites (even college educated blacks earn only 75% of their white counterparts), and the net worth of an African-American (that is, assets minus liabilities) is one tenth that of a white: blacks find it disproportionately more difficult to get mortgages and small business loans than whites, thus ensuring that capital not only is white, but will remain so. Nearly half of all black children live below the poverty line, against only 16% of white ones, and not only is the black poverty rate three times that of whites, but the black poor are poorer than the white poor.

About one in four black men between the ages of twenty and twenty-nine are in prison—more black men are in prison than in college, and the United States continues to lock them up at four times the rate even of pre-revolution South Africa. Black people convicted of similar crimes to whites will receive harder and longer sentences, and up to 80% of black men will be arrested at least once in their lifetime. Black people suffer disproportionately aggressive policing in arrest rates and treatment during and after arrest and in court but enjoy disproportionately minimal police protection. Black people know that the military puts them in the highest risk units, but even then they are safer at war than at home, for the black male is the commonest murder victim in the country: he is also the commonest suicide victim.

The life expectancy of a black child born in Harlem is lower than that of a child born in Bangladesh, and black adults die disproportionately early from the twelve commonest preventable diseases. Sixty percent of African-Americans and Latinos live in communities polluted by uncontrolled toxic waste dumps, and a 1987 study found that the race of the neighborhood's inhabitant was the single most important factor in locating toxic waste dumps. Tobacco billboards are far more likely to be placed in black than in white neighborhoods, sometimes by a ratio of 15 to 1.

Schools in black communities receive far lower funding per student than those in white ones, and black graduation rates are both lower and decreasing as a result.[4]

These dispersed regularities of racial differentiation are steadily widening the difference between white and black America, and they structure pain into the core of everyday life. The physical effects of white power are inescapably everywhere, but the discretion of its operations makes the system invisible, except in its effects. For whites, who are largely free of its effects, the invisibility is almost total; for blacks, the struggle is to make visible that which they know is there, to give a materiality to the system and its intentionality that approximates that of its effects.

The operations of whiteness have historically produced dispersed regularities with no identifiable point of origin whose absence allows white people to deny even the existence of the regularities, let alone that of any intentionality that might inform them. By disarticulating each power effect from the others and isolating it into an individual "problem" (if it is noticed at all), white people can deny regularity and thus the systematicity of their own whiteness. The net effect of such strategic denial is to produce the truth that whiteness, as an informing regularity of the micro-physics of power, does not exist. A haunting bit of dialogue from the dénouement of the movie *The Usual Suspects* reveals the strategy:

"The greatest trick the devil ever pulled was convincing the world that he didn't exist" (for the benefit of white readers who may not know it, we should point out that, in urban slang, "the devil" is the name frequently given to whiteness).

The label "the new paranoia," then, is not simply a sneering putdown of the deluded fools supposedly subjected to it, a pathologizing of their disbelief in official knowledge; it is, more importantly, a discursive strategy of whiteness deployed upon white America whose objective is to maintain the discretion of power in the face of an imperative visibility of its effects that threatens to strip it naked and thus to destabilize its reality. Calling the black knowledge of the Illuminati "paranoid" may be more delusionary for whites than the belief it labels is for blacks. The Emperor has clothes as long as people can avoid seeing his nakedness. Power is real as long as the signs of its nonexistence are as real as those of its effects. But in crisis,

> Power . . . produces nothing but the signs of its resemblance. And at the same time, another figure of power comes into play: that of a collective demand for *signs* of power—a holy union which forms around the disappearance of power. . . . This has already given rise to fascism, that overdose of a powerful referential in a society which cannot terminate its mourning.[5]

Jean Baudrillard's melancholic scenario melds quite readily with America's paranoia-fraught political tradition. Pat Buchanan's candidacies in the past three presidential campaigns, particularly those in 1992 and 1996, offer the most extreme discursive tactics in this collective search for a nostalgic political schema which can re-materialize "the real." Playing on the basest fears of a white American public struggling to "see" itself within the mirror image offered by its increasingly darker hued neighbors, Buchanan regularly made campaign pledges to take back America for "real Americans." What this thinly disguised dogma actually revealed was a tactic of scapegoating whereby immigrants, illegal and otherwise, low-wage-earning workers of color around the world, and African-Americans were metonymically figured as the incarnation of the nation's economic and social problems. Quite cruelly, these hapless hordes were transfigured into signs of power's prevailing significance. Indeed, Buchanan's vitriol provided another link in the neo-conservative political wing's pledge to ferret out and identify the miscreant likes of "welfare queens," "deadbeat dads," "drug kingpins," and illegal aliens through superior means of surveillance and information-gathering. The obsessive demand for stronger signs of power is a strategy to hide its loss;

the white desire for an overdose of referentiality is a desire for a deterrent to the knowledge that white power is a simulacrum, and a simulacrum in crisis.

Treading a social tightrope, white power must balance its instinctual desire for self-preservation with a dizzying panoply of public interpretations as to who the "real" enemy of law and order might be. Rap's deployment of the "Illuminati" is both a diagnosis of, and an exacerbating factor in, the crisis. As Genius, a member of the popular rap group Wu-Tang Clan warns:

> G: There's a lot of shit that's about to take place. Everyone's asking about ["Illuminati"]. The thing that's frightening to some is that a lot of Illuminati's ideas are already written about in the Bible. And most of these prophecies are being fulfilled, as far as microchips in your hand or on your forehead. They've already started doing it in dogs and animals. You know, bar codes and slavery—all that shit is real. How soon they plan to execute the shit, whatever, whatever, whatever. But I *know* something's about to happen. You got biological warfare, designer diseases, AIDS . . .
>
> CHS: So how does all this make you feel?
>
> G: It makes me feel *alert!* . . . It makes me feel concerned for my children, the shit they gotta go through. Everything must change, and shit *is* changing, but it's not changing for the better. Maybe for some people. It may seem like we're doing all right, but it's getting deep, man.[6]

As deployed in rap, the "Illuminati" is a complex articulation of knowledge fragments in which the secrecy of power, the power of power to remain unseen, is necessarily predicated upon its power to see and to know. The Illuminati cast light that simultaneously enables them to see and prevents others from seeing them. Foucault was not specifically describing the Illuminati (though he might well have been), when he wrote,

> The perfect disciplinary apparatus would make it possible for a single gaze to see everything constantly. A central point would be both the source of light illuminating everything and a locus of convergence for everything that must be known.[7]

Similarly, he was not (or was he?) describing the surveillance helicopters of the Los Angeles Police Department bristling with searchlights and the high technologies of seeing, knowing, and recording. Nor was he describing the back of the dollar bill that shows an illuminating eye breaking out of the apex of a mysterious and secret pyramid surrounded by Latin mottoes bearing uncanny echoes of "New World Order." He was, however, pointing to the same power as do the rap artists when they verbalize the management of visibility, the control over who is to be made visible or kept invisible from whom and under what conditions. Defiantly, many rappers profess that they can escape the tentacles of surveillance through recourse to craftiness and evasive invisibility arising from superior knowledge of the ghetto landscape. As Prodigy from the rap group Mobb Deep claims in a lyric from an LL Cool J song, "I Shot Ya":

Illuminati wants my mind, soul, and my body
Secret society, trying to keep an eye on me
But I'mo stay incogni'
In places they can't find me
Make my moves strategically . .

The chorus of "Cell Therapy" by The Goodie Mob, a rap group hailing from Atlanta, is a simple encapsulation of the struggle over visibility: "Who's that peeking in my window? POW! . . . nobody now." As these rapping poets known well, panopticism is racialized: the all-seeing eye is white; the object of its gaze, all too often, is not. The lyrics of "Cell Therapy" rearticulate the surveillance of its chorus with some of the most dispersed effects of whiteness into a poetic evocation of their regularity that is all too visible when your viewpoint is the ghetto:

Verse 1

. . . this New World Order
Dem experimenting in Atlanta, Georgia
United Nations, overseas
They trained assassins to do search and seize
Ain't knocking or asking
Dem coming for niggas like me
Po' white trash, like they
Tricks like her back in slavery
Concentration camps lace with gas pipes lines
Inferno's outdoors like they had back when Adolph Hitler was living
    in 1945
Listen to me now, believe me
Later on in the future look it up
Where they say it? Ain't no more Constitution
In the event of a race war
Places like operation heartbreak hotel
Moments tear unit air tight vents seal off despair
Dem say expect no mercy

Fool you should be my least worries got to deal with
Where my W-2's, 1099's
Unmarked black helicopters swoop down
And try to put missiles in minds . . .

Chorus

Who's that peeking in my window? POW . . . nobody now

Verse 2

Me and my family moved in our apartment complex
A gate with the serial code was put up next
They claim that this community is so drug free
But it don't look that way to me cause I can see
The young bloods hanging out at the sto 24/7
Junkies looking for a hit of the blo it's powerful
Oh you know what else they trying to do
Make a curfew especially for me and you
The traces of the New World Order
Time is getting shorter if we don't get prepared
People it's gone be a slaughter
My mind won't allow me to not be curious
My folk don't understand so they don't
Take it serious but every now and then I wonder
If the gate was put up to keep crime out or to keep our ass in . . .

Chorus

In brilliant fashion, Goodie Mob materializes power's surreptitious strategy of incarceration and surveillance so necessary for the institution of truly global capital formations and articulates them with subaltern knowledge of racial genocide. Both the title of the song and that of the album which contains it address Foucault's description of inner consciousness, or "the soul," as a by-product of power's application of force on bodies, an effect of incessant "peeking" through the window of one's most precious sanctum of interiority.[8] Without adequate communal support for their analysis, rappers like Goodie Mob realize they have no choice but to arm themselves and be prepared to take matters into their own hands ("POW . . . nobody now").

New York–based rap artists have echoed the Mob's cryptic outlook. In 1996, Afrika Bambaataa, one of rap's South Bronx pioneers, released an album of Illuminati ideology called *Time Zone: Warlocks and Witches, Computers, Microchips and You.* That same year, the Trenton, New Jersey, crew Poor Righteous Teachers (PRT) released one of the most sustained warnings against secret societies on an album called *New World Order*. On the CD box the group can be seen gazing into the viewer's eyes from within the Freemason pyramid symbolizing illumination and knowledge, the identical schema that appears on United States currency, where it makes visible, for those who can see it, the unholy alliance of power, secrecy, whiteness, and capital. On *New World Order*, PRT advocates an Afrocentric approach to resistance that emphasizes self-respect, education, and a de-emphasis on conspicuous consumption. PRT works to flush the traces of mental colonization from within the consciousness of underclass subjects. The following year, a rap group called the BoogieMonsters released an album entitled *God Sound*, which offered a similarly Afrocentric antidote to the Illuminati's vision of a spiritually sick society.

Most frequently, however, artists sympathetic to anti-Illuminati credos aim the bulk of their wrath at white power's purveyors of law and order, like New York City's Mayor Rudolph Giuliani, as part of a concerted attempt to root out external causes for ghetto paranoia. In the published lyrics to his 1999 release "I Want to Talk to You," Nas makes a fervently political protest against the alliance between the government and capitalistic oppression that is emblematic of this broader musical commentary.

Chorus

I want to talk to the mayor or
The governor
To the mutha*uckin president
I want to talk to the FBI and CIA
And the mutha*uckin congressmen
Can I talk to you?

Verse 1

Step up to the White House, let me in
What's my reason for being?
I'm your next of kin
And we built this mutha*ucker
You want to kill me cuza my hunger?
Mr. America, young black niggas want you
I want to talk to the man, understand?
Understand this mutha*ucking 'g-pack' in my hand?
Look what happened in San Fran

Young girl hit by policeman
12 shots up in her dome damn!
Niggas thought we slept
But the architechts at the Pentagon's from Egypt
Government secret
From 99 to 2G computer's shut down, what now?
Extinction on Earth? Human cut down?
Niggas play with Playstations
They buildin' space stations on Mars
Plottin' civilizations
Dissin' us, discriminating different races
Taxpayers pay for more jails for black and Latin faces . .

Chorus

Although less sophisticated lyrical compositions may only contain fragments of globalization's underground dissent—a lyric here, a quick bit of wordplay there—when taken together within the specific historical moment of the late 1990s, these bits of street-corner wisdom have proven significant elements in a contemporary structure of feeling epitomized by the new paranoia. So many rappers have been incorporating snippets of the anti-Illuminati framework into their work that *The Source*, one of the leading magazines on rap music and hip-hop culture, recently devoted an entire issue to a consideration of the myth and the socio-economic outlook it predicts for their primarily young, black readership.[9]

Amid all the recent rap albums which cite Illuminati, *All We Got Iz Us*, by a Queens-based group called Onyx, stands out for its sustained musical treatment of the themes introduced by Goodie Mob's "Cell Therapy." *All We Got Iz Us* offers an "eye-for-an-eye" approach to the quandary posed by the consolidation of white wealth at the expense of black ghettos, a revolutionary measure that calls for closer scrutiny.

Since their debut in 1993, Onyx has been indicative of what conservatives hate most about hardcore rap. Bristling with blinding animosity, Onyx's raps are some of the most testosterone-drenched dirges of despair to be heard in the industry. The group's trademark is a modified version of that counter-cultural hippie icon of the 1960s and 70s, the "happy face," which the group has updated into a menacing, slant-eyed scowl. On the CD box for *All We Got Iz Us*, the face takes on a three-dimensional cast and appears to be made of crumbling concrete and corroded steel, perhaps signifying the deteriorating ghetto streets which the crew celebrates as the last bastion of armed black resistance. As the album's title foreshadows, *All We Got Iz Us* is an ideological manifesto that puts little faith in the feasibility of political coalitions and urges ghetto residents to perceive the hammering blows of law and order against their bodies as an outright conspiracy that only differs from pre–Civil War slavery in its high-tech sophistication. The most intriguing song on the album is perhaps the apocalyptic "Last Dayz," which plays on the same biblical end-time terminology as many of today's best-selling "Christian thrillers."[10] And like these books, "Last Dayz" is a call to battle for "unsung heroes" that articulates criminality, particularly in the drug trade, as a means of resistance against incarceration in slave labor camps. We hope that via a close reading of the song's lyrics and its accompanying video, some insight into how rappers use the Illuminati as a means of inverting the omnipotent pretensions of power will emerge.

The song begins in an ominous growl over a hypnotic drum and keyboard track. During this opening theme, the three crew members, Fredro, Son E. See, and Sticky, appear to be riding in an elevator that carries them from their murky subterranean lair to the police-patrolled streets above. This dichotomous relationship between the underground and the mainstream immediately positions the video as a futuristic meditation on a battle between "the haves and the have-nots."[11] After a brief nomination of the life-and-death stakes involved, Fredro begins the first stanza with a more detailed account of the dominant political economy of the black underclass and his adversarial daydream of a more perfect world.

Verse 1 (Fredro)

> I'm America's nightmare
> Young, black and just don't give a fuck
> I just wanna get high, live it up
> So fuck a 9 to 5, and Whitey trying to enslave us
> With minimum wages
> Slammin' my niggaz up in cages
> Changing their behaviors
> That's outrageous!
> Smokin' roaches is hopeless
> We want lazy sofas and sculptures
> Lady chauffeurs who fuck us
> Full house and royal flushes
> Roll with the Rush
> It's the official nas'

Got bitches with pistols and cash
We living in the las'
My theory is Fuck it!
Sexy niggaz get abducted
My corruption is conducted through ghettos
Sippin' Armaretto
Hand on the pedal, never settle
We want Carolina Herrera
Dirty Donna Karan sweaters
Ralph Lauren leathers and suedes
Gold-plates guns and grenades . . .

Chorus

It's life on the edge of dangerous
Where you living
Never giving a shit, cuz you living in it
. . . Official nas' motherfuckas don't give a shit . . .

During Fredro's verse a bleak world begins to take shape, one in which the urban landscape serves as nothing more than one large corral for black "cattle" caught in a perpetual battle for freedom against their keepers.[12] It's a surreal realm of barcode implantations in the necks of the surveilled, apartheid-like "pass cards," and raucous street clashes. Fredro can be seen cruising the barren cityscape in a fashionable automobile. He's positioned as a survivor living by his wits in the aftermath of a holocaust. His wraithlike ability to scratch out an existence is suggested in one scene in which he disappears while behind the wheel of his car, implying the sort of shiftiness witnessed through Prodigy's aforementioned lyric. The thoroughfares of the city are otherwise deserted. We must suppose that all other former residents have forsaken the area as a territory reserved solely for the demonized and the abnormal.

Another interesting, though perplexing, aspect of this lyric is its emphasis on high-end fashion products and other hallmarks of "the good life"—"lazy sofas" and such. This incorporation of the status quo onto black bodies as a means of resistance seems antithetical at first, but ultimately the nomination of these trinkets of the leisure class emerges as perhaps the most salient bulkhead along a racial battlefield heavily inflected by class inequities. The expression of desire for inclusion in the American dream via "Ralph Lauren leathers and suedes" can be seen as a form of discursive "looting" that highlights the market-savvy mien of the dispossessed.[13]

After a short verse by Son E. See describing an aborted drug deal with a couple of cops on the make, Sticky appears in a haunting scene that inverts the panoptic eye of whiteness that provided such memorable footage from media events such as the infamous O. J. Simpson "white Bronco" chase and the Los Angeles uprising of 1992. Perched on the edge of a tenement rooftop in a vulture-like stance, Sticky scans the turbulent pavement below, while ruminating on the meaninglessness of his ife.

Verse 3 (Sticky)

Thinking 'bout taking my own life
Might as well
'Cept they might not sell weed in hell
And that's where I'm going cuz the devil's inside of me
They make me rob from my own nationality
That's kinda ignorant
But yo, I gotta pay the rent
So, yeah, I stick a nigga, mos' definite
The degenerate
If I get caught, I'm innocent
Cuz I don't leave no sticky finga prints
For the cops
They only good if they dead
Cuz all that badge and a gun shit be going to they head
To make bread
I gotta steal for sport
So, I stole the show and made some pennies for my thoughts
And if this fuckin' rap shit don't pay
I'mo start selling drugs around my way
Killin' my own people in the USG[14]
Shit, they gonna get it from somebody—it may as well be me!
'Sides, they can't tax dirty money
And you can't trust no body, no one
I'm the scorpion
And I'll probably bite the bullet cuz I live by the gun . . .

Chorus

Upon hitting the streets, Sticky is thrown into the back of a squad car, and after an urgent tussle with several officers, he narrowly escapes arrest As the video winds to a close, computerized mug shots and data collected from black prisoners implanted with microchips flash quickly across the screen, emphasizing surveillance's knowledge-producing function.

One of the most startling and distressing aspects of Sticky's verse is his compulsion to mingle self-hatred with his venomous animosity toward the cops who occupy his neighborhood. This mental short circuit at the synapse between his conscious bodily schema and the world around him is a deleterious effect of power.[15] "The degenerate's" struggle to make meaning of his life in this netherworld spirals inexorably toward spiritual death. Fitfully, he gropes through the carnage flung about him, trying to get the outline of his *true* enemy in his sights. A violent exorcism of the "devil" in his soul may lead to his salvation. Sadly, he is unable to recognize his nemesis fully, even with his bird's-eye view, and his pondering gets lost in an extemporaneous testimony of revulsion. Back on the ground, as a matter of utter pragmatics, he remorselessly exploits other ghetto dwellers through the drug trade in order to ensure his own survival. Much like DaVaughan Roper, Onyx and many other rappers view drug-related commerce as an interrelated aspect of their oppositional identity. Yet while their stated desire for social change is laudable, support for their unabashed commodification of human misery is unacceptable, particularly if such activity falls under the rubric of black emancipation.

The fact remains however, that no serious plan of action to remedy the plight of the black underclass exists, anywhere. What are we to make of this "truth?" "Absolutely nothing," say many members of the Internet Age's privileged class, belying their faith in the trickle-down effects of the bull market. When we feel similar impulses to wax self-satisfied balm on Sticky's hoarse-throated cry for the recognition of his oppression, we should pause long enough to ask ourselves what the wretched and forsaken are prepared to do, and *are* doing, to achieve a presence against the pressure of tactile erasure. Poor folks who try to explain their poverty in terms of conspiracy theory are not paranoid, as such. Is not the concept of a "conspiracy" a valid consideration for a caste that *knows* it is being disowned, since people of all sorts avoid actual contact with it, save the vicarious intimacy of punishment? Is not so-called "paranoia" the end result of having one's embodied significance construed solely as a problem? These questions become all the more urgent when we consider the lengths to which power is willing to go to defend its rule. *Last days, indeed . . .*

NOTES

Thanks to Ed Pavlić, Lee Quinby, and Jonathan Semer for their generous support and insightful criticism of earlier versions of this chapter.

1. Clifford Krauss, "Police Say Staten Island Man Stockpiled Weapons Illegally," *New York Times* (31 Aug 1996): 25. The Associated Press issued coverage of Roper's arrest that same day, and reports of the incident ran in newspapers nationwide, including the *New York Daily News* and *Newsday*, the *Jacksonville, Florida Times-Union,* and the *Chattanooga Free Press.*

2. Michiko Kakutani, "Bound By Suspicion," *New York Times Magazine* (19 Jan 1997): 16.

3. Ted Olen and Tim Stafford, "When Evangelicals Look in the Mirror, Do We See the Host of 'The 700 Club' Staring Back?" *Christianity Today* (12 Aug 1996): 27.

4. The statistical information in these paragraphs is drawn from the following sources: Andrew Hacker, *Two Nations: Black and White, Separate, Hostile, Unequal* (New York: Scribner's, 1992), chaps. 6–7; Studs Terkel, *Race: How Blacks and Whites Think and Feel about the American Obsession* (New York: New Press 1992), v; John Fiske: *Power Plays Power Works* (London: Verso 1993), chap. 11.

5. Jean Baudrillard, *Simulations* (New York: Semiotext(e), 1983), 45–46.

6. The Genius (GZA), interview by Christopher Holmes Smith, New York, New York, 11 Jan 1996.

7. Michel Foucault, *Discipline and Punish*, trans. Alan Sheridan (New York: Vintage, 1977). The second epigraph to this chapter is from this source as well, at p. 308.

8. Ibid. 29.

9. For a superb analysis of the Illuminati trend among hip-hop audiences, see Bakari Kitwana, "Future Shock," *The Source* (Aug 1996).

10. The mainstream novelist Vince Passaro reports that the sizeable revenue for "Christian thrillers" accumulates "far off the track of New York Editors' lunches" and represents a "phenomenal growth category" (64), with annual sales figures per title ranging from 150,000 to over five million copies. According to Passaro, the typical Christian thriller's "depiction of our national moment resembles a kind of medieval theme park: modern technology powers, bloodthirsty kings, dragons and plagues. The satanic presidents and demonic CEOs . . . the use of the environment as a field of oppression for the common man—all of it plays upon deep superstitions widely affecting our culture but little reported on" (65). Vince Passaro, "The Oath," *Harper's* (Sept 1996): 64–71.

11. Thanks to Darrell Newton for sharing his ideas on this above/underground dialectic in his unpublished colloquium presentation, "Black to the Future and the Fortress L.A.: An Examination of *Demolition Man*" (University of Wisconsin, Madison, 1996).

12. This livestock imagery is drawn from Robert Hayden's poem "Killing the Calves." It reads as follows:

Threatened by abundance, the ranchers
with tightfaced calculation
throw the bawling calves into a ditch and
shoot them in order to fatten the belly of cost.

The Terror of the squandered calves mingles
with the terribly agony of the starving
whom their dying will not save.
Of course, the killing is "quick and clean";
and though there is no comparison reminds us
nonetheless—men women children
forced like superfluous animals
into a pit and less than cattle
in warcrazed eyes like crazed cattle slaughtered.

Robert Hayden, *Collected Poems*, ed. Frederick Glaysher (New York: Liveright, 1985), 178.

13. John Fiske, *Media Matters: Everyday Culture and Political Change* (Minneapolis: University of Minnesota Press, 1994), 171.

14. USG: United States Ghetto.

15. Frantz Fanon, *Black Skin, White Masks*, trans. C. L. Markmann (New York: Grove Press, 1967), 110–15.

19

Music Wars: Blood and Song at the End of Yugoslavia

TOMISLAV LONGINOVIĆ

> Our folk songs are full of character, full of deeply rooted psy-
> che, full of extreme passions and one could say full of blood
> and race as well.
> (Vladimir Dvorniković, *Characterology of the Yugoslavs*, 1939)

Yugoslavia ended twice in this century: the Second World War ended the Kingdom of Yugoslavia in 1941, while the end of the Cold War indirectly led to the implosion of the Socialist Federative Republic of Yugoslavia in 1991. This essay is an attempt to tell the bloody story of these two ends, by examining the ethnomusicological theories of Vladimir Dvorniković before the end of the first Yugoslavia and by analyzing the role that popular music, as the "voice of blood," played in the cultural deconstruction of the second Yugoslavia. These two ends are marked by the loss of identity of those who forged their Yugoslav identity by accepting a shared set of values and practices that would define their community as a state of "South Slavs," although different civilizational and implicitly racial narratives informed the particular identities of various Slavic and non-Slavic populations that inhabited the last two Yugoslavias.

Combining the racial notion of "Slav-dom" with the shared histori-cal destiny of "slave-dom," Serbs, Croats, Bosniaks (Bosnian Muslims), Slovenes, Macedonians, and Montenegrins imagined their political and cultural unity along very different lines. This difference was structured by the kind of imperial and colonial power which ruled over different Balkan peoples before they began to imagine a new sense of national iden-tity during nineteenth-century struggles for independence, political self-determination, and collective territorialization of identity. The project of imagined unity not only rested on the political and social solidarity of Southern Slavs, but counted on a very strong intellectual mobilization to achieve the cultural cooperation that would result in the formation of a community of cultures within the framework of the multiethnic Slavic state.

Music was one of the key elements of the Yugoslav project, especially in its popular forms and manifestations. Since the Balkan Peninsula was for the most part inhabited by rural populations, the peasant song was regarded as the ultimate expression of the "Yugoslav character." This notion, modeled on a mixture of the romantic conception of "folk" and a specific Balkan model of "modernization," prompted the most significant Yugoslav "ethnopsychologist" to posit the peasant song as the ultimate voice of common South Slavic "blood and race." Dvorniković's *Characterology of the Yugoslavs* was published on the eve of World War II, in the same year the German Nazis and Russian Stalinists divided Poland and Croatia gained autonomy from the Yugoslav kingdom as a result of German pressure. Because external and internal projects to counter Yugoslav unity were so strong in 1939, Dvorniković's dream of a common South Slavic character has a tragic echo. The scientific idea of race obsessed this thinker whose Croat roots in Dalmatia and later Bosnia were followed by the embrace of Bosniak and South Serbian/Macedonian culture.

"Our folk song," which this enthusiastic Yugoslav imagined as a collective voice of the South Slavic "blood and race," has been fragmented twice since he wrote his monumental *Characterology* in 1939. The latest fragmentation of Yugoslavia through the formation of new state entities came about as a result of the "civilizational" differentiation of the Yugoslav idea. This differentiation was followed by the sounds of new songs, whose specific "national" flavor bears the marks of new incarnations of a "cultural" racism which has been given free reign during the latest intra-Yugoslav confrontations. It is especially tragic that Dvorniković imagined Bosnian songs as the "bottom of the soul" of all those Yugoslav peoples who suffered various forms of foreign occupation and domination.

He quotes one of the singers he interviewed in Montenegro who explains singing as a need to give expression to suffering, and not as an esthetic activity: "I don't sing because I know how, I sing to get rid of my soul's burden" (Dvorniković 1939: 429). This musical "burden" of the Yugoslav soul was imagined as the ultimate voicing of unity among different ethnicities. While trying to work out the classification of various cultural traditions, Dvorniković distinctly invokes folk music as the supreme embodiment of the Yugoslav "national spirit": "The psychology of *melos* and music leads us in the most direct, experiential manner into the deepest emotional layers, into the rhythmics and dynamics of our national psyche" (33).

While tacitly reasserting Schelling's theory of music as the most intuitive and therefore supreme of all arts, Dvorniković also "modernizes" Herder's Romantic conception of *Volksgeist* by invoking the notion of a common "national psyche." It is symptomatic that the identities of non-Slavic peoples, such as Albanians, Roma (Gypsies), Jews, and others do not figure in his more than a thousand-page-long, monumental study *Karakterologija Jugoslovena* (Characterology of the Yugoslavs) except as a negative against which the Slavic folk genius can be imagined. The tacit exclusion of non-Slavs turns into outright racism when Dvorniković turns away in disgust from the singing of the Yugoslav Roma:

> The inner being and lyricism of the Slavic song is completely alien to Gypsies. Tenderness, nostalgia, pride, manliness, heroism, subtlety, reticence, sacrifice for the loved one; all those elements of our real folk song do not come through in the Gypsy interpretation. . . . Let it be called Gypsy singing, but not the "Yugoslav folk song.". . . Our folk song should be protected from this kind of sacrilege. (399)

The singing of Roma is seen as detrimental to the development of national character, which is based on Dvorniković's theory of "integral Yugoslavism," which was promoted by the Serbian royal dynasty before World War II. War songs and turbo folk, which came into being during and after the latest Wars of Yugoslav Succession (1991–95), are cultural phenomena that work against the culturally based common identity and community promoted by both the royalist and the communist Yugoslav states. The active suppression of any discussions of racially motivated genocides of World War II during the communist period (1945–91) greatly damaged Tito's project of Yugoslavism, which could be characterized as proto-multicultural. While Roma, Albanians, Jews, and other minorities received better treatment in Yugoslavia than in any of the neighboring states in Tito's Yugoslavia, Slavic populations that shared a common language (Bosnians, Croats, Montenegrins, Serbs) ended up nurturing mutual resentments due to unresolved issues of collective crimes and punishments. The literal and figurative displacement and erasure of "cultural others" during the War of Succession has been accompanied by the sounds of "racialized" war songs, which sing about the domination and superiority of particular protagonists in the latest conflict.

While constructing the Yugoslav prototype around the "Dinaric race," the one shared by the three major religious groups which inhabit the Dinaric Mountains along the Adriatic Sea, Dvorniković obviously feels uneasy about generalizing, since cultural traditions adopted through foreign conversions and colonizations pose the greatest problem for the idea of a common "Yugoslav race." As a young man he hears the essence of the newly imagined race in the sound of Bosnian folk ballads (*sevdalinke*). Songs of love, pain, and longing for one's youth define the national soul, whose sounds at first frighten Dvorniković: "I have to admit that these songs were quite horrifying to me during my adolescent years. . . . Nasal, drawn out, with countless melismatic transitions" (376). The sounds which at first cause fear in Dvorniković's Yugoslav soul are sung in a double voice of the "Oriental and Proto-Slavic" heritage. But "Oriental" is constructed as the surface, the external, colonial layer of the song, while the Slavic heritage is seen as rooted in the racial character as the primal pain of existence.

> After transition into manhood my relationship with this type of song and folk music in general changed fundamentally: after a long incubation, the infection broke out. *Bacillus bosniensis*, although my ancestors are not Bosnian, entered my blood, and from the bottom of my soul, somewhere from its most atavistic depths, a string emerged which vibrated upon hearing the most primitive song of the porters. (376–77)

Dvorniković experiences growing appreciation of the Yugoslav folk song as an infection with a deadly disease of manhood, in his case achieved after initiation into love, sexuality, and the horrors of World War I. Longing for love combines with the longing for freedom to dominate the Yugoslav masculine imagination and is voiced in Bosnian folk ballads rooted in Ottoman, Sephardic, and Slavic heritages. The contamination of his own Croatian, Western soul with musically sounded Bosnian melancholy is the first initiation into a community whose "blood" is infected by the pain and desire of the post-colonial subject: centuries of racial segregation and gender oppression under the Ottoman *millet* system nurture a musical tradition which works to alleviate both the singer's and the audience's "burden." Yugoslavs are not only the South Slavs, but slaves from the European South as well: the continual contest between European and Asian empires to conquer and pacify these "bloodthirsty tribes" has forged a desire for Yugoslavia based on a common bond between subjects of different colonial masters.

Dvorniković's Yugoslavism could therefore be imagined primarily as a project based on the concept of race as a common historical destiny, and not so much on narratives and songs which mainly divide the South Slavs along the boundaries of former imperial domains. And now, Tito's political clones are fashioning new national cultures based on the hatred of their former "brothers" by the voicing of those cultural differences. Songs serve as a powerful tool for the formation of new collective memories, for a return to the sense of isolation from the cultures of those who no longer belong to the same birth community. The resurrection of particularized ethnicities marks a powerful return to the Romantic concepts of the people, outfitted in the 1990s with electronic media and a surplus of weapons accumulated during the Cold War paranoia which pitted Tito's Yugoslavia against both the East and the West. A return to the "old" was the easiest way to politically effect the transition into the "new," especially by populations that had been coded as "inferior races" during the World War II Nazi cleansing of Germany and Eastern Europe. When racial differences are based on a sense of civilizational belonging, the transition from the status of an "inferior" to a "superior" race is realizable with a minimum of political, social, and cultural performance of cultural differences.

That is why Dvorniković feels obliged to confront major proponents of Nordic racial superiority in 1939. Countering theories of Ludwig Woltmann, Dvorniković casts an ironic glance at his racial vision of Europe: "We should not forget that Nietzsche's *blonde Bestie* was a man who introduced organized industry, electricity and radio-waves, but also caused great anxiety by authoring such grandiose cultural advancements under the rubric of 'world war,' 'air war,' 'total war'; it is not unusual that the criterion of superiority turned against him within the soul of other races" (191–92).[1]

The turn caused by the technological utopia of Nordic racial superiority in "the soul of other races" takes the form of new fractures effected through the hygienic extermination of those below the racial divide, something that Dvorniković senses is already taking place inside his "Yugoslav soul." Since the name of Slavs already contains etymological echoes of their slave identity, their fantasies of superiority are imagined as a return to the past days of medieval glory before their respective descent into the status of subjects which were enslaved, assimilated, and colonized by imperial religions and cultures which they now consider their own. This fractured identity of slaves with the memory of kings emerges as a norm during the nineteenth-century struggles for independence from foreign domination in the Balkans.

One could reduce Dvorniković's invention of the Yugoslav race to a cultural apology for the centrist tendencies of the Karadjordjević dynasty, but a closer look at his idea of common "blood and racial filiation" among the Balkan Slavs manifests deeper internalization of the Romantic gaze:

> However, blood and racial filiation (at least in the beginning), common life through the centuries, common struggle, and historical destiny join individuals and create a common psychological type out of them, starting with daily life routines, from reactions in the most insignificant situations to those supraindividual and transgenerational leanings which bind all those individuals into one collective, into one will, into one common way of thinking and feeling, in short, into one *spirit* of the nation. (17)

South Slavic identity is constructed on the model posited by the interiorization of the Herderian gaze which imagined "the people" as an amalgam of racial and cultural categories. German Romantic imagination provided Balkan Slav literate intelligentsia with a vision of identity rooted in the songs and dances of illiterate peasants whom they identified as the supreme expression of the people's collective belonging. The 1850 Vienna agreement between the Croat Ljudevit Gaj and the Serb Vuk Karadžić defined the project of South Slavic cultural unity based on the choice of a common linguistic dialect that was supposed to be the root of the new Yugoslav identity. While searching for the spontaneous and the original in writing down the songs of the people, Vuk defined the relationship of Serbs with other Balkan Slavs as a project based on the "folkloristic" unity of the peasantry whose motto was: "One people of three faiths." Minute Balkan urban classes, steeped in racial and cultural hybridity, at this time developed a peculiar habit of imagining "the people" they belonged to on the basis of as an imaginary peasant, who spent the entire nineteenth century singing and dying for love and freedom. The Balkan urban mentality emerged as a simultaneous embrace and distancing from the "primitive" non-culture of the peasants, whose life was posited as a national ideal that counters the artifice and degradation of urban life, while such rustic life was to be personally avoided by all means.

Although blood is invoked as a basis for collectivity, the second part of Dvorniković's definition of the national spirit offers "historical destiny" as a source of the true *Volksgeist* that directs common identity. The ethnopsychologist's desperate desire to imagine the Yugoslav identity as a totality of "one will" and "one spirit of the nation" gradually slips into the discourse of racial supremacy based on the primitive power and vitality of the Dinaric type. Dvorniković proceeds to define the Dinaric type as the organic basis of the "Yugoslav race" by trying to set the issue of

superiority aside. Yet the "great anxiety" of the race slated for extermination by Hitler lingers as he explores the depths of the "Yugoslav
soul." The turn "within the soul of other races" caused by the preparation of the "total war" effort on the part of the Nordic race causes
Dvorniković to cast a superior look from the margin toward the center
of Europe. The North is imagined as the seat of "technology," as German ingenuity led astray by the stupidity of racism. This stereotypical
Romantic "gaze from the heights" is assimilated and returned from the
borderlines of Europe, where Dvorniković imagines the birth of genius
from the bosom of the Dinaric mountains. The Balkans' status of "not
quite Europe" provides him with a lens on a subject of an unacknowledged postcolonialism: the technology which fuels the modernization
of Europe is at the same time the fuel of its aggression. Although he
sets out to counter and criticize the very notion of racially based evaluation of cultures, he cannot resist the temptation of challenging the natural right of the "blond beast" to rule the world.

The Romantic gaze had been fully internalized by the thinkers of Yugoslav late modernism, which provided the "inferior races" with their
own vision of civilizational superiority. Dvorniković scorns European
musical notation systems as a "bloodless scheme of Western musical
mathematics," since its signifiers are not able to contain the fullness of
"our folk song" (391). The failure of Western transcription to grasp the
"primitive" power and melodic subtlety of the Yugoslav folk song is
the sign of an emerging complex of superiority rooted in the internalized gaze of the Romantics, which places the Balkan musical heritage at
the imagined "primitive origins" of Europe's identity.

By essentializing the folk song as the collective expression of Yugoslavism, this racial thinker develops a counter-discourse of Yugoslav power based on the shared destiny of historical victimization.
Dvorniković imagines the plenitude that exudes from the population
which creates songs full of melancholy and sorrow. The "extreme passions" are sounded by the collectivity that participates in the performance of the folk song as a ritual "unburdening" of the soul of those Yugoslavs whose identity has been rooted in historical memories of five to
ten centuries of foreign oppression.

Dvorniković locates the most intense expression of people's pain in
the territories where Turkish colonization lasted the longest in Yugoslavia. Folk song represents the bottom of the soul, an abyss from which
emanates the pain of unfulfilled desire and destiny. Dvorniković hears
the most acute expression of the Yugoslav soul in the songs that invokes
dert and *sevdah*. These two Ottoman Turkish words, which denote the

pain of perpetual frustration and *melancholy* caused by the loss or distance of the desired object, have been assimilated into the vocabulary of Bosnian, Serbian, and Macedonian populations as the supreme signifiers of collective suffering.

Dvorniković imagines the Balkan combination of café, restaurant, and bar, the *kafana*, as an "orientalized" site where men gather to vent their individual and communal frustrations by drinking plum brandy, occasionally smashing glasses on the floor to relieve their "burden" while listening to and sometimes participating in the performance of the folk song. The fact that women (invariably perceived as fallen) and "Gypsies" continue to be the main performers of Balkan folk songs manifests the enmeshed cultural coding of race and gender. The descendants of European and Asian slaves revel in their injured masculinity, while listening to the songs which evoke the sweet pain of longing. To use a word coming from the same Arabic root as the Portuguese *saudade*, the folk song evokes *sevdah*, the black bile of melancholy that lingers in the singing of Bosnians: "*Sevdah* languishes in the soul; a muffled pain which can erupt with mad and limitless intensity" (385). The mad and limitless intensity with which communist Yugoslavia imploded in 1991 (Croatia) and 1992 (Bosnia and Herzegovina) gave voice to the suppressed pain of Serbs, Croats, and Bosniaks as they fought to affirm their particular "racial-cultural" identities during the wars for independence and ethnic territorialization.

"The Yugoslav soul" imagined by Dvorniković as a sounding of people's historical and racial pain was severely fractured shortly after the 1939 publication of Dvorniković's characterology: under combined German Nazi and Italian Fascist occupation, Yugoslavs were divided along old civilizational lines into Serbs, Croats, Slovenes, etc. The bond of "common blood" was broken as a result of foreign occupation, but first Yugoslavia did not survive because the Serbs, who imagined themselves as the "integral" rulers of Yugoslavia, had a very different conception of "Yugoslavism" than Croats and Slovenes, who saw it as a transitional structure on the road to full national independence.

Following the sequence of events that caused the implosion of the second Yugoslavia in 1991, one could posit a hierarchy of musical differences that was constructed as a tool of "racial/cultural" separation from the common state. The process of "civilizational" differentiation began with the Slovenes, whose yodeling call from the snowy Alps immediately identified them with their Austro-Germanic colonial past. Slovene embrace of *Mitteleuropa* and "civil" society served as a strategic tool for the ostensible rejection of "communism," reinforced by the separation from the concepts of "Slavdom" and "Balkans." The Croats were the first to hear the yodeling call from the heights of the North and the light of the West. Their persistent struggle to stake out their belonging to Europe and the white race had been perpetually frustrated by the presence of Serbs in Croatia, whom they constructed as a doubly "orientalized" Other: first as "cunning Byzantines" who obstinately cling to their Cyrillic alphabet and Orthodox Christian religion, and second as former Ottoman slaves whose race and culture have been contaminated by the presence of Asia-in-Europe. Dr. Peter Tancig, a Slovene Minister of Science at the outset of the latest war, sent a circular message to fellow Slovenes on the Internet, clearly articulating the main features of the dominant form of Western racism which today guides the policies of both the European Union and the United States:

> The basic reason for all the past/present mess is the incompatibility of two main frames of reference/civilization, unnaturally and forcibly joined in Yugoslavia. On one side you have a typical violent and crooked oriental-bizantine [sic] heritage, best exemplified by Serbia and Montenegro. . . . On the other side (Slovenia, Croatia) there is a more humble and dilligent [sic] western-catholic tradition. . . . Trying to keep Yugoslavia afloat . . . is also very bad geostrategic thinking, as independent (and westernized) Slovenia (and Croatia) could and would act as a "cordon sanitaire" against the eastern tide of chaos. (Hayden and Bakić-Hayden 1992: 12)

It is important to emphasize the often misunderstood point about the conceptions of collective identity of various peoples in former Yugoslavia. Since most of the ethnic definitions in the United States are based on race as an extension of "color," I am often asked to point out the differences between Serbs, Croats, and Muslims based on those "visible" criteria. Since all the Balkan peoples are more or less "white" according to American racial criteria, the conceptions of race are largely based on the "invisible" notions of cultural superiority derived from a sense of belonging initiated as a result of the colonization of the Balkan peninsula by different imperial powers. These identifications are largely based on territorializations of one's religious confession: Croats see themselves as part of the culture based on Roman Catholicism, Serbs as part of Eastern Orthodox culture stemming from Byzantium, while Bosniak identity is defined by their conversion to Islam during five centuries of Ottoman rule in the Balkans.

The latest Yugoslav war was indeed fueled by the new type of racism which seems to permeate Europe at the moment, based on what Taguieff has called *differentialist racism* and Balibar has defined as a current belief that "you have to respect the 'tolerance thresholds,' maintain 'cultural distances' or, in other words, in accordance with the postulate that individuals are the exclusive heirs and bearers of a single culture, segregate collectives (the best barrier in this regard still being national frontiers)" (Balibar and Wallerstein 1991: 22–23) This new form of "racism without race" naturalizes cultural differences to such an extent that members of a given community perceive their differences from cultures of their neighbors as insurmountable and therefore better kept at a distance. Indeed, the case of former Yugoslavia is the most extreme "acting out" of the symptoms of this very European disease. The Yugoslav tragedy was augmented by the opened eyes and "closed noses" of West Europeans, whose own version of cultural and moral superiority instituted distance between themselves and Yugoslavs, whose country was represented as a site of savage butchery by "lesser Europeans." Indeed, all of "Eastern" Europe has been excised from "Europe proper" on the basis of this new brand of racism.

The case of the most widely spoken language of former Yugoslavia is a good indicator of how differentialist racism operates on the concrete level. While Bosniaks, Croats, and Serbs speak basically the same language, with some regional variations, use of a mutually intelligible communication code is obviously not a guarantee of political unity, as the latest Yugoslav implosion demonstrates with sobering clarity. The speed with which the language once called "Serbo-Croatian" has been transformed into "Bosnian," "Croatian," and "Serbian" shows how wars can drive nations to embrace cultural projects which reject mutually intelligible communication in favor of mutual misunderstanding, fear, hatred, and aggression.

Croats and Bosniaks had especially wished to distance themselves linguistically from the Serbs, whose territorial presence in Croatia and Bosnia stood in the way of "pure Croatia" and "multicultural Bosnia." Regional variants are stressed to establish and naturalize cultural difference, with Croats resurrecting the linguistic heritage from the Ustashe period and Bosniaks stressing the Arabic and Ottoman vocabulary and inflection. Books written in Cyrillic script are destroyed by Croatian libraries, since they mark the presence of the impure Serb culture within pure, Western, Roman Catholic Croatia. At the same type, Cyrillic is adopted as the official alphabet of Serbia, Montenegro, and Bosnian Serb territories and Latin script purged from school programs. Serbian cultural belonging to the sphere of Orthodoxy makes them seek support among Greeks and Russians, who are imagined as the only allies because of their rootedness in Byzantine civilization. These cultural links with past colonial masters and "friendly nations" are the main source of differentialist racism, which revives the suppressed discourse of race-as-culture which currently fuels the nationalist revivals in the Balkans. The escape from Yugoslav identity, which Croats, Bosniaks, and Slovenes have accomplished with the help of "friendly nations," has been represented by the media as the end of domination by the "Serbo-communists." This escape has been achieved by playing on the collective fantasies of superiority which Freud called "the narcissism of minor differences."[2]

Another complication in understanding the relationship between "blood and song" is added by half a century of military-party dictatorship that imposed itself under the title of "communism." After the emergence of Tito and the Communist Party as the leaders of socialist Yugoslavia, Dvorniković's "integralist" theory was seen as unitarian and reactionary. Yugoslavism was no longer defined as a concept based on the "Dinaric race" shared by Bosniaks, Croats, Montenegrins, and Serbs, but as a project which emerged from the common struggle against fascist occupation and the class interest of "workers and peasants" which joined in a "national liberation struggle" during World War II. The troubled history of racism fueled by Hitler's doctrines transformed the 1941 Independent State of Croatia (NDH) into a mass extermination site for Serbs, Jews, and Gypsies as humans of lesser quality. This often neglected aspect of the Nazi holocaust is what determined the identity of the currently disappearing populations which the West has termed "Croatian Serbs" and "Bosnian Serbs." These populations have been "racialized" as victims of Croat Ustashe who implemented their notorious solution of the "Serbian problem" by thirds: one third exterminated, one third converted to Roman Catholicism, one third expelled from the territories of Croatia, Bosnia, and Herzegovina. These "borderline Serbs" who survived the holocaust were brought up on communist ideology and hatred of "fascism," a term that originally lumped together Croat Ustashe, German Nazis, and Italian Fascists but later came to include the entire world of "Western imperialism." These two populations contributed more than anyone during Tito's "national liberation struggle" against "foreign occupation and domestic traitors."

After the war, communist propaganda never properly addressed the problem of mutual slaughter, making collective grievances almost impossible to work through openly. Tito's soft totalitarianism imposed the official ideology of "brotherhood and unity" which managed to suppress dissidence and discussion in any direction. That is why Serbs in Bosnia and Croatia saw any move toward the breakup of Yugoslavia as a return of "fascism" and implemented their own version of genocidal revenge on Bosniak and Croat populations at the beginning of the latest war. The Slovene call from the Alpine heights resounded with frightening clarity in the blood of those whose ancestors were sacrificed on the altar of Hitler's "new European order" (Debeljak 1994).

In contrast to Dvorniković, folk song was often seen by the communist "cultural workers" as a separatist or chauvinist tool that could undermine political unity, since folk song was rooted in the "blood and soil" of local, regional identity. Folk songs were often identified as Serbian, Croatian, Bosnian, Macedonian, or Slovene and participated in the creation of folkloristic performances which displayed "civilizational" particularities. In order to produce "proletarian culture," the Yugoslav communist establishment often masked differences by sponsoring folk music societies and professional folk singing and dancing ensembles (Čolović 1984, 1994).

Yugoslavs living outside urban centers usually identified with the local folkloric heritage as the essence of their being and belonging, while the state tried to promote the concept of "Yugoslav" folklore through local "cultural-artistic societies." Their performances usually began with the performance of a "Yugoslav" number, which was supposed to accent the official "brotherhood and unity." Each of the constituent nations was represented by a song or a dance which was then choreographed into a medley with musical transitions between them, forming what came to be known as a "plait of folk songs and dances." This musical version of the Communist Party platform was supposed to promote inter-ethnic confidence and understanding by blending the folk songs of various ethnic groups. After the "fall of communism," the musical plait was disentangled along "civilizational" fault lines, producing a new staging of a mix of racial and cultural pride which accompanied mass political rallies of the late 1980s. The rise of turbo folk in Serbia was part of the same political current that countered the Titoist version of multicultural communism in the name of Pan-Serbian self-determination. Thus the tremendous popularity of Lepa Brena came at the same time as the communist system began to fade away under the pressures exerted by the emergent nationalist leadership in Serbia. This Serbian version of a folk Madonna with a Barbie look was the first one to introduce synthesizers and rhythm machines along with the traditional accordions and violins, co-opting musical technology from rock culture to reinforce dynamism and eroticism in her recordings and performances. Lepa Brena could be called the mother of turbo folk, which now dominates the musical scene in Serbia and parts of the eastern Balkans (Dragićević-Šešić 1994).

The appropriation of rock idiom and instrumentation in Serbia was preceded by the rise of the currently best known alternative band from the "other" Europe. Musical articulations of Slovenian cultural supremacy appeared in pseudo-parodic performances of Laibach in the decade preceding the latest Yugoslav war. This post-punk band used a variety of totalitarian images to promote itself. The Yugoslav communist identity was built on the premise of fighting German Nazism, so the insistence of Slovene performers on giving themselves a German name was very controversial. With strong roots in conceptual art, Laibach's musical performances featured overidentification with the political power in the form of military uniforms, calls for abolition of individuality, and submission to the will of the state. Laibach is a German name for Ljubljana, the capital of Slovenia. Thriving on the ambivalent reactions of the cultural and political establishment, Laibach grew into a hierarchically organized art movement which also gave itself a German name: Neue slowenische Kunst.

By invoking Austrian and German colonial presence in Slovenia, the band caused an uncanny feeling among general audiences. Most of the urban youth took it as sarcastic retro-fitting, while some officials protested, threatening bans and legal action. By displaying swastika-like symbols and singing almost exclusively in German, Laibach not only performed Slovene cultural separation from the Balkans and its embrace of *Mitteleuropa*, but also laid bare the trappings of communist totalitarianism. The critical distance that rock culture nurtured in the 1960s and 1970s was replaced by the erasure of distance and parodic identification with the aggressor. This is how Laibach answered the question about the Slovene character of their music:

> The creative ability of the artist identifies with the national spirit. Every artist carries within him certain (ethnic) characteristics, which are the result of a common origin and kindred lifestyle of a group of people over a longer historical period. These characteristics are reflected in his work. It is impossible to imagine Cervantes or Leonardo as Russians, Voltaire and Verdi as Germans, Dostoyevski and Wagner as Italians or LAIBACH as Yugoslavs. (New Collectivism 1991: 43–44)

By identifying themselves as protagonists of Slovene and not Yugoslav art, Laibach offered the best articulation of a model of cultural separation in all parts of the country toward the end of the decade. Laibach's call became clear only after Slovenia demanded separation from the "eastern tide of chaos": we are part of white Europe and the West because "our," Slovene, music is much more sophisticated than that of the other, "primitive" Yugoslavs. Interestingly, Laibach's statement uses the same theories of "national character" invoked by Dvorniković, except that the sense of "our" song is now applicable only to Slovenia, not to all of Yugoslavia.

During the last decade of communist rule in Yugoslavia, belonging to a different cultural and civilizational framework became the central metaphor of a new type of ethnic totalitarianism with tacit racial undertones. Naturalized cultural differences which stood in the way of Dvorniković when he tried to provide an inclusive definition of "our" song as a collective voice of the Yugoslav race reappeared as the communist control over public life gradually weakened after Tito's death. Cultural differentiation in the realm of folk music is based on a claim that Slovene polkas and accordions are part of the Germanic-dominated Central European heritage, while Macedonian songs reflect half a millennium of Ottoman Turkish influences based on *zurle* and drums. By contrasting Slovene Northwest with Macedonian Southeast, racial differentialists claim that there can be no common life between Europe and Asia, between the West and the East, between the North and the South. Although all of the territory of former Yugoslavia was geographically situated in Europe, the symbolic geography instituted by multiple invasions, occupations, and colonizations structured a differential identity for each member of a particular Yugoslav ethnic group. For example, Bosniaks' horizon of identity could always be extended to include Istanbul as "one's own" site, Croats' to include Rome and Berlin, and Serbs' to include Athens and Moscow. This extension of Slavic racial identity made the possibility of a Yugoslav breakup along "civilizational" fault lines realizable within a framework of this new "differentialist" form of racism.

These particular identities have been internalizing the gaze of West European Romantics who envisioned them as "noble savages" striving toward independence from empires that were slowly ending their presence during the nineteenth century. After the formation of the first Yugoslav state, the attempt was made to imagine a culture based on common Slavic "brotherhood" which tried to "integrally" assimilate non-Slavic races by imagining a cultural vision of Dinaric-based identity of shared historical destiny of subjugated peoples. Dvorniković's work was a crown of that effort published way too late, as is often the case in the Balkans, since Yugoslavia had only two years of life before it was dismembered as part of Hitler's vision of the "new European order" ruled by Nordic races. The North and the West reasserted themselves as superior terms within the racist symbolic geography that continues to structure Eurocentric conceptions of identity and otherness. Yugo-Slavs remain locked within this classification as Yugo-Slaves, as peoples whose songs and dances entertain and provoke nostalgia for an imaginary originality of being which belongs to the East, while their dreadful bloodsheds awaken the need of the West to simultaneously distance itself culturally while imposing military order on these unruly races of the South.

During the Second World War, "brotherly" blood was shed along "civilizational" lines, proving that Balibar's theory that *culture replaces nature* functions in ordinary racism as well: Ustashe exterminated hundreds of thousands of Serbs during the Second World War because they were perceived as people of a lower civilizational standard who occupied Croatian *Lebensraum*. What defined Serbs as racial others was their adherence to Christian Orthodoxy and the use of the Cyrillic script. The common language was replaced by Croatian, books in Cyrillic were burned and Serbs converted to Catholicism (becoming Croats), expelled across the river Drina into Serbia, or exterminated in Jasenovac or elsewhere.

Serbian conquests in the Wars of Yugoslav Succession (1991–95) were culturally coded through the discourse of revenge for all past injustices, including Croat and Bosniak collaboration with the Nazis in the Second World War. The creation of detention camps and mass slaughter of Bosnian and Croat civilians is a repetition of a scenario that Serbs in Bosnia and Croatia implemented as a result of their own "identification with the aggressor." With strength in numbers and weapons provided by years of Tito's buildup to protect his brand of communist "Yugoslavism," the Serbs set out to create a common state structure by occupying "their own" territories in Croatia and Bosnia, after these two Yugoslav republics demanded full independence and excluded Serbs from their vision of the new state. Serbs imagined themselves as the adhesive that made Yugoslavia possible, while assimilating differences into their notion of an "integral" sense of cultural identity. When the end of communism left nothing of Yugoslavia to adhere to, they began to wage war for a common Serbian state and sing about their own superiority as lovers and warriors who fight not only against the brothers who betrayed the dream of a common state, but also against the whole world (Morgan 1995).

War songs foreground Freud's "narcissism of minor differences" with horrifying symptoms of that particular European disease that burdens the Balkan singer. Ever since Yugoslavia began to come apart in the late

1980s and imploded in 1991, folk song underwent a drastic redefinition. An uncanny hybridization of musical forms and traditions has taken place as a result of new music technologies. While accordion and violin remain dominant instruments, musical arrangements now include electric guitars, rhythm machines, and synthesizers. An especially frightening hybrid entitled "Srbi supermeni" (Serbs supermen), which could be characterized as war rap, concludes a recently released CD entitled *Srpske omiljene ratne pesme* (Serbian favorite war songs). After the main theme has been introduced on the accordion, the rap segment with vocals and rhythm machine proclaims in a refrain:

> We are Serbs supermen
> We wage war against the whole world
> we are ready for the holy war
> even if it lasts a hundred years. (track 20)

These lines demonstrate how a culture nurtured on stories of racial and historical victimization can easily transform their status of "international pariah" into a position of "superhuman" strength.

This song is the most sobering example of what the unresolved consequences of World War II genocide and present global isolation and Western diplomatic and military intervention have done to the collective identity of the Serbs in Bosnia. Regarded as the main perpetrators of genocide in the Bosnian war, they further embrace xenophobic cultural values and prepare for the "holy war" against the rest of the world. The notion of Islamic *jihad* was assimilated into the culture of colonized Christian "serfs" during half a millennium of Ottoman rule in the Balkans. The postcolonial appropriation of the master's metaphors of domination becomes most obvious in war songs, as race and gender are performed as signs of one's own superiority.

A subculture of ethnic war songs sprouted overnight, especially among the more extreme wings of the Serbian and Croatian paramilitary groups. The musical content was often very similar, with the texts offering diametrically opposed visions of the war. The format for the dissemination of war songs was the home-made audio cassette, which was easy to record and distribute through vendors on city streets. Alongside the new arrangements of the Serbian Chetnik and Croatian Ustashe songs that were banned in socialist Yugoslavia, this genre contained a lot of newly composed war songs as well. One of the pearls of Croatian home recording production is UNPROFOR Big Band, whose cassette title invokes the vagina of someone's mother, the most common curse in Serbo-Croatian: "Svima njima pizda materina." The illustration on the cassette cover shows a monkey with a blue United Nations helmet holding an automatic rifle, which is an obvious commentary on the number of black soldiers in the United Nations Protection Force in the Serb-held territories of Croatia. It is symptomatic that the Croatian authorities have even demanded that all UN soldiers from African countries be removed from Croatia, because of their "incompatible cultural values."

The problematic masculinity, tied to ethnic identity, is revealed in these songs with frightening clarity. The songs of UNPROFOR Big Band are saturated with obscenities, whose gender component reveals some of the cultural mechanisms that have been deeply suppressed before the war. The song "Oj, Šešelju, pederska guzico" (Hey, Šešelj, you faggot asshole), devoted to the leader of the extreme right-wing Serbian Radical Party, brings into the dialectic of war the play of the active–passive partners in homosexual intercourse.

> Hey Šešelj, hey Šešelj
> concerning Karlobag [a city in Croatia]
> you can get, you can get
> a prick up your ass. (Luković 1992: 31)

The passivization and feminization of the political opponent, who is then defiled through rape, serves to enhance and strengthen the Croatian sense of masculinity and racial superiority. The symbolic rape of Vojislav Šešelj, whose aim was to incorporate the Serbian ethnic territories in Croatia and Bosnia, is a message of what is awaiting Serbs who do not submit to Croat rule. The deeper cultural layer of homophobia reveals the affinity between the ethnic rivals; Croatian and Serbian right-wingers actually share the same set of values, which makes them lust for the racial Other of the same sex. This repression of homoeroticism leads to the literal killing of those whom they really lust for, since the "civilizational" prohibitions will not allow such a coupling within the extremely patriarchal Balkan environment. Another song from this cassette, devoted to the leaders of the Bosnian Serbs, "Karadžiću, majmune sa grane" (Karadžić, monkey on a branch), has a stanza that confirms this repressed homoerotic fascination with the racial "Other":

> My prick is piercing the long-johns
> hey Mladić, give me a blow job
> the flak jacket may save you
> but certainly not from the back. (ibid. 30)

This time, General Ratko Mladić, the military commander of the Bosnian Serbs, is invited to perform sexual acts that are perceived as demeaning to his manhood and heroism.

While the Ustashe seem keen on demonstrating their masculine power to the Serbs, the Chetnik songs are usually saturated with a sense of resentment that gives rise to the historical alibis for their "ethnic cleansing" operations. A song entitled "Znaš, Srbine, kad smo bili mali" (Remember, Serb, when we were little) goes back to the First World War to find roots of Serbian suffering:

> You know, Serb, when we were little
> in 1914 when we were whispering
> we could not get together in groups of two or three
> but had to say that we were all Croats. (ibid. 31)

The song describes the situation in Bosnia during the Austrian occupation, when Serbs could not freely exhibit their national identity but had to pretend that they were Croats in order not to be killed or sent to prison. The singer, Veselin Grujić Vesa, insists on "Orthodox religion and the Cyrillic script" as the signs of national difference from the Croats. Another singer, Baja Mali Knindža, sings that

> ever since God created humans
> always others come to judge us
> always someone bothers the Serbs
> that's why in Bosnia there's no peace. (ibid. 30)

Most of the new "war songs" created by the Serbs have a tendency to assign the blame for the Yugoslav conflict to someone else, who is usually outside the Balkans.

The central metaphor that informs the process of political and cultural "postmodernization" after Yugoslavia is a return to the neomedieval conceptions of one's own identity. In Serbia proper, the new political elites who desired separation did everything to promote a return of identity based on patriotism, Orthodox Christianity, and national pride. At the same time, "new folk" music was intentionally given more air time on the radio and television at the expense of domestic and foreign rock music. The triumph of nationalism caused not only a return to religious fundamentalism, racist stereotyping, and intolerance, but also a cultural domination of a new folk music which appropriated elements of rock and hip-hop idioms to broaden its appeal to Serbian urban audiences. This process resulted in the appearance of turbo folk, a musical genre which prevails in Serbia today.

The most conspicuous fact about turbo folk is the ease with which it absorbs and blends cultural elements which appear to be mutually exclusive. The singing is almost entirely in the tradition of the "new folk" that has been present in the Yugoslav popular culture since the 1960s. The rhythm is borrowed from techno and hip-hop, its abundant use of machines and synthesizers derived from the global influence of African-American rhythm. This is blended with the accompaniment of instruments typically used in traditional folk songs, dominated by the accordion and violin. The preferred medium for the dissemination of turbo folk is a music video, with an entire television channel *(Palma)* devoted to the songs of turbo folk stars. Consequently, the image of the performers becomes much more important than it used to be in the "new folk" music before the 1990s. As a rule, the turbo folk singer is female, with looks that fit into the race and gender demands of Western musical performers: short skirts, screaming makeup, heavy golden chains, rings, and bracelets, with the local addition of the obligatory Orthodox cross around her neck. To contrast this surface image of whiteness, the singing is distinctly "oriental," with an abundance of vibrato punctuated by eroticized dancing in the combination of "folk" and "techno" styles.

Most of the music videos display longing for European economic "whiteness" by grotesque emulations of the "lifestyles of the rich and famous" in the country which lived through an undeclared war and a global economic embargo. The dress of the performers is conspicuously "Western," modeled on images borrowed from foreign television commercials. Music spots feature women taking bubble baths, posing in front of the latest models of Porsches or BMWs, or revealing sexy black lace underwear. By creating a tele-musical fantasy structure about Serbs as "heavenly people" who remain beautiful and vital despite all the hardships imposed from the outside, turbo folk enables the Serbs to feel they are participating in the "Western" construction of whiteness and Europe at the same time as they are economically, politically and culturally excluded from it (Tompson 1995).

One of the stranger characteristics of these new songs is the fact that they ignore the "original" Serbian folk songs by openly displaying the "oriental" musical heritage rooted in Ottoman colonial presence on the Balkan peninsula. Most of the singers use a particular technique of nasal singing, which provides their songs with a specific "oriental" color. Most of the initial mega-stars of the "new folk" music were in fact Muslims— the "two Halids" as they were called in the 1980s, Halid Bešlić and Halid Muslimović. The female superstar from this initial period, Lepa Brena, was also a Muslim by heritage; her real name is Fahreta Jahić. The "oriental" character of the songs and their performers is paradoxical, since the Serbs have regarded Turks and Muslims in general as their national "other" ever since their own post-colonial sense of tragedy after the loss at Kosovo.[3]

Half a millennium later, Serbian popular favorites sounded as if they were produced in the heart of an "oriental" empire. During the past five years, the Serbs have historically and culturally been identified with the role Europe had reserved for the Ottomans during the nineteenth century. They represent the "sick man of Europe," whose slavery to the Turks had transformed them into a collectivity of living dead who sing about love and pain in the voice of their former colonial masters. The song represents a connection to "heavenly Serbia," a realm attained by the collective spilling of blood on the Kosovo field in 1389 which is historically invested with the anger of those whose desires had been frustrated by betrayal by both their women and their ethnic Others. Only a couple of years after the introduction of the "oriental" sound in the form of turbo folk, the tide of nationalist euphoria pushed the Serbs into "ethnic cleansing" operations against Muslims in Bosnia, making the popularity of the "two Halids" even more ironic. How could the eruption of "orientalism" in folk music coincide with the extermination of those whose ancestors converted to Islam centuries ago (Vgrešić 1994)?

Turbo folk is the sound of an unacknowledged postcolonial culture that had been dormant under the communist veil of forgetfulness until the latest war. The techno rhythms are embraced from the colonial cultures to the North and the West (Europe proper) as markers of racial/cultural superiority, while the wailing voice of the singer articulates a suppressed, shameful legacy of one's slavery to the Turks who are regarded as a part of the inferior cultures and races of the East and South. At the same time, this music reveals the emptiness of myths of racial and ethnic authenticity, since turbo folk almost features a hybrid culture produced by the combination of musical importations from the past and present colonial masters. Turbo folk fit perfectly into the emergent nationalist culture of the late 1980s and the war culture of the early 1990s, since it foregrounded a zero-degree identity of technological dynamism and emotional depth, which could easily be blended with the political rhetoric about age-old Serbian pride and desire for independence.

This new identity is defined by the desire for inclusion into the symbolic realm of European "whiteness" which is manifested in the presence of the adjective "turbo" in the name of the musical genre. The incessant repetition of the techno beat is a ritual meant to insure their belonging to the West, which has never recognized them as its own part. The place of the Serbs within the West is defined by the Latin etymology of their proper name (*servus*, Lat. "servant, serf, slave"). This abject position makes them "black" despite their genetic "whiteness" in the eyes of the West. In order to entice the gaze of the West, new Serbian singers engage in musical performances rooted in the combination of the most archaic and the most modern. On the one hand, Serbian treatment of the Ottoman colonial heritage comes from the Christian crusading mythology which manifests European fear of contamination with an alien, "oriental" civilization. At the same time, turbo folk features the "oriental" sound as the essence of racial being and belonging, which it appropriates from the culture of Ottoman invaders as a metaphor of its own colonial power over other Yugoslav ethnic groups. Dvorniković's vision of the Yugoslav race voiced by the wailing song of Dinaric highlanders has been "balkanized" by the particular voices of new "cultural racism" which predominates after the latest Yugoslav war. As Croats sing "Danke Deutchland" (Thank you, Germany) to the sponsors of their secession from Yugoslavia and Serbs glorify the "ethnic cleansing" of Muslims with songs like "Miloš tera stoku preko Save" (Miloš drives the cattle across the Sava River), (*SORP*, track 4), the uncanny presence of hatred of other "Yugoslavs" and megalomaniac glorification of one's own newly invented "people" bears witness to the direction that European conceptions of folk music and race will take in the next millennium.

NOTES

1. Most of Dvorniković's critique of the superiority of Nordic "racial style" comes from reading Ludvig F. Clauss, *Rasse und Seele: Eine Einführung in den Sinn der leiblichen Gestalt* (Munich, 1934), and *Die nordische Seele: Eine Einführung in die Rassenseelenkunde* (Munich, 1936).

2. "Serbo-communist" is term used by the Croatian state media in responding to "aggression" by the local Serb population, which was forced into the embrace of their brethren east of the river Drina. Freud's famous definition of nationalism fits well into the Yugoslav picture since the differences are truly minor in comparison to other postcolonial moments (*Civilisation and Its Discontents* [London: Hogarth, 1961], 114).

3. The Serbian vision of national identity is rooted in the discourse of revenge for the loss of independence after the battle of Kosovo in 1389. The target of revenge is Turks and local converts to Islam in Bosnia, Sandžak, Montenegro, and Kosovo itself.

BIBLIOGRAPHY

Balibar, Etienne, and Immanuel Wallerstein. 1991. *Race, Nation, Class: Ambiguous Identities.* London: Verso.

Čolović, Ivan. *Divlja književnost: etnolingvističko proučavanje paraliterature* [Wild literature: Ethnolinguistic study of paraliterature]. Belgrade: Nolit.

———. 1994. *Pucanje od zdravlja* Belgrade: Beogradski krug.

Debeljak, Aleš. 1994. *Twilight of the Idols: Recollections of a Lost Yugoslavia.* Fredonia: White Pine Press.

Dragićević-Šešić, Milena. 1994. *Neofolk kultura: publika i njene zvezde* [Neofolk culture: The audience and its stars]. Sremski Karlovci: Zoran Stojanović.

Dvorniković, Vladimir. 1939. *Karakterologija Jugoslovena.* [The characterology of the Yugoslavs]. Belgrade: Geca Kon.

Hayden, Robert, and Milica Bakić-Hayden. 1992. "Orientalist Variations on 'The Balkans.'" *Slavic Review* 13: 1–15.

Luković, Petar. 1992. "Šta pevaju Srbi i Hrvati?" [What Do Serbs & Croats Sing?]. *Vreme* (30 Nov): 29–32.

Morgan, Peter. 1995. "War Music." *Planet* 114: 32–38.

New Collectivism, ed. 1991. *Neue slowenische Kunst.* Los Angeles: AMOK Books.

Ramet, Pedro. 1985. "Apocalypse Culture and Social Change in Yugoslavia." In *Yugoslavia in the 1980's*, ed. Pedro Ramet. Boulder, Colo.: Westview.

Tompson, Mark. 1995. *Proizvodnja rata: mediji u Srbiji, Hrvatskoj i Bosni i Hercegovini.* Belgrade: Radio B92.

Trifunović, Brano. 1993. *Omiljene srpske ratne pesme* [Favorite Serbian war songs], vol. 1, CD-9308.

Ugrešić, Dubravka. 1994. "Folksies." *Erewhon* 1: 121–43.

UNPROFOR Big Band. 1991. *Svima njima pizda materina* [May they all go back to their mothers' cunts]: *Special Song from Slavonia.* Audiocassette. Home production.

Žižek, Slavoj. 1994. *The Metastases of Enjoyment: Six Essays on Women and Causality.* London: Verso.

20

The Remembrance of Things Past: Music, Race, and the End of History in Modern Europe

PHILIP V. BOHLMAN

"Ah, here comes Herr Klesmer," said Mrs Arrowpoint, rising; and presently bringing him to Gwendolen she left them to a dialogue which was agreeable on both sides, Herr Klesmer being a felicitous combination of the German, the Sclave, and the Semite, with grand features, brown hair floating in artistic fashion, and brown eyes in spectacles. His English had little foreignness except in its fluency; and his alarming cleverness was made less formidable just then by a certain softening air of silliness which will sometimes befall even Genius in the desire of being agreeable to Beauty.

Music was soon begun.[1]

(George Eliot, *Daniel Deronda*)

FACING RACE

The faces of Muslim refugees, lining the aisles of the buses taking them from Srebrenica and Žepče in the wake of the fall of those Bosnian cities in the summer of 1995, are silently and shockingly familiar as they appear in front-page newspaper photographs. Gazing at the photograph—one of many on the front pages of countless newspapers in the summer of 1995, a specter that would be all too familiar when seen again in the spring and summer of 1999, when Kosovar faces replaced Bosnian faces—we follow these faces toward the back of the bus, as they retreat row upon row, until they turn into shadows and then simply disappear into shapelessness. In the last decade of the twentieth century, these are the faces of race. That they are Bosnians or Kosovars makes them also Europeans, but they are Europeans without place. Their placelessness results from the convergence of many histories. They are Muslims, and the historical construction of Europe has been Christian, with the Islamic world undeniably the most threatening historical other. They are residents of places where, for centuries, Europe's politics of otherness has played itself out. The capital city of the Bosnian refugees, Sarajevo, symbolizes Europe's explosive mixture of imperialism and nationalism, framing the historical moment, the twentieth century, when that mixture proved most deadly. It is the bus that reminds us of the placelessness of the Bosnian Muslims or the Kosovar Albanians, for the bus takes them from a place denied to one now promised. But there are other buses waiting, other places to go.

At the end of the twentieth century the bus plying the border regions of Europe has become the latest in a series of vehicles that serve as a metaphor mobilizing the imagination of race in Europe. Buses provide transportation for those who do not belong and who cannot afford the federal railways. It is buses that guest workers take as they return home to Slovakia or Turkey or Macedonia. Buses are the vehicle of choice for pilgrims in search of faith and healing. Above all, the buses plying the European racial imagination pass silently across the map of modern Europe. When we notice them at all, it is at border crossings, where they stand, packed into their own special lane, making it easier for border guards to prevent them from taking something that belongs in one place to another place. Even at the border crossings, the faces of the travelers remain largely unknown, for there is a certain danger in disembarking before reaching the final destination. Rather than explain oneself, it's simply easier to stay in the bus.

The European buses with the placeless aboard in effect make a place for race by creating alternatives, however fragile and deadly, for those not fitting the prevailing models of nationalism, ethnicity, religious community, and citizenship. In this essay I turn frequently to this lack of belonging as I concern myself with the European racial imagination, not because that lack of belonging defines race but because it contains the conditions for race. Throughout European history, race has been a problem of defining and enforcing distances between those who belong and those who do not. The ultimate act of racializing is the denial of place, that is, the removal of conditions of belonging.[2] Denied the possibility of land ownership in most of Europe until the nineteenth century, Jews constituted a race apart. In the European imagination constantly in motion, Roma, Sinti, and other Gypsy groups fitted the fundamental characteristics of race.[3] European history is filled with other rhetorical denials of place, for example the Western European claims that government and civilization were impossible in Eastern Europe, which in turn remained amorphous terra incognita on the maps of Europe itself (Wolff 1994; see also Applebaum 1994). With no place to go, race became an obsessive nuisance in Europe's imagination of itself.

In this essay I examine the place and placelessness of race in Europe as components of the struggle to find space for competing histories, particularly in the New Europe that is being charted on the map of a new century. Historically, music has provided one of the most powerful languages for the inscription of this struggle. As a performative medium, music fills and then empties a temporal moment; depending on what experience that performativity evokes, music may give very different meanings to history itself. More traditionally, music is thought to possess the capacity to undergird memory. Just as memory requires that the space of history be filled with information sufficiently explanatory to bound that space, it may force out other information, thereby depending equally on forgetting. Europe's racial imagination, I argue, also forms in the competition between remembering and forgetting to claim space in history.

Music functions powerfully to facilitate both remembering and forgetting, but it is precisely that contradiction that makes it so suggestive as a means of interpellating the European racial imagination. This essay will initially seem unusual in its emphasis on music as a means to forget. Far more commonly, music is important to the interpretation of culture and history as a mnemonic device, literally a tool for remembering. Oral and written traditions dovetail in music, one undergirding the other; what notation does not capture with its inscription of the surface, the deeper structures of style communicate. These are the traits of music that folklorists describe and privilege as narrative and then construct as genres, such as ballads and epics, both of which are further valued for their capacity to narrate history itself.[4] Even such commonplace assumptions about music as a language for remembering bear witness to it as a force for forgetting. The musical landscapes of Europe form around this uneasy dialectic and more often than not admit to its irreconcilability. As a means of negotiating between past and present, then, music allows us both to enter into history and to exit from it, or, more aptly, in Eva Hoffman's ironic turn of phrase, to "exit into history" (1993).

PLACING RACE

Race occupies an elusive position in the historiographical competition for remembered and forgotten pasts. On one hand, the categories of race simplistically define the other, the outsider, those who by definition of their race do not belong. For medieval Europeans and in many parts of Europe well into the nineteenth century, race was not a particularly problematic distinction, because there was no question that those marked by racial difference, for example, Jews or Muslims, could own land; by law, the racially different could not acquire a place in Europe. Only when the racially different began to find a place in Europe—physically, geographically, and culturally—did the hard and fast categories of race begin to deteriorate. Deterioration, however, did not lead to disappearance, but rather race began to find its way into other constructions of place in Europe: in the nineteenth and early twentieth century, nationalism; and in the late twentieth century, ethnicity. Lurking behind the constructions of nation and ethnic group in Europe, race waits for contested moments to be remembered back into history, for example when "ethnic cleansing" provides the Balkan Serbs with a racial claim to Croatian, Bosnian, and Kosovar lands.

As the military enjoinder for ethnic cleansing makes all too clear, the competition for place that race mobilizes further results from the fear of pollution and contamination, processes of racial mixture that occur at the border. Contamination, therefore, jars the nationalist on the radical right into recognizing that the war against race is being lost, for cultural pollution is only possible when the borders that separate self from other are permeable. The problem of contamination has plagued European constructions of music to an inordinate degree. Musical categories were only possible when they remained unpolluted, when the Italian style was completely unlike the French style, each bearing witness to histories (as opposed to music histories) in which pure, national style asserted itself.[5] Music makes ethnic and racial contestation legible precisely because of its imprecision. By claiming that a particular stylistic trait is also a racial marker, the conditions for the disintegration or absence of that marker also enter the representational vocabulary of the racial imagination.[6] Race, as Larry Wolff has observed in Enlightenment accounts about Eastern Europe, emerges as a form of comprehension that grows from incomprehensibility (1994: 18–19, 332–55).

Race does not have single forms in Europe, past or present, nor does it lend itself to single definitions. Because it is elusive, it may have other names: nationalism, ethnicity, religious group, even family and civilization. Names and the ideological strategies they muster and mask, therefore, ensure that race is many things in Europe and that the agendas of racializing constantly shift. These shifts between remembering and forgetting ascribe agency to the European racial imagination, and it is this process of imagining race that I interrogate in this essay. Rhetorically, I organize the essay as a representation of sites of remembering and forgetting, charting the musical landscape of Europe. In particular, I consider the problems of remembering and forgetting that characterize boundary regions and border conflicts, those areas of the map in which it is most difficult to lay claim to place.[7] Music on the border and in the boundary regions is hybridized and contaminated, a mix of competing sounds and languages that bears witness to the paradoxical ability of music to ascribe and alter identity.

Borders and boundary regions, moreover, provide the most visible demarcations on maps, therefore ascribing to maps a metonymic quality that will be important throughout this essay. That a map is a construction, of course, and not a form of reality goes without saying (see Turnbull 1993). The roads and borderlines of the map are mere inscriptions, so approximate as to rely on a considerable degree of imagination (Wetherell and Potter 1992). The inscription of imagination on a map, I wish to suggest, is akin to the notations of music and the inscription of music through notation. Our experience of music, then, requires that we imagine the relation between the sonic experience of the present and the ways in which those of the past have been mapped.

By suggesting the metonymic connections between mapping the landscapes of Europe and inscribing representations of music, I follow a traditional practice, developed by musical scholars during the nineteenth century precisely at the moment when nationalism was becoming particularly important and significant. Locating music on the maps of Europe produced atlases for folklorists and "folk-song landscapes" (Volksliedlandschaften) for folk-song scholars. These musical maps not only projected the racial imagination onto the political maps of Europe, but in many ways provided the front guard for their implementation through political, even military, action. Demonstrating where the national and linguistic borders were, the folk-song landscapes revealed that music ignored those borders, thereby justifying a need to reconsider their placement.

EFFACING RACE

Just as the place of music and race begins to produce a map with roads and boundaries that, in turn, yield other forms of identity, so does the map of racial identity begin to evoke a sense of reality, asserting that the place of performed music really belongs to those songs filling it. The sense of ownership especially accrues to songs that have occupied a place the longest. Longevity itself, measured by an early form of scale or style of melody known nowhere else, or maintained by the persistence of dialect or ritual practices that seemingly refuse to change,[8] justifies the claim to space, overriding other claims with insufficient evidence from the past. Music not only makes history in this way, it inscribes it directly onto the map of the imagination. The spaces in a scale or those required for ritual and social performances of the community undergo a process of translation, making them isomorphic with the places of the culture itself. Historically, the place of culture marks time in different ways, ranging from the timeless past of the Celtic periphery of Europe, embedded in its repertories of pentatonic *a cappella* choral music (Chapman 1994), to the roots of civilization that the pentatonic scales and church modes of German folk song in Eastern Europe have maintained (Waldmann 1938b).

By concerning myself with the ways in which music maps race onto the places of Europe, I join Martin Stokes and others (see especially the essays in Stokes 1994), but I extend the notion that music performs a place into being even further. Racializing agendas powerfully motivate the ways musical evidence claims space. Music draws the map for one community, group, or nation but leaves no space for others. This inscriptional move, I argue, racializes the use of musical evidence by tying it specifically to space. Music becomes an agent for effacing race.

I have written this essay so that my text itself becomes metonymic with the entry into and exit from history, that is, the competition for spaces in which the racial imagination shapes itself as a means of mapping the landscapes of the past, present, and future. There is surely an ambiguous quality that such rhetorical positioning reveals, namely that the boundary between my theorizing and my descriptions of the theorizing of others will at times be blurred. The connections I draw between music's capacity to remember and forget, and a map's capacity representationally to draw our attention to a claim for reality or away from it—these connections arise from the intentional use of musical maps to represent alternative Europes. The fact remains that musical scholars use maps to create knowledge and power, and the musical landscapes of Europe bear stark witness to these practices.

The juxtaposition of maps and music, moreover, inevitably juxtaposes space and time. Or rather, mapping music on the landscape gives the latter a temporal quality while returning a spatial quality to the former. When used to define Europe and locate its historically meaningful places, mapping acquires a temporal quality, which derives even more power from music's inherently temporal quality. A musical map allows one, therefore, to pass between the present and the past, as in the eighteenth-century traveler's journey to Eastern Europe (Wolff 1994) or the nineteenth-century collector's journey into the most distant mountain valley, where the true origins of folk song are to be found (Bruinier 1927). The question that arises, then, is whether the place claimed by music acquires or loses its human inhabitants. And if there are human inhabitants, are they, by their nature, able to claim the place when civilization makes its claim? Music may resolve the conflict between nature and civilization, but only after the evidence it provides substitutes one group's claim to place for another's. In its journeys on the maps of Europe, then, music erases and effaces, it justifies the power that creates placelessness, and it takes its place in the European racial imagination.

SITES OF MUSIC IN EUROPE

Upon defeat in World War I, Germany not only lost its military claims to lands taken through the expansionist politics of Bismarck and Wilhelm I, it was also severed from the regions and communities of German-speaking residents, the *Sprachinseln* (speech islands), which had been an essential component in the imagination of Europe as culturally German. The music of speech islands had long provided fundamental evidence for connecting Germanness to the speech islands: music preserved repertories and dialects from the past; it possessed both the regional markers of the place from which colonists[9] came, yet also songs in High German that symbolized the common denominator of civilization;[10] songs in speech islands both contained local place references yet, at least if one took repertories as a whole, persisted in retaining place references in Germany; and, finally, German repertories presumably failed to show traces from the music of surrounding communities. Song, especially, entered into the ideological claims made for speech islands, for the texts of song epitomized the function of speech itself, as a means of transporting the past to the present and giving it a modern context.

German musical scholarship, particularly the fields of folklore and folk-song research, had depended on the German musical evidence beyond the drastically reduced borders of a Germany defeated in World War I. The dependence was at some levels entirely practical. The German Folk-Song Archive in Freiburg im Breisgau (see Holzapfel 1989), founded by John Meier in 1914, did not actually include a staff of researchers who themselves collected folk songs, that is, who undertook fieldwork, but rather the archive benefited from individuals in German-speaking groups or living in German speech islands throughout Europe who sent examples of songs, from printed sources or transcribed from performance. Germany's defeat in World War I meant, in effect, that the opportunity to build a central repository with evidence from the peripheries had become impossible. The loss of the sources for evidence, furthermore, thwarted the historical agendas of German folk-song scholarship, which had depended on creating a seamless philological fabric whose very seamlessness connected the emergence of Germanic culture in the Middle Ages with the present and created a narrative of Germanic history that enveloped early modern and modern Europe.[11] German musical scholars, then, were confronted with the problem of recuperating and reinvigorating the evidence for the place of Germany in modern European history.

It was to redress this attenuated connection to the evidence and the shrunken map of Germany that Johannes Bolte, Max Friedländer, and John Meier launched the publishing project they called *Landschaftliche Volkslieder* (Folk songs in their landscapes) in 1924. Based at the German Folk-Song Archive and sponsored by national scholarly organizations, the *Landschaftliche Volkslieder* took shape as a series of individual volumes, each pocket-sized, indeed in exactly the practical format used commonly for the ubiquitous songbooks of German singing societies. Each volume would represent a single place, that is, a single landscape, with its distinctive musical map. Though initiated in the wake of World War I, the volumes of *Landschaftliche Volkslieder* continued to appear until 1971, reaching a total of 43 volumes. The history of this mapping of German culture, therefore, intersected with the most dramatic and devastating periods of twentieth-century

European history, indeed, musically representing that history (see Bohlman 2000).

The volume that mapped each landscape bore as many connections to that landscape as possible. Each volume, for example, should be published by a press located in that landscape, whenever possible, of course. Volume 1 fulfilled this goal, appearing in Breslau (Polish Wrocław), the capital of Silesia (Siebs and Schneider 1924). Silesia had long been one of the most contested areas on the eastern border of Prussia, with a very plural population of Poles, Germans, and Jews. The songs forming the Silesian landscape show no evidence of this contestation, except insofar as they conform entirely to the stereotypical map of German historical influence. The first half of the volume contains songs in High German; the second half balances the first by including German dialect songs, many with local place references. In order to evoke and specify place more intensely, that is, to make place unforgettable, many of the volumes devoted to speech islands employed drawings of the cities and streets where the songs had been collected (cf. Brandsch and Schullerus 1932 and Deutsches Volksliedarchiv 1930, the first devoted to the Siebenbürgen [Transylvania/western Romania] Colonies of Eastern Europe, the second to the Gottschee Colonies in Slovenia). These images of place strengthened the connection of song to place and also succeeded in locating both in the historical past, by using *Fraktur* typeface and depicting cityscapes as if to suggest that they should look like any place in Central Europe; each image, for example, was identified only by its German name, with no reference whatsoever to its non-German name.[12]

As in many songbooks for German youth and social organizations, this one contains accompaniments for lute or guitar, lending the collection an international character and making it possible for anyone to learn the songs. Other volumes in the *Landschaftliche Volkslieder* also used lute and guitar accompaniment, thereby also stressing the functional relation of the songbooks to the Wandervogel youth movement, whose symbol was the "Zupfgeigenhansl," the "guitar-playing Hans," who took German folk song with him on the paths of Europe, which took shape in the streets pictured in the pages of many of the books (e.g., Brandsch and Schullerus 1932: 43 and 47). The very feeling of portability mobilized the singer's ability to approach the distant landscape through musical performance.

Subsequent volumes of the landscape series fulfilled its goals to various degrees, depending on historical circumstances and competing ideological motivations. The economic crisis engulfing Europe in the late 1920s and early 1930s meant that only landscapes inside Germany could realistically publish their own volumes.[13] During the 1930s, the series more deliberately extended its gaze to the most contested areas of German settlement, with volume 25 for example devoted to the music of the so-called Volga Colonies, that is, settlements of German-speaking farmers in the Ukrainian lowlands of the Soviet Union (Dinges 1932) and volume 35 containing songs from "middle Poland" (Klatt and Horak 1940). The landscapes represented by these volumes were part of a much larger cartographic fabric. The woof of the fabric resulted from the various threads that covered the whole of Germanic Europe. The warp connected each volume to the individual landscape and the other attempts to map that landscape. Volume 31, for example (1937), contained songs from Lorraine edited by Louis Pinck, a local priest and collector, whose publications remain the standard collection of songs in the Lothringian dialect of German. The volume itself, through the preface of Josef Müller-Blattau,[14] reminded users that it was Goethe who first collected German folk songs in Alsace-Lorraine, establishing the region as the paradigm for the classical quality of German folk culture. The folk songs in Pinck's volume, then, held the place of German culture, as if to wait for the invasion of France a few years later that would again attempt to lay claim to Lorraine as German.

The individual volumes of the landscape projects mobilized German history through complex representational practices. The songs appear on the page as if taken from the past, but the illustrations and arrangements for modern performance deliberately recontextualize them for the future. The landscape, therefore, is culturally fertile, waiting for the replanting that a new generation of singers might provide.[15] It is perhaps most striking that the project should have continued after World War II, even if the expansionist agendas are deliberately stripped away. The final volumes gathered evidence in a presumably apolitical way, simply completing the project so that no regions of the map would be left uncharted. The final volume, devoted to southern Moravia, includes songs collected during a series of festivals from 1929 to 1939 (Max 1971). The German Moravian landscape of these songs had disappeared into history, albeit metaphorically according to the editor, who stresses the connection of southern Moravia through smaller rivers to the flood plain of the Danube and farther to Vienna. The German history of southern Moravia, therefore, followed a natural route across the face of Europe, not really passing into the past, but rather merging with a different map and crossing the borders of Cold War Europe.

MAPPING MUSIC

Maps represent the unrepresentable: place and the desire to own it. Like music, which also does not represent through direct or isomorphic signification, maps represent iconically. Maps and music thus become effective interpretive tools, in fact stages in an interpretive process that possesses enormous ideological potential to reconfigure space and the ways it historicizes European nations and regions. European musical scholars nonetheless have frequently represented music with maps, as if to translate the non-representable with the non-representational. The penchant to map music onto the European imagination inevitably leads to a proliferation of historical meanings. Different musical maps therefore represent different histories, which in turn claim place for different reasons. The many histories emerging from such processes of representation make many Europes possible, each one as contested as the next.

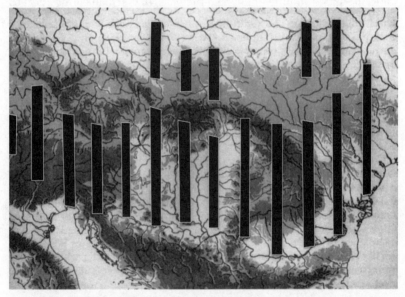

Figure 20.1. Distribution of hammered dulcimers in the Pannonian and Carpathian Mountain Regions of Central and East Central Europe. The bars represent heavy concentration of the hammered dulcimer. (Reproduced with permission from Mačák 1990: 206)

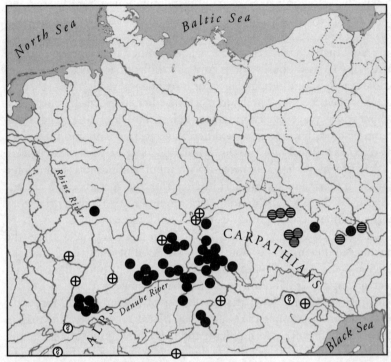

⊘ Presumably present in this area, according to surviving dance songs
⊕ Extinct prior to World War I
● Still actively danced in 1938
⊜ Documented by Czech sources

Figure 20.2. Distribution of dances with mixed meters in Central and East Central Europe. The different symbols represent the relative survaval of dances with mixed meters in the twentieth century, before and after World War I. (Zoder 1938, map 3)

Each musical map contains a precise image of a specific time and place. It was when the image of one map is compared to or challenged by another that the true extent of historical contestation really emerges. The first two maps (figs. 20.1–20.2) locate musical practices on the borders between Central and Eastern Europe, illustrating the different ways in which musical evidence coalesces around the historical processes that have located and relocated those borders. The maps share certain cartographic traits. Both are physical maps, in which nature rather than politics determines place. The viewer recognizes the dulcimer's location by comparing it to a proximate river or the mountainous or forested regions. Both maps rely on dance and instrumental music to sketch musical geography; linguistic boundaries, at least on the surface of the maps, play no role. Finally, both cartographers have avoided the evidence of political maps so assiduously—it is probably difficult for most viewers to know exactly where certain dances or instruments "really" are—that the maps evoke a feeling of prehistory, a time when music itself determined where it was played.[16] The maps in figures 20.1 and 20.2 nonetheless claim place with music in very different ways, thus imbuing them with distinctive political motivations. Raimund Zoder maps the distribution of dance forms with mixed meters. With a central concentration in alpine southern Germany and Austria, the distribution spreads eastward, appearing in the Carpathian and Tatra mountains, with their trajectory that continues across Eastern Europe into Ukraine.

In figure 20.1, the great basin of the Pannonian Region envelops the hammered dulcimer's distribution.[17] The flood plain of the Pannonian Region is the physical counterpart of the mountains in the figure, in effect making the distribution of dulcimers the counterpart of dance forms with mixed meter. Two parts—a region of instruments, a region of dance styles—complete the whole. Ivan Mačák constructed the map in figure 20.1, however, to highlight the determining musical factors in Eastern Europe, most specifically those that overlapped in Slovakia. His research for this map, moreover, was conducted during the final years of Czechoslovak unification, and the political message of Slovak connection to Eastern Europe through the Pannonian Region rather than to Central Europe through Czech-speaking areas motivates many of the representational decisions that connect dulcimer distribution to place. The juxtaposition of a physical landscape, photographed from an orbiting satellite, with no less scientific distribution charts should therefore serve as an even more politically powerful justification for the new nationalism of the 1990s (for yet another cartographic solution to the musical boundaries between Central and Eastern Europe, see Farwick 1986: 117).

The musical contestation of borders portends the entrance of race. As one musical landscape overlaps with another, as the distribution of instruments conflicts with the mixing of meters, the meanings of musical maps become increasingly exclusive and confused. By the twentieth century, the musical mapping of Europe had progressed to the point of overflowing beyond the continent itself, urging musical cartographers at once to privilege the long history of European music and to explain its privileged position in relation to the rest of the world. Musical landscapes, if imported in this way, had untapped colonial potential. The twentieth century promised to be a moment of global remapping.

Figures 20.3 and 20.4 illustrate two different motivations for remapping the musics of the world from the European perspective. Their differences notwithstanding, again we see that similarities are striking. Figure 20.3 is a reproduction of one of the most overt applications of Nazi scientism to explain the racial superiority of the so-called Nordic peoples of Central and Northern Europe. The theories that Fritz Metzler (1938) maps onto the "racial areas" *(Rassenkreise)* of the Eastern Hemisphere are at once simple and so utterly complex as to convince the reader that they must represent truth. At the simplest level, Metzler espouses the view that the major and minor tonalities, a hierarchical system of tonal relations, provide the basis for German folk song, by extension unifying, indeed producing, Nordic and Germanic music histories. Other races use smaller intervals with hierarchies lacking or independent of intervallic distance, wherefore they have never benefited from the same unity of history. The key, both literally and figuratively, to understanding the unleashing of scientism by this map lies in the left-hand corner, in which the distance of intervals is explicitly related to the cranial sizes of the different races given their places by Metzler's map.

The computer-driven scientism of a different era guided the cartographic concept for figure 20.4, for which Alan Lomax's cantometric project[18] had designed the "world distribution of European strophic singing" (Lomax 1968: 17). Strophic singing surely functions as a much less violent measuring principle than cranial size, although its implicit suggestion that complex musical forms give Europe a certain sense of musical privilege are highly suspect in themselves. This map of strophic-song distribution is not so overtly racial as Metzler's map, and if Europe is privileged, it is as a continent whose musical practices potentially influence global music-making rather than take their identities because they are distinct from global music-making. Still, the scientific categories of the cantometrics landscape are so many that they confuse by their fundamental differences. Some categories have political and historical contexts (e.g. Ethiopia and Western Europe), whereas others have ethnic, if not racial contexts (e.g. Tribal India and Northeast Bantu). Boundaries overlap and disappear, have exaggerated presence or inexplicable invisibility.[19] What is the meaning of all this global remapping? Does the distribution of European strophic singing really keep the Afro-American cultural area in Africa? Does it shift pueblo-dwelling Native Americans from the Southwest to the Southeast? Music, this cantometrics map argues, acts powerfully on these places in the racial

Figure 20.3. Basic forms of musical thinking within major racial areas. (Reproduced after Metzler 1938: map between pp. 24 and 25)

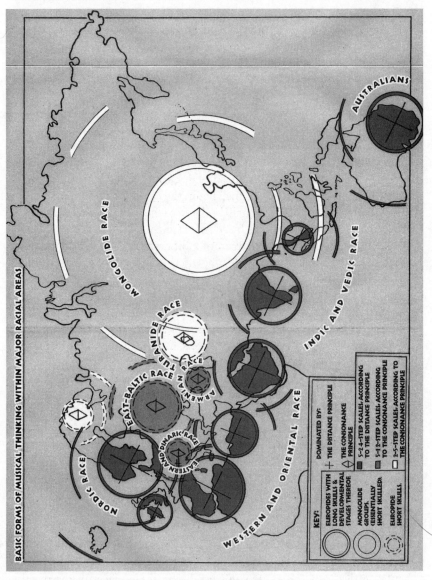

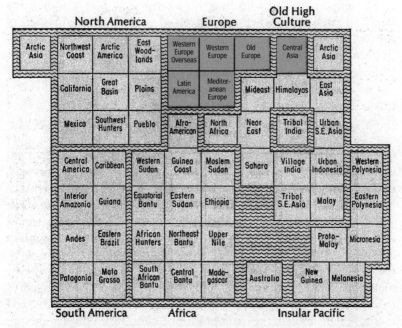

Figure 20.4. World distribution of European stropic singing (Lomax 1968: 17). Reprinted with permission from Alan Lomax, *Folk Song Style and Culture*. Copyright 1968 American Association for the Advancement of Science.

imagination, reshuffling their borders and reinscribing identities that privilege the historical forces that have distributed strophic singing. Among those forces, race is omnipresent.

COLLECTING/RECOLLECTING

Before music could be enlisted to map the racial landscapes of Europe, it was necessary to collect. Collecting was an act of finding evidence and then ordering it in such ways that it would be incontrovertible. Evidence became incontrovertible, moreover, because it was removed from its source, both temporally and geographically, and the distance between the collected object and the place in time and space that it signified effectively became impassable. The distance created by collecting, therefore, empowered the collector to seek out new forms of representing the place of music on the map of Europe. By the mid nineteenth century, that form of representation acquired the name "musical landscape," and its most highly articulated form was the folk-music landscape.[20]

The importance of collecting was lost on few interested in reinforcing the connections between music and race. The earliest folk-song collections were not, in fact, nationalistic. In Herder's seminal collections "*Stimmen der Völker in Liedern*" (1778) and *Volkslieder* (1779), for example, English and Gaelic songs (53) actually outnumber German songs (38), with numerous other regional repertories tapped for this first collecting effort. Herder used his collection to map the whole of Europe, rather than the parts of Europe. As collecting underwent processes of refinement, driven by technological advances (e.g. recording devices) and by the funding available from national sources, its focus became increasingly specific.[21] Competition also entered as a factor, with no nation, region, or ethnic and religious group wishing to be left behind in the attempts to place itself musically on the maps of Europe.[22]

Collecting was the initial stage in a process of ascribing narrative and historical potential to music and inscribing that potential through the classificatory procedures employed in storing, analyzing, and publishing the collection. In the collection, a song had mobility, which is to say it moved across space and through time. An example is Wilhelm Tappert's theory of "wandering melodies," in which individual melodies and motifs literally took to the roads of Europe, showing up throughout the continent and beyond (Tappert 1890). New collecting efforts only confirmed the historical and geographical mobility of music, affixing art and folk music to regional, national, and international landscapes (cf. Danckert 1970, Wiora 1971).

Collecting, moreover, was not simply historical. It had the power to historicize. It not only collected evidence from the past; it recollected the past itself. Firing the collector's passion was the urge to find the "oldest" evidence, which in turn would allow one to recuperate authenticity. The "oldest" had its place on the musical landscape, but that place was never in the center but rather inevitably at the edges, indeed so situated that it defined the edges. Ideally, the place of the oldest was inaccessible to all but the collector, as in the mountains of southern Germany or Austria, which became the most highly valued goals for the German folk-song collector (e.g. Bruinier 1927). Here early melodic forms were found, usually no more than four lines,[23] and non-diatonic scales with a small complement of pitches, whenever possible pentatonic, provided the basis for measurement and the establishment of age (see Wittrock 1969). Collected song, therefore, signified age and authenticity, thereby calibrating history.

The potential of collecting to recollect history was not lost on Europeans in search of their history. As Jewish communities increasingly sought a place in the cultural geography of urbanizing Europe in the late nineteenth century, they also felt an acute need to determine the shape of modern Jewish history. By the turn of the century, collecting projects were well underway, particularly those in Eastern Europe's Yiddish-speaking regions. Yiddish folk-song collectors did not want to be left out of the race to collect, and they became particularly concerned by the massive emigration that was changing the face of Jewish culture in the Pale. The first major collection of Yiddish songs, Ginsburg and Marek's *Jewish Folk Songs from Russia* (1901), made explicit its intent to gather the oldest level of Jewish folk song before it dispersed from the shtetl to the New World. *Jewish Folk Songs from Russia*, in fact, became the collector's collection, for subsequent anthologies relied on the authentic evidence in the turn-of-the-century anthology. Central European collectors, for example, turned directly to Ginsburg and Marek when making a place in collections for German social and Zionist groups (see Bohlman in press).

Age and authenticity for European Jews, however, could not simply reside at the fringes of the Pale: ultimately, only Israel could provide the evidence to provide Jews a place in modernity. With this in mind, Abraham Zvi Idelsohn embarked in 1908 on the most ambitious collecting project in twentieth-century Jewish history. A German-trained cantor from Latvia, Idelsohn acquired a wax-cylinder recorder from the Austrian Academy of Science and set off for Jerusalem, where, during much of the next decade, he recorded the music that filled the ten volumes of his *Hebräisch-orientalischer Melodienschatz* (1914–32), usually translated in English as *Thesaurus of Hebrew-Oriental Melodies*. Idelsohn based his collections, which included European (e.g. vol. 6–10) as well as "oriental" Jewish music, on the premise that oral tradition, particularly in "isolated" communities such as Yemen and Baghdad, preserved the music of biblical Israel. Armed with the reproductive technology afforded by cylinder recording, he could translate that evidence in the *Thesaurus*, inscribing it on a framework both scientific and practical. The *Thesaurus* collapsed both time and place.[24] With mounting pressures on European Jews to establish a physical home in the twentieth century, the *Thesaurus* itself collected a series of musical moments that together recollected the meanings of Jerusalem and Israel from the past for the future.

SITES OF MEMORY/MEMORIAL SITES

Quite literally, the collection of music assumed monumental proportions in the late nineteenth century. Indeed, it was as monuments that the memorializing potential of music was most visibly recognized by anthologizers and publishers alike. Whether a collection of quintessentially national compositions or a systematic canon of folk songs, music's monuments increasingly emblematized the unity of European musical landscapes. The monuments of music bore different names—in German, for example, there is a diverse range, including *Liederschatz* (treasury of songs), *Liederhort* (protective gathering of songs), *Volksliedwerk* (folk-song works), and, quite commonly, *Denkmal* (monument)—but each expressed some aspect of the validation and valuation of its musical contents, as well as its solidity and impenetrability as an object defining the place of culture. Some acts of naming left the exact physical nature of the musical monument in question, for example "Werk," which describes published national collections and the places where national collections are held.[25]

That music achieves monumental status, however, seems to contradict its performative nature, that is, its existence within time. Because it takes its meaning within time, music would seem to lose that meaning when ossified as a monument. Or stated more specifically in the terms of this essay: music, when monumentalizing, makes an ontological shift, from time to place. As James E. Young has argued in his reflections on monuments to the Holocaust, monuments are not that simple (1993). Monuments are places of both memory and meaning, indeed, of a plurality of memories that transform the monument into a memorial site at which meanings multiply (11–15; see also Kaplan 1994). Musical monuments are like Holocaust memorials in this sense. Arguably, they are memorial sites that significantly accelerate and augment the proliferation of meanings, which we witness in the ways recorded music contextualizes monuments.[26] Music, filling the spaces of the Holocaust memorial, functions to displace and replace the memories that each individual wishes the monument to evoke.

The monuments of nineteenth-century folk-song scholarship functioned to transform local spaces into national identities. Gathering the songs of earlier German collections and ordering them according to past and present, the Erk–Böhme *Deutscher Liederhort* (1893–94) reached into the historical past, establishing a repertory of medieval German music whose connections to the present formed the texture of the three-volume collection itself.[27] Erk–Böhme succeeded in compressing and consolidating German history at a moment when Germany itself was asserting its centralized statehood for the first time. In contrast, Austrian folk-song scholars erected their monuments to memorialize the Habsburg Monarchy. In 1904, Josef Pommer, supported by the Imperial Ministry for Culture and Education and the music publishing house,

Universal Edition, embarked on a project to collect and anthologize the folk music of every province in the empire, in each of the so-called "Kronländer," or lands of the crown. Each province, within or without the borders of Austria-Hungary, would receive its own monument in this project, called simply "Das Volkslied in Österreich," "Folk Song in Austria." Whereas initial research for these monuments produced several of them and led to considerable research for others, World War I terminated the project, just as it ended Austrian control over its empire. The English folk-song monument is, of course, the well-known Child ballads, *The English and Scottish Popular Ballads* (Child 1882–98), a five-volume collection that assumes not only a corpus shared by England and Scotland, but also by other regions of the British Isles and North America. The Child ballads remain until this day the quintessential memorial for the past, a guide to discovering the oldest traces of British domination of the world.[28]

As the musical monuments of nation and power spread across the musical landscape of nineteenth-century Europe, that landscape became increasingly contested; and alternative, even resistant, sites of memory responded accordingly. Some of these directly confronted the geographic encroachment that the nationalistic monuments were claiming. Jewish musical monuments, for example, claimed alternative spaces. In Central Europe, these were urban, the sacred spaces for the synagogue that the cantorial repertory (*ḥazzanut*) filled, historically reproduced by generation after generation of cantor but published in sumptuous volumes in the late nineteenth century. The cantorial monuments were local, but they filled out a map of local traditions, for example the Viennese rite of Salomon Sulzer or the Königsberg rite of Eduard Birnbaum. In Eastern Europe, the site of musical memory was the village, the shtetl, in which Yiddish folk songs survived. The Jewish intelligentsia of St. Petersburg discovered in Yiddish folk song perhaps the most lasting monument to rural Jewish culture in Europe, publishing it with the simple and unforgettable title *Jewish Folk Songs from Russia* (Ginsburg and Marek 1901).

Sites of memory and monuments might seem, at first glance, to embody ossified musical practices. Published musical monuments, after all, remove music from its place of performance and from the processes of transmission. Nothing, however, could be further from reality. Precisely because monuments arrest the ways in which one experiences the past, they also unleash the dynamic practices that multiply meaning. The memorial sites of pilgrimage offer a clear example of the dynamic tension between memory and meaning. Pilgrims from diverse backgrounds and places travel to the site of memory, a shrine or monument to a miracle, discovering in that place the possibility of changing the future by remembering the event that led to the placement of the monument, for example an act of healing. Pilgrims perform this dynamic encounter with memory through song, in Europe largely repertories of Marian songs, as well as through the ritualized paths that lead to the site of sacred memory itself.[29]

There is no single type of memorial or site for the memory that music unleashes. The monuments I describe in this section take on different shapes, just as they need to create different types of memory. The memory that musical monuments make possible may take aggressive forms, deliberately manipulating a perception of the past to shape actions in the future. The memory created by music may only evoke a sense of place, a nostalgia about a place that can no longer be recovered. The sites of memory nonetheless empower music to connect individual experiences to place. If indeed that place is not immediately retrievable, the memory that the musical monument represents is insistently a reminder that the possibility for such retrieval is not entirely lost.

SITES OF FORGETTING/SIGHTING SILENCE

Forgetting takes place most effectively at the fringes, at borders or "frontiers," at the edges and peripheries. At the edges, memory holds less firmly to the center and its symbols, and there is an increased potential for challenging the meaning of symbols at all. The cultures at the edges and frontiers of Europe, likewise, are less definite and more difficult to define than those claiming the place of center, and it is therefore to the edges and frontiers that we first turn to observe the sites of forgetting.

Celtic music lays claim to an area of Europe that exists entirely at the fringes, in fact determining much of the western edge of the map of Europe itself. Celtic regions at the end of the twentieth century are unified in the European imagination, by both language and music. Clinging to the land bordering the Atlantic and the North Sea, as if driven there by a Europe moving westward to the sea, the Celtic regions of Scotland, Ireland, Wales, Cornwall, and Brittany contain populations who speak— or spoke—related languages. Historically, it has been an arbitrary choice whether or not to claim Celtic culture as a unity or a confederacy, as connected or disconnected. When race and nation enter into the historical equation, especially in modernity, it has been unity that prevails. Most modern Celts, by and large, do not speak Celtic languages; in the popular imagination, only those at the farthest fringes (e.g. on the Hebrides off the coast of Scotland) really maintain currency and fluency (Chapman 1994: 34–35). Learning Celtic languages, moreover, has proved to be no easy task for native English-speakers, either in local language programs or in the national experiments to support bilingualism, for example in the Republic of Ireland.

Those who inhabit Celtic lands, in short, have forgotten their culture; or, at the very least, attempts to remember the culture through the language have largely failed. To stem the ineluctable pull of forgetting, promoters of Celtic identity have mustered a wide variety of musical practices (Chapman 1994; cf. Trevor-Roper 1983). A tradition of instrumental music has been molded into an instrumentarium with harps and bagpipes, both of which had been almost entirely forgotten by the beginning of the nineteenth century (Chapman 1994: 37–38). In the twentieth century, Celtic culture brokers realized that the forgotten languages were most easily acquired as song texts, particularly in choral settings, which offered the further advantage of undergirding the sense of community. The institutionalization of Celtic music through choral and dance competitions, bagpipe and harp revivals, and the commoditization and international dissemination of recordings claiming to be "Celtic music" have created a way of performing what it means to be Celtic (ibid.).

The musician at the fringe may also become the chief agent of forgetting and remembering. The Slavic minorities in German-speaking Central Europe have repeatedly negotiated their forgotten history by using music to mediate the ways in which it has been remembered. The Sorbs in the east German state of Saxony, for example, have stemmed the processes of forgetting by contributing extensively to public music-making and the professionalization of the musician in Saxony (Raupp 1963). By the eighteenth century, Sorb musicians dominated dance ensembles and were among the most distinguished organists. Sorb music, then, became a *bricolage* of other different musics, with Sorb musicians serving as the *bricoleurs* who controlled forgetting and remembering. At the frontier between Central and Eastern Europe, German- and Slavic-speaking Europe, Sorb music achieved a place for Sorb culture, if indeed an indigenous Sorb sound had largely been forgotten by the twentieth century.[30]

If the geographical fringes of the old Europe connect forgetting to the past, the public spaces of the new Europe give it a place in the present. It is the growing presence of public music-making—the concert on the street, in the stadium, or on Eurovision—that has spawned a growing tendency to explain and explain away Europe as a "Tower of Babel" (e.g. Leggewie 1990), a continent so full of competing sounds as to become incomprehensible. Music-making in the public space claims that space and contextualizes it, even if the complex music-making in that space forces one to hear at the expense of listening. The din of public sound becomes the white noise of history, which envelops one even while walking on the streets of the New Europe.

Blanketing the centers of modern European cities are pedestrian zones, many of which were built in the wake of the destruction in World War II that erased the cityscape of the nineteenth-century European city. If, however, the pedestrian zone re-placed the past, it could not erase the conditions that located race on the contested spaces of the cityscape. Whereas the spaces of racial differentiation—synagogues, Roma and Sinti settlements, new arrivals from the provinces, and, above all, ceme- teries—formed the fringes of the nineteenth-century city, the openness of the pedestrian zone locates those spaces in the urban center. Musi- cians from throughout Europe and elsewhere, especially Latin America, vie for these spaces, most of which are granted to them by the local au- thorities for only a few hours each day. Passersby experience the music of the pedestrian as disembodied fragments rendered foreign by language, musical style, or the retreat of musicians into the shadows of nearby win- dows. The music is everywhere and nowhere, unavoidable yet incompre- hensible. Music transforms the everyday experience of shopping or traveling to and from the office through a wash of racial differences.[31] Music becomes a site for the racial contestation of urban spaces (cf. Bohlman 1994).

European history is full of moments in which music was everywhere, marking race by masking it. Observers of public policy in the former communist governments of East European nations repeatedly described the surfeit of music-making that these governments supported. Opera throve, as did contests for the best folk-dance troupes in a region. Radio music filled the air, and opportunities for music education were abun- dant. Public performances by state-sponsored folk-music ensembles, *de rigueur* for every tourist visiting Budapest or Bucharest, combined bits and pieces from all the provinces, weaving them into the folk fabric— the most common metaphor—of the nation. The superabundance of music deliberately confronted one with difference by insisting that these differences did not make a difference. In the new socialist state, they all occupied the same space, a space distanced from the past and placed on the public stage of the present. It was easier and more pleasant to forget that one was witnessing difference at all.

The public sphere makes it possible to forget because of its insistence on competition. No one owns the public sphere—the streets or stadi- ums—but music affords competing groups the power to occupy it, if even for the moment of performance. The streets of Paris, for example, have provided the forum for competing ideals and ideologies, and in recent years they have particularly served as the space in which organizations for racism (e.g. Jean-Marie Le Pen's National Front) or against racism (e.g. Harlem Désir's SOS Racisme) have competed for national attention (Smoltczyk 1990, Kristeva 1993). And music is the medium for remembering and forgetting as concerts punctuate parade routes.[32] The pubic image mixing ethnic difference as musical unity in Eastern Europe, too, was the product of competition, in fact in the most literal sense, for the folk musicians who appeared publicly at regional, provincial, and national levels had to have passed through competition after competition after competition. Only the fittest survived in these competitions. Competition, however, makes it easier to forget, for some musician always occupies the stage. Music always has a place. Competition, by its very nature, creates placelessness, but then allows music to occupy the place of placelessness. And so, music returns again and again to fill the spaces opened by the competition for modern Europe and its history.

THE MYTH OF ETERNAL RETURN

The summer of 1995 proved to be a time of return in Europe, with echoes returning and resonating all too clearly again in the summer of 1999. One ethnic or national enclave after another vies for land lost during the return of heightened war in the Balkans. Bosnian Serbs return to claim cities only recently claimed by Bosnian Muslims, that is, the post-Yugoslav nation of Bosnia and Hercegovina. In 1995 the Croatian army has returned to Krajina, forcing the Serbs living there to return to Serbia, or at least to Serb-controlled lands. In 1999 Albania looked across its borders into the growing human misery and vacuum of Kosovo, a place of once and future Albanianness. Marking the welter of returning former residents is the rhetorical return of the designation "the former Yugoslavia," which had signaled liberation in the wake of Yugoslavia's 1991 disintegration but now is the best available marker of the lands to which Serbs, Croats, Bosnians, and Kosovars want to return.

Elsewhere in Europe, return is also in the air. The renaissance of pilgrimage is unabated, as modern pilgrims return to the sites visited by preceding groups and generations of pilgrims. Just as the sacred symbols of pilgrimage accrue to each other, so do the more secular and narrative, with the carnivalesque attributes and tales of healing at each site multiplying, thereby stimulating return after return. Eastern Europe, too, is ever more a site of return. Those whose ancestors lost their place in

Eastern Europe return to find them and to remember the memories lost when places such as Galicia, the Bukovina, and the Banat emigrated with those who held them in European history, or perished as their neighbors were destroyed in war and holocaust. Blazing the path for those undertaking the return to Eastern Europe is a new literature, some of it reflective and thoughtful about the impossibility of real return (e.g. Applebaum 1994, Hoffman 1993), some of it practical and factual, as if to enable the return itself (e.g. Gruber 1992).

Characteristic of this new literature is that it chronicles real journeys of return, the trips made by the authors to the land of their ancestors (e.g. Hoffman 1993) or to the lands imagined into the history of European empire by their ancestors (e.g. Dohrn 1991, Wischenbart 1992). With memories and guidebooks in hand, the authors of these narratives of return follow the physical paths that served as the foundations of modern European history. They layer return upon return upon return, transforming the very act of return into an everyday practice. Photographs from the present, artificially given a black-and-white patina, deliberately emulate the touched-up photographs from the past, as if the former could capture the images of the latter (see Baselgia 1993). Tourists, pilgrims, and refugees alike experience the return to Eastern Europe as a commonplace marker of modernity.

At the same moment when experiences of return were proliferating to reconfigure the map of Europe in the summer of 1995, a volume with South Slavic epics collected by Milman Parry in 1935 appeared in print (Erdely 1995). In almost 650 pages, this volume represents transcribed performances of three epics, with detailed notations of the hours and hours of singing that accompanied the oral tradition. That these transcriptions represent performance traditions of the Bihać region of Bosnia passes without remark in the prefatory and introductory matter of the book; the authors of these sections could hardly have known that Bihać would be the focus of world attention when their book appeared, that is, one of the few remaining "UN safe zones" for Bosnian Muslims, which, however, the Croatian attack on surrounding Serbian positions succeeded in liberating.[33] For Milman Parry and Albert B. Lord who originally collected the epics, for Béla Bartók who tried his hand at transcribing them in the United States,[34] and for the late twentieth-century guardians of the epic collections at Harvard University, the more remarkable issue was historical, namely, that the Balkans and the Bihać were safe zones for the preservation of epics, "where the singing of heroic poems, already extinct in Europe, was still flourishing in the oral tradition of several Balkan peoples" (Erdely 1995: 5).

Milman Parry, collecting epics in 1935, was returning to the past himself, for his interest was in the Homeric epics, to which he believed Balkan epics bore similarities, especially in the use of formulae in composition. The epic was the genre of returning. Composed through combinations of stanzas, single lines, syllabic patterns, and small formulaic units, the motifs and patterns return again and again, for hours and hours, in page after page. The narrative of the epic, too, is one of returning. The Balkan epics recounted the tales of heroes from Balkan history, the great deeds of military encounters between the residents of the Balkans and the Ottoman Empire. In 1995, these historical collections of history itself, raging in the safe zones of the past around Bihać, were available in detailed transcription, affording the reader the chance to return to those places that so fired the imaginations of Parry, Bartók, and the scholars of Southeast European folk song. In 1999, there would again be echoes of those safe zones in another Balkan land rich in epic traditions, Montenegro.

Music serves as a powerful metaphor for return, not only accompanying it but also giving it structure. The return that forms the representational power of music—its ability to create memory, its capacity to replace one performance with another, thereby bringing about forgetting—makes for music a place in the narrative imagination. This place of musical return in narrative imagination, when inscribed and transcribed onto the cultural geography of the past, becomes the place of history. Return has become the modern surrogate for place in Europe at the end of the twentieth century, with the music of return becoming a sound-mix of place for European modernity.

The experiences of placelessness coalesce around the sound-mix of return. That sound-mix takes us to the lost worlds of European epic singers; it accompanies us as we take stock of the horrors of concentration camps; it fills the sacred spaces of mountain basilicas as procession after procession of pilgrims performs in passing; it envelops the parades supporting racial tolerance in France and Germany; it fills the buses of refugees waiting to be allowed to cross yet another border. Music redefines these places of return and reinscribes placelessness onto the map of modernity. The music of this modern placelessness ensures that race, too, retains its place in the European imagination.

NOTES

1. It is no accident of literary history that George Eliot's "Jewish" novel, *Daniel Deronda* (1876), should juxtapose issues of music and race in one of its

Jewish characters, whose name, Klesmer, is well known at the end of the twentieth century as a designation for Jewish instrumental folk music (it literally refers to one who performs as the "vessel of sound") but was entirely unfamiliar to English readers in the late nineteenth century. In *Daniel Deronda* "Herr Klesmer" consistently racializes a mix of European musical repertories through the magic of his teaching and performing.

2. Murder and genocide, by extension, are the most brutal implementation of this denial of belonging.

3. In fact, Gypsies in Europe are overwhelmingly sedentary; it is only the image of Roma and Sinti as constantly on the move that exaggerates the racialization of their culture.

4. The historical potential of folk song to serve as evidence of and from the past led nineteenth-century folk-music scholars, notably Rochus Freiherr von Liliencron, to establish a subdiscipline devoted to *historische Volkslieder* (historical folk songs). See e.g. Liliencron 1865 and Schmidt 1971.

5. In one of the earliest systematic attempts to extend linguistic, national, and ethnic characteristics to music, Jean-Jacques Rousseau's *Dictionnaire de la musique*, definition results primarily from difference as determined by nature (see, e.g., *ranz-des-vaches*, a Swiss "air" produced by peasants calling their cattle from the mountains with alphorns, 1768: 398). National style simply ceases to exist at boundary areas where there is overlap, thus rendering these areas musically contested.

6. Hungarian folk-music scholars, for example, translated the presence of melodic transposition by perfect fifth in the musics of different Finno-Ugric–speaking peoples in Eastern Europe and Central Asia into a fundamental marker of Hungarianness in what Béla Bartók and Zoltán Kódaly called the "Old Style." When this presumably ur-Hungarian trait gave way to more tonal harmonic structure, hence to contamination by urban and Gypsy influences, Hungarian music entered new phases: the "New Style" and, against the backdrop of nineteenth-century nationalism, the "Mixed Style."

7. The German designation for boundary areas, *Grenzlandschaften* (boundary landscapes) holds special significance, for it suggests ways of exiting into history, that is into the past when a boundary landscape such as Galicia, now straddling Poland, Ukraine, and Romania, could claim forms of cultural and political unity, neither of which (e.g. the Yiddish language or Habsburg administration) can be recovered. For personal reflections on the boundary landscapes of Eastern Europe see Applebaum 1994; Dohrn 1991 and Baselgia 1993 contain modern reflections on the traces of Galicia that still survive at the end of the twentieth century.

8. The more such claims can be mustered, the stronger the evidence of ownership. Nazi musical scholars, for example, systematically gathered and listed such evidence prior to mounting the argument that the "speech islands" (*Sprachinseln*) of German-speaking residents in Eastern Europe were more German than anything else. It was important to some claims, even, that the age of the musical evidence from the speech islands was more German than the evidence in Germany, extending longevity even more. See Waldmann 1938a.

9. Those living in the speech islands most commonly bore the designation colonists (e.g. in the "Gottscheer Kolonien" in Slovenia, settled in the late Middle Ages), suggesting clearly that such colonies were surrogates for the colonies outside Europe that Germany failed to win in significant number because of its relatively late entrance into colonial competition.

10. Bounding the narrative genre of ballads was the use of texts that were only in High German. Local inflections and pronunciation might produce local variants, but these did not undermine the role of High German. When folk-song collectors found ballads in speech islands or beyond the borders of Germany, this symbolized the presence of German civilization and signaled that German oral tradition had competed successfully for the place in which the ballad repertories survived.

11. Richard Wagner's *Die Meistersinger* is a clear example of the ways in which this historical agenda took shape in a self-consciously Germanic art music during the nineteenth century.

12. Although some villages and regions had German-speaking majorities, few were without significant populations that spoke other languages. Many of the speech islands (e.g., those musically mapped in Brandsch and Schullerus 1932 and Deutsches Volksliedarchiv 1930) had been multilingual for centuries.

13. Volume 10, for example, included songs from Schleswig-Holstein and the Hanseatic cities of northern Germany and was published in Münster (Tardel 1928). All songs in the volume are in a Low German dialect, representing in particular the contested linguistic region overlapping Schleswig-Holstein and Denmark (cf. Holzapfel 1993).

14. Müller-Blattau, a musical scholar, also gave the volume a musicological legitimacy, which was inseparable from the racialized scientism of his other scholarly work (cf. Müller-Blattau 1938).

15. Images of land and agriculture are rarely absent from the folk-song landscapes. Many songs are seasonal, others celebratory of nature and the farmer's harmony with it. Farming practices, in essence, ritualize the land itself and the landscape that represents it.

16. These notions also underlie the theories of "wandering melodies" in Tappert 1890.

17. The Pannonian Region (called Pannonia by the Romans) forms roughly the extended flood plain of the lower Danube, hence including parts of Austria, Slovakia, Hungary, Romania, and Serbia.

18. Using a complex of data collected from field studies of music throughout the world, the cantometric project classified and transformed data into cultural profiles of world cultures using the computer technology of the 1960s (see Lomax 1968). The "measurement of song," at which cantometrics aimed, derived from earlier comparative approaches in the social sciences (e.g., the Human Resources Area Files) and ethnomusicology.

19. Continental shift and dispersion is considerable. Latin America, for example, belongs to Europe, Mexico to North America, and Central America and the Caribbean to South America. "Western Europe Overseas" is, nonetheless, separated by the sea from overseas.

20. The concept of a musical landscape appeared first in German *(Volksmusiklandschaft)*, and it carried primarily regional connotations. The concept of a musical landscape, nonetheless, spread to other languages and beyond folk-music scholarship to other types of musical scholarship. The concept has as much currency today as in the nineteenth century, with new and variegated uses, for example, in the description of musical cityscapes.

21. This process of transforming collection through the introduction of new technologies to create new musical discourses parallels the discourses of language examined in Kittler 1987.

22. In the introduction to the first volume of the German-language ballad collection *Deutsche Volkslieder mit ihren Melodien*, established in 1935 and completed in the 1990s, John Meier justifies the project of gathering all German ballads in a series of volumes by addressing the need to match the achievements of Frances James Child for the Anglo-Scottish ballads and Svend Grundtvig for Scandinavian ballads. See Meier 1935.

23. Genres such as the *Schnaderhüpfl*, or *Vierzeiler* (lit. "four-liner," or quatrain), are considered to be virtually mountain-specific (see, e.g., Holzapfel 1991–93).

24. Berlin, Leipzig, and Jerusalem all served as official venues of publication, making the printed volumes even more symbolic of collapsed diaspora. The final stages of the project, completed in the United States, were financially supported by the American Council of Learned Societies.

25. John Meier, Director of the German Folk-Song Archive (DVA) in Freiburg im Breisgau, began publishing volumes of German ballads in 1935, calling this project with an indefinite future *Balladenwerk*. The DVA completed this project only in the 1990s. The central institution for the collection and cataloguing of Austrian folk songs is the Volksliedwerk, located in the 16th District of Vienna, Ottakring.

26. The power of music to enhance the memory of tragedy is seldom lost on the planners of Holocaust monuments, who create a soundscape for the further stimulation of memory. Whereas most scholars examining Holocaust monuments do not mention music as one of the ancillary monuments at these sites, I should like to argue that it is precisely because music does not seem to be noticeably a part of the monument that it functions so powerfully to accelerate the proliferation of meanings.

27. In addition to remaining the standard collection of German folk songs even today—some songs are referred to by their "E-Nummer," that is, their ordinal listing in Erk–Böhme—the *Deutscher Liederhort* provides a valuable compendium of Renaissance *cantus firmi* and Baroque chorale tunes.

28. The children of the English colonists in New Zealand in Jane Campion's 1993 film *The Piano* sing Child ballad 84, "Barbara Allen," at several points in the film, therefore reminding the viewer/listener of the extent of the Empire's presence. "Barbara Allen" thus inflects the powerful monumentality of the film's primary symbol of empire and its destruction, the piano.

29. In the early 1990s, an estimated 100 million Europeans annually went on pilgrimages, still at a moment prior to the renaissance of pilgrimage that

accompanied a resacralization of European spaces after the dissolution of communist governments in Eastern Europe. For an examination of the use of music to perform the journey to the site of sacred memory, see Bohlman 1996, 1999.

30. Sorb culture enjoyed a special status in the German Democratic Republic, which encouraged the external signs of bilingualism and supported institutions of Sorb folk culture.

31. Michael Ignatieff has observed that subway musicians in urban Eastern Europe have functioned in the same way for decades (Ignatieff 1993: 108).

32. Reports of concerts against racism rarely report on the exact contents of the concerts but rather seek to impress by exaggerating the number of spectators in the audience. Even Julia Kristeva adapts such techniques of reportage: "A magnificent concert on June 15, 1985, attended by hundreds of thousands in the Place de la Concorde, succeeded in engraving in the minds of all Frenchmen *SOS Racisme*'s image and message" (1993: 14).

33. I first wrote these lines on 11 August 1995, and I reflect upon them at the time of another Balkan war on 22 May 1999.

34. Stephen Erdely reports that Bartók made it known in 1942 that "one of the reasons for my return to the United States was the possibility of a careful study of this material which I had badly missed in Europe" (from the *New York Times*, 28 June 1942; quoted in Erdely 1995: 5), as if World War II and the German occupation of the Balkans would not have been factors.

REFERENCES

Applebaum, Anne. 1994. *Between East and West: Across the Borderlands of Europe.* New York: Pantheon.

Baselgia, Guido. 1993. *Galizien.* Frankfurt am Main: Jüdischer Verlag.

Bohlman, Philip V. 1994. "Music, Modernity, and the Foreign in the New Germany." *Modernism/Modernity* 1, 1: 121–52.

———. 1996. "The Final Borderpost." *The Journal of Musicology* 14, 2: 427–52.

———. 1999. "Die Verkörperung des musikalischen Textes—Zum Verständnis der Musik als Wallfahrt." In *Musik als Text,* ed. Hermann Danuser, 200–206. Laaber: Laaber-Verlag.

———. in press. "*Jüdische Volksmusik*"—*Eine europäische Geistesgeschichte.* Vienna: Böhlau Verlag.

———. 2000. "Region/Nation/Reich: German Folk Song in the Nexus of Nationalism." Manuscript.

Brandsch, Gottlieb, and Adolf Schullerus, eds. and colls. 1932. *Siebenbürgische Volkslieder.* Landschaftliche Volkslieder, no. 21. Berlin: Walter de Gruyter.

Bruinier, J. W. 1927. *Das deutsche Volkslied: Über Wesen und Werden des deutschen Volksgesanges,* 7th ed. Aus Natur und Geisteswelt, no. 7. Leipzig: Teubner.

Chapman, Malcom. 1994. "Thoughts on Celtic Identity." In *Ethnicity, Identity and Music: The Musical Construction of Place,* ed. Martin Stokes, 29–44. Providence, R.I.: Berg.

Child, Frances James. 1882–98. *The English and Scottish Popular Ballads.* 5 vols. Boston: Houghton Mifflin.

Danckert, Werner. 1970. *Das europäische Volkslied*. Bonn: Bouvier.

Deutsches Volksliedarchiv, ed. 1930. *Gottscheer Volkslieder mit Bildern und Weisen*. Landschaftliche Volkslieder, no. 24. Berlin: Walter de Gruyter.

Dinges, Georg, ed. 1932. *Wolgadeutsche Volkslieder mit Bildern und Weisen*. Landschaftliche Volkslieder, no. 25. Berlin: Walter de Gruyter.

Dohrn, Verena. 1991. *Reise nach Galizien: Grenzlandschaften des alten Europa*. Frankfurt am Main: Fischer.

Eliot, George. 1876. *Daniel Deronda*. Edinburgh: William Blackwood.

Erdely, Stephen. 1995. *Music of Southslavic Epics from the Bihać: Region of Bosnia*. Milman Parry Studies in Oral Tradition. New York: Garland.

Erk, Ludwig. 1893–94. *Deutscher Liederhort*. 3 vols. Ed. and expanded by Franz Magnus Böhme. Leipzig: Breitkopf und Härtel.

Farwick, Petra. 1986. *Deutsche Volksliedlandschaften: Landschaftliches Register der Aufzeichnungen im Deutschen Volksliedarchiv*, vol. 3. Studien zur Volksliedforschung, no. 1. Bern: Peter Lang.

Ginsburg, S. M., and P. S. Marek. 1901. *Evreiskie narodnye pesni v Rossii* (Jewish folk songs from Russia). St. Petersburg: Voskhod.

Gruber, Ruth Ellen. 1992. *Jewish Heritage Travel: A Guide to Central & Eastern Europe*. New York: Wiley.

Herder, Johann Gottfried. 1778–79. "*Stimmen der Völker in Liedern*" and *Volkslieder*. Repr. in 1 vol. Stuttgart: Reclam, 1975.

Hoffman, Eva. 1993. *Exit into History: A Journey through the New Eastern Europe*. New York: Viking.

Holzapfel, Otto. 1989. *Das Deutsche Volksliedarchiv, Freiburg im Breisgau*. Studien zur Volksliedforschung, no. 3. Bern: Peter Lang.

————. 1991–93. *Vierzeiler-Lexikon*. 5 vols. Studien zur Volksliedforschung, nos. 7–11. Bern: Peter Lang.

————. 1993. *Das deutsche Gespenst: Wie Dänen die Deutschen und sich selbst sehen*. Kiel: Wolfgang Butt.

Idelsohn, A. Z. 1914–32. *Hebräisch-orientalischer Melodienschatz*. 10 vols. Berlin, Leipzig, and Jerusalem: Benjamin Harz and Friedrich Hofmeister.

Ignatieff, Michael. 1993. *Blood and Belonging: Journeys into the New Nationalism*. New York: Farrar, Straus and Giroux.

Kaplan, Harold. 1994. *Conscience and Memory: Meditations in a Museum of the Holocaust*. Chicago: University of Chicago Press.

Kittler, Friedrich A. 1987. *Aufschreibesysteme 1800/1900*. 2d, expanded ed. Munich: Fink.

Klatt, Robert, and Karl Horak, eds. 1940. *Deutsche Volkslieder aus Mittelpolen mit Bildern und Weisen*. Landschaftliche Volkslieder, no. 35. Cassel: Bärenreiter.

Kristeva, Julia. 1993. *Nations without Nationalism*. Trans. Leon S. Roudiez. European Perspectives. New York: Columbia University Press.

Leggewie, Claus. 1990. *Multi Kulti: Spielregeln für die Vielvölkerrepublik*. Berlin: Rotbuch Verlag.

Liliencron, Rochus Freiherr von. 1865. *Die historischen Volkslieder der Deutschen vom 13. bis 16. Jahrhundert*. Leipzig: Vogel.

Lomax, Alan. 1968. *Folk Song Style and Culture*. Washington, D.C.: American Association for the Advancement of Science.

Mačák, Ivan. 1990. "Zur Entwicklung der Musikinstrumente im westpannonischen Raum aus der Sicht der geographischen Determination." In *Dörfliche Tanzmusik im westpannonischen Raum*, ed. Walter Deutsch, 189–207. Vienna: Schendl.

Max, Wenzel, ed. 1971. *Deutsche Volksweisen aus Südmähren*. Landschaftliche Volkslieder, no. 43. Cassel: Bärenreiter.

Meier, John. 1935. *Deutsche Volkslieder mit ihren Melodien*, vol. 1. With Wilhelm Heiske, Fred Quellmalz, Harry Schewe, and Erich Seemann. Berlin: Walter de Gruyter.

Metzler, Fritz. 1938. "Dur, Moll und 'Kirchentöne' als musikalischer Rassenausdruck." In *Zur Tonalität des deutschen Volksliedes*, ed. Guido Waldmann, 1–27. Wolfenbüttel: Kallmeyer.

Moser, Hans. 1938. "Volksschauspiel." In *Deutsches Volkstum*, ed. John Meier, 3: 1–136. Berlin: Walter de Gruyter.

Müller-Blattau, Josef, ed. 1938. *Germanisches Erbe in deutscher Tonkunst*. Musikalische Volksforschung, no. 2. Berlin-Lichterfelde: Chr. Friedrich Vieweg.

Pinck, Louis, ed. 1937. *Lothringer Volkslieder mit Bildern und Weisen*. Landschaftliche Volkslieder, no. 31. Cassel: Bärenreiter.

Raupp, Jan. 1963. *Sorbische Volksmusikanten und Musikinstrumente*. Schriftenreihe des Instituts für sorbische Volksforschung, no. 17. Bautzen: VEB Domowina-Verlag.

Rousseau, Jean-Jacques. 1768. *Dictionnaire de la musique*. Paris: Duchesne.

Sachs, Curt. 1959. *Vergleichende Musikwissenschaft: Musik der Fremdkulturen*. 2d ed. Musikpädogogische Bibliothek, no. 2. Heidelberg: Quelle & Meyer.

Sauermann, Dietmar. 1968. *Historische Volkslieder des 18. und 19. Jahrhunderts: Ein Beitrag zur Volksliedforschung und zum Problem der volkstümlichen Geschichtsbetrachtung*. Münster: Aschendorff.

Schmidt, Leopold. 1971. *Historische Volkslieder aus Österreich vom 15. bis zum 19. Jahrhundert*. Vienna: Österreichischer Bundesverlag. (Wiener Neudrucke, 1)

Siebs, Theodor, and Max Schneider, eds. 1924. *Schlesische Volkslieder mit Bildern und Weisen*. Landschaftliche Volkslieder, no. 1. Breslau: Bergstadtverlag.

Smoltczyk, Alexander. 1990. "Beurs—Ästhetik als Widerstand." In Leggewie 1990: 37–45.

Stokes, Martin, ed. 1994. *Ethnicity, Identity and Music: The Musical Construction of Place*. Providence, R.I.: Berg.

Tappert, Wilhelm. 1890. *Wandernde Melodien*, 2d ed. Leipzig: List und Francke.

Tardel, Hermann, ed. 1928. *Niederdeutsche Volkslieder aus Schleswig-Holstein und den Hansestädten*. Landschaftliche Volkslieder, no. 10. Münster i.W.: Aschendorfsche Verlagsbuchhandlung.

Trevor-Roper, Hugh. 1983. "The Invention of Tradition: The Highland Tradition of Scotland." In *The Invention of Tradition*, ed. Eric Hobsbawm and Terence Ranger, 15–41. Cambridge: Cambridge University Press.

Turnbull, David. 1993. *Maps Are Territories: Science Is an Atlas.* Chicago: University of Chicago Press.

Waldmann, Guido. 1938a. "Tonalitätsfragen im Volkslied der deutschen Sprachinseln." In Waldmann 1938b: 61–72.

———, ed. 1938b. *Zur Tonalität des deutschen Volksliedes.* Wolfenbüttel: Kallmeyer.

Wallascheck, Richard. 1893. *Primitive Music: An Inquiry into the Origin and Development of Music, Song, Instruments, Dances and Pantomimes of Savage Races.* London: Longmans, Green.

Wetherell, Margaret, and Jonathan Potter. 1992. *Mapping the Language of Racism: Discourse and the Legitimation of Exploitation.* New York: Columbia University Press.

Wiora, Walter. 1971. *Das deutsche Lied: Zur Geschichte und Ästhetik einer musikalischen Gattung.* Wolfenbüttel: Möseler.

Wischenbart, Rüdiger. 1992. *Karpaten: Die dunkle Seite Europas.* With essays by Monika Czernin, Renate Heilig, Peter Klein, Herta Müller, Peter Polanski, Martin Pollack, Michael Schrott, Tilman Spengler, and Jan Tabor. Vienna: Kremayr & Scheriau.

Wittrock, Wolfgang. 1969. *Die ältesten Melodietypen im ostdeutschen Volksgesang.* Marburg: Elwert.

Wolff, Larry. 1994. *Inventing Eastern Europe: The Map of Civilization on the Mind of the Enlightenment.* Stanford, Calif.: Stanford University Press.

Young, James E. 1993. *The Texture of Memory: Holocaust Memorials and Meaning.* New Haven, Conn.: Yale University Press.

Zoder, Raimund. 1938. "Der deutsche Volkstanz." In *Deutsches Volkstum,* ed. John Meier, 3: 137–80. Berlin: Walter de Gruyter.

CONTRIBUTORS

Frances R. Aparicio is the Arthur F. Thurnau Professor and professor of Spanish and American Culture/Latino Studies at the University of Michigan, Ann Arbor. She is the author of *Listening to Salsa: Gender, Latin Popular Music, and Puerto Rican Cultures* (Wesleyan University Press, 1998) and co-editor, with Susana Chavez-Silverman, of *Tropicalizations: Transcultural Representations of Latinidad.*

Philip V. Bohlman is professor of Music and Jewish Studies at the University of Chicago. He is the author of *The Study of Folk Music in the Modern World* (Indiana University Press, 1988), *The World Centre for Jewish Music and Palestine, 1936–1940: Jewish Music on the Eve of World War II* (Oxford University Press, 1992), and *"Jüdische Volksmusik": Eine europäische Geistesgeschichte* (Böhlau Verlag, forthcoming), and co-editor, with Bruno Nettl, of *Comparative Musicology and Anthropology of Music* (1991) and, with Katherine Bergeron, of *Disciplining Music* (1992), the latter two volumes published by the University of Chicago Press.

Brian Currid is the author of several articles on topics including house music, world beat, and popular music and film. He teaches film studies and American studies at the Free University and Humboldt University in Berlin, and is at work on a manuscript, provisionally entitled "The Acoustics of National Publicity," on music in German mass culture during the Weimar and Nazi periods.

John Fiske is professor of Communication Arts at the University of Wisconsin-Madison. He is the author of nine books on cultural studies, of which the most recent is *Media Matters* (University of Minnesota Press, 1996).

Kevin Gaines teaches in the Center for African American Studies and the Department of History at the University of Michigan. He is the author of *Uplifting the Race: Black Leadership, Politics and Culture during the Twentieth Century* (1996) and of the forthcoming *From Black Power to Civil Rights: African American Expatriates in Nkrumah's Ghana*, both published by the University of North Carolina Press.

Sander L. Gilman is the Henry R. Luce Distinguished Service Professor of the Liberal Arts in Human Biology and chair of the Department of Germanic Studies at the University of Chicago. He holds positions there as professor of Germanic Studies, Comparative Literature, and Psychiatry and is a member of the Fishbein Center for the History of Science, the Committee on Jewish Studies, and the Committee on the History of Culture. His most recent book is *Making the Body Beautiful: A Cultural History of Aesthetic Surgery* (Princeton University Press, 1999).

Jocelyne Guilbault is professor of ethnomusicology in the Music Department, University of California, Berkeley. She is the author of *Zouk: World Music in the West Indies* (University of Chicago Press, 1993) and is currently working on two book projects, one concerned with musical bonds, boundaries, and borders ("Traditions and Challenges of a World Music: The Music Industry of Calypso"), and the other a study of a selected number of superstars of the English Caribbean in connection with the politics of difference in world music.

Tera W. Hunter is associate professor of history at Carnegie Mellon University. She is the author of *To 'Joy My Freedom: Southern Black Women's Lives and Labors after the Civil War* (Harvard University Press, 1997).

Margaret J. Kartomi is professor of music at Monash University, Melbourne. She is the author of many articles, as well as books on and recordings of Indonesian and other music cultures, and on organology and other aspects of ethnomusicological theory. She is a fellow of the Australian Academy of the Humanities and was awarded the Order of Australia for services to music.

Tomislav Z. Longinović is associate professor of Slavic and Comparative Literature and director of the Cultural Translation Project at the University of Wisconsin–Madison. He is the author of *Borderline Culture* (University of Arkansas Press, 1993) and of works of fiction in English (*Moment of Silence*, 1990) and Serbo-Croatian (*Sama Amerika*, 1994).

Peter Manuel has researched and published extensively on traditional and contemporary musics of North India and the Hispanic and Indic Caribbean. He is co-author, with Michael Largey and Kenneth Bilby, of *Caribbean Currents: Caribbean Music from Rumba to Reggae* (Temple University Press, 1995) and author of the forthcoming *East Indian Music in the West Indies*.

D. A. Masolo taught in the philosophy department at the University of Nairobi from 1980 to 1991. Currently he is professor of philosophy at the University of Louisville. He is the author of *African Philosophy in Search of Identity* (Indiana University Press, 1994) and co-editor, with Ivan Karp, of *African Philosophy as Cultural Inquiry* (Indiana University Press, forthcoming).

Zoila S. Mendoza is assistant professor of Native American Studies at the University of California, Davis. Among her recent publications are contributions to the *Journal of Latin American Anthropology*, the *Bulletin of Latin American Research*, and the book *Shaping Society through Dance: Mestizo Ritual Performance in the Peruvian Andes* (University of Chicago Press, forthcoming).

Rafael Pérez-Torres is associate professor of English at UCLA. He studies the social configurations of race, ethnicity, and gender and their intersection with contemporary U.S. culture. He is the author of *Movements in Chicano Poetry: Against Myths, Against Margins* (Cambridge University Press, 1995) and is currently at work on a book-length study of the relationship between ethics and the aesthetics of Chicano fiction.

Ronald Radano teaches in the School of Music and the Department of Afro-American Studies at the University of Wisconsin–Madison. He is author of the award-winning book *New Musical Figurations: Anthony Braxton's Cultural Critique* and the forthcoming study, *"Lying up a Nation": Race and the Origins of Black Music*, both published by the University of Chicago Press.

Larry Scanlon is associate professor of English at Rutgers, the State University of New Jersey, and editor of *Studies in the Age of Chaucer*. He is the author of *Narrative, Authority and Power: The Medieval Exemplum and the Chaucerian Tradition* (Cambridge, 1994) and is at work on a study of medieval sexuality and its relation to modernity entitled "The Long Shadow of the Patriarchs: Sodomy and Incest in Medieval Writing and Postmodern Theory."

Christopher Holmes Smith is a Ph.D. candidate in Media and Cultural Studies at the University of Wisconsin–Madison. His research interests include the globalization of media and popular culture, modern and postmodern social theory, and cultural studies. His recent publications include "Method and Madness: Exploring the Boundaries of Identity in Hip-Hop Performativity," in *Social Identities* 3 (October 1997) and "Freeze Frames: Frozen Foods and Memories of the Postwar American Family," in *Kitchen Culture in America: Representations of Food, Gender, and Race*, edited by Sherrie A. Inness (University of Pennsylvania Press, forthcoming).

Katie Trumpener is associate professor of Germanic Studies, Comparative Literature, English, and Cinema and Media Studies at the University of Chicago. Her first book, *Bardic Nationalism: The Romantic Novel and the British Empire* (Princeton University Press, 1997) won the British Academy's Rose Mary Crawshay Prize and the MLA Prize for a First Book; her second, *The Divided Screen: The Postwar German Cinemas*, is forthcoming from Princeton University Press.

Thomas Turino is associate professor of musicology and anthropology at the University of Illinois at Urbana-Champaign. He is the author of *Moving Away from Silence: The Music of the Peruvian Altiplano and the Experience of Urban Migration* (1993) and of the forthcoming *Nationalists, Cosmopolitans, and Popular Music in Zimbabwe*, both published by the University of Chicago Press. Currently, he is working on the semiotic theories of C. S. Peirce as they apply to music.

Christopher Waterman is professor of culture and performance and chair of the Department of World Arts and Cultures at UCLA. He is the author of *Jùjú: A Social History and Ethnography of an African Popular Music* (University of Chicago Press, 1990), and co-author of a forthcoming book on the history of American popular music, to be published by Oxford University Press.

Deborah Wong is associate professor of Music and director of the Center for Asian Pacific America at the University of California, Riverside. She is an ethnomusicologist specializing in Asian American music and the music of Thailand.

INDEX

Locators in boldface refer to pages with illustrations.